THE BENTLEY COLLECTION
OF
BRITISH SOVEREIGNS

BALDWIN'S
2013

BALDWIN'S

The Name for Numismatics

The BENTLEY Collection

of

British Milled Sovereigns

A H Baldwin & Sons Ltd, 11 Adelphi Terrace, London WC2N 6BJ
Telephone: +44 (0)20 7930 9808, Fax: +44 (0)20 7930 9450, email: auctions@baldwin.co.uk
www.baldwin.co.uk
twitter @BaldwinsCoins facebook /BaldwinsCoins

Published by A H Baldwin & Sons Ltd,
11 Adelphi Terrace,
London WCN 6BJ

ISBN 978-0-906919-25-8

British Library Cataloguing in Publication data
A CIP catalogue record is available from the British Library
Designed and set by Edward Baldwin and Seth Freeman
Printed in Great Britain by Pardy & Son (Printers) Ltd, Ringwood, UK

Welcome to this special edition catalogue of the Bentley Collection.
We have combined the three parts of the auction catalogue (which was sold with a 100% success rate 2012-2013) into a chronological run directly reflecting how the whole collection was kept before it was divided into three parts for sale by auction. Each entry appears with its full catalogue description with the relevant lot number beside, and the price realised under the estimation price, including the 20% buyer's premium. Statistical tables of prices for different sections of the collection, all three parts, appears in an appendix at the end of this book.
The lot number is a unique identifying number for each coin in the Bentley collection, but a numismatist using this catalogue who may only have the lot number to identify a coin will also need the page number too. Therefore there is a concordance of which page each lot number from the Bentley Collection appears upon from 1 to 1238

What a journey the Bentley Collection has been from start to finish, not only for the vendor in forming it from 1978, but also for the key numismatic dealers around the world who were involved heavily in helping to shape and build the collection from the "acorn" of a 1913 Sovereign purchased in 1978, to a world class, record breaking collection of over 1200 pieces, which sold for a total of just over £4million, in three parts over 18 months.
Never before this event had there been such a large private collection of numismatic sovereigns formed into as comprehensive a collection as the Bentley group, with so many proofs and patterns, and including the best attempt at collecting the die number series of Queen Victoria numbering 586 pieces alone.
Over the three parts the momentum kept on growing as world-wide interest was developed, especially in the Colonial pieces where the highlight of the three sales lay.

The 1920 Sydney Mint Sovereign exceeded all expectation to fetch a new world record price not only for a British Imperial type sovereign but also for a British Colonial coin, and an Australian currency coin. The hammer eventually fell after a heated battle involving three bidders at £650,000 (£780,000 including buyer's premium). It caused quite a stir in the Australian media. A television crew came to the Baldwin office the day before the sale, to film the coin before it went on the block, in anticipation that an Australian buyer would secure it. The successful telephone bidder after the epic battle was Sydney based dealer Robert Jaggard (on behalf of a client) who appeared on the "ABC" Newscast the next day as the buyer, overlaid with the images of the coin taken at 11 Adelphi Terrace. CNN also featured a short item about the sale in their news coverage.
Other good printed media coverage of these record breaking sales was in British newspapers such as the "Sunday Telegraph", "The Times" and "City AM". Antiques publications also featured the collection, including "The Australian" and the "Antiques Trade Gazette" and all the principal numismatic publications like "Coin World", "World Coin News", and the British "Coin News" amongst others.
The other major highlight of the three parts was the sale of the 1819 London Mint Sovereigns which was by far the finest of the known examples, and fetched an impressive £186,000 including buyer's premium, more than trebling in price in the 15 years since its purchase. With today's quality sensitive marketplace, it was proven once again that it is the quality and rarity that counts, not just for these two highlights, but for key coins across the whole scope of the Bentley Collection. The collection was worthy of a special effort in cataloguing, to record in detail all the varieties present and the weights and dimensions of each coin where appropriate.
The anonymous vendor of the Bentley Collection was needless to say delighted with the overall result of the sale of the whole collection and we can quote from an email to the cataloguer:-

"I again want to thank you and the whole Baldwin staff for the fantastic effort put into making these sales so positive."

We were flattered to receive many pleasing comments from collectors around the world in reaction to receiving each part, as a refreshing approach to such an important collection, with expert division into the component parts, and a mark of reference for the future in the Sovereign series, which leads us full circle to the tome in your hand now.
Thank you to all those numismatists who contributed towards the success of these sales.

Steve Hill
July 2013

Before running into the full catalogue of the Collection, here are some of the most interesting statistics now garnered from the results with top prices achieved.

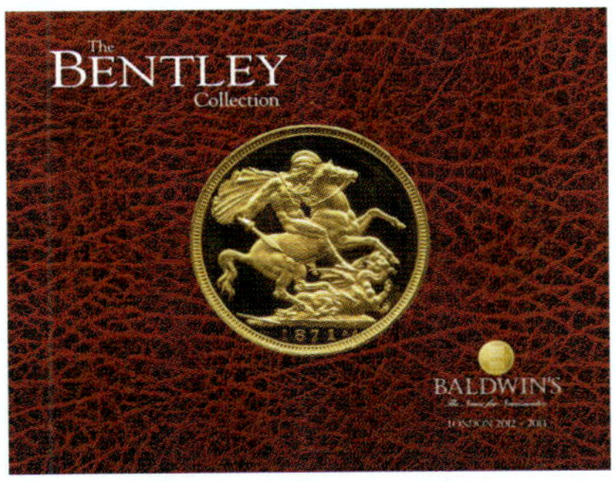

The Bentley Collection
sold for a hammer price of £3,377,795 (= £4,05**3,540** with premium) against a pre-sale estimate of £2,388,025.

Therefore the final price result was approximately 70% over the pre-sale estimate.
The collection as a whole consisted of 1241 coins, including the component coins in the 1937 matt gold set.

Part One
sold for a hammer price of £749,455 (= £899,346 with premium) against a pre-sale estimate of £545,125.

Therefore the final result was approximately 65% over the pre-sale estimate.
This part contained 382 coins.

Part Two
sold for a hammer price of £1,883,970 (= £2,260,764 with premium) against a pre-sale estimate of £1,287,450.

Therefore the final hammer price result was approximately 75% over the pre-sale estimate.
This part contained 549 coins.

Part Three
sold for a hammer price of £704,370 (= £845,244 with premium) against a pre-sale estimate of £555,750.

Therefore the final hammer price result was approximately 52% over the pre-sale estimate.
This part contained 310 coins including the component coins in the 1937 matt gold set.

The highest price result in the entire collection and a new world record was Lot 736, the **1920 Sydney Sovereign** which had a low estimate of £300,000 and realised a final sale price of £780,000 (160% over the pre-sale estimate).

For further breakdowns of statistics please see the appendices at the end of the catalogue.

Contents

Appendices

The BENTLEY Collection

A Very British Affair

The outstanding Bentley Collection began as a casual exploration into the possibility of owning some gold in the form of coin in the late seventies. Gold has always been viewed traditionally as a safe haven in times of economic woe. This quickly became a passionate quest to formulate one of the greatest collections assembled of the British Gold Sovereign. The Sovereign was the denomination that pleased the then owner the most, not only from its stand-point in history as one of the most long-lived, respected and widely distributed gold coins in the world, but also for its pleasing dimensions and size, being 22mm in diameter, weighing 7.98g and being struck in 22 carat gold.

First introduced by King Henry VII (1485-1509), in 1489, the denomination was current throughout the hand-struck hammered Tudor and Stuart periods. In various later guises the denomination was as diversely termed as "Pound", "Unite", "Laurel", and more importantly the staple coin of the 18th Century, the gold "Guinea". It was the need for a reformation of the Coinage Act in 1816 that led to the introduction of the Modern Gold Sovereign.

The coin that started it all - the George V 1913 London Sovereign

Formed over 34 years, the first purchase was made for the embryonic Bentley Collection in 1978, a George V London Sovereign dated 1913. From this foundation coin, the acorn as it were, a structured and concise "mighty oak" of a collection blossomed and matured, with an emphasis on quality and unparalleled rarity.

The interest being established by this initial purchase, nurtured a thirst for the best quality from the start. The first aim was to form a complete run of dates, not just those dates usually of a more common bullion nature in top condition, but to take the series of the modern currency Sovereign back to its introduction in 1817 under King George III (1760-1820). It was decided early on to not go back in history any further, as the priority was the modern Sovereign which presented a series with more than enough to concentrate upon, as finding the best state of preservation was paramount. Decimalisation was seen as a fitting close to the collection, as since that time, the regular issue of mint condition sovereigns has perhaps made the denomination too commemorative.

During the latter part of Queen Victoria's reign (1837-1901), the Royal branch mints began to open in the Colonial Empire; and it was at an early stage that the then owner realised that many of the Gold Sovereigns carry a small mint mark letter either under the bust or shield, or on the ground-line under St George, which indicates which Colonial branch mint that the coin has emanated from. If no letter is apparent it is a London Royal Mint issue. A decision was made to add as many of the dated pieces of these Branch Mints as possible to the collection, from Sydney (1855-1926), Melbourne (1872-1931) and Perth (1899-1931) in Australia; Ottawa (1908-1919) in Canada; Bombay in India (1918), and Pretoria in South Africa (1923-1932).

Throughout the eighties quality coins began to be added mainly in the currency series, and trusted numismatic contacts with a sharp eye began to be established not just domestically, but on all the continents where the Royal branch mints existed, in the hope of tracking down the rarest and best quality pieces from their respective geographical locations.

It was sometime in this decade that the Victorian Die Number Series of Sovereigns became a further focus for the collection. From 1863 until 1874 inclusive, the Royal Mint in London individually numbered the shield type reverse dies used to strike the currency Sovereigns as a means of "quality control" in assessing the efficiency of use of the dies, and in tracing any weakness in the production process. Some of the dates in this period number over 100 individual dies alone; therefore the scope of the Bentley Collection became even more wide-reaching, and the prospect of collecting anything other than the modern Gold Sovereign never came to fruition. The die number series has only ever been attempted by a handful of previous collectors, and nobody has ever achieved as complete a run in private ownership as demonstrated in the Bentley Collection.

Into the nineties many more important pieces were added as some of the major collections formed in earlier decades began to be dispersed both by private treaty and by public auction. Some of the rarest "Pattern" and "Proof" issues (literally prototypes of coinage) were added to the Bentley Collection during this time. The detail of the collection became therefore even more focused as it became an illustrative history of the gold Sovereign, specialising from gestation in 1816 until decimalisation under Queen Elizabeth II.

The South African ZAR gold Pond series from the late 19th Century until the Boer War, was of a similar dimension to the gold Sovereign. As it was a short run, relatively speaking, though some varieties very rare, it was decided to add as many of these pieces to the collection, as an interesting forerunner to the British colonisation of the Boer republics.

It was during this period that the crowning piece of the London Royal Mint series was acquired at public auction. The very impressive 1819 Sovereign, the most significant coin in the Bentley Collection was added at the end of the last Century. Still the finest known specimen by far, it has proven to be the most valuable London Sovereign.

Moving into the 21st Century further valuable additions were made to the collection. It did however take until 2006 to find the final date-piece required for the currency part of the collection: the most elusive and coveted of all the Colonial Sovereign Series, the fabled 1920 Sydney Mint Sovereign. This is the crown jewel of the Bentley Collection, sourced from Australia, and has proven to be the most valuable currency coin in the entire Australian Series.

This special edition Bentley Collection catalogue is not only form a lasting record of the achievement of the collector, but also an informative reference for the advanced Sovereign connoisseur; a major guide-book to the Sovereign aficionado who is forming a collection; and most importantly a tremendous inspiration to the novice collector of what can be achieved from an initial passing interest in gold bullion as coin. With patience and an appreciation for quality and rarity, it is hoped the new custodians of the coins that were sold in the Bentley Collection will be able to build similar or perhaps even more complete collections of Sovereigns.

More importantly, the Bentley Collection forms an important historical record of the British Empire for the economic historian and a physical illustration of artistic merit in coin design for the art historian. The Benedetto Pistrucci design of St George slaying the dragon has been the most enduring coin design in the world. Inspired perhaps by the George Noble of King Henry VIII (1509-1547), and in its current form for the last 190 years with minimal change, and over this period more often in use than not.

Collections of the calibre of the Bentley Collection only come along once in a numismatic generation and this special edition catalogue will last as an endearing record of that achievement.

A. H. Baldwin & Sons Ltd are proud to publish the Bentley Collection in this special limited edition.

A Brief History of the British Gold Sovereign

Introduced by King Henry VII (1485-1509), in 1489 the gold Sovereign in the hand made hammered period of our Tudor Coinage formed the grandest and most impressive coin ever issued in the English series at that date. This was a direct result of the influence of the Renaissance style that had emanated from Italy and a distinct display at how wealthy King Henry VII had become after the closure of the 100 years war and his own victory over King Richard III (1483-1485) at the Battle of Bosworth Field. Henry's first sovereign was partly influenced by the issue in 1487 of the gold Real d'Or struck in the Netherlands by the Holy Roman Emperor Maximilian.

One of the latter issues of the Henry VII Gold Sovereign

The British gold Sovereign issued at 30 Shillings and struck in 23 carat 3⅞ grains fine gold, was approximately 38mm in diameter and weighing some 30g was a most impressive issue. It was a most illustrious coin depicting the King seated on his throne with orb and sceptre, surrounded by a tressure of many arcs and a legend abbreviated in Latin, declaring him King of England, France and Lord of Ireland. The reverse showing a full bloom Tudor rose, it is a most impressive coin and went through five incarnations in Henry VII's reign alone, which is a great deal for a denomination that was not used in everyday transactions, and never really seen by the majority of the population.

Henry VIII Second Coinage Gold Sovereign

A Tudor centrepiece, the Sovereign continued to be issued in fine gold into the reign of Henry VIII (1509-1547) through three coinages and from varying mints, but due to the extravagant spending of the King, the coinage suffered and latter issues of the gold Sovereign endured being reduced in weight, and eventually in fineness to as low as 20 carats. It was only through the efforts of Henry's son, the "boy" King Edward VI (1547-1553), that the fineness of the gold Sovereign was eventually restored to a 30 Shilling face value in the last of three different issues of Sovereign in his short reign.

Henry VIII Second Coinage Gold Sovereign

[Baldwin Library images]

Queen Mary Gold Sovereign **Queen Elizabeth I, Sixth Issue, Gold Sovereign**

Edward's older sister Queen Mary (1553-1558), continued the issue of the fine gold Sovereign in her reign, as did her younger sister Queen Elizabeth I (1558-1603), though latterly Elizabeth also introduced a lower 22 carat 20 Shilling gold piece, the Pound, c.1592-1595 which ran concurrently at first and then from 1595 solely to the end of her reign. During the reign of Queen Elizabeth the first experimentation began with striking by machine, which did result in at least one "Pattern" Pound, but this method of production proved too controversial to be introduced over the traditional hammered ways at this time circa 1561-1570.

The last hammered Gold Sovereign for King James I

The Stuart King James I (1603-1625), already King of Scotland since 1567, issued a fine gold Sovereign for the first two years of his reign of a different design to Elizabeth. However from 1605 James demonstrated how he was King of both England and Scotland by introducing a new 20 Shilling denomination the "Unite" and latterly in his final coinage the "Laurel" where he is depicted laureate and draped like a Roman Emperor. The 30 Shilling Sovereign had become the Rose Ryal from now until the last coinage and the two types depict the King quite life-like seated on the throne similar to the Tudor Sovereigns.

King James I Gold Laurel

Commonwealth Gold Unite dated 1654

The Unite denomination was continued as the staple gold coin into the reign of his son King Charles I (1625-1649). During the Civil War the gold coins were issued provincially for the first time and we see the issue of the largest hammered gold denomination ever, the magnificent Triple Unite from both Shrewsbury and Oxford. The Puritans under Oliver Cromwell continued the issue of the Unite in the name of the Commonwealth (1649-1660), though by now the concept of machinery was being entertained in the Mint once again and there was a Pattern milled "Broad" of 20 Shillings produced bearing the portrait of Oliver Cromwell in 1656.

[Baldwin Library images]

Charles II hammered Gold Unite

Charles II milled Gold Guinea, dated 1663 with elephant below bust

At the Restoration, King Charles II (1660-1685) expressed his wish for mechanisation of the Mint, however the controversial machinery based at Drury House on The Strand, London where it had been housed through fear of sabotage from the hammered workers, was so massive that it took nigh on two years to fully move all the parts across, and set them up in the Tower of London within the Mint compound. During this delay Charles II issued his own hammered gold Unite of 20 Shillings, that was later termed a "Broad" once the milled machine-made coinage emerged from 1663. This was because the diameter of the hammered piece was larger and the flan, though much thinner than its machine made counterpart, appeared much broader.

This machine made piece was the gold Guinea and was first coined in 1663 initially at 20 Shillings face value. Officially it was a Twenty Shilling piece, but colloquially called a Guinea, so-named after the place where most of the gold supply came from, being Guinea in Africa. Any gold freshly supplied by the "African Company" was denoted with either an elephant, or elephant and castle, below the busts.

James II Gold Guinea 1685 with elephant and castle

William III 1695 Gold Guinea

Anne 1703 VIGO Gold Guinea

This successful denomination continued through the reigns of all the other Stuart Monarchs, King James II (1685-1688), William and Mary (1688-1694), King William III (1694-1702), Queen Anne (1702-1714), some issues with the African mark, and in Queen Anne's reign a very rare issue with VIGO below the bust denoting gold captured from the Spanish after the Vigo Bay conflict. Throughout all of these reigns including those back in the hammered Tudor and Stuart period, the price of gold had fluctuated as the gold to silver ratio varied over time compared with those ratios in trade in Europe, and at various times the supply of gold or silver coin maybe flowing into or out of England, hence varying the face value of the gold Guinea. This coupled with the poor state of the silver coinage before the Great Recoinage of silver in 1696, meant the value of the "Guinea" fluctuated as high as 30 Shillings.

The Master of the Mint in the reign of Queen Anne was Mr Isaac Newton (later knighted), who recognised the problem of a lack of fixed face value on the gold and it was in a Proclamation of 1717 in the succeeding reign that the value was set at 21 Shillings for a Guinea, so officially termed for the first time, with which we are still familiar today (thinking of traditions like the 10,000 Guineas horse race). This set the mark for the 100 year period until the introduction of the modern gold Sovereign.

[Baldwin Library images]

George II 1745 LIMA Gold Guinea

George III 1774 Proof Gold Guinea

[Baldwin Library images]

The Guinea continued to be issued by the Hanoverian dynasty, from King George I (1714-1727), King George II (1727-1760), and King George III (1760-1820). In 1733 during the reign of King George II, all the old hammered gold was finally withdrawn and recoined as milled gold, the old hammered silver having already been through a similar process back in the reign of William III, the Great Recoinage.

However there was still a long-standing issue with the import and export of silver and gold coin and the lack of harmonisation in Europe of the gold and silver ratio. Towards the end of the 18th Century there had become a distinct lack of small change in silver, as there was no limit to the specie of how coin and bullion payments were made up in transactions, both here and overseas. This major problem was relieved in part by the Bank of England who released their stocks of silver Spanish Colonial dollars to be countermarked with a head of King George III and circulate, however these countermarked Dollars were unfortunately easily copied. This problem was solved in the short term by Matthew Boulton of the Soho Mint, who used James Watt's steam presses to totally overstrike the Spanish Dollars with a Bank of England design. However the lack of a law of legal tender still meant that large payments could be tendered in large quantity of silver, and it was subsequently drained out of England and onto the Continent.

After much deliberation in Parliament this led to the Coinage Act of 22 June 1816, in which the involvement of Lord Liverpool was instrumental, where a limit of 40 shillings was set upon payments made in silver, with gold remaining legal tender for payments of any size. This immediately helped the flow and ratio of gold and silver, and made the use of European and foreign coin illegal. A newly anticipated "recoinage" was in gestation and preparation work was underway with proposals starting in 1816. The Chief Engraver was Thomas Wyon Jnr (died 22 September 1817), who submitted designs as well as the Italian Second Engraver Benedetto Pistrucci (1783-1855). The Master of the Mint was William Wellesley Pole, later Lord Maryborough, brother of the Duke of Wellington who was instrumental in bringing Pistrucci to the Mint whose work was eventually adopted for the new coinage. Pistrucci's successful design was approved on 18 June 1817, the Prince Regent having seen it on the 31 May with its innovative straight grained milled edge.

The modern gold Sovereign was first issued on 5 July 1817 at a weight of 7.98g and 22mm in diameter with a face value of One Pound or Twenty Shillings. The gold Half-Sovereign of Ten Shillings followed later in the year on the 11 October.

The Bentley Collection commences with examples of the pattern and trial issues of 1816 starting with the most significant piece of gold of the new weight standard adopted as part of the 1816 Act of Coinage.

There are many sources for the history of the gold Sovereign some of which are given in the Bibliography but one of the more recent, succinct and accurate is that which this cataloguer would recommend in the Royal Mint publication "The Gold Sovereign 1489-1989" essays "The Fifteenth Century Revival" by John Pourteous, and "The Early Story" by C E Challis, published 1989.

The Bentley Collection is catalogued in chronological order as per date upon each coin for the London series. The Colonial issue Sovereigns are catalogued in chronological order within each of their individual mints. The original Bentley lot number is retained in this book with the final price achieved beneath the original pre-auction estimate.

A Note on Mintage Figures

All quoted calendar year mintages or numbers issued have been cross checked between two publications:-
The History of the Gold Sovereign – Sir Geoffrey Duveen and H G Stride – published Oxford University Press, 1962
Sovereigns of the British Empire - Captain J J Cullimore-Allen OBE - published Spink & Son, 1965.

A Note on the Weighing of Coins

All Sovereigns are struck in 22 carat gold (916.66 fineness) unless otherwise stated.
The standard weight of a Sovereign is 7.98805g or 123.27447 grains as dictated by the Coinage Act of 1870.
One gram = 15.4323 grains.

A unique opportunity occurs with the Bentley Collection to weigh accurately a large sample of surviving sovereigns even though their manufacture is quite uniform and weights very similar. It is interesting to see how accurately they were made and to examine how wear and tear takes its toll upon the more circulated examples, some of which are currently below the accepted legal tender weight as dictated by the later 1890 Coinage Act.

In practice the weight can vary between 7.97g and 8.00g when rounded to two decimal places for a good quality coin. The more wear a coin exhibits the lower the weight can be. A sovereign was deemed non-legal tender once its weight diminished to under 122.5 grains, about 7.937g.
All coins were weighed on a Sartorius scientific balance to three decimal places and rounded up or down accordingly to two decimal places for publication.

A Note on Grading

All Sovereigns in the Bentley Collection have been graded on strict and conservative British standards. It should be borne in mind that gold, being the softest metal used in the manufacture of coinage, will always generally show some hairlines or light contact marks of some kind, and every effort has been made to mention all such instances.

For a true FDC Victoria Sovereign see lot 289 (page 260) which sets a standard for uncirculated grade that all the other Sovereigns in this collection are compared to.

Some of the coins in the Bentley Collection were originally obtained "encapsulated and graded", encased in plastic, from which the owner arranged removal of the coins. Where the original grade from the various companies involved is known it is mentioned in the cataloguing along with our own strict British grading. However, we cannot advise or predict what any coin in the Bentley Collection may or may not be graded as by a third party grading service in the future.

A Note on Varieties

Varieties of coins and differences upon them can take many different forms and some are much more significant than others. There has been a trend in the numismatic trade recently to call any slight difference from one coin to another "a newly discovered" variety or more crassly an "error", when clearly this is not always the case. To be a true error upon a coin, the engraver who made it must have made a mistake when preparing the die which is clearly evident on the struck coins from those particular dies. This can take the form of a wrong letter used in the legend whether the right way up or rotated (or correct letter but rotated), or even more seriously a wrong bust or other design element used which is different to other current coins of the time. The use of Roman style true capital letter I punches can be deemed an error, but may just have been used for necessity if the Arabic style number 1 punch was missing or broken on the day of preparing the die. These sorts of striking are all true varieties, as they differ markedly to what is normally encountered.

Overdates are another significant variety, not a product of an error, although it is possible an engraver picked up the wrong figure to punch in the date on the die and then had to correct it. A much more likely reason is that when a new year began, and it was time to strike coins bearing the new date, if any dies from the year before were still in perfectly serviceable condition, they would be reused, and the new date figure punched over the top of the previous one. This happened with at least one die for the Sovereign in 1843. However, this does not happen often in the sovereign series and is surprising it did not happen for instance in 1828, when 1827 dated dies continued to be used until November of that year. It would seem from looking at evidence of other coinage denominations that overdating to reuse older dies was not common practice until the reign of Queen Victoria. During the reigns of George III, IV and William IV all the overdated coins in all metals add up to a very small total number indeed.

What should be termed as more of a **"sub-variety"** is the instance of small differences in design or legend that are not due to the engraver, but the fault of the striking process as a whole. That is to say any weak or blocked areas of a design or legend, such as weak punctuation or partly filled or slightly broken letters. If grease or dirt adhere to the dies while the machinery is striking and deposits itself into the design elements, or legend, this can block that part of the design, making the struck coins appear weaker at the blocked parts. This commonly occurs in the legends, not so much on Sovereigns but on silver and copper coins. This probably accounts for some of the "absent serif" varieties on many of the George III Sovereigns as they appear to become weaker and weaker across successive coins of certain dates. Some of the broken serif sub-varieties may also be due to damaged punches being used by the engraver, where the serif has become detached from the punch being used. These are not errors as some have called them, or even inverted number 1's but are merely the result of faulty punches being employed or blockages upon the dies.

Another manifestation often seen on the earlier Victorian Sovereigns, especially in the second larger young head series and sometimes in the first head, is the occurrence of "**dual-hubbed dies**" which appears on the coins as the doubling of letters in the legend or date figures below. In more severe cases the design can show light doubling too. This can occur when the dies are being manufactured and they go through the "hubbing" process, when the design and main legends are pressed into the blank die using a positive form of master die called a hub. The dies are often hubbed two or more times and if the die or hub rotates or moves slightly between successive pressings it will show a slight doubling of elements where the movement has occurred. This problem seems to be solved around the time of the introduction of a re-engraved "third" young head design in 1870. Of course doubling can also be due to elements being punched into a die twice to firm up a weak initial impression or to correct an error, but dual hubbing is on a grander scale involving consecutive letters and even elements of the design.

Other more serious faults on the die designs occur as the dies near the end of their useful life and start to degrade and break down. Small hairline cracks start to appear which over successive further high pressure striking begin to open up until the die is no longer of service. In extreme cases they can break apart or explode under high pressure. Hairline die fractures become cracks, and cracks become fissures which eventually break down the dies. These die cracks manifest as raised die flaws upon the coin usually connecting many elements of the design and letters in the legend. They also seem to most commonly occur in the Victorian Sovereigns of the second young head dating back to 1848, which also covers the majority of the die number series.

A Note on Provenances

Every effort has been made to include provenance when available in the time allowed to prepare this catalogue. Most of them are present due to the records kept of the acquisitions to the collection over many years. These generally consist of old dated invoices from the individuals and companies concerned.

The Reign of King George III (1760-1820)
House of Hanover

Born: 4 June 1738

Accession: 25 October 1760

Married: Charlotte of Mecklenburg-Strelitz 8 September 1761 the day they met for the first time.

Coronation: Tuesday, 22 September 1761

Children: nine sons, six daughters

Died: 29 January 1820, aged 81

Introduction of the new Gold Sovereign

The standard design for the initial currency Sovereigns depicting King George III and the classic design of St George slaying the dragon engraved by Benedetto Pistrucci was received with great acclaim at the eventual introduction of the modern milled gold Sovereign to the British public on the 5 July 1817, as published in the London Gazette of that date.

The first type obverse depicts the King facing right with a laurel wreath upon his head showing ten leaves to the viewer with coarse hair. The date appears below and the legend reads GEORGIUS III D: G: BRITANNIAR: REX F: D: with a descending colon after BRITANNIAR:. The lettering of the legend is clear of the raised rim. The currency coins are struck with an inverted die axis, the proof versions are usually struck with an upright (en médaille) die axis. The reverse depicts St George attempting to slay the dragon with a broken lance, a fuller classical type description follows at the end of this introduction. The other part of the broken lance lays on the left ground-line with the designers initials BP incuse below it. The Order of the Garter surrounds the design with the motto of the Order upon it HONI. SOIT. QUI. MAL. Y. PENSE. There is an outer raised rim both sides. The edges are always straight grained milled, which is the first time such an edge appears on a British gold coin. The first time this description applies is at lot 3, the 1817 Proof Sovereign.

Original Design of the St. George and Dragon, by Pistrucci.

The classic figure of St George slaying the dragon was modelled from life based on an Italian servant working at Brunet's Hotel, No.25 Leicester Square, where Pistrucci lodged when he first came to work for the Mint in London. This depiction has gone down in numismatic history as one of the most enduring designs ever used upon a coin.

BENEDETTO PISTRUCCI.

It is worth repeating here the very detailed classical description of this reverse by Captain J J Cullimore-Allen OBE, author of "Sovereigns of the British Empire" published Spink & Son 1965.

"The saintly knight is mounted on horseback, his left hand holding the bridle rein. He wears a crested helmet with a plume of hair floating behind. A chlamys flows freely behind him, and is fastened in front by a fibula. On his right shoulder is a baltens for suspending the gladius. His feet and lower legs are protected by armour, except the toes, which are unprotected. The horse appears to half advance, half shrink from the dragon at its feet. St George has broken his lance in wounding the winged monster, and a portion of the lance remains in the animal's body."

The Unique Standard Sovereign Weight as defined by Act of Parliament 1816

932 **George III (1760-1820),** Trial Gold Flan for a Sovereign, 1816, 22 Carat uniface piece of gold inscribed in italic script on obverse in four lines, *Stand. Sovereign Wt. by Act of Part. 1816,* plain reverse and edge with bevelled rims, 7.99g, 19.6mm, thickness 1mm (unpublished in standard reference works). *Quite heavily hairlined, otherwise as made and engraved, unique.* £8000-10,000

Price Realised : £18,600

ex "125 Years of Baldwin's 1872-1997", Baldwin's Auction 15, 13 October 1997, lot 42, sold for £4000
ex An Important Collection of Gold Sovereigns 1816-2000, offered as one lot, Sothebys, November 2000, lot 525 (part)

After the Battle of Waterloo a reform of the coinage was required and the Government at first thought to reintroduce the Guinea and its fractions. However, the general feeling of the public was that they had become used to banknotes in round figures of a Pound and Two Pounds, rather than the more inconvenient calculations required with multiples of gold Guinea coins. Though the Prime Minister, Lord Liverpool, desired a return to the Guinea personally (he was briefly Master of the Mint 1799-1801), he was more practically minded and gave no resistance to the concession progressing through Act of Parliament, on the recommendation of the then Master of the Mint William Wellesley Pole. The Privy Council Committee duly recommended coinage of Ten Shilling, Twenty Shilling, Forty Shilling and Five Pound Pieces which was approved by the Prince Regent, 3 August 1816. For further reading see *Royal Sovereign 1489-1989,* edited by G P Dyer, specifically Chapter 3 *The Modern Sovereign.*

This intriguing piece is of the utmost historical significance. No doubt it would have been produced for the earliest stage of the process of the introduction of the new Sovereign denomination, once it had been passed by Act of Parliament, 22 June 1816. It is easy to imagine such a piece being passed around a meeting of council members for the committee on coin and such a piece helping visualise the new dimensions for the new Sovereign that came to fruition as currency 1 July 1817.
Such trial pieces do not usually survive or even leave such meetings, the first time this piece ever appeared in public for sale was at the Baldwin's 125 Years celebrations auction in 1997 and remains unpublished in standard works on the subject of the Sovereign. It has only appeared once since, in the Sotheby sale in 2000 for the Important Collection of Sovereigns which was offered by sale as a single lot, but remained unsold. The Bentley collector was later introduced to this gentleman and a great many Sovereigns changed hands privately including this piece which is now offered for sale for only the third time in 15 years.

Extremely Rare Proposal for a Sovereign Struck in Silver

1 **George III,** Pattern Sovereign 1816, struck in silver, engraved by Thomas Wyon Jnr after Pistrucci's model, laureate head right, with ties at back, four leaves at top of laurel wreath that consists of 13 leaves, toothed border both sides, legend GEORGIUS III DEI GRATIA, no punctuation, *rev* struck en médaille, crowned square shield of arms, quartered with the arms of Hanover as an escutcheon, five strings to Irish harp, crown with eleven jewels on left arch, twelve on right arch, central crown upright with parallel vertical lines of jewels, five to left and six to right, date 18 16 below arms, legend BRITTANIARUM REX FID: DEF: with colon stops, edge obliquely grained milling, 5.57g, 23.1mm (cf WR 187; Montagu 587). *Once polished and lacquered, as is typical of King Farouk provenance pieces, and a little unevenly toned, otherwise good extremely fine and of the highest rarity.* £4000-6000

Price Realised : £5,040

ex King Farouk, Palace Collections of Egypt, Sothebys, from 24 February 1954, Cairo, Egypt, lot 2334 (part)
Herman Selig Collection (part II), Coins of George III, Spink Auction 131, 2 March 1999, lot 1168
The key features of this early pattern are Wyon's George III portrait as used and adopted for the silver Shilling, the 13 leaf wreath with four leaves at the top, five strings to the Irish harp, and the crown on shield with 11/12 pearl arrangement with a 5/6 arrangement on the central vertical.

Extremely Rare Silver Pattern for a Sovereign, Undated, c.1816

933 **George III,** Pattern Sovereign, undated, struck in silver, engraved by Thomas Wyon Jnr after Pistrucci's model, laureate head right, with ties at back, four leaves at top of laurel wreath that consists of 13 leaves, toothed border on obverse only, legend GEORGIUS III DEI GRATIA no punctuation, *rev* struck en médaille, crowned square shield of arms, quartered with the arms of Hanover as an escutcheon, five strings to Irish harp, crown with twelve jewels on left arch, twelve on right arch, central crown upright with parallel vertical lines of jewels, seven to left and seven to right, legend BRITTANIARUM REX FIDEI DEFENSOR, no punctuation, last word weak so that upper serifs on letters absent or weak, edge straight grained milling, 5.64g, 23.7mm (cf WR 183; Montagu 588; Murdoch 253; ESC 1245 R6). *With an attractive dark tone, apart from weakness in striking of legend, good extremely fine and of the highest rarity.* £4000-5000

Price Realised : £8,160

ex B A Seaby Ltd, February 1977

ex Herman Selig collection (part II), Coins of George III, Spink Auction 131, 2 March 1999, lot 1169

The key features of this early undated pattern are Wyon's George III portrait as used and adopted for the silver Shilling, the 13 leaf wreath with 4 leaves at the top, 5 strings to the Irish harp, as the dated silver pattern from the Bentley Collection (lot 1, page 15), though this rendering is perhaps earlier as it is undated and the reverse has a different arrangement of the crown jewel band and arches.

Extremely Rare Gold Pattern for a Sovereign, dated 1816

934 **George III,** Pattern Sovereign, 1816, engraved by Thomas Wyon Jnr after Pistrucci's model, laureate head right, with ties at back, four leaves at top of laurel wreath that consists of 13 leaves, toothed border both sides, legend GEORGIUS III DEI GRATIA, no punctuation, *rev* inverted die axis, crowned square shield of arms, quartered with the arms of Hanover as an escutcheon, five strings to Irish harp, crown with eleven jewels on left arch, twelve on right arch, central crown upright with parallel vertical lines of jewels, six to left and seven to right, date 18 16 below arms, legend commences at lower left, BRITTANIARUM REX FID: DEF:, with colon stops, edge plain, 9.67g, 23mm (WR 187 R6, *this coin*; Montagu 538; Murdoch 181; Douglas-Morris 125; Selig 1167, *this coin*). *Quite hairlined with some tiny blemishes, otherwise practically as struck and of the highest rarity, the plate coin in the Wilson and Rasmussen publication.* £15,000-20,000

Price Realised : £22,800

ex J G Brooker collection, milled gold collection, sold privately to Spink and Son, c.1970
ex Herman Selig collection (part II), Coins of George III, Spink Auction 131, 2 March 1999, lot 1167
The key features of this early pattern are Wyon's George III portrait as used and adopted for the silver Shilling, the 13 leaf wreath with 4 leaves at the top, 5 strings to the Irish harp, and the crown on shield with 11/12 pearl arrangement with a 6/7 arrangement on the central vertical.

Extremely Rare Pattern Sovereign of 1816 Engraved by Thomas Wyon

2 **George III,** Pattern Sovereign 1816, engraved by Thomas Wyon Jnr after Pistrucci's cameo, larger laureate head right, with ties at rear, four distinct leaves at top of laurel wreath that consists of 14 leaves, toothed border both sides, obverse struck slightly off-centre, legend in small letters both sides, GEORGIUS III D: G: BRITT: REX F: D:, *rev* struck en médaille, die flaw into crown and another in legend, crowned square shield of arms quartered with the arms of Hanover as an escutcheon, five strings to Irish harp, crown with twelve jewels on each arch, central crown upright with parallel vertical lines of six jewels, taller cross on crown with horizontal line separating it from orb below, date 18 16 below arms lightly double struck, legend BRITTANIARUM REX FID: DEF:, edge plain, 9.53g, 22.1mm (WR 185 R6; Murdoch 185; Nobleman 43; Douglas-Morris 126). *Red tone spot by chin and smaller one below truncation, some light raised die flaws on the reverse, some hairlines, otherwise mint state and extremely rare.* £15,000-20,000

Price Realised : £21,600

ex R E Plumbridge collection, sold privately to A H Baldwin & Sons Ltd, c.1980
ex A H Baldwin & Sons Ltd, 125th Anniversary Sale, Baldwin's Auction 15, 13 October 1997, lot 43
The key features of this proposed pattern engraved by Wyon are the portrait with 14 leaf wreath, five strings to the Irish harp, and the crown arranged with pearls on the arches evenly balanced at twelve per side and six on each side of the central vertical. Note also the heavy weight of this impressive pattern.

An Extremely Rare Pattern Sovereign of 1816, Milled Edge Engraved by Thomas Wyon

382 **George III,** Pattern Sovereign 1816, engraved by Thomas Wyon Jnr. after Pistrucci's cameo, larger laureate head right, with ties at rear, four distinct leaves at top of laurel wreath that consists of 14 leaves, toothed border both sides, obverse struck slightly off-centre, legend in small letters both sides, GEORGIUS III D: G: BRITT: REX F: D:, *rev* struck en médaille, die flaw into crown and another in legend, crowned square shield of arms quartered with the arms of Hanover as an escutcheon, 5 strings to Irish harp, crown with 12 jewels on each arch, central crown upright with parallel vertical lines of 6 jewels, taller cross on crown with horizontal line separating it from orb below, date 18 16 below arms lightly double struck, legend BRITTANIARUM REX FID: DEF: edge, straight grained milled, 7.97g, 22.1mm (WR 186 R6 *this coin*; Murdoch 187; DM -). *Tiny pin-point sized black spots below ear lobe, lightly toned, otherwise mint state and extremely rare.* £15,000-20,000

Price Realised : £25,200

ex Virgil M Brand collection, dispersed post mortem from 1932
ex Herman Selig collection, Spink Auction 131, 2 March 1999, lot 1171 – the plate coin in Wilson and Rasmussen
The key features of this proposed pattern engraved by Wyon are the portrait with 14 leaf wreath, five strings to the Irish harp and the crown arranged with pearls on the arches evenly balanced at twelve per side and six on each side of the central vertical. This is the companion piece to Lot 2 of the Bentley Collection (above) which has a plain edge; we note that the milled edge piece offered here is of a significantly lower weight than the heavy weight plain edge piece.

Uniface Trial Reverse for a Pattern Sovereign struck in Gold, c.1817

935 **George III,** Uniface Gold Trial Reverse Sovereign, undated, struck c.1817, engraved by Benedetto Pistrucci, St George, helmeted with flowing streamer and cloak, slaying dragon right with broken lance, unlike currency issue, left forearm visible holding rein of horse, dragon at an unfinished stage, no tongue, with filled mouth, dragon claws triangular and stubby, groundline with BP incuse to left, all within horizontally crudely ruled garter with buckle, W W P incuse on sides of buckle, garter motto HONI . SOIT . QUI . MAL . Y . PENSE ., letter I of first word fully apparent, all struck slightly off-centre, edge plain, 7.97g, 22.9mm, thickness 0.75mm (WR 190 R7; Murdoch 189; BDM vol. IV, pp.586-589, 600-601). *Toned, as struck and the only known specimen, unique.* £10,000-15,000

Price Realised : £11,040

most likely ex Benedetto Pistrucci collection and subsequently J G Murdoch collection, Sothebys, 15 March 1904, lot 189, sold for £2/12/-
ex Sotheby, 26 April 1996, lot 640

This piece is of the utmost historical significance and is very unusual, being a uniface piece struck in gold. Such uniface trials were usually made in base metals, gold flans were not generally used for uniface trials unless of the highest importance. This piece was probably used by Pistrucci himself to show how close the design was to acceptable currency, it depicts St George and dragon at a very late design stage. The most interesting aspect being the treatment of the left forearm of St George gripping the rein of the horse. Other unfinished aspects are also noted upon the dragon, otherwise the rest of the design is as adopted for currency. No doubt the piece was produced in early 1817. The Sotheby catalogue of 1996 suggests this coin may be associated with a group of coins known to have been ordered by the Master of the Mint, William Wellesley Pole, for presentation to Pistrucci as way of consolation, the latter being a very volatile character. This piece was in Pistrucci's collection as "No.3" and later found its way to the Murdoch collection where it was sold without a plate illustration. Pistrucci's notes were quoted in part in the catalogue and in relation to this piece his notes translate as:-

This St George is the finest work I have done in my life with the graving-tool, and for this reason the public will excuse if it is not so fine as the later ones; besides, it was spoiled through mechanical operations at the Mint, or by accident, or maliciously, in order that my work should appear before the public more imperfect than that which I knew to be without taste.

A sense of his mood is clearly seen by his comments. Another relevant comment in Pistrucci's notes subsequent to the piece offered here and in relation to the eventual current coin reverse design is:-

...they made me change the hand, which was at first showing a portion of the arm, to what is now seen on the current coins....

It is highly likely this piece is the one that was in the Murdoch sale, the research suggests such a uniface piece in gold would be a one-off if trying to console Pistrucci. Any original Pistrucci notes offered with such a coin in the Murdoch collection in 1904 are now sadly detached.

Uniface Trial Reverse for a Sovereign struck in Lead, c.1817

936 **George III,** Uniface Base Metal Trial Reverse for a Sovereign, undated, c.1816-1817, struck in lead, engraved by Benedetto Pistrucci, St George, helmeted with thin streamer and cloak, slaying dragon right without broken lance, only left hand visible griping rein as currency piece, design cruder and unfinished, groundline incomplete at left, and tail of horse incomplete and truncated, neck of horse thinner, dragon crude and of thin appearance, 6.06g, 22.6-23.3mm, thickness 1.5mm (WR -; Douglas-Morris -). *Unrecorded in all the standard works of reference, as made with usual associated weaknesses for a lead striking, a little ovoid in shape, rim nicks and scratches on plain side, extremely fine and possibly unique.* £800-1000

Price Realised : £720

This piece appears to be an earlier rendering of the reverse, perhaps an initial phase as many aspects are either incomplete or more basically rendered. Trials of this nature are usually only ever "squeezed" from a working die in uniface format in base metal because impressions can be taken from an unhardened die. Silver and gold require a hardened die, after which further work on the die is not possible.

A Wonderful Proof Sovereign of the Initial Year of Issue of King George III

3 **George III,** Proof Sovereign, 1817, engraved by Benedetto Pistrucci, first laureate head right, coarse hair, laurel wreath of 10 leaves, date below, descending colon after BRITANNIAR:, lettering clear of raised rim, legend GEORGIUS III D: G: BRITANNIAR: REX F: D:, third I of III missing its top left serif, *rev* struck with inverted die axis, St George on horseback slaying dragon right with broken lance, helmet with flowing streamer, ground-line with BP incuse to left, all within horizontally ruled garter with buckle, W W P incuse on sides of buckle, garter motto HONI. SOIT. QUI. MAL. Y. PENSE., I of HONI missing its top left serif, edge milled, 8.00g (WR 197 R5; Murdoch 192; Nobleman 47; DM 140; S 3785). *Some red tone spots and tiny associated hairline surface marks, otherwise brilliant as struck and extremely rare.* £15,000-20,000

Price Realised : £27,600

ex Randy Weir Numismatics, Unionville, Ontario, Canada, purchased c.1990 – appropriately the first major proof rarity purchased for the collection.
One of the key features of the design of this proof as adopted and engraved for currency by Pistrucci are the wreath of 10 leaves and the date below the bust, coupled of course with St George slaying the dragon. Some of the letters in the legend lack serifs, no doubt due to blockages or faulty letter punches with corner serifs broken off being employed. A discussion about these is highlighted in a note on varieties at the start of this catalogue.

4 **George III,** Sovereign, 1817, first laureate head right, coarse hair, date below, no upper serifs to first I of legend, no upper right serif to penultimate I, *rev* St George slaying dragon right with broken lance, the last three words of motto double struck, no upper left serif to I of HONI, raised die flaw on H, T and Q of motto, 7.97g (Marsh 1; MCE 464; S 3785). *Brilliant uncirculated.* £2000-2500

Price Realised : £4,320

ex Randy Weir Numismatics, Unionville, Ontario, Canada, purchased 5 January 1989
Calendar year mintage 3,235,239
Some of the letters in the legend lack serifs, no doubt due to blockages or the employment of faulty letter punches with corner serifs broken off to prepare the dies. A discussion about these is highlighted in a note on varieties at the start of this catalogue.

Extremely Rare 1817 Sovereign Struck with an Upright Die Axis

5 **George III,** Sovereign, 1817, struck with an upright die axis, first laureate head right, coarse hair, date below, *rev* struck en médaille, St George slaying dragon right with broken lance, the last three words of motto double struck, no upper left serif to I of HONI, no bottom left serif to I of SOIT, 7.98g (Marsh 1; MCE 464; S 3785). *Cleaned and gilt, good fine and extremely rare.* £1200-1500

Price Realised : £1,320

ex Spink and Son Ltd, March 2004
Calendar year mintage 3,235,239
This cataloguer has seen no more than four specimens of this die axis variety.

1817 Sovereign with Absent Serifs on Numerals and Letters

383 **George III,** Sovereign, 1817, engraved by Benedetto Pistrucci, second 1 with no serifs top or bottom, no upper serifs to figures I in king's name and numerals, first laureate head right, coarse hair, date below, raised rim both sides, *rev* inverted die axis, St George slaying dragon right with broken lance, the last three words of motto double struck, no upper left serif to I of HONI, no bottom left serif to I of SOIT, weak MAL Y, 7.99g (Marsh 1; MCE 464; S 3785). *Brilliant, some light marks, extremely fine and rare.* £1500-1800

Price Realised : £2,400

ex Noble Investments (UK) PLC, London, 21 November 2005
The missing serifs seem to be a product of weak striking and preparation of the dies. This was highlighted under "a note on varieties" in the introduction.
Calendar year mintage 3,235,239

937

938

937 **George III,** Sovereign, 1817, first laureate head right, coarse hair, date below, no upper serifs to fourth and fifth I's of obverse legend, other serifs weak, *rev* St George slaying dragon right with broken lance, the last three words of motto double struck, no upper left serif to I of HONI, raised rim both sides, 7.91g (Marsh 1; MCE 464; S 3785). *Toned, bold fine with associated marks and hairlines.* £300-400

Price Realised : £360

purchased via A H Baldwin & Sons Ltd, March 2006
Some of the letters in the legend lack serifs, no doubt due to blockages or the employment of faulty letter punches, with corner serifs broken off, to prepare the dies. See the introduction to this catalogue for a discussion about this. It is also interesting to note that the weight of this coin in its lower grade is under the legal tender limit as dictated by the Coinage Acts of 1816-1891.
Calendar year mintage 3,235,239

938 **George III,** Sovereign, 1817, first laureate head right, coarse hair, date below, no upper right serif to fifth I of obverse legend, *rev* St George slaying dragon right with broken lance, the last three words of motto double struck, no upper left serif to I of HONI, raised rim both sides, 7.98g (Marsh 1; MCE 464; S 3785). *Brilliant, lightly toned in reverse legend, otherwise good very fine.* £600-800

Price Realised : £1,032

purchased via A H Baldwin & Sons Ltd, April 2009
Some of the letters in the legend lack serifs, no doubt due to blockages or the employment of faulty letter punches, with corner serifs broken off, to prepare the dies. See the introduction to this catalogue for a discussion about this.
Calendar year mintage 3,235,239

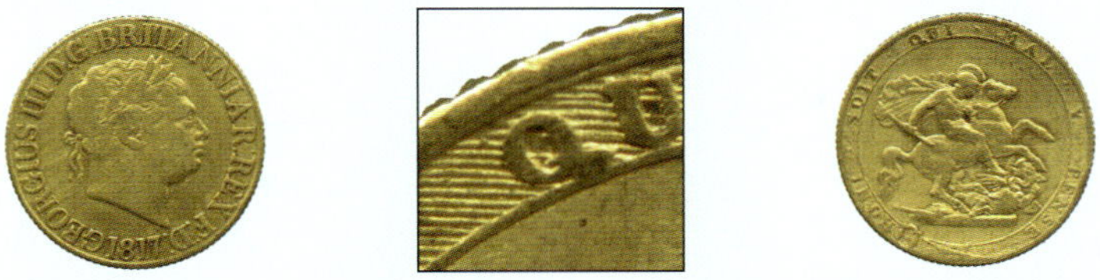

939 **George III,** Sovereign, 1817, first laureate head right, coarse hair, date below, *rev* St George slaying dragon right with broken lance, the last three words of motto double struck, no upper left serif to I of HONI, thick tailed Q in legend, due to a die flaw, raised rim both sides, 7.87g (Marsh 1; MCE 464; S 3785). *Almost fine with associated marks and hairlines, unusual.* £300-400

Price Realised : £384

purchased via A H Baldwin & Sons Ltd, March 2006
It would appear that a slight imperfection in the die opened up on the tail of the letter Q and metal filled the area giving a thicker tail on the coin struck from this reverse die. The die probably was reaching the end of its useful service anyway and this imperfection may well have sealed its fate. It is also interesting to note that the weight of this coin in its lower grade is under the legal tender limit as dictated by the Coinage Acts of 1816-1891. Calendar year mintage 3,235,239

Extremely Rare Proof Sovereign, dated 1818

940 **George III,** Proof Sovereign, 1818, engraved by Benedetto Pistrucci, first laureate head right, coarse hair, laurel wreath of 10 leaves, date below, ascending colon after BRITANNIAR, with no lower right serif to first I, no upper serifs to last four letters, lettering clear of raised rim, legend GEORGIUS III D: G: BRITANNIAR: REX F: D:, I of King's name missing lower right serif, *rev* struck with inverted die axis, St George on horseback slaying dragon right with broken lance, helmet with flowing streamer, ground-line with BP incuse to left, all within horizontally ruled garter with buckle, W W P incuse on sides of buckle, garter motto HONI. SOIT. QUI. MAL. Y. PENSE., I of HONI missing top left serif, raised rim both sides, edge milled, 7.98g (WR 198 R6; Murdoch 193; Nobleman 49/50; Douglas-Morris 142; S 3785A). *Tiny pinhead sized black spot on nape of neck and on temple, some hairlines, otherwise brilliant as struck and extremely rare.* £15,000-20,000

Price Realised : £26,400

ex Property of Gentleman collection, Spink Auction 117, 19 November 1997, lot 1961
One of the key features of the design of this proof as adopted and engraved for currency by Pistrucci are the wreath of 10 leaves and the date below the bust, coupled with St George slaying the dragon. Some of the letters in the legend lack serifs, no doubt due to blockages or faulty letter punches, with corner serifs broken off, being employed. See the introduction to this catalogue for a discussion about this.

descending colon variety

6 **George III,** Sovereign, 1818, first laureate head right, coarse hair, date below, descending colon variety, *rev* St George slaying dragon right with broken lance, no upper left serif to I of HONI, 7.98g (Marsh 2; MCE 465; S 3785). *A few light tiny digs on the obverse, one small rim nick, otherwise good extremely fine and rare.* £4000-5000

Price Realised : £7,680

ex Randy Weir Numismatics, Unionville, Ontario, Canada, purchased 2 April 1990
Calendar year mintage 2,347,230
The other variety in the Bentley Collection is the "ascending colon" type is listed as lot 384 below.

Very Rare 1818 Gold Sovereign with Ascending Colon

ascending colon in legend

384 **George III,** Sovereign, 1818, ascending colon variety, first laureate head right, coarse hair, date below, a mere trace of lower right serif to second 1 of date, raised rim both sides, *rev* St George slaying dragon right with broken lance, no upper left serif to I of HONI, 7.97g (Marsh 2A; MCE 465; S 3785A). *Red tone with underlying brilliance, very pleasing, good extremely fine and rare.* £4000-5000

Price Realised : £6,960

Calendar year mintage 2,347,230
A proof quality striking of this variety is listed as lot 940 above.

The Finest Known Example of the Legendary 1819 Sovereign

941 **George III,** Sovereign, 1819, by Benedetto Pistrucci, laureate head right, coarse hair, date below, descending colon after BRITANNIAR:, legend GEORGIUS III D: G: BRITANNIAR: REX F: D:, *rev* struck with inverted die axis, St George slaying dragon right with broken lance, groundline with BP incuse to left, all within horizontally ruled garter with buckle, W W P incuse on sides of buckle, garter motto HONI . SOIT . QUI . MAL . Y . PENSE ., no upper left serif to I of HONI, raised rim both sides, edge milled, 7.97g (Marsh 3 R6, *this coin illustrated,* plate 3; MCE 466; S 3785; BDM vol. IV, p.601, *1819 illustrated*). *Light red tone, lightly hairlined with a few tiny spots and flecks, about extremely fine and the finest known specimen extant, the key date to the entire series of British Sovereigns minted by the Royal Mint, of the highest rarity.* £150,000-200,000

Price Realised : £186,000

ex Sothebys auction, 15 October 1998, lot 286, sold for £55,000 (including premium)
Calendar year mintage 3,574

The classic rarity of the London series. The Bentley Collection specimen is the finest known in private ownership by a full British grading step. All other known specimens are in the region of poor to fair or fine condition, with only one approaching very fine.

There are still fewer than ten specimens known to be in private hands, and the purported proof version (if correctly identified as such) is unknown to modern numismatists (Murdoch 194 = WR199). Having not been seen for over 70 years since the "North Country Collector" sale of 1939.

Duveen and Stride, in the their 1962 publication *The History of the Gold Sovereign,* throw some light on the matter of the rarity of 1819 Sovereigns and the very low calendar year mintage when they say that specie payments by the Bank of England were suspended so only £3,574 worth of sovereigns were produced in that calendar year.

In the publication *Royal Sovereign 1489-1989,* edited by G P Dyer, there is an 1819 Sovereign in good fine quality illustrated on page 44. In the chapter on *The Modern Sovereign,* Graham Dyer remarks that in 1819 the Norfolk Banker Hudson Gurney told a Parliamentary Committee that he had never seen a new Sovereign in circulation. The preference of the public at that time was for spending and saving with banknotes instead of gold. It has been suggested that most of the new sovereigns of 1817 found their way overseas, with tourists wanting to spend freely on the continent, and therefore the subsequent demand diminishing into the 1818 issue and beyond. Once restrictions on payment of gold were removed by the Bank of England from 1820-1823, the Sovereign became more firmly established and took over as the payment medium from banknotes.

For further reading see *The Mint,* by John Craig, page 289, where he mentions that the minting of Sovereigns in 1819 and early 1820 was negligible. More up to date, Kevin Clancy, in his article on *The Ricardo Ingot* in the British Numismatic Journal 2001, p.172-174, alludes to there being only six known specimens of the 1819 Sovereign. Interestingly the notion of an ingot of gold in 1819 was raised by David Ricardo and progressed as far as an 1819 tin ingot being produced (an example of which appeared for sale at a DNW auction in June 2009, lot 418). These high value ingots were to be used to limit gold transactions to a small sphere of institutions and companies. The ingots were to feature four current coin designs, that of the gold Sovereign obverse dated 1819 which matches the obverse of the known currency 1819 Sovereigns, silver Crown reverse, Halfcrown reverse and Shilling obverse which also carried the date 1819.

Further work, in collaboration with the Royal Mint, has revealed some more interesting factual evidence about the issue of 1819 Sovereigns. 3,574 were struck, a very small total that could easily have been produced in one "journey" at the Mint (one day striking). However unusually the records show this total was struck over five instalments from August to November 1819 and not from gold supplied by the Bank of England in the usual way. The gold to strike the 1819 Sovereigns all emanated from private sources, most likely firms in the City of London. There is a written record of "Haldimand and Co." converting gold into current coin, perhaps to pay suppliers or Director's salaries. We know the coins did circulate, not just on the evidence of the worn coins seen today, but also other contemporary evidence.

In 1829 the Mint, in collaboration with the Bank of England, conducted a survey of the gold Sovereigns in circulation to investigate how much silver was alloyed with the gold. The Mint asked the Bank of England to locate 100 examples of each date of the Sovereign then in circulation from 1817 onward. The Bank managed to locate all that was asked for from its reserves, except for the date of 1819, of which it could only find **two** circulated examples in its holdings, this only ten years after issue. As a consequence, these two examples were excluded from the alloy melting experiment, though their later fate is unknown, perhaps finding their way to collectors.

Further evidence of circulation was provided by another survey carried out by a private banker named Martin in 1882. He conducted a huge survey of some 105,000 Sovereigns then in circulation to see how they were faring and the condition and state of the coin, in a move to have earlier worn coin withdrawn from circulation, which it subsequently was when pre-1838 dated Sovereigns were made non-legal tender. Mr Martin sourced details on dates and weights of Sovereigns nationally from banks, post offices, railway stations and anywhere else gold sovereigns were transacted, perhaps 100 pieces or more were surveyed by clerks from each source. Of the 105,000 Sovereigns surveyed only **two** pieces were reported dated 1819, this only 63 years after their issue.

At the meeting of the Numismatic Society in London, 17 December 1891, Mr J Clark exhibited examples of the 1817 and 1819 Sovereigns in "fine" condition for all attendees to see, this is mentioned in the proceedings from the 1892 volume of the Numismatic Chronicle. Perhaps this 1819 was one of the pieces surveyed in 1882 or 1829?

Interestingly, an article by Dr Philip Nelson appeared in the Spink Numismatic Circular of July 1904 listing English gold coins a mere four months after the Murdoch Sale; in the tabulation of gold coins the 1819 Sovereign is absent. This is later pointed out by correspondent Henry Garside in the November 1904 Numismatic Circular who remarks he once had a circulated example which he later lost! The Proof 1819 Sovereign appears for sale in the Spink Numismatic Circular of December 1905.

In *Sovereigns of the British Empire*, published in 1965 by Spink, Capt J J Cullimore Allen remarks that he had been unable to trace the existence of any example until the October before publication of the book, which he viewed and purchased. His collection was sold in Spink Auction 90 in 1992, as featured below. He also remarks that he had heard of an 1819 Proof Sovereign, no doubt a reference to the Murdoch lot 194 example, but of course he never confirmed or saw such a coin. Finally he confirms the National Collection in the British Museum does not contain one.
In the Seaby Coin and Medal Bulletin of July 1964 (page 256) there is a contemporary theory that the 1819 Sovereign was not struck for currency, and the only one publicly sold was the proof example. Some numismatists theorised that perhaps the £3,574 were all dated 1818, but the listing of a circulated example in the Bulletin (G1652) spoke for itself. Subsequent later research as detailed above has of course proven it was a small issue only for currency, all dated 1819.
Graham Dyer of the Royal Mint also confirms he has not come across any examples of the 1819 Sovereign in institutional collections. The cataloguer acknowledges the assistance of Mr Dyer and Chris Barker of the Royal Mint for their assistance in detailing some of the facts behind the issue of this, the rarest London Sovereign.

We attempt to list all the publicly sold 1819 Sovereigns proven to be in private hands as of 2013:

1) 1819 Sovereign, *extremely fine*
The Bentley Collection part III, lot 941 – ex Sothebys auction, 15 October 1998, lot 286, where mentioned there were five specimens known to the cataloguers at that time.

2) 1819 Sovereign, *good fine*
ex Seaby Coin and Medal Bulletin, July 1964 front cover coin, G1652 for £1000, sold to Capt J J Cullimore Allen (author of *Sovereigns of the British Empire*)
sold later as "Property of a Lady", Spink Auction 90, 15 March 1992, lot 334 for £15,500 hammer
offered in Mark Rasmussen List 12, Spring 2007, item S2 for £35,000
offered St James's Auction 7, 8 February 2008, lot 559, unsold
sold St James's Auction 11, 8 May 2009, lot 357, for £46,000 hammer.

3) 1819 Sovereign, *fine*
Classical Numismatic Group, Auction 36, 5 December 1995, lot 1604, for $18,000
later Spink Numismatic Circular, December 2007, item MG1882, *brushed with scratch on cheek, good fine*, £48,500
later appeared at Spink Auction 197, November 2008, lot 548, sold to A H Baldwin & Sons Ltd and offered and sold on their Summer 2009 Fixed Price List, item BM021 at £40,000.

4) 1819 Sovereign, *poor, ex-mount with solder around the edge*
offered with scroll mount attached in Spink Auction 140, 16 November 1999, lot 973 as sixth specimen known, *gilt and fair*
then appeared minus scroll mount in Spink Numismatic Circular October 2000, item 1995 for £8500, sold to a private collector
later appearing on Mark Rasmussen Numismatist List 3, September 2002, £9000 retail
not recorded on the market publicly since.

5) 1819 Sovereign, *ex-ring mount with solder and sweated, otherwise poor to fair*
sold Prof. R E Gibson Collection, Spink auction 40, 6th December 1984, lot 505 for £3,100 hammer to Spink Zürich and sold on to a German private collection. The cataloguers of 1984 said "very few specimens known" and the Baldwin marked copy of the catalogue has "(3?)" noted by hand.

6) 1819 Sovereign, *holed with porous surfaces, poor to fair*
first appeared un-illustrated in Glendinings, 12 February 1970, lot 75, when Michael Marsh missed a chance to purchase it as he laments in his first edition of the *Gold Sovereign*
next appeared in Glendinings, 10 February 1999, lot 66, sold for £4100 hammer to the collector who, as he completed his date run, promptly consigned his collection as one lot to Sothebys, An Important Collection of Gold Sovereigns 1816-2000, 16 November 2000, lot 525, which was unsold and later dispersed within the trade
next appeared at the "Tood Collection", DNW Sale 67, 28 September 2005, lot 165, £7,200 hammer
the next public appearance was in the "Horan" collection on Mark Rasmussen list 14, winter 2007/8, item S3, offered for £12,000
then after at St James's Auction 9, 18 June 2008, lot 423, £5100 hammer, this coin is now in a private collection.

7) Should the 1819 Proof Sovereign listed as WR199 ever come to light again it does have a fuller provenance:
ex Marmaduke Trattle, Sothebys, 30 May 1832, lot 3301, sold with an 1820 Proof for 3-Guineas to Baron Boland
then Baron Boland, Sothebys, 21 April 1841, lot 403, lotted with an 1820 Sovereign but not mentioned as proofs, for £2/5/- to the dealer Cureton
Research is on-going for a further appearance in the interim, but the next occasion seems to be
ex J G Murdoch, Sothebys, 15 March 1904, lot 194, sold for £3/7/- to Spink
then Spink Numismatic Circular December 1905, item 22445, illustrated for the first time (same illustration used in the Biographical Dictionary, published in 1909), offered for £5/5/-
then a final appearance to date in North Country Collector collection, Glendinings, 23 May 1939, lot 134, sold to A H Baldwin & Sons Ltd for £10, no trace after this date.

8) The 1819 Sovereign illustrated in the *Royal Sovereign 1489-1989*, page 44, does not match any of those listed in private ownership, and is not in the Royal Mint Collection.
It appears that most, if not all, of the Institutional coin collections in the UK, do not possess an 1819 Sovereign. The coin pictured in the *Royal Sovereign* is from the Royal Mint photographic records of coins shown to them for authentication. The piece in question was shown to the Mint personnel, via B A Seaby, in June 1974, seemingly on behalf of a private individual on the Continent. A cursory check of Seaby Coin Bulletins subsequent of that that time to the end of 1975 has not revealed any more information on this coin or any example for sale. If this coin still exists in private ownership today it takes the tally of coins to seven currency examples extant that have been photographed, of which the Bentley example is the finest known.

Second Laureate Head of King George III

Second bust type with finer engraved hair

Pistrucci took the opportunity from 1818-1820 to update his first obverse design for George III, with a second rendition of the bust of George III with different treatment of the hair strands upon the head. The legend variety is always with the ascending colon, the rim beyond the legend is also rendered differently to the previous issues. A note must be added concerning the mintage figures as those always quoted in publications only ever represent what the Mint struck from January to December of any given year. It is a well known fact that much of the mintage of 1820 dated coins continued well into 1821 and Marsh quotes an adjusted figure of estimation of 1820 Sovereigns of 2,101,994.
Some publications suggest that an 1818 dated Sovereign exists with this second type of bust, however the Bentley Collection does not contain an example of this new bust on an 1818 dated Sovereign, and this cataloguer has never seen one (yet). Therefore this second bust on an 1818 Sovereign must be extremely rare. The only other major rarity of the reign of George III the Bentley Collection lacks is the 1820 Sovereign with Roman letter I in date, as illustrated in one of the plates in Marsh's Gold Sovereign publication. The cataloguer has only ever seen three specimens of this variety.

The Extremely Rare Proof Sovereign of 1820

385 **George III,** Proof Sovereign, 1820, open 2, normal date arrangement, second laureate head right, finer engraved hair tightly curled, date below, date with 20 larger than 18, the initial G of legend turned more in line with date, ascending colon after BRITANNIAR:, lettering clear of thinner raised rim, only a trace of outer linear circle on obverse, *rev* St George slaying dragon right with broken lance, trace of upper left serif to I of HONI, weak MAL Y, 8.00g (WR 200 R7; S 3785C). *A few light hairlines and tiny dig on cheek, otherwise mint state and of the highest rarity according to Wilson and Rasmussen.* £15,000-20,000

Price Realised : £15,600

It is interesting to note in the finer detail of this proof issue that the upper left serif of I in HONI is not absent as it always seems to be on the currency examples. Perhaps this is a diagnostic of the true proof issue.
ex Sothebys, 17 November 2000, lot 525 (part), illustrated as No.7

normal date with open 2

7 **George III,** Sovereign, 1820, open 2, normal date arrangement, second laureate head right, finer engraved hair, date below, large date with high 8 and open 2, with spread 20 larger than 18, the initial G of legend turned more in line with date, 0 of date more angled and facing to right, ascending colon after BRITANNIAR:, slightly doubled lettering in obverse legend, larger space between X and F with double cut F colon, lettering clear of thinner raised rim, only a trace of outer linear circle, *rev* St George slaying dragon right with broken lance, no upper left serif to I of HONI, hairline flaw in garter and at T of SOIT, 7.99g (cf Marsh 4; MCE 466; S 3785C). *Light black streak on exergue, otherwise practically as struck with just a few light hairlines, rare this nice.* £2000-2500

Price Realised : £4,080

ex Randy Weir Numismatics, Unionville, Ontario, Canada, purchased 22 March 1990
Calendar year mintage 931,994

942 **George III,** Sovereign, 1820, open 2, normal date arrangement, second laureate head right, finer engraved hair, date below, large date with high 8 and open 2, with spread 20 larger than 18, the initial G of legend turned more in line with date, 0 of date more angled and facing to right, ascending colon after BRITANNIAR:, slightly doubled lettering in obverse legend, larger space between X and F with double cut F colon, lettering clear of thinner raised rim, only a trace of outer linear circle, *rev* St George slaying dragon right with broken lance, no upper left serif to I of HONI, or I of QUI, thin raised rim with a trace of linear circle, 8.00g (cf Marsh 4; MCE 466; S 3785C). *Quite hairlined, extremely fine.* £1200-1500

Price Realised : £1,620

ex Northeast Numismatics, Massachusetts, purchased 14 January 2005
Calendar year mintage 931,994

387 **George III,** Sovereign, 1820, open 2, normal date arrangement, second laureate head right, finer engraved hair, date below, thin top heavy open 2 in date with tail upward, higher than 0, 8 and 2 spaced apart, 20 out of line from 18, the initial G of legend halfway turned towards date, ascending colon after BRITANNIAR:, lettering clear of thinner raised rim, some obverse letters slightly doubled, only a trace of outer linear circle on obverse, *rev* St George slaying dragon right with broken lance, trace of upper left serif to I of HONI, S of SOIT with broken upper curve, 7.92g (cf Marsh 4B R; MCE 466; S 3785C). *Surface marks, some light deposits of dirt removed, fine to good fine.* £500-600

Price Realised : £480

ex Reserve Bank of Australia Sale, Downies, 29-30th November 2005, lot 1134
purchased via Winsor and Sons, Jamberoo, Australia and through A H Baldwin & Sons Ltd, 4 December 2006
Calendar year mintage 931,994
It is interesting to note that, as one of the lower grade Sovereigns in the Bentley Collection, this coin is well under the legal tender weight limit that was set in successive Coinage Acts from 1816-1891.

neater date arrangement with closed 2

8 **George III,** Sovereign, 1820, closed 2, neater smaller date arrangement, second laureate head right, finer engraved hair, slight raised die flaw from nape of neck, finer date below, the initial G of legend halfway turned towards date, closed 2 with thinner finer engraved 0, 8 and 2 spaced apart, 20 slightly smaller than 18 and in line, ascending colon after BRITANNIAR:, larger space between X and F, some obverse letters slightly doubled, lettering clear of thinner raised rim, only a trace of outer linear circle, *rev* St George slaying dragon right with broken lance, no upper left serif to I of HONI, S of SOIT with broken upper curve, no upper right serif to I of QUI, 7.98g (cf Marsh 4B R; MCE 466; S 3785C). *Two digs in obverse field, light rim nicks, good extremely fine and a rare date variety.* £1800-2200

Price Realised : £2,400

ex Property of a Gentleman, Spink Auction 117, 19 November 1997, lot 1979
Calendar year mintage 931,994

386 **George III,** Sovereign, 1820, closed 2, neater smaller date arrangement, second laureate head right, finer engraved hair, with misstruck rim milling encroaching onto obverse from 10-1 o'clock, finer date below, the initial G of legend halfway turned towards date, closed 2 with thinner finer engraved 0, 8 and 2 spaced apart, 20 slightly smaller than 18 and in line, ascending colon after BRITANNIAR:, larger space between X and F, some obverse letters slightly doubled, lettering clear of thinner raised rim, only a trace of outer linear circle, *rev* St George slaying dragon right with broken lance, no upper left serif to I of HONI, S of SOIT with broken upper curve, 7.81g (cf Marsh 4B R; MCE 466; S 3785C). *Only fair and well below the legal weight for tender due to wear, nevertheless rare.* £400-500

Price Realised : £480

purchased via A H Baldwin & Sons Ltd, July 2010
Calendar year mintage 931,994
It is interesting to note that, as one of the lower grade Sovereigns in the Bentley Collection, this coin is well under the legal tender weight limit that was set in successive Coinage Acts from 1816-1891.

943 **George III,** Sovereign, 1820, practically closed 2, neater smaller date arrangement, thinner 0, second laureate head right, finer engraved hair, date below, the initial G of legend turned more in line with legend, but distant from date, ascending colon after BRITANNIAR:, lettering in obverse legend clear of thinly ruled raised rim, no linear circle, larger space between X and F, no doubling in legend, *rev* St George slaying dragon right with broken lance, no upper left serif to I of HONI, broken first S in legend, no upper right serif to U of QUI, 7.99g (cf Marsh 4; MCE 466; S 3785C). *One short scratch with light hairlining, otherwise proof-like, practically as struck.* £2500-3000

Price Realised : £4,560

Calendar year mintage 931,994

short date figures, closed 2

9 **George III,** Sovereign, 1820, short date figures, laureate head right, finer engraved hair, shorter thicker date below, with 2 that is almost closed, 8 and 2 spaced apart, 2 doubled, the initial G of legend turned in more in line with date, ascending colon after BRITANNIAR:, larger space between X and F, slightly doubled lettering in obverse legend, lettering clear of rim, no outer linear circle, *rev* St George slaying dragon right with broken lance, no upper left serif to I of HONI, S of SOIT with broken upper curve, 8.00g (Marsh 4A R; MCE 466; S 3785C). *Proof-like with just a few light hairlines, practically as struck, good extremely fine, a wonderful example of the rarest date variety in superb condition.* £2500-3000

Price Realised : £4,320

ex Randy Weir Numismatics, Unionville, Ontario, Canada, purchased 22 March 1990
Calendar year mintage 931,994

Short date figures, open 2

388 **George III,** Sovereign, 1820, short date figures, laureate head right, finer engraved hair, shorter thicker date below, high spread short date figures with open 2, 8 and 2 widely spaced apart, the initial G of legend close to 1 and turned in more in line with date, ascending colon after BRITANNIAR:, larger space between X and F, colon after double-cut, I and V in king's name touch at top, doubled lettering both sides, lettering clear of rim, and trace of outer linear circle, *rev* St George slaying dragon right with broken lance, no upper left serif to I of HONI, U of QUI flawed, 7.97g (Marsh 4A R; MCE 466; S 3785C). *Has been once lightly gilt and mounted, edge repair in milling, otherwise detail very good, better than extremely fine, the rarest date variety for 1820.* £800-1000

Price Realised : £792

purchased via Spink and Son, March 2004
Calendar year mintage 931,994

944 **George III,** Sovereign, 1820, short date figures, by Benedetto Pistrucci, laureate head right, coarse hair, date below, spread short date figures with open 2 almost closed, 8 and 2 widely spaced apart, first G of legend close to date, ascending colon after BRITANNIAR:, lettering clear of thin raised rim and linear circle, larger space between X and F, GEORGIUS III D: G: BRITANNIAR: REX F: D:, some letters of legend doubled, *rev* struck with inverted die axis, St George slaying dragon right with broken lance, groundline with BP incuse to left, all within horizontally ruled garter with buckle, W W P incuse on sides of buckle, garter motto HONI . SOIT . QUI . MAL . Y . PENSE ., no upper left serif to I of HONI, first S of legend broken, with letter U die flawed, 7.96g (cf Marsh 4; MCE 466; S 3785C). *Some brilliance, rim nick on reverse, about very fine and the rarest date variety.* £400-600

Price Realised : £792

Calendar year mintage 931,994

945 **George III,** Sovereign, 1820, short close date figures, date doubled, by Benedetto Pistrucci, laureate head right, coarse hair, date below, closer short date figures with open 2, 182 all in a line, the 0 die-flawed, G of legend close to 1 of date and turned toward it, ascending colon after BRITANNIAR:, lettering clear of thin worn rim, larger space between X and F, GEORGIUS III D: G: BRITANNIAR: REX F: D: F, colon double cut, *rev* struck with inverted die axis, St George slaying dragon right with broken lance, groundline with BP incuse to left, all within horizontally ruled garter with buckle, W W P incuse on sides of buckle, garter motto HONI . SOIT . QUI . MAL . Y . PENSE ., no upper left serif to I of HONI, S of legend complete, edge milled, 7.72g (cf Marsh 4; MCE 466; S 3785C). *Scratched on bust, mediocre to poor but a differing variety of date to that usually seen for the rare short date figures.* £250-300

Price Realised : £312

Calendar year mintage 931,994
It is also interesting to note that the weight of this coin in its lower grade is under the legal tender limit as dictated by the Coinage Acts of 1816-1891.

946 **George III,** Sovereign, 1820, open 2, date figures close though of normal arrangement, angled lower 0 with die flaw to rim, 2 nearly touches 8, second laureate head right, finer engraved hair, date below, the initial G of legend turned more in line with legend, but distant from date, ascending colon after BRITANNIAR:, lettering in obverse legend clear of thinly ruled raised rim, no linear circle, larger space between X and F, no doubling in legend, *rev* St George slaying dragon right with broken lance, no upper left serif to I of HONI, broken first S in legend, parts of motto wording weakly struck, no upper right serif to U of QUI, 7.94g (cf Marsh 4; MCE 466; S 3785C). *Edge knock, surface marks and hairlines, otherwise good fine.* £300-400

Price Realised : £432

Calendar year mintage 931,994
George III died 29 January 1820

open 2, 8 and 2 nearly touch

10 **George III,** Sovereign, 1820, large close date figures with open 2, laureate head right, finer engraved hair, date below, 8 and 2 nearly touching, raised die flaw between them, the initial G of legend turned in more in line with date, ascending colon after BRITANNIAR:, lettering clear of rim, the first A with filled top, larger space between X and F, *rev* struck with inverted die axis, St George slaying dragon right with broken lance, no upper left serif to I of HONI, 7.96g (Marsh 4; MCE 466; S 3785C). *Many light hairline marks, nearly extremely fine.* £1500-1800

Price Realised : £1,680

ex St James's Auction 5, 27 September 2006, lot 548
Calendar year mintage 931,994
George III died 29 January 1820

The Reign of King George IV (1820-1830)
House of Hanover

Born: 12 August 1762

Accession: 29 January 1820

Married: Caroline of Brunswick 8 April 1795
later separated and banned from attending the Coronation

Coronation: Thursday, 19 July 1821

Child: one daughter Charlotte
who predeceased her Father 6 November 1817

Died: 26 June 1830, aged 67

First Type

The reign of King George IV marks the highly significant introduction of the classic design of St George slaying the dragon with a sword by Benedetto Pistrucci we are all familiar with today. Pistrucci's depiction of the first bust of George IV is very Roman in its style with the King wearing a 13 leaf laurel wreath. Pistrucci's initials are for a gold coin, significantly prominent on each side of the coin, whereas with his previous George III issue they were incuse and quite well hidden under the broken lance. The initials of the Master of the Mint, William Wellesley Pole, who was instrumental in commissioning Pistrucci to the Mint in the first place, has his initials placed under the broken lance. The WWP appears quite squiggle-like and indistinct, and amazingly lasts in this position into the reign of George V over a hundred years later. These initials were on the Garter buckle on the reverse in the previous issue of George III.

First Type Obverse and Reverse of the George IV Currency Sovereign

Other features of the first standard design for the currency Sovereigns of King George IV from 1821-1825 are an unusual style of lettering in the legend which reads GEORGIUS IIII D: G: BRITANNIAR: REX F: D:, each letter has an incuse central compartment upon its limbs ruled with raised horizontal lines. A new type of outer border is employed with fine raised teeth between an inner and outer concentric linear circle, giving quite a square indent between each tooth. The currency coins are struck with an inverted die axis as usual for this period, the figure of St George now brandishes a sword to slay the dragon, his helmet has a crested plume only, and the horse's tail terminates in three strands. The broken lance with the initials beneath lies on the ground-line to the left, the date and B.P. initials are in the exergue below and the edge is straight grained milled.

947 **George IV (1820-1830),** Uniface Base Metal Trial Reverse for a Sovereign, undated (c.1821), struck in lead on an oversize flan, by Benedetto Pistrucci, crude design with thin aspects to figures, St George, helmeted with streamer and cloak, slaying dragon right with incomplete sword blade, held by a left hand only, thin broken lance on ground, all within crudely ruled quadruple concentric circle, 6.44g, 28.3mm to 29.8mm, thickness 1mm (WR -; Douglas-Morris -). *Light series of scratches at lower right quarter, otherwise as made with associated weaknesses from being "squeezed" in lead from the die and of ovoid form, some light corrosion and raised spots on plain side, extremely fine, perhaps unique.* £800-1000

Price Realised : £720

This piece appears to be an earlier rendering of the reverse, perhaps an initial phase as many aspects are either incomplete or more basically rendered. Trials of this nature are usually only ever "squeezed" from a working die in uniface format in base metal because impressions can be taken from an unhardened die. Silver and gold require a hardened die, after which further work on the die is not possible.

948 **George IV,** Uniface Base Metal Trial Reverse for a Sovereign, undated (c.1821), struck in lead on a slightly oversize thick flan, by Benedetto Pistrucci, St George, helmeted with streamer and cloak, slaying dragon right with sword, held by a left hand only, thin broken lance on ground, trace of *WWP* on ground-line, B.P. in exergue, all within a linear raised circle, 10.87g, 24mm to 24.3mm, thickness 2mm (WR -; Douglas-Morris -). *Lightly corroded, "squeezed" in lead from the die and of ovoid form, otherwise very fine, perhaps unique.* £800-1000

Price Realised : £240

This piece appears to be a later rendering of the reverse and appears to be close to the final design used for currency. Trials of this nature are usually only ever "squeezed" from a working die in uniface format in base metal because impressions can be taken from an unhardened die. Silver and gold require a hardened die, after which further work on the die is not possible.

A Very Attractive Proof Sovereign of 1821

11 **George IV,** Proof Sovereign, 1821, engraved by Benedetto Pistrucci, first laureate head left, 13 leaves in laurel wreath, B.P. below, lettering with horizontally ruled interior compartments, GEORGIUS IIII D: G: BRITANNIAR: REX F: D:, milled border between linear concentric circles both sides, *rev* struck with inverted die axis, St George on horseback slaying dragon right with sword, helmet with crest only, horse tail terminates in three strands, broken lance on ground to left, with *WWP* in relief below, date in exergue, 8 doubled, with B.P. to upper right, edge milled, 7.99g (WR 231 R3; Montagu 926; Murdoch 378; Nobleman 132/5; S 3800). *Tiny black spot in front curl of hair and one on rim, a few other light blemishes, hairlines and tiny nicks on neck, otherwise good extremely fine and very rare.* £4000-4500

Price Realised : £6,000

ex Spink Numismatic Circular, March 1999, item 788, via Randy Weir Numismatics, Unionville, Ontario, Canada
Interestingly these 1821 proofs have the same die axis as the currency Sovereigns. All the denominations issued for the Coronation year of George IV in 1821 were also produced to proof quality, no doubt to present to officials and very important persons. Additionally Pistrucci himself would be able to supply proofs to whomever he pleased or to those who would commission him to do so. This practice later developed into the sale of entire Proof Sets in cases from 1826 for special occasions; though an 1821 Proof Set could theoretically be formed, and this cataloguer did once handle such a set for sale in a contemporary round fitted case, some 15 years ago.

Extremely Rare Bronzed Copper Proof Sovereign of 1821

949 **George IV,** Proof Sovereign, 1821, struck in bronzed copper, engraved by Benedetto Pistrucci, first laureate head left, 13 leaves in laurel wreath, B.P. below, lettering with horizontally ruled interior compartments, GEORGIUS IIII D: G: BRITANNIAR: REX F: D:, milled border between linear concentric circles both sides, *rev* struck with inverted die axis, St George on horseback slaying dragon right with sword, helmet with crest only, horse tail terminates in three strands, broken lance on ground to left, WWP in relief below, date in exergue, 8 doubled, B.P. to upper right, edge milled, 4.67g, 22.1mm (cf WR 231; Montagu -; Murdoch -; S 3800). *Toned with golden hints to milling, extremely fine and of the highest rarity.* £3000-4000

Price Realised : £5,040

ex DNW auction, 21 June 2011, lot 205
Interestingly other denominations for 1821, like the silver Crown, also exist with copper proof strikings of great rarity. Perhaps they were final trials before committing to using more precious metal, in this case, the making of gold proofs of the Sovereign. Pistrucci would have had the right to strike special orders for coins, so it is even possible he acted upon a "VIP" commission to strike examples of certain coins in bronzed copper.

12 **George IV,** Sovereign, 1821, first laureate head left, B.P. below, B over a higher B doubled, a number of small raised die flaws in lettering, filled in A's and B's last R has continuous serifs, *rev* St George slaying dragon right with sword, date in exergue, with B.P. to upper right, 7.98g (Marsh 5; MCE 471; S 3800). *Light cabinet friction evident with some light nicks and hairlines in fields and upon bust, otherwise good extremely fine and most unusual with the double struck BP.* £1800-2200

Price Realised : £1,920

ex Randy Weir Numismatics, Unionville, Ontario, Canada, purchased 22 March 1990
Calendar year mintage 9,405,114
Looking at this calendar year total, if we allow for Marsh's estimate of 1,170,000 of these being 1820 dated coins of George III, then we must reduce this total to 8,235,114.
It is interesting to note that the first type Sovereign of King George IV are the only sovereigns ever issued with decorative style lettering with "hatched" compartments. Note also the die degradation that is demonstrated by the raised flaws and hairlines.

Rare Off-centre Die Axis 1821 Sovereign

389 **George IV,** Sovereign, 1821, off-centre die axis, first laureate head left, B.P. below, slightly doubled, a number of small raised die flaws in lettering, lettering with horizontally ruled interior compartments, GEORGIUS IIII D: G: BRITANNIAR: REX F: D:, milled border between linear concentric circles both sides, *rev* struck with inverted die axis off-centre by about 45 degrees, broken lance on ground to left, with WWP in relief below, date in exergue, with B.P. to upper right, edge milled, 7.98g (Marsh 5; MCE 471; S 3800). *Light scratch above head, hairlined, almost extremely fine and unusual.* £1000-1200

Price Realised : £960

ex A H Baldwin & Sons Ltd sourced via Paul Davies Ltd, October 2010
Calendar year mintage 9,405,114

13 **George IV,** Sovereign, 1822, first laureate head left, B of legend filled as are A's and R's, last R with continuous serifs, *rev* St George slaying dragon right with sword, date in exergue, only a trace of upper serif on the 1, 7.99g (Marsh 6; MCE 472; S 3800). *Light surface marks, some light raised die flaws evident with matt textured fields, good extremely fine.* £1800-2200

Price Realised : £3,600

Calendar year mintage 5,356,787

950 **George IV,** Sovereign, 1822, first laureate head left, B.P. below with quite dramatic doubling of the B, B over a B, *rev* St George slaying dragon right with sword, date in exergue, no upper serif on the 1, and no lower serif on B of B.P. in exergue, 7.98g (Marsh 6; MCE 472; S 3800). *Light surface marks of a parallel formation with textured fields, otherwise good extremely fine and unusual.* £1200-1500

Price Realised : £1,740

ex Dr Jacob Y Terner collection, Goldberg, Hollywood, USA, 26-27 May 2003, lot 267
Calendar year mintage 5,356,787

The Extremely Rare 1823 Currency Sovereign of King George IV

14 **George IV,** Sovereign, 1823, first laureate head left, *rev* St George slaying dragon right with sword, date in exergue, only a trace of upper serif on the 1, 7.97g (Marsh 7 R3; MCE 473; S 3800). *A myriad of tiny light surface marks in fields and upon bust, pleasing good extremely fine and very attractive, the finest specimen the cataloguer is aware of in private hands and of the highest rarity.* £8000-10,000

Price Realised : £18,000

ex Dr Jacob Y Terner collection, Goldberg, Hollywood, USA, 26-27 May 2003, lot 269 – was graded MS63 by NGC
Calendar year mintage 616,770

951 George IV, Uniface Base Metal Trial Reverse for a Sovereign, 1824, struck in lead on a very thick flan, by Benedetto Pistrucci, St George, helmeted with streamer and cloak, slaying dragon right with sword, broken lance on ground, initials *WWP* on ground-line, date in exergue, no upper serif on the 1, BP without stops in exergue, all within a linear raised circle, 10.43g, 21.8mm to 22mm, thickness 2.5mm (WR -; Douglas-Morris -; cf S 3800). *Scratched and striated on plain side, "squeezed" in lead from the die and of ovoid form, rim bruise with a number of tiny digs and a patina of light oxidation, otherwise extremely fine, perhaps unique.* £800-1000

Price Realised : £744

bought A H Baldwin & Sons Ltd, March 2006
Trials of this nature are usually only ever "squeezed" from a working die in uniface format in base metal because impressions can be taken from an unhardened die. Silver and gold require a hardened die, after which further work on the die is not possible.

15 George IV, Sovereign, 1824, first laureate head left, *rev* St George slaying dragon right with sword, date in exergue, no upper serif on 1 in date, 7.98g (Marsh 8; MCE 474; S 3800). *A myriad of tiny light surface marks, extremely fine, the reverse better.* £1800-2200

Price Realised : £1,680

ex Randy Weir Numismatics, Unionville, Ontario, Canada, purchased 27 September 1990.
Calendar year mintage 3,767,904
It is interesting to note that the following year of 1825, with the first type reverse design of St George slaying the dragon, is the last year this design is used for 46 years until it is revived in 1871.

The Unique First Type 1825 Pattern Sovereign of King George IV with Plain Edge

16 George IV, Pattern Sovereign, 1825, engraved by Benedetto Pistrucci, first laureate head left, B.P. below, lettering with horizontally ruled interior compartments, GEORGIUS IIII D: G: BRITANNIAR: REX F: D:, letters O and T die-flawed with other letters slightly doubled, milled border between linear concentric circles both sides, bevelled rims both sides, *rev* struck en médaille, St George slaying dragon right with sword, broken lance on ground to left, with WWP in relief below, date in exergue, only a trace of the upper serif on the 1 in date, with B.P. to upper right, edge plain, 8.47g, 21.8mm (WR 234 R7; Murdoch 381; Nobleman 136; S 3800). *Light handling marks with many light hairlines, otherwise good extremely fine and the only known specimen, unique.* £18,000-22,000

Price Realised : £19,200

ex Marshall Collection, Spink Auction 167, 31 March 2004, lot 177
This is probably the same coin from Nobleman and Murdoch, we cannot confirm this because it is not illustrated in either catalogue. Note the unusually heavy weight for this presentation pattern. The cataloguer calls this a pattern as it has a plain edge and is far heavier than the currency coinage. The Wilson and Rasmussen reference book does not even carry an illustration of this one-off coin, where they call it a plain edge proof. The authors of that weighty tome did not even see a specimen of this pattern in any of the many museums and institutions they visited over a 10 year period of gestation for this book that was published in 2000.

The Very Rare Currency First Type Sovereign of 1825

952 **George IV,** Sovereign, 1825, engraved by Benedetto Pistrucci, first laureate head left, B.P. below, lettering with horizontally ruled interior compartments, GEORGIUS IIII D: G: BRITANNIAR: REX F: D:, milled border between linear concentric circles both sides, *rev* St George slaying dragon right with sword, broken lance on ground to left, light die flaw from tail to lance, *WWP* in relief below, date in exergue, only a trace of the upper serif on the 1 in date, with B.P. to upper right, edge plain, 7.98g (Marsh 9 R3; MCE 475; S 3800). *Some light surface marks with a textured tone, otherwise pleasing extremely fine and extremely rare.* £4000-5000

Price Realised : £7,440

Calendar year mintage 4,200,343
The calendar year mintage figure unfortunately provides no split between the first and second types for this year. It is well known that the first type for 1825 is very rare indeed, and must have only been produced up to, or around, Easter 1825 and accounts for a small fraction of the mintage for the calendar year.

Second Type

William Wyon

Jean Baptiste Merlen

[Baldwin Library images]

The second standard design for the currency Sovereigns of King George IV from 1825-1830 inclusive had an obverse designed by William Wyon based upon the sculpted model bust by Francis Legatt Chantrey (1781-1841). A marble bust that the King was particularly pleased with, and which was first used as an inspirational model for the coinage on the gold Two Pound piece of 1823 engraved by Jean Baptiste Merlen shown here.

The Second Type Obverse and Reverse of King George IV

The former abbreviated legend used on the first type obverse, now appears across both sides of the second type coins and in a fuller form, on obverse GEORGIUS IV DEI GRATIA and continuing on the reverse BRITANNIARUM REX FID: DEF: The lettering no longer has any decorative compartments. The reverse of the Sovereigns of this type, also engraved by Merlen, have a crowned quartered shield of arms, with an escutcheon of the Hanoverian Arms. It has been noted in the Bentley Collection catalogue for the first time that the semee of hearts in these Hanoverian Arms generally contains eight hearts. However it has been noted the 1825 plain edge proof only has seven, meaning it was an earlier pattern rendering of the reverse. Otherwise the reverse always depicts nine strings in the Irish harp, and some inner upper lis of the Scottish arms are detached from their frame. The straight grained milled edge continues.

Unrecorded 1825 Plain Edge Pattern Sovereign with Only a Seven Heart Semée in The Hanoverian Arms

Seven Heart Semée

17 **George IV,** Pattern Sovereign, 1825, engraved by William Wyon after Francis Chantrey's model, second bare head left, date below, rosette either side, toothed border and raised rim both sides, GEORGIUS IV DEI GRATIA, *rev* struck with inverted die axis, by Jean Baptiste Merlen, crowned quartered shield of arms, with the arms of Hanover as an escutcheon, seven hearts in semee of Hanoverian lion, upper left lis of frame around Scottish lion detached only, Irish arms with nine harp strings, BRITANNIARUM REX FID: DEF:, edge plain, 7.98g, 21.8mm (WR 235 R5; Montagu 929; Murdoch 382; Nobleman 137; DM 158; S 3801). *Light tone, with some light hairlines and handling marks, two light scratches on cheek, otherwise good extremely fine and extremely rare.* £8000-10,000

Price Realised : £10,080

ex Property of a Gentleman, Spink Auction 117, 19 November 1997, lot 1979

We note for the first time in print that the lis of the Scottish arms on the second type of George IV are generally always detached. Also the semée of hearts in the Hanoverian Arms only displays seven hearts whereas the current version displays eight. Therefore this piece is an earlier pattern with a different reverse and edge to currency.

The milled edge 1825 proof carries eight hearts in the Hanoverian Arms like the currency pieces and is therefore struck later and is different to the plain edge piece above.

All the denominations issued for the current new coinage of the second type of George IV in 1825 were also produced to proof quality, no doubt to present to officials and very important persons and in addition included a pattern gold Five Pounds, Two Pounds and silver Crown that were not current this year. Additionally Wyon himself would be able to supply proofs to whomever he pleased or to those who would commission him to do so. These rare proofs of 1825, were obviously in demand as they led directly to the sale of entire Proof Sets in cases from the next year of 1826. Proof Sets then began to be produced on a more regular basis for Coronations, Jubilees and new coinages.

Extremely Rare George IV Barton's Metal Pattern Obverse Sovereign

390 **George IV,** Pattern Uniface Sovereign, 1825, struck in Barton's Metal (gold electrolysed copper), engraved by William Wyon after Francis Chantrey's model, second bare head left, date below, rosette either side, toothed border and raised rim, bold raised lettering GEORGIUS IV DEI GRATIA, *rev* blank with a raised rim, edge plain showing copper with gold borders, 4.09g, 21.7mm (cf S 3801). *Speckling of black tone in bottom third of obverse, otherwise as struck and extremely rare.* £1500-2000

Price Realised : £1,680

Experimental patterns struck in Barton's metal exist in most denominations usually of gold and silver dated 1825. Bartons Metal is gold electrolysed copper where a thin sheet of gold has been laid over a copper core and struck as method to show how a token coinage could be produced. The Deputy Comptroller of the mint at this time was John Barton (1771-1834) who was an engineer and responsible for inventing new more efficient machinery at the Royal Mint. Many of the new methods and machines were written up in detail in the Mechanic's Magazine, volume III – 1824 in issues 63-67. The Bartons Metal patterns of 1825 are all uniface obverse and reverse designs and are extremely rare.

Extremely Rare George IV Barton's Metal Pattern Reverse Sovereign

953 **George IV,** Uniface Pattern Reverse Striking for a Sovereign, 1825, struck in Barton's Metal (gold electrolysed copper), engraved by Jean Baptiste Merlen, crowned quartered shield of arms, with the arms of Hanover as an escutcheon, seven hearts in semée of Hanoverian lion, upper left lis of frame around Scottish lion detached only, Irish arms with nine harp strings, BRITANNIARUM REX FID: DEF:, edge, plain showing copper with gold borders, 4.08g, 21.8mm (Murdoch 417; Nobleman 129; cf S 3801). *Speckling of black tone both sides, otherwise as struck and very rare.* £1500-2000

Price Realised : £2,640

Experimental patterns struck in Barton's metal exist in most denominations usually of gold and silver dated 1825. Bartons Metal is gold electrolysed copper where a thin sheet of gold has been laid over a copper core and struck as method to show how a token coinage could be produced. The Deputy Comptroller of the mint at this time was John Barton (1771-1834) who was an engineer and responsible for inventing new more efficient machinery at the Royal Mint. Many of the new methods and machines were written up in detail in the Mechanic's Magazine, volume III – 1824 in issues 63-67. The Bartons Metal patterns of 1825 are all uniface obverse and reverse designs and are extremely rare.

Very Rare 1825 Milled Edge Proof Sovereign with Eight Heart Semée in the Arms

391 **George IV,** Proof Sovereign, 1825, engraved by William Wyon after Francis Chantrey's model, second bare head left, date below, rosette either side, toothed border and raised rim both sides, GEORGIUS IV DEI GRATIA, *rev* struck with inverted die axis, by Jean Baptiste Merlen, crowned quartered shield of arms, with the arms of Hanover as an escutcheon, eight hearts in semée of Hanoverian lion, two upper lis of inner frame around Scottish lion incomplete, Irish arms with nine harp strings, re-touched frosting on design elements, leaving finest detail indistinct, evident on crown band, BRITANNIARUM REX FID: DEF:, edge milled, 8.03g (WR 236 R5; Montagu 930; Murdoch 382 (part); Nobleman 137 (part); DM 159; S 3801). *Lightly hairlined, otherwise as struck and very rare.* £6000-8000

Price Realised : £9,360

This milled edge 1825 proof carries eight hearts in the Hanoverian Arms like the currency pieces, as opposed to the seven heart semée plain edge piece (published for the very first time in the Bentley Collection).

All the denominations issued for the current new coinage of the second type of George IV in 1825 were also produced to proof quality, no doubt to present to officials and very important persons, and included a pattern gold Five Pounds, Two Pounds and silver Crown that were not current this year. Additionally, Pistrucci himself would be able to supply proofs to whomever he pleased or to those who would commission him to do so. These very rare proofs of 1825 were obviously in demand, as they led directly to the sale of entire Proof Sets in cases from the following year (1826). Proof Sets then began to be produced on a more regular basis for Coronations, Jubilees and new coinages.

Extremely Rare Bronzed Copper Proof Sovereign of 1825, Second Type

954 **George IV,** Proof Sovereign, 1825, struck in bronzed copper, engraved by William Wyon after Francis Chantrey's model, second bare head left, date below, rosette either side, toothed border and raised rim both sides, GEORGIUS IV DEI GRATIA, lower left serifs absent in first four letters of King's name, *rev* struck with inverted die axis, by Jean Baptiste Merlen, crowned quartered shield of arms, with the arms of Hanover as an escutcheon, eight hearts in semée of Hanoverian lion, two upper lis of inner frame around Scottish lion incomplete and detached, Irish arms with nine harp strings, BRITANNIARUM REX FID: DEF:, edge milled, 4.78g, 22.1mm (cf WR 236; Montagu -; Murdoch -; Douglas-Morris 159; S 3801). *One or two tiny digs, otherwise toned, practically as struck and extremely rare.* £3000-4000

Price Realised : £4,800

ex Randy Weir Numismatics, Unionville, Ontario, Canada, purchased 14 July 2003

This milled edge 1825 proof in bronzed copper carries eight hearts in the Hanoverian Arms like the currency pieces, as opposed to the seven heart semée Barton's metal piece in the previous lot, discovered in the Bentley Collection for the first time.

Perhaps such a copper striking was a final trial before committing to using more precious metal for the making of gold proofs of the Sovereign. Wyon would have had the right to strike special orders for coins, so it is even possible he acted upon a "VIP" commission to strike examples of certain coins in bronzed copper.

Eight Heart Semée in Hanoverian Arms

18 **George IV,** Sovereign, 1825, second bare head left, date below, lower left serif absent on first R of legend, *rev* crowned quartered shield of arms, with the arms of Hanover as an escutcheon, eight hearts in semee of Hanoverian lion, upper inner lis of frame around Scottish lion detached, edge milled, 7.97g (Marsh 10; MCE 476; S 3801). *Some light digs on cheek, hairlines and handling marks in fields and upon bust, otherwise good extremely fine.* £1800-2200

Price Realised : £1,680

ex Randy Weir Numismatics, Unionville, Ontario, Canada, purchased 10 June 1991
Calendar year mintage 4,200,343
The calendar year mintage figure unfortunately provides no split between the first and second types for this year, it is well known that the first type for 1825 is very rare, and must have only been produced up to, or around Easter 1825.

Very Pleasing Example of the 1826 Proof Gold Sovereign

392 **George IV,** Proof Sovereign, 1826, second bare head left, date below, lower left serif of first R absent, *rev* crowned shield of arms, quartered with the arms of Hanover as an escutcheon, eight hearts in semée of Hanoverian lion, two upper lis of inner frame around Scottish lion detached, tiny hairline flaw below shield to right, 7.99g (WR 237; S 3801). *Light tone, a little hairlined, otherwise practically as struck.* £3000-4000

Price Realised : £6,960

ex Stacks, New York, USA, 7-8 December 1994, lot 2455
The 1826 proof Sovereign was one of the coins included in commemorative sets made to present to officials and very important persons and included a pattern gold Five Pounds, Two Pounds and Half-Sovereign as well as the silver and copper denominations from Crown to Farthing. Additionally, Pistrucci himself had the right to supply single proofs to whomever he pleased or to those who would commission him to do so. Proof Sets then began to be produced on a more regular basis for Coronations, Jubilees and new coinages.

19 **George IV,** Sovereign, 1826, second bare head left, date below, 1 of date slightly double struck, *rev* die axis a touch off-centre, crowned shield of arms, quartered with the arms of Hanover as an escutcheon, 8.03g (Marsh 11; MCE 477; S 3801). *Perhaps a little softly struck with appealing surfaces, pleasing good extremely fine.* £1800-2200

Price Realised : £4,320

ex Randy Weir Numismatics, Unionville, Ontario, Canada, purchased 24 May 1990
Calendar year mintage 5,724,046
It is interesting to note that this is one of the heaviest currency Sovereigns in the entire Collection.

955 **George IV,** Sovereign, 1826, 6 of date struck over a tilted 6, 26 of date more spread than usual, second bare head left, date below, *rev* crowned shield of arms, quartered with the arms of Hanover as an escutcheon, 8.02g (Marsh 11; MCE 477; S 3801). *Short scratch on neck, hairlined, very fine, reverse better and unusual.* £600-800

Price Realised : £648

bought A H Baldwin & Sons Ltd, July 2009
Calendar year mintage 5,724,046

Very Rare 1826 Sovereign with 6 of Date over a Small 6

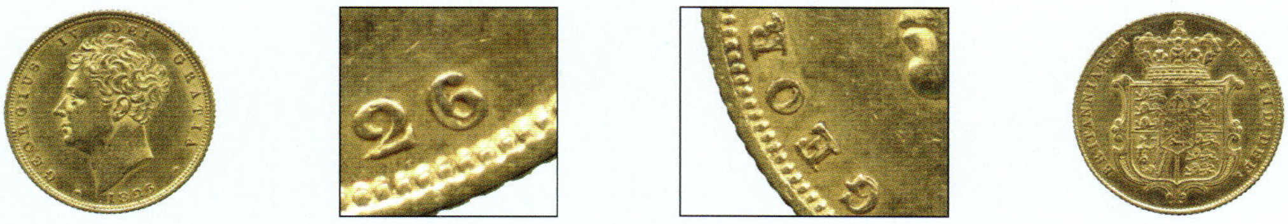

956 **George IV,** Sovereign, 1826, 6 of date struck over a small Half-Sovereign sized 6, whole legend show evidence of being overstruck on smaller sized letter punched legend, especially start of King's name, second bare head left, date below, *rev* crowned shield of arms, quartered with the arms of Hanover as an escutcheon, 7.98g (Marsh 11; MCE 477; S 3801). *Bagmarked and hairlined, almost extremely fine, the finest known of the very few so far discovered of this relatively new variety, extremely rare.* £1000-1500

Price Realised : £1,860

bought Mark Rasmussen Numismatist, list 8, item 279
Calendar year mintage 5,724,046
This intriguing variety was only discovered about six years ago and the cataloguer has still not seen more than four specimens, the others being in lower grades than the example here. It appears as if an engraver at the Mint had before him the wrong set of letter and number punches as would normally be used on the smaller coins like the Half-Sovereign and only realised once most of the obverse legend had been punched into the die. Dies by their very nature being too valuable to waste, the engraver then seems to have obtained the correct size punches and proceeded to correct the small size letters as carefully as possible. The 6 of the date is the most obvious part of this variety, along with the initial four letters of the legend, but others are evident too.

20 **George IV,** Sovereign, 1827, second bare head left, date below, first word of legend lightly die flawed, *rev* crowned shield of arms, quartered with the arms of Hanover as an escutcheon, 8.00g (Marsh 12; MCE 478; S 3801). *Light scuff at rear of neck, other light hairline marks, otherwise as struck and very appealing.* £1800-2200

Price Realised : £4,320

ex Randy Weir Numismatics, Unionville, Ontario, Canada, purchased 25 October 1991
Calendar year mintage 2,266,629

The Extremely Rare King George IV 1828 Currency Sovereign

21 **George IV,** Sovereign, 1828, second bare head left, date below, *rev* crowned shield of arms, quartered with the arms of Hanover as an escutcheon, 7.95g (Marsh 13 R4; MCE 479; S 3801). *Heavy surface marks and scuffing, nearly very fine, reverse very fine and an extremely rare date.* £12,000-15,000

Price Realised : £13,200

ex Randy Weir Numismatics, Unionville, Ontario, Canada, purchased c.1998
Calendar year mintage 386,182
The 1828 Sovereign is considered the key date for the reign of George IV and is one of the hardest to find in the London series issued by the Royal Mint. Only the 1819 Sovereign of George III is rarer, see lot 941, pages 23-25.
The reason why the 1828 Sovereign is so rare is not widely known and it came down to economics at the Royal Mint. To make a new dated die is an intensive and laborious process, in both time and cost, and considering the average longevity of a die, the Mint considered itself very lucky at the dawn of 1828 when it found a number of 1827 obverse dies were still in perfectly good working order. Therefore, rather than make new dies for 1828 immediately, it was decided to wait until the supply of 1827 dated dies dwindled. This did not finally occur until November of 1828 as it seems there was only a low demand for gold sovereigns this year. It was only in December that 1828 Sovereigns started to be minted and this probably did not last long into 1829, therefore the actual number made dated 1828 can be considered to be a fraction of the calendar year mintage quoted above, perhaps a mere twelfth as an educated estimate. It is surprising that the 1827 dies were not simply overstruck to convert them to display 1828, but it seems that overstamping dates was not common practice until the reign of Queen Victoria. Overdates during this period are few and far between in all denominations.

22 **George IV,** Sovereign, 1829, second bare head left, date below, *rev* crowned shield of arms, quartered with the arms of Hanover as an escutcheon, 7.96g (Marsh 14; MCE 480; S 3801). *Lightly hairlined, dig on neck, extremely fine, the reverse better.* £1800-2200

Price Realised : £1,680

ex Randy Weir Numismatics, Unionville, Ontario, Canada, purchased 2 March 1990
Calendar year mintage 2,444,652

Extremely Rare George IV 1830 Proof Sovereign Struck en médaille

957 **George IV,** Proof Sovereign, 1830, engraved by William Wyon after Francis Chantrey's model, second bare head left, date below, rosette either side, toothed border and raised rim both sides, GEORGIUS IV DEI GRATIA, *rev* struck en médaille, by Jean Baptiste Merlen, crowned quartered shield of arms, with the arms of Hanover as an escutcheon, eight hearts in semée of Hanoverian lion, two upper lis of inner frame around Scottish lion incomplete, Irish arms with nine harp strings, re-touched frosting on design elements leaving finest detail indistinct evident on crown band, BRITANNIARUM REX FID: DEF:, edge milled, 7.99g (WR -; Montagu -; Murdoch -; Nobleman -; Douglas-Morris -; S 3801). *Some very light surface marks on obverse, one tiny spot above legend on reverse, otherwise toned, as struck and the only known example in private hands, a superb coin.* £25,000-30,000

Price Realised : £43,200

ex DNW auction, 28 September 2005, lot 951
This milled edge proof of 1830 carries eight hearts in the Hanoverian Arms like the currency pieces, as opposed to the seven heart semée plain edge piece published in part one of the Bentley Collection for the very first time, it also has an upright axis. The 1830 Proof was only discovered, confirmed by the Royal Mint and sold for the first time publicly in 2005 at DNW where Noble Investments bought it on behalf of the Bentley collector. The coin was unknown to Wilson and Rasmussen and it was reported that the vendor at the auction had owned it since the 1960s when it was purchased from a coin dealer. Unique in private hands and preserved in the best of quality, this is one of the key pieces of George IV in the collection.

23 **George IV,** Sovereign, 1830, second bare head left, date below, *rev* crowned shield of arms, quartered with the arms of Hanover as an escutcheon, 7.95g (Marsh 15; MCE 481; S 3801). *Some very light surface marks on obverse, extremely fine, reverse better.* £1800-2200

Price Realised : £1,680

ex Randy Weir Numismatics, Unionville, Ontario, Canada, purchased 2 March 1990
Calendar year mintage 2,387,881

393 **George IV,** Sovereign, 1830, struck with en médaille die axis, second bare head left, date below, *rev* crowned shield of arms, quartered with the arms of Hanover as an escutcheon, 7.91g (Marsh 15; MCE 481; S 3801). *Once cleaned, almost very fine and rare, the only specimen the cataloguer has seen, extremely rare.* £1000-1500

Price Realised : £1,320

ex St James's Auction 4, 8 May 2006, lot 362
The occurrence of a true opposite die axis to that usually encountered is a real oddity in the gold series of currency coinage. The upright die axis is usually reserved for medals in this period or rare proof strikings (hence the term "en médaille" - like a medal) and though slightly off-centre die axis strikes do rarely occur, true opposite is a real rarity. In the Bentley Collection as a whole it is only this coin of 1830 and one dated 1817, lot 5, page 20, that have an opposite to the normal die axis. The possibly unique 1830 proof Sovereign of George IV also has this dies axis. It is interesting to note that, as one of the lower grade Sovereigns in the Bentley Collection, this coin is well under the legal tender weight limit that was set in successive Coinage Acts from 1816-1891.
Calendar year mintage 2,387,881
George IV died on 26 June 1830

The Reign of King William IV (1830-1837)
House of Hanover

Born: 21 August 1765

Accession: 26 June 1830

Married: Adelaide of Saxe-Coburg and Meiningen, 11 July 1818
after first meeting a week before,
a double wedding with his brother,
Prince Edward the Duke of Kent.

Coronation: Thursday, 8 September 1831

Children: two daughters who both died in childhood,
ten illegitimate children previously

Died: 20 June 1837, aged 71

The standard design for the currency Sovereigns of King William IV from 1830-1837 inclusive was engraved by William Wyon after Francis Chantrey's model, and consists of two bare headed bust types and one standard reverse. Both bust types have the same legend reading GULIELMUS IIII D: G: BRITANNIAR REX F: D:

First Bust

Second Bust

William IV Reverse

The first bust obverse has more finely engraved hair most noticeable on the top of his head and a more rounded ear. The position of the bust in relation to the legend dictates that his nose points to the second letter N in BRITANNIAR. The first bust obverse has border teeth that are quite fine and tall, and more in number when compared with obverse two.

The second obverse has coarser hair, a flat top to the ear and the nose points to the second I in BRITANNIAR. The border teeth also differ from the first bust as the obverse teeth are of a coarser wide spread rendering, with less depth. The majority of the coinage of William IV Sovereigns, depict this obverse, including the very first pattern piece of 1830. It seems the demarcation of second bust relates really to its use ending with the reign in 1837, as the first bust type finishes first by 1832. The reverse teeth on the second bust obverse coins are similar to the first bust obverse ones, and are taller and finer than those on the obverse of the second bust coins.

The reverses of William IV engraved by Jean Baptiste Merlen, always carry eight strings in the Irish harp with a diagonal line running through them depicting the rear of the bottom harp body. The inner arches of the crown above have thirteen pearls on each side, and five more run diagonally up each side of the central upright. There are nine varied jewels on the crown band. There is a short legend reading to the lower left ANNO and the date to the lower right. The edges are milled as usual. There was no issue in or dated 1834.

Extremely Rare William IV Barton's Metal Pattern Reverse Sovereign dated 1830

958 **William IV (1830-1837),** Uniface Pattern Reverse Striking of a Sovereign, 1830, struck in Barton's Metal, by Jean Baptiste Merlen, crowned shield of arms, quartered with the arms of Hanover as an escutcheon, eight harp strings, ANNO 1830 below, border beads with fine teeth surrounding, edge plain, showing copper as does plain side, 4.79g, 21.8mm (cf WR 260; Murdoch -). *Lightly toned, hairlined, practically as struck and extremely rare.* £1500-2000

Price Realised : £2,640

ex Randy Weir Numismatics, Unionville, Ontario, Canada, purchased 14 July 2003

Very few other experimental patterns struck in Barton's metal exist for other denominations for William IV but seem rarer than those of George IV. Bartons Metal is gold electrolysed copper where a thin sheet of gold has been laid over a copper core and struck as method to show how a token coinage could be produced. The Deputy Comptroller of the mint at this time was John Barton (1771-1834) who was an engineer and responsible for inventing new more efficient machinery at the Royal Mint. Many of the new methods and machines were written up in detail in the Mechanic's Magazine, volume III – 1824 in issues 63-67. The George IV Bartons Metal patterns of 1825 (lots 390 and 953, page 38) are uniface obverse and reverse designs and are extremely rare.

Extremely Rare William IV Pattern Sovereign Dated 1830

394 **William IV,** Pattern Sovereign, 1830, by William Wyon after Francis Chantrey's model, second bare head right with coarse hair and flat topped, deeply engraved ear, W.W. incuse fully on truncation, nose points to second I in BRITANNIAR, GULIELMUS IIII D: G: BRITANNIAR REX F: D:, finely toothed border and raised rim both sides, coarse bead like border teeth, *rev* struck with inverted die axis, by Jean Baptiste Merlen, crowned quartered shield of arms, with the arms of Hanover as an escutcheon, seven heart semée, Irish arms with eight harp strings, crown with 13 pearls on each arch and five pearls each side of vertical facing upright, inner crown band with nine jewels, ANNO 1830 below, finer taller border teeth, edge plain, 7.68g, 21.8mm (WR 260 R5; Montagu 1083; Murdoch 440 (part); Nobleman 203; DM 178; S 3829B). *Small tiny striking flaw in reverse field to left of shield, some very light hairlines, otherwise mint state and extremely rare.* £10,000-15,000

Price Realised : £19,200

Note the lighter weight of this pattern coin which ensured it would not go far if inadvertently passed into circulation.

It is interesting to see that the "second bust" rendition was used for this initial pattern dating from the year of accession in 1830. Most currency coins from 1831 carry the first bust. The second bust in currency for 1831 is extremely rare being more wholly adopted from 1832. Therefore the chronology does not follow in reality as their referencing suggests. The second bust turned out to be the most prolific in this reign, used consistently from 1832 until the end of the reign. Both busts must have been used concurrently at times but the only reason they can accurately be called first and second bust is based on when they were phased out rather than when they were first introduced. For further reading see the introduction to the reign of King William IV.

The Coronation of King William IV took place 8 September 1831. All the denominations issued for the current new coinage for the Coronation year of William IV in 1831 were also produced to proof quality in Coronation proof sets. These undoubtedly were made to present to officials and very important persons, and in addition to current 1831 dated denominations, included a proof gold Two Pounds and silver Crown, Halfcrown and Shilling that were not current that year. Additionally, William Wyon himself would be able to supply proofs to whomever he pleased or to those who would commission him to do so. The 1831 proof set is generally accepted as the second proof set available from the Royal Mint, the first being 1826, though unofficial "sets" can be put together of coins of 1821 and 1825 as well.

Extremely Rare WW No Stops Sovereign, dated 1831
ex Douglas-Morris Collection

959 **William IV,** "Proof" Sovereign, 1831, by William Wyon after Francis Chantrey's model, first bare head right with finer hair and round topped ear, WW incuse fully on truncation without stops, first W meets field, nose points to second N in BRITANNIAR, GULIELMUS IIII D: G: BRITANNIAR REX F: D:, second and third I missing top serifs, M in King's name mispunched on die and corrected, finer toothed border and raised rim both sides, *rev* struck with inverted die axis, by Jean Baptiste Merlen, crowned quartered shield of arms, with the arms of Hanover as an escutcheon, Irish arms with eight harp strings, ANNO 1831 below, finer taller border teeth, edge milled, 8.00g, 22mm (WR 262 R6; Douglas-Morris 180, *this coin*; S 3829A). *Heavily hairlined in fields, design with frosted elements, light raised die flaw in field by forehead, as defined on the coin on the Wilson Rasmussen plate, otherwise brilliant, good extremely fine and extremely rare.* £6000-8000

Price Realised : £15,000

ex Capt K J Douglas-Morris collection, Sothebys, 26 November 1974, lot 180
ex Leu Numismatik, Zürich, Switzerland, 26 October 2004, lot 441
This coin was featured in the Douglas-Morris sale in 1974 as a proof and has been later included and illustrated in the Wilson and Rasmussen publication, also as a proof gold Sovereign with ww only on the truncation without stops. In this cataloguer's experience all the ww without stops seem to be struck to similar high quality, just like the coin offered in the next lot, which is another of this variety that was bought as the currency piece. This coin is also brilliant with raised rims but perhaps not as frosted and also missing the die flaw by the forehead in the field. It would seem the flaw by forehead is diagnostic of WR262 - the proof variety. It seems that the obverse die then had the flaw polished out and continued to be used for striking, rendering the later non-die flawed coins "proof-like" as struck from proof dies. Milled edge proofs at this period 1825-1839 do not seem to have bold square rims to their edges as some later proof coins do. However, they do have a rim that is proud of the field of the coin. Therefore, it is a case of two sub-varieties for a coin struck to superior definition to that seen in currency, but perhaps not as clear-cut a proof as, say, the 1832 proof offered in lot 961.
It is interesting to see that the second bust rendition was used for the proof coin, as issued for the Coronation proof sets in 1831. Most current coins of 1831 carry the first bust, while the second bust in currency for 1831 is extremely rare. Strangely the 1830 Pattern also carries the second bust portrait (see Bentley Collection, part two) and the 1832 proof offered as lot 961 carries the first bust. There are also extremely rare first bust Sovereigns of 1832 struck as currency. Therefore the chronology does not follow in reality as their referencing suggests. The second bust turned out to be the most prolific in this reign, being used consistently from 1832 till the end of the reign. Both busts must have been used concurrently at times but the only reason they can accurately be called first and second bust is based on when they were phased out rather than when they were first used. For further reading, see an article by Harold Mountain in the Spink Numismatic Circular October 1984, page 255, *Two Kinds of William IIII Sovereigns*.
The Coronation of William IV took place 8 September 1831 and all the denominations issued for the current new coinage for the Coronation year of William IV in 1831 were also produced to proof quality in Coronation proof sets. These undoubtedly were made to present to officials and VIPs, and, in addition to current 1831 dated denominations, included a proof gold Two Pounds and silver Crown, Halfcrown and Shilling that were not current that year. Additionally William Wyon himself would be able to supply proofs to whomever he pleased or to those who would commission him to do so.

The Very Rare WW No Stops Variety Sovereign of William IV, dated 1831

960 **William IV,** Sovereign, 1831, by William Wyon after Francis Chantrey's model, first bare head right with finer hair and round topped ear, WW incuse fully on truncation without stops first W meets field, nose points to second N in BRITANNIAR, GULIELMUS IIII D: G: BRITANNIAR REX F: D:, second and third I missing top serifs, M in King's name mispunched on die and corrected, finer toothed border and raised rim both sides, *rev* struck with inverted die axis, by Jean Baptiste Merlen, crowned quartered shield of arms, with the arms of Hanover as an escutcheon, Irish arms with eight harp strings, ANNO 1831 below, date out of alignment, finer taller border teeth, edge milled, 8.00g, 22mm (Marsh 16A R5; cf MCE 489; S 3829A). *Lightly hairlined in fields, die flaw by forehead not evident, tiny black spot by top left lion on reverse, tiny scratch on cheek, design with less frosted elements than previous lot, though likely the proof obverse die was reused to strike this piece, proof-like, otherwise practically as struck and extremely rare.* £3000-4000

Price Realised : £10,560

ex Randy Weir Numismatics, Unionville, Ontario, Canada, purchased 12 February 1993
Calendar year mintage 598,547

William IV Proof Sovereign of 1831 with Second Bust

Second Bust Characteristics

24 **William IV,** Proof Sovereign, 1831, by William Wyon after Francis Chantrey's model, second bare head right with coarse hair and flat topped, deeply engraved ear, W.W. incuse fully on truncation, nose points to second I in BRITANNIAR, GULIELMUS IIII D: G: BRITANNIAR REX F: D:, finely toothed border and raised rim both sides, coarse bead like border teeth, *rev* struck with inverted die axis, by Jean Baptiste Merlen, crowned quartered shield of arms, with the arms of Hanover as an escutcheon, Irish arms with eight harp strings, ANNO 1831 below, finer taller border teeth, edge plain, 8.04g, 21.8mm (WR 261 R3; Montagu 1084; Murdoch 440; Nobleman 205/6; DM 179; S 3829B). *Lightly hairlined in fields and toned, otherwise mint state and rare.* £4000-4500

Price Realised : £5,520

ex Spink Numismatic Circular, March 1995, item 1118
It is interesting to see that the second bust rendition was used for the proof coin as issued for the Coronation proof sets in 1831. Most current coins of 1831 carry the first bust, as in the next lot, whilst the second bust in currency for 1831 is extremely rare, see lot 26 for an example of this. Strangely the 1830 Pattern also carries the second bust portrait (lot 394, page 45) and the 1832 proof (lot 961, page 49) carries the first bust. There are also extremely rare first bust Sovereigns of 1832 in currency, see lot 27, page 48. Therefore the chronology does not follow in reality as their referencing suggests. The second bust turned out to be the most prolific in this reign, being used consistently from 1832 till the end of the reign. Both busts must have been used concurrently at times but the only reason they can accurately be called first and second bust is based on when they were phased out rather than when they were first used. For further reading, see an article by Harold Mountain in the Spink Numismatic Circular October 1984 page 255 "Two Kinds of William IIII Sovereigns"
The Coronation of William IV took place on 8 September 1831 and all the denominations issued for the current new coinage were also produced to proof quality in Coronation proof sets. These undoubtedly were made to present to officials and very important persons, and in addition to current 1831 dated denominations included a proof gold Two Pounds and silver Crown, Halfcrown and Shilling that were not current that year. Additionally William Wyon himself would be able to supply proofs to whomever he pleased or to those who would commission him to do so. The 1831 Proof Set is generally accepted as the second Proof Set available from the Royal Mint, the first being 1826, though "sets" can be put together of coins of 1821 and 1825 as well.

First Bust Characteristics

25 **William IV,** Sovereign, 1831, first bare head right with finer hair and round topped ear, nose points to second N in BRITANNIAR, W.W., incuse on truncation meets field, finer toothed border and raised rim both sides, *rev* crowned quartered shield of arms, with the arms of Hanover as an escutcheon, date below, edge milled, 7.98g (Marsh 16 R2; MCE 489; S 3829). *Light die flaw on reverse to right of shield, scuff in field behind head, some hairlines, light tone, good extremely fine and very rare this nice.* £2800-3200

Price Realised : £3,840

ex Property of a Gentleman, Spink Auction 117, 19 November 1997, lot 1993
Calendar year mintage 598,547
Even though 1831 is the initial year of mintage for William IV it is also the lowest calendar output from the Mint for this reign and the first bust is therefore very rare. This output is not even five times higher than the extremely rare Victorian 1841 issue.

The Extremely Rare William IV Second Bust 1831 Sovereign

26 **William IV,** Sovereign, 1831, second bare head right with coarse hair and flat topped, deeply engraved ear, W.W. fully incuse on truncation, nose points to I in BRITANNIAR, coarse border teeth, *rev* crowned quartered shield of arms, with the arms of Hanover as an escutcheon, date below, finer border teeth, 7.92g (Marsh -; MCE 489; S 3829B). *Die flaw raised to right of shield and additionally at lower left to rim on reverse, two small rim nicks, good fine, reverse better, of the highest rarity, very few specimens known and much rarer than indicated in the catalogues.* £6000-8000

Price Realised : £6,960

ex St James's Auction 6, 8 June 2007, lot 515
There is no further breakdown in the calendar year mintage as to how the first and second busts were apportioned. It is interesting to note that the weight of this coin is below that of legal tender as proclaimed by the Coinage Acts from 1816-1890.
The second bust on an 1831 Sovereign was unknown to the late Michael Marsh and not recorded in his 2002 publication.

The Extremely Rare William IV First Bust 1832 Sovereign

27 **William IV,** Sovereign, 1832, first bare head right with finer hair and round topped ear, W.W. fully incuse on truncation, nose points to second N in BRITANNIAR, finer toothed border and raised rim both sides, *rev* crowned quartered shield of arms, with the arms of Hanover as an escutcheon, date below, 7.98g (Marsh 17A; MCE 490; S 3829). *Light die flaw to lower right of shield on reverse, some tiny light marks and scuffs on obverse, heavily hairlined, proof-like nearly extremely fine, reverse better than extremely fine, a pleasing coin and very rare, much rarer than indicated by Marsh.* £2000-2500

Price Realised : £3,120

ex Spink and Son Ltd, August 2001
Calendar year mintage 3,737,065
There is no further breakdown in the calendar year mintage as to how the first and second busts were apportioned, however the bulk of 1832 Sovereigns encountered tend to be of the second bust variety rendering the first bust very rare.

Extremely Rare William IV 1832 Proof Sovereign with First Bust

961 **William IV,** Proof Sovereign, 1832, by William Wyon after Francis Chantrey's model, first bare head right with finer hair and round topped ear, W.W. incuse fully on truncation, first W meets field, nose points to second N in BRITANNIAR, GULIELMUS IIII D: G: BRITANNIAR REX F: D:, finer toothed border and raised rim both sides, *rev* struck with inverted die axis, by Jean Baptiste Merlen, crowned quartered shield of arms, with the arms of Hanover as an escutcheon, Irish arms with eight harp strings, ANNO 1831 below, lettering doubled, finer taller border teeth, edge milled, 7.97g, 22mm (WR 263 R7, *this coin*; Douglas-Morris -; S 3829). *Lightly hairlined in fields both sides, otherwise practically as struck and of highest rarity, only two examples known to cataloguer, this coin being the plate coin in Wilson and Rasmussen.* £10,000-15,000

Price Realised : £18,600

ex Spink Auction 107, 22 November 1994, lot 428

28 **William IV,** Sovereign, 1832, second bare head right with coarse hair and flat topped, deeply engraved ear, W.W. fully incuse on truncation, nose points to second I in BRITANNIAR, coarse border teeth, *rev* crowned quartered shield of arms, with the arms of Hanover as an escutcheon, date below, finer border teeth, 7.98g (Marsh 17; MCE 490; S 3829B). *Two light die flaws in date, legend lightly die flawed, light surface marks on bust, otherwise good extremely fine.* £2000-2500

Price Realised : £3,120

ex Randy Weir Numismatics, Unionville, Ontario, Canada, purchased 12 February 1993
Calendar year mintage 3,737,065

395 **William IV,** Sovereign, 1832, M over small m or V variety, second bare head right with coarse hair and flat topped, deeply engraved ear, W.W. fully incuse on truncation, nose points to second I in BRITANNIAR, second M possibly over a V or small half-sovereign sized m and double punched, coarse border teeth, *rev,* crowned quartered shield of arms, with the arms of Hanover as an escutcheon, date below, finer border teeth, 7.97g (Marsh 17; MCE 490; S 3829B). *Rim bruise, nearly very fine, reverse better, a very unusual die variety, rare.* £800-1000

Price Realised : £660

ex St James's Auction 7, 8 February 2008, lot 602
Calendar year mintage 3,737,065

396 **William IV,** Sovereign, 1832, high off-set 2 in date, second bare head right with coarse hair and flat topped, deeply engraved ear, w.w. fully incuse on truncation, nose points to second i in BRITANNIAR, second M possibly over a V or small half-sovereign sized m and double punched, coarse border teeth, *rev* crowned quartered shield of arms, with the arms of Hanover as an escutcheon, date out of alignment below, finer border teeth, 7.87g (Marsh 17; MCE 490; S 3829B). *Surface marks, good fine, an unusual die variety, scarce.* £500-600

Price Realised : £624

purchased via A H Baldwin & Sons Ltd, March 2006
Calendar year mintage 3,737,065
It is interesting to note that, as one of the lower grade Sovereigns in the Bentley Collection, this coin is well under the legal tender weight limit that was set in successive Coinage Acts from 1816-1891.

29 **William IV,** Sovereign, 1833, second bare head right, w.w. slightly doubled incuse on truncation, *rev* crowned quartered shield of arms, with the arms of Hanover as an escutcheon, date below, doubled 33, 7.97g (Marsh 18; MCE 491; S 3829B). *Die flaw raised to left side of shield, light obverse bagmarks, otherwise extremely fine and a rare date.* £1800-2200

Price Realised : £2,160

Calendar year mintage 1,225,269

962 **William IV,** Sovereign, 1833, the second 3 die flawed and possibly over a 2, second bare head right, with flat topped ear, nose points to second i in legend, w.w. slightly doubled incuse on truncation, coarse border teeth, *rev* crowned quartered shield of arms, with the arms of Hanover as an escutcheon, date below, doubled 33, fine border teeth, legend flawed, 7.94g (Marsh 18; MCE 491; S 3829B). *The date too worn to tell if overstruck conclusively, reverse die flawed in other parts, nearly very fine, reverse better, unusual.* £600-800

Price Realised : £672

bought at London Coin Fair, June 2007, via A H Baldwin & Sons Ltd
Calendar year mintage 1,225,269

30 **William IV,** Sovereign, 1835, second bare head right, w.w. slightly doubled incuse on truncation, *rev* crowned quartered shield of arms, with the arms of Hanover as an escutcheon, date below, 7.99g (Marsh 19 R; MCE 492; S 3829B). *Some light digs and scuffs at rear of neck and onto field, otherwise extremely fine / good extremely fine, a rare date.* £2000-2500

Price Realised : £2,640

ex Randy Weir Numismatics, Unionville, Ontario, Canada, purchased 25 October 1991
Calendar year mintage 723,441
This year represents the second lowest calendar year mintage.

963 **William IV,** Sovereign, 1835, 5 struck possibly over a 3 that is die flawed, second bare head right, w.w. slightly doubled incuse on truncation, B of legend with top half filled, *rev* crowned quartered shield of arms, with the arms of Hanover as an escutcheon, date below, 7.99g (Marsh 19 R; MCE 492; S 3829B). *Struck from a rusted reverse die with many raised tiny spots on field, hence date variety inconclusive, good very fine, reverse better.* £600-800

Price Realised : £1,260

Calendar year mintage 723,441
This year represents the second lowest calendar year mintage.

964 **William IV,** Sovereign, 1836, second bare head right, w.w. incuse on truncation slightly doubled, only a trace of coarse border teeth, many teeth absent, *rev* crowned quartered shield of arms, with the arms of Hanover as an escutcheon, date below, 36 die flawed, 7.99g (Marsh 20; MCE 493; S 3829B). *Softly struck in hair and top of ear flat, otherwise extremely fine, reverse better.* £1500-2000

Price Realised : £2,760

ex Randy Weir Numismatics, Unionville, Ontario, Canada, purchased December 1990
Calendar year mintage 1,714,349

The Extremely Rare N in Shield Variety William IV 1836 Sovereign

N in Shield

31 **William IV,** Sovereign, 1836, extra letter N in shield variety, second bare head right, w.w. slightly doubled incuse on truncation, first W meets field, coarse border teeth, *rev* crowned quartered shield of arms, with the arms of Hanover as an escutcheon, extra letter N struck in lower left of shield frame, date below, upper right of 3 broken, 7.99g (Marsh 20A R3; MCE 493; S 3829B). *Some light surface marks, good very fine, reverse better and extremely rare, fewer than ten specimens known of which this is amongst the finest.* £12,000-15,000

Price Realised : £14,400

ex Spink Auction 5014, 28 September 2005, lot 1701
Calendar year mintage 1,714,349
The most striking rarity in the currency series of William IV is the "N in shield" variety discovered just over a decade ago, and still numbering to less than ten specimens known. An engraver's die error, the N of ANNO has been misplaced too high on the die and intrudes the shield design giving a spectacular error of which this example is amongst the finest known. The error in the die must have been discovered quickly at the time as not many survive from what is a relatively high mintage. This specimen was one of the first two discovered and the second to ever appear for sale, the other was a lesser grade specimen.

32 **William IV,** Sovereign, 1837, second bare head right, w.w. slightly doubled incuse on truncation, raised die flaw from top of head to BR of legend, *rev* crowned quartered shield of arms, with the arms of Hanover as an escutcheon, O of ANNO with raised die flaw to shield, date below, 8 and 3 doubled, 7.98g (Marsh 21; MCE 494; S 3829B). *Small hint of wear to hair, good extremely fine and a rare date.* £2000-2500

Price Realised : £2,640

ex Randy Weir Numismatics, Unionville, Ontario, Canada, purchased 22 March 1990
Calendar year mintage 1,172,984

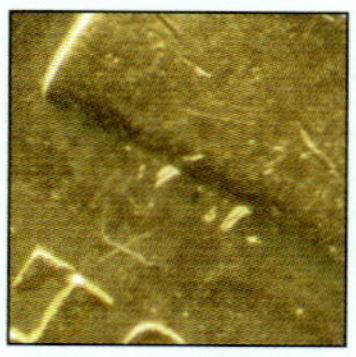

965 **William IV,** Sovereign, 1837, second bare head right, w.w. slightly doubled incuse on truncation, lower part of WW open and "flows" into field, *rev* die axis slightly off-centre, crowned quartered shield of arms, with the arms of Hanover as an escutcheon, date below, lightly doubled, 7.98g (Marsh 21; MCE 494; S 3829B). *Hairlined, pleasing extremely fine and a rare date.* £1500-2000

Price Realised : £3,240

bought A H Baldwin & Sons Ltd, August 2007
Calendar year mintage 1,172,984
William IV died 20 June 1837

The Reign of Queen Victoria (1837-1901)
House of Hanover

Born: 24 May 1819
Accession: 20 June 1837
Married: Albert of Saxe-Coburg and Gotha, 10 February 1840
Coronation: Thursday 28 June 1838
Children: four sons, five daughters
Died: 22 January 1901, aged 81

The First Young Head Sovereigns 1838-1848

Victoria First Small Young Head Type Currency Sovereign

The currency Sovereigns of Queen Victoria begin with a standard Young head design engraved by William Wyon with date below. The head does not quite fill the field as a later depiction does from 1848, and has the hair bound with a double fillet. It also has a large bun at the rear of the head that drops down into a "ponytail," which on this earlier issue terminates at the bottom in a single strand ring-like curl. The engraver's initials W.W. appear raised on the truncation. The legend reads VICTORIA DEI GRATIA. The border is finely toothed with a linear circle around the raised border which features both sides with a milled edge. The young head obverse design in basic from runs from 1838 till 1887. There are no Sovereigns dated 1840. However, this first young head is of a smaller design and only lasts for ten years inclusive from 1838-1848.

The reverse engraved by Jean Baptiste Merlen features a new crowned shield design with a laurel wreath surrounding to left and right of 24 leaves per side, the top of each wreath each side terminates in two leaves. The bottom stalks are tied together with a ribbon and emblematic plants are depicted below. A central rose with a thistle to the left and a shamrock to the right. A small rosette appears either side. The majority of currency reverses of Victoria carry seven strings in the Irish harp with a faint diagonal line running through them depicting the rear of the bottom harp body. The shorter left string generally emanates at the top from the scroll on the back of the female figure on the harp body. The inner arches of the crown above have eleven pearls on each side, and five more run up the central upright. There are nine varied jewels on the crown band. The legend reads BRITANNIARUM REGINA FID: DEF:. The reverse is struck with an inverted die axis in relation to the obverse.

The shield type reverse design endures in the London series from 1838 till 1874 with just a few varieties. In the Colonial Australian series this reverse lasted until 1887 as it proved popular and acceptable in trade with Asia, a narrative to be continued in the colonial section of this special edition of the Bentley Collection.

The Extremely Rare Small Bust Pattern Sovereign of 1837

33 **Victoria (1837-1901),** Pattern Sovereign, 1837, engraved by William Wyon, very small young head left, hair bound with double fillet, rear lower fillet finely ruled with horizontal incuse lines, plain truncation, date below slightly double struck, rosette either side, fine toothed border and raised rim both sides, VICTORIA DEI GRATIA around upper half of field, from 9 to 3 o'clock, *rev* struck with inverted die axis, engraved by Jean Baptiste Merlen, crowned quartered narrow shield of arms within laurel wreath tied with bow below shield, twelve pearls on each arch of crown, four pearls vertically arranged on central upright, nine pellets visible on ermine below jewel band, laurel wreath each side consists of 30 leaves per side and terminates in three leaves at top, six harp strings in Irish arms, left string emanates from back of female figure, emblems below, rose at centre, thistle to left, shamrock to right, small rosette either side, BRITANNIARUM REGINA FID: DEF:, edge plain, 7.75g, 21.8mm (WR 295 R5; Montagu 1564; Murdoch 497/8; Nobleman 261/2; DM 198). *Striking flaw in obverse field, some light hairlines, otherwise mint state and extremely rare.* £15,000-20,000

Price Realised : £28,800

ex Bank Leu, Zürich, Switzerland, 26 October 2004, lot 442

This is considered to be the first proposed pattern Sovereign for the young Queen Victoria for which she granted William Wyon multiple portrait sittings. The head is of a small stature, the rear hair fillet lightly ruled with horizontal lines and the legend closely spaced; the reverse by Merlen being very similar to that adopted for currency. Note the light weight too, so that such a piece would not go very far should it escape into circulation.

The Extremely Rare Victoria Pattern Sovereign of 1837

397 **Victoria,** Pattern Sovereign, 1837, engraved by William Wyon, small young head left, hair bound with plain double fillet, with raised line depicting edges of fillets, plain truncation ruled with fine lines, close spaced date below slightly double struck, rosette either side, fine toothed border and high raised rim both sides, VICTORIA DEI GRATIA more widely spaced from 8 to 4 o'clock, *rev* struck with inverted die axis, engraved by Jean Baptiste Merlen, crowned quartered narrow shield of arms within laurel wreath tied with bow below shield, twelve pearls on each arch of crown, four pearls vertically arranged on central upright, nine pellets visible on ermine below jewel band, laurel wreath each side consists of 30 leaves per side and terminates in three leaves at top, six harp strings in Irish arms, left string emanates from back of female figure, emblems below, rose at centre, thistle to left, shamrock to right, small rosette either side, BRITANNIARUM REGINA FID: DEF:, edge plain, 8.00g, 21.9mm (WR 296 R5; Montagu 1566; Murdoch 499; DM 199). *Lightly toned with some light hairlines, otherwise mint state and extremely rare.* £15,000-20,000

Price Realised : £25,200

ex Spink and Son, 17 April 1997

This is considered to be the second obverse for the proposed pattern Sovereign for young Queen Victoria for which she granted William Wyon multiple portrait sittings. The head is of a small stature, though larger than the first proposal (see lot 33, page 54), with plain fillets the legend more widely spaced. Note that this pattern is of the correct weight for issue for circulation, unlike the other smaller young head patterns in the Bentley Collection, which suggests this proposed design ran a close second to the adopted young head as used for currency.

Extremely Rare Victoria Small Young Head Pattern Sovereign

966 **Victoria,** Pattern Sovereign, 1837, engraved by William Wyon, small young head left, hair bound with two plain fillets, thinly defined ponytail hair with some disjointing, wispy lock of hair from head to ponytail halfway down, W.W. incuse on truncation, date below slightly double struck, rosette either side, fine toothed border and high raised rim both sides, VICTORIA DEI GRATIA more widely spaced from 8 to 4 o'clock, *rev* struck with inverted die axis, engraved by Jean Baptiste Merlen, crowned quartered narrow shield of arms within laurel wreath tied with bow below shield, twelve pearls on each arch of crown, four pearls vertically arranged on central upright, nine pellets visible on ermine below jewel band, laurel wreath each side consists of 30 leaves per side and terminates in three leaves at top, six harp strings in Irish arms, left string emanates from back of female figure, emblems below, rose at centre, thistle to left, shamrock to right, small rosette either side, BRITANNIARUM REGINA FID: DEF:, edge plain, 7.71g, 21.8mm (WR 298 R6; Montagu 1565; Murdoch 500; Douglas-Morris 200). *Lightly toned with light hairlines, tiny rim imperfection on the reverse, otherwise good extremely fine and extremely rare.* £15,000-20,000

Price Realised : £33,600

This is considered to be the second obverse for the proposed pattern Sovereign for young Queen Victoria for which she granted William Wyon multiple portrait sittings. The obverse design has the same rendering as the head that is considered to be the first design, lot 33, page 54. This second proposed pattern has the legend more widely spaced, though the date width is a little narrower. The reverse is the same design as lot 33 and with the same die axis orientation.

The Extremely Rare Small Bust Pattern Sovereign of 1838

34 **Victoria,** Pattern Sovereign, 1838, very small young head left, hair bound with double fillet, rear fillet plain, top of front and rear fillets defined with a double incuse line, W.W. incuse on truncation, date below, date lightly double struck, rosette either side, fine toothed border and raised rim both sides, VICTORIA DEI GRATIA more widely spaced, from 8 to 4 o'clock, *rev* struck with inverted die axis, crowned quartered narrow shield of arms within laurel wreath tied with bow below shield, laurel wreath each side consists of 30 leaves per side and terminates in three leaves at top, six strings in Irish arms, left string emanates from back of female figure, emblems below, rose at centre, thistle to left, shamrock to right, small rosette either side, small rosette either side, BRITANNIARUM REGINA FID: DEF:, legend lightly doubled, edge plain, 7.84g, 21.9mm (WR 299 R5; Montagu 1567; Murdoch 501; Nobleman 263; DM 201). *Hairline raised flaw on bust from cheek to truncation, tiny dig by mouth, hairlines in fields, otherwise lightly toned mint state and extremely rare.* £15,000-20,000

Price Realised : £24,000

ex Reginald Huth collection, Sothebys, 5 April 1927, lot 264
ex S A H Whetmore collection, Glendinings, 24 March 1943, lot 114
ex Spink Auction 157, 18 November 2001, lot 575, illustrated on front cover.
The proposals for the new coinage took some time to effect and the new currency did not come to fruition until at least 1838 for most denominations. This further proposal for the Sovereign dated 1838 carries the smaller head, the fillets in the hair are now rendered with incuse outlines, and the engraver's initials W.W. appear raised on the truncation. The legend is more widely spaced surrounding the head more effectively. Note the light weight too, so that such a piece would not go very far should it escape into circulation.

The Extremely Rare First Bust Pattern Sovereign of 1838 with Adopted Reverse

35 **Victoria,** Pattern Sovereign, 1838, first young head left, fine hair bound with double fillet, extra line depicting lower rear fillet, ponytail terminates in single curved strand of hair, W.W. raised on truncation, date below lightly double struck, fine toothed border and raised rim both sides, VICTORIA DEI GRATIA, *rev* struck en médaille, crowned shield of arms within laurel wreath tied with bow below shield, narrow crown arches not so acutely angled, each with eleven pearl adornment, five pearls vertically arranged on central upright, wreath of 24 leaves each side, each terminate with two leaves at top, seven harp strings in taller Irish arms, first left string from scroll at back of female figure, emblems below, small rosette either side, BRITANNIARUM REGINA FID: DEF:, edge plain, 7.33g, 21.9mm (WR 300 R4; Montagu 1568; Murdoch 502; DM 202). *Some light hairlines, nick on neck, otherwise mint state and extremely rare.* £12,000-15,000

Price Realised : £19,200

ex Sothebys, 9 October 1995, lot 814

This final proposal pattern is of the design adopted for currency, the differences being that this coin carries a plain edge and is struck to a much lower weight than used for currency. It is therefore technically a pattern struck to proof quality from highly polished dies. This successful final proposal is highly significant as the forerunner of the shield reverse Sovereign of Queen Victoria.

Victoria 1838 Milled Edge Sovereign, Probably Struck From Proof Dies

967 **Victoria,** Sovereign, 1838, first young head left, hair bound with double fillet, ponytail terminates in single curved strand of hair, w.w. raised on truncation, narrow date below, some light die flaws in last word of legend, border teeth very finely rendered on both sides, *rev* struck with inverted die axis, crowned shield of arms within laurel wreath, seven harp strings to Irish harp, emblems below, edge milled, 8.00g, 22.1mm (cf WR 300; S 3852). *Well defined striking with proof-like fields, no doubt struck from highly polished dies, but impaired with multiple hairlines, rim knock, some signs of polishing, extremely fine and extremely rare.* £4000-5000

Price Realised : £4,080

bought A H Baldwin & Sons Ltd, March 2006
Only discovered in the last ten years, the 1838 milled edge proof Sovereign does not exist in true FDC condition. The finest known and initial discovery piece was recently sold on the A H Baldwin Winter Fixed Price List 2012 for £17,500. This slightly lesser coin was the second piece to come to light and is struck from the same proof dies, if somewhat impaired.

Off-centre Die Axis Victoria Sovereign of 1838 of Superb Quality

968 **Victoria,** Sovereign, 1838, struck with an off-centre die axis, first young head left, hair bound with double fillet, ponytail terminates in thicker upper strand of hair, w.w. raised on truncation, wider date below very lightly double struck as is legend, *rev* die alignment off-centre by 45°, crowned shield of arms within laurel wreath, emblems below, edge milled, 7.99g (Marsh 22 R; MCE 499; S 3852). *Light surface marks and hairlines, good extremely fine and one of the finest off-centre die strikes the cataloguer has seen for a Sovereign.* £3000-3500

Price Realised : £6,000

bought A H Baldwin & Sons Ltd, July 2006
Calendar year mintage 2,718,694

single hair strand terminal to ponytail

36 **Victoria,** Sovereign, 1838, first young head left, hair bound with double fillet, ponytail terminates in single curved strand of hair, w.w. raised on truncation, date below very lightly double struck as is legend, *rev* struck with inverted die axis, crowned shield of arms within laurel wreath, emblems below, edge milled, 7.99g (Marsh 22 R; MCE 499; S 3852). *Slightly uneven tone with a couple of tiny bagmarks, otherwise as struck, rare this nice.* £3000-3500

Price Realised : £4,800

ex Randy Weir Numismatics, Unionville, Ontario, Canada, purchased 3 November 1992
Calendar year mintage 2,718,694
Two slight variations upon the hair of the young Queen have been noticed in cataloguing the Bentley Collection, in that the termination of the ponytail either ends in a single strand of hair curving in a circle like that offered here, or this hair strand is absent and the termination is the bunch of hairs above where the single strand would be as in lot 46, page 68.

398 **Victoria,** Sovereign, 1838, doubled date, first young head left, hair bound with double fillet, ponytail terminates in single curved strand of hair, W.W. raised on truncation, date below heavily double struck, queen's name less so, fine toothed border and raised rim both sides, VICTORIA DEI GRATIA, *rev* struck with inverted die axis, crowned shield of arms within laurel wreath tied with bow below shield, narrow crown arches not so acutely angled, each with eleven pearl adornment, five pearls vertically arranged on central upright, wreath of 24 leaves each side, each terminate with two leaves at top, seven harp strings in taller Irish arms, first left string from scroll at back of female figure, emblems below, small rosette either side, BRITANNIARUM REGINA FID: DEF:, edge milled, 7.99g (Marsh 22 R; MCE 499; S 3852). *Light surface marks, good extremely fine.* £2000-2500

Price Realised : £3,000

ex Spink and Son, August 2001
Calendar year mintage 2,718,694

37 **Victoria,** Sovereign, 1838, first young head left, ponytail terminates in single curved strand of hair, date below, *rev* struck with off-set die axis, crowned shield of arms within laurel wreath, emblems below, 7.94g (Marsh 22 R; MCE 499; S 3852). *Surface marks and scuffs, good fine and very unusual with the misaligned die axis, rare.* £800-1000

Price Realised : £1,080

ex St James's Auction 14, 30 September 2009, lot 414
Calendar year mintage 2,718,694

The Extremely Rare "Narrow Shield" Sovereign of 1838

38 **Victoria,** Sovereign, 1838, "narrow shield" variety, first young head left, with double fillet, ponytail terminates in single curved strand of hair, date below, 3 in date double struck, *rev* struck with inverted die axis, possibly engraved by Jean Baptiste Merlen, narrow crowned quartered shield of arms within laurel wreath of different leaf arrangement tied with bow below shield, 21 leaves each side of wreath, top of each side terminates in three leaves, twelve pearls on each arch of crown, four pearls vertically arranged on central upright, nine pellets visible on ermine below jewel band, top of wreath each side terminates in three leaves, crown with more prominent acutely angled arches, six harp strings in Irish arms which emanate from back of female figure above the lower scroll, emblems below, die flaw to right to rim, small rosette either side, BRITANNIARUM REGINA FID: DEF:, 7.99g (Marsh 22A R3; MCE 499; S 3852A). *Proof-like underlying brilliance, some light scuffing, extremely fine, reverse better and extremely rare, one of the finest extant of this great rarity.* £10,000-12,000

Price Realised : £21,600

ex Randy Weir Numismatics, Unionville, Ontario, Canada, purchased 28 June 1993
This interesting variety of reverse was only discovered a few decades ago and is perhaps an unused proposal die that was too valuable not to use. The main differences are really the lesser amount of leaves in the wreath and their arrangement and the differently rendered crown on the narrower shield. This unusual reverse found its way onto the current Sovereign of 1838, it may well be the work of an apprentice engraver working under Merlen. The variety is of the highest rarity with most of the few examples only surviving in the lower grades. This piece is the best quality example we are aware of in private hands.

Beautiful 1839 Proof Sovereign Struck with Plain Edge and Inverted Die Axis

39 **Victoria,** Proof Sovereign, 1839, first young head left, finely engraved hair bound with double fillet, ponytail terminates in single curved strand of hair, date below, date and legend lightly double struck as well as fine border teeth, *rev* struck with inverted die axis, crowned quartered shield of arms within laurel wreath, wreath of 24 leaves each side, each terminate with two leaves at top, eleven pearls on each arch of crown, five pearls vertically arranged on central upright, top of wreath each side terminates in two leaves, seven harp strings in Irish Arms, first left string from scroll at back of female figure, emblems below, absent serif on upper left of second I of BRITANNIARUM, edge plain, 7.90g, 21.9mm (WR 303; Douglas-Morris 203; S 3852). *Previously encapsulated by PCGS as a PR63, very light contemporary hairlines, otherwise very pleasing mint state.* £4000-4500

Price Realised : £5,760

ex Randy Weir Numismatics, Unionville, Ontario, Canada, purchased December 1995, NYINC, Sheraton Hotel, New York.
The 1839 Proof Sovereign was produced for presentation to very important persons, and William Wyon himself would have been able to supply proofs to whomever he pleased, or to those who would commission him to do so. These proof Sovereigns were produced with either an inverted or upright die axis, whether this was intentional or not is uncertain. The 1839 proofs were included as part of the "Coronation" Proof Sets showing proof quality coins struck from highly polished dies of all the denominations to be issued for currency if they had not done so already. Some of the proof denominations occur in these sets with either one die axis or the other, but to be a true set, all coins should feature the same die axis. As the Crown and Five Pounds always occur with the same upright die axis this would seem to dictate that all the proofs in the set from the Sovereign to Farthing of 1839 should also be upright. The Bentley Collection upright (en médaille – struck like a medal) die axis 1839 Proof Sovereign is listed as lot 399, page 61. Note the light weight of this proof, so that such a piece would not go very far should it escape into circulation.
As mentioned above the impressive Proof Set also included the magnificent Five Pounds with the impressive depiction of the Queen as Una leading the British Lion. The set also included a Crown and both of these coins featured the full signature of William Wyon, as W WYON R.A. the letters showing his membership of admission to the Royal Academy. This was the first time an artist's surname had appeared in full since Pistrucci's full name on the George III Crowns and gold Five Pounds and Two Pounds patterns of 1820. Wyon had attempted this previously with the pattern Crown for William IV in 1831, but this did not make it to production for the 1831 Proof Set, having been abbreviated to WW as usually seen on the currency coinage. It seems by 1839 the advisory committee to the Royal Mint had relented. The 1839 Proof Set is generally accepted as the third Proof Set available from the Royal Mint and deluxe fitted cases could be supplied to house the coins.

969 **Victoria,** Proof Sovereign, 1839, first young head left, finely engraved hair bound with double fillet, ponytail terminates in single curved strand of hair, date below, date and legend lightly double struck as well as fine border teeth, penultimate A of legend unbarred, last A with partial bar, hair at bun of a coarser weaker rendering, *rev* struck with inverted die axis, crowned quartered shield of arms within laurel wreath, wreath of 24 leaves each side, each terminate with two leaves at top, eleven pearls on each arch of crown, five pearls vertically arranged on central upright, top of wreath each side terminates in two leaves, seven harp strings in Irish Arms, first left string from scroll at back of female figure, emblems below, absent serif on upper left of second I of BRITANNIARUM, edge plain, 7.91g, 21.9mm (WR 303; Douglas-Morris 203; S 3852). *Very light hairlines both sides, otherwise very pleasing, practically as struck.* £4000-5000

Price Realised : £7,440

For a narrative footnote about the 1839 proof sovereigns, please see lot 39 above.

Victoria 1839 Proof Sovereign Struck En Médaille

399 **Victoria,** Proof Sovereign, 1839, first young head left, ponytail termination less detailed, no single strand, date below, last A of legend slightly disjointed, *rev* struck en médaille, crowned quartered crowned shield of arms within laurel wreath, emblems below, Irish Arms with diagonal depiction of rear of harp body visible through strings, some legend letters lightly filled with raised die flawing, second I of legend with broken upper left serif, edge plain, 7.89g, 21.8mm (WR 302 R4; S 3852). *Very light contemporary hairlines, tiny nicks over head, otherwise, as struck and rare.* £3500-4500

Price Realised : £6,000

ex Spink Auction 129, 17 November 1998, lot 277

Note the lighter weight of this proof coin, which ensured it would not go far if inadvertently passed into circulation.

The 1839 Proof Sovereign was produced for presentation to very important persons and William Wyon himself would have been able to supply proofs to whomever he pleased, or to those who would commission him to do so. These proof Sovereigns were produced with either an inverted or upright die axis, whether this was intentional or not is uncertain. The 1839 proofs were included as part of the "Coronation" Proof Sets showing proof quality coins struck from highly polished dies of all the denominations to be issued for currency, if not already in circulation. Some of the proof denominations occur in these sets with either one die axis or the other but, to be a true set, all coins should feature with the same die axis. As the Crown and Five Pounds always occur with the same upright die axis it would seem to dictate that all the proofs in the set from the Sovereign to Farthing of 1839 should also be upright (as per the example here).

For further information on the proof issue of 1839 see the footnote to Lot 39, page 60.

The 1839 proof set is generally accepted as the third proof set available from the Royal Mint and at the time deluxe fitted cases could be supplied to house the coins.

Extremely Rare 1839 Proof Sovereign Struck with a Milled Edge

40 **Victoria,** Proof Sovereign, 1839, first young head left, ponytail terminates in single curved strand of hair, date below, last A of legend slightly disjointed, *rev* struck en médaille, crowned quartered crowned shield of arms within laurel wreath, emblems below, Irish Arms lacking diagonal depiction of rear of harp body visible through strings, some legend letters lightly filled with raised die flawing, edge milled, 7.91g, 22mm (WR 304 R6; Douglas-Morris 204; S 3852). *Very light contemporary hairlines, otherwise very pleasing, mint state and of the highest rarity.* £10,000-12,000

Price Realised : £16,800

ex Captain K J Douglas-Morris collection, Sothebys, 26 November 1974, lot 204

ex Property of a Gentleman, Spink Auction 117, 19 November 1997, lot 2006

This is a proof Sovereign struck from highly polished dies of the currency design with the milled edge, the reverse die seems to be a slightly different design where the Irish Arms are given less of a three dimensional look with the strings meeting the base of the harp directly with no attempt to show perspective beyond them. The milled edge proof is so much rarer when compared to the plain edge version. Note the light weight too, so that such a piece would not go very far should it escape into circulation.

The Very Rare Victoria 1839 Currency Sovereign

400 **Victoria,** Sovereign, 1839, first young head left, ponytail terminates in single curved strand of hair, date below, last A of legend slightly disjointed, *rev* inverted die axis, crowned quartered crowned shield of arms within laurel wreath, emblems below, some legend letters lightly doubled, edge milled, 7.99g (Marsh 23; S 3852). *Some very light bagmarks, small scratches by F of reverse legend, otherwise good extremely fine and very rare.* £4000-5000

Price Realised : £8,880

ex Randy Weir Numismatics, Unionville, Ontario, Canada, purchased 14 September 1993

The Extremely Rare "Key Date" Victoria 1841 Sovereign

41 **Victoria,** Sovereign, 1841, first young head left, with single strand of hair at terminal of ponytail which is disjointed, date below, toothed border both sides, normal A's in GRATIA, *rev* struck with inverted die axis, crowned quartered shield of arms within laurel, emblems below, 7.94g (Marsh 24 R3; MCE 501; S 3852). *Fine / almost very fine, the reverse stronger than obverse, the key date for the London young head currency series, extremely rare.* £6000-8000

Price Realised : £8,640

ex St James's Auction 5, 27 September 2006, lot 582
Calendar year mintage 124,054
This coin exhibits a weaker rendering of the ponytail terminal, which in the first smaller young head usually has a single curving strand of hair to finish it off, and with the two multi-strand turnings of hair above fully jointed. This 1841 Sovereign has only a trace of the single strand termination and shows a multi-strand ending at the part above. The next part above that, is only partially joined on one side rather than both. This weaker rendering occurs very rarely.
There being no sovereigns minted bearing the date 1840, the whole calendar year figure presumably represents 1841 dated coins only, though unspent 1839 dies may have continued at first but is unlikely due to the gap in production.
With a relatively low mintage, the 1841 Sovereign does not survive in any quantity, the supply of this date in the coin market has always been out-stripped by demand and examples in recent years for sale have been few and far between. When offered for sale by auction the 1841 Sovereign has garnered higher and higher realisations recently, as was seen for a mint state example at Bonham's in December 2011, sold for £34,800 including buyer's premium.
Even though few coins exist there are two significant varieties, the full letter A's in the last word on the obverse and the unbarred A variety, only noted and published within the last decade. The Bentley Collection contains both varieties, this is the lesser quality example herewith albeit with the full A's in legend. The unbarred A variety, lot 970, page 63, survives in a higher grade of preservation.

Extremely Rare High Grade 1841 Sovereign with Unbarred A's in Legend

970 **Victoria,** Sovereign, 1841, first young head left, no single strand of hair at terminal of ponytail which is disjointed, date below, toothed border both sides, unbarred A's in GRATIA, *rev* struck with inverted die axis, crowned quartered shield of arms within laurel, emblems below, 7.98g (Marsh 24 R3; MCE 501; S 3852). *Raised die flaw on crown on the reverse, some very light bagmarks, otherwise practically extremely fine, reverse stronger, the key date for the London young head currency series, and the third finest the cataloguer has seen, extremely rare.* £10,000-15,000

Price Realised : £22,800

ex Randy Weir Numismatics, Unionville, Ontario, Canada, purchased September 1990
Calendar year mintage 124,054
For further reading on the 1841 Sovereign See footnotes to lot 41, page 62.

42 **Victoria,** Sovereign, 1842, first young head left, ponytail terminates in single curved strand of hair, date below with nearly closed 2, *rev* crowned quartered shield of arms within laurel wreath, emblems below, edge milled, 7.98g (Marsh 25; MCE 502; S 3852). *Light surface marks, a little weak of strike at Irish harp, otherwise very pleasing, good extremely fine.* £800-1000

Price Realised : £1,440

ex Randy Weir Numismatics, Unionville, Ontario, Canada, purchased 29 June 1992
Calendar year mintage 4,865,375
Much more common than the 1841, the more closed 2 variety exists of 1842 also with normal or unbarred A's in the last word of the obverse legend. The other more significant variety of 1842 is the much rarer open 2 type where the curve of the top of the 2 is not so rounded and shorter. Marsh does not list any of the varieties of 1842 in his publication as these have only been noted in the last decade.

The Extremely Rare Unbarred A Variety of 1842 Currency Sovereign

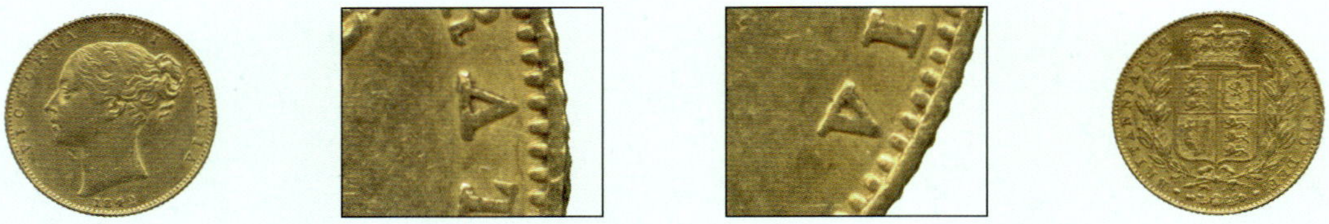

401 **Victoria,** Sovereign, 1842, unbarred A's in GRATIA, first young head left, ponytail terminates in single curved strand of hair, date below with nearly closed 2, *rev* crowned quartered shield of arms within laurel wreath, emblems below, edge milled, 7.97g (Marsh 25; MCE 502; S 3852). *Surface marks, good fine to nearly very fine and extremely rare with the unbarred A's in legend.* £800-1000

Price Realised : £792

ex St James's Auction 10, 6-7 November 2008, lot 526
Calendar year mintage 4,865,375
It is interesting to note that this is the same obverse die used for the 1841 Sovereign with unbarred A's and it was the 1842 version that was noted in print first. There are three varieties of the 1842 Sovereign in the Bentley Collection, normal 1842, the very rare "open 2" and the piece shown here, the extremely rare "unbarred A" variety which appears to be a product of weak cross-bars in the A's rather than an inverted "V" as some thought previously.

Very Nice Victoria 1842 Sovereign with Open 2

971 **Victoria,** Sovereign, 1842, open 2 in date, first young head left, ponytail terminates in single curved strand of hair, date below, tall sharp pointed 4, *rev* crowned quartered shield of arms within laurel wreath, emblems below, edge milled, 7.97g (Marsh 25; MCE 502; S 3852). *Once cleaned, scuffed very fine and very rare.* £600-800

Price Realised : £792

ex St James's Auction 6, 9 June 2007, lot 531
Calendar year mintage 4,865,375
The more significant variety of 1842 is the rarer open 2 type where the curve of the top of the 2 is not so rounded and shorter. The 4 in this date variety is also a taller and sharper topped figure than the normal 1842 date. Marsh does not list any of the varieties of 1842 in his publication as these have only been noted in the last decade.
For further reading on date varieties of 1842 Sovereign See footnote for lot 42, page 63.

43 **Victoria,** Sovereign, 1843, first young head left, ponytail terminates in single curved strand of hair, date below, *rev* crowned quartered shield of arms within laurel wreath, emblems below, upper left serif of second I absent in BRITANNIARUM, 8.00g (Marsh 26; MCE 503; S 3852). *Light surface marks, otherwise good extremely fine.* £700-900

Price Realised : £1,560

ex Randy Weir Numismatics, Unionville, Ontario, Canada, purchased 7 January 1995
Calendar year mintage 5,981,968

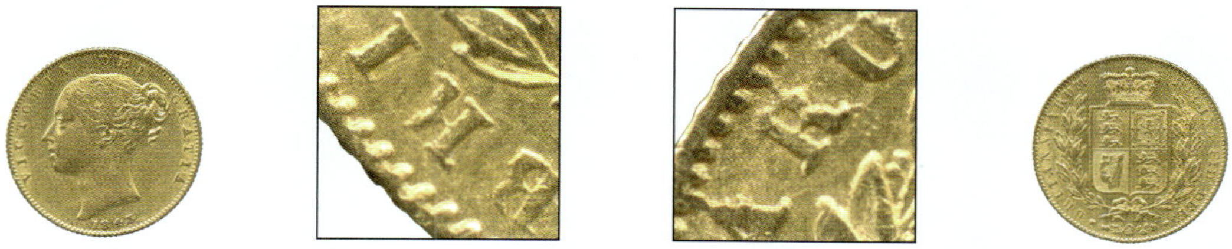

402 **Victoria,** Sovereign, 1843, first young head left, ponytail terminates in single curved strand of hair, date below, die flaw between 4 and 3, other light flaws in legend, penultimate A of legend filled, *rev* crowned quartered shield of arms within laurel wreath, emblems below, upper left serif of second I absent and first letter R in BRITANNIARUM broken and resembling a K, 7.95g (Marsh 26; MCE 503; S 3852). *Scuffed with surface marks, otherwise good fine.* £300-400

Price Realised : £360

ex St James's Auction 14, 30 September 2010, lot 417
Calendar year mintage 5,981,968

The Extremely Rare 1843, 3 over 2 Overdate Sovereign

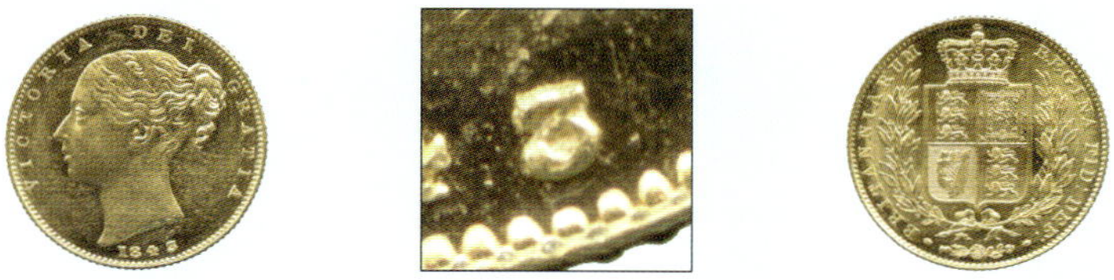

44 **Victoria,** Sovereign, 1843, 3 struck over a 2, spread date with 3 distant from 4, first young head left, ponytail terminates in single curved strand of hair, date below, *rev* crowned quartered shield of arms within laurel wreath, emblems below, 7.98g (Marsh 26B R5; MCE 503; S 3852). *Proof-like, the obverse lightly scuffed with surface marks, hairlined both sides, otherwise good extremely fine and extremely rare.* £800-1000

Price Realised : £2,280

ex Spink and Son Ltd, March 2001
Calendar year mintage 5,981,968
This extremely rare overdate was only discovered in 1980 by the late Michael Marsh, according to his publication. From the scant few survivors evident it is therefore likely that only one or perhaps two obverse dies dated 1842 were in serviceable enough use at the end of their production run not to be scrapped and overstruck with the new date figure 3 to continue into the issue of 1843 dated sovereigns.

The Only Known Example of the Victoria 1843 Sovereign with "3" over an "8"

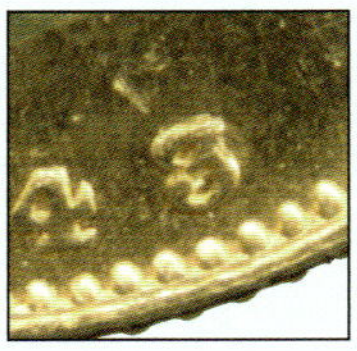

403 **Victoria,** Sovereign, 1843, 3 struck over an 8, first young head left, ponytail terminates in single curved strand of hair, date below, *rev* crowned quartered shield of arms within laurel wreath, emblems below, 7.99g (cf Marsh 26B; MCE 503; S 3852). *Proof-like some hairline marks, good extremely fine, extremely rare, the only specimen currently known.* £2000-2500

Price Realised : £3,120

purchased via A H Baldwin & Sons Ltd, 28 July 2010
Calendar year mintage 5,981,968
This extremely rare overdate was only discovered two years ago and is not dissimilar to the 1843 with 3 over 2 (discovered and published in 1980 by Michael Marsh, see Lot 44, page 65). However, unlike the 3 over 2, which was clearly using a left-over die from 1842 to prolong its life and therefore intentional, this coin depicts a true engraving error. It seems that the date was punched incorrectly with an 8 at first instead of a 3 and had to be corrected. It remains the only specimen known to the cataloguer thus far and is in superb condition

Rare Victoria 1843 Overdate Sovereign

972 **Victoria,** Sovereign, 1843, 3 struck over a 2 or rotated 2, first young head left, ponytail terminates in single curved strand of hair, date below, shorter stubby 4 in date spread away from 3, O of Queen's name with slight break at lower right from die, *rev* crowned quartered shield of arms within laurel wreath, emblems below, 7.98g (cf Marsh 26B R5; MCE 503; S 3852). *Cleaned, light surface marks, very fine and very rare.* £600-800

Price Realised : £984

bought A H Baldwin & Sons Ltd, 28 July 2010
Calendar year mintage 5,981,968
This extremely rare overdate was only discovered in 1980 by the late Michael Marsh, according to his publication. From the scant few survivors evident it is therefore likely that only one or perhaps two obverse dies dated 1842 were in serviceable enough use at the end of their production run not to be scrapped and overstruck with the new date figure 3 to continue into the issue of 1843 dated sovereigns. This example does not appear to be a straight forward 2, but one that is perhaps slightly rotated.
For other examples of date varieties of 1843 Sovereigns see lots 43 and 44, pages 64-65.

973 **Victoria,** Sovereign, 1843, Roman letter I in date for figure 1, first young head left, ponytail terminates in single curved strand of hair, date below, T of Queen's name die flawed, *rev* crowned quartered shield of arms within laurel wreath, emblems below, upper left serif of second I of legend broken off, 7.98g (cf Marsh 26; MCE 503; S 3852). *Cleaned, some heavy scuffs and surface marks, bold very fine and very rare.* £800-1000

Price Realised : £1,056

ex St James's Auction 6, 9 June 2007, lot 533
Calendar year mintage 5,981,968
The third ranked of the more interesting varieties of 1843 Sovereign after the narrow shield and overdate varieties, it is interesting to note that a true capital letter I punch has been used instead of an Arabic figure 1 to date the obverse die. Some of the other so-called "Roman I" date varieties are actually Arabic 1's over inverted Arabic 1's there are not so many that are a true letter I punch. Again this is another sign of how the quality of the engraving was becoming more careless at this time, but not too serious as to not make it into circulation. The variety for 1843 discovered only in the last ten years, therefore not described by Marsh for this date.
For other examples of date varieties of 1843 Sovereigns see lots 43 and 44, pages 64-65.

The Extremely Rare "Narrow Shield" Sovereign of 1843

45 **Victoria,** Sovereign, 1843, "narrow shield" variety, first young head left, with double fillet, ponytail terminates in single curved strand of hair, date below, *rev* possibly engraved by Jean Baptiste Merlen, "narrow" crowned quartered shield of arms within laurel wreath of different leaf arrangement, crown with more prominent and acutely angled arches, tied with bow below shield with smaller ribbon ends, twelve pearls on each arch of crown, four pearls vertically arranged on central upright, nine pellets visible on ermine below jewel band, wreath of 21 leaves each side, top of wreath each side terminates in three leaves, seven harp strings in Irish arms, left string emanates from back of female figure above lower scroll, narrower spaced taller emblems below, double shamrock head to right of large central rose, thistle to left, no rosettes, small hyphen either side, 7.97g (Marsh 26A R4; MCE 504; S 3852B). *Light surface marks, flaw to left of reverse through second N of legend, extremely fine and extremely rare.* £12,000-15,000

Price Realised : £20,400

ex Randy Weir, Unionville, Ontario, Canada, purchased 29 April 1992
The "narrow shield" variety of 1843 is different to the 1838 version and is perhaps the result of use of another unspent proposed reverse die from storage. The 1843 shield differs in a few design elements from the 1838 version most noticeable from the fact it has seven strings as opposed to six on the 1838 version. The leaf arrangements are similar and both consist of 21 leaves in each side of the wreath. The emblems below are quite different however and are much thicker and narrower on the 1843 reverse and have a mere hyphen each side rather than a rosette. The shamrock has two of its distinctive leaves rather than one, the central rose much larger and the thistle appears to have distant thistles beyond. Some of the leaves of the left hand wreath are not fully struck up or more faintly engraved.
The reason for striking the 1843 "narrow shield" is perhaps lost to history, but the legacy are these extremely rare narrow shield pieces most of which survive in lower grade. The Bentley Collection example is one of the finest extant.

thicker hair terminal to ponytail **normal date 1844**

46 **Victoria,** Sovereign, 1844, first young head left, no single strand of hair at terminal of ponytail which is partly disjointed, date below, date evenly spread, 18 doubled, last A of legend filled, *rev* crowned quartered shield of arms within laurel wreath, emblems below, small rosette either side, upper left serif of second I absent in BRITANNIARUM, a few light raised flaws in reverse lettering, 7.99g (Marsh 27; MCE 505; S 3852). *Three tiny scratches in shield by crown and in lower right quarter, small light scratch under truncation, otherwise a little weakly struck at shield, pleasing extremely fine.* £600-800

Price Realised : £1,500

ex Randy Weir Numismatics, Unionville, Ontario, Canada, purchased 12 November 1990
Calendar year mintage 3,000,445
This coin exhibits a weaker rendering of the ponytail terminal, which in the first smaller young head usually has a single curving strand of hair to finish it off, and with the two multi-strand turnings of hair above fully jointed. This 1844 Sovereign does not have the single strand termination and shows a multi-strand ending at the part above. The next part above that is only partially joined on one side rather than both. This weaker rendering occurs very rarely.
There are various differing date arrangements for the 1844 dated sovereign, some are more widely spaced than others; some have dates arranged in a smooth arc, whereas others may have the 44 markedly higher than the 18. The cataloguer feels that it was about this time that the consistency of the quality control in the production of dies started to slip, but this may be because the output of coins produced is consistently on the high side in the 1840s compared to previous decades and the number of dies that would have been required to strike such amounts commensurately greater. Still higher mintages were yet to come in succeeding years and the Bentley Collection will continue to demonstrate many of the varieties that resulted from this seemingly rushed work at the Mint. 1844 also marks the year that Leonard C Wyon, son of William becomes second engraver.

Victoria 1844 Sovereign with Normal Date Arrangement

974 **Victoria,** Sovereign, 1844, first young head left, no single strand of hair at terminal of ponytail which is partly disjointed, date below, date evenly spread, 44 smaller than 18, *rev* crowned quartered shield of arms within laurel wreath, emblems below, upper left serif of second I absent and foot of previous N in BRITANNIARUM, 7.95g (Marsh 27; MCE 505; S 3852). *Scratch above head, other heavy surface marks and scuffs, otherwise good fine.* £250-300

Price Realised : £288

Bought A H Baldwin & Sons Ltd, June 2008
Calendar year mintage 3,000,445. For further reading on date varieties of 1844 Sovereigns see footnote for lot 46 above.

closer date, small "44"

47 **Victoria,** Sovereign, 1844, smaller 44, closer spaced date**,** first young head left, ponytail terminates in single curved strand of hair, date below, 18 doubled, last A of legend filled, *rev* crowned quartered shield of arms within laurel wreath, emblems below, upper left serif of second I absent and disjointed first N and I in BRITANNIARUM, 7.98g (cf Marsh 27; MCE 505; S 3852). *Scratch across neck, with other light scuffs and hairlines, good very fine, reverse better.* £500-600

Price Realised : £552

ex Property of a Gentleman, Spink Auction 124, lot 2016
Calendar year mintage 3,000,445
A different date variety of 1844, which was shown and verified by Michael Marsh after the publication of his last book and was to be assigned the reference number 27B, however no further editions of *The Gold Sovereign* are forthcoming since the passing of Mr Marsh. Therefore the only 1844 variety in Marsh is the more spectacular 4 over inverted 4, an example of which is lot 975, page 69.

closer date, small "44"

404 **Victoria,** Sovereign, 1844, smaller 44 higher than 18, closer spaced date, first young head left, ponytail terminates in single curved strand of hair, date below, *rev* crowned quartered shield of arms within laurel wreath, emblems below, upper left serif of second I absent and disjointed first N and I in BRITANNIARUM, 7.97g (cf Marsh 27; MCE 505; S 3852). *Cleaned, nearly very fine.* £300-350

Price Realised : £384

Calendar year mintage 3,000,445
For further reading on date varieties of 1844 Sovereigns see footnote for entry above.

The Very Rare 4 Over Inverted 4 Date Variety Victoria 1844 Sovereign

975 **Victoria,** Sovereign, 1844, first 4 struck over inverted 4, small close date, first young head left, date below, *rev* crowned quartered shield of arms within laurel wreath, emblems below, upper left serif of second I absent and foot of previous N in BRITANNIARUM, 7.96g (Marsh 27A R2; MCE 505; S 3852). *Surface marks, bold very fine and extremely rare.* £1000-1200

Price Realised : £2,640

ex Spink and Son Ltd, July 2004
Calendar year mintage 3,800,845
This is the most spectacular variety shared by 1844, 1845 and 1846 Sovereigns, and the overstrike and undertype are very apparent and clear on the example offered here.
The variety was first discovered on the 1844 version way back in September 1974 when a certain "Goldfinger" wrote to the Spink Numismatic Circular (page 341) alerting readers to the variety with a clear illustration.
Most collectors ask how such a striking can occur. This is due to a true engraver's error, punching in the date, the 4 punch was obviously entered inverted on the first attempt and then shoddily corrected with a second punching over the top. In the numismatic trade such errors and corrections are fondly referred to as "after lunch" coins, in that it is assumed the engraver made such an error for today's collectors to enjoy, when working after a hearty lunch and maybe having imbibed too much ale. More likely though was that it was perhaps easy to mistake the orientation of the 4 punch, or perhaps working under candle-light or the poorer light of a dark day such a mistake could occur. The fact that the error and correction exists for three consecutive years suggests someone working at the Mint may have made the same mistake three times, and another sign of workmanship slipping, though at least it was corrected before any coins could be struck for circulation. This variety remains very elusive.
For further reading on date varieties of 1844 Sovereigns see footnotes to lots 46 and 47, page 68.

closer date

48 **Victoria,** Sovereign, 1845, smaller closer date in arc, first young head left, ponytail terminates in single curved strand of hair, date below, *rev* crowned quartered shield of arms within laurel wreath, emblems below, raised die flaw at bottom to right of emblems to wreath stalk, 7.98g (Marsh 28; MCE 506; S 3852). *A little weakly struck at shield, reverse rim nick, some very light bagmarks, otherwise practically as struck.* £800-1000

Price Realised : £1,560

ex Randy Weir Numismatics, Unionville, Ontario, Canada, purchased 29 June 1990
Calendar year mintage 3,800,845
There are varying date arrangements and varieties for 1845 too, for the same reasons as in 1844. Normal date and close date are the main two varieties, the larger more top-heavy 5 as in the next lot being another. Marsh only features again the more spectacular 4 over inverted 4 variety, see lot 50, page 71.

small close date

405 **Victoria,** Sovereign, 1845, small close date, first young head left, ponytail does not terminate in single strand of hair, date below in an arc, slight doubling of legend both sides, *rev* crowned quartered shield of arms within laurel wreath, emblems below, top of E in DEI incomplete, 8.01g (Marsh 28; MCE 506; S 3852). *A little weakly struck at shield, otherwise uncirculated.* £800-1000

Price Realised : £6,240

Calendar year mintage 3,800,845. For further reading on varieties of 1845 Sovereigns see footnote for Lot 50, page 71.

spread date

49 **Victoria,** Sovereign, 1845, spread date with larger bulbous 5, first young head left, ponytail terminates in single curved strand of hair, date below, first A in GRATIA unbarred, last A disjointed, *rev* crowned quartered shield of arms within laurel wreath, emblems below, top of E in DEI incomplete, 7.98g (Marsh 28; MCE 506; S 3852). *Heavily scuffed in fields with scratch by mouth, almost very fine.* £350-400

Price Realised : £480

ex St James's Auction 11, 8 May 2009, lot 392
Calendar year mintage 3,800,845
Not only has this coin a more unusual 5 with a spread date but the second A in the obverse legend has no bar and the last A is not complete. Jean Baptiste Merlen had been superannuated from the Mint in July 1844 at the age of 75 so all die work on reverses from 1845 can be considered firmly as being "after" J B Merlen. For further reading on varieties of 1845 Sovereigns see footnote for Lot 50, page 71.

spread date large "5"

406 **Victoria,** Sovereign, 1845, spread date large 5, first young head left, ponytail does not terminate in single strand of hair, date below, first A unbarred and last A broken in obverse legend, *rev* crowned quartered shield of arms within laurel wreath, emblems below, top of E in DEI incomplete, die flaw on N and A of first word, 7.94g (Marsh 28; MCE 506; S 3852). *Once cleaned, good fine to nearly very fine.* £300-350

Price Realised : £312

purchased via A H Baldwin & Sons Ltd, 8 February 2008
Calendar year mintage 3,800,845. For further reading on varieties of 1845 Sovereigns see footnote for Lot 50, page 71.

976 **Victoria,** Sovereign, 1845, spread date with flat-topped 8 with larger upper loop than lower, perhaps inverted, first young head left, date below, *rev* crowned quartered shield of arms within laurel wreath, emblems below, 7.93g (Marsh 28; MCE 506; S 3852). *Heavily surface marked in fields, good fine and unusual.* £300-400

Price Realised : £264

bought A H Baldwin & Sons Ltd, June 2008
Calendar year mintage 3,800,845
This unusual variety appears to have the figure 8 inverted in the date. Note that the weight of this coin is on the limit of what was legally acceptable for trade at face value according to the Acts of Coinage 1816-70. Jean Baptiste Merlen had been superannuated from the Mint in July 1844 at the age of 75 so all die work on reverses from 1845 can be considered firmly as being "after" J B Merlen. For further reading on varieties of 1845 Sovereigns see footnote for Lot 50, page 71.

4 over inverted 4

50 **Victoria,** Sovereign, 1845, 4 struck over inverted 4, closer date, larger 5, first young head left, ponytail terminates in single curved strand of hair, date below, light raised flaw between 8 and 4, last A of legend partly filled, *rev* crowned quartered shield of arms within laurel wreath, emblems below, 7.98g (Marsh 28A R2; MCE 506; S 3852). *A little weakly struck at shield, some very light bagmarks and hairlines, otherwise extremely fine / good extremely fine and very rare.* £800-1000

Price Realised : £1,920

ex Spink and Son Ltd, November 2000
Calendar year mintage 3,800,845
This is the most spectacular variety shared by 1844, 1845 and 1846 Sovereigns, and the overstrike and undertype are very apparent and clear on the example offered here. The variety was first discovered on the 1844 version way back in September 1974 when a certain "Goldfinger" wrote to the Spink Numismatic Circular (page 341) alerting readers to the variety with a clear illustration. In fact this coin was the first that turned up of this date for this variety, and was shown to the late Michael Marsh so it could be included in the most recent published version of the Gold Sovereign. Most collectors ask how such a striking can occur. This is due to a true engravers error, punching in the date, the 4 punch was obviously entered inverted on the first attempt and then shoddily corrected with a second punching over the top. In the numismatic trade such errors and corrections are fondly referred to as "after lunch" coins, in that it is assumed the engraver made such an error for today's collectors to enjoy, when working after a hearty lunch and maybe having imbibed too much ale. More likely though was that it was perhaps easy to mistake the orientation of the 4 punch, or perhaps working under candle-light or the poorer light of a dark day such a mistake could occur. The fact that the error and correction exists for three consecutive years suggests someone working at the Mint may have made the same mistake three times, and another sign of workmanship slipping, though at least it was corrected before any coins could be struck for circulation. This variety remains very elusive.

1845 Sovereign with Angled Date

978 **Victoria,** Sovereign, 1845, spread date in an arc, 4 weak and die flawed, larger 5, first young head left, date below, V of Queen's name very weakly rendered, last of legend filled, *rev* crowned quartered shield of arms within laurel wreath, emblems below, some letters of legend a little weak, 8.00g (Marsh 28; MCE 506; S 3852). *Weak on harp on the reverse, some die flaws and surface marks, scuff on neck, otherwise extremely fine and unusual.* £600-800

Price Realised : £2,280

bought Spink and Son Ltd, January 2005
Calendar year mintage 3,800,845
For further reading on varieties of 1845 Sovereigns see footnote for lot 50 above.

Roman I

51 **Victoria,** Sovereign, 1845, Roman letter I in date for figure 1, first young head left, ponytail terminates in single curved strand of hair, date below, spread even date, light raised flaw in some letters of VICTORIA, *rev* crowned quartered shield of arms within laurel wreath, emblems below, 7.98g (cf Marsh 28; MCE 506; S 3852). *Once cleaned, now lightly toned, with associated surface marks and hairlines, fine, very rare.* £800-1000

Price Realised : £1,080

ex St James's Auction 4, 8 May 2006, lot 375
Calendar year mintage 3,800,845
The second ranked of the more interesting varieties of 1845 Sovereign and another that has only been discovered in the last decade and is unrecorded by Marsh. Interesting in that a true capital letter I punch has been used instead of an Arabic style figure 1 to date the obverse die. Some of the other so-called "Roman I" date varieties are actually Arabic figure 1's over inverted Arabic figure 1's there are not so many that are a true letter I punch. Again this is another sign of how the quality of the engraving was becoming more careless at this time, but not too serious as to not make it into circulation.

Obverse Legend with E Over Tilted E in DEI

977 **Victoria,** Sovereign, 1845, spread date, first young head left, date below, E of DEI over a tilted E, last A of legend filled, *rev* crowned quartered shield of arms within laurel wreath, emblems below, 7.97g (Marsh 28; MCE 506; S 3852). *Surface marks, good fine and unusual.* £250-300

Price Realised : £240

ex Paul Davies Ltd, Ilkley, via A H Baldwin & Sons Ltd, October 2006
Calendar year mintage 3,800,845
For further reading on varieties of 1845 Sovereigns see footnote to lots 48-51, pages 69-71.

407 **Victoria,** Sovereign, 1846, first young head left, date below, curvy 6 with sharp end, hairline raised flaw by 4, *rev* crowned quartered shield of arms within laurel, emblems below, some doubling in part of reverse legend, 7.98g (Marsh 29; MCE 507; S 3852). *Light surface marks, good extremely fine, previously graded by NGC as MS63.* £600-800

Price Realised : £2,520

ex Randy Weir Numismatics, Unionville, Ontario, Canada, purchased 2 June 1995
Calendar year mintage 3,802,947

Rare Victoria 1846 Sovereign with 1 Over Inverted 1 in Date

979 **Victoria,** Sovereign, 1846, figure 1 in date over inverted 1 giving impression of a Roman I, date doubled, 6 bulbous, first young head left, date below, Queen's name lightly die flawed, *rev* crowned quartered shield of arms within laurel wreath, emblems below, broken foot on first N of legend, flaw by third R, broken limb on last E with F doubled, 7.99g (cf Marsh 29; MCE 507; S 3852). *Heavily cleaned, some heavy surface marks and edge bruise, otherwise nearly extremely fine and very rare.* £600-800

Price Realised : £1,560

bought Spink and Son Ltd, May 2005
Calendar year mintage 5,981,968
The second most interesting variety of 1846 Sovereign, after the 4 over inverted 4 variety. It will be noted the "Roman I" is actually a product of a figure 1 at first being entered upon the die inverted and then corrected with one the right way up, giving a serif at all four corners, albeit with the upper right one being the one underneath and therefore with a step down from the correct figure on top. Again this is another sign of how the quality of the engraving was becoming more careless at this time, but not too serious as to not make it into circulation. The variety for 1846 discovered only in the last ten years and therefore not described by Marsh for this date.
For further reading on varieties of 1846 Sovereigns see footnote for lot 52, page 73.

The Extremely Rare 4 over Inverted 4, 1846 Sovereign

4 over inverted 4

52 **Victoria,** Sovereign, 1846, 4 struck over inverted 4, first young head left, ponytail terminates in single curved strand of hair, date below, curvy 6 with sharp end, *rev* crowned quartered shield of arms within laurel, emblems below, 7.98g (cf Marsh 29; MCE 507; S 3852). *Once cleaned, now lightly toned, light surface marks and hairlines, good very fine and extremely rare.* £1000-1200

Price Realised : £960

Calendar year mintage 3,802,947

This is the most spectacular variety shared by 1844, 1845 and 1846 Sovereigns, and one of three varieties known for 1846 Sovereigns, the others being the normal date and Roman letter I for Arabic figure 1 in date. The 4 over inverted 4 is due to a true engraver's error, punching in the date the 4 punch was obviously entered inverted on the first attempt and then shoddily corrected with a second punching over the top. The fact the error and correction exists for three consecutive years suggests someone working at the Mint may have made the same mistake three times and another sign of workmanship slipping, as the mintage for the calendar year is very similar to 1845. This variety on the 1846 Sovereign has only been discovered in the last ten years and since Michael Marsh passed away so it is not listed in his publication like the 1844 and 1845 and is considered to be the rarest of the three dates with this variety.

53 **Victoria,** Sovereign, 1847, first young head left, ponytail terminates in single curved strand of hair, date below, date with doubled figures, *rev* crowned quartered shield of arms within laurel wreath, emblems below, 8.00g (Marsh 30; MCE 508; S 3852). *Light surface marks and hairlines, pleasing, good extremely fine.* £600-800

Price Realised : £1,080

Calendar year mintage 4,667,126

54 **Victoria,** Sovereign, 1847, date out of alignment, first young head left, ponytail terminates in a trace of a single curved strand of hair, date below, misaligned date with lower 1 and higher 8 and 4, the 4 slightly doubled, *rev* crowned quartered shield of arms within laurel, emblems below, 7.94g (Marsh 30; MCE 508; S 3852). *Once cleaned, some surface deposits remain around rim, now lightly toned, scuffed, good fine.* £300-350

Price Realised : £336

ex Spink and Son Ltd, November 2003

Calendar year mintage 4,667,126

A slight variance in date variety for 1847, again due to the high output this calendar year, many dies were required and so some dates appear differently arranged to others. The only more significant varieties of 1847 are all centred on the figure 1 in the dates, the most interesting being the Roman letter I variety, see lot 980, page 74, as well as other dates that have missing serifs on the 1.

Rare Victoria 1847 Sovereign with 1 Over Inverted 1 in Date

980 **Victoria,** Sovereign, 1847, figure 1 in date over inverted 1 giving impression of a Roman I, the inverted 1 appears to be on top of the correct 1, 4 doubled therefore appears quite tall, first young head left, date below, Queen's name lightly die flawed, *rev* crowned quartered shield of arms within laurel wreath, emblems below, broken foot on first N of legend, flaw by third R, broken limb on last E with F doubled, 7.92g (cf Marsh 30; MCE 508; S 3852). *Light surface marks and rim nick, cleaned, almost fine to fine and very unusual.* £300-500

Price Realised : £360

bought Spink and Son Ltd, May 2005
Calendar year mintage 5,981,968
Perhaps the most interesting variety of 1847 Sovereign. It will be noted the "Roman I" is actually a product of a figure 1 over another of the opposite inversion. However in this case the inverted figure appears to be over a correctly placed 1. The lower left serif being the one that steps down from the figure on top, indicating the correct figure underneath. This may well have been an attempt to correct the die that had the broken lower right serif that had been used for other 1847 Sovereigns, an example of which is lot 409 below. This is another sign of how the quality of the engraving was becoming more careless at this time, but not too serious as to not make it into circulation. The variety for 1847 discovered only in the last ten years and therefore not described by Marsh for this date. Note the weight of this coin is under the limit of what was legally acceptable for trade at face value according to the Acts of Coinage 1816-70.
For further reading on varieties of 1847 Sovereigns see footnote for lot 54, page 73.

Unusual Inverted 1 in Date 1847 Sovereign

inverted figure "1"

408 **Victoria,** Sovereign, 1847, no lower left serif to 1 in date as an inverted figure 1, struck over another figure 1 perhaps also inverted, first young head left, ponytail terminates in a trace of a single curved strand of hair, date below doubled, last I of legend without lower right serif, *rev* crowned quartered shield of arms within laurel, emblems below, die flaw by second A in legend, another by letter G, 7.92g (Marsh 30; MCE 508; S 3852). *Once cleaned, fine, very unusual and rare.* £400-500

Price Realised : £408

ex St James's Auction 7, 8 February 2008, lot 647
It is interesting to note that, as one of the lower grade Sovereigns in the Bentley Collection, this coin is well under the legal tender weight limit that was set in successive Coinage Acts from 1816-1891. This coin seems genuinely to have the "1" of the date inverted which is very unusual.
Calendar year mintage 4,667,126. For further reading on varieties of 1847 Sovereigns see footnote for Lot 54, page 73.

missing serif in date

409 **Victoria,** Sovereign, 1847, no lower right serif to 1 in date, 4 with tiny serif, first young head left, ponytail does not terminate in a single strand of hair, date below doubled, last I of legend without lower right serif, *rev* crowned quartered shield of arms within laurel, emblems below, 7.96g (Marsh 30; MCE 508; S 3852). *Once cleaned, good fine, very unusual and rare.* £400-500

Price Realised : £408

Calendar year mintage 4,667,126
For further reading on varieties of 1847 Sovereigns see footnote for Lot 54, page 73.

Contemporary Copper Imitation of a Sovereign, dated 1847

981 **Victoria,** Trial Sovereign, 1847, struck in copper, after William Wyon, coarse second larger style young head left, with thin double fillet in hair ruled with double incuse lines, open inner ear, hair bun touches G of legend, W.W. raised on truncation, date below, squat type 4 with double serif in date, toothed border both sides separate from rim, VICTORIA DEI GRATIA, *rev* struck with inverted die axis, crowned shield of arms within laurel wreath tied with bow below shield, six harp strings in thinner harp, lions in shield disjointed, emblems below, ribbons closer to emblems, small rosette either side, BRITANNIARUM REGINA FID: DEF:, first A with raised die flaw, edge milled, 4.62g, 22.4mm. *Black spot by date, good extremely fine and unusual.* £300-500

Price Realised : £816

Possibly a fantasy or forger's piece, or maybe an apprentice's rendering for the second larger bust that followed in 1848. From the crudity of the design and inconsistency of it, compared to Mint product, it most likely is a forgery which, when covered with a thin layer of gilding, could pass as a Sovereign to the unwary.

The Extremely Rare 1848 First Smaller Young Head Sovereign

55 **Victoria,** Sovereign, 1848, first young head left, ponytail terminates in single curved strand of hair, date below, doubled date figures out of alignment, toothed border both sides, *rev* crowned quartered shield of arms within laurel wreath, emblems below, 7.98g (Marsh 31A R2; MCE 509; S 3852). *Light surface marks and nicks, small black spot on reverse rim and by Scottish lion, otherwise good extremely fine and extremely rare.* £4000-5000

Price Realised : £8,880

ex Spink and Son Ltd, May 2001
Calendar year mintage 2,246,701
One of the unsung great rarities in the shield sovereign series of Queen Victoria is the first small young head upon the 1848 Sovereign. The majority of the surviving 1848 coins usually exhibit the second larger young head and the first small head is extremely rare in this cataloguer's experience, more so than the rating put upon it by Marsh. The calendar year mintage is much lower in 1848 and there was a Royal Mint Commission that year to look into ways to improve the die and matrix production at which William Wyon was required to give evidence. This maybe why the output was lower and the reason why the larger young head was introduced as a result of the deliberations of this committee and would explain why the first head is rare for this year. Perhaps the wear and tear on dies was considered to be less if the design more evenly filled the available field with less of a gap between it and the legend, perhaps resulting in less strain on the dies and increasing their longevity in striking. This is worthy of further research. The legacy we are left with today is an obvious juncture in the transition of the two types of bust, the first one being so much rarer for 1848.

The Second Larger Young Head type Sovereign of Queen Victoria (1837-1901)

Victoria Second Small Young Head Type Currency Sovereign
From 1848 the size of Victoria's young head bust increases to fill more of the available field and is therefore rendered closer to the legend lettering. This may have been an attempt to prolong the life of the dies, which are subjected to multiple tons of pressure in use, and as conjectured in the footnote for the previous lot after a Royal Mint Commission in this year investigated the die and matrix production. The Chief Engraver, William Wyon was called to give evidence on die production to this commission.
This second larger young head type sovereign was in use from 1848-1855 inclusive and is of the same general design as the previous smaller bust with the engravers initials W.W. raised with stops on the bust. The easiest way to tell the sizes of the bust, particularly when looking at the changeover year of 1848, is to look how close the front hair band fillet is to the legend as it is this point that differs most in the sizing of the busts.
In 1853 there was a slight change on some dies produced and the engravers initials WW are incuse on the truncation without stops and this runs concurrently from 1853-1855 with the first type and then alone from 1856-1870 inclusive. Strangely the 1853 proof has one stop between the letter W's only on the truncation.
From 1863 until 1874 the reverses of the shield type feature an additional "die" number below the shield. These will be discussed at the relevant point in the catalogue as they form quite an extensive series.

56 **Victoria,** Sovereign, 1848, second larger young head left, hair bound with double fillet, W.W. raised on truncation, ponytail terminates in single curved strand of hair, legend surrounding, date below, 8 and 4 date figures doubled, *rev* crowned quartered shield of arms within laurel wreath, F of DEF with a weak top bar, 7.99g (Marsh 31; MCE 509; S 3852C). *Only the lightest of surface marks, a superb coin, uncirculated.*
£800-1000
Price Realised : £3,840

ex Randy Weir Numismatics, Unionville, Ontario, Canada, purchased 2 June 1995
Calendar year mintage 2,246,701
This is the most prolific of the 1848 coins carrying the new second larger young head, the change over occurred perhaps for the reasons discussed above in the introduction to the second young head of Queen Victoria.

410 **Victoria,** Sovereign, 1848, second larger young head left, hair bound with double fillet, W.W. raised on truncation, legend surrounding, date below, date and legend doubled, *rev* crowned quartered shield of arms within laurel wreath, E of DEF with a weak top bar, 7.98g (Marsh 31; MCE 509; S 3852C). *Prooflike though scuffed, extremely fine.*
£400-600
Price Realised : £1,560

Calendar year mintage 2,246,701
This is the most prolific of the 1848 coins carrying the new second larger young head (albeit with some doubling of date and legend), the change-over may have occurred for the reasons discussed in the introduction to the second young head of Queen Victoria. See also "a note on varieties" in the introduction, specifically the part about dual-hubbed dies.

411 **Victoria,** Sovereign, 1848, first I of queen's name with no lower serifs, second larger young head left, hair bound with double fillet, W.W. raised on truncation, legend surrounding, date below, date and legend doubled, *rev* crowned quartered shield of arms within laurel wreath, 7.97g (Marsh 31; MCE 509; S 3852C). *Hairlined, almost extremely fine and very unusual.* £300-400

Price Realised : £480

ex A H Baldwin & Sons Ltd sourced via Paul Davies Ltd, October 2010
Calendar year mintage 2,246,701

982 **Victoria,** Sovereign, 1848, unusual rendering of 4 with bulbous top, second larger young head left, hair bound with double fillet, W.W. raised on truncation, legend surrounding, date below, squat 4 with flawed top, *rev* crowned quartered shield of arms within laurel wreath, F of FID doubled, 7.97g (Marsh 31; MCE 509; S 3852C). *Cleaned with surface marks, otherwise very fine and unusual.* £300-400

Price Realised : £288

ex St James's Auction 11, 8 May 2009, lot 401
This is the most prolific of the 1848 coins carrying the new second larger young head, albeit with some doubling of date and legend. The change occurred, perhaps, for the reasons discussed in the introduction to the second young head of Queen Victoria. See also "a note on varieties" in the introduction, specifically the part about dual-hubbed dies which is responsible for the doubling of date and legend.
Calendar year mintage 2,246,701

983 **Victoria,** Sovereign, 1848, second larger young head left, hair bound with double fillet, W.W. raised on truncation, legend surrounding, date below, neater pointed 4, second and third I's of legend and first T and R without lower left serifs, *rev* crowned quartered shield of arms within laurel wreath, emblems below, weak top to last E of legend, weak upper serif to first I of legend, 7.92g (Marsh 31; MCE 509; S 3852C). *Cleaned with surface marks, otherwise good fine and unusual.* £250-300

Price Realised : £264

bought Paul Davies Ltd, via A H Baldwin & Sons Ltd, October 2006
Calendar year mintage 2,246,701. It is interesting to note that the weight of this coin in its lower grade is under the legal tender limit as dictated by the Coinage Acts of 1816-1891.

57 **Victoria,** Sovereign, 1849, second larger young head left, no single strand of hair at terminal of ponytail which is partly disjointed, date below, date figures and latter half of legend doubled, *rev* crowned quartered shield of arms within laurel wreath, emblems below, thin topped letters in DEF, 7.98g (Marsh 32 R; MCE 510; S 3852C). *A few light marks and hairline scratches, otherwise extremely fine.* £500-600

Price Realised : £1,020

ex Randy Weir Numismatics, Unionville, Ontario, Canada, purchased 29 June 1990
As with other dates of the 1840s variation occurs again in the alignment and layout of the dates for this relatively low mintage. The above coin can be considered the normal variety. This coin exhibits a weaker rendering of the ponytail terminal, which in the first smaller young head usually has a single curving strand of hair to finish it off, and with the two multi-strand turnings of hair above fully jointed. This 1849 Sovereign does not have the single strand termination and shows a multi-strand ending at the part above. The next part above that is only partially joined on one side rather than both. This weaker rendering occurs very rarely.
Calendar year mintage 1,755,399. For further reading on varieties of 1849 Sovereigns see footnotes to lots 57 and 58, pages 77-78.

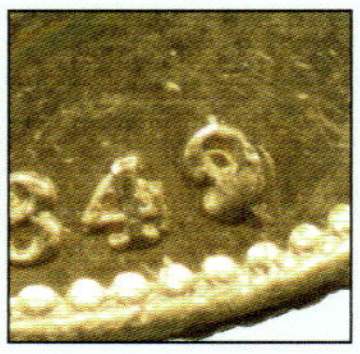

rotated "9" in date

412 **Victoria,** Sovereign, 1849, 9 rotated out of line and doubled, second larger young head left, date below, date figures and latter half of legend doubled, *rev* crowned quartered shield of arms within laurel wreath, die flawed emblems below, 7.99g (Marsh 32 R; MCE 510; S 3852C). *Once cleaned, otherwise extremely fine.* £500-600

Price Realised : £624

ex Spink and Son, purchased November 2003
Calendar year mintage 1,755,399
For further reading on varieties of 1849 Sovereigns see footnote for Lots 57-58, pages 77-78.

The Very Rare Roman Style I Dated 1849 Sovereign

Roman I

58 **Victoria,** Sovereign, 1849, Roman letter I in date for figure 1, second larger young head left, no single strand of hair at terminal of ponytail which is partly disjointed, date below, *rev* crowned quartered shield of arms within laurel wreath, emblems below, light raised die flaw to right of rose, 7.98g (cf Marsh 32 R; MCE 510; S 3852C). *Hairline surface marks, extremely fine and very rare.* £1500-1800

Price Realised : £1,320

ex A H Baldwin & Sons Ltd, November 2008
Calendar year mintage 1,755,399
The most interesting and rarest variety of 1849 Sovereign, one that has only been discovered in the last decade and is unrecorded by Marsh. Interesting in that a true capital letter I punch has been used instead of an Arabic style figure 1 to date the obverse die. Some of the other so-called "Roman I" date varieties are actually Arabic figure 1's over inverted Arabic figure 1's. There are not so many that are a true letter I punch. The piece in the Bentley Collection is the finest known to the cataloguer of this extremely rare variety. For further reading on varieties of 1849 Sovereigns see footnotes to lots 57 and 58, pages 77-78.

1849 Sovereign with Small Date

984 **Victoria,** Sovereign, 1849, second larger young head left, date below, clear date with bulbed 9 nearly closed, neater 4, *rev* crowned quartered shield of arms within laurel wreath, emblems below, flawed A in first word of reverse legend, third I with weak lower serif, 7.97g (Marsh 32 R; MCE 510; S 3852C). *Cleaned, rim nick, very fine.* £250-300

Price Realised : £312

bought A H Baldwin & Sons Ltd, 28 July 2010
Calendar year mintage 1,755,399
For further reading on varieties of 1849 Sovereigns see footnotes to lots 57 and 58, pages 77-78.

59 **Victoria,** Sovereign, 1850, second larger young head left, ponytail terminates in single curved strand of hair, date below, *rev* crowned quartered shield of arms within laurel wreath, emblems below, 7.97g (Marsh 33 R; MCE 511; S 3852C). *Only the lightest of surface marks, a superb coin, uncirculated and very rare in this quality.*

£800-1000

Price Realised : £1,320

ex Randy Weir Numismatics, Unionville, Ontario, Canada, purchased 22 March 1990
Calendar year mintage 1,402,039
With a relatively low calendar year mintage the 1850 Sovereign has always been considered a rare date in the series, and was perhaps more highly thought of in dealer's lists of some 50 or 60 years ago, where it is rated as very rare. Other specimens must have come to light since then, as in this cataloguer's experience the date is merely rare and is on par for availability with the 1849 Sovereign, which is of a similar quantity of mintage, and rated therefore the same by Marsh. Of course in the top grades, as we have demonstrated here, any Sovereign, even for a more common mintage, can be considered rare or even very rare.

985 **Victoria,** Sovereign, 1850, second larger young head left, date below, die flaw from 0 of date to neck, doubled legend, *rev* crowned quartered shield of arms within laurel wreath, emblems below, third I of legend with no upper left serif, 7.94g (Marsh 33 R; MCE 511; S 3852C). *Cleaned, nearly very fine.*

£250-300

Price Realised : £312

ex St James's Auction 11, 8 May 2009, lot 402
Calendar year mintage 1,402,039
For further reading on varieties of 1850 Sovereigns see footnotes to lots 59, 60 and 61, pages 79-81.

missing serif in date

413 **Victoria,** Sovereign, 1850, thin topped 1 in date with no upper serif, second larger young head left, date below, doubled legend and date, *rev* crowned quartered shield of arms within laurel wreath, emblems below, 7.97g (Marsh 33 R; MCE 511; S 3852C). *Once cleaned, nearly extremely fine and very unusual.*

£800-1000

Price Realised : £912

ex A H Baldwin & Sons Ltd sourced via Paul Davies Ltd, October 2010
Calendar year mintage 1,402,039
For further reading on varieties of 1850 Sovereigns see footnote for lots 59, 60 and 61, pages 79-81.

The Extremely Rare Inverted A for V in VICTORIA, 1850 Sovereign

inverted A

60 **Victoria,** Sovereign, 1850, inverted A for V at start of legend, second larger young head left, no single strand of hair at terminal of ponytail which is partly disjointed, date below, some doubling of legend letters both sides, hairline raised flaw in GRATIA, *rev* crowned quartered shield of arms within laurel wreath, emblems below, 7.96g (cf Marsh 33 R; MCE 511; S 3852C). *Surface marks, once cleaned now lightly toned, a couple of digs on bust, otherwise bold very fine and extremely rare.* £800-1000

Price Realised : £1,020

ex St James's Auction 13, 6 May 2010, lot 958
Calendar year mintage 1,402,039
Another variety only discovered in the last decade since the publication of Marsh's "The Gold Sovereign", this most interesting variety is still only demonstrated by a few specimens. The engraver in haste, or due to lack of sharpness in eyesight, or daylight, has obviously selected an A punch rather than a V when stamping in the letters onto the obverse die, or perhaps the correct punch could not be located in the time allowed. He and his superiors either never noticed, and / or could not afford to waste a valuable die for a tiny error the legacy of which has passed to us as an interesting true variety in the coinage of 1850.
Additionally this coin exhibits a weaker rendering of the ponytail terminal, which in the first smaller young head usually has a single curving strand of hair to finish it off, and with the two multi-strand turnings of hair above fully jointed. This 1850 Sovereign does not have the single strand termination and shows a multi-strand ending at the part above. The next part above that is only partially joined on one side rather than both. This weaker rendering occurs very rarely.

Dramatic 1850 Sovereign with 5 Clearly Over the 8 of the Date

986 **Victoria,** Sovereign, 1850, 5 struck over 8, second larger young head left, date below, *rev* crowned quartered shield of arms within laurel wreath, emblems below, 7.97g (cf Marsh 33 R; MCE 511; S 3852C). *Cleaned, good very fine and of the highest rarity, the cataloguer has only heard of one other specimen extant, extremely rare.* £1000-1500

Price Realised : £2,520

ex Clark Smith collection, San Rafael, California, July 2010
Calendar year mintage 1,402,039
This is one of the most recent discoveries in the Sovereign series, first noted about 8 years ago. The Bentley collector had to wait some five years before finally acquiring this piece three years ago.
The product of an engraver's error, the date figure 5 was punched in at first as an 8 and had to be corrected. In the numismatic trade such errors and corrections are fondly referred to as "after lunch" coins, in that it is assumed the engraver made such an error when working after a hearty lunch and maybe having imbibed too much ale. More likely though was that it was perhaps easy to mistake the 5 punch for an 8, or perhaps working under candle-light or the poorer light of a dark day such a mistake could occur. This variety remains most elusive.
For further reading on varieties of 1850 Sovereigns see footnotes to lots 59, 60 and 61, pages 79-81.

The Extremely Rare Roman Style I Dated 1850 Sovereign

Roman I

61 **Victoria,** Gold Sovereign, 1850, Roman letter I in date for figure 1, second larger young head left, ponytail terminates in a mere trace of single curved strand of hair, date below, figures slightly doubled giving a I over a smaller I effect to the initial figure, legend doubled, *rev* crowned quartered shield of arms within laurel wreath, emblems below, 7.98g (cf Marsh 33 R; MCE 511; S 3852C). *Once lightly cleaned, now lightly toned, good extremely fine and extremely rare.* £1500-1800

Price Realised : £1,320

ex St James's Auction 4, 8 May 2006, lot 383
Calendar year mintage 1,402,039
The other interesting and rare variety of 1850 Sovereign, the Roman letter I date variety, has only been discovered in the last decade and is unrecorded by Marsh. Interesting in that a true capital letter I punch has been used instead of an Arabic style figure 1 to date the obverse die. The doubling of the date caused by "dual-hubbing" in cutting the die has added interest in that the letter I appears to be over a smaller letter I caused by the judder in the die cutting process. The piece in the Bentley Collection, though once cleaned, is the finest known to the cataloguer of this extremely rare variety. For more information about "dual-hubbing" of dies please see the varieties section of the introduction.

spread date

62 **Victoria,** Sovereign, 1851, spread date, second larger young head left, no single strand of hair at terminal of ponytail which is partly disjointed, date below, gap between 18 and 51, die flaw through second 1 from rim to neck, *rev* crowned quartered shield of arms within laurel wreath, emblems below, 7.97g (Marsh 34; MCE 512; S 3852C). *Light bagmarks, some light raised die flaws, otherwise extremely fine.* £400-500

Price Realised : £552

ex Randy Weir Numismatics, Unionville, Ontario, Canada, purchased 22 March 1990
Calendar year mintage 4,013,624
For a relatively high mintage for calendar year not many varieties seem to exist for 1851, in fact the Bentley Collection only contains two date varieties, a spread date as here and a closer narrower date, see lot 63, page 82.
Additionally this coin exhibits a weaker rendering of the ponytail terminal, which in the first smaller young head usually has a single curving strand of hair to finish it off, and with the two multi-strand turnings of hair above fully jointed. This 1851 Sovereign does not have the single strand termination and shows a multi-strand ending at the part above. The next part above that is only partially joined on one side rather than both. This weaker rendering occurs very rarely.
29 October 1851 marks the day that William Wyon dies aged about 56 and still in the post of Chief Engraver. His son Leonard C Wyon succeeds him. Leonard's cousin James Wyon became resident engraver at this time too – he being later called upon to design the first portrait of the Queen at the Sydney Mint.

1851 Sovereign with 5 Struck Over a Lower 5 in Date

987 **Victoria,** Sovereign, 1851, 5 struck over a lower 5, spread date between 18 and 51, second larger young head left, date below, *rev* crowned quartered shield of arms within laurel wreath, emblems below, 7.98g (Marsh 34; MCE 512; S 3852C). *A few trifling hairlines, otherwise good extremely fine.* £400-500

Price Realised : £2,280

Calendar year mintage 4,013,624
For further reading on variety of 1851 Sovereigns see footnote for lot 62 above.

63 **Victoria,** Sovereign, 1852, second larger young head left, ponytail terminates in single curved strand of hair, date below, die flaw raised on 1 of date, *rev* crowned quartered shield of arms within laurel wreath, light raised die flaws by crown, emblems below, 7.98g (Marsh 35; MCE 513; S 3852C). *A very pleasing coin, uncirculated.* £700-900

Price Realised : £1,860

ex Randy Weir Numismatics, Unionville, Ontario, Canada, purchased 7 January 1995
Calendar year mintage 8,053,435
Representing the highest mintage thus far of Victoria's reign and the highest since 1821, the 1852 Sovereign sees its fair share of varieties in date and legend, of which there are six in total in the Bentley Collection. This coin is considered the normal variety. William Wyon, having died 29 October 1851 aged about 56, can no longer be considered as having a hand in engraving the obverse dies, so from now onward dies originally designed by Wyon are engraved "after" him.

414 **Victoria,** Sovereign, 1852, second larger young head left, date below doubled, die flaw at end of legend, *rev* crowned quartered shield of arms within laurel wreath, emblems below, 7.98g (Marsh 35; MCE 513; S 3852C). *Once cleaned, lightly hairlined nearly extremely fine.* £300-400

Price Realised : £312

purchased via A H Baldwin & Sons Ltd, 28 July 2010
Calendar year mintage 8,053,435
For further reading on varieties of 1852 Sovereigns see footnote for lot 63 above.

415 **Victoria,** Sovereign, 1852, second larger young head left, date below doubled, die flaw at end of legend, *rev* crowned quartered shield of arms within laurel wreath, emblems below, E of DEF with a weak top bar, penultimate I of legend without upper left serif, 7.97g (Marsh 35; MCE 513; S 3852C). *Some surface marks, nearly extremely fine and unusual.* £300-400

Price Realised : £336

ex St James's Auction 13, 6 May 2010, lot 965
Calendar year mintage 8,053,435
For further reading on varieties of 1852 Sovereigns see footnotes to lot 63 above.

989 **Victoria,** Sovereign, 1852, second larger young head left, date below, *rev* crowned quartered shield of arms within laurel wreath, emblems below, penultimate D over a lower D in legend, 7.92g (Marsh 35; MCE 513; S 3852C). *Short scratch in obverse field, otherwise good fine.* £250-300

Price Realised : £264

ex G K Coins, London, early 2005
Calendar year mintage 8,053,435
It is interesting to note that the weight of this coin in its lower grade is under the legal tender limit as dictated by the Coinage Acts of 1816-1891. For further reading on varieties of 1852 Sovereigns see footnote for lot 63 above.

The Extremely Rare Roman Style I Dated 1852 Sovereign

64 **Victoria,** Sovereign, 1852, Roman letter I in date for figure 1, raised die flaw in I, second larger young head left, ponytail terminates in a mere trace of single curved strand of hair, date below, back of neck and some letters in legend doubled, first I of legend over a higher I, *rev* crowned quartered shield of arms within laurel wreath, emblems below, 7.98g (cf Marsh 35; MCE 513; S 3852C). *Tiny dig over hair bun and light rim bruise, almost extremely fine, the reverse better, extremely rare.* £1000-1200

Price Realised : £1,020

ex St James's Auction 6, 8 June 2007, lot 548
Calendar year mintage 8,053,435. Even though the calendar year mintage is high the 1852 with Roman letter I in date is extremely rare, only being discovered in the last decade and not published in Marsh.

988 **Victoria,** Sovereign, 1852, 5 struck over a lower 5, date doubled, second larger young head left, date below, legend lightly doubled, *rev* crowned quartered shield of arms within laurel wreath, emblems below, light raised die flaws rose and between R and G in legend, 8.00g (Marsh 35; MCE 513; S 3852C). *Lightly hairlined, good extremely fine.* £500-600

Price Realised : £1,680

Calendar year mintage 8,053,435
For further reading on varieties of 1852 Sovereigns see footnote for lot 63, page 82.

The Impressive and Very Elusive 1853 Proof Sovereign

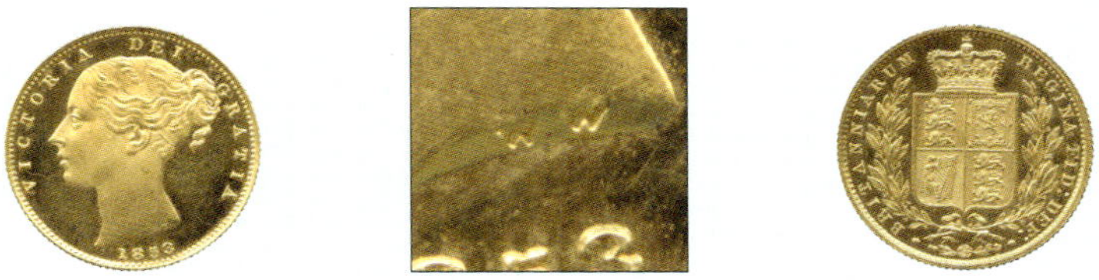

65 **Victoria,** Proof Sovereign, 1853, engraved after William Wyon, second larger young head left, no single strand of hair at terminal of ponytail, hair bound with double fillet, W.W incuse on truncation, spread date below slightly doubled, VICTORIA DEI GRATIA slightly doubled, toothed border and raised linear outer rim both sides, *rev* engraved after Jean Baptiste Merlen, struck with inverted die axis, crowned quartered shield of arms within laurel wreath tied with bow below shield, seven harp strings in Irish arms, emblems below, small rosette either side, BRITANNIARUM REGINA FID: DEF:, edge milled, 7.99g, 22.1mm (WR 305 R3; Montagu 1570; Murdoch 505; DM 205; S 3852D). *Light hairline scratch by first I of VICTORIA, toned, otherwise very pleasing as struck and very rare.* £10,000-12,000

Price Realised : £16,800

ex Spink Auction 119, 4 March 1997, lot 74
The 1853 Proof Sovereign struck from highly polished dies is a coin that was included in the very rare "Proof Sets" of all the coinage that were available for purchase from the Court Jeweller "Hunt and Roskell". The coins were available to purchase singly too and this is one of the rarer Proof Sovereigns of the reign. The Proof Sets of 1853 are the rarest the Mint has ever produced in pre-decimal times and are generally considered the fourth set to have been officially issued. With this Proof Sovereign note the new rendition of W.W on the truncation with only the single stop between the letters. It is questionable if perhaps these sets were produced as a memorial to their designer William Wyon who died 29 October 1851, aged about 56, and the incuse letters perhaps could be a metaphor for him being deceased, and under the level plain rather than living and above it. Such an intention would never have been recorded, but further research into the reasoning for issue of the 1853 Proof Sets and the differing WW treatment on the truncation of the Sovereign would be very useful.
The 1853 Proof Set is one of the most attractive sets, containing arguably one of Wyon's finest designs, the silver Gothic style Crown, first produced as an excessively rare pattern in 1846 and then as a proof for sale in 1847, with supposedly about 8000 struck. Estimates of issue for the 1853 Proof Set have ranged from 150 to 400, though it is still an unknown quantity for sure. The Sovereign for the first time, is the highest value coin in the 1853 Proof Set when compared with the three previous official Proof Sets.

1853 spread date

416 **Victoria,** Sovereign, 1853, spread date, second larger young head left, W.W. raised on truncation, date below, 5 struck over a lower 5, 18 doubled, legend slightly doubled, *rev* crowned quartered shield of arms within laurel wreath, emblems below, some light die flaws, 7.99g (Marsh 36; MCE 514; S 3852C). *Some hairline surface marks mainly on obverse, otherwise good extremely fine.* £400-500

Price Realised : £840

ex Douro Cargo, Spink Auction 118, 20-21 November 1996, lot 294
Calendar year mintage 10,597,993
For further reading on varieties of 1853 Sovereigns see footnote for lot 66, page 85.

990 **Victoria,** Sovereign, 1853, wide spread date, second larger young head left, W.W. raised on truncation, date below slightly out of line, legend doubled especially DEI, raised die flaw at end of legend, *rev* crowned quartered shield of arms within laurel wreath, emblems below, 7.97g (Marsh 36; MCE 514; S 3852C). *Some light bagmarks, mainly on neck, otherwise good extremely fine.* £400-500

Price Realised : £2,760

Calendar year mintage 10,597,993
For further reading on varieties of 1853 Sovereigns see footnote for lot 66, page 85.

1853 Sovereign with Wide Date

992 **Victoria,** Sovereign, 1853, second larger young head left, W.W. raised on truncation, obverse slightly double struck, raised die flaw in date, first I of Queen's name over a higher I, last A of legend die flawed to rim, *rev* crowned quartered shield of arms within laurel wreath, emblems below, whole reverse lightly double struck, 7.98g (Marsh 36; MCE 514; S 3852C). *Some light nicks and scratches, otherwise lightly toned with underlying brilliance, about extremely fine.* £300-400

Price Realised : £504

Calendar year mintage 10,597,993
For further reading on varieties of 1853 Sovereigns see footnote for lot 66, page 85.

66 **Victoria,** Sovereign, 1853, second larger young head left, W.W. raised on truncation, no single strand of hair at terminal of ponytail which is partly disjointed, date below, raised flaw between A and T of last word of legend that is slightly doubled, *rev* crowned quartered shield of arms within laurel wreath, emblems below, 7.98g (Marsh 36; MCE 514; S 3852C). *Previously graded by NGC as MS63, a few tiny surface marks, otherwise practically as struck.* £600-800

Price Realised : £1,260

ex St James's Auction 5, 27 September 2006, lot 610
Calendar year mintage 10,597,993
The calendar year output for 1853 represents the highest mintage in over 30 years at this point in time, and is the highest mintage for the modern milled sovereign since its inception in 1817. The date is therefore rife with variety not only with aspects like the W.W. on the neck, but also in the date and, rarely, in the legend. The variety depicted here is considered the normal type encountered for 1853 with the raised W.W. in relief on the truncation of the neck.
Additionally this coin and the next three exhibit a weaker rendering of the ponytail terminal, which in the first smaller young head usually has a single curving strand of hair to finish it off, and with the two multi-strand turnings of hair above fully jointed. This 1853 Sovereign and from this date forward, do not have the single strand termination and shows a multi-strand ending at the part above. The next part above that is only partially joined on one side rather than both. This weaker rendering occurs normally from here on.

991 **Victoria,** Sovereign, 1853, 3 struck over a 5, second larger young head left, W.W. raised on truncation, obverse slightly double struck, raised die flaw from tip of truncation to rim, *rev* crowned quartered shield of arms within laurel wreath, emblems below, 7.96g (cf Marsh 36; MCE 514; S 3852C). *With a clear overstrike, heavily surface marked and scuffed, otherwise about very fine and unusual, very rare.* £400-600

Price Realised : £840

ex St James's Auction 13, 6 May 2010, lot 979, erroneously catalogued as 5 over 3
Calendar year mintage 10,597,993
The product of an engraver's error, the date figure 3 was punched in at first as an 5 and had to be corrected. In the numismatic trade such errors and corrections are fondly referred to as "after lunch" coins, in that it is assumed the engraver made such an error when working after a hearty lunch and maybe having imbibed too much ale. More likely though was that it was perhaps easy to mistake the 3 punch for an 5, or perhaps working under candle-light or the poorer light of a dark day such a mistake could occur. This variety remains quite elusive.
For further reading on varieties of 1853 Sovereigns see footnote for lot 66 above.

The Extremely Rare DEF over DEE 1853 Sovereign

67 **Victoria,** Sovereign, 1853, F over E in DEF, reads DEE, second larger young head left, W.W. raised on truncation, no single strand of hair at terminal of ponytail which is partly disjointed, date below, *rev* crowned quartered shield of arms within laurel wreath, emblems below, REGINA with raised die flaw, 7.94g (cf Marsh 36; MCE 514; S 3852C). *Of bright appearance, hairlined and scuffed, very fine, the reverse better, extremely rare.* £800-1000

Price Realised : £1,104

ex Spink Auction, 27 June 2007, lot 31
Calendar year mintage 10,597,993
One of the more interesting and significant varieties, the "DEE" variety made its public debut in the Spink auction where it was purchased in June 2007. Scant few have turned up since and it remains an extremely rare variety. It is another example of engraver's error with correction, that is worth looking out for on any other 1853 dated Sovereigns.

993 **Victoria,** Sovereign, 1853, figure 1 in date over inverted 1 giving impression of a Roman I, second larger young head left, ww incuse on truncation without stops, obverse legend double struck, raised die flaw from tip of truncation to rim, *rev* crowned quartered shield of arms within laurel wreath, emblems below, 7.96g (cf Marsh 36; MCE 514; S 3852C). *Cleaned with surface marks and heavy hairlines, otherwise good very fine and very rare.* £800-1000

Price Realised : £984

ex St James's Auction 5, 27 September 2006, lot 611
Calendar year mintage 10,597,993
The most interesting variety of 1853 Sovereign with rare incuse WW. It will be noted the "Roman I" is actually a product of a figure 1 at first being entered upon the die inverted and then corrected with one the right way up, giving a serif at all four corners, albeit with the upper right one being the one underneath and therefore with a step down from the correct figure on top. Again this is another sign of how the quality of the engraving was becoming more careless at this time, but not too serious as to not make it into circulation. The variety for 1853 discovered only in the last ten years and therefore not described by Marsh for this date.
For further reading on varieties of 1853 Sovereigns see footnote for lot 66, page 85.

68 **Victoria,** Sovereign, 1853, first letter of legend is an inverted A, Roman letter I in date for figure 1, second larger young head left, w.w. raised on truncation, no single strand of hair at terminal of ponytail which is partly disjointed, date below, raised flaw on I of date and doubled 5, inverted A for V in VICTORIA, *rev* crowned quartered shield of arms within laurel wreath, emblems below, some letters doubled, 7.97g (cf Marsh 36; MCE 514; S 3852C). *Unrecorded by Marsh, only discovered six years ago, once cleaned, now lightly toned, heavy surface marks on obverse, otherwise very fine and extremely rare.* £800-1000

Price Realised : £960

ex A H Baldwin & Sons Ltd sourced via Paul Davies Ltd, September 2006
Calendar year mintage 10,597,993
Two significant varieties upon one coin, not only was a letter I punch selected rather than a figure 1 for the date but a letter A was used instead of a V for the initial letter of the Queen's name. As the numismatic trade would say this is a real "after lunch" coin, from the engravers of the Mint and is of the highest rarity.

The Very Rare 1853 WW Incuse on Truncation Sovereign

69 **Victoria,** Sovereign, 1853, ww incuse on truncation without stops, engraved after William Wyon, second larger young head left, no single strand of hair at terminal of ponytail which is partly disjointed, date below, raised die flaw in 1 of date, *rev* crowned quartered shield of arms within laurel wreath, emblems below, raised die flaw on rose, small rosette either side, legend lightly doubled, 7.99g (cf Marsh 36; MCE 514; S 3852D). *Light surface marks on obverse, some hairlines and bagmarks, otherwise as struck, very pleasing and very rare.* £800-1000

Price Realised : £2,640

Calendar year mintage 10,597,993
The most significant variety and the rarest in top grade, the ww incuse on truncation, noting the lack of stops, must have been produced in only small quantity as it was gradually phased in concurrently with the phasing out of the w.w. raised on truncation from 1853 to 1855. Perhaps it was to mark the end of William Wyon's involvement with die work at the Mint, he having died 29 October 1851. Marsh does not record in his tabulations or discuss the varieties of the initials on the truncation from 1853 to 1855 in his publication. His only mere mention of them is one sentence when describing the obverse of his type "IA" where he says that the letters only "appear incuse on some coins", when in reality from 1856-1869 they are all incuse!
The ww incuse variety does turn up most often in fine to near very fine condition, however, the piece in the Bentley Collection is the finest the cataloguer is aware of in private hands.

The Very Rare 1854 W.W. in Relief on Truncation Sovereign

70 **Victoria,** Sovereign, 1854, w.w. raised on truncation, second larger young head left, with double fillet, date below, slightly closer date figures, 8 and 5 lightly doubled, *rev* crowned quartered shield of arms within laurel wreath, emblems below, slight raised die flaw on G in legend, 7.97g (Marsh 37; MCE 515; S 3852C). *Light scratch behind head in field, otherwise good extremely fine and very rare.* £800-1000

Price Realised : £2,880

ex Spink and Son Ltd, January 2005
Calendar year mintage 3,589,611
The most significantly rare variety of 1854 Sovereign is the w.w. raised on truncation variety as it is seemingly being phased out and the incuse ww is more prominent amongst surviving examples. In addition to the initials being raised the date is more closely spaced than the incuse initial varieties. As mentioned in the footnote to the previous lot, Marsh does not record the varieties on the truncation and all are assumed to be raised initials.

71 **Victoria,** Sovereign, 1854, ww incuse on truncation without stops, second larger young head left, date below, lightly doubled legend both sides, *rev* crowned quartered shield of arms within laurel wreath, emblems below, 7.98g (cf Marsh 37; MCE 515; S 3852D). *Light surface marks and scuffs on obverse, otherwise extremely fine / good extremely fine.* £600-700

Price Realised : £744

ex Randy Weir Numismatics, Unionville, Ontario, Canada, purchased 22 March 1990
Calendar year mintage 3,589,611
The ww incuse variety for 1854 is that which is usually encountered for this date.

"4" over a smaller "4"

417 **Victoria,** Sovereign, 1854, 4 over a higher smaller 4, second larger young head left, ww incuse on truncation without stops, die flaw from truncation tip to rim, date below, the small 4 either a product of double strike, or possibly correcting a Half-Sovereign size 4, lightly doubled legend both sides, penultimate A with blobby die flaw to right foot, *rev* crowned quartered shield of arms within laurel wreath, emblems below, 7.95g (cf Marsh 37; MCE 515; S 3852D). *Once cleaned, light surface marks, nearly very fine.* £300-350

Price Realised : £288

Calendar year mintage 3,589,611
The ww incuse variety for 1854 is that which is usually encountered for this date; the unusual date is not. For further reading on varieties of 1854 Sovereigns see footnote for lot 70 above.

Very Rare 1854 Sovereign C Over Rotated C in VICTORIA

994 **Victoria,** Sovereign, 1854, letter C over rotated C in Queen's name, second larger young head left, ww incuse on truncation without stops, date below, spread date with crosslet 4, flaw between 1 and 8 of date, further flaw in last I of legend, *rev* crowned quartered shield of arms within laurel wreath, emblems below, 7.99g (cf Marsh 37; MCE 515; S 3852D). *Light surface marks on obverse, otherwise extremely fine and extremely rare.* £1000-1200

Price Realised : £1,980

ex St James's Auction 13, 6 May 2010, lot 975
Calendar year mintage 3,589,611
The ww incuse variety for 1854 is that which is usually encountered for this date. When preparing this die the engraver must have first sunk the letter C punch a full right angle or two out of usual alignment which then had to be corrected with the letter C the right way up.
For further reading on varieties of 1854 Sovereigns see footnote for lot 70, page 87.

The Very Rare 1855 WW in Relief on Truncation Sovereign

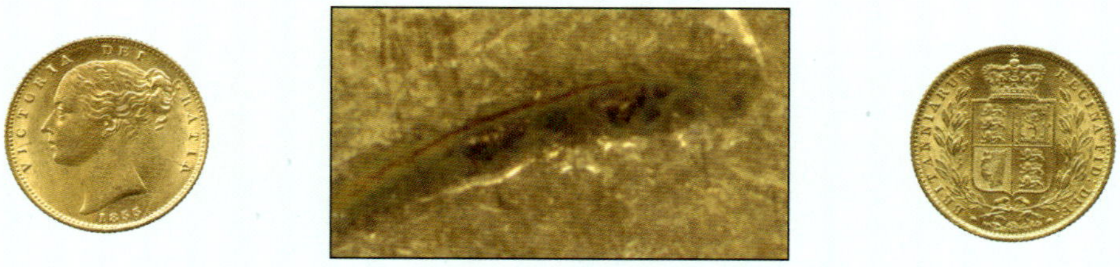

72 **Victoria,** Sovereign, 1855, w.w. raised on truncation, second larger young head left, date below, die flawed 5's and last A of legend, *rev* crowned quartered shield of arms within laurel wreath, emblems below, 7.98g (Marsh 38; MCE 516; S 3852C). *Hairline scratch on obverse field, toned, pleasing extremely fine and very rare.* £600-700

Price Realised : £864

ex Randy Weir Numismatics, Unionville, Ontario, Canada, purchased 13 August 1992
Calendar year mintage 8,448,482
The most significantly rare variety of 1855 Sovereign is the w.w. raised on truncation variety as this is the last year it occurs before being phased out, at least until a re-appearance from 1870 with a new variety of bust, and the incuse ww is more prominent for 1855 amongst surviving examples. As mentioned previously Marsh does not record the varieties on the truncation and he assumed all had raised initials.

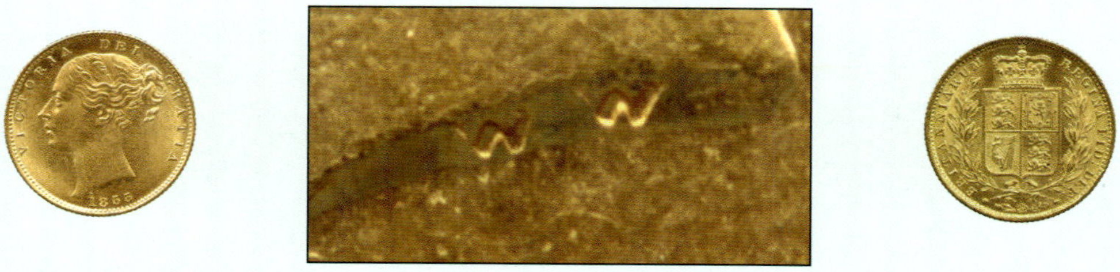

73 **Victoria,** Sovereign, 1855, ww incuse on truncation without stops, second larger young head left, date below, figure 1 with raised die flaw onto neck, 8 doubled, *rev* crowned quartered shield of arms within laurel, emblems below, 7.98g (cf Marsh 37; MCE 516; S 3852D). *A few light surface marks, otherwise pleasing, practically as struck.* £600-700

Price Realised : £1,560

ex St James's Auction 4, 8 May 2006, lot 386
Calendar year mintage 8,448,482
The ww incuse variety for 1855 is that which is usually encountered for this date which is relatively common due to the high calendar year mintage.

The Rare 1855 Sovereign with 1 of Date Struck over Inverted 1

74 **Victoria,** Sovereign, 1855, Arabic 1 over an inverted Arabic 1 giving the impression of a Roman I in date, ww incuse on truncation without stops, second larger young head left, date below very slightly double struck especially second 5, *rev* die axis off-centre, crowned quartered shield of arms within laurel wreath emblems below, 7.91g (cf Marsh 38; MCE 516; S 3852D). *Small scratch on reverse, once cleaned, fair to fine and rare.*
£600-700
Price Realised : £624

ex St James's auction 10, 6-7 November 2008, lot 541
Calendar year mintage 8,448,482
This is the second most significant variety of 1855, not a true letter I in the date but rather the engraver having punched the figure 1 on the die upside down at first, realising the error, then correcting it with the figure 1 the right way round over the top. The upper right of the double punched figure has a trace of the serif from the inverted 1, which is obviously not part of the correctly placed figure 1 over the top. It is also interesting to note as one of the lower grade Sovereigns in the Bentley Collection, that this coin is well under the legal tender weight limit that was set in successive Coinage Acts from 1816-1891. It is one of the lightest currency coins in the entire collection.

995 **Victoria,** Sovereign, 1855, the 5's of date dis-jointed, ww incuse on truncation without stops, second larger young head left, date below, legend lightly double struck, penultimate A unbarred, no serif to lower part of first I and R in legend and die flaw to left of first letter T, *rev* crowned quartered shield of arms within laurel wreath, emblems below, 7.99g (Marsh 38; MCE 516; S 3852C). *Cleaned with associated surface marks, extremely fine.*
£300-400
Price Realised : £456

ex St James's Auction 13, 6 May 2010, lot 982
Calendar year mintage 8,448,482
The ww incuse variety for 1855 is that which is usually encountered for this date which is relatively common due to the high calendar year mintage.
For further reading on varieties of 1855 Sovereigns see footnote for lots 72 and 74, pages 88-89.

broken 5's in date

418 **Victoria,** Sovereign, 1855, broken figure 5's in date, second larger young head left, ww incuse on truncation without stops, date below, date and legend doubled both sides, *rev* crowned quartered shield of arms within laurel, emblems below, 7.98g (cf Marsh 37; MCE 516; S 3852D). *Nicely toned, a few tiny digs, otherwise extremely fine and unusual.*
£400-500
Price Realised : £552

ex Randy Weir Numismatics, Unionville, Ontario, Canada, purchased 20 November 1989
Calendar year mintage 8,448,482
For further reading on varieties of 1855 Sovereigns see footnote for lots 72 and 74, pages 88-89.

connected 5's in date

419 **Victoria,** Sovereign, 1855, connected though doubled figure 5's in date, second larger young head left, ww incuse on truncation without stops, date below, date and legend doubled both sides, flaw from first I in legend towards rim, *rev* crowned quartered shield of arms within laurel, emblems below, 7.98g (cf Marsh 37; MCE 516; S 3852D). *Once cleaned, light surface marks, nearly very fine.* £300-350

Price Realised : £288

ex St James's Auction 13, 6 May 2010, lot 979
Calendar year mintage 8,448,482
For further reading on varieties of 1855 Sovereigns see footnote for lots 72 and 74, pages 88-89.

996 **Victoria,** Sovereign, 1855, second 5 of date over a smaller 5, the 5's disconnected, ww incuse on truncation without stops, second larger young head left, date below, legend lightly double struck, *rev* crowned quartered shield of arms within laurel wreath, emblems below, 7.89g (Marsh 38; MCE 516; S 3852C). *Cleaned with associated surface marks, the doubled 5 very clear and unusual, fair to fine.* £250-300

Price Realised : £336

ex Paul Davies Ltd, Ilkley, via A H Baldwin & Sons Ltd, January 2008
Calendar year mintage 8,448,482
The ww incuse variety for 1855 is that which is usually encountered for this date and is relatively common due to the high calendar year mintage. It is also interesting to note that the weight of this coin in its lower grade is under the legal tender limit as dictated by the Coinage Acts of 1816-1891. For further reading on varieties of 1855 Sovereigns see footnote for lots 72 and 74, pages 88-89.

75 **Victoria,** Sovereign, 1856, ww incuse on truncation without stops, second larger young head left, date below, curvy 6 with bulbous top, *rev* crowned quartered shield of arms within laurel wreath, emblems below, legend slightly doubled, 7.97g (Marsh 39; MCE 517; S 3852D). *Rim nick, many light surface marks with underlying brilliance, otherwise good extremely fine.* £500-600

Price Realised : £624

ex Randy Weir Numismatics, Unionville, Ontario, Canada, purchased 31 July 1990
Calendar year mintage 4,806,160
The calendar year mintage is nearly halved from the previous year but still on the high side, however there are not as many varieties as one would expect when comparing with previous similar mintage years within the scope of the Bentley Collection. This 1856 Sovereign can be considered the normal variety.

997 **Victoria,** Sovereign, 1856, ww incuse on truncation without stops, second larger young head left, date below, doubled with curvy 6 with bulbous top, last word of legend doubled, *rev* crowned quartered shield of arms within laurel wreath, emblems below, legend slightly doubled, 7.97g (Marsh 39; MCE 517; S 3852D). *Scratch across mouth, cleaned with surface marks, good fine.* £250-300

Price Realised : £240

ex AH Baldwin and Sons Ltd, November 2008
Calendar year mintage 4,806,160

Extremely rare 1856 Sovereign with 6 of date over 5

clashed "6" over "5"

420 **Victoria,** Sovereign, 1856, 6 struck over a 5, second larger young head left, WW incuse on truncation without stops, date below, curvy 6 with bulbous top, *rev* crowned quartered shield of arms within laurel wreath, emblems below, reverse legend slightly doubled, 7.96g (Marsh 39; MCE 517; S 3852D). *Once cleaned, light surface marks, otherwise good very fine and extremely rare.* £700-800

Price Realised : £768

purchased via A H Baldwin & Sons Ltd, November 2008
Calendar year mintage 4,806,160
This coin clearly has a figure 5 within the 6; the figure 5 is showing through part of the 6 rather than showing only around the outline. The upper interior of the 6 clearly shows elements of a 5 shaped interior too. A highly unusual coin.
For further reading on varieties of 1856 Sovereigns see footnote for lot 75, page 90.

A Spectacular and Extremely Rare Brockage Sovereign of 1856

76 **Victoria,** Brockage obverse, Sovereign, 1856, WW incuse on truncation without stops, second larger young head left, date below, curvy 6 with bulbous top, toothed border, VICTORIA DEI GRATIA, *rev* with an incuse and reflected impression of the obverse, 8.01g (cf Marsh 39; MCE 517; S 3852D). *Previously graded by PCGS as MS63, a few light surface marks and hairlines, short scratch on reverse, a little off-centre, superb proof-like with a red copper tone, otherwise as struck and of the highest rarity.* £2000-2500

Price Realised : £15,000

ex Heritage Long Beach Sale, Dallas, Texas, California, 2 June 2006, lot 13173
Calendar year mintage 4,806,160
A true one-off. A brockage occurs when the striking process goes awry. When a coin is struck, one die is static and fixed in position, usually the obverse as in this case when made in 1856. The glitch in the process occurs with the feeding in of the blanks of gold. A blank flan previous to the brockage we have here, would have entered the striking chamber and not seated quite on target, therefore it would be unable to exit easily after striking. This coupled with the tonnage of pressure of the reverse die coming down to strike its design, the blank adhered to the moving reverse die, instead of exiting the chamber automatically. The next blank gold flan to be struck, our soon to be brockage coin herewith, will have entered the chamber and the reverse die with the previous coin stuck to it, will have struck this newly entered flan with an obverse impression on its reverse, as well as receiving the obverse impression as usual. At this point the problem in the process is usually discovered, and it is likely the scratch on the reverse is perhaps from a tool used to prise the coin off the dies where it was stuck. Brockages are often spectacular and occur in gold coinage with much less frequency than the silver and copper due to the higher quality control in working with gold flans.

spread date

77 **Victoria,** Sovereign, 1857, spread date figures, WW incuse on truncation without stops, second larger young head left, date below, doubled date and legend with some border teeth flawed, *rev* crowned quartered shield of arms within laurel wreath, emblems below, 7.99g (Marsh 40; MCE 518; S 3852D). *A few light surface marks, otherwise pleasing good extremely fine.* £500-600

Price Realised : £600

ex Randy Weir Numismatics, Unionville, Ontario, Canada, purchased December 1995, NYINC, Sheraton Hotel, New York.
Calendar year mintage 4,495,748
With the relatively high calendar year mintage, varieties of date whether spread, normal or close occur for 1857.

1000 **Victoria,** Sovereign, 1857, spread date figures, die flawed 5 with angled top, and figure 7 distant from one another, WW incuse on truncation without stops, second larger young head left, date below, some letters of legend out of rotational alignment, *rev* crowned quartered shield of arms within laurel wreath, emblems below, 7.95g (Marsh 40; MCE 518; S 3852D). *Once cleaned with scuffs and surface marks, otherwise good fine.* £250-300

Price Realised : £240

ex Paul Davies Ltd, Ilkley, via A H Baldwin & Sons Ltd, June 2008
Calendar year mintage 4,495,748
Examples of both the spread and normal dates were sold in part one of the Bentley Collection, lots 77 and 78

close date

421 **Victoria,** Sovereign, 1857, closer date figures, second larger young head left, WW incuse on truncation without stops, date below, 7 with small tailed die flaw on upper bar, die flaw on first and third I's of legend, EI of DEI out of rotational alignment, *rev* crowned quartered shield of arms within laurel wreath, emblems below, die flaw on last A and rose of emblems, 7.95g (Marsh 40; MCE 518; S 3852D). *Once cleaned, reverse toned, light surface marks, extremely fine and unusual.* £300-400

Price Realised : £432

Calendar year mintage 4,495,748

normal date arrangement

422 **Victoria,** Sovereign, 1857, normal date figures, tailed 7 over a smaller 7, second larger young head left, WW incuse on truncation without stops, date below, *rev* crowned quartered shield of arms within laurel wreath, emblems below, 7.97g (Marsh 40; MCE 518; S 3852D). *A few light surface marks and digs, otherwise extremely fine and unusual.* £300-350

Price Realised : £432

ex Randy Weir Numismatics, Unionville, Ontario, Canada, purchased in the late 1990s
Calendar year mintage 4,495,748

78 **Victoria,** Sovereign, 1857, normal date figures, WW incuse on truncation without stops, second larger young head left, date below, last A in VICTORIA struck high over another lower A, letters A's in GRATIA with weak cross-bars, *rev* crowned quartered shield of arms within laurel wreath, emblems below, 7.95g (Marsh 40; MCE 518; S 3852D). *Cleaned, very fine, the reverse better and unusual.* £400-500

Price Realised : £360

ex Randy Weir Numismatics, Unionville, Ontario, Canada, purchased December 1995, NYINC, Sheraton Hotel, New York.
Calendar year mintage 4,495,748

unusual overstruck I in VICTORIA

423 **Victoria,** Sovereign, 1857, normal date figures, double struck second I in queen's name, possibly over a Half-Sovereign-sized I, second larger young head left, WW incuse on truncation without stops, date below, some obverse letters out of alignment and doubled, *rev* crowned quartered shield of arms within laurel wreath, emblems below, last F with die flaw to rim, 7.98g (Marsh 40; MCE 518; S 3852D). *Light short scratch in field behind neck, otherwise almost extremely fine, unusual.* £300-400

Price Realised : £312

ex A H Baldwin & Sons Ltd sourced via Paul Davies Ltd, June 2008
Calendar year mintage 4,495,748

998 **Victoria,** Sovereign, 1857, normal date figures, with 7 quite die flawed and closed so it appears like a triangle, WW incuse on truncation without stops, second larger young head left, date below, some letters of legend out of rotational alignment, last A of legend quite die flawed, *rev* crowned quartered shield of arms within laurel wreath, emblems below, 7.93g (Marsh 40; MCE 518; S 3852D). *Cleaned, now toned with surface marks, otherwise good fine and unusual.* £250-300

Price Realised : £264

ex AH Baldwin and Sons Ltd, April 2009
Calendar year mintage 4,495,748
It is interesting to note that the weight of this coin in its lower grade is upon the legal tender limit as dictated by the Coinage Acts of 1816-1891.

999 **Victoria,** Sovereign, 1857, normal date figures, 5 over a lower 5 with a tail to 7, WW incuse on truncation without stops, second larger young head left, date below, some letters of legend out of rotational alignment, with some doubling, *rev* crowned quartered shield of arms within laurel wreath, emblems below, 7.95g (Marsh 40; MCE 518; S 3852D). *Toned with surface marks, otherwise good fine.* £250-300

Price Realised : £240

ex AH Baldwin and Sons Ltd, March 2006
Calendar year mintage 4,495,748

79 **Victoria,** Sovereign, 1858, WW incuse on truncation without stops, second larger young head left, date below, high 5 in date and figures out of line, GRATIA doubled, *rev* crowned quartered shield of arms within laurel wreath, emblems below, legend lightly doubled, 8.00g (Marsh 41 R; MCE 519; S 3852D). *Lightly scuffed and hairlined, extremely fine / good extremely fine and rare.* £600-700

Price Realised : £1,800

Calendar year mintage 803,234
A dramatically lower calendar year mintage figure than previous years, in fact the fourth lowest for the Victoria shield London series, and only seven times higher than the 1841 output. The 1858 Sovereign can be considered rare but does seem to be readily available. This is either because of a high survival rate as perhaps a quantity of the issue was hoarded, coming to the market-place many years later, or some of the 1859 output was dated 1858. However the 1859 output is not that high either being not even double that of 1858. The hoarding theory is most likely.

1858 Sovereign with Second 8 Struck Over a 7 in Date

1001 **Victoria,** Sovereign, 1858, with second 8 struck over a 7, WW incuse on truncation without stops, second larger young head left, date below, C of Queen's name out of rotational alignment, penultimate A of legend unbarred, *rev* crowned quartered shield of arms within laurel wreath, emblems below, 7.99g (cf Marsh 41 R; MCE 519; S 3852D). *Once cleaned, lightly hairlined, fine, reverse better and very rare.* £300-400

Price Realised : £576

ex Spink and Son Ltd, March 2005
Calendar year mintage 803,234
Not listed by Marsh, the 8 over 7 overdate is a relatively recent discovery and very seldom encountered. The only evidence of the 7 under the 8 is the top right where the "elbow" of the upper right of the 7 is revealed. This is how an 8 over 7 appears in other coinages, such as the Jubilee head shilling of 1888 which all appear to be overdates and even the Oliver Cromwell Crown of 1658.
A dramatically lower calendar year mintage figure than previous years, in fact the fourth lowest for the Victoria shield London series, and only seven times higher than the 1841 output. The 1858 Sovereign can be considered rare but does seem to be readily available. This is either because of a high survival rate, perhaps a quantity of the issue was hoarded, coming to the market place many years later, or some of the 1859 output was dated 1858. However the 1859 output is not that high either being not even double that of 1858. The hoarding theory is more likely.

The Extremely Rare Unbarred A's in Obverse Legend 1858 Sovereign

424 **Victoria,** Sovereign, 1858, incomplete 5 and unbarred A's in legend, second larger young head left, WW incuse on truncation without stops, date below, high 5 in date and figures out of line, unbarred A's in GRATIA, some doubling both sides, die flaw in legend and C out of rotational alignment, *rev* crowned quartered shield of arms within laurel wreath, emblems below, reverse legend lightly doubled, 7.95g (Marsh 41 R; MCE 519; S 3852D). *Once cleaned, good fine and extremely rare, very few examples known.* £300-400

Price Realised : £600

purchased via A H Baldwin & Sons Ltd, 28 July 2010
Calendar year mintage 803,234
The unbarred A's in GRATIA variety is only seen on the dates 1841, 1842 and 1858.
For further reading on varieties of 1858 Sovereigns see footnote for lot 79 above.

1002 **Victoria,** Sovereign, 1858, unbarred A's in last word of legend, WW incuse on truncation without stops, second larger young head left, weakly struck rear to hair bun, date below, incomplete 5 in date, weak top to first E in legend, R of Queen's name doubled, *rev* crowned quartered shield of arms within laurel wreath, emblems below, M of legend doubled, 7.98g (Marsh 41 R; MCE 519; S 3852D). *Scuffed with surface marks, good fine, reverse better, about very fine, rare.* £300-400

Price Realised : £504

Calendar year mintage 803,234
For further reading on varieties of 1858 Sovereigns see footnote for lot 79, page 94.

80 **Victoria,** Sovereign, 1859, incomplete 5 in date, WW incuse on truncation without stops, second larger young head left, date below, first I of legend die flawed and letter O doubled, *rev* crowned quartered shield of arms within laurel wreath, emblems below, 8.00g (Marsh 42; MCE 520; S 3852D). *A few light surface marks, rim nick, otherwise good extremely fine.* £600-700

Price Realised : £2,160

Calendar year mintage 1,547,603
Another lower mintage, though this figure was quite normal when you look at say the reign of William IV. The calendar year output also includes 167,539 Sovereigns of the "Ansell" variety with the extra line in the lower hair fillet. So-called as a quantity of Australian mined, but quite brittle gold, was successfully strengthened and hardened enough to strike coin from, through experimentation, by the mint's Mr G F Ansell. See lot 426, page 96, for the beautiful Bentley Collection specimen of the 1859 Ansell Sovereign.

425 **Victoria,** Sovereign, 1859, incomplete 5 in date, second larger young head left, WW incuse on truncation without stops, date below, *rev* crowned quartered shield of arms within laurel wreath, emblems below, 7.95g (Marsh 42; MCE 520; S 3852D). *Fine to good fine with associated surface marks.* £300-350

Price Realised : £312

purchased from Andrew Holds at an unspecified date c.2002
Calendar year mintage 1,547,603

1003 **Victoria,** Sovereign, 1859, higher 59 in date, WW incuse on truncation without stops, second larger young head left, date below, 9 over a lower 9, the 5 disjointed, R of Queen's name out of rotational alignment, first E of legend doubled, *rev* crowned quartered shield of arms within laurel wreath, emblems below, die flaw in first T and M of legend with some doubling, 7.97g (Marsh 42; MCE 520; S 3852D). *Some light deposit on reverse legend, cleaned with light surface marks, deep scratch on neck, otherwise about very fine.* £250-300

Price Realised : £312

ex Douro Cargo, Spink Auction 118, 20-21 November 1996, lot 391 (part)
ex Spink Numismatic Circular, July 1998, item 4725
Calendar year mintage 1,547,603
Another low mintage, though this figure was quite normal when you look at, say, the reign of William IV. The calendar year output also includes 167,539 Sovereigns of the "Ansell" variety with the extra line in the lower hair fillet.

The Finest Known "Ansell" Variety Sovereign Dated 1859

the Ansell ribbon

426 **Victoria,** Sovereign, 1859, "Ansell" second larger young head left, with extra line depicted on lower fillet of hair, indicating struck from Australian "brittle" gold, WW incuse on truncation without stops, date below, complete 5, small bulb type 9, die flaw from neck to field to left of date, another long flaw from top rim over head vertical to cheek, unbarred last A in legend, *rev* crowned quartered shield of arms within laurel wreath, emblems below, 7.99g (Marsh 42A R4; MCE 520; S 3852E). *Good extremely fine and the finest Ansell Sovereign known to the Cataloguer.* £6000-8000

Price Realised : £15,600

ex Dr David Aboav collection of Sovereigns and Half-Sovereigns, Spink Auction 147, 5 October 2000, lot 376
ex "A Collection of Sovereigns", Mark Rasmussen, List No.3 supplement, Autumn 2002, 7 November 2002
"Ansell" variety mintage 167,539 of a total calendar year of 1,547,603
In 1859 this quantity of coin from the regular mintage was found to be of inferior "brittle" quality and, on melting, was found to have been annealed with quantities of antimony, arsenic and lead. Mr George Frederick Ansell, who was employed in the Rolling Room at the mint and had a scientific background, was given permission to experiment with this inferior batch of sovereigns. He was successful in adjusting the alloy mix to reproduce them in a much stronger form which resulted in the whole quantity being re-coined and denoted with the extra line in the hair fillet. Today they are very rare indeed, especially in the high grade seen here.

81 **Victoria,** Sovereign, 1860, curvy rounded 6 with bulbous top, second larger young head left, WW incuse on truncation without stops, date below, die flaw to right of zero, E of DEI possibly over rotated E, burr of extra metal at rear of E, *rev* crowned quartered shield of arms within laurel wreath, emblems below, 7.99g (Marsh 43; MCE 521; S 3852D). *Once cleaned, now lightly toned with associated scuffing and hairlines on obverse, otherwise about extremely fine with a stronger reverse.* £700-800

Price Realised : £744

ex Spink and Son Ltd, March 2005
Calendar year mintage 2,555,958
As we enter the 1860s we start to find more engraving oddities than ever, as the quality of workmanship in the gold striking department seems to become more lax, which may partly explain why the introduction of the die number system occurred, as a means of new quality control. Once that occurred, engraving errors suddenly seem to all but disappear, as will be seen later in the chronology of the Bentley Collection.
The oddity we have here is the E in DEI which is showing extra metal around its central limb. This has been theorised to be E over a rotated E as a best fit suggestion, however this still does not seem to be the explanation. It may just be as simple as a faulty E punch entered onto the die, perhaps with a burr of metal attached to the E when the punch was engraved which was forgotten to be filed away and that has also therefore been punched into the die. When that die strikes a new flan, the burr which is incuse on the die also fills with metal giving a hairline of raised metal attached to the E. Small T shaped raised burrs have been seen on other letters and figures on other denominations in the silver series, and some copper around this time in the life of the Mint. For instance, figure 1's seem to be susceptible in the Shilling series to have a small T shape flaw underneath them occasionally. These have been theorised to be figure 1's over a lower figure 1 or even a smaller figure 1 from the Maundy series, but is more likely something that has emanated from a faulty punch.
1860 marks the year that James Wyon retires as resident engraver at the Mint and is succeeded by his son George Wyon.

427 **Victoria,** Sovereign, 1860, curvy rounded 6 with bulbous top, letter O-like zero, second larger young head left, WW incuse on truncation without stops, date below, doubled legend on obverse, *rev* crowned quartered shield of arms within laurel wreath, emblems below, second N in legend with raised die flaw, 7.99g (Marsh 43; MCE 521; S 3852D). *Rim nick, surface marks and hairlines, otherwise extremely fine.* £350-450

Price Realised : £888

ex Noble Numismatics (UK) PLC, direct purchase, 3 October 2005
Calendar year mintage 2,555,958
As we enter the 1860s we start to find more engraving oddities than ever. As the quality of workmanship in the gold striking department seems to become more lax, the introduction of the die number system occurred as a new means of quality control. After which, engraving errors suddenly seem to all but disappear, as will be seen later in the chronology of the Bentley Collection.
The large wide O in the date of this coin was once thought to be rarer than a normal thinner zero. However the cataloguer has seen more 1860 dated Sovereigns with this letter O type zero than normal figure 0. Perhaps the zero punch went missing for a time at the mint in 1860 or broke beyond repair.
1860 marks the year that James Wyon retires as resident engraver at the mint and is succeeded by his son George Wyon.

428 **Victoria,** Sovereign, 1860, curvy rounded 6 with bulbous top, second larger young head left, WW incuse on truncation without stops, date below, first I in queen's name with no lower serifs and letter R without lower left serif, as well as D and I in DEI, some light raised die flaws, penultimate A on obverse unbarred, *rev* crowned quartered shield of arms within laurel wreath, emblems below, reverse legend doubled, 7.93g (Marsh 43; MCE 521; S 3852D). *Cleaned fine, very unusual with so many serifs missing.* £300-350

Price Realised : £312

ex A H Baldwin & Sons Ltd sourced via Paul Davies Ltd, June 2008
Calendar year mintage 2,555,958
This 1860 Sovereign with the absent serifs is most likely explained by the blockage upon the obverse die by either dirt or grease in the corners of many of the letters. This would occur if either the obverse die had been newly reset in position and had been recently greased, or if the die had endured a production journey (a days die work) when, nearing the end of the day, dirt from the dies or metal from the blanks was starting to clog the serifs on the obverse die. This leaves us with several small details missing on the letters of the struck coin. Dirt and grease tend to end up on the periphery of the coin rather than nearer the centre upon the design, as the centre receives the full blow of the strike where the highest relief occurs, whilst the metal (and dirt and grease) tends to spread outwards towards the margins of the coin. This is why it gathers in small depressions of the lettering only, such as the serifs and cross-bars.

1004 **Victoria,** Sovereign, 1860, curvy rounded 6 with bulbous top, 60 higher than 18, second larger young head left, WW incuse on truncation without stops, date below, second I of legend missing lower right serif and R with lower left serif absent, no lower left serifs to letters in second word, unbarred first A in last word of legend, *rev* crowned quartered shield of arms within laurel wreath, emblems below, no lower left serif to last I of legend, 7.95g (Marsh 43; MCE 521; S 3852D). *Once cleaned, good fine with associated surface marks.* £250-300

Price Realised : £360

ex St James's Auction 11, 8 May 2009, lot 407
Calendar year mintage 2,555,958
As we enter the 1860s we start to find more engraving oddities than ever as the quality of workmanship in the gold striking department seems to become more lax, which may part-explain why the introduction of the die number system occurred, as a means of new quality control. Once that occurred, engraving errors suddenly seem to all but disappear, as has been demonstrated in other parts of the chronology of the Bentley Collection.
1860 marks the year that James Wyon retires as resident engraver at the Mint and is succeeded by his son George Wyon.

The Rare 1860 O over C in VICTORIA Sovereign

82 **Victoria,** Sovereign, 1860, with O struck over C in obverse legend, second larger young head left, WW incuse on truncation without stops, date below, curvy rounded 6 with bulbous top, taller 0 in date, die flaw to right of 0 in date, *rev* crowned quartered shield of arms within laurel wreath, emblems below, doubled legend, raised die flaw at top right of crown to rim and at A of BRITANNIARUM, 7.99g (cf Marsh 43; MCE 521; S 3852D). *Thin streak of black tone on reverse, a few light surface marks, otherwise about extremely fine, reverse better and rare.* £800-1000

Price Realised : £1,320

ex Spink and Son Ltd, May 2002
Calendar year mintage 2,555,958
The coin in the Bentley Collection was the "discovery piece", the first to be seen and demonstrated to have the O in the Queen's name struck over a letter C some ten years ago. Therefore it is not recorded in Marsh. The overstrike is not obvious and manifests as only a protrusion of metal at the top right of the O. This metal is the upper serif of a letter C. The engraver must have selected the letter C punch to place on the die when arranging the Queen's name, having only just used it two letters before. Having realised the error, the engraver has very carefully covered the entire C using the correct O punch which fortunately has the same curvature as a C, almost completely extinguishing it, leaving just the serif sticking out of the top right of the O. This is as obvious as the variety gets, it must have occurred on only the one die and known specimens have grown in number since discovery to somewhere in the order of ten to fifteen today.

1005 **Victoria,** Sovereign, 1860, curvy rounded 6 with bulbous top, larger taller 0 in date, second larger young head left, WW incuse on truncation without stops, date below, *rev* crowned quartered shield of arms within laurel wreath, emblems below, E of second word over a higher E, 7.95g (Marsh 43; MCE 521; S 3852D). *Some surface marks, almost very fine, reverse better.* £250-300

Price Realised : £312

ex DNW auction, 7 October 2003, lot 489, bought via Spink and Son Ltd
Calendar year mintage 2,555,958
For further reading on varieties of 1860 Sovereigns see footnote for lots 427 and 428, page 97.

Inverted A for V in VICTORIA coupled with a 1 over Inverted 1 in Date

83 **Victoria,** Sovereign, 1860, inverted A for V in VICTORIA, Arabic 1 over an inverted Arabic 1 giving the impression of a Roman I in date, second larger young head left, WW incuse on truncation without stops, date below, curvy rounded 6 with bulbous top, die flaw to right of date, legend doubled and I of DEI with raised die flaw, *rev* crowned quartered shield of arms within laurel wreath, emblems below, 7.97g (cf Marsh 43; MCE 521; S 3852D). *Once cleaned, almost very fine / very fine and very rare.* £1000-1200

Price Realised : £1,080

ex A H Baldwin & Sons Ltd sourced via Paul Davies Ltd, October 2006
Calendar year mintage 2,555,958
Two significant varieties upon the one coin is a very unusual thing to occur. Looking at the two engraving errors only one of which has been corrected, perhaps demonstrates that dates were punched in at a different stage to legends. The Roman I depiction is not a true letter I but made up from an engraver's error of placing the figure 1 inverted at first with a correction over the top of the figure 1 the right side up. There is a marked step at the upper right of the correct figure down onto the serif of the inverted figure 1 below. This error is then coupled with the uncorrected inverted letter A instead of a V in the Queen's name which is seen on a few other dates and all are very rare.

1860 Sovereign with Inverted A for V in Queen's Name

1006 **Victoria,** Sovereign, 1860, letter o for 0 in date, inverted A for V in Queen's name, second larger young head left, WW incuse on truncation without stops, date below, raised die flaw to left of 1 in date, *rev* crowned quartered shield of arms within laurel wreath, emblems below, E of second word over a higher E, 7.94g (cf Marsh 43; MCE 521; S 3852D). *Heavily surface marked, cleaned fine, very rare and unusual.* £800-1000

Price Realised : £1,080

ex Noble Investments plc, 21 November 2005
Calendar year mintage 2,555,958
Another variety only discovered in the last decade since the publication of Marsh's *The Gold Sovereign*. This most interesting variety is still only demonstrated by a few specimens. The engraver in haste, or due to lack of sharpness in eyesight, or daylight, has obviously selected an A punch rather than a V when stamping in the letters onto the obverse die, or perhaps the correct punch could not be located in the time allowed. He and his superiors either never noticed, and / or could not afford to waste a valuable die for a tiny error the legacy of which has passed to us as an interesting true variety in the coinage of 1860. Interestingly it must have occurred on at least two obverse dies for 1860 as this is one of two variations of the inverted A for V in the Bentley Collection. The piece here has a letter "o" for "0" in the date, the other, lot 83 above, had the inversion coupled with a Roman style I in the date.

spread date

429 **Victoria,** Sovereign, 1861, spread date especially 8 and 6, lightly doubled, curvy rounded 6 with bulbous top higher in date, date out of alignment, second larger young head left, WW incuse on truncation without stops, date below, doubled date and obverse legend, *rev* crowned quartered shield of arms within laurel wreath, emblems below, 7.99g (Marsh 44; MCE 522; S 3852D). *Some light surface marks, otherwise good very fine.* £300-400

Price Realised : £360

purchased via A H Baldwin & Sons Ltd, July 2006
Calendar year mintage 7,624,736
The Mint output for the calendar year is back up to higher levels. Statistically, therefore, this dictates more variety than ever and is apparent on date and legends for 1861 dated Sovereigns - there are over ten different varieties in the Bentley Collection alone.

1008 **Victoria,** Sovereign, 1861, spread date lightly doubled, second larger young head left, WW incuse on truncation without stops, date below, die flaw at first 1 of date, first four letters of legend doubled, the first I over a higher I, *rev* crowned quartered shield of arms within laurel wreath, emblems below, last A of second word doubled, 7.97g (Marsh 44; MCE 522; S 3852D). *Scratch beside* 1 *of date, cleaned with surface marks, very fine.* £250-300

Price Realised : £312

ex St James's Auction 6, 8 June 2007, lot 559
Calendar year mintage 7,624,736

closer date

431 **Victoria,** Sovereign, 1861, curvy rounded 6 with bulbous top, second larger young head left, WW incuse on truncation without stops, date below, light die flaw to left of date, 8 doubled, very light legend doubling both sides, *rev* crowned quartered shield of arms within laurel wreath, emblems below, 7.96g (Marsh 44; MCE 522; S 3852D). *Once cleaned, good very fine, reverse better.* £300-400

Price Realised : £288

ex St James's Auction 5, 27 September 2006, lot 628
Calendar year mintage 7,624,736

1009 **Victoria,** Sovereign, 1861, curvy open 6 in date, second larger young head left, WW incuse on truncation without stops, date below, D of second word over a lower D, doubled date and legend, *rev* crowned quartered shield of arms within laurel wreath, emblems below, heavy raised die flaw to left of rose, 7.97g (Marsh 44; MCE 522; S 3852D). *Cleaned, mainly on obverse, with surface marks, almost extremely fine.* £300-400

Price Realised : £384

ex Paul Davies Ltd, Ilkley, via Spink and Son Ltd, January 2005
Calendar year mintage 7,624,736

1011 **Victoria,** Sovereign, 1861, curvy open 6 in date, second larger young head left, WW incuse on truncation without stops, date below, third I of legend without lower left serif, die flaw in first C of legend, *rev* crowned quartered shield of arms within laurel wreath, emblems below, first N in legend doubled, 7.95g (Marsh 44; MCE 522; S 3852D). *A little scuffed with surface marks, good fine.* £250-300

Price Realised : £240

ex Paul Davies Ltd, Ilkley, via A H Baldwin & Sons Ltd, January 2008
Calendar year mintage 7,624,736

1012 **Victoria,** Sovereign, 1861, curvy open 6 in date, second 1 over a much lower 1, second larger young head left, WW incuse on truncation without stops, date below, raised die flaw from tip of truncation to rim, *rev* crowned quartered shield of arms within laurel wreath, emblems below, 7.98g (Marsh 44; MCE 522; S 3852D). *Cleaned, with light surface marks, very fine, reverse better.* £250-300

Price Realised : £432

Calendar year mintage 7,624,736

IA over tilting IA

430 **Victoria,** Sovereign, 1861, curvy rounded 6 with bulbous top, loop of 6 does not meet upright, IA of queen's name struck over tilting figures, second larger young head left, ww incuse on truncation without stops, date below, all letters of queen's name out of alignment, light die flaw on V and last A of legend, *rev* crowned quartered shield of arms within laurel wreath, emblems below, doubled reverse legend, 7.96g (Marsh 44; MCE 522; S 3852D). *Once cleaned, nearly very fine.* £300-350

Price Realised : £312

ex A H Baldwin & Sons Ltd sourced via Paul Davies Ltd, October 2006
Calendar year mintage 7,624,736
This 1861 Sovereign appears to have suffered from shoddy engraving of the legend on the obverse die, in that the queen's name is out of alignment and there is even a correction on the last two letters, where they appear more out of line than ever.
This could have occurred for a number of reasons, perhaps an inexperienced apprentice engraver made a real hash of the legend and was stopped from working further on this die and a more skilled worker stepping in to re-punch the last two letters and complete the legend. Or perhaps it was the product of a skilled engraver on an off-day, feeling unwell, or after a hearty lunch in the last hour or two of the day and tiredness had crept in. The engraver then corrected and finished off the die the next day when feeling fresher. There are a myriad of reasons, it is nice to speculate why.

1861 Sovereign with T Over a Tilted T in Queen's Name

1007 **Victoria,** Sovereign, 1861, T over a tilting T in Queen's name, second larger young head left, ww incuse on truncation without stops, date below, curvy rounded 6 with bulbous top, *rev* crowned quartered shield of arms within laurel wreath, emblems below, last A of second word doubled, 7.95g (Marsh 44; MCE 522; S 3852D). *Once cleaned, with hairlines and surface marks, otherwise very fine, unusual.* £300-400

Price Realised : £336

ex St James's Auction 5, 27 September 2006, lot 629
Calendar year mintage 7,624,736
Another variety of legend with double punched letters in places, some more carelessly applied than others and with the T of VICTORIA correctly punched over the top of a quite tilted letter T at a diagonal angle.

87 **Victoria,** Sovereign, 1861, second larger young head left, ww incuse on truncation without stops, date below, curvy rounded incomplete 6 with bulbous top, some legend letters doubled on both sides, C therefore appears nearly closed, *rev* crowned quartered shield of arms within laurel wreath, emblems below, E of DEF over a higher E, 7.96g (Marsh 44; MCE 522; S 3852D). *Once cleaned, scuffed mainly on obverse, nearly very fine.* £300-400

Price Realised : £264

Calendar year mintage 7,624,736
Another variety of legend with double punched letters in places, some more carelessly applied than others and with an incomplete 6 in the date where the centre curve does not meet the upright, rendering it an "open" 6.

84 **Victoria,** Sovereign, 1861, 61 higher than 18, date out of alignment, second larger young head left, ww incuse on truncation without stops, date below, 1 and 6 slightly double struck, curvy rounded 6 with bulbous top, *rev* crowned quartered shield of arms within laurel wreath, emblems below, 7.98g (Marsh 44; MCE 522; S 3852D). *Some streaks of tone on reverse, a couple of tiny digs, otherwise good extremely fine.* £500-600

Price Realised : £4,560

ex Bruce Lorich, State College, Pennsylvania, USA, 2002
Calendar year mintage 7,624,736
The Mint output for the calendar year is back up to higher levels and therefore statistically this dictates more variety than ever, which is apparent on date and legends for 1861 dated Sovereigns. There are over ten different varieties in the Bentley Collection alone.

85 **Victoria,** Sovereign, 1861, VI of VICTORIA over a smaller "half-sovereign" sized VI, G of GRATIA over a rotated G or from a faulty G punch, extra burrs of metal at top, second larger young head left, ww incuse on truncation without stops, date below, curvy rounded 6 with bulbous top, *rev* crowned quartered shield of arms within laurel wreath, emblems below, die flaw on first N of legend, 7.98g (Marsh 44; MCE 522; S 3852D). *Once cleaned, now toned, some surface marks and scuffs, bold very fine, very unusual and rare.* £400-500

Price Realised : £672

ex A H Baldwin & Sons Ltd sourced via Paul Davies Ltd, October 2010
Calendar year mintage 7,624,736
This interesting variation is the result of the engraver starting to punch the obverse legend with the wrong set of letter punches, those that should perhaps be used on Half-Sovereign sized coins and smaller. Perhaps the die worked on before this was one for the Half-Sovereign hence the punches being to hand. The engraver has fixed the error with the correct size letter punches on the die, but the smaller letters still show. Another instance of such an error occurs on a variety of the 1826 Sovereign of George IV where some letters of the legend and the 6 in the date are corrected over smaller figures. See lot 956, page 41.
The other oddity on this coin is the G over a rotated G in GRATIA which may well be a faulty G punch an explanation for which is in the footnote to lot 81, page 96.

86 **Victoria,** Sovereign, 1861, inverted top-heavy 8, second larger young head left, ww incuse on truncation without stops, date below, curvy rounded 6 with bulbous top, E of DEI struck over a rotated or faulty E, large burr of metal at back of E, *rev* crowned quartered shield of arms within laurel wreath, emblems below, legend with some doubled letters mainly on reverse, 7.95g (Marsh 44; MCE 522; S 3852D). *Some surface marks, nearly very fine and unusual.* £350-400

Price Realised : £432

ex St James's Auction 5, 27 September 2006, lot 631
Calendar year mintage 7,624,736
This is a similar legend error to that which occurred on one of the 1860 obverses as demonstrated in lot 81, page 96, where the footnote there goes into detail about the use of a faulty E punch which may have again been used for this 1861 dated Sovereign. The 8 in the date appears to be quite top-heavy and may well be inverted to what is normally seen. It does seem strange that with the frequency of engraving inconsistency at this time, that top heavy 8's are not encountered more often. Perhaps the tooling of the punches was such that it was nigh on impossible to invert it or that this particular 8 punch was engraved this way.

1861 Sovereign with Unbarred A in GRATIA

1010 **Victoria,** Sovereign, 1861, curvy closed 6 in date, second larger young head left, WW incuse on truncation without stops, date below, 6 of date flawed shut, no lower serifs to first I and R of legend with some doubling, penultimate A of legend unbarred, other serifs in legend weak, *rev* crowned quartered shield of arms within laurel wreath, emblems below, 7.97g (Marsh 44; MCE 522; S 3852D). *A little scuffed with surface marks, almost extremely fine.* £300-400

Price Realised : £744

ex St James's Auction 6, 8 June 2007, lot 558
Calendar year mintage 7,624,736

The Extremely Rare C over a Rotated C in VICTORIA, 1861 Sovereign

88 **Victoria,** Sovereign, 1861, C of VICTORIA struck over rotated C, second larger young head left, WW incuse on truncation without stops, date below, curvy rounded 6 with bulbous top, 8 doubled, R over a lower R correcting alignment of arc in VICTORIA, *rev* crowned quartered shield of arms within laurel wreath, emblems below, some light doubling of lettering, 7.96g (cf Marsh 44; MCE 522; S 3852D). *Once cleaned, light surface marks and hairlines, very fine, reverse better and extremely rare.* £1000-1200

Price Realised : £960

ex A H Baldwin & Sons Ltd sourced via Paul Davies Ltd, January 2008
Calendar year mintage 7,624,736
One of the more spectacular engraving errors of 1861 still with only few specimens known, the C of the Queen's name was entered at first a whole right angle out of alignment and was then corrected over the top. The C therefore appears closed not unlike a letter O. This is another variety that was discovered only in the last ten years and therefore is unpublished in Marsh. Most of these more recent varieties have been added to the Spink Standard Catalogue in this period of time at the instigation of this cataloguer.

89 **Victoria,** Sovereign, 1861, O of VICTORIA struck over figure zero, second larger young head left, WW incuse on truncation without stops, date below, raised die flaw through 1, figure 8 doubled, curvy rounded 6 with bulbous top, some light doubling of letters on obverse, *rev* crowned quartered shield of arms within laurel, emblems below, some light raised die flaws in some letters, 7.98g (cf Marsh 44; MCE 522; S 3852D). *Once cleaned, now lightly toned, about very fine, reverse stronger and rare.* £400-500

Price Realised : £384

ex A H Baldwin & Sons Ltd, July 2010
Calendar year mintage 7,624,736
This corrected error seems to have occurred where a figure zero punch for dates has been used to stamp the letter O on the die in the Queen's name at first in error. The correct letter O has then been stamped over the top seemingly a couple of times to make sure the legend reads correctly. The variety was only recently discovered and has yet to make it into any publication.

The Extremely Rare Roman Style I Dated 1861 Sovereign

90 **Victoria,** Sovereign, 1861, Roman letter I in date for figure 1, second larger young head left, WW incuse on truncation without stops, date below, figure 8 doubled, curvy rounded 6 with bulbous top, raised die flaw from tip of neck to rim, no lower left serif to E in DEI, R in Queen's name with twin tales and other light doubling of lettering evident both sides, *rev* crowned quartered shield of arms within laurel wreath, emblems below, 7.99g (Marsh 44A R2; MCE 522; S 3852D). *A few light surface marks, otherwise good extremely fine and the finest known specimen extant, pleasing and extremely rare.* £1000-1200

Price Realised : £2,880

ex Spink and Son Ltd, January 2002
Calendar year mintage 7,624,736
This true letter I for figure 1 in date variety is the only such instance recorded by Marsh, though it exists for other dates. Most of these have only been noted in recent years and still more varieties may be waiting to be discovered. The engraver has used a letter I instead of a figure 1 in date and is arguably one of the more spectacular varieties of the many for 1861.

91 **Victoria,** Sovereign, 1862, second larger young head left, WW incuse on truncation without stops, date below, curvy rounded 6 with bulbous top, whole legend and date doubled and with some lesser doubling evident on reverse, *rev* crowned quartered shield of arms within laurel wreath, emblems below, 8.00g (Marsh 45; MCE 523; S 3852D). *Tiny red spot at terminal of ponytail and another on reverse over crown, otherwise uncirculated and very pleasing.* £700-900

Price Realised : £4,320

ex Randy Weir Numismatics, Unionville, Ontario, Canada, purchased 18 October 1993
Calendar year mintage 7,836,413
A similar calendar year mintage to the previous year, 1862 is also rife with variety, though the coin we have here is quite normal for the ilk. There are nine varieties of 1862 in the Bentley Collection.
1862 marks the year at the Mint that resident engraver George Wyon dies and the post becomes vacant until 1865.

large "1" over smaller "1" with small "8"

432 **Victoria,** Sovereign, 1862, curvy rounded 6 with bulbous top, loop of 6 does not meet upright, large 1 appears to be over a smaller 1, small 8 over small 8, 2 die flawed, second larger young head left, WW incuse on truncation without stops, date below, some doubling in parts of legend both sides, *rev* crowned quartered shield of arms within laurel wreath, emblems below, some raised die flaws on reverse, noticeably between R and I and E and G at start and end of legend respectively, 7.98g (Marsh 45; MCE 523; S 3852D). *Some light black surface marks, good very fine and unusual.* £300-400

Price Realised : £312

purchased via A H Baldwin & Sons Ltd, July 2010.
Calendar year mintage 7,836,413
The 8 appears to be the size used for the Half-Sovereign denomination. The 1 and the 2 of the date are much larger, the 6 is somewhere in between. The 1 appears to be struck over a small 1 of the same sort of stature as the 8. An unusual date overall.

hooked type "6" in date

433 **Victoria,** Sovereign, 1862, larger wider date with hooked type 6, second larger young head left, WW incuse on truncation without stops, date below, some doubling in parts of obverse legend more so in last word, *rev* crowned quartered shield of arms within laurel wreath, emblems below, 7.97g (Marsh 45; MCE 523; S 3852D). *Some light surface marks, very fine and unusual.* £300-350

Price Realised : £288

purchased via A H Baldwin & Sons Ltd, November 2008
Calendar year mintage 7,836,413
This 1862 Sovereign features the more open and sharper "hooked" 6 which begins to make an appearance from this date onwards into the die number series. The more curvy bulb type 6 is still more prevalent for the 1860 decade as a whole but this hooked 6 seems to appear toward the end of the 1862 production run and goes as far as die number 7 consecutively and then die number 9 for 1863 once the die number series commences. In the Bentley Collection it does not make another appearance until die number 15 of 1864 and then appears sporadically until die number 30 of that year. After that, at least within the confines of the Bentley Collection, it does not appear again making the hooked 6 a bit of a rarity.

high "62" in date

434 **Victoria,** Sovereign, 1862, larger wider date with hooked type 6, 62 very high compared to 18, second larger young head left, WW incuse on truncation without stops, date below, legend doubled both sides, *rev* crowned quartered shield of arms within laurel wreath, emblems below, some raised die flaws on reverse, noticeably between R and I and E and G at start and end of legend respectively, 7.97g (Marsh 45; MCE 523; S 3852D). *Some light black surface marks, very fine and unusual.* £300-350

Price Realised : £288

purchased Spink and Son, May 2005
Calendar year mintage 7,836,413

1014 **Victoria,** Sovereign, 1862, wider spread date with hooked 6, second larger young head left, WW incuse on truncation without stops, date below, die flaw in 2, doubled legend, *rev* crowned quartered shield of arms within laurel wreath, emblems below, second word doubled, 7.99g (Marsh 45; MCE 523; S 3852D). *Some light surface marks, good very fine.* £300-400

Price Realised : £312

ex Randy Weir Numismatics, Unionville, Ontario, Canada, purchased 25 August 1993
Calendar year mintage 7,836,413

The Rare 1862 Sovereign with 1 Struck over Inverted 1

92 **Victoria,** Sovereign, 1862, Arabic 1 over an inverted Arabic 1 giving the impression of a Roman I in date, second larger young head left, ww incuse on truncation without stops, date below, closer date figures, incomplete 6 and 2, curvy rounded 6 with bulbous top, obverse legend with some doubling of letters, *rev* crowned quartered shield of arms within laurel wreath, emblems below, some raised die flaws, noticeably between R and I and E and G at start and end of legend respectively, 8.00g (Marsh 45; MCE 523; S 3852D). *Some light surface marks, nearly extremely fine and rare.* £800-1000

Price Realised : £864

ex St James's Auction 10, 6-7 November 2008, lot 551
Calendar year mintage 7,836,413
One of the more significant varieties of 1862 though the engraver's error does not involve the use of a true letter I in the date but the inversion of a figure 1 corrected by a normal figure 1. This has been quite successful as the upper right serif of the inverted figure beneath is barely visible, but is there. See footnote for lot 74 for a longer explanation of the corrected erroneous 1.

1862 Sovereign with R Over Inverted R in Queen's Name

1013 **Victoria,** Sovereign, 1862, with R struck over an inverted R in Queen's name, second larger young head left, ww incuse on truncation without stops, date below, curvy rounded open 6 with bulbous top, 1 over a lower 1, last A of legend doubled, *rev* crowned quartered shield of arms within laurel wreath, emblems below, 7.99g (cf Marsh 45; MCE 523; S 3852D). *Toned with lustre, pleasing extremely fine and still the finest known of this variety to the cataloguer, not many more have appeared for sale, very rare.* £1000-1500

Price Realised : £3,000

ex Northeast Numismatics, via Spink and Son, Atlanta ANA show, August 2002
Calendar year mintage 7,836,413
This example of the very rare R over inverted R variety was the very first discovered by the cataloguer. It was originally housed in a PCGS holder, graded as MS62, but the variety not noted. The cataloguer pointed out the new discovery to James Ricks of Northeast Numismatics and a deal was struck to have the coin find its way to the Bentley Collection. It was discoveries such as this that continued to excite the Bentley collector and has helped the Standard Catalogue of British Coins to harvest more and more varieties well beyond the scope of Marsh, which does not record this more recent discovery.
It would seem the engraver of this die punched the letter R in upside down and then corrected it over the top.
1862 marks the year at the Mint that resident engraver George Wyon dies, the post becomes vacant until 1865.

93 **Victoria,** Sovereign, 1862, A of GRATIA over a tilting A, second larger young head left, WW incuse on truncation without stops, date below, raised die flaw through 8, curvy rounded 6 with bulbous top, *rev* crowned quartered shield of arms within laurel wreath, emblems below, 7.92g (Marsh 45; MCE 523; S 3852D). *Once cleaned, fine, unusual and rare.* £300-350

Price Realised : £312

ex A H Baldwin & Sons Ltd sourced via Paul Davies Ltd, June 2008
Calendar year mintage 7,836,413
Another unusual corrected engraving error in the legend, this time with a V at first entered inverted instead of a letter A punch which has been punched over the top. It is also interesting to note that the weight of this coin in its lower grade is under the legal tender limit as dictated by the Coinage Acts of 1816-1891.

The Very Rare R over E on Reverse Sovereign of 1862

94 **Victoria,** Sovereign, 1862, sharper more hooked 6, first R of BRITANNIARUM over an E, second larger young head left, WW incuse on truncation without stops, date more spread below, *rev* crowned quartered shield of arms within laurel wreath, emblems below, 7.95g (Marsh 45; MCE 523; S 3852D). *Once cleaned, now lightly toned, very fine, the reverse a little stronger, a nice obvious corrected engraving error and extremely rare.* £800-1000

Price Realised : £864

ex A H Baldwin & Sons Ltd sourced via Paul Davies Ltd, October 2007
Calendar year mintage 7,836,413
This coin was purchased at the annual London Coinex in 2007 and was the first time the variety was noted. Another corrected engraver's error, a letter E punch at first mistakenly used after the B and then corrected with the letter R. Quality of engraving of dies at this time was shoddy, perhaps due to many apprentices involved on account of higher workloads with the greater outputs, but at least the errors in legends on dies were being discovered and corrected before coins were struck from them for circulation. The other point about this coin is it marks the first appearance of a sharper and hooked looking figure 6 in the date as opposed to the more usual and bulbous curvy 6 seen otherwise.

1015 **Victoria,** Sovereign, 1862, spread date with hooked open 6, second larger young head left, WW incuse on truncation without stops, date below, last A die flawed with some doubling, *rev* crowned quartered shield of arms within laurel wreath, emblems below, some doubling of legend in first word, last F of legend over indeterminate figure, perhaps a rotated F, but is the variety Marsh recognises as F over inverted A, 7.97g (Marsh 45A R2; MCE 523; S 3852D). *Once cleaned, good very fine, reverse a little better and very rare.* £800-1000

Price Realised : £792

ex Spink Auction, 24 September 2003, lot 1524
Calendar year mintage 7,836,413
This intriguing variety has puzzled numismatists for some time. Marsh recognised the variety early on and lists it as F over inverted A. The letter F of DEF clearly has two raised prongs sticking out of the top bar. The best conclusion when this was first discovered was that this could only be an inverted A. However, the width between the prongs is too narrow for the feet of an A or a V for that matter. This cataloguer often though it could be the result of a rotated character underneath, but nothing seems to fit the narrow width between the prongs. More recent thought by this cataloguer in the light of other Sovereign varieties seen tends to swing thinking towards merely an unfinished F punch used for this final F on this die, with extra burrs of unfinished metal adhered to the top of the F. Note however the previous F in the legend shows no such characteristic. It is still not conclusive what this last letter F is over or not as the case may be. It seems likely to be excess metal of some kind and is nevertheless a rarely seen variety.

Uniface Copper Obverse Pattern Possibly for a Sovereign, circa 1863

1016 Victoria, Uniface Pattern Obverse Trial, 1863, 63 double struck with curvy bulbed 6, struck in copper and gilt lightly on obverse only, by Charles Wiener, young head left with emblematic wreath of shamrocks, rose and thistle in hair, long ribbon ties at rear, C.W below truncation, date below, VICTORIA REGINA, toothed border and raised rim, *rev* plain, edge plain, 5.74g, 22.3mm, thickness 2mm (cf ESC 1372, with legend of 1377). *Gilding wearing through, some blank filing on plain side and on rim, good extremely fine and perhaps unique.* £600-800

Price Realised : £1,056

ex Patina collection, Spink Auction 1298, 11 July 2001, lot 1028
This unusual uniface pattern was added to the Bentley Collection because it could have been for a Sovereign proposal, it not being exactly recorded in the usual references for silver coinage. It is worthy of further research, perhaps in collaboration with the Royal Mint.

An Excessively Rare Copper Pattern Sovereign by Wiener dated 1863

95 Victoria, Pattern Sovereign, 1863, struck in copper, engraved by Charles Wiener, young head left with wreath of shamrocks, rose and thistle in hair, long ribbon ties at rear, C.W below truncation, date below, 63 double struck, raised die flaw runs through 8 then up to ear, gap between 18 and 63, curvy rounded 6 with bulbous top, VICTORIA REGINA, coarse toothed border, *rev* struck with slightly off-centre inverted die axis, engraved after Jean Baptiste Merlen, crowned quartered shield of arms within laurel wreath tied with bow below shield, 24 leaves in wreath, crown with eleven pearls upon each arch, five pearl on central upright, seven harp strings in Irish arms, left string emanates from scroll, emblems below, small rosette either side, BRITANNIARUM REGINA FID: DEF:, fine border teeth, edge plain, 4.15g, 21.8mm, thickness 1.9mm (Nobleman 282, *this coin illustrated*; see Forrer, volume VI, page 480). *Patchy tone on the reverse, toned, good extremely fine and of the highest rarity.* £1500-2000

Price Realised : £2,160

ex H Montagu collection, Spink and Son Ltd, sales list 1891, lot 1744
ex Nobleman collection, Sothebys, 27 March 1922, lot 282 (part)
ex Sothebys, 19 November 1969, lot 255
ex Baldwin's Auction 13, 28 May 1997, lot 2044
This unusual pattern is struck in copper and was engraved by the Belgian Charles Wiener (25 March 1832- 15 August 1888). In 1863 he proposed a number of new designs to the Mint of Shilling and Sovereign size, all of which are unadopted for currency and are at least rare and many are described in English Silver Coinage. This piece however is not listed in English Silver Coinage and seems firmly aimed at the Sovereign in that it carries Merlen's design on the reverse as used on currency sovereigns. A printed note in the cataloguing of it in the Montagu sales list reveals that "this portrait was rejected by the Queen at once." This piece is also mentioned in the Biographical Dictionary of Medallists on page 480. It should perhaps be considered as some kind of mule as the border teeth between obverse and reverse do not even match. There is one other similar pattern piece in the Bentley Collection struck in gilt copper, a uniface obverse, see lot 1016 above.

96 **Victoria,** Sovereign, 1863, 63 higher than 18, second larger young head left, ww incuse on truncation without stops, date out of alignment below, sharper more hooked 6, Queen's name doubled, last A of legend over a lower A, *rev* die axis off-centre, crowned quartered shield of arms within laurel wreath, emblems below, 7.98g (Marsh 46; MCE 524; S 3852D). *Very light surface marks, good extremely fine.* £600-700

Price Realised : £840

Calendar year mintage 5,921,669
A slight drop in calendar year output, perhaps signifies the introduction of a new system of numbering the reverse dies employed at the Mint to keep a check on the efficiency and longevity of dies. The 1863 coin as we have here and in lot 97, page 110, are the last dated coins of the London shield reverse type to not have a die number below the wreath. As the reverse die is the moving one in the press the operator using the machinery containing that die will be the only person responsible for coinage of that particular die number. Quality control of engraving suddenly seems to vastly improve as the engraver would know that a certain die number would trace the die straight back to his handiwork. For more information see the following die number section.

The Extremely Rare 1863 Sovereign with 827 Die Number on Truncation

1017 **Victoria,** Sovereign, 1863, numbers 827 in relief on truncation meets field, second larger young head left, date below, sharper more hooked incomplete open 6, doubled date especially 8, legend lightly doubled with last I flawed to rim, *rev* crowned quartered shield of arms within laurel wreath tied with bow below shield, no die number below, emblems below, 7.99g (Marsh 48A R5; MCE 524; S 3853A). *Very light surface marks and scuffs, about very fine, better than usually encountered for this great rarity, extremely rare.* £8000-10,000

Price Realised : £18,000

ex Randy Weir Numismatics, Unionville, Ontario, Canada, purchased 28 June 1993
The intriguing "827"variety first came to light in 1954 when an 827 numbered truncation with die number 22 reverse appeared in the Hatton Hoard of gold found in Derbyshire. This initial coin ended up in the British Museum Collection.
The variety here is termed the "first" variety of the "827" Sovereign without a die number on the reverse. The "second" die number 22 variety was sold in part one of the Bentley Collection for £11,000 hammer.
These first variety 827 die number Sovereigns are thought to have been produced and struck from a first batch of re-melted "scissel" and scrap emanating from some Rothschild brittle ingots delivered to the Mint circa November-December 1863. Of the very few specimens known, the Bentley specimen is amongst the finer.
For further reading about the 827 Sovereigns see Spink Numismatic Circular, October 1977, page 421, article by G P Dyer.

The Rare 1863 Sovereign with 1 Struck over an Inverted 1

97 **Victoria,** Sovereign, 1863, Arabic figure 1 over an inverted Arabic figure 1 giving the impression of a Roman I in date, second larger young head left, ww incuse on truncation without stops, date below, sharper more hooked 6, legend doubled, especially Queen's name, *rev* crowned quartered shield of arms within laurel wreath, emblems below, start of legend with doubled lettering, 7.99g (cf Marsh 46; MCE 524; S 3852D). *Scuff on cheek and other light surface marks, otherwise extremely fine and rare.* £800-1000

Price Realised : £840

ex St James's Auction 5, 27 September 2006, lot 633
Another instance of the date figure 1 being entered inverted at first, then corrected after with the figure the right way up. This is evident from the step down at the top right of the correct figure 1, to the serif below from the inverted one beneath. See footnote of lot 74 for a fuller explanation of how this occurs. A very rare corrected error and one of the last before the stricter quality control of the die number series begins.

The Victorian Die Number Series of Gold Sovereigns 1863-1874 at the Royal Mint London

From 1863 to 1874 inclusive, seemingly as a new drive for quality control, the Royal Mint in London added a tiny die number to the reverse die of gold Sovereigns. There were however no Sovereigns issued in, or dated 1867 in this time-frame. This die numbering occurred additionally on gold Half-Sovereigns from 1863 till 1880, and also in the silver coinage, on Shillings from 1864 till 1879, and Sixpences from 1864 till 1879. There is correlation in these denominations all being of a similar size and stature, which may mean similar minting presses being employed and perhaps worked by the same teams of operators. They were now seemingly subject to a stricter regime where work in production could be individually traced back to a worker on a given day. Equally the engravers with their apprentices in their respective department could also be traced from the tiny number on the die they had worked upon. Within the Mint itself in 1865 the vacant post (since 1862) of Resident Engraver is taken up by T J Minton.
This is discussed further by E G V Newman in his essay *"The Model of Accuracy"* in the *"Royal Sovereign 1489-1989"* published by the Royal Mint.

One of the serious passions of the owner of the Bentley Collection, for the last twenty years, was the quest to find as many of the known die numbers as possible on the reverse of the Victorian London shield Sovereigns from 1863-1874 inclusive. This has resulted today in a total accumulation of 565 different die number pieces in the whole collection, by far the most ever assembled by a private collector. Only an illustrious few have ever attempted such an undertaking.

For the first five years of attempting this, the best quality was only accepted for the various die numbers, however it became readily apparent that many of the die numbers were just not obtainable in top grade, this being at a time when a collector was doing well to merely obtain a date in top grade. With the sale of the Douro Cargo of gold Sovereigns in November 1996, a sale in which your present writer was one of the principle cataloguers (four different people catalogued Douro as it was such a Herculean task by quantity within the deadline), a massive opportunity arose to obtain many die numbers at one fell swoop, with most well preserved after their time on the seabed of the Bay of Biscay.

The Bentley Collector ended up securing over 130 pieces at once through an agent at this momentous sale, which increased the collection of die numbers at this time to 216 pieces. A further large addition was made in 2001 from a collection of Sovereigns that was previously unsuccessfully offered for sale as one lot at Sotheby, 16-17 November 2000, an "Important Collection of Gold Sovereigns 1816-2000." This collector had also attempted the die number series and had also bought many in the Douro Cargo auction, managing to amass a total of 195 die numbers. The two collectors eventually were put in touch and a great many Sovereigns changed hands, thus adding many to the Bentley holding.

Since the auction of the Douro Cargo in 1996, other parcels of Douro coins have come to the market, which were groups that were shared out to other individuals involved with the salvaging of the cargo. These have been the richest source for obtaining further die numbers in more recent years, mainly through the auspices of Paul Davies Ltd.

Michael Marsh has been the only author to attempt to record as many of the die numbers as possible, presumably from those either seen by him or reported to him in commerce or in institutional records or collections, and these are listed in his book.

With the Bentley Collection we have produced a never before attempted tabulation of all the die numbers against their respective dates. Those that are not recorded by Marsh are highlighted, and the gaps in the collection that Marsh claims exist are denoted as "M".

VICTORIAN DIE NUMBER SOVEREIGNS

Die No.	1863	1864	1865	1866	1868	1869	1870	1871	1872	1873	1874
1	✓	✓	✓	✓	✓	✓	✓	✓	✓	✓	
2	✓	✓	✓	✓	✓	✓	M	✓	✓	✓	
3	✓	✓	✓	✓	✓	✓	M	✓	✓	✓	
4	✓	✓	✓	✓	✓	✓	M	✓	✓	✓	
5	✓	✓	✓	✓	✓	✓	M	✓	✓	✓	
6	✓	✓	✓	✓	✓	✓	M	✓	✓	✓	
7	✓	✓	M	✓	✓	✓	M	✓	✓	✓	
8	✓	✓	✓	✓	✓	✓	M	✓	✓	✓	
9	✓	✓	✓	✓	✓	✓	M	✓	✓	✓	
10	✓	✓	✓	✓	✓	✓	M	✓	✓	✓	
11	✓	M	✓	✓	✓	✓	M	✓	✓	✓	
12	✓	✓	✓	M	✓	✓	M	✓	✓	✓	M
13	✓	✓	✓	✓	✓	✓	M	✓	✓	✓	
14	✓	M	✓	✓	✓	✓	M	✓	✓	✓	
15	✓	✓	✓	✓	✓	✓	M	✓	✓	✓	M
16	✓	M	✓	✓	✓	✓	M	✓	✓	✓	
17	✓	M	✓	✓	✓	✓	M	✓	✓	M	
18	✓	M	✓	✓	✓	✓	M	✓	✓	✓	
19	✓	✓	✓	✓	✓	✓	M	✓	✓	✓	
20	✓	M	✓	✓	✓	✓	M	✓	✓	✓	
21	✓	✓	✓	✓	✓	✓	M	✓	✓	✓	
22	✓+827	✓	✓	✓	✓	✓	M	✓	✓	✓	
23	✓	✓	✓	✓	✓	M	M	✓	✓	M	
24	✓	✓	✓	✓	✓	✓	M	✓	✓	M	
25	M	✓	M	✓	✓	✓	M	✓	✓	M	
26	M	✓	✓	✓	✓	✓	M	✓	✓	M	
27		✓	✓	✓	✓	✓	M	✓	✓	M	
28		✓	✓	✓	✓	✓	M	✓	✓	M	✓
29		✓	✓	✓	✓	✓	M	✓	✓	M	
30		✓	M	✓	✓	✓	M	✓	✓	M	
31		✓	✓	✓	✓	✓	M	✓	✓	✓	
32		✓	✓	✓	✓	✓	M	✓	✓	M	✓
33		✓	✓	✓	✓	✓	M	✓	✓	M	✓
34		✓	M	✓	✓	✓	M	✓	✓	M	M

Die No.	1863	1864	1865	1866	1868	1869	1870	1871	1872	1873	1874
35		✓	✓	✓	✓	✓	M	✓	✓		M
36		✓	✓	✓	✓	✓	M	✓	✓	✓	
37		✓	✓	✓	✓	✓	M	✓	✓	M	
38	M	✓	M	✓	✓	✓	M	✓	✓	M	
39		✓	M	✓	✓	✓	M	✓	✓	M	
40		✓	✓	✓	M	✓	M	✓	✓	M	
41		✓	M	✓	✓	✓	M	✓	✓	M	
42		✓	M	✓		✓	M	✓	✓	M	
43		✓		✓		✓	M	✓	✓	M	
44		✓	M	✓		✓	M	✓	✓	M	
45		✓	M	✓		✓	M	✓	✓	M	
46		✓		✓		✓	M	M	✓	M	
47		M		✓	M	✓	M	✓	✓	M	
48		✓		✓	M	✓	M	✓	✓	M	
49		✓		✓		✓	M	M	✓	M	
50		✓		✓		✓	M	M	✓	M	
51		✓	M	✓		✓	M	M	✓	M	
52		✓		✓		✓	M	M	✓	M	
53		✓		✓		✓	M	M	✓	M	
54		✓	M	✓		✓	M	✓	✓	M	
55		✓		✓		M	M	M	✓	M	
56		✓		✓		✓	M	M	✓	M	
57		✓		✓		✓	M	M	✓	M	
58		✓		✓		✓	M	M	✓	M	
59		M		✓		✓	M	M	✓	M	
60		✓		✓		✓	M	M	✓	M	
61		✓		✓		✓	M	M	✓	M	
62		✓		✓		✓	M	M	✓	M	
63		✓		✓		✓	M	M	✓	M	
64		✓		✓		✓24K	M	M	✓	M	
65		✓		✓		M	M	M	✓	M	
66		✓		✓		M	M	✓	✓	M	
67				✓		M	M	✓	✓	M	
68		M		✓		M	M	✓	✓	M	
69		✓		✓		✓	M	M	✓	M	
70				✓		M	M	✓	✓	M	
71		✓		✓		M	M	✓	✓	M	
72		✓		✓		M	M	✓	✓	M	
73		✓		✓		M	M	✓	✓	M	
74		✓		✓		M	M	✓	✓	M	
75		✓		✓		M	M	✓	✓	M	
76		✓		✓		M	M	✓	✓	M	
77		✓		✓			M	✓	✓	M	
78		✓		✓			M	✓	✓	M	
79		✓		M			M	✓	✓	M	
80		✓					✓		✓	M	
81		✓					✓		✓	M	
82		✓					✓		✓	M	
83		✓					✓	M	✓	M	
84		✓					✓		✓	M	
85		✓					✓		✓	M	
86		✓					✓		✓	M	
87		✓					✓		✓	M	
88		✓					✓	M	✓	M	
89		✓					✓		✓	M	
90		✓					✓		✓	M	
91		✓					✓		✓	M	
92		✓					✓		✓	M	
93		✓					✓		✓	M	
94		✓					✓	M	✓	M	
95		✓					✓		✓	M	
96		✓					✓	M	✓	M	
97		✓						✓	✓	M	
98		✓						✓	✓	M	
99		✓					M	✓	✓	M	
100		✓					M	✓	✓	M	
101		✓						✓	✓		

Die No.	1863	1864	1865	1866	1868	1869	1870	1871	1872	1873	1874
102		✓						✓	✓		
103		✓						✓	M	✓	
104		✓						✓	✓	M	
105		✓						✓	✓		
106		M						✓	✓		
107								M		✓	
108								✓	✓		
109								✓	✓		
110								✓	✓		
111								✓	✓		
112							✓		✓		
113							✓				
114							✓				
115							✓				
116							✓				
117							✓				
118							✓				
119							✓				
120							✓				
121							✓				
122							✓				
123							✓				

KEY:-

black	✓	Bentley Collection
red	✓	Bentley Collection contains; but Marsh does not record
red	M	Marsh records number that is not present in the Bentley Collection
1863	✓+827	Bentley Collection contains examples of the regular die number and one with the 827 obverse
1869	✓24K	Bentley Collection contains a proof Sovereign in 24 Carat gold only for this die number

TOTAL of Differently die numbered Sovereigns

	1863	1864	1865	1866	1868	1869	1870	1871	1872	1873	1874
✓	24	94	34	77	40	63	18	75	110	27	3
M	3	10	12	2	3	13	80	23	1	75	4
Total	**27**	**104**	**46**	**79**	**43**	**76**	**98**	**98**	**111**	**102**	**7**

In the table above all the Bentley die numbers are ticked and the ones Marsh records additionally as "known" are marked with a red M. On some occasions the Bentley collection contains a die number not recorded in Marsh. These are marked with a red tick. It is interesting to note patterns in this table, of what runs of numbers exist for which date side by side with other adjacent dates. Looking at the end of the period where the numbers run to over 100 in a given year, it is interesting to see there is no die number 107 in the Bentley Collection for 1871 or 1872, but there is for 1873. Marsh claims it should exist for 1871, but we wonder if perhaps it was intended to be used for 1871 originally but ended up being stored until use for 1873 dated coins, perhaps the Mint record reflects this and is where Marsh obtained information about it being for 1871 originally as he also records it for 1873.

It should be noted that the Bentley Collector supplied information on die numbers in this collection to Marsh for publication in the latest edition of the book in 2002. If the 2002 edition is compared to the edition before it will be seen how many die numbers have been added! However this cataloguer cannot help but feel that there are a few inaccuracies in the Marsh listings of die numbers in his book "The Gold Sovereign", not only because he recorded numbers given to him in correspondence from others which are always open to misinterpretation without Mr Marsh seeing the reported coin for himself; but also because it seems that some consecutive runs of numbers listed as "known" just do not seem to turn up on the marketplace. This is demonstrated where the Bentley Collector has taken 20 years, without finding a single die number in a consecutive sequence, for a date like 1870 from die 2 until 79 inclusive which Marsh claims all exist. Knowing that some of the mintage figures in Marsh's tabulations have typographic errors, it follows that the listings of die numbers could be flawed also. Mr Marsh was in touch with the Royal Mint at times so it may be that records there will show which numbers should exist and perhaps this sort of information was incorporated in the listings. These anomalies remain to be proven with continued research, but it should be noted that with these tiny die numbers, it is notoriously easy to mistake a 5 for a 3 and vice versa. Human error will always creep in though it is hoped the physical recording of the Bentley die numbers herewith are 100% accurate.

98 **Victoria,** Sovereign, 1863, die number 1, second larger young head left, ww incuse on truncation without stops, date below, sharper more hooked incomplete 6, raised die flaw to the right side of 1, some letters doubled in obverse legend, VIC of VICTORIA seemingly struck over smaller letters, *rev* crowned quartered shield of arms within laurel wreath tied with bow below shield, die number 1 below, emblems below, small rosette either side, 7.98g (Marsh 48; MCE 524; S 3853). *Toned with some light surface marks, good very fine.* £300-350

Price Realised : £264

Calendar year mintage 5,921,669
As mentioned previously, the calendar year mintage above also includes the last of the non-die number coins dated 1863. This coin is die number 1 of 24 numbered dies in the Bentley Collection plus the 827 numbered piece with die 22 reverse. Marsh claims three other numbers exist making 27 reverse dies with numbers in total, plus some more of the non-die numbered variety, to strike nearly 6 million Sovereigns. This shows good die longevity.

99 **Victoria,** Sovereign, 1863, die number 2, second larger young head left, ww incuse on truncation without stops, date below, 8 slightly doubled, sharper more hooked incomplete 6, some lettering doubled, raised die flaw evident between E and I in DEI, *rev* crowned quartered shield of arms within laurel wreath, die number 2 below, emblems below, 7.97g (Marsh 48; MCE 524; S 3853). *Light rim bruise and surface marks, about extremely fine, reverse better.* £350-450

Price Realised : £288

ex Randy Weir Numismatics, Unionville, Ontario, Canada, purchased 5 December 1989
Calendar year mintage 5,921,669
See footnote for lot 98 (above) for a brief synopsis of the 1863 die numbers.

435 **Victoria,** Sovereign, 1863, die number 3, second larger young head left, ww incuse on truncation without stops, date below, 8 slightly doubled, sharper more hooked incomplete 6, die flaw on 1 of date, raised die flaw evident on C of queen's name, *rev* crowned quartered shield of arms within laurel wreath, die number 3 below, emblems below, hairline raised die flaw around most of legend, especially on second word, 7.97g (Marsh 48; MCE 524; S 3853). *Light rim nick, hairlines, a pleasing extremely fine.* £300-400

Price Realised : £504

ex An Important Collection of Gold Sovereigns 1816-2000, offered as one lot, Sothebys, November 2000, lot 525 (part)
Calendar year mintage 5,921,669
See footnote for lot 98 (above) for a brief synopsis of the 1863 die numbers.

436 **Victoria,** Sovereign, 1863, die number 4, second larger young head left, ww incuse on truncation without stops, date below, sharper more hooked incomplete 6, die flaw on 1 of date running to neck, raised die flaw evident from last A of legend to rim, *rev* crowned quartered shield of arms within laurel wreath, die number 4 below, emblems below, hairline raised die flaw on first A of reverse legend, 7.97g (Marsh 48; MCE 524; S 3853). *Light hairlines, good very fine.* £300-350

Price Realised : £312

ex Bennie Linden collection, DNW, 7 October 2003, lot 493
Calendar year mintage 5,921,669
See footnote for lot 98, page 114, for a brief synopsis of the 1863 die numbers

1018 **Victoria,** Sovereign, 1863, die number 5, second larger young head left, ww incuse on truncation without stops, date below, sharper more hooked incomplete 6, last word of legend die flawed, second I of Queen's name die flawed to rim, *rev* crowned quartered shield of arms within laurel wreath, die number 5 below, emblems below, hairline die flaw in penultimate word, 7.98g (Marsh 48; MCE 524; S 3853). *Light surface marks, scuffs and hairlines, almost extremely fine.* £300-400

Price Realised : £336

ex An Important Collection of Gold Sovereigns 1816-2000, offered as one lot, Sothebys, November 2000, lot 525 (part)
Calendar year mintage 5,921,669
For further reading on varieties of 1863 die number Sovereigns see footnote for lot 98, page 114

1019 **Victoria,** Sovereign, 1863, die number 6, second larger young head left, ww incuse on truncation without stops, date below, curvy 6 with bulb top, date lightly die flawed, *rev* crowned quartered shield of arms within laurel wreath, die number 6 below, emblems below, 7.98g (Marsh 48; MCE 524; S 3853). *Light surface marks, once cleaned, about very fine to very fine.* £250-300

Price Realised : £240

ex Douro Cargo, Spink Auction 118, 20-21 November 1996, uncertain lot number
ex An Important Collection of Gold Sovereigns 1816-2000, offered as one lot, Sothebys, November 2000, lot 525 (part)
Calendar year mintage 5,921,669
See footnote for lot 98, page 114, for a brief synopsis of the 1863 die numbers.

100 **Victoria,** Sovereign, 1863, die number 7, second larger young head left, ww incuse on truncation without stops, date below, 8 slightly doubled, sharper more hooked incomplete 6, first I of legend die flawed, some doubling of legend, *rev* die axis off-centre, crowned quartered shield of arms within laurel wreath, die number 7 below, emblems below, legend partly die flawed, 7.98g (Marsh 48; MCE 524; S 3853). *Streaky tone on obverse, toned, about extremely fine.* £400-450

Price Realised : £360

ex Douro Cargo, Spink Auction 118, 20-21 November 1996, uncertain lot number
ex An Important Collection of Gold Sovereigns 1816-2000, offered as one lot, Sothebys, 16-17 November 2000, lot 525 (part)
Calendar year mintage 5,921,669. See footnote for lot 98, page 114, for a brief synopsis of the 1863 die numbers.

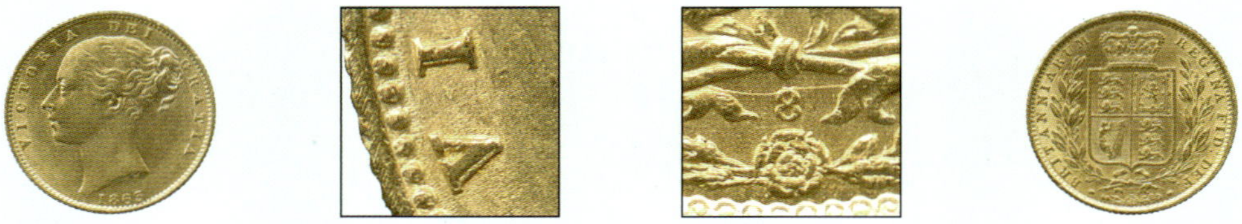

437 **Victoria,** Sovereign, 1863, die number 8, second larger young head left, WW incuse on truncation without stops, raised die flaw from tip of neck to rim, date below, curvy rounded 6 with bulbous top, queen's name doubled especially VI, V possibly over a small V, *rev* crowned quartered shield of arms within laurel wreath, die number 8 below, emblems below, some light doubling in reverse legend, raised die flaw in second word, 7.96g (Marsh 48; MCE 524; S 3853). *Light surface marks, extremely fine, unusual with the* V *over a seemingly smaller* V, *a result of the double strike.* £300-400

Price Realised : £432

Calendar year mintage 5,921,669
See footnote for lot 98, page 114, for a brief synopsis of the 1863 die numbers.

101 **Victoria,** Sovereign, 1863, die number 9, second larger young head left, WW incuse on truncation without stops, date below, sharper more hooked incomplete 6, some doubling of obverse legend, *rev* crowned quartered shield of arms within laurel wreath, die number 9 below, emblems below, some letters with a trace of doubling, 7.96g (Marsh 48; MCE 524; S 3853). *Surface marks and scuffs, otherwise toned, good very fine.* £300-350

Price Realised : £264

ex Paul Davies Ltd. This coin was purchased from one of the groups of coins from the wreck of the RMS *Douro* that were not sold by auction and within the last 10 years.
Calendar year mintage 5,921,669
See footnote for lot 98, page 114, for a brief synopsis of the 1863 die numbers.

1020 **Victoria,** Sovereign, 1863, die number 10, second larger young head left, WW incuse on truncation without stops, date below, curvy 6 with bulb top, legend lightly doubled both sides, *rev* crowned quartered shield of arms within laurel wreath, die number 10 below, 0 weaker than 1, emblems below, 7.99g (Marsh 48; MCE 524; S 3853). *Light surface marks on cheek, hairlines, otherwise extremely fine.* £300-400

Price Realised : £456

Purchased via Spink and Son Ltd, November 2003
Calendar year mintage 5,921,669. See footnote for lot 98, page 114, for a brief synopsis of the 1863 die numbers.

102 **Victoria,** Sovereign, 1863, die number 11, second larger young head left, WW incuse on truncation without stops, date below, 3 with raised die flaw to rim, curvy rounded 6 with bulbous top, *rev* crowned quartered shield of arms within laurel wreath, die number 11 below, emblems below, some hairline raised flaws in lettering, 7.96g (Marsh 48; MCE 524; S 3853). *Once cleaned, reverse rim nick, surface marks with hairlines, otherwise extremely fine.* £350-400

Price Realised : £360

ex Ebay purchase, April 2002
Calendar year mintage 5,921,669
See footnote for lot 98, page 114, for a brief synopsis of the 1863 die numbers.
The curvy rounded 6 has returned from die number 10 onwards, as we have here on die 11.

438 **Victoria,** Sovereign, 1863, die number 12, second larger young head left, ww incuse on truncation without stops, date below, curvy rounded 6 with bulbous top, raised die flaw on 1 of date, lightly doubled legend, *rev* crowned quartered shield of arms within laurel wreath, die number 12 below, emblems below, 7.99g (Marsh 48; MCE 524; S 3853). *Light streak of tone, good extremely fine.* £400-500

Price Realised : £1,056

Calendar year mintage 5,921,669
See footnote for lot 98, page 114, for a brief synopsis of the 1863 die numbers.

439 **Victoria,** Sovereign, 1863, die number 13, second larger young head left, ww incuse on truncation without stops, date below, curvy rounded 6 with bulbous top, *rev* crowned quartered shield of arms within laurel wreath, die number 13 below, emblems below, reverse legend lightly doubled, 8.00g (Marsh 48; MCE 524; S 3853). *Some light scuffs, extremely fine.* £300-400

Price Realised : £624

ex Douro Cargo, Spink Auction 118, 20-21 November 1996, lot 894 (part)
Calendar year mintage 5,921,669
See footnote for lot 98, page 114, for a brief synopsis of the 1863 die numbers.

1021 **Victoria,** Sovereign, 1863, die number 14, second larger young head left, ww incuse on truncation without stops, date below, curvy 6 with bulb top, third I of legend die flawed, *rev* crowned quartered shield of arms within laurel wreath, die number 14 below, emblems below, 7.99g (Marsh 48; MCE 524; S 3853). *Once cleaned, light hairlines mainly around reverse legend, otherwise about extremely fine, reverse better.* £300-400

Price Realised : £432

ex G K Coins, London, via Spink and Son Ltd, August 2003
Calendar year mintage 5,921,669
See footnote for lot 98, page 114, for a brief synopsis of the 1863 die numbers.

1022 **Victoria,** Sovereign, 1863, die number 15, second larger young head left, ww incuse on truncation without stops, date below, curvy 6 with bulb top die flawed shut, Queen's name lightly doubled, *rev* crowned quartered shield of arms within laurel wreath, die number 15 below, emblems below, 7.98g (Marsh 48; MCE 524; S 3853). *Light hairlines, otherwise toned, practically as struck.* £400-600

Price Realised : £840

ex An Important Collection of Gold Sovereigns 1816-2000, offered as one lot, Sothebys, November 2000, lot 525 (part)
Calendar year mintage 5,921,669
See footnote for lot 98, page 114, for a brief synopsis of the 1863 die numbers.

103 **Victoria,** Sovereign, 1863, die number 16, second larger young head left, ww incuse on truncation without stops, date below, curvy rounded 6 with bulbous top, *rev* crowned quartered shield of arms within laurel wreath, die number 16 below, emblems below, some hairline raised flaws, 7.97g (Marsh 48; MCE 524; S 3853). *Some light scuffs and hairlines, good extremely fine.* £400-500

Price Realised : £408

ex Douro Cargo, Spink Auction 118, 20-21 November 1996, uncertain lot number
Ex An Important Collection of Gold Sovereigns 1816-2000, offered as one lot, Sothebys, 16-17 November 2000, lot 525 (part)
Calendar year mintage 5,921,669
See footnote for lot 98, page 114, for a brief synopsis of the 1863 die numbers.

440 **Victoria,** Sovereign, 1863, die number 17, second larger young head left, ww incuse on truncation without stops, date below, curvy rounded 6 with bulbous top, die flawed and doubled date, *rev* crowned quartered shield of arms within laurel wreath, die number 17 below, emblems below, 7.91g (Marsh 48; MCE 524; S 3853). *Scuffed with surface marks, very fine.* £300-350

Price Realised : £288

ex London Coins Auction 103, November 2003
Calendar year mintage 5,921,669
It is interesting to note that, as one of the lower grade Sovereigns in the Bentley Collection, this coin is well under the legal tender weight limit that was set in successive Coinage Acts from 1816-1891.
See footnote for lot 98, page 114, for a brief synopsis of the 1863 die numbers.

1023 **Victoria,** Sovereign, 1863, die number 18, second larger young head left, ww incuse on truncation without stops, date below, curvy 6 with bulb top die flawed shut, Queen's name lightly doubled, *rev* crowned quartered shield of arms within laurel wreath, die number 18 below, emblems below, 7.97g (Marsh 48; MCE 524; S 3853). *Light hairlines and some scuffs, discoloured, otherwise about very fine.* £250-300

Price Realised : £240

ex Paul Davies Ltd, Ilkley. This coin was purchased from one of the groups of coins from the wreck of the RMS *Douro* that were not sold by auction and within the last 10 years.
Calendar year mintage 5,921,669
See footnote for lot 98, page 114, for a brief synopsis of the 1863 die numbers.

104 **Victoria,** Sovereign, 1863, die number 19, second larger young head left, ww incuse on truncation without stops, date below, doubled figures in date, curvy rounded 6 with bulbous top, *rev* crowned quartered shield of arms within laurel wreath, die number 19 below lightly die flawed, emblems below, legend lightly die flawed, 7.95g (Marsh 48; MCE 524; S 3853). *Once cleaned, now lightly toned, nearly very fine.* £300-350

Price Realised : £264

Calendar year mintage 5,921,669
See footnote for lot 98, page 114, for a brief synopsis of the 1863 die numbers.

441 **Victoria,** Sovereign, 1863, die number 20, second larger young head left, WW incuse on truncation without stops, date below, curvy rounded 6 with bulbous top, queen's name doubled, *rev* crowned quartered shield of arms within laurel wreath, die number 20 below, with larger 2 and smaller round higher O, emblems below, 7.99g (Marsh 48; MCE 524; S 3853). *Light surface marks, from being bagged when new, good extremely fine.* £400-500

Price Realised : £768

ex Randy Weir Numismatics, Unionville, Ontario, Canada, purchased May 1990
Calendar year mintage 5,921,669
The arrangement of the die number on the reverse seems a little haphazard compared to others.
See footnote for lot 98, page 114, for a brief synopsis of the 1863 die numbers.

105 **Victoria,** Sovereign, 1863, die number 21, second larger young head left, WW incuse on truncation without stops, date below, 3 slightly die flawed, curvy rounded 6 with bulbous top, Queen's name is slightly out of alignment in its arc, *rev* crowned quartered shield of arms within laurel wreath, die number 21 below emblems below, 7.93g (Marsh 48; MCE 524; S 3853). *Once cleaned, with light surface marks and scuffs and hairline scratches, otherwise nearly very fine.* £300-350

Price Realised : £264

ex Paul Davies Ltd. This coin was purchased from one of the groups of coins from the wreck of the RMS *Douro* that were not sold by auction and within the last 10 years.
Calendar year mintage 5,921,669
See footnote for lot 98, page 114, for a brief synopsis of the 1863 die numbers.
This coin from its wear and tear falls just below the legal tender weight limit set by the Coinage Acts from 1816-1891.

442 **Victoria,** Sovereign, 1863, die number 22, second larger young head left, WW incuse on truncation without stops, date below, curvy rounded 6 with bulbous top, *rev* crowned quartered shield of arms within laurel wreath, die number 22 below, emblems below, 7.96g (Marsh 48; MCE 524; S 3853). *Once cleaned, very fine, reverse a little better.* £300-400

Price Realised : £288

ex G K Coins, purchased via Spink and Son, November 2003
Calendar year mintage 5,921,669
See footnote for lot 98, page 114, for a brief synopsis of the 1863 die numbers.

The Extremely Rare 827 on Truncation 1863 Sovereign with Die Number 22 Reverse

106 **Victoria,** Gold Sovereign, 1863, numbers 827 in relief on truncation meets field, second larger young head left, date below, sharper more hooked incomplete 6, *rev* crowned quartered shield of arms within laurel wreath tied with bow below shield, die number 22 in relief below, the second 2 weaker than first, emblems below, 7.99g (Marsh 48A R5; MCE 524; S 3853A). *Light surface marks and hairlines, extremely fine, reverse better, extremely rare.* £8000-10,000

Price Realised : £13,200

ex Spink and Son Ltd, May 2001
This intriguing variety first came to light in 1954 when an 827 numbered truncation with die number 22 reverse turned up in the Hatton Hoard of gold found in Derbyshire. This initial coin ended up in the British Museum Collection. This variety is termed the "second" variety of the "827" Sovereign coupled with the die number 22 reverse. The "first" non-die number variety is listed as lot 1017, page 109. These are called the second variety as it is thought that this die numbered "827" Sovereign was produced and struck from a second batch of re-melted "scissel" and scrap emanating from the Rothschild brittle ingots delivered to the Mint around November to December 1863. Of the very few specimens known the Bentley specimen is one of the finest extant.
For further reading about the 827 Sovereigns see Spink Numismatic Circular, October 1977, p.421, article by G P Dyer.

1024 **Victoria,** Sovereign, 1863, die number 23, second larger young head left, ww incuse on truncation without stops, date below, curvy 6 with bulb top die flawed shut, *rev* crowned quartered shield of arms within laurel wreath, die number 23 below, emblems below, hairline die flaws in reverse legend, 7.98g (Marsh 48; MCE 524; S 3853). *Some light hairlines, otherwise lightly toned, pleasing extremely fine.* £300-400

Price Realised : £312

Calendar year mintage 5,921,669
See footnote for lot 98, page 114, for a brief synopsis of the 1863 die numbers.

1025 **Victoria,** Sovereign, 1863, die number 24, second larger young head left, ww incuse on truncation without stops, date below, curvy 6 with bulb top, date doubled as are some letters in Queen's name, *rev* crowned quartered shield of arms within laurel wreath, die number 24 below, 4 higher than 2, emblems below, hairline die flaws in reverse legend, 7.96g (Marsh 48; MCE 524; S 3853). *Some light hairlines, otherwise lightly toned, pleasing extremely fine.* £300-400

Price Realised : £288

ex Paul Davies Ltd, Ilkley. This coin was purchased from one of the groups of coins from the wreck of the RMS *Douro* that were not sold by auction and within the last 10 years.
Calendar year mintage 5,921,669. See footnote for lot 98, page 114, for a brief synopsis of the 1863 die numbers.

107 **Victoria,** Sovereign, 1864, die number 1, second larger young head left, ww incuse on truncation without stops, date below, stub top to 4, curvy rounded 6 with bulbous top, raised die flaw through 1 of date, raised die flaw in IA of GRATIA, *rev* crowned quartered shield of arms within laurel wreath, die number 1 below, emblems below, 8.00g (Marsh 49; MCE 525; S 3853). *Toned, extremely fine with just a few very light marks.* £350-450

Price Realised : £504

ex Spink and Son Ltd, November 2003
Calendar year mintage 8,656,352
This coin is die number 1 of 94 different numbered dies in the Bentley Collection, running from 1 to 105. Four of these are unrecorded by Marsh in his listing of numbers known. Marsh claims ten other numbers exist making 104 reverse dies in total to strike more than 8 million Sovereigns, showing not such a good die longevity. However it must always be borne in mind that the calendar year mintages are exactly that, and do not reflect the dates upon the coins in that period, some of them could have been 1863 dated coins, and 1864 date coins were probably made into the first part of 1865. A statistician should be able to make more sense of the figures given more time and research, perhaps in collaboration with the Royal Mint Museum.

108 **Victoria,** Sovereign, 1864, die number 2, second larger young head left, ww incuse on truncation without stops, date below, stub top to 4, curvy rounded 6 with bulbous top, V and last I of legend with raised die flaws, Queen's name doubled, *rev* crowned quartered shield of arms within laurel wreath, die number 2 below, emblems below, 7.95g (Marsh 49; MCE 525; S 3853). *Once cleaned, heavily scuffed surfaces, nearly very fine, reverse better.* £300-350

Price Realised : £288

ex Spink and Son Ltd, July 2003
Calendar year mintage 8,656,352
See footnote for lot 107 (above) for a brief synopsis of the 1864 die numbers.

443 **Victoria,** Sovereign, 1864, die number 3, second larger young head left, ww incuse on truncation without stops, date below, stub top to 4, curvy rounded 6 with bulbous top, light raised die flaw through 1 of date, raised die flaw in V and A of queen's name and last I of obverse legend, *rev* crowned quartered shield of arms within laurel wreath, die number 3 below, emblems below, 7.99g (Marsh 49; MCE 525; S 3853). *A few very light marks, red patch of tone on the reverse, very fine, reverse extremely fine and brilliant.* £300-400

Price Realised : £312

ex Randy Weir Numismatics, Unionville, Ontario, Canada, purchased late 1990s
Calendar year mintage 8,656,352
See footnote for lot 107 (above) for a brief synopsis of the 1864 die numbers.

444 **Victoria,** Sovereign, 1864, die number 4, second larger young head left, WW incuse on truncation without stops, date below, stub top to 4, curvy rounded 6 with bulbous top, light raised die flaw through 4 of date, queen's name doubled, *rev* crowned quartered shield of arms within laurel wreath, die number 4 below, emblems below, 7.98g (Marsh 49; MCE 525; S 3853). *Rim nick on reverse, a pleasing extremely fine, reverse good extremely fine.* £350-450

Price Realised : £552

ex Douro Cargo, Spink Auction 118, 20-21 November 1996, lot 549 (part)
Calendar year mintage 8,656,352. See footnote for lot 107, page 121, for a brief synopsis of the 1864 die numbers.

1026 **Victoria,** Sovereign, 1864, die number 5, second larger young head left, WW incuse on truncation without stops, date below, stub top to 4, curvy rounded 6 with bulbous top, heavy raised die flaw through 1 of date, some light doubling of legend both sides, *rev* crowned quartered shield of arms within laurel wreath, die number 5 below, the 5 filled, emblems below, 7.98g (Marsh 49; MCE 525; S 3853). *A few very light marks, toned, extremely fine.* £300-400

Price Realised : £288

Calendar year mintage 8,656,352.
See footnote for lot 107, page 121, for a brief synopsis of the 1864 die numbers.

109 **Victoria,** Sovereign, 1864, die number 6, second larger young head left, WW incuse on truncation without stops, date below, more pointed 4, curvy rounded 6 with bulbous top, last I of legend die flawed, some light doubling of legend both sides, *rev* crowned quartered shield of arms within laurel, die number 6 below, emblems below, 7.98g (Marsh 49; MCE 525; S 3853). *Light surface marks, nearly extremely fine, reverse better.* £350-400

Price Realised : £300

ex Ebay purchase, August 2009
The figure 4 in the date does not have a flat top like most of the 1864 dated Sovereigns do, and is more pointed.
Calendar year mintage 8,656,352. See footnote for lot 107, page 121, for a brief synopsis of the 1864 die numbers.

1027 **Victoria,** Sovereign, 1864, die number 7, second larger young head left, WW incuse on truncation without stops, date below, stub top to 4, curvy rounded 6 with bulbous top flawed shut, first I of legend die flawed, some light doubling of legend both sides, more evident on reverse, *rev* crowned quartered shield of arms within laurel wreath, die number 7 below, emblems below, hairline raised flaws in double N of legend, 7.98g (Marsh 49; MCE 525; S 3853). *Once cleaned, red spot on reverse with some light red patches both sides, surface marks, otherwise nearly extremely fine.* £250-300

Price Realised : £336

ex Paul Davies Ltd. Ilkley. This coin was purchased from one of the groups of coins from the wreck of the RMS *Douro* that were not sold by auction and within the last 10 years.
Calendar year mintage 8,656,352. See footnote for lot 107, page 121, for a brief synopsis of the 1864 die numbers.

110 **Victoria,** Sovereign, 1864, die number 8, second larger young head left, WW incuse on truncation without stops, date below, stub top to 4, curvy rounded 6 with bulbous top, R in Queen's name appears out of alignment, only a trace of bottom serifs of I in DEI, lightly doubled legend both sides, *rev* crowned quartered shield of arms within laurel wreath, die number 8 below, emblems below, 7.95g (Marsh 49; MCE 525; S 3853). *Once cleaned, now lightly toned with hairline surface marks, very fine.* £300-350

Price Realised : £264

ex Spink and Son Ltd, March 2005
Calendar year mintage 8,656,352
See footnote for lot 107, page 121, for a brief synopsis of the 1864 die numbers.

445 **Victoria,** Sovereign, 1864, die number 9, second larger young head left, WW incuse on truncation without stops, date below doubled, stub top to 4, curvy rounded 6 with bulbous top, queen's name quite doubled, as are other words in legend, raised die flaw on first I, *rev* crowned quartered shield of arms within laurel wreath, die number 9 below, emblems below, 7.97g (Marsh 49; MCE 525; S 3853). *Some pin-point sized black spots, once lightly cleaned, rim nick, otherwise extremely fine.* £300-400

Price Realised : £360

Calendar year mintage 8,656,352
See footnote for lot 107, page 121, for a brief synopsis of the 1864 die numbers.

446 **Victoria,** Sovereign, 1864, die number 10, second larger young head left, WW incuse on truncation without stops, date below, stub top to 4, curvy rounded 6 with bulbous top, some letters of obverse legend doubled, smaller letter A's or maybe inverted V's over A's in last word, *rev* crowned quartered shield of arms within laurel wreath, die number 10 below, 10 lightly flawed, emblems below, die flaw in last R of legend, 7.95g (Marsh 49; MCE 525; S 3853). *Once lightly cleaned, rim nick, otherwise good very fine / almost extremely fine and unusual.* £300-400

Price Realised : £312

Calendar year mintage 8,656,352
The doubling of the A's in the last word could be a case of the engraver correcting smaller A's underneath from the erroneous use of Half-Sovereign punches. See footnote for lot 107, page 121, for a brief synopsis of the 1864 die numbers.

1028 **Victoria,** Sovereign, 1864, die number 12, second larger young head left, WW incuse on truncation without stops, date below, stub top to 4, curvy rounded 6 with bulbous top, die flawed 1 in date from neck to rim, some light doubling of legend, *rev* crowned quartered shield of arms within laurel wreath, die number 12 below, emblems below, 7.95g (Marsh 49; MCE 525; S 3853). *Once cleaned, more brilliant on the reverse, with surface marks and scuffs with hairlines, otherwise about very fine.* £250-300

Price Realised : £264

Purchased via Spink and Son Ltd, November 2003
Calendar year mintage 8,656,352
See footnote for lot 107, page 121, for a brief synopsis of the 1864 die numbers.

111 **Victoria,** Sovereign, 1864, die number 13, second larger young head left, ww incuse on truncation without stops, date below, stub top to 4, curvy rounded 6 with bulbous top, *rev* crowned quartered shield of arms within laurel wreath, die number 13 below, emblems below, 7.94g (Marsh 49; MCE 525; S 3853). *Once cleaned with residual deposit on reverse, good fine / very fine and a die number not recorded by Marsh.* £300-350

Price Realised : £288

ex Paul Davies Ltd. This coin was purchased from one of the groups of coins from the wreck of the RMS *Douro* that were not sold by auction and within the last 10 years.
Calendar year mintage 8,656,352
See footnote for lot 107, page 121, for a brief synopsis of the 1864 die numbers. This is another die number that is not recorded by Marsh in his extensive listing.

447 **Victoria,** Sovereign, 1864, die number 15, second larger young head left, ww incuse on truncation without stops, date below doubled, sharp top to 4, sharper more hooked incomplete 6, die flaw to left of 8 running from rim to neck, some very light doubling in legend both sides, *rev* crowned quartered shield of arms within laurel wreath, die number 15 below, emblems below, 7.95g (Marsh 49; MCE 525; S 3853). *Once lightly cleaned, nearly very fine.* £300-350

Price Realised : £288

ex A H Baldwin & Sons Ltd sourced via Paul Davies Ltd, October 2006
Calendar year mintage 8,656,352
This coin shows a reversion to the sharper hooked type 6 in the date along with a more sharply topped figure 4. The hooked type 6 was discussed further at lot 433, page 105, it is quite a rarity especially in 1864 dated Sovereigns in the Bentley collection.
See footnote for lot 107, page 121, for a brief synopsis of the 1864 die numbers.

1029 **Victoria,** Sovereign, 1864, die number 19, second larger young head left, ww incuse on truncation without stops, date below, sharp top to 4, hooked 6 with sharper top, die flawed 1 in date, with flaw to right from neck to rim, some light doubling of legend, *rev* crowned quartered shield of arms within laurel wreath, die number 19 below, emblems below, 7.93g (Marsh 49; MCE 525; S 3853). *Once cleaned, with surface marks and scuffs with hairlines, fine, this die number unlisted by the most recent edition of Marsh, presumably very rare.* £250-300

Price Realised : £360

ex Paul Davies Ltd, Ilkley, via A H Baldwin & Sons Ltd, June 2007
Calendar year mintage 8,656,352
See footnote for lot 107, page 121, for a brief synopsis of the 1864 die numbers.
This die number is one of four for 1864 unlisted by Marsh, the others are dies 13, 73 and 77 in the Bentley Collection.
It is also interesting to note that the weight of this coin in its lower grade is upon the legal tender limit as dictated by the Coinage Acts of 1816-1891.

112 **Victoria,** Sovereign, 1864, die number 21, second larger young head left, WW incuse on truncation without stops, date below, more pointed 4, curvy rounded 6 with bulbous top, die flawed O and last A in obverse legend, trace of doubling to legend both sides, *rev* crowned quartered shield of arms within laurel wreath, die number 21 below, emblems below, 7.96g (Marsh 49; MCE 525; S 3853). *Once cleaned with associated digs and surface marks, very fine / good very fine.* £300-350

Price Realised : £264

ex Randy Weir Numismatics, Unionville, Ontario, Canada, purchased c.2000
The figure 4 in the date does not have a flat top like most the 1864 dated Sovereigns do, and is more pointed.
Calendar year mintage 8,656,352. See footnote for lot 107, page 121, for a brief synopsis of the 1864 die numbers.

1030 **Victoria,** Sovereign, 1864, die number 22, second larger young head left, WW incuse on truncation without stops, date below, sharp top to 4, curvy rounded 6 with only a trace of top bulb, some light die flaws in last word and last few letters of Queen's name, *rev* crowned quartered shield of arms within laurel wreath, die number 22 below, emblems below, 7.99g (Marsh 49; MCE 525; S 3853). *Hairline scratch below bun of hair, red spot on neck, once cleaned with some light surface marks, patchy tone on reverse, otherwise extremely fine.* £300-400

Price Realised : £312

ex Douro Cargo, Spink Auction 118, 20-21 November 1996, lot 322 (part)
Calendar year mintage 8,656,352. See footnote for lot 107, page 121, for a brief synopsis of the 1864 die numbers.

113 **Victoria,** Sovereign, 1864 die number 23, second larger young head left, WW incuse on truncation without stops, date below, more pointed 4, sharper more hooked incomplete 6, last I flawed into field, obverse legend lightly doubled, *rev* crowned quartered shield of arms within laurel wreath, die number 23 below, emblems below, hairline raised die flaws in lettering, 7.99g (Marsh 49; MCE 525; S 3853). *Very light surface marks, toned, good extremely fine.* £500-600

Price Realised : £480

ex Randy Weir Numismatics, Unionville, Ontario, Canada, purchased 7 January 1995
Not only does this coin have the mare unusual pointed 4 but also the rarer sharper hooked 6 in date.
Calendar year mintage 8,656,352. See footnote for lot 107, page 121, for a brief synopsis of the 1864 die numbers.

448 **Victoria,** Sovereign, 1864, die number 24, second larger young head left, WW incuse on truncation without stops, date below doubled, sharp top to 4, sharper more hooked complete 6, die flaw running from rim to neck via 6, last A of legend doubled, last R with raised die flaw, *rev* crowned quartered shield of arms within laurel wreath, die number 24 below, emblems below, some doubling of reverse legend, 7.99g (Marsh 49; MCE 525; S 3853). *Small spot at mouth and top of hair bun, more red spots on reverse, otherwise extremely fine / good extremely fine.* £350-450

Price Realised : £672

ex Douro Cargo, Spink Auction 118, 20-21 November 1996, lot 549 (part)
This coin shows a refinement of the hooked 6 in that it is now complete, the loop is attached to the body of the 6. The hooked type 6 was discussed further at lot 433, page 105. It is quite a rarity, especially in 1864 dated Sovereigns in the Bentley collection.
Calendar year mintage 8,656,352. See footnote for lot 107, page 121, for a brief synopsis of the 1864 die numbers.

1031 **Victoria,** Sovereign, 1864, die number 25, second larger young head left, ww incuse on truncation without stops, date below, sharp top to 4, curvy rounded 6, third I of legend doubled, *rev* crowned quartered shield of arms within laurel wreath, die number 25 below, emblems below, 7.97g (Marsh 49; MCE 525; S 3853). *Hairline scratch on cheek, tiny black spot on each side of coin, once cleaned with some light surface marks, scuffs and uneven tone, otherwise extremely fine.* £300-400

Price Realised : £336

Purchased via Spink and Son Ltd, November 2003
Calendar year mintage 8,656,352
See footnote for lot 107, page 121, for a brief synopsis of the 1864 die numbers.

114 **Victoria,** Sovereign, 1864, die number 26, second larger young head left, ww incuse on truncation without stops, date below, more pointed 4, curvy rounded 6 with bulbous top and die flawed, *rev* crowned quartered shield of arms within laurel wreath, die number 26 below, emblems below, 7.97g (Marsh 49; MCE 525; S 3853). *Once cleaned, a few light nicks and surface marks, good very fine, reverse better.* £300-400

Price Realised : £264

ex Paul Davies Ltd. This coin was purchased from one of the groups of coins from the wreck of the RMS *Douro* that were not sold by auction and within the last 10 years.
Calendar year mintage 8,656,352
See footnote for lot 107, page 121, for a brief synopsis of the 1864 die numbers.
The figure 4 in the date does not have a flat top like most the 1864 dated Sovereigns do, and is more pointed.

449 **Victoria,** Sovereign, 1864, die number 27, second larger young head left, ww incuse on truncation without stops, date below doubled, sharp top to 4, curvy rounded 6 with bulbous top, a hint of doubling of legend both sides, *rev* crowned quartered shield of arms within laurel wreath, die number 27 below, emblems below, 7.98g (Marsh 49; MCE 525; S 3853). *Once cleaned, some light surface marks and scuffs, extremely fine.* £300-400

Price Realised : £360

ex Randy Weir Numismatics, Unionville, Ontario, Canada, purchased 18 September 1995
Calendar year mintage 8,656,352
This coin shows a reversion to the curvy 6 but this time it is coupled with the sharp topped 4 which is usually seen with the hooked 6. There are only seven instances of this combination in 1864 die number sovereigns in the Bentley Collection, with sporadic occurrences between die numbers 21 and 36.
See footnote for lot 107, page 121, for a brief synopsis of the 1864 die numbers and lot 433, page 105, for the types of 6

450 **Victoria,** Sovereign, 1864, die number 28, second larger young head left, WW incuse on truncation without stops, date below doubled, sharp top to 4, sharper more hooked incomplete 6, some doubling of legend both sides, *rev* crowned quartered shield of arms within laurel wreath, die number 28 below, emblems below, light flaw above end of penultimate word of legend, 7.98g (Marsh 49; MCE 525; S 3853). *Once cleaned, some red spots on reverse and patch by date, good fine, reverse better.* £300-350

Price Realised : £288

This coin was purchased from one of the groups of coins from the wreck of the RMS *Douro* that were not sold by auction and within the last 10 years.
Calendar year mintage 8,656,352
The hooked type 6 was discussed further at lot 433, page 105. It is quite a rarity especially in 1864 dated Sovereigns in the Bentley collection. The hooked type 6 in date seems to disappear, never to be used again, in the shield Sovereign series after die number 30 of 1864. See footnote for lot 107, page 121, for a brief synopsis of the 1864 die numbers.

1032 **Victoria,** Sovereign, 1864, die number 29, second larger young head left, WW incuse on truncation without stops, date below, sharp top to 4, sharper hooked open 6, *rev* crowned quartered shield of arms within laurel wreath, die number 29 below, emblems below, hairline raised die flaw in second word, 7.99g (Marsh 49; MCE 525; S 3853). *Rim nick, two tiny red spots on the reverse, once cleaned with some light surface marks, otherwise extremely fine.* £300-400

Price Realised : £312

ex Douro Cargo, Spink Auction 118, 20-21 November 1996, lot 549 (part)
Calendar year mintage 8,656,352
See footnote for lot 107, page 121, for a brief synopsis of the 1864 die numbers.

115 **Victoria,** Sovereign, 1864, die number 30, second larger young head left, WW incuse on truncation without stops, date below, 8 doubled, stub top to 4, sharper more hooked incomplete 6, slightly doubled legend, first A of legend over a higher A, penultimate A die flawed, *rev* crowned quartered shield of arms within laurel wreath, die number 30 below, emblems below, 7.98g (Marsh 49; MCE 525; S 3853). *Lightly scuffed with surface marks and hairlines, extremely fine / good extremely fine.* £400-500

Price Realised : £552

ex Douro Cargo, Spink Auction 118, 20-21 November 1996, lot 549 (part)
Calendar year mintage 8,656,352
See footnote for lot 107, page 121, for a brief synopsis of the 1864 die numbers.
Note this coin has the rarer sharper hooked 6 in date. Research into the types of 6 and 4 has not been published before, though this cataloguer first noticed it about ten years ago.

1033 **Victoria,** Sovereign, 1864, die number 31, second larger young head left, WW incuse on truncation without stops, date below, stub top to 4, curvy closed 6 with top bulb, last two words doubled, penultimate I die flawed, *rev* crowned quartered shield of arms within laurel wreath, die number 31 below, emblems below, top left serif of B absent, 7.91g (Marsh 49; MCE 525; S 3853). *Some surface marks, toned fine / good fine.* £250-300

Price Realised : £264

ex An Important Collection of Gold Sovereigns 1816-2000, offered as one lot, Sothebys, November 2000, lot 525 (part)
It is interesting to note that the weight of this coin in its lower grade is under the legal tender limit as dictated by the Coinage Acts of 1816-1891.
Calendar year mintage 8,656,352
See footnote for lot 107, page 121, for a brief synopsis of the 1864 die numbers.

116 **Victoria,** Sovereign, 1864, die number 32, second larger young head left, WW incuse on truncation without stops, date below, die flaw through figure 1, doubled 64, stub top to 4, curvy rounded 6 with bulbous top, legend doubled, more lightly in Queen's name, D of DEI flawed, *rev* die axis off-centre, crowned quartered shield of arms within laurel wreath, die number 32 below, emblems below, upper left serif of B absent, legend lightly doubled, 7.99g (Marsh 49; MCE 525; S 3853). *Once cleaned, patchy light tone and surface marks, good very fine.* £300-350

Price Realised : £240

ex Paul Davies Ltd. This coin was purchased from one of the groups of coins from the wreck of the RMS *Douro* that were not sold by auction and within the last 10 years.
Calendar year mintage 8,656,352
See footnote for lot 107, page 121, for a brief synopsis of the 1864 die numbers.

451 **Victoria,** Sovereign, 1864, die number 33, second larger young head left, WW incuse on truncation without stops, date below, stub top to 4, curvy rounded 6 with bulbous top, hint of doubling to legend, *rev* crowned quartered shield of arms within laurel wreath, die number 33 below, UM of legend out of alignment, 7.99g (Marsh 49; MCE 525; S 3853). *Once lightly cleaned, light bagmarks evident, extremely fine.* £300-400

Price Realised : £360

Calendar year mintage 8,656,352
See footnote for lot 107, page 121, for a brief synopsis of the 1864 die numbers.

1034 Victoria, Sovereign, 1864, die number 34, second larger young head left, ww incuse on truncation without stops, date doubled below, stub top to 4, curvy rounded 6 with bulbous top flawed shut, legend doubled, *rev* crowned quartered shield of arms within laurel wreath, die number 34 below, emblems below, slight doubling of legend, 7.98g (Marsh 49; MCE 525; S 3853). *Once cleaned, rim nick each side, otherwise pleasing extremely fine.* £300-400

Price Realised : £360

This coin was purchased from one of the groups of coins from the wreck of the RMS *Douro* that were not sold by auction and within the last 10 years.
Calendar year mintage 8,656,352.
See footnote for lot 107, page 121, for a brief synopsis of the 1864 die numbers.

117 Victoria, Sovereign, 1864, die number 35, second larger young head left, ww incuse on truncation without stops, date below, more pointed 4, curvy rounded 6 with bulbous top, raised die flaw to left of date, *rev* crowned quartered shield of arms within laurel wreath, die number 35 below, emblems below, I of FID out of alignment, 7.99g (Marsh 49; MCE 525; S 3853). *Surface marks, toned, extremely fine.* £350-450

Price Realised : £384

ex Ebay purchase May 2004
Calendar year mintage 8,656,352
See footnote for lot 107, page 121, for a brief synopsis of the 1864 die numbers.
The figure 4 in the date does not have a flat top like most the 1864 dated Sovereigns do, and is more pointed.

452 Victoria, Sovereign, 1864, die number 36, second larger young head left, ww incuse on truncation without stops, date below, sharp top to 4, curvy rounded 6 with bulbous top, R of queen's name out of alignment, hint of doubling to legend, *rev* crowned quartered shield of arms within laurel wreath, die number 36 below, emblems below, 7.97g (Marsh 49; MCE 525; S 3853). *Once lightly cleaned, almost very fine / good very fine.* £300-350

Price Realised : £288

ex Spink Numismatic Circular, February 1998, item 518
ex An Important Collection of Gold Sovereigns 1816-2000, offered as one lot, Sothebys, November 2000, lot 525 (part)
Calendar year mintage 8,656,352
See footnote for lot 107, page 121, for a brief synopsis of the 1864 die numbers.

1035 Victoria, Sovereign, 1864, die number 37, second larger young head left, WW incuse on truncation without stops, date below, stub top to 4, curvy rounded 6 with bulbous top flawed shut, *rev* crowned quartered shield of arms within laurel wreath, die number 37 below, emblems below, top left serif of B in legend absent, 7.94g (Marsh 49; MCE 525; S 3853). *Once cleaned, two red spots on the obverse, otherwise about very fine.* £250-300

Price Realised : £240

This coin was purchased from one of the groups of coins from the wreck of the RMS *Douro* that were not sold by auction and within the last 10 years.
Calendar year mintage 8,656,352. See footnote for lot 107, page 121, for a brief synopsis of the 1864 die numbers.

453 Victoria, Sovereign, 1864, die number 38, second larger young head left, WW incuse on truncation without stops, date below, stub top to 4, curvy rounded 6 with bulbous top, R of queen's name out of alignment, some doubling to legend both sides, *rev* crowned quartered shield of arms within laurel wreath, die number 38 below, emblems below, 7.99g (Marsh 49; MCE 525; S 3853). *Some light hairlines, a pleasing extremely fine.* £350-450

Price Realised : £408

ex Randy Weir Numismatics, Unionville, Ontario, Canada, purchased c.1995
Calendar year mintage 8,656,352. See footnote for lot 107, page 121, for a brief synopsis of the 1864 die numbers.

1036 Victoria, Sovereign, 1864, die number 39, second larger young head left, WW incuse on truncation without stops, date below, stub top to 4, curvy rounded 6 with bulbous top flawed shut, R of Queen's name out of rotational alignment, *rev* crowned quartered shield of arms within laurel wreath, die number 39 below, emblems below, top left serif of B in legend absent, 7.97g (Marsh 49; MCE 525; S 3853). *Some surface marks and uneven tone, otherwise extremely fine.* £300-400

Price Realised : £264

purchased via Spink and Son Ltd, November 2003
Calendar year mintage 8,656,352. See footnote for lot 107, page 121, for a brief synopsis of the 1864 die numbers.

118 Victoria, Sovereign, 1864, die number 40, second larger young head left, WW incuse on truncation without stops, date below, stub top to 4, curvy rounded 6 with bulbous top, raised die flaw to left of date, R in Queen's name out of alignment, *rev* crowned quartered shield of arms within laurel wreath, die number 40 below, emblems below, upper left serif of B absent, 7.98g (Marsh 49; MCE 525; S 3853). *Once cleaned with a few red spots each side, more on the reverse, light surface marks, otherwise extremely fine.* £350-450

Price Realised : £384

ex Douro Cargo, Spink Auction 118, 20-21 November 1996, lot 549 (part)
Calendar year mintage 8,656,352
See footnote for lot 107, page 121, for a brief synopsis of the 1864 die numbers.

119 **Victoria,** Sovereign, 1864, die number 41, second larger young head left, WW incuse on truncation without stops, raised hairline flaw from bun of hair to rim, date below, 4 die flawed, stub top to 4, curvy rounded 6 with bulbous top, obverse legend doubled especially last word, hairline die flaw at end of Queen's name, *rev* crowned quartered shield of arms within laurel wreath, die number 41 below, emblems below, 7.99g (Marsh 49; MCE 525; S 3853). *Hairline surface marks, pleasing extremely fine.* £350-450

Price Realised : £504

ex Douro Cargo, Spink Auction 118, 20-21 November 1996, lot 323
Calendar year mintage 8,656,352
See footnote for lot 107, page 121, for a brief synopsis of the 1864 die numbers.

454 **Victoria,** Sovereign, 1864, die number 42, second larger young head left, WW incuse on truncation without stops, date below, stub top to 4, curvy rounded 6 with bulbous top, penultimate I die flawed, *rev* crowned quartered shield of arms within laurel wreath, die number 42 below doubled, emblems below, raised die flaw to right of crown runs to rim, 7.98g (Marsh 49; MCE 525; S 3853). *Once lightly cleaned, otherwise extremely fine.* £300-400

Price Realised : £552

ex Douro Cargo, Spink Auction 118, 20-21 November 1996, lot 1348 (part)
Calendar year mintage 8,656,352. See footnote for lot 107, page 121, for a brief synopsis of the 1864 die numbers.

455 **Victoria,** Sovereign, 1864, die number 43, second larger young head left, WW incuse on truncation without stops, date below, stub top to 4, curvy rounded 6 with bulbous top, light doubling of legend both sides, *rev* crowned quartered shield of arms within laurel wreath, die number 43 below doubled, emblems below, raised die flaw to right of crown runs to rim, 7.98g (Marsh 49; MCE 525; S 3853). *Once cleaned, two scuffs on face, good fine to almost very fine.* £300-350

Price Realised : £264

Calendar year mintage 8,656,352
See footnote for lot 107, page 121, for a brief synopsis of the 1864 die numbers. This coin was purchased from one of the groups of coins from the wreck of the RMS *Douro* that were not sold by auction and within the last 10 years.

1037 **Victoria,** Sovereign, 1864, die number 44, second larger young head left, WW incuse on truncation without stops, date below, stub top to 4, curvy rounded 6 with bulbous top flawed shut, *rev* crowned quartered shield of arms within laurel wreath, die number 44 below, emblems below, some slight short raised die flaws within reverse and E of second word, 7.98g (Marsh 49; MCE 525; S 3853). *Some surface marks, cleaned, otherwise good fine to about very fine.* £250-300

Price Realised : £240

ex Spink and Son Ltd, November 2003
Calendar year mintage 8,656,352
See footnote for lot 107, page 121, for a brief synopsis of the 1864 die numbers.

120 **Victoria,** Sovereign, 1864, die number 45, second larger young head left, WW incuse on truncation without stops, date below, stub top to 4, curvy rounded 6 with bulbous top, *rev* crowned quartered shield of arms within laurel wreath, die number 45 below, blundered flawed and double struck, emblems below, 7.96g (Marsh 49; MCE 525; S 3853). *Brightly cleaned, light surface marks and rim bruise, fine to nearly very fine.* £300-350

Price Realised : £264

ex Dr Arnold R Saslow, Ye Olde Curiositie Shoppe, New Jersey, USA, August 2003
Calendar year mintage 8,656,352. See footnote for lot 107, page 121, for a brief synopsis of the 1864 die numbers.

456 **Victoria,** Sovereign, 1864, die number 46, second larger young head left, WW incuse on truncation without stops, date below, 18 doubled, stub top to 4, curvy rounded 6 with bulbous top, last two words doubled in legend, *rev* crowned quartered shield of arms within laurel wreath, die number 46 below doubled, emblems below, raised die flaw to right of crown runs to rim, 7.98g (Marsh 49; MCE 525; S 3853). *Once cleaned, dig on neck, toned very fine.* £300-350

Price Realised : £288

Calendar year mintage 8,656,352
See footnote for lot 107, page 121, for a brief synopsis of the 1864 die numbers. This coin was purchased from one of the groups of coins from the wreck of the RMS *Douro* that were not sold by auction and within the last 10 years.

121 **Victoria,** Sovereign, 1864, die number 48, second larger young head left, WW incuse on truncation without stops, date below lightly doubled, stub top to 4, curvy rounded 6 with bulbous top, *rev* crowned quartered shield of arms within laurel wreath, die number 48 below, emblems below, legend lightly doubled, 7.99g (Marsh 49; MCE 525; S 3853). *Some light nicks and surface marks, otherwise good extremely fine.* £400-500

Price Realised : £504

ex An Important Collection of Gold Sovereigns 1816-2000, offered as one lot, Sothebys, 16-17 November 2000, lot 525 (part)
Calendar year mintage 8,656,352. See footnote for lot 107, page 121, for a brief synopsis of the 1864 die numbers.

1038 **Victoria,** Sovereign, 1864, die number 49, second larger young head left, WW incuse on truncation without stops, date below, lightly doubled, stub top to 4, curvy rounded 6 with bulbous top flawed shut, light trace of doubling in legend, *rev* crowned quartered shield of arms within laurel wreath, die number 49 below, emblems below, hairline raised die flaw connects tops of some letters in legend, 7.98g (Marsh 49; MCE 525; S 3853). *Once cleaned with associated surface marks, red tone, otherwise practically extremely fine.* £300-400

Price Realised : £288

ex Abbatucci Cargo, Christies, 10 July 1997, untraced lot number
ex Spink Numismatic Circular, April 1998, item 2183
ex An Important Collection of Gold Sovereigns 1816-2000, offered as one lot, Sothebys, November 2000, lot 525 (part)
Calendar year mintage 8,656,352. See footnote for lot 107, page 121, for a brief synopsis of the 1864 die numbers.

1039 Victoria, Sovereign, 1864, die number 50, second larger young head left, WW incuse on truncation without stops, date below, lightly doubled, stub top to 4, curvy rounded 6 with bulbous top flawed shut, *rev* crowned quartered shield of arms within laurel wreath, die number 50 below, emblems below, 7.95g (Marsh 49; MCE 525; S 3853). *Once cleaned with associated surface marks and digs, otherwise almost very fine.* £250-300

Price Realised : £240

Ebay purchase, March 2002
Calendar year mintage 8,656,352. See footnote for lot 107, page 121, for a brief synopsis of the 1864 die numbers.

122 Victoria, Sovereign, 1864, die number 51, second larger young head left, WW incuse on truncation without stops, date below, stub top to 4, curvy rounded 6 with bulbous top, I, T, and IA of Queen's name with absent upper serifs, the A die flawed, I of DEI with only a trace of upper serifs, *rev* crowned quartered shield of arms within laurel wreath, die number 51 below, emblems below, 7.99g (Marsh 49; MCE 525; S 3853). *Once cleaned, now lightly toned, surface marks, extremely fine / good extremely fine.* £350-450

Price Realised : £336

ex Spink and Son Ltd, November 2003
Calendar year mintage 8,656,352
See footnote for lot 107, page 121, for a brief synopsis of the 1864 die numbers.

457 Victoria, Sovereign, 1864, die number 52, second larger young head left, WW incuse on truncation without stops, date below, stub top to 4, curvy rounded 6 with bulbous top, *rev* crowned quartered shield of arms within laurel wreath, die number 52 below, emblems below, raised die flaw connects upper parts of letters in legend, 7.98g (Marsh 49; MCE 525; S 3853). *Once cleaned, rim nick, surface marks, otherwise extremely fine.* £300-400

Price Realised : £360

ex Randy Weir Numismatics, Unionville, Ontario, Canada, purchased 27 September 1990
Calendar year mintage 8,656,352. See footnote for lot 107, page 121, for a brief synopsis of the 1864 die numbers.

123 Victoria, Sovereign, 1864, die number 53, second larger young head left, WW incuse on truncation without stops, date below, stub top to 4, curvy rounded 6 with bulbous top, *rev* crowned quartered shield of arms within laurel wreath, die number 53 below, emblems below, reverse legend lightly die flawed, 7.95g (Marsh 49; MCE 525; S 3853). *Cleaned, some tiny black spots on obverse, red spots on reverse, light surface marks, bold very fine.* £300-350

Price Realised : £264

ex Paul Davies Ltd. This coin was purchased from one of the groups of coins from the wreck of the RMS *Douro* that were not sold by auction and within the last 10 years.
Calendar year mintage 8,656,352
See footnote for lot 107, page 121, for a brief synopsis of the 1864 die numbers.

458 **Victoria,** Sovereign, 1864, die number 54, second larger young head left, WW incuse on truncation without stops, date below, die flaw from stub top 4 to neck, curvy rounded 6 with bulbous top, slight die flaw in first I of legend, *rev* crowned quartered shield of arms within laurel wreath, die number 54 below, emblems below, absent upper serif to B in legend, 7.97g (Marsh 49; MCE 525; S 3853). *Once cleaned, now lightly toned, almost extremely fine.* £300-400

Price Realised : £288

ex Douro Cargo, Spink Auction 118, 20-21 November 1996, lot 1348 (part)
Note the lack of upper serif on the letter B
Calendar year mintage 8,656,352. See footnote for lot 107, page 121, for a brief synopsis of the 1864 die numbers.

1040 **Victoria,** Sovereign, 1864, die number 55, second larger young head left, WW incuse on truncation without stops, date below, stub top to 4, curvy rounded 6 with bulbous top flawed shut, last A of Queen's name die flawed, *rev* crowned quartered shield of arms within laurel wreath, die number 55 below, emblems below, absent upper left serif on B of legend, 7.95g (Marsh 49; MCE 525; S 3853). *Once cleaned with associated surface marks, otherwise bold fine.* £250-300

Price Realised : £240

purchased via Spink and Son Ltd, November 2003
Calendar year mintage 8,656,352. See footnote for lot 107, page 121, for a brief synopsis of the 1864 die numbers.

124 **Victoria,** Sovereign, 1864, die number 56, second larger young head left, WW incuse on truncation without stops, raised die flaw from tip of neck to rim, flaw from bun of hair to rim, date below, stub top to 4, curvy rounded 6 with bulbous top, trace of doubling in Queen's name, *rev* crowned quartered shield of arms within laurel wreath, die number 56 below, emblems below, 7.98g (Marsh 49; MCE 525; S 3853). *Some red spots on reverse and other tiny specks and surface marks, otherwise nearly extremely fine.* £350-400

Price Realised : £288

ex Douro Cargo, Spink Auction 118, 20-21 November 1996, lot 1348 (part)
Calendar year mintage 8,656,352. See footnote for lot 107, page 121, for a brief synopsis of the 1864 die numbers.

459 **Victoria,** Sovereign, 1864, die number 57, second larger young head left, WW incuse on truncation without stops, date below, stub top to 4, curvy rounded 6 with bulbous top, weak tops to some letters with a trace of doubling, no top serif to D in obverse legend, *rev* crowned quartered shield of arms within laurel wreath, die number 57 below, emblems below, 7.94g (Marsh 49; MCE 525; S 3853). *Light red tone with some surface marks, otherwise almost very fine.* £300-350

Price Realised : £264

This coin was purchased from one of the groups of coins from the wreck of the RMS *Douro* that were not sold by auction and within the last 10 years. Note the lack of upper serif on the letter D.
Calendar year mintage 8,656,352
See footnote for lot 107, page 121, for a brief synopsis of the 1864 die numbers.

1041 **Victoria,** Sovereign, 1864, die number 58, second larger young head left, WW incuse on truncation without stops, date below, stub top to 4, curvy rounded 6 with bulbous top flawed shut, *rev* crowned quartered shield of arms within laurel wreath, die number 58 below, emblems below, second R of legend with die flaw to rim, 7.94g (Marsh 49; MCE 525; S 3853). *Once cleaned with associated surface marks and red spots, otherwise bold fine.* £250-300

Price Realised : £240

This coin was purchased from one of the groups of coins from the wreck of the RMS *Douro* that were not sold by auction and within the last 10 years.
Calendar year mintage 8,656,352
See footnote for lot 107, page 121, for a brief synopsis of the 1864 die numbers.

1042 **Victoria,** Sovereign, 1864, die number 60, second larger young head left, WW incuse on truncation without stops, date below, stub top to 4, curvy rounded 6 with bulbous top flawed shut, die flaw from lower part of 4 to rim, die flaw from V of legend and penultimate A to rim, *rev* crowned quartered shield of arms within laurel wreath, die number 60 below, emblems below, 7.99g (Marsh 49; MCE 525; S 3853). *Some black marks by tip of neck and other light hairlines, otherwise toned, practically extremely fine.* £250-300

Price Realised : £384

ex Douro Cargo, Spink Auction 118, 20-21 November 1996, lot 1348 (part)
Calendar year mintage 8,656,352
See footnote for lot 107, page 121, for a brief synopsis of the 1864 die numbers.

125 **Victoria,** Sovereign, 1864, die number 61, second larger young head left, WW incuse on truncation without stops, date below, stub top to 4, curvy rounded 6 with bulbous top, flawed R in VICTORIA and heavier between last I and A of legend, *rev* crowned quartered shield of arms within laurel wreath, die number 61 below, emblems below, upper left serif of B absent, 7.98g (Marsh 49; MCE 525; S 3853). *Dig on "6" of date, some red spots and scuffs, other light surface marks, bold very fine.* £300-350

Price Realised : £264

ex Paul Davies Ltd. This coin was purchased from one of the groups of coins from the wreck of the RMS *Douro* that were not sold by auction and within the last 10 years.
Calendar year mintage 8,656,352
See footnote for lot 107, page 121, for a brief synopsis of the 1864 die numbers.

460 **Victoria,** Sovereign, 1864, die number 62, second larger young head left, ww incuse on truncation without stops, date below, die flaw from 1 to neck, stub top to 4, curvy rounded 6 with bulbous top, last A and 4 doubled, *rev* crowned quartered shield of arms within laurel wreath, die number 62 below, wide spaced 62, emblems below, absent upper serif to B in legend, raised die flaw from left of centre of crown to rim, 7.93g (Marsh 49; MCE 525; S 3853). *Scratch in field in front of neck, other scuffs and nicks, fine, reverse better.* £300-350

Price Realised : £264

Calendar year mintage 8,656,352
See footnote for lot 107, page 121, for a brief synopsis of the 1864 die numbers. This coin was purchased from one of the groups of coins from the wreck of the RMS *Douro* that were not sold by auction and within the last 10 years.

126 **Victoria,** Sovereign, 1864, die number 63, second larger young head left, ww incuse on truncation without stops, raised die flaw from tip of neck to rim, date below, stub top to 4, curvy rounded 6 with bulbous top, *rev* crowned quartered shield of arms within laurel wreath, die number 63 below, emblems below, hairline raised flaws in legend, 7.99g (Marsh 49; MCE 525; S 3853). *Once cleaned, now lightly toned, some scuffing and light surface marks, otherwise good very fine.* £300-350

Price Realised : £264

Calendar year mintage 8,656,352
See footnote for lot 107, page 121, for a brief synopsis of the 1864 die numbers.

461 **Victoria,** Sovereign, 1864, die number 64, second larger young head left, ww incuse on truncation without stops, date below, stub top to 4, curvy rounded 6 with bulbous top, doubled date and legend, *rev* crowned quartered shield of arms within laurel wreath, die number 64 below, emblems below, absent upper serif to B in legend, 7.99g (Marsh 49; MCE 525; S 3853). *A few light bagmarks, otherwise as struck with a very pleasing obverse, previously graded by NGC as MS63 CAMEO.* £500-600

Price Realised : £1,500

ex Jacob Y Terner collection, Goldberg, Hollywood, USA, 26-27 May 2003, lot 360
Calendar year mintage 8,656,352
See footnote for lot 107, page 121, for a brief synopsis of the 1864 die numbers. Note the lack of upper serif on the letter B.

462 **Victoria,** Sovereign, 1864, die number 65, second larger young head left, WW incuse on truncation without stops, date below, stub top to 4, curvy rounded 6 with bulbous top, light die flaw to left of 1 in date, *rev* crowned quartered shield of arms within laurel wreath, die number 65 below, emblems below, absent upper serif to B in legend, 7.98g (Marsh 49; MCE 525; S 3853). *Uneven tone, very fine, the reverse better.* £300-350

Price Realised : £288

ex Douro Cargo, Spink Auction 118, 20-21 November 1996
ex Spink Numismatic Circular, October 1997, item 5024
ex An Important Collection of Gold Sovereigns 1816-2000, offered as one lot, Sothebys, November 2000, lot 525 (part)
Calendar year mintage 8,656,352
See footnote for lot 107, page 121, for a brief synopsis of the 1864 die numbers.
Note the lack of upper serif on the letter B.

1043 **Victoria,** Sovereign, 1864, die number 66, second larger young head left, WW incuse on truncation without stops, date below, stub top to 4, curvy rounded 6 with bulbous top flawed shut, trace of doubling in legend, *rev* crowned quartered shield of arms within laurel wreath, die number 66 below, emblems below, 7.93g (Marsh 49; MCE 525; S 3853). *Scratch above date with other surface marks, otherwise about fine.* £250-300

Price Realised : £240

purchased via Spink and Son Ltd, November 2003
Calendar year mintage 8,656,352
See footnote for lot 107, page 121, for a brief synopsis of the 1864 die numbers.
It is interesting to note that the weight of this coin in its lower grade is upon the legal tender limit as dictated by the Coinage Acts of 1816-1891.

1044 **Victoria,** Sovereign, 1864, die number 69, second larger young head left, WW incuse on truncation without stops, date below, stub top to 4, curvy rounded 6 with bulbous top flawed shut, G of legend doubled, *rev* crowned quartered shield of arms within laurel wreath, die number 69 below, emblems below, last I of legend with raised blob of excess metal upon it, legend lightly doubled, 7.96g (Marsh 49; MCE 525; S 3853). *Once cleaned, a weaker strike, surface marks, toned, extremely fine.* £300-400

Price Realised : £360

ex Spink Numismatic Circular, February 1998, item 520
ex An Important Collection of Gold Sovereigns 1816-2000, offered as one lot, Sothebys, November 2000, lot 525 (part)
Calendar year mintage 8,656,352
See footnote for lot 107, page 121, for a brief synopsis of the 1864 die numbers.

127 **Victoria,** Sovereign, 1864, die number 71, second larger young head left, ww incuse on truncation without stops, date below, stub top to 4, curvy rounded 6 with bulbous top, *rev* crowned quartered shield of arms within laurel wreath, die number 71 below, emblems below, upper left serif of B on reverse absent, hairline raised flaws in legend, 7.98g (Marsh 49; MCE 525; S 3853). *Once cleaned, now lightly toned, obverse with underlying brilliance, reverse matt, scuffed fields, light surface marks, otherwise good very fine to nearly extremely fine.* £300-350

Price Realised : £264

ex Paul Davies Ltd. This coin was purchased from one of the groups of coins from the wreck of the RMS *Douro* that were not sold by auction and within the last 10 years.
Calendar year mintage 8,656,352. See footnote for lot 107, page 121, for a brief synopsis of the 1864 die numbers.

463 **Victoria,** Sovereign, 1864, die number 72, second larger young head left, ww incuse on truncation without stops, date below, lightly die flawed stub top 4, curvy rounded 6 with bulbous top, light die flaw between AT of last word, *rev* crowned quartered shield of arms within laurel wreath, die number 72 below, emblems below, weak upper serif on first R in legend, 7.98g (Marsh 49; MCE 525; S 3853). *Good very fine, the reverse better.* £300-350

Price Realised : £288

This coin was purchased from one of the groups of coins from the wreck of the RMS *Douro* that were not sold by auction and within the last 10 years.
Calendar year mintage 8,656,352. See footnote for lot 107, page 121, for a brief synopsis of the 1864 die numbers.

1045 **Victoria,** Sovereign, 1864, die number 73, second larger young head left, ww incuse on truncation without stops, date below, stub top to 4, curvy rounded 6 with bulbous top flawed shut, *rev* crowned quartered shield of arms within laurel wreath, die number 73 below, emblems below, lightly doubled legend, 7.94g (Marsh 49; MCE 525; S 3853). *Once cleaned with surface marks and rim bruise, bold fine, this die number unlisted by the most recent edition of Marsh, presumably very rare.* £250-300

Price Realised : £240

ex A H Baldwin & Sons Ltd, May 2006
Calendar year mintage 8,656,352. See footnote for lot 107, page 121, for a brief synopsis of the 1864 die numbers.
This die number is one of four for 1864 unlisted by Marsh, the others are dies 13, 19 and 77 in the Bentley Collection.

128 **Victoria,** Sovereign, 1864, die number 74, second larger young head left, ww incuse on truncation without stops, date below lightly doubled, stub top to 4, curvy rounded 6 with bulbous top, first A of GRATIA flawed to rim, *rev* die axis off-centre, crowned quartered shield of arms within laurel wreath, die number 74 below, emblems below, 7.97g (Marsh 49; MCE 525; S 3853). *Light surface marks, good very fine.* £300-350

Price Realised : £264

Calendar year mintage 8,656,352
See footnote for lot 107, page 121, for a brief synopsis of the 1864 die numbers.

129 **Victoria,** Sovereign, 1864, die number 75, second larger young head left, ww incuse on truncation without stops, date below, stub top to 4, curvy rounded 6 with bulbous top, *rev* crowned quartered shield of arms within laurel wreath, die number 75 below, emblems below, light doubling on parts of legend, 7.98g (Marsh 49; MCE 525; S 3853). *A few light surface marks, pleasing good extremely fine.* £350-450

Price Realised : £960

Calendar year mintage 8,656,352
See footnote for lot 107, page 121, for a brief synopsis of the 1864 die numbers.

464 **Victoria,** Sovereign, 1864, die number 76, second larger young head left, ww incuse on truncation without stops, date below, stub top to 4, curvy rounded 6 with bulbous top, obverse legend doubled, *rev* crowned quartered shield of arms within laurel wreath, die number 76 below, emblems below, 7.99g (Marsh 49; MCE 525; S 3853). *Some red deposit of lower right quarter of reverse, otherwise toned extremely fine.* £300-400

Price Realised : £384

This coin was purchased from one of the groups of coins from the wreck of the RMS *Douro* that were not sold by auction and within the last 10 years.
Calendar year mintage 8,656,352. See footnote for lot 107, page 121, for a brief synopsis of the 1864 die numbers.

465 **Victoria,** Sovereign, 1864, die number 77, second larger young head left, ww incuse on truncation without stops, date below, stub top to 4, curvy rounded 6 with bulbous top, doubled date and start of legend, *rev* crowned quartered shield of arms within laurel wreath, die number 77 below, emblems below, absent upper serif to B in legend, some doubling and die flaw at first I and T, 7.97g (Marsh 49; MCE 525; S 3853). *Once cleaned, good fine, reverse much better, this die number unlisted in Marsh.* £300-350

Price Realised : £264

Calendar year mintage 8,656,352
Within the Bentley Collection, this is one of only eight die number coins in the entire series that was not recorded as a known die number by Marsh, three of which occur in 1864 dated die number Sovereigns. It is therefore quite a rarity. For further information please refer to the die number table at the start of the die number section. Note the lack of upper serif on the letter B.
See footnote for lot 107, page 121, for a brief synopsis of the 1864 die numbers.

1046 **Victoria,** Sovereign, 1864, die number 78, second larger young head left, ww incuse on truncation without stops, date below, stub top to 4, curvy rounded 6 with bulbous top flawed shut, die flaw from lower part of 4 to neck, trace of doubling of legend both sides, *rev* crowned quartered shield of arms within laurel wreath, die number 78 below, emblems below, 7.99g (Marsh 49; MCE 525; S 3853). *Scuff on cheek with other light surface marks, otherwise good extremely fine.* £400-500

Price Realised : £456

ex Douro Cargo, Spink Auction 118, 20-21 November 1996, lot 1350 (part)
Calendar year mintage 8,656,352. See footnote for lot 107, page 121, for a brief synopsis of the 1864 die numbers.

1047 **Victoria,** Sovereign, 1864, die number 79, second larger young head left, WW incuse on truncation without stops, date below, stub top to 4, curvy rounded 6 with bulbous top flawed shut, hint of doubling to legend, *rev* crowned quartered shield of arms within laurel wreath, die number 79 below, emblems below, 7.94g (Marsh 49; MCE 525; S 3853). *Surface marks and hairlines, toned, good fine.* £250-300

Price Realised : £240

This coin was purchased from one of the groups of coins from the wreck of the RMS *Douro* that were not sold by auction and within the last 10 years.
Calendar year mintage 8,656,352. See footnote for lot 107, page 121, for a brief synopsis of the 1864 die numbers.

130 **Victoria,** Sovereign, 1864, die number 80, second larger young head left, WW incuse on truncation without stops, date below, stub top to 4 with raised die flaw to neck, curvy rounded 6 with bulbous top, obverse legend lightly doubled, *rev* die axis off-centre, crowned quartered shield of arms within laurel wreath, die number 80 below, emblems below, hairline die flaws in reverse legend, 7.97g (Marsh 49; MCE 525; S 3853). *Surface marks, light red spots on reverse, nearly very fine, reverse better.* £300-350

Price Realised : £264

ex Paul Davies Ltd. This coin was purchased from one of the groups of coins from the wreck of the RMS *Douro* that were not sold by auction and within the last 10 years.
Calendar year mintage 8,656,352. See footnote for lot 107, page 121, for a brief synopsis of the 1864 die numbers.

466 **Victoria,** Sovereign, 1864, die number 81, second larger young head left, WW incuse on truncation without stops, date below, stub top to 4, curvy rounded 6 with bulbous top, some light doubling in legend, last A die flawed, *rev* crowned quartered shield of arms within laurel wreath, die number 81 below, emblems below, 8.00g (Marsh 49; MCE 525; S 3853). *Unevenly toned, almost extremely fine.* £300-350

Price Realised : £576

This coin was purchased from one of the groups of coins from the wreck of the RMS *Douro* that were not sold by auction and within the last 10 years.
Calendar year mintage 8,656,352. See footnote for lot 107, page 121, for a brief synopsis of the 1864 die numbers.

1048 **Victoria,** Sovereign, 1864, die number 82, second larger young head left, WW incuse on truncation without stops, date below, stub top to 4, curvy rounded 6 with bulbous top flawed shut, hint of doubling to legend both sides, *rev* crowned quartered shield of arms within laurel wreath, die number 82 below, emblems below, 7.99g (Marsh 49; MCE 525; S 3853). *Hairline scratch to cheek and light surface marks, retaining brilliance, good extremely fine.* £400-500

Price Realised : £504

ex Randy Weir Numismatics, Unionville, Ontario, Canada, purchased 5 December 1989
Calendar year mintage 8,656,352
See footnote for lot 107, page 121, for a brief synopsis of the 1864 die numbers.

1049 Victoria, Sovereign, 1864, die number 83, second larger young head left, WW incuse on truncation without stops, date below, stub top to 4, curvy rounded 6 with bulbous top flawed shut, date doubled along with last word, *rev* crowned quartered shield of arms within laurel wreath, die number 83 below, emblems below, upper left serif of B in legend absent, 7.95g (Marsh 49; MCE 525; S 3853). *Once cleaned with surface marks, toned, good fine / about very fine.* £250-300

Price Realised : £216

Purchased via Spink and Son Ltd, November 2003
Calendar year mintage 8,656,352. See footnote for lot 107, page 121, for a brief synopsis of the 1864 die numbers.

131 Victoria, Sovereign, 1864, die number 84, second larger young head left, WW incuse on truncation without stops, date below, 1 of date die flawed to neck, stub top to 4, curvy rounded 6 with bulbous top, G of GRATIA doubled, *rev* crowned quartered shield of arms within laurel wreath, die number 84 below, emblems below, hairline die flaws in legend, 7.98g (Marsh 49; MCE 525; S 3853). *Some red specks and surface marks, nearly extremely fine / extremely fine.* £300-350

Price Realised : £408

ex Paul Davies Ltd. This coin was purchased from one of the groups of coins from the wreck of the RMS *Douro* that were not sold by auction and within the last 10 years.
Calendar year mintage 8,656,352. See footnote for lot 107, page 121, for a brief synopsis of the 1864 die numbers.

132 Victoria, Sovereign, 1864, die number 85, second larger young head left, WW incuse on truncation without stops, date below lightly doubled, die flaw in figure 1, stub top to 4, curvy rounded 6 with bulbous top, obverse lettering doubled, *rev* crowned quartered shield of arms within laurel wreath, die number 85 below, emblems below, upper left serif of B absent, 7.94g (Marsh 49; MCE 525; S 3853). *Once cleaned with associated surface marks and scuffs, bold fine.* £300-350

Price Realised : £264

ex Paul Davies Ltd. This coin was purchased from one of the groups of coins from the wreck of the RMS *Douro* that were not sold by auction and within the last 10 years.
Calendar year mintage 8,656,352. See footnote for lot 107, page 121, for a brief synopsis of the 1864 die numbers.

467 Victoria, Sovereign, 1864, die number 86, second larger young head left, WW incuse on truncation without stops, die flaw from tip of neck to rim, date below, stub top to 4, curvy rounded 6 with bulbous top, obverse legend doubled, I of DEI flawed to head, *rev* crowned quartered shield of arms within laurel wreath, die number 86 below, emblems below, 8.00g (Marsh 49; MCE 525; S 3853). *Some light surface marks, pleasing good extremely fine.* £400-500

Price Realised : £552

ex Douro Cargo, Spink Auction 118, 20-21 November 1996, lot 1350 (part)
Calendar year mintage 8,656,352. See footnote for lot 107, page 121, for a brief synopsis of the 1864 die numbers.

1050 **Victoria,** Sovereign, 1864, die number 87, second larger young head left, ww incuse on truncation without stops, date below, stub top to 4, curvy rounded 6 with bulbous top flawed shut, date doubled along with first three letters of legend, *rev* crowned quartered shield of arms within laurel wreath, die number 87 below, emblems below, N's in legend doubled, 7.97g (Marsh 49; MCE 525; S 3853). *Once cleaned with surface marks, toned, bold very fine.* £250-300

Price Realised : £288

Purchased via Spink and Son Ltd, November 2003
Calendar year mintage 8,656,352
See footnote for lot 107, page 121, for a brief synopsis of the 1864 die numbers.

133 **Victoria,** Sovereign, 1864, die number 88, second larger young head left, ww incuse on truncation without stops, date below lightly doubled, die flaw in figure 1, stub top to 4, curvy rounded 6 with bulbous top, trace of doubling in legend, all obverse letter R's die flawed, *rev* crowned quartered shield of arms within laurel wreath, die number 88 below, emblems below, 8.00g (Marsh 49; MCE 525; S 3853). *Nick behind bust and spot on neck, a few surface marks, extremely fine.* £350-400

Price Realised : £552

ex Douro Cargo, Spink Auction 118, 20-21 November 1996, lot 1350 (part)
Calendar year mintage 8,656,352
See footnote for lot 107, page 121, for a brief synopsis of the 1864 die numbers.

468 **Victoria,** Sovereign, 1864, die number 89, second larger young head left, ww incuse on truncation without stops, die flaw in field near neck, date below, stub top to 4, curvy rounded 6 with bulbous top, last I die flawed, trace of doubling in legend, *rev* crowned quartered shield of arms within laurel wreath, die number 89 below, emblems below, 7.98g (Marsh 49; MCE 525; S 3853). *Some spots and light speckling both sides, extremely fine.* £400-500

Price Realised : £624

ex Douro Cargo, Spink Auction 118, 20-21 November 1996, lot 1350 (part)
Calendar year mintage 8,656,352
See footnote for lot 107, page 121, for a brief synopsis of the 1864 die numbers.

1051 **Victoria,** Sovereign, 1864, die number 90, second larger young head left, ww incuse on truncation without stops, date below, stub top to 4, curvy rounded 6 with bulbous top flawed shut, *rev* crowned quartered shield of arms within laurel wreath, die number 90 below, emblems below, upper left serif of B in legend absent, G of legend with flawed lower part right, 7.98g (Marsh 49; MCE 525; S 3853). *Black spot on obverse, two red spots on reverse, otherwise good extremely fine.* £400-500

Price Realised : £528

ex Douro Cargo, Spink Auction 118, 20-21 November 1996, lot 1350 (part)
Calendar year mintage 8,656,352. See footnote for lot 107, page 121, for a brief synopsis of the 1864 die numbers.

134 **Victoria,** Sovereign, 1864, die number 91, second larger young head left, WW incuse on truncation without stops, date below lightly doubled, die flaw in figure 1, stub top to 4, curvy rounded 6 with bulbous top, first I and last A die flawed to rim, trace of doubling in legend, *rev* crowned quartered shield of arms within laurel wreath, die number 91 below, emblems below, upper left serif of B absent, 7.98g (Marsh 49; MCE 525; S 3853). *Light surface marks, extremely fine / good extremely fine.* £400-500

Price Realised : £552

Calendar year mintage 8,656,352
See footnote for lot 107, page 121, for a brief synopsis of the 1864 die numbers.

135 **Victoria,** Sovereign, 1864, die number 92, second larger young head left, WW incuse on truncation without stops, date below, die flaw in figure 8, stub top to 4, curvy rounded 6 with bulbous top, first I of legend die flawed into field from rim and nearly to mouth, small flaw inside D of DEI, *rev* crowned quartered shield of arms within laurel wreath, die number 92 below, emblems below, 7.99g (Marsh 49; MCE 525; S 3853). *Few trifling marks, obverse rim nick, otherwise good extremely fine.* £400-500

Price Realised : £624

ex Douro Cargo, Spink Auction 118, 20-21 November 1996, lot 324
Calendar year mintage 8,656,352. See footnote for lot 107, page 121, for a brief synopsis of the 1864 die numbers.

469 **Victoria,** Sovereign, 1864, die number 93, second larger young head left, WW incuse on truncation without stops, date below, stub top to 4, curvy rounded 6 with bulbous top, trace of doubling in obverse legend, *rev* crowned quartered shield of arms within laurel wreath, die number 93 below, emblems below, absent upper serif to B in legend, 7.94g (Marsh 49; MCE 525; S 3853). *Uneven tone, good fine.* £300-350

Price Realised : £264

ex An Important Collection of Gold Sovereigns 1816-2000, offered as one lot, Sothebys, November 2000, lot 525 (part)
Note the lack of upper serif on the letter B
Calendar year mintage 8,656,352. See footnote for lot 107, page 121, for a brief synopsis of the 1864 die numbers.

470 **Victoria,** Sovereign, 1864, die number 94, second larger young head left, WW incuse on truncation without stops, die flaw from tip of neck to rim, date below, stub top to 4, curvy rounded 6 with bulbous top, some doubling in legend both sides, *rev* crowned quartered shield of arms within laurel wreath, die number 94 below, emblems below, absent upper serif to B in legend, 7.97g (Marsh 49; MCE 525; S 3853). *Toned, some light marks, a pleasing extremely fine.* £350-450

Price Realised : £408

ex An Important Collection of Gold Sovereigns 1816-2000, offered as one lot, Sothebys, November 2000, lot 525 (part)
Note the lack of upper serif on the letter B.
Calendar year mintage 8,656,352. See footnote for lot 107, page 121, for a brief synopsis of the 1864 die numbers.

1052 **Victoria,** Sovereign, 1864, die number 95, second larger young head left, ww incuse on truncation without stops, date below, stub top to 4, curvy rounded 6 with bulbous top flawed shut, first and last letters of legend lightly die flawed, some letters doubled, *rev* crowned quartered shield of arms within laurel wreath, die number 95 below, emblems below, hairline raised die flaw across the tops of some letters, 7.97g (Marsh 49; MCE 525; S 3853). *Surface marks and blemishes, some scuffs, otherwise very fine.* £250-300

Price Realised : £288

This coin was purchased from one of the groups of coins from the wreck of the RMS *Douro* that were not sold by auction and within the last 10 years.
Calendar year mintage 8,656,352
See footnote for lot 107, page 121, for a brief synopsis of the 1864 die numbers.

1053 **Victoria,** Sovereign, 1864, die number 96, second larger young head left, ww incuse on truncation without stops, date below, lightly doubled, stub top to 4, curvy rounded 6 with bulbous top flawed shut, light trace of doubling in legend, *rev* crowned quartered shield of arms within laurel wreath, die number 96 below, emblems below, lightly doubled legend, 7.99g (Marsh 49; MCE 525; S 3853). *A couple of rim nicks, light surface marks and scuffs, obverse prooflike, pleasing extremely fine.* £300-400

Price Realised : £360

ex Abbatucci Cargo, Christies, 10 July 1997, untraced lot number
ex Spink Numismatic Circular, April 1998, item 2187
ex An Important Collection of Gold Sovereigns 1816-2000, offered as one lot, Sothebys, November 2000, lot 525 (part)
Calendar year mintage 8,656,352
See footnote for lot 107, page 121, for a brief synopsis of the 1864 die numbers.

471 **Victoria,** Sovereign, 1864, die number 97, second larger young head left, ww incuse on truncation without stops, die flaw from tip of neck to rim, date below, stub top to 4, curvy rounded 6 with bulbous top, trace of doubling in obverse legend, *rev* crowned quartered shield of arms within laurel wreath, die number 97 below, emblems below, absent upper serif to B in legend, 7.98g (Marsh 49; MCE 525; S 3853). *Scratch on obverse from mouth towards start of legend, patches of red tone on reverse, otherwise a pleasing good extremely fine.* £400-500

Price Realised : £504

ex Douro Cargo, Spink Auction 118, 20-21 November 1996, lot 1351 (part)
Note the lack of upper serif on the letter B.
Calendar year mintage 8,656,352
See footnote for lot 107, page 121, for a brief synopsis of the 1864 die numbers.

136 **Victoria,** Sovereign, 1864, die number 98, second larger young head left, WW incuse on truncation without stops, date below, die flaw in figure 4 with stub top, curvy rounded 6 with bulbous top, first A of GRATIA doubled, *rev* crowned quartered shield of arms within laurel wreath, die number 98 below, emblems below, 7.94g (Marsh 49; MCE 525; S 3853). *Toned, some red spots on reverse, light surface marks and scuffs, good fine, the reverse better.* £300-350

Price Realised : £264

ex Paul Davies Ltd. This coin was purchased from one of the groups of coins from the wreck of the RMS *Douro* that were not sold by auction and within the last 10 years.
Calendar year mintage 8,656,352. See footnote for lot 107, page 121, for a brief synopsis of the 1864 die numbers.

1054 **Victoria,** Sovereign, 1864, die number 99, second larger young head left, WW incuse on truncation without stops, date below, stub top to 4, curvy rounded 6 with bulbous top flawed shut, hint of doubling to legend both sides and date, raised die flaw between last two letters, *rev* crowned quartered shield of arms within laurel wreath, die number 99 below, emblems below, 7.99g (Marsh 49; MCE 525; S 3853). *Some nicks and light surface marks, otherwise good extremely fine.* £400-500

Price Realised : £1,560

ex Randy Weir Numismatics, Unionville, Ontario, Canada, purchased 7 June 1996
Calendar year mintage 8,656,352. See footnote for lot 107, page 121, for a brief synopsis of the 1864 die numbers.

137 **Victoria,** Sovereign, 1864, die number 100, second larger young head left, WW incuse on truncation without stops, date below quite doubled, stub top to 4, curvy rounded 6 with bulbous top, obverse legend doubled, trace of doubling on reverse, *rev* crowned quartered shield of arms within laurel wreath, die number 100 slightly double struck below, emblems below, 7.97g (Marsh 49; MCE 525; S 3853). *Red spot in obverse legend, a few more red spots and rim nick on the reverse, other light marks, extremely fine / good extremely fine.* £400-500

Price Realised : £432

ex Douro Cargo, Spink Auction 118, 20-21 November 1996, lot 1351 (part)
Calendar year mintage 8,656,352. See footnote for lot 107, page 121, for a brief synopsis of the 1864 die numbers.

472 **Victoria,** Sovereign, 1864, die number 101, second larger young head left, WW incuse on truncation without stops, die flaw through 1 of date from neck to rim, date below, stub top to 4, curvy rounded 6 with bulbous top, *rev* crowned quartered shield of arms within laurel wreath, die number 101 below, emblems below, hint of doubling in reverse legend, 7.99g (Marsh 49; MCE 525; S 3853). *Surface marks, extremely fine / good extremely fine.* £350-450

Price Realised : £432

ex Douro Cargo, Spink Auction 118, 20-21 November 1996, lot 1351 (part)
Calendar year mintage 8,656,352. See footnote for lot 107, page 121, for a brief synopsis of the 1864 die numbers.

1055 **Victoria,** Sovereign, 1864, die number 102, second larger young head left, ww incuse on truncation without stops, date below, stub top to 4, curvy rounded 6 with bulbous top flawed shut, hint of doubling to legend both sides and 64 of date, raised die flaw to left of D in legend and across brow of portrait to front fillet, *rev* crowned quartered shield of arms within laurel wreath, die number 102 below, emblems below, 8.00g (Marsh 49; MCE 525; S 3853). *Once cleaned, with light surface marks, otherwise extremely fine / good extremely fine.* £300-400

Price Realised : £312

ex Harlan J Berk, Chicago, during 2003
Calendar year mintage 8,656,352
See footnote for lot 107, page 121, for a brief synopsis of the 1864 die numbers.

138 **Victoria,** Sovereign, 1864, die number 103, second larger young head left, ww incuse on truncation without stops, date below, stub top to 4, curvy rounded 6 with bulbous top, last I die flawed, obverse legend lightly doubled, *rev* crowned quartered shield of arms within laurel wreath, die number 103 below, emblems below, 8.00g (Marsh 49; MCE 525; S 3853). *Short scratch over "6" in date, with light surface marks, extremely fine / good extremely fine, previously graded by PCGS as MS64.* £350-450

Price Realised : £696

ex Douro Cargo, Spink Auction 118, 20-21 November 1996, lot 1351 (part)
Calendar year mintage 8,656,352
See footnote for lot 107, page 121, for a brief synopsis of the 1864 die numbers.

473 **Victoria,** Sovereign, 1864, die number 104, second larger young head left, ww incuse on truncation without stops, date below, stub top to 4, curvy rounded 6 with bulbous top, last I of legend with weak upper serifs, *rev* crowned quartered shield of arms within laurel wreath, die number 104 below, emblems below, 7.97g (Marsh 49; MCE 525; S 3853). *Cleaned with light scuffs and hairlines, extremely fine.* £300-400

Price Realised : £312

Calendar year mintage 8,656,352
See footnote for lot 107, page 121, for a brief synopsis of the 1864 die numbers.

1056 **Victoria,** Sovereign, 1864, die number 105, second larger young head left, ww incuse on truncation without stops, date below, stub top to 4 with die flaw from neck to rim, curvy rounded 6 with bulbous top flawed shut, doubling to legend and front of portrait, *rev* crowned quartered shield of arms within laurel wreath, die number 105 below, emblems below, legend gently doubled, 7.99g (Marsh 49; MCE 525; S 3853). *Some light surface marks, otherwise toned, extremely fine.* £300-400

Price Realised : £792

ex Randy Weir Numismatics, Unionville, Ontario, Canada, during 1998
Calendar year mintage 8,656,352
See footnote for lot 107, page 121, for a brief synopsis of the 1864 die numbers.

139 **Victoria,** Sovereign, 1865, die number 1, second larger young head left, ww incuse on truncation without stops, date below lightly doubled, curvy rounded 6 with bulbous top, toothed border both sides, obverse legend lightly doubled, *rev* crowned quartered shield of arms within laurel wreath, die number 1 below, emblems below, 7.99g (Marsh 50; MCE 526; S 3853). *Reverse of more of a matt appearance, light surface marks, toned, nearly extremely fine.* £300-350

Price Realised : £264

ex An Important Collection of Gold Sovereigns 1816-2000, offered as one lot, Sothebys, 16-17 November 2000, lot 525 (part)
Calendar year mintage 1,450,238
This coin is die number 1 of 34 different numbered dies in the Bentley Collection running from 1 to 40. Marsh claims twelve other numbers exist making 52 reverse dies in total to strike about one and a half million Sovereigns. This suggests poor die longevity, however it must always be borne in mind that the calendar year mintages are exactly that, and do not reflect the dates upon the coins in that period, some of them could have been 1864 dated coins, and 1865 date coins were probably made into the first part of 1866. A statistician should be able to make more sense of the figures, given more time and research, perhaps in collaboration with the Royal Mint.

474 **Victoria,** Sovereign, 1865, die number 2, second larger young head left, ww incuse on truncation without stops, date below, curvy rounded 6 with bulbous top, last three letters of legend and penultimate I die flawed, *rev* crowned quartered shield of arms within laurel wreath, die number 2 below, emblems below, some doubling of reverse legend, 7.98g (Marsh 50; MCE 526; S 3853). *Light surface marks and hairlines, pleasing good extremely fine.* £400-500

Price Realised : £744

ex An Important Collection of Gold Sovereigns 1816-2000, offered as one lot, Sothebys, November 2000, lot 525 (part)
Calendar year mintage 1,450,238
See footnote for lot 139 (above) for a brief synopsis of the 1865 die numbers.

1057 **Victoria,** Sovereign, 1865, die number 3, second larger young head left, ww incuse on truncation without stops, date below, 5 with incomplete loop, curvy rounded 6 with bulbous top flawed shut, raised die flaw to the left of 1 in date, obverse legend lightly doubled, penultimate I and last A of legend die flawed, *rev* crowned quartered shield of arms within laurel wreath, die number 3 below, emblems below, hairline raised die flaw at last colon of legend, 7.99g (Marsh 50; MCE 526; S 3853). *Light surface marks and hairlines, otherwise good extremely fine.* £400-500

Price Realised : £528

ex Randy Weir Numismatics, Unionville, Ontario, Canada, 13 August 1992
Calendar year mintage 1,450,238
See footnote for lot 139 (above) for a brief synopsis of the 1865 die numbers.

1058 **Victoria,** Sovereign, 1865, die number 4, second larger young head left, WW incuse on truncation without stops, date below, 5 with incomplete loop, curvy rounded 6 with bulbous top flawed shut, raised die flaw to the left of 1 in date, *rev* crowned quartered shield of arms within laurel wreath, die number 4 below, emblems below, 7.94g (Marsh 50; MCE 526; S 3853). *Heavy scuffs and surface marks with hairlines, otherwise good fine / very fine.* £250-300

Price Realised : £216

This coin was purchased from one of the groups of coins from the wreck of the RMS *Douro* that were not sold by auction and within the last 10 years.
Calendar year mintage 1,450,238
See footnote for lot 139, page 147, for a brief synopsis of the 1865 die numbers.

140 **Victoria,** Sovereign, 1865, die number 5, second larger young head left, WW incuse on truncation without stops, date below, curvy rounded 6 with bulbous top, incomplete bottom loop to 5 with a squarer top, toothed border both sides, trace of doubling of legend both sides, *rev* crowned quartered shield of arms within laurel wreath, die number 5 below, emblems below, 7.98g (Marsh 50; MCE 526; S 3853). *Once cleaned with associated surface marks and hairlines, otherwise good very fine.* £300-350

Price Realised : £264

ex Paul Davies Ltd. This coin was purchased from one of the groups of coins from the wreck of the RMS *Douro* that were not sold by auction and within the last 10 years.
Calendar year mintage 1,450,238
See footnote for lot 139, page 147, for a brief synopsis of the 1865 die numbers.

141 **Victoria,** Sovereign, 1865, die number 6, second larger young head left, WW incuse on truncation without stops, date below, angled top to 5, curvy rounded 6 with bulbous top, flaw from top of 1 in date, raised die flaw from V to rim, *rev* crowned quartered shield of arms within laurel wreath, die number 6 below, emblems below, 7.98g (Marsh 50; MCE 526; S 3853). *Very light surface marks, hairline scratch by ponytail in field, toned, extremely fine.* £350-400

Price Realised : £432

ex Douro Cargo, Spink Auction 118, 20-21 November 1996, lot 390 (part)
ex Spink Numismatic Circular, October 1997, item 5025
ex An Important Collection of Gold Sovereigns 1816-2000, offered as one lot, Sothebys, 16-17 November 2000, lot 525 (part)
Calendar year mintage 1,450,238
See footnote for lot 139, page 147, for a brief synopsis of the 1865 die numbers.

475 **Victoria,** Sovereign, 1865, die number 8, second larger young head left, ww incuse on truncation without stops, die flaw from bun of hair to rim to left of G, date below, incomplete bottom loop to 5 which has a square top half, curvy rounded 6 with bulbous top, hint of doubling to obverse legend, *rev* crowned quartered shield of arms within laurel wreath, die number 8 below, emblems below, 7.99g (Marsh 50; MCE 526; S 3853). *Light surface marks toned extremely fine / good extremely fine.* £350-450

Price Realised : £432

ex Douro Cargo, Spink Auction 118, 20-21 November 1996, lot 1315 (part)
Calendar year mintage 1,450,238. See footnote for lot 139, page 147, for a brief synopsis of the 1865 die numbers.

1059 **Victoria,** Sovereign, 1865, die number 9, second larger young head left, ww incuse on truncation without stops, date below, square top 5 with incomplete loop, curvy rounded 6 with bulbous top flawed shut, *rev* crowned quartered shield of arms within laurel wreath, die number 9 below, emblems below, 7.98g (Marsh 50; MCE 526; S 3853). *Once cleaned, scuffed obverse with surface marks and hairlines, spot on reverse rim, otherwise good very fine / extremely fine.* £250-350

Price Realised : £288

ex Douro Cargo, Spink Auction 118, 20-21 November 1996, lot 1316 (part)
ex Spink Numismatic Circular, July 1998, item 4734
ex An Important Collection of Gold Sovereigns 1816-2000, offered as one lot, Sothebys, November 2000, lot 525 (part)
Calendar year mintage 1,450,238. See footnote for lot 139, page 147, for a brief synopsis of the 1865 die numbers.

142 **Victoria,** Sovereign, 1865, die number 10, second larger young head left, ww incuse on truncation without stops, date below, raised die flaw to left of 1, curvy rounded 6 with bulbous top, 5 with a squarer top, die flawed second I in first word, *rev* crowned quartered shield of arms within laurel wreath, die number 10 below, emblems below, 7.98g (Marsh 50; MCE 526; S 3853). *Some scuffs and hairlines on obverse, retaining a proof-like underlying brilliance, nearly extremely fine / extremely fine.* £300-400

Price Realised : £384

ex Spink and Son Ltd, November 2003
Calendar year mintage 1,450,238. See footnote for lot 139, page 147, for a brief synopsis of the 1865 die numbers.

143 **Victoria,** Sovereign, 1865, die number 11, second larger young head left, ww incuse on truncation without stops, date below, curvy rounded 6 with bulbous top, incomplete bottom loop to 5 with a squarer top lightly die flawed, *rev* crowned quartered shield of arms within laurel wreath, die number 11 below, emblems below, hint of doubling in legend, 8.00g (Marsh 50; MCE 526; S 3853). *A few tiny nicks and hairlines, otherwise practically as struck.* £500-600

Price Realised : £744

ex Randy Weir Numismatics, Unionville, Ontario, Canada, 14 September 1993
Calendar year mintage 1,450,238
See footnote for lot 139, page 147, for a brief synopsis of the 1865 die numbers.

476 **Victoria,** Sovereign, 1865, die number 12, second larger young head left, WW incuse on truncation without stops, date below, square top 5, curvy rounded 6 with bulbous top, last I of legend die flawed, *rev* crowned quartered shield of arms within laurel wreath, die number 12 below, die flaw at top of 12, emblems below, reverse legend doubled, 7.98g (Marsh 50; MCE 526; S 3853). *Some light hairlines, pleasing good extremely fine.* £400-500

Price Realised : £432

ex Randy Weir Numismatics, Unionville, Ontario, Canada, purchased c.1995
Calendar year mintage 1,450,238
See footnote for lot 139, page 147, for a brief synopsis of the 1865 die numbers.

477 **Victoria,** Sovereign, 1865, die number 13, second larger young head left, WW incuse on truncation without stops, date below, square top 5, curvy rounded 6 with bulbous top, last I of legend die flawed, doubled date and legend both sides, *rev* crowned quartered shield of arms within laurel wreath, die number 13 below, emblems below, 7.97g (Marsh 50; MCE 526; S 3853). *Some traces of black deposit, once cleaned, very fine.* £300-350

Price Realised : £264

Calendar year mintage 1,450,238
See footnote for lot 139, page 147, for a brief synopsis of the 1865 die numbers.

144 **Victoria,** Sovereign, 1865, die number 14, second larger young head left, WW incuse on truncation without stops, date below, angled top to 5, curvy rounded 6 with bulbous top, die flaw in field between end of legend and date, *rev* crowned quartered shield of arms within laurel wreath, die number 14 below, emblems below, trace of doubling in legend, 7.99g (Marsh 50; MCE 526; S 3853). *A couple of tiny spots on obverse rim and another near die number on reverse, a few light hairlines, otherwise as struck.* £500-600

Price Realised : £1,104

ex Randy Weir Numismatics, Unionville, Ontario, Canada, 3 November 1992
Calendar year mintage 1,450,238
See footnote for lot 139, page 147, for a brief synopsis of the 1865 die numbers.

478 **Victoria,** Sovereign, 1865, die number 15, second larger young head left, WW incuse on truncation without stops, date below, angled top 5, die flawed curvy rounded 6 with bulbous top, light die flaw from penultimate A into field, lightly doubled obverse legend, *rev* crowned quartered shield of arms within laurel wreath, die number 15 below, emblems below, die flaw at NIA of legend, 7.97g (Marsh 50; MCE 526; S 3853). *Some light hairlines, good extremely fine.* £400-500

Price Realised : £576

ex An Important Collection of Gold Sovereigns 1816-2000, offered as one lot, Sothebys, November 2000, lot 525 (part)
Calendar year mintage 1,450,238
See footnote for lot 139, page 147, for a brief synopsis of the 1865 die numbers.

1060 Victoria, Sovereign, 1865, die number 16, second larger young head left, ww incuse on truncation without stops, date below, angled top 5, curvy rounded 6 with bulbous top, 65 doubled, raised die flaw through 1, legend doubled, *rev* crowned quartered shield of arms within laurel wreath, die number 16 below, emblems below, traces of raised die flaw across some letters, 7.98g (Marsh 50; MCE 526; S 3853). *Lustrous with some light hairlines, otherwise uneven tone, extremely fine.* £300-400

Price Realised : £384

ex Randy Weir Numismatics, Unionville, Ontario, Canada, 5 May 1989
Calendar year mintage 1,450,238. See footnote for lot 139, page 147, for a brief synopsis of the 1865 die numbers.

1061 Victoria, Sovereign, 1865, die number 17, second larger young head left, ww incuse on truncation without stops, date below, angled top 5, curvy open 6 with bulbous top, die flaw from tip of truncation to rim, *rev* crowned quartered shield of arms within laurel wreath, die number 17 below, emblems below, die flaw in field by M of legend, 7.93g (Marsh 50; MCE 526; S 3853). *Once cleaned, now toned, with some light hairlines and rim nick, otherwise good fine, reverse better.* £250-300

Price Realised : £240

This coin was purchased from one of the groups of coins from the wreck of the RMS *Douro* that were not sold by auction and within the last 10 years.
Calendar year mintage 1,450,238. See footnote for lot 139, page 147, for a brief synopsis of the 1865 die numbers.

145 Victoria, Sovereign, 1865, die number 18, second larger young head left, ww incuse on truncation without stops, date below, angled top to 5, curvy rounded 6 with bulbous top, lightly doubled legend both sides, *rev* crowned quartered shield of arms within laurel wreath, die number 18 below, emblems below, 7.96g (Marsh 50; MCE 526; S 3853). *Some light surface marks and hairlines, nearly very fine / good very fine.* £300-350

Price Realised : £264

ex Paul Davies Ltd. This coin was purchased from one of the groups of coins from the wreck of the RMS *Douro* that were not sold by auction and within the last 10 years.
Calendar year mintage 1,450,238. See footnote for lot 139, page 147, for a brief synopsis of the 1865 die numbers.

1062 Victoria, Sovereign, 1865, die number 19, second larger young head left, ww incuse on truncation without stops, date below, square top complete 5, curvy 6 with bulbous top die flawed shut, trace of die flaw in last A of legend, *rev* crowned quartered shield of arms within laurel wreath, die number 19 below, emblems below, 7.99g (Marsh 50; MCE 526; S 3853). *Only lightest of hairlines, rim nick, otherwise good extremely fine.* £400-500

Price Realised : £1,560

ex Randy Weir Numismatics, Unionville, Ontario, Canada, 27 July 1994.
Calendar year mintage 1,450,238. See footnote for lot 139, page 147, for a brief synopsis of the 1865 die numbers.

146 **Victoria,** Sovereign, 1865, die number 20, second larger young head left, ww incuse on truncation without stops, date below lightly doubled, angled top to 5, curvy rounded 6 with bulbous top, light raised die flaw in last word, *rev* crowned quartered shield of arms within laurel wreath, die number 20 below, emblems below, trace of doubling in legend, 7.97g (Marsh 50; MCE 526; S 3853). *Some nicks, hairlines and scuffs, otherwise practically extremely fine.* £300-400

Price Realised : £360

ex St James's Auction 5, 27 September 2006, lot 637
Calendar year mintage 1,450,238
See footnote for lot 139, page 147, for a brief synopsis of the 1865 die numbers.

479 **Victoria,** Sovereign, 1865, die number 21, second larger young head left, ww incuse on truncation without stops, date below, angled top 5, die flawed curvy rounded 6 with bulbous top, light die flaw between T and I of last word, hint of doubling both sides, *rev* crowned quartered shield of arms within laurel wreath, die number 21 below, emblems below, 7.98g (Marsh 50; MCE 526; S 3853). *Heavily scuffed on obverse, hairlined, about extremely fine.* £300-400

Price Realised : £360

Calendar year mintage 1,450,238
See footnote for lot 139, page 147, for a brief synopsis of the 1865 die numbers.

1063 **Victoria,** Sovereign, 1865, die number 22, second larger young head left, ww incuse on truncation without stops, date below, square top complete 5, curvy 6 with bulbous top die flawed shut, die flaw from first T to rim, hint of doubling both sides, *rev* crowned quartered shield of arms within laurel wreath, die number 22 below, emblems below, 7.98g (Marsh 50; MCE 526; S 3853). *A few light digs, rim nick, otherwise extremely fine.* £300-400

Price Realised : £336

ex Douro Cargo, Spink Auction 118, 20-21 November 1996, lot 1353 (part)
Calendar year mintage 1,450,238
See footnote for lot 139, page 147, for a brief synopsis of the 1865 die numbers.

147 **Victoria,** Sovereign, 1865, die number 23, second larger young head left, ww incuse on truncation without stops, date below, angled top to 5, curvy rounded 6 with bulbous top, last A in legend die flawed, *rev* crowned quartered shield of arms within laurel, die number 23 below, smaller 3 than the 2, emblems below, hint of doubling to legend, 7.97g (Marsh 50; MCE 526; S 3853). *Uneven tone with some light surface marks and scuffs, otherwise extremely fine.* £300-400

Price Realised : £312

ex Douro Cargo, Spink Auction 118, 20-21 November 1996, lot 1353 (part)
Calendar year mintage 1,450,238
See footnote for lot 139, page 147, for a brief synopsis of the 1865 die numbers.

480 **Victoria,** Sovereign, 1865, die number 24, second larger young head left, ww incuse on truncation without stops, date below, angled top 5, curvy rounded 6 with bulbous top, *rev* crowned quartered shield of arms within laurel wreath, die number 24 below, emblems below, hint of doubling in legend, 7.98g (Marsh 50; MCE 526; S 3853). *Toned extremely fine / good extremely fine.* £300-400

Price Realised : £360

Calendar year mintage 1,450,238
See footnote for lot 139, page 147, for a brief synopsis of the 1865 die numbers.

1064 **Victoria,** Sovereign, 1865, die number 26, second larger young head left, ww incuse on truncation without stops, date below, square top complete 5, curvy 6 with bulbous top die flawed shut, die flaw at first I of legend, *rev* crowned quartered shield of arms within laurel wreath, die number 26 below, 6 with digs, emblems below, 7.98g (Marsh 50; MCE 526; S 3853). *Light surface marks, the "6" of the die number with digs which means this coin was at first mistaken for die 28, otherwise toned, bold fine.* £250-300

Price Realised : £216

Purchased via Spink and Son Ltd, November 2003
Calendar year mintage 1,450,238
See footnote for lot 139, page 147, for a brief synopsis of the 1865 die numbers.

148 **Victoria,** Sovereign, 1865, die number 27, second larger young head left, ww incuse on truncation without stops, date below, closed 6, lightly doubled date, angled top to 5, curvy rounded 6 with bulbous top, hint of doubling to legend both sides, *rev* crowned quartered shield of arms within laurel wreath, die number 27 below, emblems below, 7.98g (Marsh 50; MCE 526; S 3853). *A few tiny nicks and surface marks, pleasing good extremely fine.* £400-500

Price Realised : £504

Calendar year mintage 1,450,238
See footnote for lot 139, page 147, for a brief synopsis of the 1865 die numbers.

481 **Victoria,** Sovereign, 1865, die number 28, second larger young head left, ww incuse on truncation without stops, date below, angled top 5, curvy rounded 6 with bulbous top, *rev* crowned quartered shield of arms within laurel wreath, die number 28 below, 8 higher than 2, emblems below, 7.96g (Marsh 50; MCE 526; S 3853). *Toned nearly very fine / good very fine.* £300-350

Price Realised : £264

ex Spink Numismatic Circular, February 1998, item 521
ex An Important Collection of Gold Sovereigns 1816-2000, offered as one lot, Sothebys, November 2000, lot 525 (part)
Calendar year mintage 1,450,238
See footnote for lot 139, page 147, for a brief synopsis of the 1865 die numbers.

1065 **Victoria,** Sovereign, 1865, die number 29, second larger young head left, ww incuse on truncation without stops, date below, square top complete 5, curvy 6 with bulbous top die flawed shut, die flaw at first I of legend, *rev* crowned quartered shield of arms within laurel wreath, die number 29 below, 9 smaller than 2, emblems below, hint of doubling to legend, 7.97g (Marsh 50; MCE 526; S 3853). *A few light surface marks, toned, about extremely fine.* £300-400

Price Realised : £288

This coin was purchased from one of the groups of coins from the wreck of the RMS *Douro* that were not sold by auction and within the last 10 years.
Calendar year mintage 1,450,238
See footnote for lot 139, page 147, for a brief synopsis of the 1865 die numbers.

149 **Victoria,** Sovereign, 1865, die number 31, second larger young head left, ww incuse on truncation without stops, date below lightly doubled, curvy rounded 6 with bulbous top, angled top to 5, trace of doubling in legend both sides, *rev* crowned quartered shield of arms within laurel wreath, die number 31 below, emblems below, 7.95g (Marsh 50; MCE 526; S 3853). *Once cleaned with associated surface marks and hairlines, nearly very fine / very fine.* £300-350

Price Realised : £264

ex Spink and Son Ltd, March 2005
Calendar year mintage 1,450,238
See footnote for lot 139, page 147, for a brief synopsis of the 1865 die numbers.

482 **Victoria,** Sovereign, 1865, die number 32, second larger young head left, ww incuse on truncation without stops, date doubled below, angled top 5, curvy rounded 6 with bulbous top, legend doubled both sides, *rev* crowned quartered shield of arms within laurel wreath, die number 32 below, emblems below, 7.99g (Marsh 50; MCE 526; S 3853). *Some scuffs and hairlines, extremely fine, reverse better.* £300-400

Price Realised : £408

Calendar year mintage 1,450,238
See footnote for lot 139, page 147, for a brief synopsis of the 1865 die numbers.

1066 **Victoria,** Sovereign, 1865, die number 33, second larger young head left, ww incuse on truncation without stops, date below, square top complete 5, curvy 6 with bulbous top die flawed shut, die flaw through 1 of date from neck to rim, *rev* crowned quartered shield of arms within laurel wreath, die number 33 below, emblems below, 7.98g (Marsh 50; MCE 526; S 3853). *A few light hairlines, otherwise good extremely fine.* £400-500

Price Realised : £480

ex Douro Cargo, Spink Auction 118, 20-21 November 1996, lot 1353 (part)
Calendar year mintage 1,450,238
See footnote for lot 139, page 147, for a brief synopsis of the 1865 die numbers.

150 **Victoria,** Sovereign, 1865, die number 35, second larger young head left, ww incuse on truncation without stops, date below lightly doubled, curvy rounded 6 with bulbous top, angled top to 5, last word die flawed, trace of doubling in legend both sides, *rev* crowned quartered shield of arms within laurel wreath, die number 35 below, emblems below, 7.98g (Marsh 50; MCE 526; S 3853). *Dig on cheek with two light hairline scratches, spot on obverse legend, otherwise extremely fine.* £300-350

Price Realised : £384

ex Douro Cargo, Spink Auction 118, 20-21 November 1996, lot 1353 (part)
Calendar year mintage 1,450,238. See footnote for lot 139, page 147, for a brief synopsis of the 1865 die numbers.

483 **Victoria,** Sovereign, 1865, die number 36, second larger young head left, ww incuse on truncation without stops, date below, 8 doubled, angled top 5, curvy rounded 6 with bulbous top, trace of legend doubling both sides, light die flaw at start and end of legend, flaw from neck into field, *rev* crowned quartered shield of arms within laurel wreath, die number 36 below, emblems below, 7.99g (Marsh 50; MCE 526; S 3853). *Scratch by nose, dig by first R on reverse, light hairline marks, tiny red spot both sides, otherwise extremely fine.* £300-350

Price Realised : £528

ex Douro Cargo, Spink Auction 118, 20-21 November 1996, lot 1353 (part)
Calendar year mintage 1,450,238. See footnote for lot 139, page 147, for a brief synopsis of the 1865 die numbers.

1067 **Victoria,** Sovereign, 1865, die number 37, second larger young head left, ww incuse on truncation without stops, date below, square top complete 5 die flawed from neck to rim, curvy 6 with bulbous top die flawed shut, second I of legend die flawed, trace of doubling on obverse, *rev* crowned quartered shield of arms within laurel wreath, die number 37 below, emblems below, 7.99g (Marsh 50; MCE 526; S 3853). *Rim nick on reverse, patch of tone on lower left of reverse, otherwise about extremely fine.* £300-400

Price Realised : £336

This coin was purchased from one of the groups of coins from the wreck of the RMS *Douro* that were not sold by auction and within the last 10 years.
Calendar year mintage 1,450,238. See footnote for lot 139, page 147, for a brief synopsis of the 1865 die numbers.

151 **Victoria,** Sovereign, 1865, die number 40, second larger young head left, ww incuse on truncation without stops, date below, curvy rounded 6 with bulbous top die flawed shut, angled top to 5, *rev* crowned quartered shield of arms within laurel wreath, die number 40 below, emblems below, 7.98g (Marsh 50; MCE 526; S 3853). *Some light nicks and hairlines, nearly extremely fine.* £300-350

Price Realised : £336

ex Douro Cargo, Spink Auction 118, 20-21 November 1996, lot 1319 (part)
Calendar year mintage 1,450,238
See footnote for lot 139, page 147, for a brief synopsis of the 1865 die numbers.
This coin concludes the 1865 die number coins in the Bentley Collection, 13 pieces in total.

484 **Victoria,** Sovereign, 1866, die number 1, second larger young head left, ww incuse on truncation without stops, date doubled below, die flaw between 1 and 8, curvy rounded 6's with bulbous top, last I of legend die flawed, trace of doubling in obverse legend, *rev* crowned quartered shield of arms within laurel wreath, die number 1 below, emblems below, 7.98g (Marsh 51; MCE 527; S 3853). *Once cleaned with associated nicks and hairlines, red patch of tone on caul of crown, otherwise extremely fine.* £300-400

Price Realised : £384

ex Douro Cargo, Spink Auction 118, 20-21 November 1996, lot 552 (part)
Calendar year mintage 4,047,288
This coin is die number 1 of 77 different numbered dies in the Bentley Collection running from 1 to 78. Marsh claims that die numbers 12 and 79 also exist, which are absent from this collection, making a total of 79 reverse dies to strike just over four million Sovereigns, suggesting good longevity. One die number in the Bentley Collection run of 1866 is not recorded by Marsh, number 67.

152 **Victoria,** Sovereign, 1866, die number 2, second larger young head left, ww incuse on truncation without stops, date below with raised die flaws, 1 die flawed, curvy rounded 6's with bulbous top die flawed, *rev* crowned quartered shield of arms within laurel wreath, die number 2 below, emblems below, raised die flaw on last word of legend, 7.99g (Marsh 51; MCE 527; S 3853). *Previously graded by PCGS as MS64, some rim nicks with a few hairlines, otherwise pleasing good extremely fine.* £400-500

Price Realised : £1,056

ex Ebay purchase, April 2002
Calendar year mintage 4,047,288. See footnote for lot 484 (above) for a brief synopsis of the 1866 die numbers.

485 **Victoria,** Sovereign, 1866, die number 3, second larger young head left, ww incuse on truncation without stops, date doubled below, curvy rounded 6's with bulbous top, some doubling in obverse legend, *rev* crowned quartered shield of arms within laurel wreath, die number 3 below, emblems below, 7.96g (Marsh 51; MCE 527; S 3853). *Once cleaned, with scuffs and hairlines, very fine / extremely fine.* £300-350

Price Realised : £264

This coin was purchased from one of the groups of coins from the wreck of the RMS *Douro* that were not sold by auction and within the last 10 years.
Calendar year mintage 4,047,288. See footnote for lot 484 (above) for a brief synopsis of the 1866 die numbers.

1068 **Victoria,** Sovereign, 1866, die number 4, second larger young head left, ww incuse on truncation without stops, date below, lightly doubled, die flaw to left of 1, curvy rounded 6's with bulbous top die flawed shut, last three letters of legend die flawed, *rev* crowned quartered shield of arms within laurel wreath, die number 4 below, 4 filled, emblems below, 7.97g (Marsh 51; MCE 527; S 3853). *A few red spots both sides, mainly on lower portion of reverse, toned, nearly good very fine.* £300-400

Price Realised : £312

This coin was purchased from one of the groups of coins from the wreck of the RMS *Douro* that were not sold by auction and within the last 10 years.
Calendar year mintage 4,047,288. See footnote for lot 484 (above) for a brief synopsis of the 1866 die numbers.

1069 Victoria, Sovereign, 1866, die number 5, second larger young head left, ww incuse on truncation without stops, date below, curvy rounded 6's with bulbous top die flawed shut, trace of doubling to legend, *rev* crowned quartered shield of arms within laurel wreath, die number 5 below, emblems below, 7.98g (Marsh 51; MCE 527; S 3853). *With underlying proof-like brilliance, some hairlines, otherwise good extremely fine.* £400-500

Price Realised : £1,320

ex Douro Cargo, Spink Auction 118, 20-21 November 1996, lot 552 (part)
This coin was previously graded by PCGS as MS64
Calendar year mintage 4,047,288. See footnote for lot 484, page 156, for a brief synopsis of the 1866 die numbers.

486 Victoria, Sovereign, 1866, die number 6, second larger young head left, ww incuse on truncation without stops, date below, curvy rounded 6's with bulbous top, second 6 die flawed, C of queen's name die flawed to rim, *rev* crowned quartered shield of arms within laurel wreath, die number 6 below, emblems below, 7.96g (Marsh 51; MCE 527; S 3853). *Once cleaned, toned with light surface marks, nearly very fine / good very fine.* £300-350

Price Realised : £264

This coin was purchased from one of the groups of coins from the wreck of the RMS *Douro* that were not sold by auction and within the last 10 years.
Calendar year mintage 4,047,288.
See footnote for lot 484, page 156, for a brief synopsis of the 1866 die numbers.

153 Victoria, Sovereign, 1866, die number 7, second larger young head left, ww incuse on truncation without stops, date below, raised die flaw in field to left of 1 running to neck, curvy rounded 6's with bulbous top die flawed shut, hairline die flaw from letter O to rim and in last word on obverse, *rev* crowned quartered shield of arms within laurel wreath, die number 7 below, emblems below, R of second word flawed and trace of doubling in legend, 7.99g (Marsh 51; MCE 527; S 3853). *Light nicks and hairlines, some surface marks, otherwise good extremely fine.* £350-450

Price Realised : £480

ex Randy Weir Numismatics, Unionville, Ontario, Canada, 12 November 1990
Calendar year mintage 4,047,288. See footnote for lot 484, page 156, for a brief synopsis of the 1866 die numbers.

154 Victoria, Sovereign, 1866, die number 8, second larger young head left, ww incuse on truncation without stops, date below lightly doubled, curvy rounded 6's with bulbous top die flawed shut, *rev* crowned quartered shield of arms within laurel wreath, die number 8 below, emblems below, 7.98g (Marsh 51; MCE 527; S 3853). *Once cleaned with associated surface scuff marks and hairlines, extremely fine.* £300-350

Price Realised : £408

Calendar year mintage 4,047,288
See footnote for lot 484, page 156, for a brief synopsis of the 1866 die numbers.

487 **Victoria,** Sovereign, 1866, die number 9, second larger young head left, ww incuse on truncation without stops, date below, curvy rounded 6's with bulbous top, last I of legend die flawed, *rev* crowned quartered shield of arms within laurel wreath, die number 9 below, die flaw on top of 9, emblems below, 7.97g (Marsh 51; MCE 527; S 3853). *Lightly toned, extremely fine.* £350-450

Price Realised : £408

Calendar year mintage 4,047,288
See footnote for lot 484, page 156, for a brief synopsis of the 1866 die numbers.

1070 **Victoria,** Sovereign, 1866, die number 10, second larger young head left, ww incuse on truncation without stops, date below, curvy rounded 6's with bulbous top, second 6 lightly die flawed from neck to rim, *rev* crowned quartered shield of arms within laurel wreath, die number 10 below, emblems below, light die flaw across some letters in latter half of legend, 7.99g (Marsh 51; MCE 527; S 3853). *Some scuffs on a brilliant obverse, a few other hairlines and surface marks, matt appearance to reverse, otherwise good extremely fine.* £300-400

Price Realised : £312

ex Douro Cargo, Spink Auction 118, 20-21 November 1996, lot 552 (part)
Calendar year mintage 4,047,288. See footnote for lot 484, page 156, for a brief synopsis of the 1866 die numbers.

155 **Victoria,** Sovereign, 1866, die number 11, second larger young head left, ww incuse on truncation without stops, date below, curvy rounded 6's with bulbous top lightly die flawed shut, raised die flaw at last I of legend, *rev* crowned quartered shield of arms within laurel wreath, die number 11 below, emblems below, 8.00g (Marsh 51; MCE 527; S 3853). *A few light hairlines and surface marks, obverse with underlying brilliance, good extremely fine.* £350-450

Price Realised : £552

ex Spink and Son Ltd, November 2003
Calendar year mintage 4,047,288. See footnote for lot 484, page 156, for a brief synopsis of the 1866 die numbers.

Very Rare "6" over "5" Overdate on an 1866 Die Number Sovereign

488 **Victoria,** Sovereign, 1866, second 6 struck over 5, die number 11, second larger young head left, ww incuse on truncation without stops, date doubled below, curvy rounded 6's with bulbous top, die flaw to left of 1 in date, trace of doubling to legend both sides, *rev* crowned quartered shield of arms within laurel wreath, die number 11 below, emblems below, 7.99g (Marsh 51; MCE 527; S 3853). *A few tiny nicks on obverse otherwise, as struck and very unusual with the overstruck date, very rare.* £600-800

Price Realised : £1,800

ex Randy Weir Numismatics, Unionville, Ontario, Canada, purchased May 1990
The phenomenon of an overstruck date in the die number series is very seldom seen. Die number 11 for this date exists in non overdate format too, an example of which is listed as lot 155 in the Bentley Collection.
Calendar year mintage 4,047,288. See footnote for lot 484, page 156, for a brief synopsis of the 1866 die numbers.

489 **Victoria,** Sovereign, 1866, die number 13, second larger young head left, ww incuse on truncation without stops, date below, curvy rounded 6's with bulbous top and die flawed, *rev* crowned quartered shield of arms within laurel wreath, die number 13 below, emblems below, 7.97g (Marsh 51; MCE 527; S 3853). *Lightly scuffed and hairlined, nearly very fine, reverse better.* £300-350

Price Realised : £264

ex Spink and Son, purchased March 2005
Calendar year mintage 4,047,288. See footnote for lot 484, page 156, for a brief synopsis of the 1866 die numbers.

1071 **Victoria,** Sovereign, 1866, die number 14, second larger young head left, ww incuse on truncation without stops, date below, curvy rounded 6's with bulbous top die flawed shut, trace of doubling in legend, *rev* crowned quartered shield of arms within laurel wreath, die number 14, below, emblems below, light die flaw to right of crown from arch to rim, 7.95g (Marsh 51; MCE 527; S 3853). *Once cleaned, now toned with some scuffs and surface marks, otherwise almost very fine, reverse better.* £250-300

Price Realised : £240

This coin was purchased from one of the groups of coins from the wreck of the RMS *Douro* that were not sold by auction and within the last 10 years.
Calendar year mintage 4,047,288. See footnote for lot 484, page 156, for a brief synopsis of the 1866 die numbers.

490 **Victoria,** Sovereign, 1866, die number 15, second larger young head left, ww incuse on truncation without stops, date below, curvy rounded open 6's with bulbous top, *rev* crowned quartered shield of arms within laurel wreath, die number 15 below, emblems below, 7.99g (Marsh 51; MCE 527; S 3853). *Two small red patches of tone on reverse, light surface marks and scuffs, otherwise extremely fine.* £300-400

Price Realised : £384

Calendar year mintage 4,047,288
See footnote for lot 484, page 156, for a brief synopsis of the 1866 die numbers.

Unusual 1866 Sovereign with Roman Style I in Die Number 16 on Reverse

156 **Victoria,** Sovereign, 1866, die number 16, second larger young head left, ww incuse on truncation without stops, date below with doubled figures, 1 of date die flawed, curvy rounded 6's with bulbous top, trace of doubling to obverse legend, *rev* crowned quartered shield of arms within laurel wreath, die number 16 below, Roman I in 16, emblems below, 7.98g (Marsh 51; MCE 527; S 3853). *A little scuffed and hairlined, good very fine / nearly extremely fine, very unusual with Roman I style figure in die number.* £400-500

Price Realised : £384

ex A H Baldwin & Sons Ltd sourced via Paul Davies Ltd, December 2009
This coin was purchased from one of the groups of coins from the wreck of the RMS *Douro* that were not sold by auction and within the last 10 years. It is unusual in that it demonstrates a Roman style letter I in the tiny die number on the reverse, which is seen very rarely in the die number series, it is an oddity.
Calendar year mintage 4,047,288. See footnote for lot 484, page 156, for a brief synopsis of the 1866 die numbers.

1072 **Victoria,** Sovereign, 1866, die number 17, second larger young head left, WW incuse on truncation without stops, date below, curvy rounded 6's with bulbous top die flawed shut, raised die flaw through last 6, further flaw from letter C to rim in legend, *rev* crowned quartered shield of arms within laurel wreath, die number 17, below, emblems below, light die flaw connects some letters of reverse legend, 7.98g (Marsh 51; MCE 527; S 3853). *Once cleaned, with some scuffs and surface marks, otherwise brilliant, almost extremely fine, reverse better.* £300-400

Price Realised : £264

Purchased via Spink and Son Ltd, November 2003
Calendar year mintage 4,047,288
See footnote for lot 484, page 156, for a brief synopsis of the 1866 die numbers.

1073 **Victoria,** Sovereign, 1866, die number 18, second larger young head left, WW incuse on truncation without stops, date below, curvy rounded 6's with bulbous top die flawed shut, *rev* crowned quartered shield of arms within laurel wreath, die number 18, below, emblems below, 7.97g (Marsh 51; MCE 527; S 3853). *Some black deposit in borders with light surface marks, otherwise toned, about extremely fine.* £300-400

Price Realised : £264

Purchased via Spink and Son Ltd, November 2003
Calendar year mintage 4,047,288
See footnote for lot 484, page 156, for a brief synopsis of the 1866 die numbers.

157 **Victoria,** Sovereign, 1866, die number 19, second larger young head left, WW incuse on truncation without stops, date below, curvy rounded 6's with bulbous top, raised die flaw from tip of neck to rim, other flaws to rim from D of DEI and last R, a further flaw in hair near ear, *rev* crowned quartered shield of arms within laurel wreath, die number 19 below, emblems below, 7.98g (Marsh 51; MCE 527; S 3853). *Surface marks, toned, extremely fine.* £350-450

Price Realised : £624

ex Douro Cargo, Spink Auction 118, 20-21 November 1996, lot 326
Calendar year mintage 4,047,288. See footnote for lot 484, page 156, for a brief synopsis of the 1866 die numbers.

491 **Victoria,** Sovereign, 1866, die number 20, second larger young head left, WW incuse on truncation without stops, date below, curvy rounded 6's with bulbous top, *rev* crowned quartered shield of arms within laurel wreath, die number 20 below, emblems below, trace of doubling in reverse legend, 7.95g (Marsh 51; MCE 527; S 3853). *Some red patches of tone on reverse and spots, light surface marks and scuffs, otherwise nearly very fine / good very fine.* £300-350

Price Realised : £264

This coin was purchased from one of the groups of coins from the wreck of the RMS *Douro* that were not sold by auction and within the last 10 years.
Calendar year mintage 4,047,288. See footnote for lot 484, page 156, for a brief synopsis of the 1866 die numbers.

1074 **Victoria,** Sovereign, 1866, die number 21, second larger young head left, ww incuse on truncation without stops, date below, curvy rounded 6's with bulbous top die flawed shut, die flaw through 1 of date to rim, further die flaw through last I of obverse legend, *rev* crowned quartered shield of arms within laurel wreath, die number 21 below, emblems below, trace of doubling to legend, light die flaws in penultimate word, 7.96g (Marsh 51; MCE 527; S 3853). *Some scuffing and surface marks on obverse, otherwise about very fine / good very fine.* £250-300

Price Realised : £288

This coin was purchased from one of the groups of coins from the wreck of the RMS *Douro* that were not sold by auction and within the last 10 years.
Calendar year mintage 4,047,288. See footnote for lot 484, page 156, for a brief synopsis of the 1866 die numbers.

158 **Victoria,** Sovereign, 1866, die number 22, second larger young head left, ww incuse on truncation without stops, date below, curvy rounded 6's with bulbous top lightly die flawed shut, *rev* crowned quartered shield of arms within laurel wreath, die number 22 below die flawed, emblems below, trace of doubling of legend, 7.98g (Marsh 51; MCE 527; S 3853). *Toned, with only the lightest trace of surface marks, a very pleasing coin, practically as struck.* £600-800

Price Realised : £840

ex Douro Cargo, Spink Auction 118, 20-21 November 1996, lot 329
Calendar year mintage 4,047,288. See footnote for lot 484, page 156, for a brief synopsis of the 1866 die numbers.

159 **Victoria,** Sovereign, 1866, die number 23, second larger young head left, ww incuse on truncation without stops, date below, curvy rounded 6's with bulbous top lightly die flawed shut, *rev* crowned quartered shield of arms within laurel wreath, die number 23 below lightly die flawed, emblems below, 7.96g (Marsh 51; MCE 527; S 3853). *Surface marks, some scuffing and blemishes, brilliant obverse with matt reverse, good very fine.* £300-350

Price Realised : £264

ex Paul Davies Ltd. This coin was purchased from one of the groups of coins from the wreck of the RMS *Douro* that were not sold by auction and within the last 10 years.
Calendar year mintage 4,047,288. See footnote for lot 484, page 156, for a brief synopsis of the 1866 die numbers.

492 **Victoria,** Sovereign, 1866, die number 24, second larger young head left, ww incuse on truncation without stops, date below doubled and die flawed, curvy rounded 6's with bulbous top, some doubling of legend both sides, *rev* crowned quartered shield of arms within laurel wreath, die number 24 below, emblems below, die flaw from left crown arch to rim, 7.98g (Marsh 51; MCE 527; S 3853). *Some haymarking and hairlines, good extremely fine.* £400-500

Price Realised : £504

ex Randy Weir Numismatics, Unionville, Ontario, Canada, purchased October 1991
Calendar year mintage 4,047,288. See footnote for lot 484, page 156, for a brief synopsis of the 1866 die numbers.

1075 Victoria, Sovereign, 1866, die number 25, second larger young head left, ww incuse on truncation without stops, date below, curvy rounded 6's with bulbous top die flawed shut, *rev* crowned quartered shield of arms within laurel wreath, die number 25 below, emblems below, 7.98g (Marsh 51; MCE 527; S 3853). *Very scuffed and hairlined both sides, otherwise brilliant proof-like extremely fine, reverse better.* £300-400

Price Realised : £288

ex Randy Weir Numismatics, Unionville, Ontario, Canada, July 1993
Calendar year mintage 4,047,288
See footnote for lot 484, page 156, for a brief synopsis of the 1866 die numbers.

493 Victoria, Sovereign, 1866, die number 26, second larger young head left, ww incuse on truncation without stops, date below doubled and die flawed, low 1 in date, curvy rounded 6's with bulbous top, *rev* crowned quartered shield of arms within laurel wreath, die number 26 below widely spaced, emblems below, 7.96g (Marsh 51; MCE 527; S 3853). *Some light surface marks, short scratch by eye, bold very fine, reverse better.* £300-350

Price Realised : £288

This coin was purchased from one of the groups of coins from the wreck of the RMS *Douro* that were not sold by auction and within the last 10 years.
Calendar year mintage 4,047,288. See footnote for lot 484, page 156, for a brief synopsis of the 1866 die numbers.

1076 Victoria, Sovereign, 1866, die number 27, second larger young head left, ww incuse on truncation without stops, date below, curvy rounded 6's with bulbous top die flawed shut, *rev* crowned quartered shield of arms within laurel wreath, die number 27 below, emblems below, trace of doubling to legend, 7.98g (Marsh 51; MCE 527; S 3853). *Once cleaned, now toned, some scratches to cheek, bold very fine.* £250-300

Price Realised : £216

This coin was purchased from one of the groups of coins from the wreck of the RMS *Douro* that were not sold by auction and within the last 10 years.
Calendar year mintage 4,047,288
See footnote for lot 484, page 156, for a brief synopsis of the 1866 die numbers.

494 Victoria, Sovereign, 1866, die number 28, second larger young head left, ww incuse on truncation without stops, date below, curvy rounded open 6's with bulbous top, *rev* crowned quartered shield of arms within laurel wreath, die number 28 below, emblems below, first N of legend doubled, 7.98g (Marsh 51; MCE 527; S 3853). *Some light surface marks, extremely fine / good extremely fine.* £350-450

Price Realised : £504

ex Randy Weir Numismatics, Unionville, Ontario, Canada, purchased 14 November 1990
Calendar year mintage 4,047,288
See footnote for lot 484, page 156, for a brief synopsis of the 1866 die numbers.

1077 **Victoria,** Sovereign, 1866, die number 29, second larger young head left, ww incuse on truncation without stops, date below, curvy rounded 6's with bulbous top, *rev* crowned quartered shield of arms within laurel wreath, die number 29 below, emblems below, trace of doubling to legend, hairline die flaw connects some letters at end of first word and the second, 7.99g (Marsh 51; MCE 527; S 3853). *Hairlined both sides, with underlying proof-like lustre on obverse, matt reverse, otherwise extremely fine, reverse better.* £300-400

Price Realised : £264

purchased via Spink and Son Ltd, November 2003
This coin was previously graded by NGC as MS60
Calendar year mintage 4,047,288. See footnote for lot 484, page 156, for a brief synopsis of the 1866 die numbers.

160 **Victoria,** Sovereign, 1866, die number 30, second larger young head left, ww incuse on truncation without stops, date below, curvy rounded 6's with bulbous top, last 6 with raised die flaw, penultimate A flawed, *rev* struck with inverted die axis, crowned shield of arms within laurel wreath, die number 30 below, emblems below, some light die flaws in legend and near die number, 7.98g (Marsh 51; MCE 527; S 3853). *Once cleaned, light surface marks, nearly extremely fine.* £350-400

Price Realised : £300

ex Randy Weir Numismatics, Unionville, Ontario, Canada, c.2000
Calendar year mintage 4,047,288. See footnote for lot 484, page 156, for a brief synopsis of the 1866 die numbers.

161 **Victoria,** Sovereign, 1866, die number 31, second larger young head left, ww incuse on truncation without stops, date below, curvy rounded 6's with bulbous top lightly die flawed shut, *rev* crowned quartered shield of arms within laurel wreath, die number 31 below, emblems below, 7.98g (Marsh 51; MCE 527; S 3853). *Red spot on obverse, black spot on reverse rim, light hairline marks and scratch on cheek, otherwise extremely fine.* £350-450

Price Realised : £336

ex Douro Cargo, Spink Auction 118, 20-21 November 1996, uncertain lot number.
ex An Important Collection of Gold Sovereigns 1816-2000, offered as one lot, Sothebys, 16-17 November 2000, lot 525 (part)
Calendar year mintage 4,047,288. See footnote for lot 484, page 156, for a brief synopsis of the 1866 die numbers.

495 **Victoria,** Sovereign, 1866, die number 32, second larger young head left, ww incuse on truncation without stops, date below, second 6 die flawed, curvy rounded 6's with bulbous top, last A of legend die flawed, *rev* crowned quartered shield of arms within laurel wreath, die number 32 below, emblems below, hint of doubling in reverse legend, die flaw by G, 7.98g (Marsh 51; MCE 527; S 3853). *Some light surface marks and scuffs, extremely fine, reverse better.* £300-400

Price Realised : £384

ex Douro Cargo, Spink Auction 118, 20-21 November 1996, lot 330 (part)
Calendar year mintage 4,047,288. See footnote for lot 484, page 156, for a brief synopsis of the 1866 die numbers.

162 **Victoria,** Sovereign, 1866, die number 33, second larger young head left, ww incuse on truncation without stops, date below, curvy rounded 6's with bulbous top, *rev* crowned quartered shield of arms within laurel wreath, die number 33 below, emblems below, hint of doubling in legend, 7.97g (Marsh 51; MCE 527; S 3853). *Toned, light surface marks, nearly very fine, reverse better.* £300-350

Price Realised : £264

ex Paul Davies Ltd. This coin was purchased from one of the groups of coins from the wreck of the RMS *Douro* that were not sold by auction and within the last 10 years.
Calendar year mintage 4,047,288
See footnote for lot 484, page 156, for a brief synopsis of the 1866 die numbers.

1078 **Victoria,** Sovereign, 1866, die number 34, second larger young head left, ww incuse on truncation without stops, date below, curvy rounded 6's with bulbous top, last I of legend die flawed to rim, *rev* crowned quartered shield of arms within laurel wreath, die number 34 below, 3 of number die flawed, emblems below, hint of doubling to legend, 7.99g (Marsh 51; MCE 527; S 3853). *Surface marks and hairlines both sides, otherwise extremely fine, reverse better.* £300-400

Price Realised : £264

ex Randy Weir Numismatics, Unionville, Ontario, Canada, 18 April 1994
Calendar year mintage 4,047,288
See footnote for lot 484, page 156, for a brief synopsis of the 1866 die numbers.

163 **Victoria,** Sovereign, 1866, die number 35, second larger young head left, ww incuse on truncation without stops, date below, curvy rounded 6's with bulbous top, last I in legend die flawed to rim, *rev* crowned quartered shield of arms within laurel wreath, die number 35 below, emblems below, hint of doubling in legend, 7.98g (Marsh 51; MCE 527; S 3853). *Light surface marks, extremely fine, reverse better.* £350-400

Price Realised : £432

ex Douro Cargo, Spink Auction 118, 20-21 November 1996, uncertain lot number.
ex An Important Collection of Gold Sovereigns 1816-2000, offered as one lot, Sothebys, 16-17 November 2000, lot 525 (part)
Calendar year mintage 4,047,288
See footnote for lot 484, page 156, for a brief synopsis of the 1866 die numbers.

496 **Victoria,** Sovereign, 1866, die number 36, second larger young head left, ww incuse on truncation without stops, date below, curvy rounded 6's with bulbous top, C of queen's name die flawed, *rev* crowned quartered shield of arms within laurel wreath, die number 36 below, emblems below, 7.96g (Marsh 51; MCE 527; S 3853). *Some light spots on reverse good very fine.* £300-350

Price Realised : £264

This coin was purchased from one of the groups of coins from the wreck of the RMS *Douro* that were not sold by auction and within the last 10 years.
Calendar year mintage 4,047,288. See footnote for lot 484, page 156, for a brief synopsis of the 1866 die numbers.

497 **Victoria,** Sovereign, 1866, die number 37, second larger young head left, WW incuse on truncation without stops, date below, curvy rounded open 6's with bulbous top, *rev* crowned quartered shield of arms within laurel wreath, die number 37 below, emblems below, 7.98g (Marsh 51; MCE 527; S 3853). *Rim nick on obverse, old light scratch on face, otherwise extremely fine / good extremely fine.* £350-450

Price Realised : £432

ex Warwick and Warwick Auction, before 2000, lot 479
ex An Important Collection of Gold Sovereigns 1816-2000, offered as one lot, Sothebys, November 2000, lot 525 (part)
Calendar year mintage 4,047,288
See footnote for lot 484, page 156, for a brief synopsis of the 1866 die numbers.

498 **Victoria,** Sovereign, 1866, die number 38, second larger young head left, WW incuse on truncation without stops, date below, curvy rounded open 6's with bulbous top, *rev* crowned quartered shield of arms within laurel wreath, die number 38 below, emblems below, 7.98g (Marsh 51; MCE 527; S 3853). *Some light surface marks, otherwise good extremely fine.* £400-500

Price Realised : £504

ex Randy Weir Numismatics, Unionville, Ontario, Canada, purchased 6 July 1990
Calendar year mintage 4,047,288
See footnote for lot 484, page 156, for a brief synopsis of the 1866 die numbers.

1079 **Victoria,** Sovereign, 1866, die number 39, second larger young head left, WW incuse on truncation without stops, date below, curvy rounded 6's with bulbous top die flawed shut, both 6's lightly die flawed, further die flaw by first four letters of legend, *rev* crowned quartered shield of arms within laurel wreath, die number 39 below, emblems below, hint of doubling in legend, 7.99g (Marsh 51; MCE 527; S 3853). *A few black spots and surface marks on the reverse, otherwise extremely fine.* £300-400

Price Realised : £264

ex Douro Cargo, Spink Auction 118, 20-21 November 1996, lot 1315 (part)
Calendar year mintage 4,047,288
See footnote for lot 484, page 156, for a brief synopsis of the 1866 die numbers.

164 **Victoria,** Sovereign, 1866, die number 40, second larger young head left, WW incuse on truncation without stops, date below, curvy rounded 6's with bulbous top, *rev* crowned quartered shield of arms within laurel wreath, die number 40 below, emblems below, 7.99g (Marsh 51; MCE 527; S 3853). *An early strike with proof-like surfaces, a few light surface marks and two light scratches on neck, otherwise good extremely fine and very pleasing.* £400-500

Price Realised : £480

ex An Important Collection of Gold Sovereigns 1816-2000, offered as one lot, Sothebys, 16-17 November 2000, lot 525 (part)
Calendar year mintage 4,047,288
See footnote for lot 484, page 156, for a brief synopsis of the 1866 die numbers.

499 **Victoria,** Sovereign, 1866, die number 41, second larger young head left, WW incuse on truncation without stops, date below, curvy rounded open 6's with bulbous top, *rev* crowned quartered shield of arms within laurel wreath, die number 41 below, emblems below, 7.98g (Marsh 51; MCE 527; S 3853). *Some light hairlines, extremely fine / good extremely fine.* £400-500

Price Realised : £432

ex Randy Weir Numismatics, Unionville, Ontario, Canada, purchased 13 June 1997
Calendar year mintage 4,047,288
See footnote for lot 484, page 156, for a brief synopsis of the 1866 die numbers.

1080 **Victoria,** Sovereign, 1866, die number 42, second larger young head left, WW incuse on truncation without stops, date below, curvy rounded 6's with bulbous top, the second 6 die flawed shut, die flaw at first O of legend to rim, further flaw at last A of legend, *rev* crowned quartered shield of arms within laurel wreath, die number 42 below, emblems below, 7.97g (Marsh 51; MCE 527; S 3853). *Small red spot at rear of neck and other surface marks, rim nick, otherwise extremely fine / good extremely fine.* £300-400

Price Realised : £312

ex Douro Cargo, Spink Auction 118, 20-21 November 1996, lot 332 (part)
Calendar year mintage 4,047,288
See footnote for lot 484, page 156, for a brief synopsis of the 1866 die numbers.

165 **Victoria,** Sovereign, 1866, die number 43, second larger young head left, WW incuse on truncation without stops, date below lightly doubled, curvy rounded 6's with bulbous top, 1 with raised die flaw, obverse legend doubled, *rev* crowned quartered shield of arms within laurel wreath, die number 43 below lightly flawed, emblems below, last N flawed, legend more heavily doubled with some light raised die flaws running to leaves, 7.98g (Marsh 51; MCE 527; S 3853). *Toned with some hairlines, pleasing, good extremely fine.* £400-500

Price Realised : £552

Calendar year mintage 4,047,288
See footnote for lot 484, page 156, for a brief synopsis of the 1866 die numbers.

1081 **Victoria,** Sovereign, 1866, die number 44, second larger young head left, WW incuse on truncation without stops, date below, curvy rounded 6's with bulbous top, die flaw through 1 of date from neck to rim, further flaw at last letter T to rim, with some doubling of legend, *rev* crowned quartered shield of arms within laurel wreath, die number 44 below, the 4's filled, emblems below, first N of legend with die flaw to rim, 7.96g (Marsh 51; MCE 527; S 3853). *Some surface marks, tiny spots on obverse, otherwise toned, bold very fine.* £250-300

Price Realised : £240

ex Douro Cargo, Spink Auction 118, 20-21 November 1996, lot 1319 (part)
Calendar year mintage 4,047,288
See footnote for lot 484, page 156, for a brief synopsis of the 1866 die numbers.

166 **Victoria,** Sovereign, 1866, die number 45, second larger young head left, ww incuse on truncation without stops, date below, curvy rounded 6's with bulbous top, *rev* crowned quartered shield of arms within laurel wreath, die number 45 below, emblems below, 7.97g (Marsh 51; MCE 527; S 3853). *Some patches of tone on obverse and black spots on reverse, scratch across neck and face onto field at top, light surface marks, bold very fine.* £300-350

Price Realised : £288

ex Douro Cargo, Spink Auction 118, 20-21 November 1996, uncertain lot number.
ex An Important Collection of Gold Sovereigns 1816-2000, offered as one lot, Sothebys, 16-17 November 2000, lot 525 (part)
Calendar year mintage 4,047,288. See footnote for lot 484, page 156, for a brief synopsis of the 1866 die numbers.

500 **Victoria,** Sovereign, 1866, die number 46, second larger young head left, ww incuse on truncation without stops, date below, curvy rounded open 6's with bulbous top, die flaw from I of queen's name to cheek, *rev* crowned quartered shield of arms within laurel wreath, die number 46 below, emblems below, trace of doubling in legend, die flaw on R of second word, 7.97g (Marsh 51; MCE 527; S 3853). *Streak of tone on reverse and other light marks, extremely fine / good extremely fine.* £350-450

Price Realised : £456

ex Douro Cargo, Spink Auction 118, 20-21 November 1996, lot 333 (part)
Calendar year mintage 4,047,288. See footnote for lot 484, page 156, for a brief synopsis of the 1866 die numbers.

501 **Victoria,** Sovereign, 1866, die number 47, second larger young head left, ww incuse on truncation without stops, date below, curvy rounded 6's with bulbous top, *rev* crowned quartered shield of arms within laurel wreath, die number 47 below, emblems below, trace of doubling in legend, 7.99g (Marsh 51; MCE 527; S 3853). *Light surface marks and hairlines, spot by throat and top of head, patch of tone and a few spots on reverse, otherwise extremely fine.* £300-400

Price Realised : £360

This coin was purchased from one of the groups of coins from the wreck of the RMS *Douro* that were not sold by auction and within the last 10 years.
Calendar year mintage 4,047,288. See footnote for lot 484, page 156, for a brief synopsis of the 1866 die numbers.

1082 **Victoria,** Sovereign, 1866, die number 48, second larger young head left, ww incuse on truncation without stops, date below, curvy rounded 6's with bulbous top die flawed shut, date doubled, along with last few letters of legend, *rev* crowned quartered shield of arms within laurel wreath, die number 48 below, emblems below, 7.97g (Marsh 51; MCE 527; S 3853). *Some surface marks and hairlines, otherwise toned, extremely fine.* £300-400

Price Realised : £264

ex Douro Cargo, Spink Auction 118, 20-21 November 1996, lot 554 (part)
Calendar year mintage 4,047,288
See footnote for lot 484, page 156, for a brief synopsis of the 1866 die numbers.

167 **Victoria,** Sovereign, 1866, die number 49, second larger young head left, WW incuse on truncation without stops, date below, curvy rounded 6's with bulbous top, *rev* crowned quartered shield of arms within laurel wreath, die number 49 below die flawed, emblems below, trace of doubling in legend, 7.97g (Marsh 51; MCE 527; S 3853). *Some spots on reverse, other light nicks and surface marks, extremely fine.* £350-450

Price Realised : £384

ex Douro Cargo, Spink Auction 118, 20-21 November 1996, lot 1357 (part)
Calendar year mintage 4,047,288
See footnote for lot 484, page 156, for a brief synopsis of the 1866 die numbers.

502 **Victoria,** Sovereign, 1866, die number 50, second larger young head left, WW incuse on truncation without stops, date below, curvy rounded 6's with bulbous top, die flawed V in legend, *rev* crowned quartered shield of arms within laurel wreath, die number 50 below, emblems below, trace of doubling in legend, 7.98g (Marsh 51; MCE 527; S 3853). *Tiny nick by nose in field, other light marks otherwise good extremely fine.* £350-450

Price Realised : £504

ex Douro Cargo, Spink Auction 118, 20-21 November 1996, lot 554 (part)
Calendar year mintage 4,047,288
See footnote for lot 484, page 156, for a brief synopsis of the 1866 die numbers.

1083 **Victoria,** Sovereign, 1866, die number 51, second larger young head left, WW incuse on truncation without stops, date below, curvy rounded 6's with bulbous top die flawed shut, last I of legend die flawed, *rev* crowned quartered shield of arms within laurel wreath, die number 51 below with die flaw, emblems below, hint of doubling to legend, last A with die flaw, 7.99g (Marsh 51; MCE 527; S 3853). *Some surface marks, almost extremely fine, reverse better.* £300-400

Price Realised : £264

ex Douro Cargo, Spink Auction 118, 20-21 November 1996, lot 1319 (part)
Calendar year mintage 4,047,288
See footnote for lot 484, page 156, for a brief synopsis of the 1866 die numbers.

1084 **Victoria,** Sovereign, 1866, die number 52, second larger young head left, WW incuse on truncation without stops, date below, curvy rounded 6's with bulbous top, obverse legend doubled, last T of legend with die flaw into field, *rev* crowned quartered shield of arms within laurel wreath, die number 52 below, emblems below, hint of doubling to legend, 7.95g (Marsh 51; MCE 527; S 3853). *Some surface marks and hairlines, otherwise good fine / very fine.* £250-300

Price Realised : £216

Calendar year mintage 4,047,288
See footnote for lot 484, page 156, for a brief synopsis of the 1866 die numbers.

168 **Victoria,** Sovereign, 1866, die number 53, second larger young head left, WW incuse on truncation without stops, date below, curvy rounded 6's with bulbous top, V of legend flawed, *rev* crowned quartered shield of arms within laurel wreath, die number 53 below, emblems below, raised die flaw between I and D and trace of doubling in legend, 7.99g (Marsh 51; MCE 527; S 3853). *Proof-like on reverse, a few light marks, extremely fine / good extremely fine.* £400-500

Price Realised : £432

Calendar year mintage 4,047,288
See footnote for lot 484, page 156, for a brief synopsis of the 1866 die numbers.

169 **Victoria,** Sovereign, 1866, die number 54, second larger young head left, WW incuse on truncation without stops, date below, curvy rounded 6's with bulbous top, 1 of date doubled, penultimate A flawed, *rev* crowned quartered shield of arms within laurel wreath, die number 54 below, emblems below, 7.93g (Marsh 51; MCE 527; S 3853). *Once cleaned, with some scuffing, now toning, good fine / very fine.* £300-350

Price Realised : £264

ex Spink and Son Ltd, November 2003
Calendar year mintage 4,047,288
See footnote for lot 484, page 156, for a brief synopsis of the 1866 die numbers.

1085 **Victoria,** Sovereign, 1866, die number 55, second larger young head left, WW incuse on truncation without stops, date below, curvy rounded 6's with bulbous top, *rev* crowned quartered shield of arms within laurel wreath, die number 55 below, emblems below, hint of doubling to legend, die flaw to right rosette at lower part of wreath, 7.97g (Marsh 51; MCE 527; S 3853). *Surface marks and hairlines both sides, of matt appearance, otherwise good extremely fine.* £300-400

Price Realised : £360

ex Randy Weir Numismatics, Unionville, Ontario, Canada, 14 June 1994
Calendar year mintage 4,047,288
See footnote for lot 484, page 156, for a brief synopsis of the 1866 die numbers.

503 **Victoria,** Sovereign, 1866, die number 56, second larger young head left, WW incuse on truncation without stops, date below, curvy rounded 6's with bulbous top, die flaw from T to rim in legend, *rev* crowned quartered shield of arms within laurel wreath, die number 56 below, emblems below, 7.95g (Marsh 51; MCE 527; S 3853). *Some hairlines, otherwise nearly extremely fine.* £300-400

Price Realised : £288

This coin was purchased from one of the groups of coins from the wreck of the RMS *Douro* that were not sold by auction and within the last 10 years.
Calendar year mintage 4,047,288
See footnote for lot 484, page 156, for a brief synopsis of the 1866 die numbers.

1086 **Victoria,** Sovereign, 1866, die number 57, second larger young head left, ww incuse on truncation without stops, date below, curvy rounded 6's with bulbous top die flawed shut, second 6 die flawed from neck to rim, *rev* crowned quartered shield of arms within laurel wreath, die number 57 below, emblems below, 7.87g (Marsh 51; MCE 527; S 3853). *Surface marks and hairlines, fair, reverse better.* £250-300

Price Realised : £216

ex Paul Davies Ltd, Ilkley, October 2006
It is interesting to note that the weight of this coin in its lower grade is well under the legal tender limit as dictated by the Coinage Acts of 1816-1891.
Calendar year mintage 4,047,288
See footnote for lot 484, page 156, for a brief synopsis of the 1866 die numbers.

170 **Victoria,** Sovereign, 1866, die number 58, second larger young head left, ww incuse on truncation without stops, date below, curvy rounded 6's with bulbous top, penultimate A flawed, *rev* struck with inverted die axis, crowned shield of arms within laurel wreath, die number 58 below, emblems below, raised die flaw between A and N of legend, 7.99g (Marsh 51; MCE 527; S 3853). *Light surface marks, toned, good extremely fine.* £500-600

Price Realised : £744

ex Douro Cargo, Spink Auction 118, 20-21 November 1996, lot 1359 (part)
Calendar year mintage 4,047,288
See footnote for lot 484, page 156, for a brief synopsis of the 1866 die numbers.

171 **Victoria,** Sovereign, 1866, die number 59, second larger young head left, ww incuse on truncation without stops, date below, curvy rounded 6's with bulbous top, die flaw from 8 to rim, *rev* crowned quartered shield of arms within laurel wreath, die number 59 below, emblems below, 7.97g (Marsh 51; MCE 527; S 3853). *Some scuffs and hairlines, very fine, reverse better.* £300-350

Price Realised : £264

ex Douro Cargo, Spink Auction 118, 20-21 November 1996, lot 1321 (part)
Calendar year mintage 4,047,288
See footnote for lot 484, page 156, for a brief synopsis of the 1866 die numbers.

504 **Victoria,** Sovereign, 1866, die number 60, second larger young head left, ww incuse on truncation without stops, date below, curvy rounded 6's with bulbous top, last A die flawed to rim, *rev* crowned quartered shield of arms within laurel wreath, die number 60 below, emblems below, trace of doubling in legend, 7.99g (Marsh 51; MCE 527; S 3853). *Nearly extremely fine / brilliant extremely fine.* £300-400

Price Realised : £312

Calendar year mintage 4,047,288
See footnote for lot 484, page 156, for a brief synopsis of the 1866 die numbers.

1087 **Victoria,** Sovereign, 1866, die number 61, second larger young head left, ww incuse on truncation without stops, date below, curvy rounded 6's with bulbous top die flawed shut, last I of legend die flawed, *rev* crowned quartered shield of arms within laurel wreath, die number 61 below with die flaw, emblems below, hint of doubling to legend, 7.98g (Marsh 51; MCE 527; S 3853). *Some surface marks and hairlines, extremely fine, reverse better.* £300-400

Price Realised : £312

ex Douro Cargo, Spink Auction 118, 20-21 November 1996, lot 1359 (part)
Calendar year mintage 4,047,288. See footnote for lot 484, page 156, for a brief synopsis of the 1866 die numbers.

505 **Victoria,** Sovereign, 1866, die number 62, second larger young head left, ww incuse on truncation without stops, date below, curvy rounded 6's with bulbous top, penultimate I die flawed to rim, *rev* crowned quartered shield of arms within laurel wreath, die number 62 below, emblems below, 7.97g (Marsh 51; MCE 527; S 3853). *Scuffed, black streak of tone on reverse, nearly extremely fine / extremely fine.* £300-400

Price Realised : £312

ex Douro Cargo, Spink Auction 118, 20-21 November 1996, lot 1321 (part)
Calendar year mintage 4,047,288. See footnote for lot 484, page 156, for a brief synopsis of the 1866 die numbers.

172 **Victoria,** Sovereign, 1866, die number 63, second larger young head left, ww incuse on truncation without stops, date below, curvy rounded 6's with bulbous top lightly die flawed shut, flaw before last A, *rev* crowned quartered shield of arms within laurel wreath, die number 63 below, emblems below, hint of doubling in legend, 7.98g (Marsh 51; MCE 527; S 3853). *Hairline scratch on neck with some tiny spots, rim nick, surface marks, otherwise good extremely fine.* £400-500

Price Realised : £552

ex Douro Cargo, Spink Auction 118, 20-21 November 1996, lot 554 (part)
Calendar year mintage 4,047,288. See footnote for lot 484, page 156, for a brief synopsis of the 1866 die numbers.

1088 **Victoria,** Sovereign, 1866, die number 64, second larger young head left, ww incuse on truncation without stops, date below, curvy rounded 6's with bulbous top die flawed shut, die flaw through 1 of date from neck to rim, first two words slightly doubled, *rev* crowned quartered shield of arms within laurel wreath, die number 64 below, emblems below, trace of doubling to legend, 7.96g (Marsh 51; MCE 527; S 3853). *Some light marks, toned, almost very fine, reverse better.* £250-300

Price Realised : £216

This coin was purchased from one of the groups of coins from the wreck of the RMS *Douro* that were not sold by auction and within the last 10 years.
Calendar year mintage 4,047,288
See footnote for lot 484, page 156, for a brief synopsis of the 1866 die numbers.

173 **Victoria,** Sovereign, 1866, die number 65, second larger young head left, WW incuse on truncation without stops, date below, curvy rounded 6's with bulbous top, last 6 lightly die flawed shut, *rev* crowned quartered shield of arms within laurel wreath, die number 65 below, emblems below, 7.96g (Marsh 51; MCE 527; S 3853). *Once cleaned, now lightly toned, light short scratch at lower right of reverse, some surface marks with some scuffs on obverse, otherwise nearly extremely fine.* £300-350

Price Realised : £264

Calendar year mintage 4,047,288
See footnote for lot 484, page 156, for a brief synopsis of the 1866 die numbers.

506 **Victoria,** Sovereign, 1866, die number 66, second larger young head left, WW incuse on truncation without stops, date below, curvy rounded 6's with bulbous top, last R die flawed to hair, *rev* crowned quartered shield of arms within laurel wreath, die number 66 below, emblems below, trace of doubling in legend, 7.99g (Marsh 51; MCE 527; S 3853). *Light hairline marks, short scratch behind neck, toned extremely fine.* £300-400

Price Realised : £528

ex Douro Cargo, Spink Auction 118, 20-21 November 1996, lot 1359 (part)
Calendar year mintage 4,047,288. See footnote for lot 484, page 156, for a brief synopsis of the 1866 die numbers.

1089 **Victoria,** Sovereign, 1866, die number 67, second larger young head left, WW incuse on truncation without stops, date below, curvy rounded 6's with bulbous top die flawed shut, *rev* crowned quartered shield of arms within laurel wreath, die number 67 below, emblems below, 7.97g (Marsh 51; MCE 527; S 3853). *Scratch in field behind bust near ponytail of hair, other light marks and scuffs, otherwise almost extremely fine, reverse better, this die number unlisted by Marsh, therefore rare.* £300-400

Price Realised : £336

This coin was purchased from one of the groups of coins from the wreck of the RMS *Douro* that were not sold by auction and within the last 10 years.
This die number is the only one in the Bentley Collection for 1866 unlisted by Marsh. Inversely the Bentley Collection does not contain a die number 12 or 79 for 1866 which are listed by Marsh as existing.
Calendar year mintage 4,047,288. See footnote for lot 484, page 156, for a brief synopsis of the 1866 die numbers.

174 **Victoria,** Sovereign, 1866, die number 68, second larger young head left, WW incuse on truncation without stops, date below, curvy rounded 6's with bulbous top lightly die flawed shut, second 6 die flawed from rim to neck, last A of legend die flawed, obverse legend doubled, *rev* crowned quartered shield of arms within laurel wreath, die number 68 below, the 8 doubled, emblems below, hint of doubling to legend, 7.98g (Marsh 51; MCE 527; S 3853). *Some scuffs and light surface marks, toned, extremely fine.* £350-450

Price Realised : £408

Calendar year mintage 4,047,288
See footnote for lot 484, page 156, for a brief synopsis of the 1866 die numbers.

507 **Victoria,** Sovereign, 1866, die number 69, second larger young head left, ww incuse on truncation without stops, date below, curvy rounded open 6's with bulbous top, hint of doubling both sides, *rev* crowned quartered shield of arms within laurel wreath, die number 69 below, emblems below, 7.99g (Marsh 51; MCE 527; S 3853). *Light hairlines and surface marks, nearly extremely fine.* £300-350

Price Realised : £312

ex Spink Numismatic Circular, February 1998, item 522
ex An Important Collection of Gold Sovereigns 1816-2000, offered as one lot, Sothebys, November 2000, lot 525 (part)
Calendar year mintage 4,047,288. See footnote for lot 484, page 156, for a brief synopsis of the 1866 die numbers.

508 **Victoria,** Sovereign, 1866, die number 70, second larger young head left, ww incuse on truncation without stops, die flaw from tip of neck into field, date below, curvy rounded 6's with bulbous top, hint of doubling in obverse legend, *rev* crowned quartered shield of arms within laurel wreath, die number 70 below, die flaw above 70, emblems below, 7.98g (Marsh 51; MCE 527; S 3853). *Light hairlines, tiny rim nick, good extremely fine.* £400-500

Price Realised : £528

Calendar year mintage 4,047,288
See footnote for lot 484, page 156, for a brief synopsis of the 1866 die numbers.

1090 **Victoria,** Sovereign, 1866, die number 71, second larger young head left, ww incuse on truncation without stops, date below, curvy rounded 6's with bulbous top die flawed shut, date and parts of legend doubled both sides, *rev* crowned quartered shield of arms within laurel wreath, die number 71 below with die flaw, emblems below, 7.97g (Marsh 51; MCE 527; S 3853). *Some light hairlines, toned, good very fine.* £250-300

Price Realised : £288

ex Douro Cargo, Spink Auction 118, 20-21 November 1996, lot 334 (part)
Calendar year mintage 4,047,288
See footnote for lot 484, page 156, for a brief synopsis of the 1866 die numbers.

175 **Victoria,** Sovereign, 1866, die number 72, second larger young head left, ww incuse on truncation without stops, date below, 1 with raised die flaw, curvy rounded 6's with bulbous top lightly die flawed shut, a mere hint of doubling to legends both sides, *rev* crowned quartered shield of arms within laurel wreath, die number 72 below, the 7 smaller than the 2, emblems below, 7.95g (Marsh 51; MCE 527; S 3853). *Red spot by D of* DEI, *toned, almost very fine.* £300-350

Price Realised : £264

ex Paul Davies Ltd. This coin was purchased from one of the groups of coins from the wreck of the RMS *Douro* that were not sold by auction and within the last 10 years.
Calendar year mintage 4,047,288
See footnote for lot 484, page 156, for a brief synopsis of the 1866 die numbers.

1091 Victoria, Sovereign, 1866, die number 73, second larger young head left, ww incuse on truncation without stops, date below, curvy rounded 6's with bulbous top, tip of neck slightly die flawed and first V of legend to rim, last two letters of legend joined by flaw, *rev* crowned quartered shield of arms within laurel wreath, die number 73 below with die flaw, emblems below, hint of legend doubling, 7.98g (Marsh 51; MCE 527; S 3853). *Some light hairlines, rim nick on reverse, almost extremely fine, reverse better.* £250-300

Price Realised : £288

Calendar year mintage 4,047,288
See footnote for lot 484, page 156, for a brief synopsis of the 1866 die numbers.

176 Victoria, Sovereign, 1866, die number 74, second larger young head left, ww incuse on truncation without stops, date below, curvy rounded 6's with bulbous top lightly die flawed shut, first V with raised die flaw to rim, last I and A of obverse legend die flawed, *rev* crowned quartered shield of arms within laurel wreath, die number 74 below die flawed, emblems below, light raised die flaw in some letters, 7.97g (Marsh 51; MCE 527; S 3853). *Short scratch on cheek, some nicks and light surface marks, good very fine.* £300-350

Price Realised : £264

Calendar year mintage 4,047,288
See footnote for lot 484, page 156, for a brief synopsis of the 1866 die numbers.

509 Victoria, Sovereign, 1866, die number 75, second larger young head left, ww incuse on truncation without stops, date below, curvy rounded 6's with bulbous top, *rev* crowned quartered shield of arms within laurel wreath, die number 75 below die flawed, emblems below, 7.95g (Marsh 51; MCE 527; S 3853). *Red patches of tone on obverse, toned nearly very fine, reverse better.* £300-350

Price Realised : £264

This coin was purchased from one of the groups of coins from the wreck of the RMS *Douro* that were not sold by auction and within the last 10 years.
Calendar year mintage 4,047,288. See footnote for lot 484, page 156, for a brief synopsis of the 1866 die numbers.

1092 Victoria, Sovereign, 1866, die number 76, second larger young head left, ww incuse on truncation without stops, date below, curvy rounded 6's with bulbous top die flawed shut, *rev* crowned quartered shield of arms within laurel wreath, die number 76 below with die flaw, emblems below, 7.90g (Marsh 51; MCE 527; S 3853). *Scuffed with surface marks, digs, pits and hairlines, toned, bold fine.* £250-300

Price Realised : £240

ex GK Coins, London, via Spink and Son Ltd, November 2003
It is interesting to note that the weight of this coin in its lower grade is under the legal tender limit as dictated by the Coinage Acts of 1816-1891.
Calendar year mintage 4,047,288
See footnote for lot 484, page 156, for a brief synopsis of the 1866 die numbers.

177 **Victoria,** Sovereign, 1866, die number 77, second larger young head left, ww incuse on truncation without stops, date below lightly doubled, curvy rounded 6's with bulbous top lightly die flawed shut, hint of doubling in legends both sides, *rev* crowned quartered shield of arms within laurel wreath, die number 77 below die flawed, emblems below, 7.99g (Marsh 51; MCE 527; S 3853). *Cleaned, with associated surface marks and scuffs, light scratch by ear, rim bruise on reverse, almost extremely fine.* £300-350

Price Realised : £264

ex Paul Davies Ltd. This coin was purchased from one of the groups of coins from the wreck of the RMS *Douro* that were not sold by auction and within the last 10 years.
Calendar year mintage 4,047,288
See footnote for lot 484, page 156, for a brief synopsis of the 1866 die numbers.

510 **Victoria,** Sovereign, 1866, die number 78, second larger young head left, ww incuse on truncation without stops, date doubled below, curvy rounded 6's with bulbous top, last word of obverse legend doubled and lightly flawed, *rev* crowned quartered shield of arms within laurel wreath, die number 78 below, emblems below, hint of doubling in legend, 7.96g (Marsh 51; MCE 527; S 3853). *Cleaned very fine / good very fine.* £300-350

Price Realised : £264

ex Stacks, 2 December 1997, lot 78
ex An Important Collection of Gold Sovereigns 1816-2000, offered as one lot, Sothebys, November 2000, lot 525 (part)
Calendar year mintage 4,047,288
See footnote for lot 484, page 156, for a brief synopsis of the 1866 die numbers.
There were no Sovereigns issued in or dated 1867.

1093 **Victoria,** Sovereign, 1868, die number 1, second larger young head left, ww incuse on truncation without stops, date below, curvy rounded 6 with bulbous top lightly die flawed, *rev* crowned quartered shield of arms within laurel wreath, die number 1 below, emblems below, hint of doubling in legend, 7.94g (Marsh 52; MCE 528; S 3853). *Scratch above date, some scuffs, cleaned, bold fine.* £250-300

Price Realised : £240

This coin was purchased from one of the groups of coins from the wreck of the RMS *Douro* that were not sold by auction and within the last 10 years.
Calendar year mintage 1,653,384
This coin is die number 1 of 40 different numbered dies in the Bentley Collection running from 1 to 41. Marsh claims that die numbers 40, 47 and 48 also exist, which are absent from this collection, making a total of 43 reverse dies to strike just over 1½ million Sovereigns. This suggests a low longevity, but as will be seen the mintage for 1869 is high, so some dies dated 1868 will probably have been used into the year 1869. One die number in the Bentley Collection run of 1868 is not recorded by Marsh, number 10.

178 **Victoria,** Sovereign, 1868, die number 2, second larger young head left, WW incuse on truncation without stops, date below, curvy rounded 6 with bulbous top lightly die flawed, hint of doubling in legends both sides, *rev* crowned quartered shield of arms within laurel wreath, die number 2 below flawed, emblems below, 7.99g (Marsh 52; MCE 528; S 3853). *A few rim nicks and surface marks, extremely fine.* £350-450

Price Realised : £480

ex Randy Weir Numismatics, Unionville, Ontario, Canada, 22 March 1990
Calendar year mintage 1,653,384
See footnote for lot 1093, page 175, for a brief synopsis of the 1868 die numbers.

1094 **Victoria,** Sovereign, 1868, die number 3, second larger young head left, WW incuse on truncation without stops, date below, curvy rounded 6 with bulbous top lightly die flawed, second 8 die flawed, date doubled, hint of doubling in legend both sides, *rev* crowned quartered shield of arms within laurel wreath, die number 3 below, emblems below, hairline raised flaw joins some letters of legend, 7.97g (Marsh 52; MCE 528; S 3853). *Toned with some scuffs, good fine.* £250-300

Price Realised : £264

This coin was purchased from one of the groups of coins from the wreck of the RMS *Douro* that were not sold by auction and within the last 10 years.
Calendar year mintage 1,653,384. See footnote for lot 1093, page 175, for a brief synopsis of the 1868 die numbers.

511 **Victoria,** Sovereign, 1868, die number 4, second larger young head left, WW incuse on truncation without stops, date below, curvy rounded 6 with bulbous top, last A die flawed, hint of doubling in legends both sides, *rev* crowned quartered shield of arms within laurel wreath, die number 4 below, emblems below, 7.99g (Marsh 52; MCE 528; S 3853). *Light scratch on neck and surface marks, extremely fine, reverse better.* £300-400

Price Realised : £480

ex An Important Collection of Gold Sovereigns 1816-2000, offered as one lot, Sothebys, November 2000, lot 525 (part)
Calendar year mintage 1,653,384. See footnote for lot 1093, page 175, for a brief synopsis of the 1868 die numbers.

179 **Victoria,** Sovereign, 1868, die number 5, second larger young head left, WW incuse on truncation without stops, date below, doubled date, curvy rounded 6 with bulbous joined top, last A of obverse flawed, hint of doubling in legends both sides, more so on reverse, *rev* crowned quartered shield of arms within laurel wreath, die number 5 below, emblems below, only a trace of upper serif of first B in legend, 7.98g (Marsh 52; MCE 528; S 3853). *Some nicks and marks on nose and face, other surface marks, bold very fine.* £300-350

Price Realised : £264

ex A H Baldwin & Sons Ltd sourced via Paul Davies Ltd, October 2006.
This coin was purchased from one of the groups of coins from the wreck of the RMS *Douro* that were not sold by auction and within the last 10 years.
Calendar year mintage 1,653,384. See footnote for lot 1093, page 175, for a brief synopsis of the 1868 die numbers.

512 **Victoria,** Sovereign, 1868, die number 6, second larger young head left, ww incuse on truncation without stops, date below, curvy rounded 6 with bulbous top, penultimate I die flawed to rim, doubled obverse legend, *rev* crowned quartered shield of arms within laurel wreath, die number 6 below die flawed, emblems below, raised die flaw between R and I of legend, 7.94g (Marsh 52; MCE 528; S 3853). *Some residual dirt around rim both sides, scuffed with surface marks, fine / good fine.* £300-350

Price Realised : £288

ex Northeast Coins and Treasures, Vermont, USA, via Ebay, September 2003
Calendar year mintage 1,653,384. See footnote for lot 1093, page 175, for a brief synopsis of the 1868 die numbers.

1095 **Victoria,** Sovereign, 1868, die number 7, second larger young head left, ww incuse on truncation without stops, date below, curvy rounded 6 with bulbous top, flaw to right of second 8, die flaw by last A of legend, *rev* crowned quartered shield of arms within laurel wreath, die number 7 below, emblems below, trace of doubling of legend, 7.98g (Marsh 52; MCE 528; S 3853). *Some light hairlines, almost extremely fine, reverse better.* £300-400

Price Realised : £384

ex Douro Cargo, Spink Auction 118, 20-21 November 1996, lot 335 (part)
Calendar year mintage 1,653,384. See footnote for lot 1093, page 175, for a brief synopsis of the 1868 die numbers.

1096 **Victoria,** Sovereign, 1868, die number 8, second larger young head left, ww incuse on truncation without stops, date below, curvy thinner and lower 6 with bulbous top, die flawed 1 in date up to neck, some doubling of legend, *rev* crowned quartered shield of arms within laurel wreath, die number 8 below, emblems below, hairline die flaw connects some letters in legend, upper serif on B weak, 7.97g (Marsh 52; MCE 528; S 3853). *Once cleaned, some red spots each side of coin, now toned, very fine.* £250-300

Price Realised : £312

This coin was purchased from one of the groups of coins from the wreck of the RMS *Douro* that were not sold by auction and within the last 10 years.
Calendar year mintage 1,653,384. See footnote for lot 1093, page 175, for a brief synopsis of the 1868 die numbers.

180 **Victoria,** Sovereign, 1868, die number 9, second larger young head left, ww incuse on truncation without stops, date below, 6 with open curvy top but no bulb, hint of doubling in legends both sides, *rev* crowned quartered shield of arms within laurel wreath, die number 9 below, emblems below, 7.97g (Marsh 52; MCE 528; S 3853). *Spot on obverse legend, scuffs, nicks and light surface marks, toned, nearly very fine / good very fine.* £300-350

Price Realised : £264

ex Spink and Son Ltd, November 2003
This coin was purchased from one of the groups of coins from the wreck of the RMS *Douro* that were not sold by auction and within the last 10 years. It demonstrates a slightly different 6 in the date probably the result of a faulty punch, where the bulb-like terminal at the top of the 6 is absent. This occurs a number of times in 1868 dated coins.
Calendar year mintage 1,653,384. See footnote for lot 1093, page 175, for a brief synopsis of the 1868 die numbers.

513 **Victoria,** Sovereign, 1868, die number 10, second larger young head left, ww incuse on truncation without stops, date below, curvy rounded open 6 without bulb, doubled legend both sides, second I die flawed to rim, *rev* crowned quartered shield of arms within laurel wreath, die number 10 below die flawed, emblems below, 7.96g (Marsh 52; MCE 528; S 3853). *Scratch to left of date and on cheek, red spot on reverse and other light surface marks, otherwise almost very fine, this die number was not known to Marsh, rare.* £300-350

Price Realised : £384

Calendar year mintage 1,653,384
This coin was purchased from one of the groups of coins from the wreck of the RMS *Douro* that were not sold by auction and within the last 10 years, hence it maybe the only known 1868 die number 10 Sovereign.
See footnote for lot 1093, page 175, for a brief synopsis of the 1868 die numbers.
This is one of only eight die number coins in the entire series in the Bentley Collection that was not recorded as a known die number by Marsh, this being the only one that occurs for 1868 dated die number Sovereigns.

1097 **Victoria,** Sovereign, 1868, die number 11, second larger young head left, ww incuse on truncation without stops, date below, curvy rounded 6 with bulbous top, *rev* crowned quartered shield of arms within laurel wreath, die number 11 below, no upper serifs to 1's of die number, emblems below, 7.93g (Marsh 52; MCE 528; S 3853). *Heavily scuffed and surface marked, otherwise almost fine, the reverse better.* £250-300

Price Realised : £216

purchased Spink and Son Ltd, November 2003
It is interesting to note that the weight of this coin in its lower grade is upon the legal tender limit as dictated by the Coinage Acts of 1816-1891.
Calendar year mintage 1,653,384
See footnote for lot 1093, page 175, for a brief synopsis of the 1868 die numbers.

181 **Victoria,** Sovereign, 1868, die number 12, second larger young head left, WW incuse on truncation without stops, date below, 6 with open curvy top but no bulb, hint of doubling in legends both sides, *rev* crowned quartered shield of arms within laurel wreath, die number 12 below die flawed with no upper serif to 1, emblems below, 7.98g (Marsh 52; MCE 528; S 3853). *Heavily scuffed, scratch on cheek, patch of tone on shield and other surface marks, otherwise good fine.* £300-350

Price Realised : £264

ex Spink and Son Ltd, November 2003
Note the lack of upper serif on the 1 of the die number, it seems it was not just the date or letter punches that had broken corners.
Calendar year mintage 1,653,384
See footnote for lot 1093, page 175, for a brief synopsis of the 1868 die numbers.

514 **Victoria,** Sovereign, 1868, die number 13, second larger young head left, WW incuse on truncation without stops, date below, die flawed 1, curvy rounded open 6 without bulb, doubled legend both sides, less so on reverse, *rev* crowned quartered shield of arms within laurel wreath, die number 13 below, no upper serif to 1, emblems below, die flaw joins the upper parts of some reverse letters, 7.97g (Marsh 52; MCE 528; S 3853). *A few tiny spots each side, very fine, reverse better.* £300-350

Price Realised : £288

ex Spink and Son, purchased July 2004
Calendar year mintage 1,653,384
See footnote for lot 1093, page 175, for a brief synopsis of the 1868 die numbers. This coin was purchased from one of the groups of coins from the wreck of the RMS *Douro* that were not sold by auction. Note the lack of upper serif on the 1 of the die number. It seems it was not just the date or letter punches that had broken corners.

1098 **Victoria,** Sovereign, 1868, die number 14, second larger young head left, WW incuse on truncation without stops, date below, curvy thinner and lower 6 with bulbous top, the second 8 higher than other figures, hint of doubling of legend both sides, *rev* crowned quartered shield of arms within laurel wreath, die number 14 below, 1 with no upper serif, emblems below, 7.97g (Marsh 52; MCE 528; S 3853). *Heavy surface marks and scuffs, almost very fine.* £250-300

Price Realised : £240

This coin was purchased from one of the groups of coins from the wreck of the RMS *Douro* that were not sold by auction and within the last 10 years.
Calendar year mintage 1,653,384
See footnote for lot 1093, page 175, for a brief synopsis of the 1868 die numbers.

182 **Victoria,** Sovereign, 1868, die number 15, second larger young head left, WW incuse on truncation without stops, date below, curvy rounded 6 with bulbous joined top, flaw below last 8 to rim, *rev* crowned quartered shield of arms within laurel wreath, die number 15 below with no upper serif, emblems below, hint of doubling in legend, 7.98g (Marsh 52; MCE 528; S 3853). *Quite scuffed with surface marks, very fine.* £300-350

Price Realised : £264

ex Douro Cargo, Spink Auction 118, 20-21 November 1996, lot 1317 (part)
ex Spink Numismatic Circular, October 1997, item 5028
ex An Important Collection of Gold Sovereigns 1816-2000, offered as one lot, Sothebys, 16-17 November 2000, lot 525 (part)
Calendar year mintage 1,653,384
See footnote for lot 1093, page 175, for a brief synopsis of the 1868 die numbers.
Note the lack of upper serif on the 1 of the die number, it seems it was not just the date or letter punches that had broken corners.

515 Victoria, Sovereign, 1868, die number 16, second larger young head left, WW incuse on truncation without stops, date below, curvy rounded open 6 without bulb, *rev* crowned quartered shield of arms within laurel wreath, die number 16 below lightly die flawed, emblems below, hint of doubling in reverse legend, 7.97g (Marsh 52; MCE 528; S 3853). *A few tiny nicks and hairlines, scratch on lower right of reverse, otherwise very fine.* £300-350

Price Realised : £288

This coin was purchased from one of the groups of coins from the wreck of the RMS *Douro* that were not sold by auction and within the last 10 years, hence it may be the only known 1868 die number 16 Sovereign.
Calendar year mintage 1,653,384. See footnote for lot 1093, page 175, for a brief synopsis of the 1868 die numbers.

183 Victoria, Sovereign, 1868, die number 17, second larger young head left, WW incuse on truncation without stops, date below, curvy rounded 6 with bulbous top, raised die flaw from tip of neck to rim, *rev* crowned quartered shield of arms within laurel wreath, die number 17 below die flawed with no upper serif, emblems below, hint of doubling in legend, 7.98g (Marsh 52; MCE 528; S 3853). *Short scratch on cheek, light raised flaws in hair and light surface marks, otherwise extremely fine.* £350-450

Price Realised : £600

ex Spink and Son Ltd, November 2003
Note the lack of upper serif on the 1 of the die number, it seems it was not just the date or letter punches that had broken corners.
Calendar year mintage 1,653,384. See footnote for lot 1093, page 175, for a brief synopsis of the 1868 die numbers.

516 Victoria, Sovereign, 1868, die number 18, second larger young head left, WW incuse on truncation without stops, raised blobby die flaw at lower curve of neck, date below, curvy rounded open 6 without bulb, *rev* crowned quartered shield of arms within laurel wreath, die number 18 below, no upper serif to 1, emblems below, hint of doubling in reverse legend, die flaw joins the upper parts of some reverse letters, 7.97g (Marsh 52; MCE 528; S 3853). *Light nicks and bagmarks, a pleasing extremely fine.* £350-450

Price Realised : £504

Calendar year mintage 1,653,384
See footnote for lot 1093, page 175, for a brief synopsis of the 1868 die numbers.
Note the lack of upper serif on the 1 of the die number, it seems it was not just the date or letter punches that had broken corners.

1099 Victoria, Sovereign, 1868, die number 19, second larger young head left, WW incuse on truncation without stops, date below, curvy thinner and lower 6 with bulbous top, hint of doubling of legend both sides, *rev* crowned quartered shield of arms within laurel wreath, die number 19 below, 1 with no upper serif, emblems below, hairline raised flaw connects some letters, 7.99g (Marsh 52; MCE 528; S 3853). *Some die clashing evident, hairlined, obverse rim nick and scuff on cheek, otherwise brilliant, extremely fine / good extremely fine.* £300-400

Price Realised : £624

ex Douro Cargo, Spink Auction 118, 20-21 November 1996, lot 556 (part)
Calendar year mintage 1,653,384. See footnote for lot 1093, page 175, for a brief synopsis of the 1868 die numbers.

184 **Victoria,** Sovereign, 1868, die number 20, second larger young head left, ww incuse on truncation without stops, date below doubled, curvy rounded 6 with bulbous top, G of obverse legend die flawed, some doubling in legends both sides, *rev* crowned quartered shield of arms within laurel wreath, die number 20 below, flaw through die number, some letters of legend die flawed, emblems below, 7.99g (Marsh 52; MCE 528; S 3853). *Short scratch to cheek, other light surface marks and nicks, extremely fine.* £350-450

Price Realised : £360

ex An Important Collection of Gold Sovereigns 1816-2000, offered as one lot, Sothebys, 16-17 November 2000, lot 525 (part)
Calendar year mintage 1,653,384
See footnote for lot 1093, page 175, for a brief synopsis of the 1868 die numbers.

1100 **Victoria,** Sovereign, 1868, die number 21, second larger young head left, ww incuse on truncation without stops, date below, curvy rounded 6 with bulbous top, *rev* crowned quartered shield of arms within laurel wreath, die number 21 below, number flawed and 1 with no upper serif, emblems below, hairline raised flaw connects some letters with a hint of doubling, 7.96g (Marsh 52; MCE 528; S 3853). *Scratch on cheek, some light marks and nicks, otherwise about extremely fine / extremely fine.* £300-400

Price Realised : £264

This coin was purchased from one of the groups of coins from the wreck of the RMS *Douro* that were not sold by auction and within the last 10 years.
Calendar year mintage 1,653,384
See footnote for lot 1093, page 175, for a brief synopsis of the 1868 die numbers.

185 **Victoria,** Sovereign, 1868, die number 22, second larger young head left, ww incuse on truncation without stops, date below, curvy rounded 6 with bulbous top, hint of doubling to obverse legend, *rev* crowned quartered shield of arms within laurel wreath, die number 22 below die flawed, emblems below, 7.95g (Marsh 52; MCE 528; S 3853). *Quite scuffed with surface marks, good fine / almost very fine.* £300-350

Price Realised : £264

Calendar year mintage 1,653,384
See footnote for lot 1093, page 175, for a brief synopsis of the 1868 die numbers.

517 **Victoria,** Sovereign, 1868, die number 23, second larger young head left, ww incuse on truncation without stops, raised die flaw from tip of neck to first I of queen's name, date below, curvy rounded open 6 without bulb, *rev* crowned quartered shield of arms within laurel wreath, die number 23 below, emblems below, hint of doubling in reverse legend, die flaw joins the upper parts of some reverse letters, 7.97g (Marsh 52; MCE 528; S 3853). *Once cleaned, now toned, almost very fine / extremely fine.* £300-350

Price Realised : £264

Calendar year mintage 1,653,384
See footnote for lot 1093, page 175, for a brief synopsis of the 1868 die numbers.

518 **Victoria,** Sovereign, 1868, die number 24, second larger young head left, WW incuse on truncation without stops, raised die flaw from V to rim, date below, curvy rounded open 6 without bulb, *rev* crowned quartered shield of arms within laurel wreath, die number 24 below, emblems below, hint of doubling in reverse legend, die flaw joins the upper parts of some reverse letters, 7.98g (Marsh 52; MCE 528; S 3853). *Hairline scratch in obverse field, shorter scratch on neck, a few scuffs and nicks otherwise, extremely fine, reverse better.* £300-400

Price Realised : £408

ex An Important Collection of Gold Sovereigns 1816-2000, offered as one lot, Sothebys, November 2000, lot 525 (part)
Calendar year mintage 1,653,384
See footnote for lot 1093, page 175, for a brief synopsis of the 1868 die numbers.

1101 **Victoria,** Sovereign, 1868, die number 25, second larger young head left, WW incuse on truncation without stops, date below, curvy 6 without bulb, date and legend doubled both sides, letter C die flawed to rim and penultimate A of legend, *rev* crowned quartered shield of arms within laurel wreath, die number 25 below, number die flawed, emblems below, hairline raised flaw connects some letters, 7.99g (Marsh 52; MCE 528; S 3853). *Some light marks, otherwise toned, almost extremely fine / extremely fine.* £300-400

Price Realised : £432

Calendar year mintage 1,653,384
See footnote for lot 1093, page 175, for a brief synopsis of the 1868 die numbers.

186 **Victoria,** Sovereign, 1868, die number 26, second larger young head left, WW incuse on truncation without stops, date below, 6 with open curvy top but no bulb, doubled A in VICTORIA, *rev* crowned quartered shield of arms within laurel wreath, die number 26 below lightly die flawed, emblems below, some light raised flaws in letters, 7.98g (Marsh 52; MCE 528; S 3853). *Light nicks and surface marks, some brilliance, otherwise extremely fine.* £350-450

Price Realised : £432

ex Douro Cargo, Spink Auction 118, 20-21 November 1996, lot 556 (part)
Calendar year mintage 1,653,384. See footnote for lot 1093, page 175, for a brief synopsis of the 1868 die numbers.

519 **Victoria,** Sovereign, 1868, die number 27, second larger young head left, WW incuse on truncation without stops, curvy rounded open 6 without bulb, doubled A in queen's name, *rev* crowned quartered shield of arms within laurel wreath, die number 27 below, emblems below, 7.99g (Marsh 52; MCE 528; S 3853). *Some nicks and hairlines otherwise, nearly extremely fine / extremely fine.* £300-400

Price Realised : £312

ex Charles Stueve, Abbeygate Coins, Westhampton Beach, New York, c.1990
Calendar year mintage 1,653,384. See footnote for lot 1093, page 175, for a brief synopsis of the 1868 die numbers.

1102 **Victoria,** Sovereign, 1868, die number 28, second larger young head left, ww incuse on truncation without stops, date below, curvy rounded 6 with bulbous top, raised die flaw from neck to rim to left of date, *rev* crowned quartered shield of arms within laurel wreath, die number 28 below, number disjointed, emblems below, upper serif of B absent, some doubling of legend, 7.97g (Marsh 52; MCE 528; S 3853). *Some light marks, patchy tone both sides, very fine / about extremely fine.* £250-300

Price Realised : £240

This coin was purchased from one of the groups of coins from the wreck of the RMS *Douro* that were not sold by auction and within the last 10 years.
Calendar year mintage 1,653,384
See footnote for lot 1093, page 175, for a brief synopsis of the 1868 die numbers.

1103 **Victoria,** Sovereign, 1868, die number 29, second larger young head left, ww incuse on truncation without stops, date below, curvy 6 without bulb, higher second 8 in date, *rev* crowned quartered shield of arms within laurel wreath, die number 29 below, emblems below, die flaw to top left corner of shield into leaves of wreath, 7.99g (Marsh 52; MCE 528; S 3853). *Heavy surface marks, scratch from neck to chin, otherwise about extremely fine.* £250-300

Price Realised : £288

ex Douro Cargo, Spink Auction 118, 20-21 November 1996, lot 337 (part)
Calendar year mintage 1,653,384. See footnote for lot 1093, page 175, for a brief synopsis of the 1868 die numbers.

187 **Victoria,** Sovereign, 1868, die number 30, second larger young head left, ww incuse on truncation without stops, date below, curvy rounded 6 with bulbous top, legend doubled both sides with some raised die flaws, *rev* crowned quartered shield of arms within laurel wreath, die number 30 below lightly die flawed, emblems below, 7.98g (Marsh 52; MCE 528; S 3853). *Cleaned with associated nicks and surface marks, nearly extremely fine / extremely fine.* £300-400

Price Realised : £264

ex Randy Weir Numismatics, Unionville, Ontario, Canada, 2 June 1995
Calendar year mintage 1,653,384. See footnote for lot 1093, page 175, for a brief synopsis of the 1868 die numbers.

520 **Victoria,** Sovereign, 1868, die number 31, second larger young head left, ww incuse on truncation without stops, curvy rounded open 6 without bulb, *rev* crowned quartered shield of arms within laurel wreath, die number 31 below, no upper serif to 1, emblems below, small upper serif to B in legend which is lightly doubled, 7.98g (Marsh 52; MCE 528; S 3853). *Some scuffs and hairlines otherwise, nearly extremely fine / extremely fine.* £300-400

Price Realised : £384

Calendar year mintage 1,653,384
See footnote for lot 1093, page 175, for a brief synopsis of the 1868 die numbers.

1104 **Victoria,** Sovereign, 1868, die number 32, second larger young head left, WW incuse on truncation without stops, date below, curvy 6 without bulb, *rev* crowned quartered shield of arms within laurel wreath, die number 32 below, number lightly flawed, emblems below, hairline raised die flaw connects some letters of reverse legend, 7.98g (Marsh 52; MCE 528; S 3853). *Dig on nose, short scratch by eye and hairlines, otherwise extremely fine.* £300-400

Price Realised : £408

ex An Important Collection of Gold Sovereigns 1816-2000, offered as one lot, Sothebys, November 2000, lot 525 (part)
Calendar year mintage 1,653,384. See footnote for lot 1093, page 175, for a brief synopsis of the 1868 die numbers.

188 **Victoria,** Sovereign, 1868, die number 33, second larger young head left, WW incuse on truncation without stops, date below, curvy rounded 6 with bulbous top, first I of obverse legend die flawed, hint of doubling to legend both sides, *rev* crowned quartered shield of arms within laurel wreath, die number 33 below, emblems below, 7.98g (Marsh 52; MCE 528; S 3853). *Hairlined with other light marks, pleasing extremely fine.* £400-500

Price Realised : £480

ex Randy Weir Numismatics, Unionville, Ontario, Canada, purchased c.1992
Calendar year mintage 1,653,384. See footnote for lot 1093, page 175, for a brief synopsis of the 1868 die numbers.

189 **Victoria,** Sovereign, 1868, die number 34, second larger young head left, WW incuse on truncation without stops, date below, date doubled, curvy rounded 6 with bulbous top, trace of doubling to legend both sides, *rev* crowned quartered shield of arms within laurel wreath, die number 34 below, emblems below, 7.98g (Marsh 52; MCE 528; S 3853). *A few red tone spots on the reverse, surface marks, otherwise good very fine.* £300-350

Price Realised : £336

ex Paul Davies Ltd. This coin was purchased from one of the groups of coins from the wreck of the RMS *Douro* that were not sold by auction and within the last 10 years.
Calendar year mintage 1,653,384. See footnote for lot 1093, page 175, for a brief synopsis of the 1868 die numbers.

521 **Victoria,** Sovereign, 1868, die number 35, second larger young head left, WW incuse on truncation without stops, curvy rounded open 6 without bulb, hint of doubling with some light flaws in legend, *rev* crowned quartered shield of arms within laurel wreath, die number 35 below lightly flawed, emblems below, 7.99g (Marsh 52; MCE 528; S 3853). *Some hairlines and surface marks, black streak on neck, tone spots on chin, otherwise extremely fine.* £300-400

Price Realised : £528

This coin was purchased from one of the groups of coins from the wreck of the RMS *Douro* that were not sold by auction and within the last 10 years.
Calendar year mintage 1,653,384. See footnote for lot 1093, page 175, for a brief synopsis of the 1868 die numbers.

522 **Victoria,** Sovereign, 1868, die number 36, second larger young head left, WW incuse on truncation without stops, curvy rounded open 6 without bulb, *rev* crowned quartered shield of arms within laurel wreath, die number 36 below widely spaced, emblems below, hairline raised flaw in some letters, 7.96g (Marsh 52; MCE 528; S 3853). *Some hairlines, good very fine.* £300-350

Price Realised : £264

Calendar year mintage 1,653,384
See footnote for lot 1093, page 175, for a brief synopsis of the 1868 die numbers.

1105 **Victoria,** Sovereign, 1868, die number 37, second larger young head left, WW incuse on truncation without stops, date below, curvy 6 without bulb, hint of doubling to legend both sides, *rev* crowned quartered shield of arms within laurel wreath, die number 37 below, emblems below, only a trace of upper left serif to B which has a dig, 7.99g (Marsh 52; MCE 528; S 3853). *Light surface marks and nicks, otherwise extremely fine.* £300-400

Price Realised : £360

Calendar year mintage 1,653,384
See footnote for lot 1093, page 175, for a brief synopsis of the 1868 die numbers.

1106 **Victoria,** Sovereign, 1868, die number 38, second larger young head left, WW incuse on truncation without stops, date below, curvy rounded 6 with bulbous top, date die flawed across top, hint of doubling to legend, last two words with raised die flaw in some letters, especially between T and I, *rev* crowned quartered shield of arms within laurel wreath, die number 38 below, the 3 and 8 spread, emblems below, 7.99g (Marsh 52; MCE 528; S 3853). *Scratch on neck and obverse scuffed, otherwise very fine.* £250-300

Price Realised : £240

This coin was purchased from one of the groups of coins from the wreck of the RMS *Douro* that were not sold by auction and within the last 10 years, bought via Spink and Son Ltd, July 2004.
Calendar year mintage 1,653,384
See footnote for lot 1093, page 175, for a brief synopsis of the 1868 die numbers.

190 **Victoria,** Sovereign, 1868, die number 39, second larger young head left, WW incuse on truncation without stops, date below, curvy rounded 6 with bulbous top, *rev* crowned quartered shield of arms within laurel wreath, die number 39 below, emblems below, only a trace of upper serif of first B in legend, 7.99g (Marsh 52; MCE 528; S 3853). *Rim nick on reverse, hairlined with light surface marks, extremely fine, reverse better.* £350-450

Price Realised : £864

ex Douro Cargo, Spink Auction 118, 20-21 November 1996, lot 556 (part)
Calendar year mintage 1,653,384
See footnote for lot 1093, page 175, for a brief synopsis of the 1868 die numbers.

523 **Victoria,** Sovereign, 1868, die number 41, second larger young head left, WW incuse on truncation without stops, curvy rounded open 6 without bulb, hint of doubling in legend, *rev* crowned quartered shield of arms within laurel wreath, die number 41 below, no upper serif to 1, emblems below, 7.98g (Marsh 52; MCE 528; S 3853). *Light surface marks, extremely fine / good extremely fine.* £350-450

Price Realised : £648

Note the lack of upper serif on the 1 of the die number, it seems it was not just the date or letter punches that had broken corners.
Calendar year mintage 1,653,384
See footnote for lot 1093, page 175, for a brief synopsis of the 1868 die numbers.

191 **Victoria,** Sovereign, 1869, die number 1, second larger young head left, WW incuse on truncation without stops, raised die flaw from tip of neck to rim, date below, 6 with open curvy top but no bulb, light raised die flaw in Queen's name, *rev* crowned quartered shield of arms within laurel wreath, die number 1 below with only a lower left serif, emblems below, only a trace of upper serif of first B in legend, some light doubling in legend, 7.98g (Marsh 53; MCE 529; S 3853). *Light scratch in hair, red spot on reverse with light hairlines and other surface marks, nearly extremely fine / extremely fine.* £300-350

Price Realised : £312

ex Randy Weir Numismatics, Unionville, Ontario, Canada, c.2000
Calendar year mintage 6,441,322
This coin is die number 1 of 63 different numbered dies in the Bentley Collection running from 1 to 69. Marsh claims that 13 other die numbers exist, which are absent from this collection, making a total of 76 reverse dies to strike nearly 6.5 million Sovereigns, although some of this total may be 1868 dated Sovereigns. This suggests good longevity for the dies. One die number in the Bentley Collection run of 1866 is not recorded by Marsh, number 63.
Note the lack of serifs on the 1 of the die number, it seems it was not just the date or letter punches that had broken corners. The unusual curved 6 without the top terminal bulb, the likely result of a faulty punch continues intermittently into 1869.

1107 **Victoria,** Sovereign, 1869, die number 2, second larger young head left, WW incuse on truncation without stops, date below, curvy rounded 6 with bulbous top, light raised die flaw between 1 and 8 of date, *rev* crowned quartered shield of arms within laurel wreath, die number 2 below, emblems below, some light doubling in reverse legend, 7.98g (Marsh 53; MCE 529; S 3853). *Surface marks and light hairlines, otherwise extremely fine.* £300-400

Price Realised : £336

ex Randy Weir Numismatics, Unionville, Ontario, Canada, 22 July 1994
Calendar year mintage 6,441,322
See footnote for lot 191 (above) for a brief synopsis of the 1869 die numbers.

192 **Victoria,** Sovereign, 1869, die number 3, second larger young head left, ww incuse on truncation without stops, date below, curvy rounded 6 with bulbous top, *rev* crowned quartered shield of arms within laurel wreath, die number 3 below, emblems below, hint of doubling to legend with raised die flaws in some letters, die flaw in field to left rosette from rim to wreath leaves, 7.98g (Marsh 53; MCE 529; S 3853). *Surface marks and hairlines, otherwise extremely fine.* £350-450

Price Realised : £360

ex Douro Cargo, Spink Auction 118, 20-21 November 1996, lot 1362 (part)
Calendar year mintage 6,441,322
See footnote for lot 191, page 186, for a brief synopsis of the 1869 die numbers.

524 **Victoria,** Sovereign, 1869, die number 4, second larger young head left, ww incuse on truncation without stops, date below, 6 with open curvy top with bulb, last A of legend die flawed, hint of doubling in legend both sides, *rev* crowned quartered shield of arms within laurel wreath, die number 4 below, emblems below, light raised die flaw connects some letters, 7.98g (Marsh 53; MCE 529; S 3853). *Some nicks and surface marks, extremely fine.* £300-350

Price Realised : £384

Calendar year mintage 6,441,322
See footnote for lot 191, page 186, for a brief synopsis of the 1869 die numbers.

1108 **Victoria,** Sovereign, 1869, die number 5, second larger young head left, ww incuse on truncation without stops, date below, curvy rounded 6 with bulbous top, trace of doubling to legend both sides, *rev* crowned quartered shield of arms within laurel wreath, die number 5 below, emblems below, light hairline flaw connects some reverse letters, 7.98g (Marsh 53; MCE 529; S 3853). *Some nicks and light hairlines, otherwise extremely fine.* £300-400

Price Realised : £384

ex Randy Weir Numismatics, Unionville, Ontario, Canada, 27 September 1990
Calendar year mintage 6,441,322
See footnote for lot 191, page 186, for a brief synopsis of the 1869 die numbers.

525 **Victoria,** Sovereign, 1869, die number 6, second larger young head left, ww incuse on truncation without stops, date below, 6 with open curvy top without bulb, hint of doubling in legend both sides, *rev* crowned quartered shield of arms within laurel wreath, die number 6 die flawed below, emblems below, 7.96g (Marsh 53; MCE 529; S 3853). *Some surface marks, very fine.* £300-350

Price Realised : £264

The unusual curved 6 without the top terminal bulb, the likely result of a faulty punch, continues intermittently through 1869.
Calendar year mintage 6,441,322
See footnote for lot 191, page 186, for a brief synopsis of the 1869 die numbers.

193 **Victoria,** Sovereign, 1869, die number 7, second larger young head left, WW incuse on truncation without stops, date below, curvy rounded 6 with bulbous top, die flaw to left of date, trace of doubling to legend both sides, *rev* crowned quartered shield of arms within laurel wreath, die number 7 below, emblems below, some light raised hairline flaws in legend, 7.98g (Marsh 53; MCE 529; S 3853). *One red spot on reverse, light surface marks, extremely fine.* £350-450

Price Realised : £456

ex Douro Cargo, Spink Auction 118, 20-21 November 1996, lot 558 (part)
Calendar year mintage 6,441,322
See footnote for lot 191, page 186, for a brief synopsis of the 1869 die numbers.

526 **Victoria,** Sovereign, 1869, die number 8, second larger young head left, WW incuse on truncation without stops, date below, 6 with open curvy top with bulb, *rev* crowned quartered shield of arms within laurel wreath, die number 8 below, emblems below, small upper serif to B in legend, 7.99g (Marsh 53; MCE 529; S 3853). *Some light hairlines, extremely fine / good extremely fine.* £400-500

Price Realised : £576

ex Randy Weir Numismatics, Unionville, Ontario, Canada, purchased 9 June 1993
Calendar year mintage 6,441,322
See footnote for lot 191, page 186, for a brief synopsis of the 1869 die numbers.

1109 **Victoria,** Sovereign, 1869, die number 9, second larger young head left, WW incuse on truncation without stops, date below, curvy rounded 6 with bulbous top, *rev* crowned quartered shield of arms within laurel wreath, die number 9 below lightly flawed, emblems below, light hint of doubling to legend, 7.96g (Marsh 53; MCE 529; S 3853). *Red spot on crown, light surface marks, otherwise about very fine, reverse better.* £300-400

Price Realised : £240

ex Spink and Son Ltd, July 2004
Calendar year mintage 6,441,322
See footnote for lot 191, page 186, for a brief synopsis of the 1869 die numbers.

1110 **Victoria,** Sovereign, 1869, die number 10, second larger young head left, WW incuse on truncation without stops, date below, curvy rounded 6 with bulbous top, third I and penultimate A die flawed, *rev* crowned quartered shield of arms within laurel wreath, die number 10 below lightly flawed, no lower right serif to 1, emblems below, light hint of doubling to legend, 7.99g (Marsh 53; MCE 529; S 3853). *Four red spots on obverse, some surface marks, otherwise extremely fine, reverse better.* £300-400

Price Realised : £408

ex Douro Cargo, Spink Auction 118, 20-21 November 1996, lot 558 (part)
Calendar year mintage 6,441,322
See footnote for lot 191, page 186, for a brief synopsis of the 1869 die numbers.

194 **Victoria,** Sovereign, 1869, die number 11, second larger young head left, ww incuse on truncation without stops, date below lightly doubled, curvy rounded 6 with bulbous top, trace of doubling to obverse legend, *rev* crowned quartered shield of arms within laurel wreath, die number 11 below with no lower right serifs, emblems below, 7.96g (Marsh 53; MCE 529; S 3853). *Light rim nicks and heavier surface marks, extremely fine.* £350-450

Price Realised : £600

ex Douro Cargo, Spink Auction 118, 20-21 November 1996, lot 1362 (part)
Note the lack of serifs on the 1's of the die number, it seems it was not just the date or letter punches that had broken corners. This faulty 1 punch continues to be used for all the 1 type die numbers of 1869.
Calendar year mintage 6,441,322
See footnote for lot 191, page 186, for a brief synopsis of the 1869 die numbers.

527 **Victoria,** Sovereign, 1869, die number 12, second larger young head left, ww incuse on truncation without stops, doubled date below, 6 with open curvy top without bulb, last A of legend and second I in queen's name die flawed, some doubling in obverse legend and a trace on reverse, *rev* crowned quartered shield of arms within laurel wreath, die number 12 below, emblems below, small upper serif to B in legend, 7.98g (Marsh 53; MCE 529; S 3853). *Dark spot on obverse, tiny black specks on reverse with some light nicks and hairlines, nearly extremely fine / extremely fine.* £300-400

Price Realised : £1,104

ex Douro Cargo, Spink Auction 118, 20-21 November 1996, lot 558 (part)
Note the unusual curved 6 in date without the top terminal bulb.
Calendar year mintage 6,441,322
See footnote for lot 191, page 186, for a brief synopsis of the 1869 die numbers.

1111 **Victoria,** Sovereign, 1869, die number 13, second larger young head left, ww incuse on truncation without stops, date below, curvy 6 without bulb, raised die flaw to left of date onto neck, *rev* crowned quartered shield of arms within laurel wreath, die number 13 below lightly flawed, only a lower left serif to 1, others absent, emblems below, end of second word lightly die flawed, 7.98g (Marsh 53; MCE 529; S 3853). *Hairlined, otherwise toned, about extremely fine, reverse better.* £300-400

Price Realised : £240

ex Douro Cargo, Spink Auction 118, 20-21 November 1996, lot 558 (part)
The unusual curved 6 without the top terminal bulb, the likely result of a faulty punch continues intermittently into 1869.Calendar year mintage 6,441,322
See footnote for lot 191, page 186, for a brief synopsis of the 1869 die numbers.

195 **Victoria,** Sovereign, 1869, die number 14, second larger young head left, WW incuse on truncation without stops, date below lightly doubled, curvy rounded 6 with bulbous top, penultimate A of legend die flawed, hint of doubling to legend both sides, *rev* crowned quartered shield of arms within laurel wreath, die number 14 below flawed with no upper and lower right serifs, emblems below, only a trace of upper serif of first B in legend, 7.99g (Marsh 53; MCE 529; S 3853). *Spot on neck, light hairlines and surface marks, otherwise extremely fine.* £350-450

Price Realised : £360

ex Douro Cargo, Spink Auction 118, 20-21 November 1996, lot 558 (part)
Note the lack of serifs on the 1's of the die number, it seems it was not just the date or letter punches that had broken corners.
Calendar year mintage 6,441,322. See footnote for lot 191, page 186, for a brief synopsis of the 1869 die numbers.

528 **Victoria,** Sovereign, 1869, die number 15, second larger young head left, WW incuse on truncation without stops, date below, 6 with open curvy top with bulb, *rev* crowned quartered shield of arms within laurel wreath, die number 15 below, no lower right serif to 1, emblems below, small upper serif to B in legend, hint of doubling to legend, 8.00g (Marsh 53; MCE 529; S 3853). *Some light hairlines and red patches of tone on obverse, some brilliance both sides, otherwise good extremely fine.* £400-500

Price Realised : £552

ex Douro Cargo, Spink Auction 118, 20-21 November 1996, lot 559 (part)
Note the lack of lower right serif on the 1 of the die number. It seems it was not just the date or letter punches that had broken corners.
Calendar year mintage 6,441,322. See footnote for lot 191, page 186, for a brief synopsis of the 1869 die numbers.

1112 **Victoria,** Sovereign, 1869, die number 16, second larger young head left, WW incuse on truncation without stops, date below, curvy 6 without bulb, doubled legend, last A die flawed, *rev* crowned quartered shield of arms within laurel wreath, die number 16 below, no lower right serif to 1, emblems below, 7.98g (Marsh 53; MCE 529; S 3853). *Hairlined, otherwise extremely fine, reverse better.* £300-400

Price Realised : £384

ex Douro Cargo, Spink Auction 118, 20-21 November 1996, lot 559 (part)
Calendar year mintage 6,441,322. See footnote for lot 191, page 186, for a brief synopsis of the 1869 die numbers.

196 **Victoria,** Sovereign, 1869, die number 17, second larger young head left, WW incuse on truncation without stops, date below, 6 with open curvy top but no bulb, *rev* crowned quartered shield of arms within laurel wreath, die number 17 below flawed no lower right serif, emblems below, hint of doubling in legend, 7.97g (Marsh 53; MCE 529; S 3853). *Toned with light surface marks and hairlines, good very fine.* £300-350

Price Realised : £264

ex Paul Davies Ltd. This coin was purchased from one of the groups of coins from the wreck of the RMS *Douro* that were not sold by auction and within the last 10 years.
Note the lack of serifs on the 1's of the die number, it seems it was not just the date or letter punches that had broken corners.
Calendar year mintage 6,441,322. See footnote for lot 191, page 186, for a brief synopsis of the 1869 die numbers.

529 **Victoria,** Sovereign, 1869, die number 18, second larger young head left, WW incuse on truncation without stops, die flawed date below, 6 with closed curvy top with bulb, *rev* crowned quartered shield of arms within laurel wreath, die number 18 below, no lower right serif to 1, emblems below, die flaw from right laurel wreath to second word, 7.98g (Marsh 53; MCE 529; S 3853). *Patchy red tone on reverse, scratch in hair, very fine / good very fine.* £300-350

Price Realised : £288

This coin was purchased from one of the groups of coins from the wreck of the RMS *Douro* that were not sold by auction and within the last 10 years.
Note the lack of lower right serif on the 1 of the die number. It seems it was not just the date or letter punches that had broken corners.
Calendar year mintage 6,441,322. See footnote for lot 191, page 186, for a brief synopsis of the 1869 die numbers.

197 **Victoria,** Sovereign, 1869, die number 19, second larger young head left, WW incuse on truncation without stops, date below, curvy rounded 6 with bulbous top, die flawed 6, *rev* crowned quartered shield of arms within laurel wreath, die number 19 below flawed no lower right serif, emblems below, 7.99g (Marsh 53; MCE 529; S 3853). *Short scratch on obverse, some nicks and hairlines in fields, nearly extremely fine, reverse better.* £350-400

Price Realised : £300

ex Ebay purchase, August 2003
Note the lack of serifs on the 1's of the die number, it seems it was not just the date or letter punches that had broken corners.
Calendar year mintage 6,441,322. See footnote for lot 191, page 186, for a brief synopsis of the 1869 die numbers.

1113 **Victoria,** Sovereign, 1869, die number 20, second larger young head left, WW incuse on truncation without stops, date below, curvy rounded 6 with bulbous top, doubled date and legend, *rev* crowned quartered shield of arms within laurel wreath, die number 20 below, small o larger 2, emblems below, 7.94g (Marsh 53; MCE 529; S 3853). *Heavily scuffed with surface marks, brilliant reverse, otherwise about very fine, reverse better.* £250-300

Price Realised : £264

ex Paul Davies Ltd, Ilkley, via A H Baldwin & Sons Ltd, June 2007
Calendar year mintage 6,441,322. See footnote for lot 191, page 186, for a brief synopsis of the 1869 die numbers.

530 **Victoria,** Sovereign, 1869, die number 21, second larger young head left, WW incuse on truncation without stops, die flawed date below, 6 with open curvy top without bulb, *rev* crowned quartered shield of arms within laurel wreath, die number 21 below, no lower right serif to 1, emblems below, 7.98g (Marsh 53; MCE 529; S 3853). *Patchy red tone both sides, otherwise extremely fine / good extremely fine.* £350-450

Price Realised : £432

This coin was purchased from one of the groups of coins from the wreck of the RMS *Douro* that were not sold by auction and within the last 10 years.
Note the unusual curved 6 in date without the top terminal bulb and the lack of lower right serif to the 1 in the die number.
Calendar year mintage 6,441,322. See footnote for lot 191, page 186, for a brief synopsis of the 1869 die numbers.

1114 **Victoria,** Sovereign, 1869, die number 22, second larger young head left, ww incuse on truncation without stops, date below, curvy 6 without bulb, light die flaw in some letters of last word, *rev* crowned quartered shield of arms within laurel wreath, die number 22 below, emblems below, 7.98g (Marsh 53; MCE 529; S 3853). *Light scratch by earlobe and other light marks, otherwise extremely fine, reverse better.* £300-400

Price Realised : £336

Calendar year mintage 6,441,322
See footnote for lot 191, page 186, for a brief synopsis of the 1869 die numbers.

198 **Victoria,** Sovereign, 1869, die number 24, second larger young head left, ww incuse on truncation without stops, date below, 6 with open curvy top but no bulb, hint of doubling on some letters both sides, *rev* crowned quartered shield of arms within laurel wreath, die number 24 below, emblems below, 7.99g (Marsh 53; MCE 529; S 3853). *Light surface marks, toned, extremely fine.* £400-450

Price Realised : £384

ex Randy Weir Numismatics, Unionville, Ontario, Canada, purchased 25 September 2001
Calendar year mintage 6,441,322
See footnote for lot 191, page 186, for a brief synopsis of the 1869 die numbers.

531 **Victoria,** Sovereign, 1869, die number 25, second larger young head left, ww incuse on truncation without stops, die flawed date below, 6 with open curvy top without bulb, *rev* crowned quartered shield of arms within laurel wreath, die number 25 below, emblems below, light raised flaw joins some letters on reverse, 7.99g (Marsh 53; MCE 529; S 3853). *Light surface marks and hairlines, otherwise almost extremely fine / extremely fine.* £300-400

Price Realised : £384

ex Randy Weir Numismatics, Unionville, Ontario, Canada, purchased 27 July 1994
Note the unusual curved 6 in date without the top terminal bulb.
Calendar year mintage 6,441,322
See footnote for lot 191, page 186, for a brief synopsis of the 1869 die numbers.

1115 **Victoria,** Sovereign, 1869, die number 26, second larger young head left, ww incuse on truncation without stops, date below, curvy 6 without bulb, legend doubled, *rev* crowned quartered shield of arms within laurel wreath, die number 26 below, small 6 larger 2, emblems below, light hairline raised flaw to some reverse letters, 7.99g (Marsh 53; MCE 529; S 3853). *Scuffed with surface marks and nicks, dig on cheek, otherwise extremely fine.* £300-400

Price Realised : £288

ex Randy Weir Numismatics, Unionville, Ontario, Canada, 13 August 1992
Calendar year mintage 6,441,322
See footnote for lot 191, page 186, for a brief synopsis of the 1869 die numbers.

199 **Victoria,** Sovereign, 1869, die number 27, second larger young head left, ww incuse on truncation without stops, date below, 6 with open curvy top but no bulb, *rev* crowned quartered shield of arms within laurel wreath, die number 27 below, emblems below, light hairline raised flaw in legend, 7.99g (Marsh 53; MCE 529; S 3853). *Light surface marks and nicks, otherwise good extremely fine.* £450-550

Price Realised : £624

ex Randy Weir Numismatics, Unionville, Ontario, Canada, purchased September 1991
Calendar year mintage 6,441,322
See footnote for lot 191, page 186, for a brief synopsis of the 1869 die numbers.

200 **Victoria,** Sovereign, 1869, die number 28, second larger young head left, ww incuse on truncation without stops, date below, light raised die flaw in date and from 1 to rim, curvy rounded 6 with bulbous top, *rev* crowned quartered shield of arms within laurel wreath, die number 28 below, emblems below, 7.99g (Marsh 53; MCE 529; S 3853). *A few light surface marks, extremely fine.* £350-450

Price Realised : £360

ex Randy Weir Numismatics, Unionville, Ontario, Canada, purchased c.1992
Calendar year mintage 6,441,322
See footnote for lot 191, page 186, for a brief synopsis of the 1869 die numbers.

532 **Victoria,** Sovereign, 1869, die number 29, second larger young head left, ww incuse on truncation without stops, die flaw between 1 and 8 of date below, 6 with open curvy top with bulb, *rev* crowned quartered shield of arms within laurel wreath, die number 29 below, larger 2 with small 9, emblems below, light raised flaw joins some letters on reverse, 8.00g (Marsh 53; MCE 529; S 3853). *A few tiny specks of toning, otherwise as struck and pleasing.* £400-600

Price Realised : £840

ex Douro Cargo, Spink Auction 118, 20-21 November 1996, lot 1369 (part)
Calendar year mintage 6,441,322
See footnote for lot 191, page 186, for a brief synopsis of the 1869 die numbers.

533 **Victoria,** Sovereign, 1869, die number 30, second larger young head left, ww incuse on truncation without stops, date below, die flaw in 1 of date, 6 with curvy top with bulb, *rev* crowned quartered shield of arms within laurel wreath, die number 30 below die flawed, emblems below, 7.99g (Marsh 53; MCE 529; S 3853). *Light surface marks and hairlines, otherwise toned extremely fine / good extremely fine.* £350-450

Price Realised : £456

ex Randy Weir Numismatics, Unionville, Ontario, Canada, purchased 6 February 1990
Calendar year mintage 6,441,322
See footnote for lot 191, page 186, for a brief synopsis of the 1869 die numbers.

1116 **Victoria,** Sovereign, 1869, die number 31, second larger young head left, ww incuse on truncation without stops, date below, curvy rounded 6 with bulbous top, legend doubled, *rev* crowned quartered shield of arms within laurel wreath, die number 31 below, 1 without lower right serif, emblems below, light hairline raised flaw to some reverse letters, 7.99g (Marsh 53; MCE 529; S 3853). *Surface marks and hairlines, otherwise about extremely fine, reverse better.* £300-400

Price Realised : £264

ex Randy Weir Numismatics, Unionville, Ontario, Canada, 1997
Calendar year mintage 6,441,322
See footnote for lot 191, page 186, for a brief synopsis of the 1869 die numbers.

201 **Victoria,** Sovereign, 1869, die number 32, second larger young head left, ww incuse on truncation without stops, date below, curvy rounded 6 with bulbous top, *rev* crowned quartered shield of arms within laurel wreath, die number 32 below, emblems below, 7.96g (Marsh 53; MCE 529; S 3853). *Some surface marks, toned, very fine.* £300-350

Price Realised : £264

ex Spink and Son Ltd, November 2003
This coin was purchased from one of the groups of coins from the wreck of the RMS *Douro* that were not sold by auction and within the last 10 years.
Calendar year mintage 6,441,322
See footnote for lot 191, page 186, for a brief synopsis of the 1869 die numbers.

534 **Victoria,** Sovereign, 1869, die number 33, second larger young head left, ww incuse on truncation without stops, date below, 6 with open curvy top with bulb, last T of legend with die flaw to rim, hint of doubling in legend, *rev* crowned quartered shield of arms within laurel wreath, die number 33 below die flawed, emblems below, 7.99g (Marsh 53; MCE 529; S 3853). *Patchy red tone on reverse, almost extremely fine / extremely fine.* £300-400

Price Realised : £312

ex Douro Cargo, Spink Auction 118, 20-21 November 1996, lot 1369 (part)
Calendar year mintage 6,441,322
See footnote for lot 191, page 186, for a brief synopsis of the 1869 die numbers.

Intriguing 1869 Sovereign Die Number 34 Struck from Very Yellow Gold

202 **Victoria,** Sovereign, struck from very yellow gold, 1869, die number 34, second larger young head left, WW incuse on truncation without stops, date below, 6 with open curvy top but no bulb, *rev* crowned quartered shield of arms within laurel wreath, die number 34 below, emblems below, 7.98g (Marsh 53; MCE 529; S 3853). *Proof-like, perhaps a very early or experimental strike, only the lightest of surface marks, otherwise as struck, highly unusual and rare.* £800-1000

Price Realised : £2,040

ex Randy Weir Numismatics, Unionville, Ontario, Canada, purchased 14 January 1992
Calendar year mintage 6,441,322
See footnote for lot 191, page 186, for a brief synopsis of the 1869 die numbers.
The very yellow gold suggests that this coin has been alloyed with silver, rather than the more usual copper which results in the typical red colour of gold as seen usually with coins that emanate from the London Royal Mint. Gold alloyed with silver is typical of what is seen at the Sydney Mint in Australia and is encountered in gold mined from the Asia and Pacific Rim areas. It could be this coin was simply made from re-constituted Australian gold, but the superb quality coupled with the proof-like finish is suggestive more of a presentation piece. It is not dissimilar, though with a slightly inferior finish, to the 24 carat gold proof of 1869 with die number 64 listed as lot 212. A specific gravity test may be worth conducting for it is truly a coin worthy of further research, perhaps in collaboration with the Royal Mint Museum.

1117 **Victoria,** Sovereign, 1869, die number 35, second larger young head left, WW incuse on truncation without stops, date below, curvy 6 without bulb, light die flaw in last few letters of legend, *rev* crowned quartered shield of arms within laurel wreath, die number 35 below, emblems below, legend lightly doubled, 7.99g (Marsh 53; MCE 529; S 3853). *Slight surface marks and hairlines, otherwise proof-like, good extremely fine.* £400-500

Price Realised : £792

ex Dr Jacob Y Terner collection, Goldbergs, Hollywood, USA, May 2003, lot 357, where the coin was graded MS62 by PCGS
Calendar year mintage 6,441,322
See footnote for lot 191, page 186, for a brief synopsis of the 1869 die numbers.

535 **Victoria,** Sovereign, 1869, die number 36, second larger young head left, WW incuse on truncation without stops, date below, 6 with open curvy top without bulb, *rev* crowned quartered shield of arms within laurel wreath, die number 36 below, emblems below, hint of doubling in reverse legend, 7.99g (Marsh 53; MCE 529; S 3853). *Obverse rim nick, toned, good extremely fine.* £350-450

Price Realised : £432

ex Douro Cargo, Spink Auction 118, 20-21 November 1996, lot 1369 (part)
Calendar year mintage 6,441,322
See footnote for lot 191, page 186, for a brief synopsis of the 1869 die numbers. Note the unusual curved 6 in date without the top terminal bulb.

1118 **Victoria,** Sovereign, 1869, die number 37, second larger young head left, WW incuse on truncation without stops, date below, curvy 6 without bulb, weak lower part to figure 9, doubled legend both sides, *rev* crowned quartered shield of arms within laurel wreath, die number 37 below, emblems below, 7.97g (Marsh 53; MCE 529; S 3853). *Red spot on caul of crown on the reverse, nick in hair with scratch into field on obverse, otherwise extremely fine, reverse better.* £300-400

Price Realised : £360

ex Douro Cargo, Spink Auction 118, 20-21 November 1996, lot 1369 (part)
Calendar year mintage 6,441,322
See footnote for lot 191, page 186, for a brief synopsis of the 1869 die numbers.

203 **Victoria,** Sovereign, 1869, die number 38, second larger young head left, WW incuse on truncation without stops, date below, curvy rounded 6 with bulbous top that is die flawed, *rev* crowned quartered shield of arms within laurel wreath, die number 38 below, emblems below, some doubling in legend with hairline raised flaw in some letters, 7.99g (Marsh 53; MCE 529; S 3853). *Light surface marks and hairlines, good extremely fine.* £400-500

Price Realised : £504

ex Douro Cargo, Spink Auction 118, 20-21 November 1996, lot 1369 (part)
Calendar year mintage 6,441,322
See footnote for lot 191, page 186, for a brief synopsis of the 1869 die numbers.

204 **Victoria,** Sovereign, 1869, die number 39, second larger young head left, WW incuse on truncation without stops, date below, curvy rounded 6 with bulbous top, hairline raised die flaw in some obverse letters, *rev* crowned quartered shield of arms within laurel wreath, die number 39 below, emblems below, 7.98g (Marsh 53; MCE 529; S 3853). *Light surface marks and scuffs, toned, extremely fine.* £350-450

Price Realised : £384

ex Randy Weir Numismatics, Unionville, Ontario, Canada, purchased c.1992
Calendar year mintage 6,441,322
See footnote for lot 191, page 186, for a brief synopsis of the 1869 die numbers.

1119 **Victoria,** Sovereign, 1869, die number 40, second larger young head left, WW incuse on truncation without stops, date below, curvy rounded 6 with bulbous top, die flaw through 1 of date from neck to rim, V of legend die flawed, trace of doubling to legend both sides, *rev* crowned quartered shield of arms within laurel wreath, die number 40 below, emblems below, only trace of upper serif to B, 7.97g (Marsh 53; MCE 529; S 3853). *Toned, light surface marks, otherwise good fine, reverse better.* £250-300

Price Realised : £240

ex DNW auction, 17 December 2007, lot 146
Calendar year mintage 6,441,322
See footnote for lot 191, page 186, for a brief synopsis of the 1869 die numbers.

536 **Victoria,** Sovereign, 1869, die number 40, second larger young head left, ww incuse on truncation without stops, date below, 6 with open curvy top without bulb, hint of doubling in obverse legend, *rev* crowned quartered shield of arms within laurel wreath, die number 40 below, emblems below, light raised flaw joins some letters on reverse, 7.99g (Marsh 53; MCE 529; S 3853). *Some hairline marks, proof-like, good extremely fine.* £500-600

Price Realised : £624

ex Douro Cargo, Spink Auction 118, 20-21 November 1996, lot 1370 (part)
Note the unusual curved 6 in date without the top terminal bulb.
Calendar year mintage 6,441,322. See footnote for lot 191, page 186, for a brief synopsis of the 1869 die numbers.

537 **Victoria,** Sovereign, 1869, die number 41, second larger young head left, ww incuse on truncation without stops, date below, 6 with open curvy top with bulb, *rev* crowned quartered shield of arms within laurel wreath, die number 41 below, 1 without lower right serif, emblems below, 7.99g (Marsh 53; MCE 529; S 3853). *Some hairlines, extremely fine / good extremely fine.* £400-500

Price Realised : £504

ex Douro Cargo, Spink Auction 118, 20-21 November 1996, lot 1370 (part)
Note the lack of lower right serif on the 1 of the die number. It seems it was not just the date or letter punches that had broken corners.
Calendar year mintage 6,441,322
See footnote for lot 191, page 186, for a brief synopsis of the 1869 die numbers.

1120 **Victoria,** Sovereign, 1869, die number 42, second larger young head left, ww incuse on truncation without stops, date below, curvy 6 without bulb, raised die flaw from tip of neck to rim, hairline flaw in last three letters of legend, *rev* crowned quartered shield of arms within laurel wreath, die number 42 below, number lightly doubled, emblems below, hairline flaw in some latter letters of first word, 7.99g (Marsh 53; MCE 529; S 3853). *Scratch under* OR *of Queen's name, hairlines and surface marks, otherwise extremely fine.* £300-400

Price Realised : £264

ex An Important Collection of Gold Sovereigns 1816-2000, offered as one lot, Sothebys, November 2000, lot 525 (part)
Calendar year mintage 6,441,322
See footnote for lot 191, page 186, for a brief synopsis of the 1869 die numbers.

205 **Victoria,** Sovereign, 1869, die number 43, second larger young head left, ww incuse on truncation without stops, date below, curvy rounded open 6 with bulbous top, *rev* crowned quartered shield of arms within laurel wreath, die number 43 below, light die flaw through 43, emblems below, 7.99g (Marsh 53; MCE 529; S 3853). *Some light hairlines and surface marks, otherwise pleasing extremely fine.* £400-500

Price Realised : £384

ex An Important Collection of Gold Sovereigns 1816-2000, offered as one lot, Sothebys, 16-17 November 2000, lot 525 (part)
Calendar year mintage 6,441,322
See footnote for lot 191, page 186, for a brief synopsis of the 1869 die numbers.

538 **Victoria,** Sovereign, 1869, die number 44, second larger young head left, WW incuse on truncation without stops, die flaws from hair bun to rim and tip of neck to rim, doubled date below, 6 with open curvy top with bulb, doubled obverse legend, *rev* crowned quartered shield of arms within laurel wreath, die number 44 below, emblems below, only a trace of the upper serif in B of legend, 7.98g (Marsh 53; MCE 529; S 3853). *Light surface marks, extremely fine.* £350-450

Price Realised : £600

ex Randy Weir Numismatics, Unionville, Ontario, Canada, purchased c.1996
Calendar year mintage 6,441,322
See footnote for lot 191, page 186, for a brief synopsis of the 1869 die numbers.

1121 **Victoria,** Sovereign, 1869, die number 45, second larger young head left, WW incuse on truncation without stops, date below, curvy rounded 6 with bulbous top, *rev* crowned quartered shield of arms within laurel wreath, die number 45 below, high 4 low 5, emblems below, 7.97g (Marsh 53; MCE 529; S 3853). *Scuffed with light, once cleaned, otherwise about very fine, reverse better.* £250-300

Price Realised : £240

ex An Important Collection of Gold Sovereigns 1816-2000, offered as one lot, Sothebys, November 2000, lot 525 (part)
Calendar year mintage 6,441,322
See footnote for lot 191, page 186, for a brief synopsis of the 1869 die numbers.

206 **Victoria,** Sovereign, 1869, die number 46, second larger young head left, WW incuse on truncation without stops, date below, curvy rounded 6 with bulbous top lightly die flawed shut, *rev* crowned quartered shield of arms within laurel wreath, die number 46 below, emblems below, 7.99g (Marsh 53; MCE 529; S 3853). *Surface nicks and hairlines, almost extremely fine.* £350-400

Price Realised : £300

Calendar year mintage 6,441,322
See footnote for lot 191, page 186, for a brief synopsis of the 1869 die numbers.

539 **Victoria,** Sovereign, 1869, die number 47, second larger young head left, WW incuse on truncation without stops, die flawed date below, 6 with open curvy top with bulb, last A die flawed to rim, hint of doubling to obverse legend, *rev* crowned quartered shield of arms within laurel wreath, die number 47 below, emblems below, hairline die flaw in second word, 7.98g (Marsh 53; MCE 529; S 3853). *Light surface marks and hairlines, bold very fine.* £300-350

Price Realised : £288

This coin was purchased from one of the groups of coins from the wreck of the RMS *Douro* that were not sold by auction and within the last 10 years.
Calendar year mintage 6,441,322
See footnote for lot 191, page 186, for a brief synopsis of the 1869 die numbers.

1122 **Victoria,** Sovereign, 1869, die number 48, second larger young head left, WW incuse on truncation without stops, date below, curvy rounded 6 with bulbous top, raised die flaw in first R of legend, *rev* crowned quartered shield of arms within laurel wreath, die number 48 below, high 4 low 8, emblems below, 7.98g (Marsh 53; MCE 529; S 3853). *Two obverse rim nicks, otherwise extremely fine, reverse better.* £300-400

Price Realised : £360

Calendar year mintage 6,441,322
See footnote for lot 191, page 186, for a brief synopsis of the 1869 die numbers.

207 **Victoria,** Sovereign, 1869, die number 49, second larger young head left, WW incuse on truncation without stops, date below lightly doubled, 6 with open curvy top but no bulb, VICTO of legend doubled, *rev* crowned quartered shield of arms within laurel wreath, die number 49 below, emblems below, 7.98g (Marsh 53; MCE 529; S 3853). *Light surface marks and hairlines, pleasing extremely fine.* £400-500

Price Realised : £480

ex Spink and Son Ltd, November 2003
Calendar year mintage 6,441,322
See footnote for lot 191, page 186, for a brief synopsis of the 1869 die numbers.

540 **Victoria,** Sovereign, 1869, die number 50, second larger young head left, WW incuse on truncation without stops, date below, 6 with open curvy top without bulb, *rev* crowned quartered shield of arms within laurel wreath, die number 50 below, emblems below, 7.99g (Marsh 53; MCE 529; S 3853). *Reverse rim nick, dig and scratch on neck, otherwise good extremely fine.* £350-450

Price Realised : £624

Note the unusual curved 6 in date without the top terminal bulb.
Calendar year mintage 6,441,322
See footnote for lot 191, page 186, for a brief synopsis of the 1869 die numbers.

1123 **Victoria,** Sovereign, 1869, die number 51, second larger young head left, WW incuse on truncation without stops, date below doubled, curvy 6 without bulb, die flaw through 1 of date to rim, last A of legend die flawed, *rev* crowned quartered shield of arms within laurel wreath, die number 51 below, 1 only with a lower left serif, emblems below, light raised die flaw in reverse legend connects some letters, 7.95g (Marsh 53; MCE 529; S 3853). *Light surface marks, very fine.* £250-300

Price Realised : £240

Calendar year mintage 6,441,322
See footnote for lot 191, page 186, for a brief synopsis of the 1869 die numbers.

208 **Victoria,** Sovereign, 1869, die number 52, second larger young head left, WW incuse on truncation without stops, date below, doubled date and bottom loop of 8 filled, 6 with open curvy top but no bulb, obverse legend lightly doubled, *rev* crowned quartered shield of arms within laurel wreath, die number 52 below lightly flawed, emblems below, legend with hairline raised die flaws, 7.97g (Marsh 53; MCE 529; S 3853). *Light scuffs and surface marks, toned, very fine / good very fine.* £300-350

Price Realised : £288

ex Spink and Son Ltd, November 2003
Calendar year mintage 6,441,322
See footnote for lot 191, page 186, for a brief synopsis of the 1869 die numbers.

1124 **Victoria,** Sovereign, 1869, die number 53, second larger young head left, WW incuse on truncation without stops, date below, curvy 6 without bulb, die flaw through 1 of date to rim, weak lower part to 9, *rev* crowned quartered shield of arms within laurel wreath, die number 53 below, emblems below, 7.98g (Marsh 53; MCE 529; S 3853). *Light surface marks and hairlines, short scratch under ponytail on the obverse, otherwise extremely fine.* £300-400

Price Realised : £264

Calendar year mintage 6,441,322
See footnote for lot 191, page 186, for a brief synopsis of the 1869 die numbers.

541 **Victoria,** Sovereign, 1869, die number 54, second larger young head left, WW incuse on truncation without stops, date below, 6 with open curvy top without bulb, D of legend and last I each with a raised die flaw running to rim, *rev* crowned quartered shield of arms within laurel wreath, die number 54 below, emblems below, 7.98g (Marsh 53; MCE 529; S 3853). *A few red spots and patches of tone, very fine, reverse better.* £300-350

Price Realised : £264

Note the unusual curved 6 in date without the top terminal bulb.
Calendar year mintage 6,441,322
See footnote for lot 191, page 186, for a brief synopsis of the 1869 die numbers.

1125 **Victoria,** Sovereign, 1869, die number 56, second larger young head left, WW incuse on truncation without stops, date below, curvy 6 without bulb, A of Queen's name doubled, last I of legend with only a trace of upper serifs, *rev* crowned quartered shield of arms within laurel wreath, die number 56 below, emblems below, 7.99g (Marsh 53; MCE 529; S 3853). *Light surface marks and scuffs, underlying brilliance both sides, proof-like in parts, about extremely fine.* £300-400

Price Realised : £240

Calendar year mintage 6,441,322
See footnote for lot 191, page 186, for a brief synopsis of the 1869 die numbers.

209 **Victoria,** Sovereign, 1869, die number 57, second larger young head left, ww incuse on truncation without stops, date below, 6 with open curvy top but no bulb, last A of legend flawed, *rev* crowned quartered shield of arms within laurel wreath, die number 57 below, emblems below, legend with light raised die flaw in some letters, 7.99g (Marsh 53; MCE 529; S 3853). *Light surface marks, nearly extremely fine / extremely fine.* £350-450

Price Realised : £360

Calendar year mintage 6,441,322
See footnote for lot 191, page 186, for a brief synopsis of the 1869 die numbers.

542 **Victoria,** Sovereign, 1869, die number 58, second larger young head left, ww incuse on truncation without stops, date below, 6 with open curvy top without bulb, hint of doubling to legend both sides, *rev* crowned quartered shield of arms within laurel wreath, die number 58 below, emblems below, second A quite doubled, 7.98g (Marsh 53; MCE 529; S 3853). *Surface marks and hairlines, almost extremely fine / extremely fine.* £300-400

Price Realised : £312

ex United Bank of Switzerland Sale 47, lot 1665
ex An Important Collection of Gold Sovereigns 1816-2000, offered as one lot, Sothebys, November 2000, lot 525 (part)
Note the unusual curved 6 in date without the top terminal bulb.
Calendar year mintage 6,441,322. See footnote for lot 191, page 186, for a brief synopsis of the 1869 die numbers.

1126 **Victoria,** Sovereign, 1869, die number 59, second larger young head left, ww incuse on truncation without stops, date below, curvy rounded 6 with bulbous top, last A of legend die flawed, *rev* crowned quartered shield of arms within laurel wreath, die number 59 below, low 5 high 9, emblems below, 7.97g (Marsh 53; MCE 529; S 3853). *Light surface marks and scuffs, once cleaned, otherwise good very fine / about extremely fine.* £300-400

Price Realised : £240

ex AH Baldwin and Sons Ltd, October 2006
Calendar year mintage 6,441,322. See footnote for lot 191, page 186, for a brief synopsis of the 1869 die numbers.

210 **Victoria,** Sovereign, 1869, die number 60, second larger young head left, ww incuse on truncation without stops, date below, 1 of date flawed, 6 with open curvy top but no bulb, first V, D and last A of legend die flawed to rim, other letters with light flaws between, *rev* crowned quartered shield of arms within laurel wreath, die number 60 below, emblems below, hairline raised die flaws on some letters, 7.98g (Marsh 53; MCE 529; S 3853). *Surface marks and hairlines, extremely fine.* £350-450

Price Realised : £552

Calendar year mintage 6,441,322
See footnote for lot 191, page 186, for a brief synopsis of the 1869 die numbers.

211 **Victoria,** Sovereign, 1869, die number 61, second larger young head left, WW incuse on truncation without stops, date below lightly doubled, curvy rounded open 6 with bulbous top, Queen's name doubled, *rev* crowned quartered shield of arms within laurel wreath, die number 61 die flawed below no lower and upper right serifs, emblems below, hairline raised die flaws on some letters of reverse, 7.96g (Marsh 53; MCE 529; S 3853). *Once cleaned with associated surface marks, scuffs and nicks, tiny red spot on reverse, very fine, reverse better.* £300-350

Price Realised : £264

ex Spink and Son Ltd, November 2003
Note the lack of serifs on the 1's of the die number, it seems it was not just the date or letter punches that had broken corners.
Calendar year mintage 6,441,322
See footnote for lot 191, page 186, for a brief synopsis of the 1869 die numbers.

543 **Victoria,** Sovereign, 1869, die number 62, second larger young head left, WW incuse on truncation without stops, date below, 6 with open curvy top without bulb, *rev* crowned quartered shield of arms within laurel wreath, die number 62 below, small 6 with larger 2, emblems below, 7.99g (Marsh 53; MCE 529; S 3853). *Some light surface marks, good extremely fine.* £400-500

Price Realised : £1,200

ex Randy Weir Numismatics, Unionville, Ontario, Canada, purchased 18 October 1993
Note the unusual curved 6 in date without the top terminal bulb.
Calendar year mintage 6,441,322
See footnote for lot 191, page 186, for a brief synopsis of the 1869 die numbers.

1127 **Victoria,** Sovereign, 1869, die number 63, second larger young head left, WW incuse on truncation without stops, date below, curvy rounded 6 with bulbous top, a hint of doubling to date and legend, *rev* crowned quartered shield of arms within laurel wreath, die number 63 below, widely spaced 6 and 3, emblems below, 7.96g (Marsh 53; MCE 529; S 3853). *Light surface marks, toned, about extremely fine, reverse better.* £300-400

Price Realised : £240

ex Douro Cargo, Spink Auction 118, 20-21 November 1996, lot 443 (part)
ex An Important Collection of Gold Sovereigns 1816-2000, offered as one lot, Sothebys, November 2000, lot 525 (part)
Calendar year mintage 6,441,322
See footnote for lot 191, page 186, for a brief synopsis of the 1869 die numbers.

The Extremely Rare 1869 Proof Sovereign Struck in 24 Carat Gold, Die Number 64

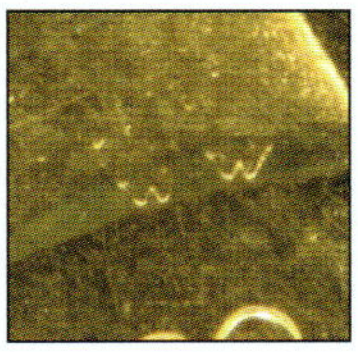

212 **Victoria,** Proof Sovereign, 1869, struck in 24 carat yellow gold, die number 64, second larger young head left, engraved after William Wyon, WW incuse on truncation without stops, date below, 6 with open curvy top but no bulb, VICTORIA DEI GRATIA, toothed border and raised linear outer rim both sides, *rev* struck with inverted die axis, after Jean Baptiste Merlen, crowned quartered shield of arms within laurel wreath, die number 64 below, emblems below, small rosette either side, BRITANNIARUM REGINA FID: DEF:, M of legend doubled, raised metal flaw on field to right of crown, edge milled, 22.1mm, 7.96g (WR 312 R7; DM 207).
Light scratch from back of head, slightly streaky tone on obverse, as struck mint state. £8000-10,000

Price Realised : £13,200

ex Captain K J Douglas-Morris collection, Sothebys, 26 November 1974, lot 207
ex Spink Numismatic Circular, April 1990, item 1646
ex An Important Collection of Gold Sovereigns 1816-2000, offered as one lot, Sothebys, 16-17 November 2000, lot 525 (part)
Calendar year mintage 6,441,322
See footnote for lot 191, page 186, for a brief synopsis of the 1869 die numbers.
This die number 64 on the 24 carat proof, does not seem to exist for a currency piece as well. The Bentley Collector never came across one in currency format in 20 years of looking. This is odd as the 827 die number 22 also exists coupled with a normal obverse.

544 **Victoria,** Sovereign, 1869, die number 69, second larger young head left, WW incuse on truncation without stops, date below, 6 with open curvy top with bulb, penultimate A die flawed, *rev* crowned quartered shield of arms within laurel wreath, die number 69 below, 7.96g (Marsh 53; MCE 529; S 3853). *Heavy surface marks and scuffs, light red spots on reverse, almost very fine, reverse better.* £300-350

Price Realised : £264

ex Randy Weir Numismatics, Unionville, Ontario, Canada, purchased 18 October 1993
Calendar year mintage 6,441,322
See footnote for lot 191, page 186, for a brief synopsis of the 1869 die numbers.

The Third Young Head type of Queen Victoria

It has always been known that the truncation again differs from 1870 onward for the young head shield reverse design Sovereigns, and they are so referenced in the Spink Standard Catalogue as S.3853B. Marsh mentions the difference in his narrative as point number 3, but did not go as so far to tabulate or study it further. The raised W.W. actually runs to the very edge of the truncation and meets the field.

However, most significantly, in the years of study by this cataloguer of the Bentley Collection, he noted that the bust is actually slightly different. There is a change to the rendering of the hair which is very evident when comparing coins of the previous type and this "new" third head. The rendering of the hair in the large bun and the strands of hair nearest the letter G are of a different arrangement and the treatment of the ponytail below also differs. Coupled with the change of the WW initials on the neck, back to being punctuated and in relief on this truncation, it makes for a more significant variety than has previously been credited. The reason for this change in engraving is open to further research, but this cataloguer feels it must be something to do with a significant Act of Coinage passed and proclaimed in 1870, where all coinage in circulation dating to before the reign of Queen Victoria was deemed to be no longer legal tender. This is coupled with the fact that change was afoot at the Sydney branch Mint in Australia with the design of the Sovereign there about to be changed to fit in with the London issues. The only difference to denote them as Sydney being the mere addition of a small letter S for Sydney where the die number appears on the London issued pieces. The Melbourne Mint was already planned and being built and that coinage too would fit in with this design with a small letter M below the shield and wreath.

Looking at further physical evidence of the Sovereigns from now onward, it will be seen with coins of this new production that the instance of "doubling" of letters on the dies striking (dual-hubbing) the coins begins to diminish through successive years and the hairline raised die flaws are all but quenched by the new strikings. Quality control is gradually climbing to a new high it seems. See a note on varieties in the introduction for further information. Cross referencing and chronology with any surviving records at the Mint would be most welcomed and prudent research to further prove these theories.

A Unique Presentation Proof Striking of an 1870 Sovereign Die Number 1

213 **Victoria,** Specimen Proof Presentation Sovereign, 1870, die number 1, third young head left, with double fillet, w.w. in relief on truncation, hair of differing arrangement in the bun of the hair with an extra strand of hair in the ponytail, date below, toothed border both sides, VICTORIA DEI GRATIA, right half of legend doubled, light raised die flaw in last word of obverse legend, *rev* struck with inverted die axis, crowned quartered shield of arms within laurel wreath, die number 1 below, no lower right serif to 1, emblems below, 7.98g (WR -; Marsh 54; MCE 530; S 3853B). *Struck with a true proof finish to the fields, with parallel die polish lines evident as with other proofs of this period, however obverse design not frosted, though with an excellent well defined strike with raised rim, mint state and the finest known 1870 Sovereign in the world, probably unique.* £8000-10,000

Price Realised : £14,400

ex Mark Rasmussen Numismatist, June 2001.
Calendar year mintage 2,189,960
This very intriguing coin was submitted to the Royal Mint for an opinion in 2000-2001 to see if any light could be shed on what it was and why it may exist. The Mint were noncommittal at the time, as their records of this period appear silent, but study photographs were taken by them for future reference as a coin of this ilk has never been seen before. Discovered too late to be considered for publication in the "WR" reference book, neither this cataloguer, or Mr Rasmussen, who sold the coin as a "special" Sovereign best described as a "specimen" in light of the Mint's response, have come across anything like it of this type or date in our careers.
This cataloguer would be so bold today as to upgrade its status to a Proof Sovereign based on the fact that the finish of the fields is uniform and compares very well with the fields on other proof pieces of the period like the 1853. The fields are actually just as characteristic as the proof fields on the 1869 piece in the previous lot, as the quality is so superb and obvious care and attention has been taken in its production. Note the faulty 1 punch appears again to strike the die number with missing serif.
As the design was changed with this issue to a w.w. in relief rendering, it seems even more of a valid reason to strike a proof presentation coin. When you couple this fact with a significant Act of Coinage being passed in 1870 as well, when all pre-Victorian coinage was deemed non-legal tender, and all the Sovereigns and other coins of William IV and before were to be called in, the great change that was afoot was appropriate for a design change, and the striking of such a "VIP" issue. It is even more appropriate from the study of the Bentley Collection that a further nuance in the design of the hair with a change of bust possibly marks the introduction of this Coinage Act. The rendering of the hair at the back of the bun is different, in addition to the truncation initial letters. From now onward it is generally noted that the quality control has improved; the weight standard of the coins leaving the Mint has increased by one to two hundredths of a gramme as best quality Sovereigns are often as high as 8.00g exactly, rather than 7.98 to 7.99g as previously when preserved in top quality.

1128 **Victoria,** Sovereign, 1870, die number 1, second larger young head left, WW incuse on truncation without stops, date below, date and legend doubled, *rev* crowned quartered shield of arms within laurel wreath, die number 1 below, only with a lower left serif, lightly die flawed as are some letters of reverse legend, emblems below, 7.99g (Marsh 54; MCE 530; S 3853). *Hairlines, surface marks and nicks, otherwise extremely fine.* £300-350

Price Realised : £1,104

ex Randy Weir Numismatics, Unionville, Ontario, Canada, 19 October 1992
Calendar year mintage 2,189,960
This coin is die number 1 of a mere 18 different numbered dies in the Bentley Collection running from 1 to 96. Marsh claims that 80 other die numbers exist! With so many absent from this collection, it makes a total of 98 reverse dies to strike just over 2 million Sovereigns. This suggests very uneconomic longevity for the dies, and this cataloguer feels that the die numbers recorded for 1870 in Marsh are unreliable and must have been some sort of human typographical error perhaps transposing 1871 known die numbers for 1870 which is more likely, especially when we see that the total number of dies for 1871 when Marsh is added to Bentley is also 98 and that is to strike over 8½ million Sovereigns in one calendar year!
What we do know is that, in twenty years of seriously looking for die numbers of 1870 for the Bentley collector, nothing numbered 2 to 79 inclusive has turned up, not even in the Douro Cargo and that is not just in the coins offered at auction in 1996 but in all the other portions that have come to the market more recently from individuals involved with the salvage operation.

1129 **Victoria,** Sovereign, 1870, die number 80, third young head left, W.W. in relief on truncation meets field, two strands of hair at bun near G of legend detached, extra curl at terminal of ponytail, date below, low 7 in date, letter C and first A of obverse legend flawed, die flaw from tip of neck, *rev* crowned quartered shield of arms within laurel wreath, die number 80 lightly flawed below, large 8, smaller o, emblems below, 7.96g (Marsh 54; MCE 530; S 3853B). *Light surface marks, otherwise good very fine, reverse better.* £300-350

Price Realised : £240

Calendar year mintage 2,189,960
See footnote for lot 1128 (above) for a brief synopsis of the 1870 die numbers.

214 **Victoria,** Sovereign, 1870, die number 81, third young head left, W.W. in relief on truncation, date below, 1 of date die flawed, last T of obverse legend flawed, *rev* crowned quartered shield of arms within laurel wreath, die number 81 below, emblems below, 7.96g (Marsh 54; MCE 530; S 3853B). *Light scuffs and surface marks, a few red spots, nearly very fine / very fine.* £300-350

Price Realised : £264

ex Paul Davies Ltd. This coin was purchased from one of the groups of coins from the wreck of the RMS *Douro* that were not sold by auction and within the last 10 years.
Calendar year mintage 2,189,960
See footnote for lot 1128 (above) for a brief synopsis of the 1870 die numbers.

545 **Victoria,** Sovereign, 1870, die number 82, third young head left, with double fillet, w.w. in relief on truncation, hair of differing arrangement in the bun of the hair with an extra strand of hair in the ponytail, date below, 1 of date doubled, penultimate A die flawed, *rev* crowned quartered shield of arms within laurel wreath, die number 82 below, smaller 8 with larger 2, emblems below, 7.98g (Marsh 54; MCE 530; S 3853B). *Rim nick on obverse, some scuffs, hairlines and other light marks, toned, good very fine / extremely fine.* £300-350

Price Realised : £288

Calendar year mintage 2,189,960
This coin is die number 82 of a mere 18 different numbered dies in the Bentley Collection running from 1 to 96. Marsh claims that 80 other die numbers exist! See the footnote to lot 1128, page 206, for further information and analysis.

1130 **Victoria,** Sovereign, 1870, die number 83, third young head left, w.w. in relief on truncation meets field, extra curl at terminal of hair, date below, letter V of obverse legend flawed into field, *rev* crowned quartered shield of arms within laurel wreath, die number 83 below, emblems below, 7.98g (Marsh 54; MCE 530; S 3853B). *Red spot on reverse, toned with surface marks, otherwise very fine, reverse better.* £250-300

Price Realised : £240

This coin was purchased from one of the groups of coins from the wreck of the RMS *Douro* that were not sold by auction and within the last 10 years.
Calendar year mintage 2,189,960. See footnote for lot 1128, pag 206, for a brief synopsis of the 1870 die numbers.

215 **Victoria,** Sovereign, 1870, die number 84, third young head left, w.w. in relief on truncation, date below, tiny die flaw to left of date, *rev* crowned quartered shield of arms within laurel wreath, die number 84 below die flawed, emblems below, hairline raised die flaws on some letters, 8.00g (Marsh 54; MCE 530; S 3853B). *Red copper tone, nick on cheek and other very light marks, good extremely fine.* £500-600

Price Realised : £672

ex Douro Cargo, Spink Auction 118, 20-21 November 1996, lot 1376 (part)
Calendar year mintage 2,189,960. See footnote for lot 1128, pag 206, for a brief synopsis of the 1870 die numbers.

216 **Victoria,** Sovereign, 1870, die number 85, third young head left, w.w. in relief on truncation, date below, some light raised die flaws in obverse legend, *rev* crowned quartered shield of arms within laurel wreath, die number 85 below die flawed, emblems below, 8.00g (Marsh 54; MCE 530; S 3853B). *Red tone, a few light hairlines, pleasing good extremely fine.* £500-600

Price Realised : £1,380

ex An Important Collection of Gold Sovereigns 1816-2000, offered as one lot, Sothebys, 16-17 November 2000, lot 525 (part)
Calendar year mintage 2,189,960
See footnote for lot 1128, pag 206, for a brief synopsis of the 1870 die numbers.

217 **Victoria,** Sovereign, 1870, die number 86, third young head left, with double fillet, w.w. in relief on truncation, raised die flaw from hair bun to rim, date below lightly doubled, die flawed 8, last T of legend flawed, *rev* struck with inverted die axis, crowned shield of arms within laurel wreath, die number 86 below die flawed, other light flaws in lettering, emblems below, 7.98g (Marsh 54; MCE 530; S 3853B). *Scratch on neck, hairlined, brilliant extremely fine.* £350-450

Price Realised : £552

ex An Important Collection of Gold Sovereigns 1816-2000, offered as one lot, Sothebys, 16-17 November 2000, lot 525 (part)
Calendar year mintage 2,189,960
See footnote for lot 1128, pag 206, for a brief synopsis of the 1870 die numbers.

546 **Victoria,** Sovereign, 1870, die number 86, third young head left, w.w. in relief on truncation, date below, trace of date doubled, last T die flawed, die flaw in hair, *rev* crowned quartered shield of arms within laurel wreath, die number 86 below die flawed, emblems below, hairline flaw at start of second word, 7.98g (Marsh 54; MCE 530; S 3853B). *Red spot on reverse, light surface marks, almost extremely fine / extremely fine.* £300-400

Price Realised : £360

Calendar year mintage 2,189,960
See footnote for lot 1128, pag 206, for a brief synopsis of the 1870 die numbers.

1131 **Victoria,** Sovereign, 1870, die number 87, third young head left, w.w. in relief on truncation meets field, date below, die flaw through 1 of date from rim to neck, a number of letters of obverse legend die flawed, *rev* crowned quartered shield of arms within laurel wreath, die number 87 below, emblems below, 8.00g (Marsh 54; MCE 530; S 3853B). *Light hairlines and surface marks, two spots on obverse, one on the reverse, obverse rim nick, brilliant reverse, otherwise extremely fine, reverse better.* £300-400

Price Realised : £360

ex Douro Cargo, Spink Auction 118, 20-21 November 1996, lot 1376 (part)
Calendar year mintage 2,189,960
See footnote for lot 1128, pag 206, for a brief synopsis of the 1870 die numbers.

218 **Victoria,** Sovereign, 1870, die number 88, third young head left, with double fillet, w.w. in relief on truncation, date below, die flaw to left of date and at first V and last A of legend, *rev* crowned quartered shield of arms within laurel wreath, die number 88 below die flawed, light doubling of legend with some light hairline raised flaws, emblems below, 7.99g (Marsh 54; MCE 530; S 3853B). *Light scratch in field above nose, toned, extremely fine.* £350-450

Price Realised : £504

ex Douro Cargo, Spink Auction 118, 20-21 November 1996, lot 1376 (part)
Calendar year mintage 2,189,960
See footnote for lot 1128, pag 206, for a brief synopsis of the 1870 die numbers.

547 **Victoria,** Sovereign, 1870, die number 89, third young head left, w.w. in relief on truncation, date below, legend doubled on obverse, die flaw in field at lower left, *rev* crowned quartered shield of arms within laurel wreath, die number 89 below, emblems below, light hairline flaws connect some reverse letters, 7.99g (Marsh 54; MCE 530; S 3853B). *Once cleaned with light surface marks and hairlines, now toned, extremely fine.* £300-350

Price Realised : £480

Calendar year mintage 2,189,960
See footnote for lot 1128, pag 206, for a brief synopsis of the 1870 die numbers.

1132 **Victoria,** Sovereign, 1870, die number 90, third young head left, w.w. in relief on truncation meets field, date below, die flaw to left of 1 from rim to neck, doubled legend, first and third I of legend and last A die flawed, *rev* crowned quartered shield of arms within laurel wreath, die number 90 below, emblems below, 7.98g (Marsh 54; MCE 530; S 3853B). *Light hairlines from being once lightly cleaned perhaps, now toned, extremely fine.* £300-400

Price Realised : £264

Calendar year mintage 2,189,960
See footnote for lot 1128, pag 206, for a brief synopsis of the 1870 die numbers.

219 **Victoria,** Sovereign, 1870, die number 91, third young head left, w.w. in relief on truncation, stops very tiny and on field, date below, date figures horizontally die flawed, 1 and 7 flaws run to rim, last I of legend die flawed to rim, legend lightly doubled, *rev* crowned quartered shield of arms within laurel wreath, die number 91 below, emblems below, some light flaws in some letters of legend, 7.98g (Marsh 54; MCE 530; S 3853B). *Black streak of tone on neck, light surface marks, almost extremely fine.* £300-350

Price Realised : £384

ex Douro Cargo, Spink Auction 118, 20-21 November 1996, lot 1376 (part)
Calendar year mintage 2,189,960
See footnote for lot 1128, pag 206, for a brief synopsis of the 1870 die numbers.

548 **Victoria,** Sovereign, 1870, die number 92, third young head left, w.w. in relief on truncation, date below, penultimate A die flawed to rim, *rev* crowned quartered shield of arms within laurel wreath, die number 92 below, emblems below, hint of doubling to reverse legend, 7.97g (Marsh 54; MCE 530; S 3853B). *Scratch on obverse from chin to nose, another to right side of bow in reverse wreath, otherwise toned almost extremely fine.* £300-350

Price Realised : £288

ex Douro Cargo, Spink Auction 118, 20-21 November 1996, lot 1376 (part)
Calendar year mintage 2,189,960
See footnote for lot 1128, pag 206, for a brief synopsis of the 1870 die numbers.

549 **Victoria,** Sovereign, 1870, die number 93, third young head left, w.w. in relief on truncation, date below, last A die flawed to rim, *rev* crowned quartered shield of arms within laurel wreath, die number 93 below die flawed, emblems below, 7.99g (Marsh 54; MCE 530; S 3853B). *Light scratch in obverse field, with other light hairlines and surface marks, otherwise extremely fine.* £300-350

Price Realised : £384

ex Douro Cargo, Spink Auction 118, 20-21 November 1996, lot 1376 (part)
Calendar year mintage 2,189,960. See footnote for lot 1128, pag 206, for a brief synopsis of the 1870 die numbers.

1133 **Victoria,** Sovereign, 1870, die number 94, third young head left, w.w. in relief on truncation meets field, date below, die flaw through 1 from rim to neck, further flaw from hair bun to rim, date and legend lightly doubled both sides, *rev* crowned quartered shield of arms within laurel wreath, die number 94 below, emblems below, 7.96g (Marsh 54; MCE 530; S 3853B). *Some red spots each side with light surface marks, otherwise bold very fine.* £250-300

Price Realised : £288

This coin was purchased from one of the groups of coins from the wreck of the RMS *Douro* that were not sold by auction and within the last 10 years.
Calendar year mintage 2,189,960. See footnote for lot 1128, pag 206, for a brief synopsis of the 1870 die numbers.

220 **Victoria,** Sovereign, 1870, die number 95, third young head left, die flaws from neck, ww in relief on truncation, stops not visible, date below, date figures very flawed especially 7, last I of legend die flawed, *rev* crowned quartered shield of arms within laurel wreath, die number 95 below, emblems below, 7.96g (Marsh 54; MCE 530; S 3853B). *Red spot on throat and one on reverse to right of die number, reverse rim nick, toned, nearly very fine / good very fine.* £300-350

Price Realised : £264

ex Paul Davies Ltd via Spink and Son Ltd, July 2004
This coin was purchased from one of the groups of coins from the wreck of the RMS *Douro* that were not sold by auction.
Note the lack of stops in the initials on truncation which should be on the field. They are absent no doubt due to a blockage on the die rather than being left out of the engraving.
Calendar year mintage 2,189,960. See footnote for lot 1128, pag 206, for a brief synopsis of the 1870 die numbers.

550 **Victoria,** Sovereign, 1870, die number 96, third young head left, w.w. in relief on truncation, date below, 8 and 0 of date doubled, *rev* crowned quartered shield of arms within laurel wreath, die number 96 below die flawed, emblems below, 7.96g (Marsh 54; MCE 530; S 3853B). *Slightly scuffed fields with underlying brilliance, nearly very fine / good very fine.* £300-350

Price Realised : £288

ex Spink and Son, purchased July 2004
Calendar year mintage 2,189,960. See footnote for lot 1128, pag 206, for a brief synopsis of the 1870 die numbers.

1134 **Victoria,** Sovereign, 1870, die number 112, third young head left, ww in relief on truncation meets field, stops not visible, date below, last A of legend die flawed, *rev* crowned quartered shield of arms within laurel wreath, die number 112 lightly flawed below, 2 larger than the figure 1's, emblems below, 7.98g (Marsh 54; MCE 530; S 3853B). *Two red spots on obverse, eight on reverse, other light surface marks and hairlines, otherwise toned, about very fine, reverse better.* £250-300

Price Realised : £240

This coin was purchased from one of the groups of coins from the wreck of the RMS *Douro* that were not sold by auction and within the last 10 years.
Calendar year mintage 2,189,960. See footnote for lot 1128, pag 206, for a brief synopsis of the 1870 die numbers.

221 **Victoria,** Sovereign, 1870, die number 113, third young head left, ww incuse on truncation without stops, date below, lightly flawed and doubled, last I of obverse legend flawed, *rev* crowned shield of arms within laurel wreath, die number 113 below lightly die flawed, emblems below, 7.96g (Marsh 54; MCE 530; S 3853). *Three short scratches on obverse field behind head, other light surface marks, otherwise almost very fine.* £300-350

Price Realised : £264

ex Paul Davies Ltd. This coin was purchased from one of the groups of coins from the wreck of the RMS *Douro* that were not sold by auction and within the last 10 years.
Calendar year mintage 2,189,960. See footnote for lot 1128, pag 206, for a brief synopsis of the 1870 die numbers.

551 **Victoria,** Sovereign, 1870, die number 114, third young head left, w.w. in relief on truncation, date below, last A die flawed to rim, *rev* crowned quartered shield of arms within laurel wreath, die number 114 below, no upper serifs to figure 1's, emblems below, hint of doubling to reverse legend, 7.95g (Marsh 54; MCE 530; S 3853B). *Once polished, toned, nearly very fine / very fine.* £300-350

Price Realised : £264

This coin was purchased from one of the groups of coins from the wreck of the RMS *Douro* that were not sold by auction and within the last 10 years.
Note the lack of upper serifs on the 1's of the die number. It seems it was not just the date or letter punches that had broken corners.
Calendar year mintage 2,189,960 . See footnote for lot 1128, pag 206, for a brief synopsis of the 1870 die numbers.

1135 **Victoria,** Sovereign, 1870, die number 115, third young head left, w.w. in relief on truncation meets field, date below, date and legend doubled, *rev* crowned quartered shield of arms within laurel wreath, die number 115 below, the die number ascends in height from left to right, emblems below, 7.96g (Marsh 54; MCE 530; S 3853B). *Cleaned with associated surface marks and hairlines, otherwise about very fine, reverse better.* £250-300

Price Realised : £240

Calendar year mintage 2,189,960. See footnote for lot 1128, pag 206, for a brief synopsis of the 1870 die numbers.

222 **Victoria,** Sovereign, 1870, die number 116, third young head left, ww in relief on truncation without stops, date below, doubled 8 and 0, *rev* crowned quartered shield of arms within laurel wreath, die number 116 below die flawed, first 1 of die number with no upper serif, second 1 with trace only, emblems below, 7.98g (Marsh 54; MCE 530; S 3853). *Toned, some surface marks, very fine / good very fine.* £300-350

Price Realised : £336

ex Paul Davies Ltd. This coin was purchased from one of the groups of coins from the wreck of the RMS *Douro* that were not sold by auction and within the last 10 years.
The weak and absent serifs on the die number, are most likely due to weak punching of the die number rather than faulty "one" punches.
Calendar year mintage 2,189,960. See footnote for lot 1128, pag 206, for a brief synopsis of the 1870 die numbers.

552 **Victoria,** Sovereign, 1870, die number 117, third young head left, w.w. in relief on truncation, date below, 1 of date die flawed to rim, *rev* crowned quartered shield of arms within laurel wreath, die number 117 below, no upper serifs to figure 1's, emblems below, 7.95g (Marsh 54; MCE 530; S 3853B). *Red tone, heavy surface marks, some residual black dirt around rim, almost very fine.* £300-350

Price Realised : £288

This coin was purchased from one of the groups of coins from the wreck of the RMS *Douro* that were not sold by auction and within the last 10 years.
Note the lack of upper serifs on the 1's of the die number. It seems it was not just the date or letter punches that had broken corners.
Calendar year mintage 2,189,960. See footnote for lot 1128, pag 206, for a brief synopsis of the 1870 die numbers.

1136 **Victoria,** Sovereign, 1870, die number 118, third young head left, w.w. in relief on truncation meets field, date below doubled, raised die flaw from tip of neck to rim, last A of legend die flawed, other light flaw in Queen's name, *rev* crowned quartered shield of arms within laurel wreath, die number 118 below, first 1 with trace of upper serif, second 1 with no upper serif, emblems below, 7.99g (Marsh 54; MCE 530; S 3853B). *Heavy surface marks and hairlines, rim bruise on reverse, otherwise extremely fine.* £300-400

Price Realised : £288

Calendar year mintage 2,189,960. See footnote for lot 1128, pag 206, for a brief synopsis of the 1870 die numbers.

223 **Victoria,** Sovereign, 1870, die number 119, third young head left, with double fillet, w.w. in relief on truncation, date below lightly doubled, penultimate A of obverse legend die flawed to T, *rev* struck with inverted die axis, crowned shield of arms within laurel wreath, die number 119 below lightly flawed, ones without upper serifs, emblems below, raised die flaw in some letters then to rim, 7.98g (Marsh 54; MCE 530; S 3853B). *Reverse rim nick, practically extremely fine, reverse better.* £350-450

Price Realised : £480

ex Randy Weir Numismatics, Unionville, Ontario, Canada, purchased 19 October 1992
The ones in the die number with absent serifs could be due to blockages on the die rather than faulty punches.
Calendar year mintage 2,189,960. See footnote for lot 1128, pag 206, for a brief synopsis of the 1870 die numbers.

1137 **Victoria,** Sovereign, 1870, die number 120, third young head left, ww in relief on truncation meets field, stops not visible, date below, date and legend doubled, raised die flaw to left of date from neck to rim, *rev* crowned quartered shield of arms within laurel wreath, die number 120 lightly flawed below, emblems below, 7.97g (Marsh 54; MCE 530; S 3853B). *Cleaned with surface marks and hairlines, otherwise good very fine, reverse better.* £250-300

Price Realised : £240

Calendar year mintage 2,189,960
See footnote for lot 1128, pag 206, for a brief synopsis of the 1870 die numbers.

1138 **Victoria,** Sovereign, 1870, die number 121, third young head left, w.w. in relief on truncation meets field, date below, 1 of date doubled, raised die flaw in first three letters of last word, *rev* crowned quartered shield of arms within laurel wreath, die number 121 lightly flawed below, first 1 with no upper serif, emblems below, raised die flaw lightly connects some letters of reverse legend, 8.00g (Marsh 54; MCE 530; S 3853B). *Some light hairlines, proof-like obverse, otherwise good extremely fine.* £400-500

Price Realised : £696

ex Randy Weir Numismatics, Unionville, Ontario, Canada, early 1993
Calendar year mintage 2,189,960
See footnote for lot 1128, pag 206, for a brief synopsis of the 1870 die numbers.

224 **Victoria,** Sovereign, 1870, die number 122, third young head left, with double fillet, w.w. in relief on truncation, date below lightly doubled and die flawed, *rev* crowned quartered shield of arms within laurel wreath, die number 122 below, emblems below, 7.93g (Marsh 54; MCE 530; S 3853B). *Cleaned, now toning, nearly very fine with surface marks, reverse better.* £300-350

Price Realised : £264

ex Spink and Son Ltd, November 2003
Calendar year mintage 2,189,960
See footnote for lot 1128, pag 206, for a brief synopsis of the 1870 die numbers.

553 **Victoria,** Sovereign, 1870, die number 123, third young head left, w.w. in relief on truncation, date below, 0 of date die flawed to rim, *rev* crowned quartered shield of arms within laurel wreath, die number 123 below, no upper serif to 1, emblems below, 7.98g (Marsh 54; MCE 530; S 3853B). *Some nicks and scuffs, hairlined with other light surface marks, brilliant extremely fine / good extremely fine.* £300-350

Price Realised : £528

ex Stacks, 5 November 1997, lot 1031
ex An Important Collection of Gold Sovereigns 1816-2000, offered as one lot, Sothebys, November 2000, lot 525 (part)
Note the lack of upper serifs on the 1 of the die number. It seems it was not just the date or letter punches that had broken corners.
Calendar year mintage 2,189,960
See footnote for lot 1128, pag 206, for a brief synopsis of the 1870 die numbers.

A Superb Specimen or Presentation Striking of Die Number 1 of the 1871 Sovereign

225 **Victoria,** Sovereign, 1871, die number 1, third young head left, W.W. in relief on truncation, date below, *rev* crowned quartered shield of arms within laurel wreath, die number 1 below, no lower right serif to die number, emblems below, 7.99g (Marsh 55; MCE 531; S 3853B). *Proof-like with the characteristic parallel die polishing lines evident on the fields, though the edge not quite as sharp as a proof, frosted design elements, most likely struck for a* VIP, *FDC and the finest known 1871 Sovereign in the world.* £3000-3500

Price Realised : £3,360

Calendar year mintage 8,767,250
This coin is a superior striking to currency and seems to represent the reuse of the proof die number 1 die as seen on the 1870 proof in lot 213, page 205, though the reverse is not as proof-like as that coin. The obverse certainly seems to be struck from a proof die, however the edge and rim is not as sharp as a true proof and it is most likely this is an early strike from die number one that was obviously saved for presentation. Further study and research perhaps in collaboration with the Royal Mint Museum may prove to be fruitful.

1139 **Victoria,** Sovereign, 1871, die number 1, third young head left, W.W. in relief on truncation, date below, raised die flaw to left of date from neck to rim, *rev* crowned shield of arms within laurel wreath, die number 1 below, no lower right serif, emblems below, 8.00g (Marsh 55; MCE 531; S 3853B). *Light surface marks on obverse, otherwise extremely fine / good extremely fine.* £400-500

Price Realised : £600

Calendar year mintage 8,767,250
This coin is die number 1 of a total of 75 different numbered dies in the Bentley Collection, running from 1 to 111. Marsh claims that 23 other die numbers exist, with so many absent from this collection, it makes a total of 98 reverse dies to strike nearly 9 million Sovereigns. Coincidentally this is the same total arrived at for 1870, if you take Marsh's extras for that year into account, which again suggests some sort of error in determining known dies of 1870. Die number 42 is present in the Bentley Collection which is a number not included in Marsh's list for 1871. The 1871 total number of dies to calendar year output suggests reasonable longevity for the dies, however it must be borne in mind that 1871 is the first calendar year where the new St George and dragon reverse Sovereign for Queen Victoria is produced and the output will include a lesser proportion for these coins too. This is why trying to analyse calendar output against die numbers and variations known is so troublesome.
It seems from now onward the evidence of dies starting to break up gradually with raised hairline die flaws, and a problem of dual-hubbing in the dies giving doubled letters and date figures, seems to diminish from now onward. See "a note on varieties" in the introduction of the catalogue to learn more about dual-hubbing.

554 **Victoria,** Sovereign, 1871, die number 2, third young head left, w.w. in relief on truncation, date below, 8 of date die flawed, some raised flaws at end of legend, *rev* crowned quartered shield of arms within laurel wreath, die number 2 below, emblems below, 8.00g (Marsh 55; MCE 531; S 3853B). *Some light surface marks, extremely fine / good extremely fine.* £350-450

Price Realised : £744

ex Randy Weir Numismatics, Unionville, Ontario, Canada, purchased 14 August 1992
Calendar year mintage 8,767,250
See footnote for lot 1139, page 214, for a brief synopsis of the 1871 die numbers.

1140 **Victoria,** Sovereign, 1871, die number 3, third young head left, w.w. in relief on truncation, date below, raised die flaw to left of date from neck to rim, further flaw between I and A of legend and from hair bun to rim, *rev* crowned shield of arms within laurel wreath, die number 3 below, emblems below, 7.99g (Marsh 55; MCE 531; S 3853B). *Light surface marks, otherwise extremely fine / good extremely fine.* £400-500

Price Realised : £384

Calendar year mintage 8,767,250
See footnote for lot 1139, page 214, for a brief synopsis of the 1871 die numbers.

226 **Victoria,** Sovereign, 1871, die number 4, third young head left, w.w. in relief on truncation, date below, 18 doubled, last I of legend flawed, *rev* struck with inverted die axis, crowned shield of arms within laurel wreath, die number 4 below, emblems below, 7.98g (Marsh 55; MCE 531; S 3853B). *Obverse and reverse rim nick, hairlined, nearly extremely fine / extremely fine.* £350-450

Price Realised : £360

ex Sahara Coins, Las Vegas, Nevada, USA, November 2001
Calendar year mintage 8,767,250
See footnote for lot 1139, page 214, for a brief synopsis of the 1871 die numbers.

555 **Victoria,** Sovereign, 1871, die number 5, third young head left, w.w. in relief on truncation, date below, doubling of date and legend, some raised flaws in parts of legend, *rev* crowned quartered shield of arms within laurel wreath, die number 5 below, emblems below, trace of doubling in legend, 7.98g (Marsh 55; MCE 531; S 3853B). *Some light surface marks, scuffed on cheek, previously graded by PCGS as MS63, extremely fine.* £300-400

Price Realised : £528

ex Douro Cargo, Spink Auction 118, 20-21 November 1996, lot 566 (part)
ex An Important Collection of Gold Sovereigns 1816-2000, offered as one lot, Sothebys, November 2000, lot 525 (part)
Calendar year mintage 8,767,250
See footnote for lot 1139, page 214, for a brief synopsis of the 1871 die numbers.

1141 **Victoria,** Sovereign, 1871, die number 6, third young head left, w.w. in relief on truncation, date lightly doubled below, hairline raised die flaw connects all letters and date figures, *rev* crowned shield of arms within laurel wreath, die number 6 below, emblems below, hairline raised die flaw connects some letters in legend, 8.00g (Marsh 55; MCE 531; S 3853B). *A couple of spots on cheek and neck, others on upper right of reverse, light surface marks and hairlined, otherwise extremely fine.* £300-400

Price Realised : £408

ex Abbeygate Coins, USA, purchased 1995, previously graded as MS62
Calendar year mintage 8,767,250
See footnote for lot 1139, page 214, for a brief synopsis of the 1871 die numbers.

556 **Victoria,** Sovereign, 1871, die number 7, third young head left, w.w. in relief on truncation, date below, lightly die flawed date, G of legend die flawed to rim, *rev* crowned quartered shield of arms within laurel wreath, die number 7 below, emblems below, raised hairline flaw connects some letters of legend, 7.94g (Marsh 55; MCE 531; S 3853B). *Some light surface marks, with nicks and scuffs, toned good fine / very fine.* £300-350

Price Realised : £264

This coin was purchased from one of the groups of coins from the wreck of the RMS *Douro* that were not sold by auction, bought in the last 10 years.
Calendar year mintage 8,767,250
See footnote for lot 1139, page 214, for a brief synopsis of the 1871 die numbers.

227 **Victoria,** Sovereign, 1871, die number 8, third young head left, w.w. in relief on truncation, date below, first 1 in date die flawed, 8 doubled, first V flawed to rim, last A of legend filled, *rev* crowned quartered shield of arms within laurel wreath, die number 8 below, emblems below, hairline raised die flaw in some letters, 7.97g (Marsh 55; MCE 531; S 3853B). *Black streak of tone on cheek, some hairlines, nearly extremely fine, reverse better.* £350-450

Price Realised : £300

ex Randy Weir Numismatics, Unionville, Ontario, Canada, purchased 12 November 1990
Calendar year mintage 8,767,250
See footnote for lot 1139, page 214, for a brief synopsis of the 1871 die numbers.

557 **Victoria,** Sovereign, 1871, die number 9, third young head left, w.w. in relief on truncation, date below, hint of doubling in legend both sides, *rev* crowned quartered shield of arms within laurel wreath, die number 9 below, emblems below, raised hairline flaw connects some letters of legend, 7.98g (Marsh 55; MCE 531; S 3853B). *Some light surface marks and nicks, otherwise extremely fine.* £350-400

Price Realised : £360

Calendar year mintage 8,767,250
See footnote for lot 1139, page 214, for a brief synopsis of the 1871 die numbers.

1142 **Victoria,** Sovereign, 1871, die number 10, third young head left, w.w. in relief on truncation, date below, raised die flaws connects some letters of legend both sides, *rev* crowned shield of arms within laurel wreath, die number 10 below, low 1, high 0, emblems below, hint of doubling in legend, 7.99g (Marsh 55; MCE 531; S 3853B). *Scuffed with many tiny surface marks, light deposit on reverse rim, otherwise toned, good very fine.* £250-300

Price Realised : £216

Calendar year mintage 8,767,250
See footnote for lot 1139, page 214, for a brief synopsis of the 1871 die numbers.

228 **Victoria,** Sovereign, 1871, die number 11, third young head left, w.w. in relief on truncation, date below, hairline raised die flaw in some obverse letters, *rev* crowned quartered shield of arms within laurel wreath, die number 11 below, emblems below, hint of doubling on lettering, 7.98g (Marsh 55; MCE 531; S 3853B). *Red spot on crown caul of reverse, some hairlines and scuffs, dig above head, almost extremely fine with underlying brilliance, reverse better.* £300-350

Price Realised : £264

ex Douro Cargo, Spink Auction 118, 20-21 November 1996, lot 1377 (part)
Calendar year mintage 8,767,250
See footnote for lot 1139, page 214, for a brief synopsis of the 1871 die numbers.

1143 **Victoria,** Sovereign, 1871, die number 12, third young head left, w.w. in relief on truncation, date below, die flaw to left of date from neck to rim, trace of doubling to legends both sides, *rev* crowned shield of arms within laurel wreath, die number 12 lightly flawed below, emblems below, 7.99g (Marsh 55; MCE 531; S 3853B). *Some light hairlines and surface marks, streak of tone on cheek, black mark over head, otherwise toned, extremely fine.* £300-400

Price Realised : £264

ex Douro Cargo, Spink Auction 118, 20-21 November 1996, lot 1377 (part)
Calendar year mintage 8,767,250
See footnote for lot 1139, page 214, for a brief synopsis of the 1871 die numbers.

229 **Victoria,** Sovereign, 1871, die number 13, third young head left, w.w. in relief on truncation, date below quite doubled, first 1 in date flawed from rim to neck, last T flawed to rim, *rev* crowned quartered shield of arms within laurel wreath, die number 13 below die flawed, the 3 over a lower 3, emblems below, trace of doubling in legend, 7.99g (Marsh 55; MCE 531; S 3853B). *Patch of tone on cheek, light hairlines and surface marks with a few nicks, tiny black spot on reverse, otherwise extremely fine / good extremely fine.* £350-450

Price Realised : £384

ex Randy Weir Numismatics, Unionville, Ontario, Canada, purchased 27 July 1994
Calendar year mintage 8,767,250
See footnote for lot 1139, page 214, for a brief synopsis of the 1871 die numbers.

558 **Victoria,** Sovereign, 1871, die number 14, third young head left, w.w. in relief on truncation, date below, hint of doubling in legend both sides, *rev* crowned quartered shield of arms within laurel wreath, die number 14 below, emblems below, raised hairline flaw in last A of legend to rim, 7.97g (Marsh 55; MCE 531; S 3853B). *Tiny obverse rim nick, otherwise pleasing good extremely fine.* £400-500

Price Realised : £480

ex Douro Cargo, Spink Auction 118, 20-21 November 1996, lot 1377 (part)
Calendar year mintage 8,767,250
See footnote for lot 1139, page 214, for a brief synopsis of the 1871 die numbers.

1144 **Victoria,** Sovereign, 1871, die number 15, third young head left, w.w. in relief on truncation, date below, die flaw at first A of legend to rim, doubled date and legend both sides, *rev* crowned shield of arms within laurel wreath, die number 15 below, 5 slightly higher than 1, emblems below, 7.99g (Marsh 55; MCE 531; S 3853B). *Some light hairlines, spots and surface marks, otherwise toned, extremely fine, reverse better.* £300-400

Price Realised : £264

ex Douro Cargo, Spink Auction 118, 20-21 November 1996, lot 1377 (part)
Calendar year mintage 8,767,250
See footnote for lot 1139, page 214, for a brief synopsis of the 1871 die numbers.

230 **Victoria,** Sovereign, 1871, die number 16, third young head left, w.w. in relief on truncation, raised die flaw from tip of neck to rim, date below, light raised die flaws in field and last I of legend flawed to rim, *rev* crowned quartered shield of arms within laurel wreath, die number 16 below die flawed, emblems below, trace of doubling in legend, 7.98g (Marsh 55; MCE 531; S 3853B). *Red spots on reverse, extremely fine, reverse better.* £350-450

Price Realised : £432

ex Douro Cargo, Spink Auction 118, 20-21 November 1996, lot 567 (part)
ex An Important Collection of Gold Sovereigns 1816-2000, offered as one lot, Sothebys, 16-17 November 2000, lot 525 (part)
Calendar year mintage 8,767,250
See footnote for lot 1139, page 214, for a brief synopsis of the 1871 die numbers.

231 **Victoria,** Sovereign, 1871, die number 17, third young head left, w.w. in relief on truncation, date below, doubled 18, 8 flawed die number 3, first T and last A of obverse legend die flawed, hint of doubling in legends both sides, *rev* crowned quartered shield of arms within laurel wreath, die number 17 below, the 7 doubled, emblems below, 7.98g (Marsh 55; MCE 531; S 3853B). *Hairline scratch behind ponytail in field, otherwise toned, pleasing good extremely fine.* £400-500

Price Realised : £1,104

ex Randy Weir Numismatics, Unionville, Ontario, Canada, purchased 12 October 1993
Calendar year mintage 8,767,250
See footnote for lot 1139, page 214, for a brief synopsis of the 1871 die numbers.

559 **Victoria,** Sovereign, 1871, die number 18, third young head left, w.w. in relief on truncation, date below, die flaw by 1 of date, *rev* crowned quartered shield of arms within laurel wreath, die number 18 below, emblems below, hint of doubling in legend, 7.99g (Marsh 55; MCE 531; S 3853B). *Surface marks and hairlines, pleasing extremely fine / good extremely fine.* £350-450

Price Realised : £432

ex Randy Weir Numismatics, Unionville, Ontario, Canada, c.1997
Calendar year mintage 8,767,250
See footnote for lot 1139, page 214, for a brief synopsis of the 1871 die numbers.

1145 **Victoria,** Sovereign, 1871, die number 19, third young head left, w.w. in relief on truncation, date below, die flaw through first 1 of date from neck to rim, another die flaw connects some letters of legend, *rev* crowned shield of arms within laurel wreath, die number 19 below, 9 slightly higher than 1, emblems below, hint of doubling to legend, 7.98g (Marsh 55; MCE 531; S 3853B). *Some light hairlines, otherwise toned, good extremely fine.* £300-400

Price Realised : £384

ex Randy Weir Numismatics, Unionville, Ontario, Canada, October 1992
Calendar year mintage 8,767,250
See footnote for lot 1139, page 214, for a brief synopsis of the 1871 die numbers.

560 **Victoria,** Sovereign, 1871, die number 20, third young head left, w.w. in relief on truncation, date below, die flaw through 8 of date to rim, *rev* crowned quartered shield of arms within laurel wreath, die number 20 below, top of 2 incomplete, emblems below, raised hairline flaw connects some letters with a hint of doubling in legend, 7.98g (Marsh 55; MCE 531; S 3853B). *Surface marks and nicks, nearly extremely fine.* £300-350

Price Realised : £288

ex Randy Weir Numismatics, Unionville, Ontario, Canada, c.1997
Calendar year mintage 8,767,250
See footnote for lot 1139, page 214, for a brief synopsis of the 1871 die numbers.

232 **Victoria,** Sovereign, 1871, die number 21, third young head left, w.w. in relief on truncation, date below, doubling of date and some letters of legend at beginning and end, *rev* crowned quartered shield of arms within laurel wreath, die number 21 below, emblems below, 7.98g (Marsh 55; MCE 531; S 3853B). *With underlying brilliance and only the lightest of marks, toned, practically as struck.* £500-600

Price Realised : £840

ex Bowers and Merena, Treasures of the World Sale, 5-6 June 2002, lot 418
Calendar year mintage 8,767,250
See footnote for lot 1139, page 214, for a brief synopsis of the 1871 die numbers.

1146 **Victoria,** Sovereign, 1871, die number 22, third young head left, w.w. in relief on truncation, date doubled below, die flaw through latter 1 of date from neck to rim, first and last letters of legend die flawed, *rev* crowned shield of arms within laurel wreath, die number 22 lightly flawed below, emblems below, hint of doubling to legend with light hairline flaw connecting some letters, 7.97g (Marsh 55; MCE 531; S 3853B). *Some light hairlines, otherwise about extremely fine, reverse better.* £300-400

Price Realised : £240

Calendar year mintage 8,767,250
See footnote for lot 1139, page 214, for a brief synopsis of the 1871 die numbers.

233 **Victoria,** Sovereign, 1871, die number 23, third young head left, w.w. in relief on truncation, date below, 18 doubled, date and last word die flawed, last 1 flawed to rim, *rev* crowned quartered shield of arms within laurel wreath, die number 23 below die flawed, emblems below, trace of doubling in legend, 7.98g (Marsh 55; MCE 531; S 3853B). *Light surface marks, good very fine, reverse better.* £300-350

Price Realised : £264

ex Randy Weir Numismatics, Unionville, Ontario, Canada, undated invoice c.2000
Calendar year mintage 8,767,250
See footnote for lot 1139, page 214, for a brief synopsis of the 1871 die numbers.

561 **Victoria,** Sovereign, 1871, die number 24, third young head left, w.w. in relief on truncation, date below, die flaw from top of head to field, another in last I of legend, doubling of date and legend both sides, *rev* crowned quartered shield of arms within laurel wreath, die number 24 below, emblems below, raised hairline flaw in second word, 7.99g (Marsh 55; MCE 531; S 3853B). *Brilliant, light surface marks, rim nick on reverse, extremely fine.* £300-350

Price Realised : £384

Calendar year mintage 8,767,250
See footnote for lot 1139, page 214, for a brief synopsis of the 1871 die numbers.

1147 **Victoria,** Sovereign, 1871, die number 25, third young head left, w.w. in relief on truncation, date below, hint of doubling to legend, *rev* crowned shield of arms within laurel wreath, die number 25 lightly flawed below, emblems below, smaller upper serif to letter B than lower one, light hairline flaw connects some letters of legend, 7.98g (Marsh 55; MCE 531; S 3853B). *Some light hairlines and marks, otherwise toned, good extremely fine.* £300-400

Price Realised : £336

ex Randy Weir Numismatics, Unionville, Ontario, Canada, 27 July 1994
Calendar year mintage 8,767,250
See footnote for lot 1139, page 214, for a brief synopsis of the 1871 die numbers.

562 **Victoria,** Sovereign, 1871, die number 26, third young head left, W.W. in relief on truncation, date below, raised die flaw at penultimate A, hint of doubling to legend, *rev* crowned quartered shield of arms within laurel wreath, die number 26 below, top of 2 incomplete, emblems below, 7.99g (Marsh 55; MCE 531; S 3853B). *Tiny dig on reverse by second letter I, some light bagmarks behind head, otherwise brilliant uncirculated.* £500-600

Price Realised : £624

Calendar year mintage 8,767,250
See footnote for lot 1139, page 214, for a brief synopsis of the 1871 die numbers.

234 **Victoria,** Sovereign, 1871, die number 27, third young head left, W.W. in relief on truncation, date below, first 1 die flawed into neck, V flawed to rim and other light flaws in some letters both sides, doubled obverse legend, *rev* crowned quartered shield of arms within laurel wreath, die number 27 below, 2 is incomplete, emblems below, 7.98g (Marsh 55; MCE 531; S 3853B). *Streak of tone under eye, black spot at D of DEF, some hairlines, toned, good extremely fine.* £350-450

Price Realised : £504

ex Randy Weir Numismatics, Unionville, Ontario, Canada, purchased 27 September 1990
Calendar year mintage 8,767,250
See footnote for lot 1139, page 214, for a brief synopsis of the 1871 die numbers.

563 **Victoria,** Sovereign, 1871, die number 28, third young head left, W.W. in relief on truncation, date below, doubling of date and legend both sides, *rev* crowned quartered shield of arms within laurel wreath, die number 28 below, top of 2 incomplete, emblems below, 7.99g (Marsh 55; MCE 531; S 3853B). *Light hairlines and surface marks, spot in field behind neck, toned good extremely fine.* £350-450

Price Realised : £624

ex Randy Weir Numismatics, Unionville, Ontario, Canada, 2 June 1995
Calendar year mintage 8,767,250
See footnote for lot 1139, page 214, for a brief synopsis of the 1871 die numbers.

1148 **Victoria,** Sovereign, 1871, die number 29, third young head left, W.W. in relief on truncation, date below, first 1 of date die flawed, *rev* crowned shield of arms within laurel wreath, die number 29 lightly flawed below, emblems below, light hairline flaw connects some letters of legend, hint of doubling to legend, 8.00g (Marsh 55; MCE 531; S 3853B). *Scratch on throat with other hairline scuffs and marks, otherwise toned, extremely fine, reverse better.* £300-400

Price Realised : £336

ex Randy Weir Numismatics, Unionville, Ontario, Canada, July 1995
Calendar year mintage 8,767,250
See footnote for lot 1139, page 214, for a brief synopsis of the 1871 die numbers.

235 **Victoria,** Sovereign, 1871, die number 30, third young head left, w.w. in relief on truncation, date below, first 1 in date flawed, *rev* crowned quartered shield of arms within laurel wreath, die number 30 below, emblems below, hint of doubling of letters both sides, 7.98g (Marsh 55; MCE 531; S 3853B). *Hairline surface marks by bridge of nose and other light nicks, otherwise good extremely fine.* £350-450

Price Realised : £336

ex Randy Weir Numismatics, Unionville, Ontario, Canada, purchased 22 March 1990
Calendar year mintage 8,767,250
See footnote for lot 1139, page 214, for a brief synopsis of the 1871 die numbers.

564 **Victoria,** Sovereign, 1871, die number 31, third young head left, w.w. in relief on truncation, date below, die flaw to left of D in legend and at last A, another to left of date, *rev* crowned quartered shield of arms within laurel wreath, die number 31 below, emblems below, hint of doubling in some letters, 8.00g (Marsh 55; MCE 531; S 3853B). *Light hairlines and surface marks, good extremely fine.* £350-450

Price Realised : £480

ex Randy Weir Numismatics, Unionville, Ontario, Canada, 6 February 1990
Calendar year mintage 8,767,250
See footnote for lot 1139, page 214, for a brief synopsis of the 1871 die numbers.

1149 **Victoria,** Sovereign, 1871, die number 32, third young head left, w.w. in relief on truncation, date below, die flaw to left of D in legend to bust and at last A, *rev* crowned shield of arms within laurel wreath, die number 32 below, the 2 double struck, emblems below, hint of doubling to legend, 7.99g (Marsh 55; MCE 531; S 3853B). *Hairline scratch to neck and other surface marks, otherwise toned with underlying brilliance, extremely fine, reverse better.* £300-400

Price Realised : £288

ex Randy Weir Numismatics, Unionville, Ontario, Canada, July 1995
Calendar year mintage 8,767,250
See footnote for lot 1139, page 214, for a brief synopsis of the 1871 die numbers.

565 **Victoria,** Sovereign, 1871, die number 33, third young head left, w.w. in relief on truncation, date below, letter C die flawed shut, doubled date and legend, *rev* crowned quartered shield of arms within laurel wreath, die number 33 below, emblems below, first E die flawed to rim, 7.96g (Marsh 55; MCE 531; S 3853B). *Light surface marks, red tone, very fine / good very fine.* £300-350

Price Realised : £264

Calendar year mintage 8,767,250
See footnote for lot 1139, page 214, for a brief synopsis of the 1871 die numbers.

236 **Victoria,** Sovereign, 1871, die number 34, third young head left, w.w. in relief on truncation, date below, first 1 die flawed from rim to neck, V and last A of legend flawed, light flaws in TO and at last T of legend, *rev* crowned quartered shield of arms within laurel wreath, die number 34 below, top of die number double struck, emblems below, left rosette die flawed, hint of doubling in reverse legend, 7.99g (Marsh 55; MCE 531; S 3853B). *Light surface marks, toned, good extremely fine.* £350-450

Price Realised : £480

ex Spink and Son Ltd, November 2003
Calendar year mintage 8,767,250
See footnote for lot 1139, page 214, for a brief synopsis of the 1871 die numbers.

566 **Victoria,** Sovereign, 1871, die number 35, third young head left, w.w. in relief on truncation, date below, die flaw to left of date onto neck, other flaws at O, third I, and last T of legend, doubled profile of bust and date and legend, *rev* crowned quartered shield of arms within laurel wreath, die number 35 below, emblems below, first D die flawed to wreath and another near letter G to rim, 7.99g (Marsh 55; MCE 531; S 3853B). *Light surface marks and nicks, extremely fine, the reverse better.* £300-400

Price Realised : £384

Calendar year mintage 8,767,250
See footnote for lot 1139, page 214, for a brief synopsis of the 1871 die numbers.

1150 **Victoria,** Sovereign, 1871, die number 36, third young head left, w.w. in relief on truncation, date below, die flaw to left date to neck and at last A of legend, *rev* crowned shield of arms within laurel wreath, die number 36 below, emblems below, hint of doubling to legend, 8.00g (Marsh 55; MCE 531; S 3853B). *Black speck by third* I *of obverse legend, other light surface marks and hairlines, otherwise good extremely fine, reverse as struck.* £400-600

Price Realised : £480

ex Randy Weir Numismatics, Unionville, Ontario, Canada, May 1990
Calendar year mintage 8,767,250
See footnote for lot 1139, page 214, for a brief synopsis of the 1871 die numbers.

237 **Victoria,** Sovereign, 1871, die number 37, third young head left, w.w. in relief on truncation, the first stop absent, date below, date lightly doubled, left of 7 die flawed, a number of letters with hairline die flaws both sides, last A on obverse flawed to rim, *rev* crowned quartered shield of arms within laurel wreath, die number 37 below, lightly flawed die number, emblems below, 7.98g (Marsh 55; MCE 531; S 3853B). *Some light hairlines, practically as struck.* £500-600

Price Realised : £960

ex Randy Weir Numismatics, Unionville, Ontario, Canada, purchased 31 July 1993
The first absent stop in the initials upon the neck is probably due to a blockage on the die striking the coin.
Calendar year mintage 8,767,250
See footnote for lot 1139, page 214, for a brief synopsis of the 1871 die numbers.

567 **Victoria,** Sovereign, 1871, die number 38, third young head left, W.W. in relief on truncation, date below, die flaw through letter C, another at tip of neck and last A of legend, *rev* crowned quartered shield of arms within laurel wreath, die number 38 below, emblems below, light raised die flaws in reverse legend, 7.99g (Marsh 55; MCE 531; S 3853B). *Light surface marks and hairlines, one rim nick each side, good extremely fine.* £350-450

Price Realised : £552

Calendar year mintage 8,767,250

See footnote for lot 1139, page 214, for a brief synopsis of the 1871 die numbers.

1151 **Victoria,** Sovereign, 1871, die number 39, third young head left, W.W. in relief on truncation, date below, die flaw by 8 and 7 to rim and at last I and A of legend, legend doubled, further die flaw from tip of neck to rim and in field below rear of neck, ultimately causing a lamination by the ponytail of the field surface, *rev* crowned shield of arms within laurel wreath, die number 39 below, emblems below, 7.99g (Marsh 55; MCE 531; S 3853B). *Streaks of tone, other light surface marks and hairlines, good extremely fine.* £300-400

Price Realised : £264

ex Randy Weir Numismatics, Unionville, Ontario, Canada, 18 April 1994

Calendar year mintage 8,767,250

See footnote for lot 1139, page 214, for a brief synopsis of the 1871 die numbers.

1152 **Victoria,** Sovereign, 1871, die number 40, third young head left, W.W. in relief on truncation, date below, letter C, first A and last I of legend die flawed, *rev* crowned shield of arms within laurel wreath, die number 40 below, emblems below, hint of doubling to legend with light raised die flaw, 7.99g (Marsh 55; MCE 531; S 3853B). *Streaks of black tone, scratch over 71 of date, otherwise extremely fine.* £300-400

Price Realised : £288

ex Randy Weir Numismatics, Unionville, Ontario, Canada, October 1992

Calendar year mintage 8,767,250

See footnote for lot 1139, page 214, for a brief synopsis of the 1871 die numbers.

1153 **Victoria,** Sovereign, 1871, die number 41, third young head left, W.W. in relief on truncation, date below, heavy die flaw between 1 and 8 from rim to neck, flaw from V to rim, *rev* crowned shield of arms within laurel wreath, die number 41 below, double struck, 4 over a low 4, 1 over a high 1, emblems below, small upper serif to B, with light raised die flaw connecting some letters, 7.99g (Marsh 55; MCE 531; S 3853B). *Deposit in O of Queen's name, two rim nicks each on obverse and reverse, otherwise good very fine.* £250-300

Price Realised : £264

This coin was purchased from one of the groups of coins from the wreck of the RMS *Douro* that were not sold by auction and within the last 10 years.

Calendar year mintage 8,767,250

See footnote for lot 1139, page 214, for a brief synopsis of the 1871 die numbers.

238 **Victoria,** Sovereign, 1871, die number 42, third young head left, w.w. in relief on truncation, date below, die flaw at 1 and flaw between last I and A, *rev* crowned quartered shield of arms within laurel wreath, die number 42 below, broken 2, emblems below, hint of doubling in legend with some raised die flaws, 7.98g (Marsh 55; MCE 531; S 3853B). *Scratch above forehead, rim bruise on obverse, other nicks, surface marks and hairlines, toned, good very fine, reverse better, die number not recorded by Marsh in his list of 2002.* £300-350

Price Realised : £288

ex Paul Davies Ltd. This coin was purchased from one of the groups of coins from the wreck of the RMS *Douro* that were not sold by auction and within the last 10 years.
Calendar year mintage 8,767,250
See footnote for lot 1139, page 214, for a brief synopsis of the 1871 die numbers.

568 **Victoria,** Sovereign, 1871, die number 43, third young head left, w.w. in relief on truncation, date below, tiny die flaw by last A of legend, *rev* crowned quartered shield of arms within laurel wreath, die number 43 below, emblems below, hint of doubling on reverse legend, 7.96g (Marsh 55; MCE 531; S 3853B). *Light surface marks, one reverse rim nick each side, toned about very fine / good very fine.* £300-350

Price Realised : £264

Calendar year mintage 8,767,250
See footnote for lot 1139, page 214, for a brief synopsis of the 1871 die numbers.

1154 **Victoria,** Sovereign, 1871, die number 44, third young head left, w.w. in relief on truncation, date below, heavy die flaw through 7 from rim to neck and at last A of legend, flaw from hair bun to rim, *rev* crowned shield of arms within laurel wreath, die number 44 below, left 4 thicker and die flawed, emblems below, hint of doubling of legend with light raised die flaw connecting some letters and wreath, 7.97g (Marsh 55; MCE 531; S 3853B). *Light surface marks, toned, otherwise about extremely fine, reverse better.* £300-400

Price Realised : £228

Calendar year mintage 8,767,250
See footnote for lot 1139, page 214, for a brief synopsis of the 1871 die numbers.

239 **Victoria,** Sovereign, 1871, die number 45, third young head left, w.w. in relief on truncation, date below, first 1 heavily die flawed to left and onto neck, first T flawed and very last A of legend, *rev* crowned quartered shield of arms within laurel wreath, die number 45 below, emblems below, hint of doubling in legend with some raised die flaws, 7.99g (Marsh 55; MCE 531; S 3853B). *Rim bruise on obverse, light surface marks, otherwise good extremely fine.* £350-450

Price Realised : £432

ex Colonial Stamp and Coin Store, Kingston, New York, USA, June 2002
Calendar year mintage 8,767,250
See footnote for lot 1139, page 214, for a brief synopsis of the 1871 die numbers.

240 **Victoria,** Sovereign, 1871, die number 47, third young head left, W.W. in relief on truncation, date below, flaw across top of date, more between 1 and 8, obverse legend lightly cross flawed in last word, *rev* crowned quartered shield of arms within laurel wreath, die number 47 below, emblems below, 7.94g (Marsh 55; MCE 531; S 3853B). *Surface marks, toned, good fine, reverse better.* £300-350

Price Realised : £264

ex Spink Numismatic Circular, February 1998, item 528
ex An Important Collection of Gold Sovereigns 1816-2000, offered as one lot, Sothebys, 16-17 November 2000, lot 525 (part)
Calendar year mintage 8,767,250
See footnote for lot 1139, page 214, for a brief synopsis of the 1871 die numbers.

569 **Victoria,** Sovereign, 1871, die number 48, third young head left, W.W. in relief on truncation, date below, 7 of date die flawed, as well as both letter A's, further die flaw from hair bun to rim, doubling of legend both sides, *rev* crowned quartered shield of arms within laurel wreath, die number 48 below, emblems below, hint of doubling on reverse legend, 7.98g (Marsh 55; MCE 531; S 3853B). *Light surface marks, nicks and hairlines, once cleaned, now toned good very fine / extremely fine.* £300-350

Price Realised : £288

Calendar year mintage 8,767,250
See footnote for lot 1139, page 214, for a brief synopsis of the 1871 die numbers.

241 **Victoria,** Sovereign, 1871, die number 54, third larger young head left, W.W. in relief on truncation, date below lightly doubled, last A of legend die flawed, *rev* crowned quartered shield of arms within laurel wreath, die number 54 below, emblems below, second I in reverse legend doubled, 7.98g (Marsh 55; MCE 531; S 3853B). *Some hairlines, toned, good extremely fine.* £350-450

Price Realised : £432

ex Randy Weir Numismatics, Unionville, Ontario, Canada, purchased 6 February 1990
Calendar year mintage 8,767,250
See footnote for lot 1139, page 214, for a brief synopsis of the 1871 die numbers.

570 **Victoria,** Sovereign, 1871, die number 66, third young head left, W.W. in relief on truncation, date below, first 1 of date die flawed to neck, last I of legend flawed to rim, doubling of legend both sides, more evident on obverse, *rev* crowned quartered shield of arms within laurel wreath, die number 66 below, emblems below, 8.00g (Marsh 55; MCE 531; S 3853B). *Light surface marks and nicks, otherwise extremely fine.* £350-400

Price Realised : £360

ex Randy Weir Numismatics, Unionville, Ontario, Canada, c.1997
Calendar year mintage 8,767,250
See footnote for lot 1139, page 214, for a brief synopsis of the 1871 die numbers.

1155 **Victoria,** Sovereign, 1871, die number 67, third young head left, w.w. in relief on truncation, date below, die flaw by 18 to neck, die flaw from hair bun to rim, hint of doubling in legend, *rev* crowned shield of arms within laurel wreath, die number 67 lightly flawed below, open 6, emblems below, second A and M of legend doubled, 7.98g (Marsh 55; MCE 531; S 3853B). *Light surface marks and hairlines, toned with a brilliant reverse, otherwise about extremely fine.* £300-400

Price Realised : £264

Calendar year mintage 8,767,250
See footnote for lot 1139, page 214, for a brief synopsis of the 1871 die numbers.

242 **Victoria,** Sovereign, 1871, die number 68, third young head left, w.w. in relief on truncation, date below lightly doubled, 8 to 7 with hairline flaw, last IA of legend die flawed to rim, hint of doubling in legend both sides, more on obverse, *rev* crowned quartered shield of arms within laurel wreath, die number 68 below, emblems below, 7.98g (Marsh 55; MCE 531; S 3853B). *Some hairlines and surface marks, reverse brilliant, toned, nearly extremely fine.* £350-450

Price Realised : £300

ex Paul Davies Ltd. This coin was purchased from one of the groups of coins from the wreck of the RMS *Douro* that were not sold by auction and within the last 10 years.
Calendar year mintage 8,767,250
See footnote for lot 1139, page 214, for a brief synopsis of the 1871 die numbers.

1156 **Victoria,** Sovereign, 1871, die number 70, third young head left, w.w. in relief on truncation, date below, die flaw at last two letters of legend, *rev* crowned shield of arms within laurel wreath, die number 70 below, emblems below, 7.93g (Marsh 55; MCE 531; S 3853B). *Some black deposit around rim and border teeth, light nicks and hairlines, otherwise toned, good fine.* £250-300

Price Realised : £216

ex Paul Davies Ltd, Ilkley, via A H Baldwin & Sons Ltd, October 2006
It is interesting to note that the weight of this coin in its lower grade is upon the legal tender limit as dictated by the Coinage Acts of 1816-1891.
Calendar year mintage 8,767,250
See footnote for lot 1139, page 214, for a brief synopsis of the 1871 die numbers.

243 **Victoria,** Sovereign, 1871 die number 71, third young head left, w.w. in relief on truncation, date below, first 1 flawed to neck, last A of legend die flawed to rim, *rev* crowned quartered shield of arms within laurel wreath, die number 71 below, 1 missing lower right serif, emblems below, 7.99g (Marsh 55; MCE 531; S 3853B). *Light surface marks, scuffs and hairlines, nearly extremely fine.* £300-350

Price Realised : £264

ex Spink and Son Ltd, November 2003
Calendar year mintage 8,767,250
See footnote for lot 1139, page 214, for a brief synopsis of the 1871 die numbers.

244 **Victoria,** Sovereign, 1871 die number 72, third young head left, w.w. in relief on truncation, date below, first 1 flawed to left, some letters in legend, last I flawed to rim, *rev* crowned quartered shield of arms within laurel wreath, die number 72 below, emblems below, 7.98g (Marsh 55; MCE 531; S 3853B). *Obverse rim nick, three red spots on reverse, surface marks, good extremely fine.* £400-500

Price Realised : £432

ex Douro Cargo, Spink Auction 118, 20-21 November 1996, lot 568 (part)
ex An Important Collection of Gold Sovereigns 1816-2000, offered as one lot, Sothebys, 16-17 November 2000, lot 525 (part)
Calendar year mintage 8,767,250
See footnote for lot 1139, page 214, for a brief synopsis of the 1871 die numbers.

571 **Victoria,** Sovereign, 1871, die number 73, third young head left, w.w. in relief on truncation, date below, die flaw to left of date from rim to neck, other tiny flaws in hair bun and at last A of legend, *rev* crowned quartered shield of arms within laurel wreath, die number 73 below, emblems below, second T of legend doubled only, 8.00g (Marsh 55; MCE 531; S 3853B). *Light surface marks, nicks and hairlines, mainly on obverse, some spots on reverse, otherwise good extremely fine.* £350-450

Price Realised : £408

This coin was purchased from one of the groups of coins from the wreck of the RMS *Douro* that were not sold by auction, bought in the last 10 years.
Calendar year mintage 8,767,250
See footnote for lot 1139, page 214, for a brief synopsis of the 1871 die numbers.

572 **Victoria,** Sovereign, 1871, die number 74, third young head left, w.w. in relief on truncation, date below, die flaw in penultimate A to rim, *rev* crowned quartered shield of arms within laurel wreath, die number 74 below, emblems below, 7.96g (Marsh 55; MCE 531; S 3853B). *Scratch on cheek, some scuffs and surface marks, rim nick on obverse, some tiny red spots, otherwise very fine.* £300-350

Price Realised : £264

This coin was purchased from one of the groups of coins from the wreck of the RMS *Douro* that were not sold by auction, bought in the last 10 years.
Calendar year mintage 8,767,250
See footnote for lot 1139, page 214, for a brief synopsis of the 1871 die numbers.

1157 **Victoria,** Sovereign, 1871, die number 75, third young head left, w.w. in relief on truncation, date below, die flaw through 7 to neck, *rev* crowned shield of arms within laurel wreath, die number 75 below, emblems below, 7.97g (Marsh 55; MCE 531; S 3853B). *Toned with light surface marks and hairlines, otherwise very fine, reverse better.* £250-300

Price Realised : £240

ex Douro Cargo, Spink Auction 118, 20-21 November 1996, lot 1381 (part)
Calendar year mintage 8,767,250
See footnote for lot 1139, page 214, for a brief synopsis of the 1871 die numbers.

1158 **Victoria,** Sovereign, 1871, die number 76, third young head left, w.w. in relief on truncation, date below, die flaw from hair bun to rim between T and I at end of legend, *rev* crowned shield of arms within laurel wreath, die number 76 below, 6 lower than 7, emblems below, penultimate F doubled, 7.97g (Marsh 55; MCE 531; S 3853B). *Dig by hair fillets, toned with light surface marks, nicks and hairlines, otherwise good very fine, reverse better.* £250-300

Price Realised : £264

Calendar year mintage 8,767,250
See footnote for lot 1139, page 214, for a brief synopsis of the 1871 die numbers.

245 **Victoria,** Sovereign, 1871 die number 77, third young head left, w.w. in relief on truncation, raised die flaw from tip of neck to rim, date below, last word doubled, last A with light die flaw, doubled obverse legend, *rev* crowned quartered shield of arms within laurel wreath, die number 77 below, emblems below, 7.97g (Marsh 55; MCE 531; S 3853B). *Obverse rim nick, light surface marks, toned, nearly very fine.* £300-350

Price Realised : £288

ex Paul Davies Ltd. This coin was purchased from one of the groups of coins from the wreck of the RMS *Douro* that were not sold by auction and within the last 10 years.
Calendar year mintage 8,767,250
See footnote for lot 1139, page 214, for a brief synopsis of the 1871 die numbers.

573 **Victoria,** Sovereign, 1871, die number 78, third young head left, w.w. in relief on truncation, date below, date doubled with die flaw by second 1 from rim to neck, further die flaw in last three letters of legend, *rev* crowned quartered shield of arms within laurel wreath, die number 78 below, emblems below, hairline raised die flaw in some letters of reverse, 7.97g (Marsh 55; MCE 531; S 3853B). *Some surface marks and hairlines, some tiny red spots, otherwise almost very fine.* £300-350

Price Realised : £264

ex Randy Weir Numismatics, Unionville, Ontario, Canada, 2 June 1995
Calendar year mintage 8,767,250
See footnote for lot 1139, page 214, for a brief synopsis of the 1871 die numbers.

246 **Victoria,** Sovereign, 1871, die number 79, third young head left, w.w. in relief on truncation, date below, first 1 heavily die flawed to neck, last A of legend die flawed to rim, hint of doubling in legend both sides, less so on reverse, *rev* crowned quartered shield of arms within laurel wreath, die number 79 below, emblems below, some letters with light flaws, 8.00g (Marsh 55; MCE 531; S 3853B). *Reverse rim nick, tiny red spot on forehead, other light nicks and marks, extremely fine.* £350-450

Price Realised : £360

ex Douro Cargo, Spink Auction 118, 20-21 November 1996, lot 1381 (part)
Calendar year mintage 8,767,250
See footnote for lot 1139, page 214, for a brief synopsis of the 1871 die numbers.

574 **Victoria,** Sovereign, 1871, die number 97, third young head left, w.w. in relief on truncation, date below, date lightly die flawed and some letters of legend, last I of legend with die flaw to rim, some doubling of date and legend both sides, *rev* crowned quartered shield of arms within laurel wreath, die number 97 below, emblems below, hairline raised die flaw in some letters of reverse, 8.00g (Marsh 55; MCE 531; S 3853B). *Some light surface marks and nicks, toned extremely fine.* £350-400

Price Realised : £360

Calendar year mintage 8,767,250
See footnote for lot 1139, page 214, for a brief synopsis of the 1871 die numbers.

1159 **Victoria,** Sovereign, 1871, die number 98, third young head left, w.w. in relief on truncation, date below, date and legend doubled, *rev* crowned shield of arms within laurel wreath, die number 98 below, larger 8 than 9, emblems below, M very thick with thin right diagonal, 7.97g (Marsh 55; MCE 531; S 3853B). *Nick on cheek, with underlying proof-like brilliance, scuffed on obverse, otherwise extremely fine, reverse better.* £300-400

Price Realised : £240

ex Randy Weir Numismatics, Unionville, Ontario, Canada, February 1999
Calendar year mintage 8,767,250
See footnote for lot 1139, page 214, for a brief synopsis of the 1871 die numbers.

247 **Victoria,** Sovereign, 1871 die number 99, third young head left, portrait lightly doubled, w.w. in relief on truncation, date below, doubled date with die flaws to neck, obverse legend doubled, *rev* crowned quartered shield of arms within laurel wreath, die number 99 below, emblems below, M and third R doubled in reverse legend, 7.99g (Marsh 55; MCE 531; S 3853B). *Light surface marks and hairlines, dig to right of date, red spot on obverse legend, otherwise proof-like, good extremely fine.* £400-500

Price Realised : £384

ex Douro Cargo, Spink Auction 118, 20-21 November 1996, lot 1381 (part)
Calendar year mintage 8,767,250
See footnote for lot 1139, page 214, for a brief synopsis of the 1871 die numbers.

575 **Victoria,** Sovereign, 1871, die number 100, third young head left, w.w. in relief on truncation, date below, last word of legend die flawed, *rev* crowned quartered shield of arms within laurel wreath, die number 100 below, 1 with weak serif and central 0 over a higher 0, emblems below, hint of doubling in legend, 7.98g (Marsh 55; MCE 531; S 3853B). *Some light surface marks, black blemish in field behind head, dig over 8 of date, otherwise toned good extremely fine.* £350-450

Price Realised : £480

ex Douro Cargo, Spink Auction 118, 20-21 November 1996, lot 1381 (part)
Calendar year mintage 8,767,250
See footnote for lot 1139, page 214, for a brief synopsis of the 1871 die numbers.

1160 Victoria, Sovereign, 1871, die number 101, third young head left, w.w. in relief on truncation, date below, *rev* crowned shield of arms within laurel wreath, die number 101 below, 1's with only a trace of upper serif, right 1 touches ribbon to right and further spread from 10, emblems below, legend partly doubled, M very thick with thin right diagonal, 7.99g (Marsh 55; MCE 531; S 3853B). *Obverse rim nick, light surface marks, otherwise good extremely fine.* £300-400

Price Realised : £336

ex Randy Weir Numismatics, Unionville, Ontario, Canada, February 1994
Calendar year mintage 8,767,250. See footnote for lot 1139, page 214, for a brief synopsis of the 1871 die numbers.

248 Victoria, Sovereign, 1871, die number 102, third young head left, ww in relief on truncation, the stops absent, date below, 187 severely cross die flawed, obverse legend lightly die flawed, *rev* crowned quartered shield of arms within laurel wreath, die number 102 below, the 1 touches the left ribbon of wreath, emblems below, doubled M in legend, 7.97g (Marsh 55; MCE 531; S 3853B). *Once cleaned, now toned, many light nicks and surface marks, nearly extremely fine.* £350-450

Price Realised : £300

ex Ebay purchase, August 2001.
The absent stops in the initials of the truncation are probably due to a blockage on what was evidently a pair of dies nearing the end of their serviceable life.
Calendar year mintage 8,767,250
See footnote for lot 1139, page 214, for a brief synopsis of the 1871 die numbers.

576 Victoria, Sovereign, 1871, die number 103, third young head left, w.w. in relief on truncation, date below, die flaw across top of 18 and in latter part of queen's name, hint of doubling to some letters both sides, *rev* crowned quartered shield of arms within laurel wreath, die number 103 below, emblems below, 7.99g (Marsh 55; MCE 531; S 3853B). *Some scuffs and surface marks with hairlines, light scratches on neck, otherwise with a black tone, good extremely fine.* £300-400

Price Realised : £360

ex Stacks, 21 February 1997, lot 1135
ex An Important Collection of Gold Sovereigns 1816-2000, offered as one lot, Sothebys, November 2000, lot 525 (part)
Calendar year mintage 8,767,250. See footnote for lot 1139, page 214, for a brief synopsis of the 1871 die numbers.

1161 Victoria, Sovereign, 1871, die number 104, third young head left, w.w. in relief on truncation, date below, light die flaw across top of date into field, second word die flawed with last A of legend flawed to rim, *rev* crowned shield of arms within laurel wreath, die number 104 below, 4 out of alignment, emblems below, legend partly doubled, 7.97g (Marsh 55; MCE 531; S 3853B). *Some light surface marks, otherwise toned, almost extremely fine.* £300-400

Price Realised : £264

Calendar year mintage 8,767,250
See footnote for lot 1139, page 214, for a brief synopsis of the 1871 die numbers.

249 **Victoria,** Sovereign, 1871, die number 105, third young head left, w.w. in relief on truncation, date below, 18 cross flawed, obverse legend with some raised die flaws, *rev* crowned quartered shield of arms within laurel wreath, die number 105 below, no upper serif to 1, emblems below, doubled M in legend, 7.98g (Marsh 55; MCE 531; S 3853B). *Short scratch on cheek, other light surface marks, toned with underlying brilliance, otherwise nearly extremely fine.* £350-450

Price Realised : £300

Note the re-emergence of the broken serif 1 punch in the die number.
Calendar year mintage 8,767,250. See footnote for lot 1139, page 214, for a brief synopsis of the 1871 die numbers.

577 **Victoria,** Sovereign, 1871, die number 106, third young head left, w.w. in relief on truncation, date below, some letters with a hint of doubling, *rev* crowned quartered shield of arms within laurel wreath, die number 106 below, 1 with weak serif, 6 higher than 10, emblems below, M of legend thick from doubling, but right upright thinner, 7.99g (Marsh 55; MCE 531; S 3853B). *Some light surface marks and nicks, otherwise good very fine.* £300-350

Price Realised : £288

This coin was purchased from one of the groups of coins from the wreck of the RMS *Douro* that were not sold by auction, bought in the last 10 years.
Calendar year mintage 8,767,250. See footnote for lot 1139, page 214, for a brief synopsis of the 1871 die numbers.

1162 **Victoria,** Sovereign, 1871, die number 108, third young head left, w.w. in relief on truncation, date below, light die flaw across top of date and in most letters of legend, *rev* crowned shield of arms within laurel wreath, die number 108 below, 8 lower out of alignment, no upper serif to 1, emblems below, legend partly doubled, 7.97g (Marsh 55; MCE 531; S 3853B). *Red blemish on obverse, spots on reverse, scuffed with hairlines and surface marks, otherwise toned, very fine.* £250-300

Price Realised : £240

This coin was purchased from one of the groups of coins from the wreck of the RMS *Douro* that were not sold by auction and within the last 10 years.
Calendar year mintage 8,767,250. See footnote for lot 1139, page 214, for a brief synopsis of the 1871 die numbers.

250 **Victoria,** Sovereign, 1871, die number 109, third young head left, w.w. in relief on truncation, date below, lightly flawed with 1 to rim, other light raised die flaws in obverse legend, *rev* crowned quartered shield of arms within laurel wreath, die number 109 below, 9 further away from 10, the 1 touches the left ribbon of wreath and die flawed, emblems below, doubled M in legend, 7.95g (Marsh 55; MCE 531; S 3853B). *Toned with small spots and blemishes, hairlines and surface marks, good fine / nearly very fine.* £300-350

Price Realised : £264

ex Paul Davies Ltd. This coin was purchased from one of the groups of coins from the wreck of the RMS *Douro* that were not sold by auction and within the last 10 years.
Calendar year mintage 8,767,250. See footnote for lot 1139, page 214, for a brief synopsis of the 1871 die numbers.

1163 **Victoria,** Sovereign, 1871, die number 110, third young head left, w.w. in relief on truncation, date below, second 1 die flawed to neck, *rev* crowned shield of arms within laurel wreath, die number 110 below, no upper serif to first 1, emblems below, legend partly doubled, 7.98g (Marsh 55; MCE 531; S 3853B). *Light scratch in obverse field behind head, other hairlines and surface marks, otherwise toned, extremely fine, reverse better.* £300-400

Price Realised : £360

Calendar year mintage 8,767,250
See footnote for lot 1139, page 214, for a brief synopsis of the 1871 die numbers.

251 **Victoria,** Sovereign, 1871 die number 111, third young head left, w.w. in relief on truncation, date below, first 1 flawed from rim to neck, I of DEI with vertical flaw from rim to bust, last word cross flawed and continues to date, *rev* crowned quartered shield of arms within laurel wreath, die number 111 below, no upper serifs, emblems below, doubled M in legend, 7.99g (Marsh 55; MCE 531; S 3853B). *Reverse rim nick, hairlined, toned, nearly extremely fine.* £350-450

Price Realised : £264

Note the use of the broken serif 1 punch in the die number.
Calendar year mintage 8,767,250. See footnote for lot 1139, page 214, for a brief synopsis of the 1871 die numbers.

Extremely Rare Unpublished Pattern Shield Reverse Sovereign of 1871 With Plain Edge

252 **Victoria,** Pattern Sovereign, 1871, engraved after William Wyon, third young head left, with double fillet, w.w. in relief on truncation intrudes onto field, date below, toothed border and raised rim both sides, VICTORIA DEI GRATIA, *rev* struck en médaille, engraved after Jean Baptiste Merlen, crowned shield of arms within laurel wreath tied with bow below shield, seven harp strings in Irish arms, left string emanates from scroll, emblems below, small rosette either side, BRITANNIARUM REGINA FID: DEF:, legend slightly doubled, edge plain, 8.04g, 21.8mm (cf WR 314; DM -; Murdoch 506; Nobleman 269, part). *Tiny nick between D and E and I and A on obverse, otherwise brilliant mint state, well defined strike and unrecorded, the only known specimen.* £15,000-18,000

Price Realised : £26,400

ex Sothebys, 9 October 1995, lot 821
This coin could possibly be the Murdoch and Nobleman specimen but there are no illustrations in these catalogues to compare it to. An unpublished Pattern Sovereign not in the standard work, the year 1871 was significant as this was when the Pistrucci St George and dragon reverse design was re-introduced to the London sovereign. Both the shield reverse and the St George reverse were struck concurrently by the Royal Mint London until 1874. These 1871 proofs struck from highly polished dies were no doubt produced as a matter of record. Only the milled edge version is published. Of the highest rarity and probably unique as Wilson and Rasmussen were not aware of it for their work which was based on ten years of visits to museum and institutional collections around the country to see what existed.

1872 Shield Reverse Victoria Sovereign without Die Number

253 **Victoria,** Sovereign, 1872, no reverse die number, third young head left, W.W. in relief on truncation, date below, raised die flaw through 1 of date, last two words of obverse legend doubled and die flawed, *rev* crowned quartered shield of arms within laurel wreath, emblems below, 7.98g (Marsh 47; MCE 533; S 3852C). *Some light streaks of red tone, very light surface marks, good extremely fine.* £600-800

Price Realised : £1,032

ex Randy Weir Numismatics, Unionville, Ontario, Canada, 20 June 1990
Calendar year mintage 13,486,708
This calendar year output figure at the Mint represents the pinnacle of production in the 19th Century. No higher figure was achieved for the gold Sovereign for more than 30 years after this. It is also a good two and a half million more than the next most prolific production year of the London Mint in the 19th Century. This could go some way to explaining why this variety of Sovereign appears without the usual die numbered reverse. It may have been left off intentionally or neglected to be added, but we consider a more likely explanation being the re-employment of an older die from storage from the non-die numbered period.

1164 **Victoria,** Sovereign, 1872, die number 1, third young head left, W.W. in relief on truncation, date below, die flaw through 1 to neck, third I of legend flawed from rim to head, last A of legend with a trace of a die flaw, *rev* crowned quartered shield of arms within laurel wreath, die number 1 lightly flawed below, emblems below, some doubling in reverse legend, hairline flaw connects some letters, 7.99g (Marsh 56; MCE 533; S 3853B). *Softly struck on high points, toned with some light marks, otherwise extremely fine.* £300-400

Price Realised : £312

Calendar year mintage 13,486,708
This coin is die number 1 of a total of 110 different numbered dies in the Bentley Collection, running from 1 to 112. Marsh claims that only one other exists - number 103. This would seem to suggest good die longevity for such a high output in the calendar year as 1872 represents the pinnacle of calendar year output for the reign of Queen Victoria and the highest mintage in a year since the inception of the modern gold Sovereign. However it must be borne in mind that this figure includes the new St George and dragon reverse Sovereign for Queen Victoria, and the non-die number Sovereigns of 1872 too. This is why trying to analyse calendar output against die numbers and variations known is so troublesome. Further study and research perhaps in collaboration with the Royal Mint Museum may prove to be fruitful.
It would be more than 35 years before this total in one calendar year was surpassed. The longevity for the dies can be considered reasonable.

578 **Victoria,** Sovereign, 1872, die number 2, third young head left, W.W. in relief on truncation, date below trace of doubling in date and legend both sides, *rev* crowned quartered shield of arms within laurel wreath, die number 2 below, lightly die flawed number and legend, emblems below, 8.00g (Marsh 56; MCE 533; S 3853B). *Short scratch by ponytail of hair, reverse rim nick, otherwise toned extremely fine.* £300-400

Price Realised : £360

ex Douro Cargo, Spink Auction 118, 20-21 November 1996, lot 1383pt.
Calendar year mintage 13,486,708
See footnote for lot 1164 (above) for a brief synopsis of the 1872 die numbers.

1165 **Victoria,** Sovereign, 1872, die number 3, third young head left, w.w. in relief on truncation, date below, die flaw from tip of neck to rim and at last T of legend, hint of doubling to legend both sides, *rev* crowned quartered shield of arms within laurel wreath, die number 3 below, emblems below, 7.99g (Marsh 56; MCE 533; S 3853B). *A few streaks of tone, two light parallel scratches in front of throat, otherwise good extremely fine.* £300-400

Price Realised : £360

ex Douro Cargo, Spink Auction 118, 20-21 November 1996, lot 1383 (part)
Calendar year mintage 13,486,708
See footnote for lot 1164, page 234, for a brief synopsis of the 1872 die numbers.

254 **Victoria,** Sovereign, 1872, die number 4, third young head left, w.w. in relief on truncation, tip of neck die flawed, raised flaw from top of hair band to rim, date below lightly doubled, first V, last T and A of legend die flawed, trace of doubling in legend both sides, more so on obverse, *rev* crowned quartered shield of arms within laurel wreath, die number 4 below, 4 over a higher 4, emblems below, raised die flaw in some letters, 7.98g (Marsh 56; MCE 533; S 3853B). *Previously graded by NGC as MS62, small scratch on cheek, otherwise toned, extremely fine.* £350-450

Price Realised : £432

ex Steinbergs of North Carolina, USA, May 2006.
Calendar year mintage 13,486,708
See footnote for lot 1164, page 234, for a brief synopsis of the 1872 die numbers.

255 **Victoria,** Sovereign, 1872, die number 5, third young head left, w.w. in relief on truncation, date below, 18 doubled, 1 die flawed to neck, *rev* crowned quartered shield of arms within laurel wreath, die number 5 below, die flawed, emblems below, light raised die flaws in legend with a hint of doubling, 7.97g (Marsh 56; MCE 533; S 3853B). *Surface marks and hairlines, toned, very fine.* £300-350

Price Realised : £264

ex Spink and Son Ltd, November 2003
Calendar year mintage 13,486,708
See footnote for lot 1164, page 234, for a brief synopsis of the 1872 die numbers.

256 **Victoria,** Sovereign, 1872, die number 6, third young head left, w.w. in relief on truncation, raised die flaw from hair bun to rim, date below, 18 doubled with a hint of doubling in legend both sides, *rev* crowned quartered shield of arms within laurel wreath, die number 6 below, emblems below, 7.98g (Marsh 56; MCE 533; S 3853B). *A very pleasing coin, toned and uncirculated.* £500-600

Price Realised : £792

ex Douro Cargo, Spink Auction 118, 20-21 November 1996, lot 1383 (part)
Calendar year mintage 13,486,708
See footnote for lot 1164, page 234, for a brief synopsis of the 1872 die numbers.

579 **Victoria,** Sovereign, 1872, die number 7, third young head left, w.w. in relief on truncation, date below, *rev* crowned quartered shield of arms within laurel wreath, die number 7 below, emblems below, 7.97g (Marsh 56; MCE 533; S 3853B). *Red blemish on reverse shield, softly struck in parts, otherwise extremely fine / good extremely fine and pleasing.* £350-450

Price Realised : £360

ex Douro Cargo, Spink Auction 118, 20-21 November 1996, lot 1383 (part)
Calendar year mintage 13,486,708. See footnote for lot 1164, page 234, for a brief synopsis of the 1872 die numbers.

580 **Victoria,** Sovereign, 1872, die number 8, third young head left, w.w. in relief on truncation, date below, hint of doubling to date and legend both sides, die flaw from V to rim, and through first A from rim to head, further flaw in hair bun to rim, *rev* crowned quartered shield of arms within laurel wreath, die number 8 below, emblems below, hairlines raised die flaw in some letters, 7.98g (Marsh 56; MCE 533; S 3853B). *Some light deposit and red spots on reverse, some hairlines, otherwise good extremely fine.* £350-450

Price Realised : £432

ex Douro Cargo, Spink Auction 118, 20-21 November 1996, lot 1383 (part)
Calendar year mintage 13,486,708
See footnote for lot 1164, page 234, for a brief synopsis of the 1872 die numbers.

1166 **Victoria,** Sovereign, 1872, die number 9, third young head left, w.w. in relief on truncation, date below, die flaw through 1 of date to neck and at last T of legend to adjacent I and A, hint of doubling to date and legend both sides, *rev* crowned quartered shield of arms within laurel wreath, die number 9 below, emblems below, 7.97g (Marsh 56; MCE 533; S 3853B). *Red spot by* V *and blemish on harp, surface marks, otherwise good very fine.* £250-300

Price Realised : £288

This coin was purchased from one of the groups of coins from the wreck of the RMS *Douro* that were not sold by auction and within the last 10 years.
Calendar year mintage 13,486,708
See footnote for lot 1164, page 234, for a brief synopsis of the 1872 die numbers.

1167 **Victoria,** Sovereign, 1872, die number 10, third young head left, w.w. in relief on truncation, date below, die flaw at last A to rim with some other traces of flaws in legend, hint of doubling to date and legend both sides, *rev* crowned quartered shield of arms within laurel wreath, die number 10 below, smaller o than 1, emblems below, 7.98g (Marsh 56; MCE 533; S 3853B). *Tiny digs on neck, proof-like with toning, otherwise extremely fine, reverse better.* £300-400

Price Realised : £312

ex Randy Weir Numismatics, Unionville, Ontario, Canada, 27 September 1990
Calendar year mintage 13,486,708
See footnote for lot 1164, page 234, for a brief synopsis of the 1872 die numbers.

257 **Victoria,** Sovereign, 1872, die number 11, third young head left, w.w. in relief on truncation, date below, lightly doubled with a hint of doubling in legend both sides, last A of legend and hair bun flawed to rim, *rev* crowned quartered shield of arms within laurel wreath, die number 11 below, emblems below, 7.99g (Marsh 56; MCE 533; S 3853B). *Some surface marks, light red tone, good extremely fine.* £350-450

Price Realised : £432

ex Douro Cargo, Spink Auction 118, 20-21 November 1996, lot 339
Calendar year mintage 13,486,708
See footnote for lot 1164, page 234, for a brief synopsis of the 1872 die numbers.

581 **Victoria,** Sovereign, 1872, die number 12, third young head left, w.w. in relief on truncation, date below, die flawed 2 in date, further raised flaws in both T's and last A of legend, hint of doubling to top part of obverse and some of reverse legend, *rev* crowned quartered shield of arms within laurel wreath, die number 12 below, emblems below, 7.99g (Marsh 56; MCE 533; S 3853B). *Red spot at bridge of nose and black blemish on reverse rim, some other red colour, hairlines on cheek and other light surface marks, otherwise good extremely fine.* £350-450

Price Realised : £528

ex Douro Cargo, Spink Auction 118, 20-21 November 1996, lot 1384 (part)
Calendar year mintage 13,486,708
See footnote for lot 1164, page 234, for a brief synopsis of the 1872 die numbers.

582 **Victoria,** Sovereign, 1872, die number 13, third young head left, w.w. in relief on truncation, date below, die flaws to last three letters in queen's name and last A of legend, hint of doubling to date and legend both sides, *rev* crowned quartered shield of arms within laurel wreath, die number 13 below, emblems below, 7.98g (Marsh 56; MCE 533; S 3853B). *A few light hairlines, otherwise pleasing, toned good extremely fine.* £400-500

Price Realised : £888

ex Douro Cargo, Spink Auction 118, 20-21 November 1996, lot 570 (part)
ex An Important Collection of Gold Sovereigns 1816-2000, offered as one lot, Sothebys, November 2000, lot 525 (part)
Calendar year mintage 13,486,708
See footnote for lot 1164, page 234, for a brief synopsis of the 1872 die numbers.

258 **Victoria,** Sovereign, 1872, die number 14, third young head left, w.w. in relief on truncation, date below, lightly die flawed the 1 to neck, last A flawed to rim, hint of doubling in legend both sides, *rev* crowned quartered shield of arms within laurel wreath, die number 14 below, emblems below, 7.97g (Marsh 56; MCE 533; S 3853B). *Once cleaned, now toned, light surface marks, good very fine.* £300-350

Price Realised : £288

ex Ebay purchase, July 2003
Calendar year mintage 13,486,708. See footnote for lot 1164, page 234, for a brief synopsis of the 1872 die numbers.

1168 **Victoria,** Sovereign, 1872, die number 15, third young head left, W.W. in relief on truncation, date below, die flaw between T and I in legend, hint of doubling to date and legend both sides, *rev* crowned quartered shield of arms within laurel wreath, die number 15 below, 5 higher than 1, emblems below, 7.98g (Marsh 56; MCE 533; S 3853B). *Some light surface marks, toned, extremely fine, reverse better.* £300-400

Price Realised : £264

ex Randy Weir Numismatics, Unionville, Ontario, Canada, late 1998
Calendar year mintage 13,486,708
See footnote for lot 1164, page 234, for a brief synopsis of the 1872 die numbers.

583 **Victoria,** Sovereign, 1872, die number 16, third young head left, W.W. in relief on truncation, date below, raised die flaw beyond last letter of legend and another from rim into field before start of legend, letter E of legend mal-formed, *rev* crowned quartered shield of arms within laurel wreath, die number 16 below, emblems below, hint of doubling to legend, flaw between I and N of second word, 7.97g (Marsh 56; MCE 533; S 3853B). *Dig on letter* E *of obverse has malformed it, light surface marks and obverse rim nick, good very fine / extremely fine.* £300-350

Price Realised : £264

Calendar year mintage 13,486,708
See footnote for lot 1164, page 234, for a brief synopsis of the 1872 die numbers.

259 **Victoria,** Sovereign, 1872, die number 17, third young head left, W.W. in relief on truncation, date below, *rev* crowned quartered shield of arms within laurel wreath, die number 17 below, emblems below, hint of doubling in some letters of legend, 7.98g (Marsh 56; MCE 533; S 3853B). *Tiny black spots on reverse, light nicks and surface marks on obverse, extremely fine / good extremely fine with underlying brilliance.* £350-450

Price Realised : £300

ex Douro Cargo, Spink Auction 118, 20-21 November 1996, lot 570
ex An Important Collection of Gold Sovereigns 1816-2000, offered as one lot, Sothebys, 16-17 November 2000, lot 525 (part)
Calendar year mintage 13,486,708
See footnote for lot 1164, page 234, for a brief synopsis of the 1872 die numbers.

1169 **Victoria,** Sovereign, 1872, die number 18, third young head left, W.W. in relief on truncation, only trace of stops visible, date below, first R, D and last A die flawed to rim, *rev* crowned quartered shield of arms within laurel wreath, die number 18 lightly flawed below, 8 higher than 1, emblems below, hint of doubling legend, die flaw at last I and E to rim, 7.95g (Marsh 56; MCE 533; S 3853B). *Some light surface marks and dig on neck, patchy tone, otherwise about very fine, reverse better.* £250-300

Price Realised : £216

Calendar year mintage 13,486,708
See footnote for lot 1164, page 234, for a brief synopsis of the 1872 die numbers.

584 **Victoria,** Sovereign, 1872, die number 19, third young head left, W.W. in relief on truncation, only a trace of stops in letters, date below, penultimate A die flawed, *rev* crowned quartered shield of arms within laurel wreath, die number 19 below, emblems below, hint of doubling to legend and flaws in some letters, 7.98g (Marsh 56; MCE 533; S 3853B). *Streak of black tone to obverse with a few light hairlines, scratch on cheek, otherwise extremely fine.* £300-400

Price Realised : £312

ex Douro Cargo, Spink Auction 118, 20-21 November 1996, lot 570 (part)
ex An Important Collection of Gold Sovereigns 1816-2000, offered as one lot, Sothebys, November 2000, lot 525 (part)
Calendar year mintage 13,486,708. See footnote for lot 1164, page 234, for a brief synopsis of the 1872 die numbers.

260 **Victoria,** Sovereign, 1872, die number 20, third young head left, W.W. in relief on truncation, small die flaw at top of head under DEI, date below, 18 die flawed, hint of doubling in legend both sides, *rev* crowned quartered shield of arms within laurel wreath, die number 20 below, emblems below, legend lightly die flawed, 7.97g (Marsh 56; MCE 533; S 3853B). *Tiny hairline scratch under bust, reverse rim nick, hairlines, otherwise toned, about very fine, reverse better.* £300-350

Price Realised : £264

ex Spink and Son Ltd, November 2003
Calendar year mintage 13,486,708
See footnote for lot 1164, page 234, for a brief synopsis of the 1872 die numbers.

585 **Victoria,** Sovereign, 1872, die number 21, third young head left, W.W. in relief on truncation, date below, doubling in legend, a hint on reverse, *rev* crowned quartered shield of arms within laurel wreath, die number 21 below, emblems below, 7.97g (Marsh 56; MCE 533; S 3853B). *Scratch to right of crown on reverse, some nicks and hairlines, otherwise toned very fine / good very fine.* £300-350

Price Realised : £264

Calendar year mintage 13,486,708
See footnote for lot 1164, page 234, for a brief synopsis of the 1872 die numbers.

1170 **Victoria,** Sovereign, 1872, die number 22, third young head left, W.W. in relief on truncation, date lightly doubled below, top right of first T flawed, *rev* crowned quartered shield of arms within laurel wreath, die number 22 lightly flawed below, emblems below, hint of doubling to legend, 7.98g (Marsh 56; MCE 533; S 3853B). *Some light scratches behind head and in front of neck, red spots and blemishes on reverse, surface marks, otherwise very fine.* £250-300

Price Realised : £240

This coin was purchased from one of the groups of coins from the wreck of the RMS *Douro* that were not sold by auction and within the last 10 years.
Calendar year mintage 13,486,708. See footnote for lot 1164, page 234, for a brief synopsis of the 1872 die numbers.

1171 **Victoria,** Sovereign, 1872, die number 23, third young head left, w.w. in relief on truncation, date lightly doubled below, 1 with die flaw to neck, last letter I flawed across to A, flaw from rim to hair bun, *rev* crowned quartered shield of arms within laurel wreath, die number 23 below, emblems below, hint of doubling to legend with light raised flaw connecting some letters, 7.98g (Marsh 56; MCE 533; S 3853B). *A few nicks at end of ponytail, other surface marks, otherwise toned, extremely fine, reverse better.* £300-400

Price Realised : £312

ex Douro Cargo, Spink Auction 118, 20-21 November 1996, lot 1386 (part)
Calendar year mintage 13,486,708
See footnote for lot 1164, page 234, for a brief synopsis of the 1872 die numbers.

261 **Victoria,** Sovereign, 1872 die number 24, third young head left, w.w. in relief on truncation, date below, 1 die flawed to neck, raised die flaws and hint of doubling in legend both sides, *rev* crowned quartered shield of arms within laurel wreath, die number 24 below, die flawed with large 2 small 4, emblems below, 7.98g (Marsh 56; MCE 533; S 3853B). *Light hairlines and surface marks, extremely fine / good extremely fine.* £350-450

Price Realised : £336

ex Randy Weir Numismatics, Unionville, Ontario, Canada, purchased c.2000
Calendar year mintage 13,486,708
See footnote for lot 1164, page 234, for a brief synopsis of the 1872 die numbers.

586 **Victoria,** Sovereign, 1872, die number 25, third young head left, w.w. in relief on truncation, date below, die flaw to right of 2 from rim to neck, further die flaw between T and I across to last A, hint doubling in some letters both sides, *rev* crowned quartered shield of arms within laurel wreath, die number 25 below, emblems below, hairline die flaw in F and M of legend, 8.00g (Marsh 56; MCE 533; S 3853B). *Scratch to right of die number on reverse, some hairlines, otherwise extremely fine / good extremely fine.* £300-400

Price Realised : £360

ex Douro Cargo, Spink Auction 118, 20-21 November 1996, lot 1386 (part)
Calendar year mintage 13,486,708
See footnote for lot 1164, page 234, for a brief synopsis of the 1872 die numbers.

1172 **Victoria,** Sovereign, 1872, die number 26, third young head left, w.w. in relief on truncation, date below, die flaw between 1 and 8 of date, last letter T with flaw to rim, hint of doubling to legend both sides, *rev* crowned quartered shield of arms within laurel wreath, die number 26 below, emblems below, legend with light raised flaw connecting some letters, 7.99g (Marsh 56; MCE 533; S 3853B). *Spot under harp, reverse rim nick and other light surface marks, otherwise toned, extremely fine, reverse better.* £300-400

Price Realised : £240

ex Douro Cargo, Spink Auction 118, 20-21 November 1996, lot 1386 (part)
Calendar year mintage 13,486,708. See footnote for lot 1164, page 234, for a brief synopsis of the 1872 die numbers.

262 **Victoria,** Sovereign, 1872, die number 27, third young head left, w.w. in relief on truncation, date below, date and legend both sides lightly doubled in parts, *rev* crowned quartered shield of arms within laurel wreath, die number 27 below, die flawed, emblems below, 7.99g (Marsh 56; MCE 533; S 3853B). *Once cleaned, now lightly toned with polished brilliance, surface marks and hairlines, nearly extremely fine, reverse better.* £300-350

Price Realised : £264

ex Spink and Son Ltd, November 2003
Calendar year mintage 13,486,708
See footnote for lot 1164, page 234, for a brief synopsis of the 1872 die numbers.

263 **Victoria,** Sovereign, 1872, die number 28, third young head left, w.w. in relief on truncation, date below, lightly flawed date and obverse legend lightly doubled, *rev* crowned quartered shield of arms within laurel wreath, die number 28 below, emblems below, light raised die flaw in part of first word on reverse, 7.97g (Marsh 56; MCE 533; S 3853B). *Light surface marks extremely fine / good extremely fine.* £350-450

Price Realised : £648

ex Douro Cargo, Spink Auction 118, 20-21 November 1996, lot 1386 (part)
Calendar year mintage 13,486,708
See footnote for lot 1164, page 234, for a brief synopsis of the 1872 die numbers.

587 **Victoria,** Sovereign, 1872, die number 29, third young head left, w.w. in relief on truncation, date below, die flaw across top of date and last A to rim, some doubling in legend, *rev* crowned quartered shield of arms within laurel wreath, die number 29 below, emblems below, some raised flaws in parts of legend, 7.98g (Marsh 56; MCE 533; S 3853B). *Rim nick on obverse, streak of black tone on reverse, some hairline scuffs, otherwise extremely fine.* £300-400

Price Realised : £360

Calendar year mintage 13,486,708
See footnote for lot 1164, page 234, for a brief synopsis of the 1872 die numbers.

1173 **Victoria,** Sovereign, 1872, die number 30, third young head left, w.w. in relief on truncation, date below, last letter A with flaw to rim, hint of doubling to legend both sides, *rev* crowned quartered shield of arms within laurel wreath, die number 30 below, emblems below, 7.97g (Marsh 56; MCE 533; S 3853B). *Light nicks and hairlines, otherwise brilliant, extremely fine.* £300-400

Price Realised : £264

ex Douro Cargo, Spink Auction 118, 20-21 November 1996, lot 340 (part)
Calendar year mintage 13,486,708
See footnote for lot 1164, page 234, for a brief synopsis of the 1872 die numbers.

588 **Victoria,** Sovereign, 1872, die number 31, third young head left, w.w. in relief on truncation, date below, die flaw across part of date and penultimate A to rim, some doubling in legend, *rev* crowned quartered shield of arms within laurel wreath, die number 31 below, small 3, large 1, emblems below, some raised flaws in parts of legend, 7.98g (Marsh 56; MCE 533; S 3853B). *Patchy tone both sides, scuffed with some hairlines, otherwise very fine.* £300-350

Price Realised : £288

ex Douro Cargo, Spink Auction 118, 20-21 November 1996, lot 1321 (part)
Calendar year mintage 13,486,708. See footnote for lot 1164, page 234, for a brief synopsis of the 1872 die numbers.

1174 **Victoria,** Sovereign, 1872, die number 32, third young head left, w.w. in relief on truncation, date lightly die flawed below, raised die flaws at letter A's of legend and letter G, hint of doubling to legend both sides, *rev* crowned quartered shield of arms within laurel wreath, die number 32 below, emblems below, legend with light raised flaw connecting some letters, 7.97g (Marsh 56; MCE 533; S 3853B). *Some deposit on legend both sides and reverse design, surface marks, otherwise toned, very fine.* £250-300

Price Realised : £240

ex Douro Cargo, Spink Auction 118, 20-21 November 1996, lot 1321 (part)
Calendar year mintage 13,486,708. See footnote for lot 1164, page 234, for a brief synopsis of the 1872 die numbers.

264 **Victoria,** Sovereign, 1872, die number 33, third young head left, w.w. in relief on truncation, date below lightly die flawed, legend lightly flawed, last A up to rim, *rev* crowned quartered shield of arms within laurel wreath, die number 33 below, flawed, emblems below, lightly flawed reverse legend with some doubling, 7.96g (Marsh 56; MCE 533; S 3853B). *A few spots and nicks with a little black residual deposit, good fine, reverse better.* £300-350

Price Realised : £264

ex A H Baldwin & Sons Ltd sourced via Paul Davies Ltd, October 2006.
Calendar year mintage 13,486,708. See footnote for lot 1164, page 234, for a brief synopsis of the 1872 die numbers.

589 **Victoria,** Sovereign, 1872, die number 34, third young head left, w.w. in relief on truncation, date below, date and legend lightly doubled both sides with some light raised die flaws, *rev* crowned quartered shield of arms within laurel wreath, die number 34 below, filled and blundered figures, emblems below, 7.99g (Marsh 56; MCE 533; S 3853B). *Patchy tone both sides, surface marks and spots, otherwise almost extremely fine.* £300-350

Price Realised : £312

ex Spink and Son, purchased September 2003
This coin was purchased via Spink from one of the groups of coins from the wreck of the RMS *Douro* that were not sold by auction, bought in the last 10 years.
Calendar year mintage 13,486,708. See footnote for lot 1164, page 234, for a brief synopsis of the 1872 die numbers.

1175 **Victoria,** Sovereign, 1872, die number 35, third young head left, w.w. in relief on truncation, date lightly die flawed below, raised die flaws in some letters like V and hint of doubling to legend both sides, *rev* crowned quartered shield of arms within laurel wreath, die number 35 below, emblems below, 7.97g (Marsh 56; MCE 533; S 3853B). *Scuffed with surface marks, otherwise toned, about very fine, reverse better.* £250-300

Price Realised : £240

ex Douro Cargo, Spink Auction 118, 20-21 November 1996, lot 1321 (part)
Calendar year mintage 13,486,708
See footnote for lot 1164, page 234, for a brief synopsis of the 1872 die numbers.

265 **Victoria,** Sovereign, 1872, die number 36, third young head left, w.w. in relief on truncation, date below, flaw to left of 1 from rim to neck, die flaw from rim to top of head, letters V, O and last A flawed to rim, legend both sides lightly doubled and die flawed, *rev* crowned quartered shield of arms within laurel wreath, die number 36 below, emblems below, 7.98g (Marsh 56; MCE 533; S 3853B). *Obverse rim nicks, two spots on reverse, other light marks, very fine / good very fine.* £300-350

Price Realised : £264

ex Douro Cargo, Spink Auction 118, 20-21 November 1996, lot 1321 (part)
Calendar year mintage 13,486,708
See footnote for lot 1164, page 234, for a brief synopsis of the 1872 die numbers.

590 **Victoria,** Sovereign, 1872, die number 37, third young head left, w.w. in relief on truncation, date below, *rev* crowned quartered shield of arms within laurel wreath, die number 37 below, emblems below, hint of doubling in some letters with some light raised flaws, 7.99g (Marsh 56; MCE 533; S 3853B). *Some light scuffing with surface marks, two red spots on reverse, otherwise very fine / good very fine.* £300-350

Price Realised : £264

Calendar year mintage 13,486,708
See footnote for lot 1164, page 234, for a brief synopsis of the 1872 die numbers.
This coin was purchased via Spink from one of the groups of coins from the wreck of the RMS *Douro* that were not sold by auction, bought in the last 10 years.

266 **Victoria,** Sovereign, 1872, die number 38, third young head left, w.w. in relief on truncation, date below, obverse legend with some die flaws and light doubling, *rev* crowned quartered shield of arms within laurel wreath, die number 38 below, lightly flawed, emblems below, legend with first N die flawed to rim, 7.97g (Marsh 56; MCE 533; S 3853B). *Surface marks and light nicks, good very fine.* £300-350

Price Realised : £264

ex An Important Collection of Gold Sovereigns 1816-2000, offered as one lot, Sothebys, 16-17 November 2000, lot 525 (part)
Calendar year mintage 13,486,708
See footnote for lot 1164, page 234, for a brief synopsis of the 1872 die numbers.

591 **Victoria,** Sovereign, 1872, die number 39, third young head left, w.w. in relief on truncation, date below, 1 of date die flawed, *rev* crowned quartered shield of arms within laurel wreath, die number 39 below, emblems below, hint of doubling in a few letters, 7.98g (Marsh 56; MCE 533; S 3853B). *Some light nicks and surface marks, extremely fine / good extremely fine.* £350-450

Price Realised : £360

ex Douro Cargo, Spink Auction 118, 20-21 November 1996, lot 1386 (part)
Calendar year mintage 13,486,708
See footnote for lot 1164, page 234, for a brief synopsis of the 1872 die numbers.

1176 **Victoria,** Sovereign, 1872, die number 40, third young head left, w.w. in relief on truncation, date below, 8 with die flaw, flaw above eye on portrait, *rev* crowned quartered shield of arms within laurel wreath, die number 40 below, emblems below, some light doubling and light flaws in reverse legend, 7.99g (Marsh 56; MCE 533; S 3853B). *Two tiny spots on the obverse, one on the reverse, short scratch in obverse field with other light with surface marks, softly struck on reverse crown, otherwise toned, extremely fine / about extremely fine.* £250-300

Price Realised : £432

ex Randy Weir Numismatics, Unionville, Ontario, Canada, 28 September 1994
Calendar year mintage 13,486,708
See footnote for lot 1164, page 234, for a brief synopsis of the 1872 die numbers.

267 **Victoria,** Sovereign, 1872, die number 41, third young head left, w.w. in relief on truncation, date below, V die flawed, date and legend lightly doubled both sides, *rev* crowned quartered shield of arms within laurel wreath, die number 41 below, emblems below, legend with light die flaws, 7.98g (Marsh 56; MCE 533; S 3853B). *Two light hairline scratches on obverse field, light surface marks, otherwise good extremely fine.* £350-450

Price Realised : £384

ex Douro Cargo, Spink Auction 118, 20-21 November 1996, lot 342
Calendar year mintage 13,486,708
See footnote for lot 1164, page 234, for a brief synopsis of the 1872 die numbers.

1177 **Victoria,** Sovereign, 1872, die number 42, third young head left, w.w. in relief on truncation, date below, V with die flaw, *rev* crowned quartered shield of arms within laurel wreath, die number 42 below, emblems below, some light doubling in reverse legend, 7.98g (Marsh 56; MCE 533; S 3853B). *Light surface marks and scuffs, brilliant, very fine, reverse better.* £250-300

Price Realised : £264

Calendar year mintage 13,486,708
See footnote for lot 1164, page 234, for a brief synopsis of the 1872 die numbers.

268 **Victoria,** Sovereign, 1872, die number 43, third young head left, w.w. in relief on truncation, date below, V die flawed, date and legend lightly doubled both sides, *rev* crowned quartered shield of arms within laurel wreath, die number 43 below, emblems below, legend lightly die flawed, 7.96g (Marsh 56; MCE 533; S 3853B). *Some scuffs and surface marks, otherwise nearly very fine, reverse better.* £300-350

Price Realised : £264

ex Ebay purchase, August 2003
Calendar year mintage 13,486,708
See footnote for lot 1164, page 234, for a brief synopsis of the 1872 die numbers.

592 **Victoria,** Sovereign, 1872, die number 44, third young head left, w.w. in relief on truncation, date below, *rev* crowned quartered shield of arms within laurel wreath, die number 44 below, emblems below, hint of doubling and light die flaws in legend, 7.99g (Marsh 56; MCE 533; S 3853B). *Some light surface marks, two red spots on reverse with rim nick, otherwise nearly extremely fine.* £300-350

Price Realised : £288

ex Douro Cargo, Spink Auction 118, 20-21 November 1996, lot 1386 (part)
Calendar year mintage 13,486,708
See footnote for lot 1164, page 234, for a brief synopsis of the 1872 die numbers.

1178 **Victoria,** Sovereign, 1872, die number 45, third young head left, w.w. in relief on truncation, date below, 1 and 8 with die flaw and flaw from hair bun to rim along with last I of legend, legend lightly doubled, *rev* crowned quartered shield of arms within laurel wreath, die number 45 lightly flawed below, emblems below, some light flaws in reverse legend, 7.98g (Marsh 56; MCE 533; S 3853B). *Reverse rim nick, red tone, about extremely fine, reverse better.* £300-400

Price Realised : £264

ex Douro Cargo, Spink Auction 118, 20-21 November 1996, lot 571 (part)
ex An Important Collection of Gold Sovereigns 1816-2000, offered as one lot, Sothebys, November 2000, lot 525 (part)
Calendar year mintage 13,486,708
See footnote for lot 1164, page 234, for a brief synopsis of the 1872 die numbers.

269 **Victoria,** Sovereign, 1872, die number 46, third young head left, w.w. in relief on truncation, date below, last A of legend die flawed, *rev* crowned quartered shield of arms within laurel wreath, die number 46 below, emblems below, legend slightly doubled with raised die flaws, 7.99g (Marsh 56; MCE 533; S 3853B). *Some light ink marks above hair bun, surface marks, very fine / good very fine.* £300-350

Price Realised : £264

ex Randy Weir Numismatics, Unionville, Ontario, Canada, undated invoice c.2000
Calendar year mintage 13,486,708
See footnote for lot 1164, page 234, for a brief synopsis of the 1872 die numbers.

593 **Victoria,** Sovereign, 1872, die number 47, third young head left, W.W. in relief on truncation, date below, 1 of date die flawed to neck and across to 8, *rev* crowned quartered shield of arms within laurel wreath, die number 47 below, emblems below, some light die flaws in legend, 7.98g (Marsh 56; MCE 533; S 3853B). *Some light surface marks, some tiny spots on reverse, small scratch to left of crown, otherwise nearly extremely fine.* £300-350

Price Realised : £264

ex Douro Cargo, Spink Auction 118, 20-21 November 1996, lot 1320 (part)
Calendar year mintage 13,486,708
See footnote for lot 1164, page 234, for a brief synopsis of the 1872 die numbers.

1179 **Victoria,** Sovereign, 1872, die number 48, third young head left, W.W. in relief on truncation, date below, hint of doubling in date and legend both sides with some hairline raised flaws, *rev* crowned quartered shield of arms within laurel wreath, die number 48 below, low 8, high 4, emblems below, 7.98g (Marsh 56; MCE 533; S 3853B). *Scratch down neck, spot on reverse and other surface marks, good very fine, reverse better.* £250-300

Price Realised : £240

This coin was purchased from one of the groups of coins from the wreck of the RMS *Douro* that were not sold by auction and within the last 10 years.
Calendar year mintage 13,486,708
See footnote for lot 1164, page 234, for a brief synopsis of the 1872 die numbers.

1180 **Victoria,** Sovereign, 1872, die number 49, third young head left, W.W. in relief on truncation, date below, hairline raised flaw from neck to letter V, *rev* crowned quartered shield of arms within laurel wreath, die number 49 below doubled, 9 struck over a lower 9, emblems below, 7.99g (Marsh 56; MCE 533; S 3853B). *Black streak of tone behind neck, otherwise brilliant, a truly uncirculated Sovereign, very pleasing.* £600-800

Price Realised : £1,980

ex Douro Cargo, Spink Auction 118, 20-21 November 1996, lot 1388 (part)
Calendar year mintage 13,486,708
See footnote for lot 1164, page 234, for a brief synopsis of the 1872 die numbers.

594 **Victoria,** Sovereign, 1872, die number 50, third young head left, w.w. in relief on truncation, date below, O, third I and last A of legend die flawed to rim, *rev* crowned quartered shield of arms within laurel wreath, die number 50 below, emblems below, raised light die flaws in legend, 7.99g (Marsh 56; MCE 533; S 3853B). *Some light surface marks, rim nick on reverse, otherwise extremely fine / good extremely fine.* £350-400

Price Realised : £432

purchased via Ebay, August 2004
Calendar year mintage 13,486,708
See footnote for lot 1164, page 234, for a brief synopsis of the 1872 die numbers.

1181 **Victoria,** Sovereign, 1872, die number 51, third young head left, w.w. in relief on truncation, die flaw by first W, date below, hairline raised flaw from last I to rim in legend, hint of doubling to legend both sides, *rev* crowned quartered shield of arms within laurel wreath, die number 51 below, emblems below, raised die flaw connects some letters, 7.98g (Marsh 56; MCE 533; S 3853B). *Many light nicks on the obverse, once cleaned with associated surface marks, now toning, otherwise extremely fine, reverse better.* £300-400

Price Realised : £312

Calendar year mintage 13,486,708
See footnote for lot 1164, page 234, for a brief synopsis of the 1872 die numbers.

270 **Victoria,** Sovereign, 1872, die number 52, third young head left, w.w. in relief on truncation, date below, flaw to left of 1 from rim to neck, other light raised die flaws in legend, *rev* crowned quartered shield of arms within laurel wreath, die number 52 below, incomplete 2, emblems below, light doubling in some letters, 7.98g (Marsh 56; MCE 533; S 3853B). *Surface marks with rim nick on reverse, almost extremely fine / extremely fine.* £300-350

Price Realised : £312

ex Douro Cargo, Spink Auction 118, 20-21 November 1996, lot 1388 (part)
Calendar year mintage 13,486,708
See footnote for lot 1164, page 234, for a brief synopsis of the 1872 die numbers.

271 **Victoria,** Sovereign, 1872, die number 53, third young head left, w.w. in relief on truncation, date below, first two A's in legend flawed to rim, *rev* crowned quartered shield of arms within laurel wreath, die number 53 below, emblems below, light doubling to letters, 7.99g (Marsh 56; MCE 533; S 3853B). *Light wispy black streaks and spot on reverse, light surface marks, good extremely fine.* £350-450

Price Realised : £528

ex Randy Weir Numismatics, Unionville, Ontario, Canada, purchased 27 September 1990
Calendar year mintage 13,486,708
See footnote for lot 1164, page 234, for a brief synopsis of the 1872 die numbers.

595 **Victoria,** Sovereign, 1872, die number 54, third young head left, w.w. in relief on truncation, date below, last word doubled with light die flaws, *rev* crowned quartered shield of arms within laurel wreath, die number 54 below, emblems below, some letters doubled, 8.00g (Marsh 56; MCE 533; S 3853B). *Scratch on neck, digs by chin, other light surface marks and nicks, obverse rim nick, otherwise toned, good extremely fine.* £350-400

Price Realised : £408

ex Stacks, 21 February 1997, lot 1139
ex An Important Collection of Gold Sovereigns 1816-2000, offered as one lot, Sothebys, November 2000, lot 525 (part)
Calendar year mintage 13,486,708
See footnote for lot 1164, page 234, for a brief synopsis of the 1872 die numbers.

596 **Victoria,** Sovereign, 1872, die number 55, third young head left, w.w. in relief on truncation, date below, *rev* crowned quartered shield of arms within laurel wreath, die number 55 below, left 5 is larger than other, emblems below, 7.95g (Marsh 56; MCE 533; S 3853B). *Scuffed with light surface marks, some black deposits on rim, otherwise almost very fine / very fine.* £300-350

Price Realised : £264

Calendar year mintage 13,486,708
See footnote for lot 1164, page 234, for a brief synopsis of the 1872 die numbers.

1182 **Victoria,** Sovereign, 1872, die number 56, third young head left, w.w. in relief on truncation, date below, hairline raised flaw at V and O in legend, other light flaws to legend both sides, *rev* crowned quartered shield of arms within laurel wreath, die number 56 below, emblems below, raised die flaw connects some letters, 7.96g (Marsh 56; MCE 533; S 3853B). *Red spot on the obverse, light surface marks, otherwise very fine, reverse better.* £250-300

Price Realised : £240

ex Douro Cargo, Spink Auction 118, 20-21 November 1996, lot 1324 (part)
Calendar year mintage 13,486,708
See footnote for lot 1164, page 234, for a brief synopsis of the 1872 die numbers.

272 **Victoria,** Sovereign, 1872, die number 57, third young head left, w.w. in relief on truncation, date below, raised die flaws in some letters of legend both sides, *rev* crowned quartered shield of arms within laurel wreath, die number 57 below, emblems below, 7.97g (Marsh 56; MCE 533; S 3853B). *Once cleaned, now lightly toned, surface marks and scuffs, a few nicks and hairlines, good very fine.* £300-350

Price Realised : £264

ex Spink and Son Ltd, March 2005
Calendar year mintage 13,486,708
See footnote for lot 1164, page 234, for a brief synopsis of the 1872 die numbers.

273 **Victoria,** Sovereign, 1872, die number 58, third young head left, w.w. in relief on truncation, date below lightly flawed, raised die flaw from rim into field at 5 o'clock to behind head, raised die flaws in legend both sides, *rev* crowned quartered shield of arms within laurel wreath, die number 58 below, with high die flaw, emblems below, 8.00g (Marsh 56; MCE 533; S 3853B). *Brilliant with light surface marks and hairlines, good extremely fine.* £400-500

Price Realised : £624

ex Randy Weir Numismatics, Unionville, Ontario, Canada, purchased 28 September 1994
Calendar year mintage 13,486,708
See footnote for lot 1164, page 234, for a brief synopsis of the 1872 die numbers.

597 **Victoria,** Sovereign, 1872, die number 59, third young head left, w.w. in relief on truncation, date below, 1 of date die flawed to rim, light die flaws in last word of legend, *rev* crowned quartered shield of arms within laurel wreath, die number 59 below, emblems below, some light flaws in reverse legend, 7.99g (Marsh 56; MCE 533; S 3853B). *Some nicks and light surface marks, very fine / good very fine.* £300-350

Price Realised : £264

Calendar year mintage 13,486,708
See footnote for lot 1164, page 234, for a brief synopsis of the 1872 die numbers.

1183 **Victoria,** Sovereign, 1872, die number 60, third young head left, w.w. in relief on truncation, date below, hairline flaws to date and legend both sides, *rev* crowned quartered shield of arms within laurel wreath, die number 60 below, emblems below, 7.97g (Marsh 56; MCE 533; S 3853B). *Two digs on neck along with other light surface marks and nicks, otherwise good very fine, reverse better.* £250-300

Price Realised : £240

Calendar year mintage 13,486,708
See footnote for lot 1164, page 234, for a brief synopsis of the 1872 die numbers.

1184 **Victoria,** Sovereign, 1872, die number 61, third young head left, w.w. in relief on truncation, date below, letter V and last A of legend die flawed, *rev* crowned quartered shield of arms within laurel wreath, die number 61 below, smaller 6 slightly lower than 1, emblems below, light hairline die flaws on reverse rim, 7.96g (Marsh 56; MCE 533; S 3853B). *Heavily surface marked and scuffed, obverse rim bruise, otherwise about very fine, reverse better.* £250-300

Price Realised : £216

ex Randy Weir Numismatics, Unionville, Ontario, Canada, October 1998
Calendar year mintage 13,486,708
See footnote for lot 1164, page 234, for a brief synopsis of the 1872 die numbers.

274 **Victoria,** Sovereign, 1872, die number 62, third young head left, w.w. in relief on truncation, date below, raised die flaws in legend from first I to rim, last I flawed and across to last A, *rev* crowned quartered shield of arms within laurel wreath, die number 62 below, emblems below, hairline raised die flaw in legend, 7.98g (Marsh 56; MCE 533; S 3853B). *A few light spots on and to the left of neck on obverse, surface marks and hairlines, extremely fine.* £300-350

Price Realised : £384

ex Douro Cargo, Spink Auction 118, 20-21 November 1996, lot 1388 (part)
Calendar year mintage 13,486,708
See footnote for lot 1164, page 234, for a brief synopsis of the 1872 die numbers.

275 **Victoria,** Sovereign, 1872, die number 63, third young head left, w.w. in relief on truncation, date below lightly doubled with light flaws as is obverse legend, *rev* crowned quartered shield of arms within laurel wreath, die number 63 below, emblems below, hairline raised die flaw in legend, 7.99g (Marsh 56; MCE 533; S 3853B). *Obverse rim nicks, light surface marks and hairlines, otherwise toned, good very fine.* £300-350

Price Realised : £330

ex Paul Davies Ltd. This coin was purchased from one of the groups of coins from the wreck of the RMS *Douro* that were not sold by auction and within the last 10 years.
Calendar year mintage 13,486,708
See footnote for lot 1164, page 234, for a brief synopsis of the 1872 die numbers.

598 **Victoria,** Sovereign, 1872, die number 64, third young head left, w.w. in relief on truncation, date below, date lightly die flawed, last A die flawed to rim, *rev* crowned quartered shield of arms within laurel wreath, die number 64 below, emblems below, some light flaws in reverse legend, 7.99g (Marsh 56; MCE 533; S 3853B). *Some nicks under chin, short scratch on neck, other light surface marks, two obverse rim nicks and one on reverse, scratch by 2 of date, otherwise nearly extremely fine.* £300-350

Price Realised : £288

ex Douro Cargo, Spink Auction 118, 20-21 November 1996, lot 1388 (part)
Calendar year mintage 13,486,708
See footnote for lot 1164, page 234, for a brief synopsis of the 1872 die numbers.

A Very Rare Occurrence of an Over-struck Die Number on a Sovereign

number "65" over "64"

599 **Victoria,** Sovereign, 1872, die number 65, 5 over 4 in die number, third young head left, w.w. in relief on truncation, date below, date lightly die flawed, last A die flawed to rim, hint of doubling to legend, *rev* crowned quartered shield of arms within laurel wreath, die number 65 below, the 5 struck over a 4, emblems below, some light flaws in reverse legend, 8.00g (Marsh 56; MCE 533; S 3853B). *Nick on cheek by mouth, some light hairline surface marks, otherwise extremely fine / good extremely fine and very rare with an overstruck die number.* £400-600

Price Realised : £1,560

ex Douro Cargo, Spink Auction 118, 20-21 November 1996, lot 345 (part), the overstrike not noted
Calendar year mintage 13,486,708
See footnote for lot 1164, page 234, for a brief synopsis of the 1872 die numbers.
We are used to seeing overstruck dates but this coin is the only overstrike of a die number that we are aware of. Presumably it has to be an engraving error on the part of the engraver preparing the numbered dies. Perhaps he had just made reverse die number 64 and still had the 4 punch to hand and used it in error when making die 65. Of course with the strict quality control now in place at the mint it had to be corrected immediately to show 65. Overdates in the die number series are practically non-existent too as the quality control was so high, this piece is therefore very unusual and very rare. For an overdate in the die number series see lot 488, page 158.

1185 **Victoria,** Sovereign, 1872, die number 66, third young head left, w.w. in relief on truncation, date below, hint of raised die flaw and some doubling in legend both sides, *rev* die axis slightly off-centre, crowned quartered shield of arms within laurel wreath, die number 66 below, emblems below, light hairline die flaws on reverse rim, 7.98g (Marsh 56; MCE 533; S 3853B). *Tiny red spot on forehead, scratch to left of* 1 *in date and reverse rim nick, otherwise bold very fine, reverse better.* £250-300

Price Realised : £240

This coin was purchased from one of the groups of coins from the wreck of the RMS *Douro* that were not sold by auction and within the last 10 years.
Calendar year mintage 13,486,708
See footnote for lot 1164, page 234, for a brief synopsis of the 1872 die numbers.

276 **Victoria,** Sovereign, 1872, die number 67, third young head left, w.w. in relief on truncation, date below, 1 with raised flaw to neck, hairline raised die flaws in some letters both sides, *rev* crowned quartered shield of arms within laurel wreath, die number 67 below, figures widely spaced, emblems below, lightly flawed, 7.96g (Marsh 56; MCE 533; S 3853B). *Scuffed with many surface marks, large dig on throat, nearly very fine, reverse better.* £300-350

Price Realised : £264

Ebay purchase c.2001 – Epsom Stamp Centre, Surrey.
Calendar year mintage 13,486,708
See footnote for lot 1164, page 234, for a brief synopsis of the 1872 die numbers.

1186 **Victoria,** Sovereign, 1872, die number 68, third young head left, w.w. in relief on truncation, date below, *rev* die axis slightly off-centre, crowned quartered shield of arms within laurel wreath, die number 68 below, emblems below, some letters lightly doubled, 7.97g (Marsh 56; MCE 533; S 3853B). *Streak of tone in hair, one obverse and one reverse rim nick, underlying brilliance both sides, otherwise proof-like extremely fine.* £300-400

Price Realised : £480

ex Douro Cargo, Spink Auction 118, 20-21 November 1996, lot 1388 (part)
Calendar year mintage 13,486,708
See footnote for lot 1164, page 234, for a brief synopsis of the 1872 die numbers.

277 **Victoria,** Sovereign, 1872, die number 69, third young head left, with double fillet, w.w. in relief on truncation, date below, hairline raised die flaws and doubling in some letters both sides, E of DEI from faulty punch with curved lower horizontal limb, *rev* crowned quartered shield of arms within laurel wreath, die number 69 below, incomplete 9, emblems below, 7.98g (Marsh 56; MCE 533; S 3853B). *Surface marks, nearly extremely fine, reverse better.* £350-400

Price Realised : £300

ex Douro Cargo, Spink Auction 118, 20-21 November 1996, lot 572 (part)
ex An Important Collection of Gold Sovereigns 1816-2000, offered as one lot, Sothebys, 16-17 November 2000, lot 525 (part)
Calendar year mintage 13,486,708. See footnote for lot 1164, page 234, for a brief synopsis of the 1872 die numbers.

600 **Victoria,** Sovereign, 1872, die number 70, third young head left, w.w. in relief on truncation, date below, date and legend slightly doubled both sides, last A of legend die flawed to rim, *rev* die axis slightly off-centre, crowned quartered shield of arms within laurel wreath, die number 70 below, emblems below, some light flaws in reverse legend, 7.97g (Marsh 56; MCE 533; S 3853B). *Obverse rim nick, short scratch on bun of hair, heavy surface marks, otherwise once cleaned, very fine, unusual with off centre die axis.* £300-350

Price Realised : £264

Calendar year mintage 13,486,708
See footnote for lot 1164, page 234, for a brief synopsis of the 1872 die numbers.

1187 **Victoria,** Sovereign, 1872, die number 71, third young head left, w.w. in relief on truncation, date below, last A of legend die flawed to rim, hint of doubling to date and legend both sides, die flaw from top of head to rim, *rev* crowned quartered shield of arms within laurel wreath, die number 71 below, 1 larger than 7, emblems below, 7.96g (Marsh 56; MCE 533; S 3853B). *Scuffs, nicks and surface marks, about very fine, reverse better.* £250-300

Price Realised : £216

This coin was purchased from one of the groups of coins from the wreck of the RMS *Douro* that were not sold by auction and within the last 10 years.
Calendar year mintage 13,486,708
See footnote for lot 1164, page 234, for a brief synopsis of the 1872 die numbers.

278 **Victoria,** Sovereign, 1872, die number 72, third young head left, w.w. in relief on truncation, date below, 18 die flawed along with die flaws in legend both sides, second and last A of obverse flawed to rim, *rev* crowned quartered shield of arms within laurel wreath, die number 72 below, incomplete 2, emblems below, hint of doubling in some letters, 7.98g (Marsh 56; MCE 533; S 3853B). *Dig on cheek, streaks of tone on reverse, uneven circle of tone on obverse, light surface marks, nearly extremely fine.* £300-350

Price Realised : £264

ex Douro Cargo, Spink Auction 118, 20-21 November 1996, lot 1324 (part)
Calendar year mintage 13,486,708
See footnote for lot 1164, page 234, for a brief synopsis of the 1872 die numbers.

601 **Victoria,** Sovereign, 1872, die number 73, third young head left, w.w. in relief on truncation, date below, date lightly doubled with 1 die flawed to neck, *rev* crowned quartered shield of arms within laurel wreath, die number 73 below, emblems below, some letters doubled in reverse legend, 7.98g (Marsh 56; MCE 533; S 3853B). *Slight metal flaw to top of left laurel wreath on reverse, some hairlines and surface marks, toned very fine, reverse better.* £300-350

Price Realised : £264

Calendar year mintage 13,486,708
See footnote for lot 1164, page 234, for a brief synopsis of the 1872 die numbers.

602 **Victoria,** Sovereign, 1872, die number 74, third young head left, w.w. in relief on truncation, date below, date with 2 die flawed to neck, another flaw at last T of legend, *rev* crowned quartered shield of arms within laurel wreath, die number 74 below, die flaws in 74, emblems below, some letters in reverse legend die flawed, 7.98g (Marsh 56; MCE 533; S 3853B). *Some nicks and short scratches on neck and cheek, obverse rim nick and other light surface marks, otherwise brilliant extremely fine.* £300-350

Price Realised : £384

ex Randy Weir Numismatics, Unionville, Ontario, Canada, 2 June 1995
Calendar year mintage 13,486,708
See footnote for lot 1164, page 234, for a brief synopsis of the 1872 die numbers.

1188 **Victoria,** Sovereign, 1872, die number 75, third young head left, w.w. in relief on truncation, date below, die flaw to left of 1 to neck, 2 flawed to rim, last I of legend die flawed to rim, *rev* crowned quartered shield of arms within laurel wreath, die number 75 below, large 5, small 7, emblems below, light hairline die flaws on reverse legend, 7.97g (Marsh 56; MCE 533; S 3853B). *Once polished, streaks of tone by date, otherwise about very fine, reverse better.* £250-300

Price Realised : £216

Calendar year mintage 13,486,708
See footnote for lot 1164, page 234, for a brief synopsis of the 1872 die numbers.

1189 **Victoria,** Sovereign, 1872, die number 76, third young head left, w.w. in relief on truncation, date below, 1 die flawed to neck, *rev* crowned quartered shield of arms within laurel wreath, die number 76 below, 6 doubled, emblems below, 7.96g (Marsh 56; MCE 533; S 3853B). *Light surface marks and hairlines, obverse rim nick, otherwise about extremely fine, reverse better.* £300-400

Price Realised : £240

ex Randy Weir Numismatics, Unionville, Ontario, Canada, 28 September 1994
Calendar year mintage 13,486,708
See footnote for lot 1164, page 234, for a brief synopsis of the 1872 die numbers.

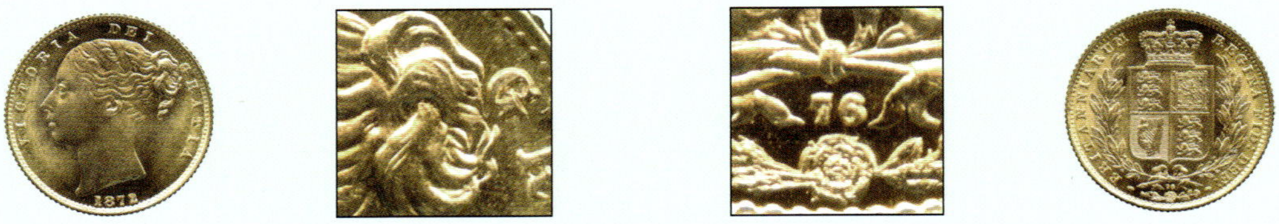

603 **Victoria,** Sovereign, 1872, die number 76, third young head left, hair in bun with more well struck attached curls, w.w. in relief fully on truncation, date below, some doubling in date and legend both sides, *rev* crowned quartered shield of arms within laurel wreath, die number 76 below, 6 doubled, emblems below, some letters in reverse legend lightly die flawed, 8.00g (Marsh 56; MCE 533; S 3853B). *Scuff on neck with light surface marks, brilliant and pleasing, good extremely fine.* £350-450

Price Realised : £576

ex Randy Weir Numismatics, Unionville, Ontario, Canada, 14 June 1992
There appears to be a touch more outline definition to the profile of this coin (evident on the rear of the hairbun and the base of the truncation), probably indicative of an early strike for the die.
Calendar year mintage 13,486,708. See footnote for lot 1164, page 234, for a brief synopsis of the 1872 die numbers.

279 **Victoria,** Sovereign, 1872, die number 77, third young head left, w.w. in relief on truncation, date below, 1 lightly flawed as well as some letters in obverse legend, *rev* crowned quartered shield of arms within laurel wreath, die number 77 below, emblems below, 7.97g (Marsh 56; MCE 533; S 3853B). *Red spot on tip of neck, spot on centre of shield with patch of deposit at* DEF, *scratch under chin with obverse rim nick, otherwise good very fine, reverse stronger.* £300-350

Price Realised : £288

ex Douro Cargo, Spink Auction 118, 20-21 November 1996, lot 1321 (part)
Calendar year mintage 13,486,708. See footnote for lot 1164, page 234, for a brief synopsis of the 1872 die numbers.

604 **Victoria,** Sovereign, 1872, die number 78, third young head left, w.w. in relief on truncation, date below, 1 of date flawed to rim, further flaw at last A of legend, some doubling in legend, *rev* crowned quartered shield of arms within laurel wreath, die number 78 below, small 7, large 8, emblems below, some letters in reverse legend lightly die flawed, 7.99g (Marsh 56; MCE 533; S 3853B). *Some surface marks, obverse rim nick, toned almost extremely fine / extremely fine.* £300-400

Price Realised : £312

ex Douro Cargo, Spink Auction 118, 20-21 November 1996, lot 572 (part)
ex An Important Collection of Gold Sovereigns 1816-2000, offered as one lot, Sothebys, November 2000, lot 525 (part)
Calendar year mintage 13,486,708. See footnote for lot 1164, page 234, for a brief synopsis of the 1872 die numbers.

280 **Victoria,** Sovereign, 1872, die number 79, third young head left, w.w. in relief on truncation, date below, very doubled with obverse legend, last A with raised die flaw to rim, *rev* crowned quartered shield of arms within laurel wreath, die number 79 below, lightly die flawed, emblems below, raised die flaw in some letters, 7.99g (Marsh 56; MCE 533; S 3853B). *Light scratch on cheek, other light surface marks, toned, extremely fine.* £300-350

Price Realised : £432

ex Douro Cargo, Spink Auction 118, 20-21 November 1996, lot 1324 (part)
Calendar year mintage 13,486,708
See footnote for lot 1164, page 234, for a brief synopsis of the 1872 die numbers.

605 **Victoria,** Sovereign, 1872, die number 80, third young head left, w.w. in relief on truncation, date below, 1 and 2 of date both die flawed to rim, some doubling in legend both sides, *rev* crowned quartered shield of arms within laurel wreath, die number 80 below, lightly die flawed, emblems below, some letters in reverse legend lightly die flawed, 7.98g (Marsh 56; MCE 533; S 3853B). *Black mark above 72, scratch on ear lobe and behind head, toned on reverse, almost extremely fine/ extremely fine.* £300-350

Price Realised : £288

ex Douro Cargo, Spink Auction 118, 20-21 November 1996, lot 1389 (part)
Calendar year mintage 13,486,708
See footnote for lot 1164, page 234, for a brief synopsis of the 1872 die numbers.

1190 **Victoria,** Sovereign, 1872, die number 81, third young head left, w.w. in relief on truncation, date below, penultimate A of legend die flawed, trace of doubling to legend both sides, *rev* crowned quartered shield of arms within laurel wreath, die number 81 below, large 1, small 8, emblems below, light hairline die flaws on reverse legend, 7.97g (Marsh 56; MCE 533; S 3853B). *Toned with light surface marks, about extremely fine, reverse better.* £300-400

Price Realised : £264

ex Douro Cargo, Spink Auction 118, 20-21 November 1996, lot 1389 (part)
Calendar year mintage 13,486,708
See footnote for lot 1164, page 234, for a brief synopsis of the 1872 die numbers.

1191 **Victoria,** Sovereign, 1872, die number 82, third young head left, w.w. in relief on truncation, date below, 7 of date flawed from rim to neck, die flaw between last IA in legend, *rev* crowned quartered shield of arms within laurel wreath, die number 82 lightly flawed below, emblems below, die flaw from top of crown to rim, 7.96g (Marsh 56; MCE 533; S 3853B). *Toned with light surface marks, very fine.* £250-300

Price Realised : £216

ex Douro Cargo, Spink Auction 118, 20-21 November 1996, lot 1389 (part)
Calendar year mintage 13,486,708
See footnote for lot 1164, page 234, for a brief synopsis of the 1872 die numbers.

281 **Victoria,** Sovereign, 1872, die number 83, third young head left, W.W. in relief on truncation, date below, very doubled along with some obverse letters, raised flaw between I and A, *rev* crowned quartered shield of arms within laurel wreath, die number 83 below, emblems below, hint of doubling of legend with raised die flaws, 7.98g (Marsh 56; MCE 533; S 3853B). *Large cross scratched each side of crown, red spots on obverse with blemishes on reverse and other light marks, very fine, reverse better.* £250-300

Price Realised : £228

ex Douro Cargo, Spink Auction 118, 20-21 November 1996, lot 1324 (part)
Calendar year mintage 13,486,708
See footnote for lot 1164, page 234, for a brief synopsis of the 1872 die numbers.

606 **Victoria,** Sovereign, 1872, die number 84, third young head left, W.W. in relief on truncation, date lightly doubled below, *rev* crowned quartered shield of arms within laurel wreath, die number 84 below, lightly die flawed large 8, small 4, emblems below, some letters in reverse legend doubled, 7.98g (Marsh 56; MCE 533; S 3853B). *Light streaks of tone with hairlines and surface marks, very fine / almost extremely fine.* £300-350

Price Realised : £288

ex Douro Cargo, Spink Auction 118, 20-21 November 1996, lot 1324 (part)
Calendar year mintage 13,486,708
See footnote for lot 1164, page 234, for a brief synopsis of the 1872 die numbers.

282 **Victoria,** Sovereign, 1872, die number 85, third young head left, hair bun with die flaw, W.W. in relief on truncation, raised die flaw from tip of neck to rim, date below, first T flawed to rim, *rev* crowned quartered shield of arms within laurel wreath, die number 85 below, 5 flawed and filled and higher than 8, emblems below, a few letters doubled in legend, 7.99g (Marsh 56; MCE 533; S 3853B). *Previously graded by PCGS as MS64, some streaks of tone with a few nicks and surface marks, nearly extremely fine, reverse better.* £300-350

Price Realised : £312

ex Randy Weir Numismatics, Unionville, Ontario, Canada, purchase 22 March 1990
Calendar year mintage 13,486,708
See footnote for lot 1164, page 234, for a brief synopsis of the 1872 die numbers.

607 **Victoria,** Sovereign, 1872, die number 86, third young head left, W.W. in relief on truncation, date lightly doubled below, 1 die flawed, last A of legend die flawed to rim, hint of doubling to legend both sides, *rev* crowned quartered shield of arms within laurel wreath, die number 86 below, emblems below, some letters in reverse legend lightly die flawed, 7.99g (Marsh 56; MCE 533; S 3853B). *Nick on cheek, light surface marks, extremely fine / good extremely fine, previously graded by PCGS as MS64.* £350-450

Price Realised : £744

ex Jacob Y Terner collection, Goldberg, Hollywood, USA, Sale 20, 26-27 May 2003, lot 364
Calendar year mintage 13,486,708
See footnote for lot 1164, page 234, for a brief synopsis of the 1872 die numbers.

1192 **Victoria,** Sovereign, 1872, die number 87, third young head left, w.w. in relief on truncation, date below, 1 of date flawed, V and last A in legend die flawed, *rev* crowned quartered shield of arms within laurel wreath, die number 87 below, emblems below, die flaw connects some letters in doubled legend, 7.98g (Marsh 56; MCE 533; S 3853B). *A number of spots by eye towards legend and light surface marks, very fine, reverse better.* £250-300

Price Realised : £240

Calendar year mintage 13,486,708
See footnote for lot 1164, page 234, for a brief synopsis of the 1872 die numbers.

283 **Victoria,** Sovereign, 1872, die number 88, third young head left, w.w. in relief on truncation, date below lightly doubled along with obverse legend, 1 flawed up into field, *rev* crowned quartered shield of arms within laurel wreath, die number 88 below, 88 lightly filled, emblems below, 7.97g (Marsh 56; MCE 533; S 3853B). *Dig in hair, light surface marks, toned, very fine, reverse better.* £300-350

Price Realised : £288

ex Spink and Son Ltd, November 2003
This coin was purchased from one of the groups of coins from the wreck of the RMS *Douro* that were not sold by auction bought in the last 10 years.
Calendar year mintage 13,486,708
See footnote for lot 1164, page 234, for a brief synopsis of the 1872 die numbers.

1193 **Victoria,** Sovereign, 1872, die number 89, third young head left, w.w. in relief on truncation, date below, date and legend both sides doubled, die flaw from first A to rim and at AT in last word, *rev* crowned quartered shield of arms within laurel wreath, die number 89 lightly flawed below, emblems below, die flaw from G of legend to rim, 7.99g (Marsh 56; MCE 533; S 3853B). *Toned with light surface marks, good extremely fine.* £400-500

Price Realised : £384

ex Randy Weir Numismatics, Unionville, Ontario, Canada, 14 August 1992
Calendar year mintage 13,486,708
See footnote for lot 1164, page 234, for a brief synopsis of the 1872 die numbers.

284 **Victoria,** Sovereign, 1872, die number 90, third young head left, raised die flaw from hair bun to rim, w.w. in relief on truncation, date below, some light doubling with raised die flaws in obverse legend, *rev* die axis slightly off-centre, crowned quartered shield of arms within laurel wreath, die number 90 below, 90 with upper raised flaw, emblems below, some flaws in legend, 7.99g (Marsh 56; MCE 533; S 3853B). *Nicks on cheek and other light surface marks, toned, good extremely fine.* £350-450

Price Realised : £480

ex Douro Cargo, Spink Auction 118, 20-21 November 1996, lot 573 (part)
Calendar year mintage 13,486,708. See footnote for lot 1164, page 234, for a brief synopsis of the 1872 die numbers.

1194 **Victoria,** Sovereign, 1872, die number 91, third young head left, w.w. in relief on truncation, date below, date and legend doubled, die flaw at last A of legend, *rev* crowned quartered shield of arms within laurel wreath, die number 91 lightly flawed below, smaller 9 lower than 1, emblems below, 8.00g (Marsh 56; MCE 533; S 3853B). *Brilliant, light surface marks, proof-like, good extremely fine.* £400-500

Price Realised : £552

ex Douro Cargo, Spink Auction 118, 20-21 November 1996, lot 1390 (part)
Calendar year mintage 13,486,708
See footnote for lot 1164, page 234, for a brief synopsis of the 1872 die numbers.

608 **Victoria,** Sovereign, 1872, die number 92, third young head left, w.w. in relief on truncation, date below, 1 of date doubled, raised die flaw to left of last I in legend, *rev* crowned quartered shield of arms within laurel wreath, die number 92 below, 9 doubled, emblems below, some letters in reverse legend doubled, 7.98g (Marsh 56; MCE 533; S 3853B). *Green spot on obverse, two red spots on reverse, other hairlines, nicks, digs and surface marks, very fine / extremely fine.* £300-350

Price Realised : £288

ex Douro Cargo, Spink Auction 118, 20-21 November 1996, lot 1320 (part)
Calendar year mintage 13,486,708
See footnote for lot 1164, page 234, for a brief synopsis of the 1872 die numbers.

285 **Victoria,** Sovereign, 1872, die number 93, third young head left, w.w. in relief on truncation, date below, date doubled, *rev* crowned quartered shield of arms within laurel wreath, die number 93 below, emblems below, die flaw between RE of REG, 7.99g (Marsh 56; MCE 533; S 3853B). *Nick behind ear, red spot on reverse, light surface marks, otherwise practically as struck.* £400-500

Price Realised : £624

ex Douro Cargo, Spink Auction 118, 20-21 November 1996, lot 573 (part)
Calendar year mintage 13,486,708
See footnote for lot 1164, page 234, for a brief synopsis of the 1872 die numbers.

609 **Victoria,** Sovereign, 1872, die number 94, third young head left, w.w. in relief on truncation, date below, date and legend doubled, third I with raised die flaw to rim, last A with a trace of die flaw, *rev* crowned quartered shield of arms within laurel wreath, die number 94 below, emblems below, some letters in reverse legend with raised die flaws, 7.99g (Marsh 56; MCE 533; S 3853B). *Some light surface marks and spots, otherwise extremely fine.* £350-400

Price Realised : £360

ex Douro Cargo, Spink Auction 118, 20-21 November 1996, lot 1390 (part)
Calendar year mintage 13,486,708
See footnote for lot 1164, page 234, for a brief synopsis of the 1872 die numbers.

1195 **Victoria,** Sovereign, 1872, die number 95, third young head left, w.w. in relief on truncation, date below, date and legend doubled, die flaw at VI and last A of legend to rim, *rev* crowned quartered shield of arms within laurel wreath, die number 95 lightly flawed below, emblems below, some light die flaws in reverse legend, 7.99g (Marsh 56; MCE 533; S 3853B). *Toned with light surface marks, good extremely fine.* £400-500

Price Realised : £408

This coin was purchased from one of the groups of coins from the wreck of the RMS *Douro* that were not sold by auction and within the last 10 years.
Calendar year mintage 13,486,708
See footnote for lot 1164, page 234, for a brief synopsis of the 1872 die numbers.

610 **Victoria,** Sovereign, 1872, die number 96, third young head left, w.w. in relief on truncation, raised die flaw from neck to rim, date below, hint of doubling to some obverse letters, *rev* crowned quartered shield of arms within laurel wreath, die number 96 below, 96 flawed, emblems below, some letters in reverse legend with raised die flaws, 7.98g (Marsh 56; MCE 533; S 3853B). *A few light surface marks, two obverse rim nicks, otherwise pleasing, good extremely fine.* £400-500

Price Realised : £480

ex Douro Cargo, Spink Auction 118, 20-21 November 1996, lot 573 (part)
Calendar year mintage 13,486,708. See footnote for lot 1164, page 234, for a brief synopsis of the 1872 die numbers.

1196 **Victoria,** Sovereign, 1872, die number 97, third young head left, w.w. in relief on truncation, date below, die flaw at V of legend, *rev* crowned quartered shield of arms within laurel wreath, die number 97 below, emblems below, 7.97g (Marsh 56; MCE 533; S 3853B). *Toned with light surface marks, very fine, reverse better.* £250-300

Price Realised : £216

This coin was purchased from one of the groups of coins from the wreck of the RMS *Douro* that were not sold by auction and within the last 10 years.
Calendar year mintage 13,486,708
See footnote for lot 1164, page 234, for a brief synopsis of the 1872 die numbers.

286 **Victoria,** Sovereign, 1872, die number 98, third young head left, w.w. in relief on truncation, date below, doubled date and some legend letters, with light die flaws on both sides, *rev* crowned quartered shield of arms within laurel wreath, die number 98 below, emblems below, lightly cross flawed, 7.97g (Marsh 56; MCE 533; S 3853B). *A few tiny spots and surface marks, extremely fine / good extremely fine.* £350-450

Price Realised : £504

ex Douro Cargo, Spink Auction 118, 20-21 November 1996, lot 575 (part)
Calendar year mintage 13,486,708. See footnote for lot 1164, page 234, for a brief synopsis of the 1872 die numbers.

287 **Victoria,** Sovereign, 1872, die number 99, third young head left, W.W. in relief on truncation, date below, *rev* crowned quartered shield of arms within laurel wreath, die number 99 quite spread below, left 9 has thicker bottom than right one, emblems below, some raised die flaws in upper half of legend, 7.95g (Marsh 56; MCE 533; S 3853B). *Once cleaned with associated surface marks and hairlines, nearly very fine.* £300-350

Price Realised : £264

ex An Important Collection of Gold Sovereigns 1816-2000, offered as one lot, Sothebys, 16-17 November 2000, lot 525 (part)
Calendar year mintage 13,486,708
See footnote for lot 1164, page 234, for a brief synopsis of the 1872 die numbers.

1197 **Victoria,** Sovereign, 1872, die number 100, third young head left, W.W. in relief on truncation, date below, die flawed 1 in date to neck, hint of doubling to legend, last A of legend die flawed, *rev* crowned quartered shield of arms within laurel wreath, die number 100 below, 1 doubled, emblems below, hairline die flaws in reverse legend, 7.99g (Marsh 56; MCE 533; S 3853B). *Surfaces of matt appearance, light surface marks, good extremely fine.* £300-400

Price Realised : £432

ex Randy Weir Numismatics, Unionville, Ontario, Canada, 29 October 1992
Calendar year mintage 13,486,708
See footnote for lot 1164, page 234, for a brief synopsis of the 1872 die numbers.

611 **Victoria,** Sovereign, 1872, die number 101, third young head left, W.W. in relief on truncation, date below, date and legend doubled both sides, last A die flawed, *rev* crowned quartered shield of arms within laurel wreath, die number 101 below, first 1 over a lower 1, second 1 touches ribbon, emblems below, some letters in reverse legend with raised die flaws, 7.99g (Marsh 56; MCE 533; S 3853B). *Red spots on reverse, obverse rim nick, light surface marks, extremely fine.* £350-400

Price Realised : £360

ex Douro Cargo, Spink Auction 118, 20-21 November 1996, lot 1320 (part)
Calendar year mintage 13,486,708. See footnote for lot 1164, page 234, for a brief synopsis of the 1872 die numbers.

612 **Victoria,** Sovereign, 1872, die number 102, third young head left, W.W. in relief on truncation, date below, date and legend doubled both sides, *rev* crowned quartered shield of arms within laurel wreath, die number 102 below, incomplete 2, emblems below, 7.98g (Marsh 56; MCE 533; S 3853B). *Some scratches and digs on reverse by crown, otherwise unevenly toned with light surface marks, good very fine.* £300-350

Price Realised : £312

ex Spink and Son, purchased July 2004
This coin was purchased via Spink from one of the groups of coins from the wreck of the RMS *Douro* that were not sold by auction, bought in the last 10 years.
Calendar year mintage 13,486,708
See footnote for lot 1164, page 234, for a brief synopsis of the 1872 die numbers.

1198 **Victoria,** Sovereign, 1872, die number 104, third young head left, w.w. in relief on truncation, date below, trace of raised die flaw in Queen's name, *rev* crowned quartered shield of arms within laurel wreath, die number 104 below, some filling on 0 and 4, emblems below, hairline die flaws in reverse legend, 7.96g (Marsh 56; MCE 533; S 3853B). *Black spot each side, red tone, surface marks and nicks, otherwise good fine, reverse better.* £300-400

Price Realised : £240

ex Paul Davies Ltd, Ilkley, January 2008
Calendar year mintage 13,486,708
See footnote for lot 1164, page 234, for a brief synopsis of the 1872 die numbers.

613 **Victoria,** Sovereign, 1872, die number 105, third young head left, w.w. in relief on truncation, date below, *rev* crowned quartered shield of arms within laurel wreath, die number 105 below, 1 weak and flawed, emblems below, 7.96g (Marsh 56; MCE 533; S 3853B). *Scratch on neck, reverse rim nick, scuffed, once cleaned, almost very fine / good very fine.* £300-350

Price Realised : £264

ex Spink and Son, purchased March 2005
Calendar year mintage 13,486,708
See footnote for lot 1164, page 234, for a brief synopsis of the 1872 die numbers.

288 **Victoria,** Sovereign, 1872, die number 105, third young head left, w.w. in relief on truncation, date below, last A of legend die flawed to rim, *rev* die axis slightly off-centre, crowned quartered shield of arms within laurel wreath, die number 105 below, emblems below, 7.96g (Marsh 56; MCE 533; S 3853B). *Scratch behind head, some surface marks and nicks, toned, good fine / nearly very fine.* £300-350

Price Realised : £264

ex Spink and Son Ltd, November 2003
Calendar year mintage 13,486,708
See footnote for lot 1164, page 234, for a brief synopsis of the 1872 die numbers.

1199 **Victoria,** Sovereign, 1872, die number 106, third young head left, w.w. in relief on truncation, date below, very light hint of doubling to date and legend both sides, *rev* crowned quartered shield of arms within laurel wreath, die number 106 below, 1 touches left ribbon and the number out of alignment in an arc, emblems below, 7.99g (Marsh 56; MCE 533; S 3853B). *Red spots each side, otherwise brilliant, good extremely fine.* £300-400

Price Realised : £336

ex Douro Cargo, Spink Auction 118, 20-21 November 1996, lot 1393 (part)
Calendar year mintage 13,486,708
See footnote for lot 1164, page 234, for a brief synopsis of the 1872 die numbers.

1200 **Victoria,** Sovereign, 1872, die number 108, third young head left, w.w. in relief on truncation, date below, very light hint of doubling to legend both sides, *rev* die axis off-centre, crowned quartered shield of arms within laurel wreath, die number 108 below, number out of alignment in an ascending arc, emblems below, hairline flaw in some letters of legend, 7.99g (Marsh 56; MCE 533; S 3853B). *Some streaks of tone, extremely fine.* £300-400

Price Realised : £384

ex Randy Weir Numismatics, Unionville, Ontario, Canada, 29 October 1992
Calendar year mintage 13,486,708
See footnote for lot 1164, page 234, for a brief synopsis of the 1872 die numbers.

289 **Victoria,** Sovereign, 1872, die number 109, third young head left, with double fillet, w.w. in relief on truncation, date below, *rev* crowned quartered shield of arms within laurel wreath, die number 109 below, 1 nearly touches left ribbon, emblems below, hint of doubling in legend, 7.98g (Marsh 56; MCE 533; S 3853B). *Toned, a true fleur de coin Sovereign, superb.* £600-800

Price Realised : £2,880

ex Douro Cargo, Spink Auction 118, 20-21 November 1996, lot 575 (part)
Calendar year mintage 13,486,708
See footnote for lot 1164, page 234, for a brief synopsis of the 1872 die numbers.
If you ever want to see a true uncirculated Victoria Sovereign this is it, anything less is not uncirculated and this is the standard that the rest of the Bentley Collection is compared to.

290 **Victoria,** Sovereign, 1872, die number 110, third young head left, w.w. in relief on truncation, date below, lightly hairlined as well as some letters of obverse legend, *rev* crowned quartered shield of arms within laurel wreath, die number 110 below, number arranged out of line in an ascending arc, emblems below, 7.96g (Marsh 56; MCE 533; S 3853B). *Scratch under chin and hairline on cheek, some spotting on reverse, toned, good very fine, reverse better.* £300-350

Price Realised : £264

ex Douro Cargo, Spink Auction 118, 20-21 November 1996, lot 1320 (part)
Calendar year mintage 13,486,708
See footnote for lot 1164, page 234, for a brief synopsis of the 1872 die numbers.

291 **Victoria,** Sovereign, 1872, die number 111, third young head left, w.w. in relief on truncation, date below, doubled 7, *rev* crowned quartered shield of arms within laurel wreath, die number 111 below, first two 1's joined by bottom serifs, emblems below, some letters doubled, 7.99g (Marsh 56; MCE 533; S 3853B). *Light nicks and surface marks, red spots both sides, more on reverse, brilliant fields, good extremely fine.* £350-450

Price Realised : £384

ex Douro Cargo, Spink Auction 118, 20-21 November 1996, lot 575 (part)
Calendar year mintage 13,486,708. See footnote for lot 1164, page 234, for a brief synopsis of the 1872 die numbers.

614 **Victoria,** Sovereign, 1872, die number 112, third young head left, w.w. in relief on truncation, date below lightly die flawed, obverse legend doubled, hint of doubling on reverse, *rev* crowned quartered shield of arms within laurel wreath, die number 112 below, incomplete 2, joined to middle 1, emblems below, 7.98g (Marsh 56; MCE 533; S 3853B). *Surface marks, patchy uneven tone, extremely fine.* £350-400

Price Realised : £360

ex Douro Cargo, Spink Auction 118, 20-21 November 1996, lot 575 (part)
Calendar year mintage 13,486,708. See footnote for lot 1164, page 234, for a brief synopsis of the 1872 die numbers.

1201 **Victoria,** Sovereign, 1873, die number 1, third young head left, w.w. in relief on truncation, date below, open lower part to 3 in date, date and legend doubled in places both sides, 1 flawed from rim to neck, V flawed to rim, *rev* crowned quartered shield of arms within laurel wreath, die number 1 below, emblems below, U of legend flawed to rim, 7.98g (Marsh 57; MCE 535; S 3853B). *Some light surface marks, extremely fine, reverse better.* £300-400

Price Realised : £336

ex Douro Cargo, Spink Auction 118, 20-21 November 1996, lot 1395 (part)
Calendar year mintage 2,368,215
This coin is die number 1 of a total of 27 different numbered dies in the Bentley Collection for 1873, running from 1 to 107. Marsh claims that 75 others exist! With so many absent from this collection, it makes a total of 102 reverse dies to strike just over 2 million Sovereigns. This suggests very uneconomic longevity indeed for the dies as this output figure also includes the St George and dragon reverse coins of 1873. This cataloguer feels that the die numbers recorded for 1873 in Marsh may be unreliable and could be some sort of human or typographical error, perhaps transposing 1872 known die numbers for 1873 which is more likely. The fact there are some rather large gaps in the die numbering of the Bentley specimens leaves the verdict open. What we can say is in twenty years of seriously looking, most of the numbers claimed to exist have just not been on the marketplace.

292 **Victoria,** Sovereign, 1873, die number 2, third young head left, w.w. in relief on truncation, date below, date and legend doubled in places both sides, 1 flawed from rim to neck, *rev* crowned quartered shield of arms within laurel wreath, die number 2 below, emblems below, 7.99g (Marsh 57; MCE 535; S 3853B). *Some light surface marks, good extremely fine.* £350-450

Price Realised : £552

Calendar year mintage 2,368,215. See footnote for lot 1201 (above) for a brief synopsis of the 1873 die numbers.

1202 **Victoria,** Sovereign, 1873, die number 3, third young head left, W.W. in relief on truncation, date below, date and legend doubled in places both sides, flaw to left of date to neck, V flawed and further flaws between D and E and between I and A, *rev* crowned quartered shield of arms within laurel wreath, die number 3 lightly flawed below, emblems below, 7.98g (Marsh 57; MCE 535; S 3853B). *Toned, good very fine, reverse better.* £300-400

Price Realised : £264

ex Douro Cargo, Spink Auction 118, 20-21 November 1996, lot 576 (part)
ex An Important Collection of Gold Sovereigns 1816-2000, offered as one lot, Sothebys, November 2000, lot 525 (part)
Calendar year mintage 2,368,215
See footnote for lot 1201, page 263, for a brief synopsis of the 1873 die numbers.

615 **Victoria,** Sovereign, 1873, die number 4, third young head left, W.W. in relief on truncation, date below, date and legend doubled in places both sides, last letter I flawed from rim, *rev* crowned quartered shield of arms within laurel wreath, die number 4 below, lightly die flawed, emblems below, 7.99g (Marsh 57; MCE 535; S 3853B). *Some light surface marks, toned almost extremely fine / extremely fine.* £350-400

Price Realised : £432

ex Douro Cargo, Spink Auction 118, 20-21 November 1996, lot 576 (part)
ex An Important Collection of Gold Sovereigns 1816-2000, offered as one lot, Sothebys, November 2000, lot 525 (part)
Calendar year mintage 2,368,215
See footnote for lot 1201, page 263, for a brief synopsis of the 1873 die numbers.

1203 **Victoria,** Sovereign, 1873, die number 5, third young head left, W.W. in relief on truncation, date below, date and legend slightly doubled, V flawed and further flaw to rim between I and A, *rev* crowned quartered shield of arms within laurel wreath, die number 5 lightly flawed below, emblems below, some letters in legend die flawed, 8.00g (Marsh 57; MCE 535; S 3853B). *Light hairlines and surface marks, otherwise good extremely fine.* £300-400

Price Realised : £456

Calendar year mintage 2,368,215
See footnote for lot 1201, page 263, for a brief synopsis of the 1873 die numbers.

293 **Victoria,** Sovereign, 1873, die number 6, third young head left, W.W. in relief on truncation, date below, 18 and some obverse letters doubled, *rev* crowned quartered shield of arms within laurel wreath, die number 6 below, emblems below, 7.96g (Marsh 57; MCE 535; S 3853B). *Scratch on cheek, other light surface marks, some black spots, toned, good very fine / almost extremely fine.* £300-350

Price Realised : £288

ex Spink Numismatic Circular, October 1997, item 5034
ex An Important Collection of Gold Sovereigns 1816-2000, offered as one lot, Sothebys, 16-17 November 2000, lot 525 (part)
Calendar year mintage 2,368,215. See footnote for lot 1201, page 263, for a brief synopsis of the 1873 die numbers.

294 **Victoria,** Sovereign, 1873, die number 7, third young head left, W.W. in relief on truncation, date below, lightly doubled along with some of the legend both sides, *rev* crowned quartered shield of arms within laurel wreath, die number 7 below, emblems below, 7.99g (Marsh 57; MCE 535; S 3853B). *Blemish above crown, light surface marks, toned, extremely fine / good extremely fine.* £350-450

Price Realised : £432

ex Douro Cargo, Spink Auction 118, 20-21 November 1996, lot 902
Calendar year mintage 2,368,215
See footnote for lot 1201, page 263, for a brief synopsis of the 1873 die numbers.

616 **Victoria,** Sovereign, 1873, die number 8, third young head left, W.W. in relief on truncation, date below, date and legend doubled in places both sides, last letter A flawed to rim, *rev* crowned quartered shield of arms within laurel wreath, die number 8 below, emblems below, 7.98g (Marsh 57; MCE 535; S 3853B). *Scratch by nose and one on throat, some other scuffs and surface marks, extremely fine / good extremely fine.* £350-400

Price Realised : £360

ex Randy Weir Numismatics, Unionville, Ontario, Canada, 2 June 1995
Calendar year mintage 2,368,215
See footnote for lot 1201, page 263, for a brief synopsis of the 1873 die numbers.

1204 **Victoria,** Sovereign, 1873, die number 9, third young head left, W.W. in relief on truncation, date below, legend slightly doubled both sides, V flawed and further flaw to rim between I and A, *rev* crowned quartered shield of arms within laurel wreath, die number 9 doubled below, emblems below, some letters in legend die flawed, 7.99g (Marsh 57; MCE 535; S 3853B). *Two hairline scratches on obverse, some scuffs, rim nick each side, otherwise toned, extremely fine.* £300-400

Price Realised : £240

ex Randy Weir Numismatics, Unionville, Ontario, Canada, October 1998
Calendar year mintage 2,368,215
See footnote for lot 1201, page 263, for a brief synopsis of the 1873 die numbers.

295 **Victoria,** Sovereign, 1873, die number 10, third young head left, W.W. in relief on truncation, date below, hint of doubling to date and legend both sides, last I with vertical die flaw to rim, *rev* crowned quartered shield of arms within laurel wreath, die number 10 below, emblems below, 7.99g (Marsh 57; MCE 535; S 3853B). *Hairline scratch on head, other light nicks and surface marks, otherwise good extremely fine.* £400-500

Price Realised : £504

ex Douro Cargo, Spink Auction 118, 20-21 November 1996, lot 1395 (part)
Calendar year mintage 2,368,215
See footnote for lot 1201, page 263, for a brief synopsis of the 1873 die numbers.

617 **Victoria,** Sovereign, 1873, die number 11, third young head left, W.W. in relief on truncation, date below, die flaws in queen's name and some light doubling on both sides, *rev* crowned quartered shield of arms within laurel wreath, die number 11 below, lightly die flawed, emblems below, 7.98g (Marsh 57; MCE 535; S 3853B). *Scratch at back of neck into field, some other surface marks, toned almost extremely fine / extremely fine.* £300-400

Price Realised : £384

ex Randy Weir Numismatics, Unionville, Ontario, Canada, c.1997
Calendar year mintage 2,368,215
See footnote for lot 1201, page 263, for a brief synopsis of the 1873 die numbers.

1205 **Victoria,** Sovereign, 1873, die number 12, third young head left, W.W. in relief on truncation, date below, date and legend slightly doubled both sides, V flawed, *rev* crowned quartered shield of arms within laurel wreath, die number 12 below, the 2 disjointed, emblems below, some letters in legend die flawed, 7.98g (Marsh 57; MCE 535; S 3853B). *Scratch above 3 of date, some light surface marks and rim nick on reverse, otherwise about extremely fine, reverse better.* £300-400

Price Realised : £240

Calendar year mintage 2,368,215
See footnote for lot 1201, page 263, for a brief synopsis of the 1873 die numbers.

296 **Victoria,** Sovereign, 1873, die number 13, third young head left, W.W. in relief on truncation, date below, light raised die flaws in date and legend both sides, first T flawed to rim, some doubling in legend both sides, *rev* crowned quartered shield of arms within laurel wreath, die number 13 below, emblems below, 7.98g (Marsh 57; MCE 535; S 3853B). *Previously graded by NGC as MS61, scratch behind hair bun, scuff behind neck, toned, extremely fine, reverse better.* £300-350

Price Realised : £384

Calendar year mintage 2,368,215
See footnote for lot 1201, page 263, for a brief synopsis of the 1873 die numbers.

618 **Victoria,** Sovereign, 1873, die number 14, third young head left, W.W. in relief on truncation, date below, trace of light doubling in date and legend on both sides, *rev* crowned quartered shield of arms within laurel wreath, die number 14 below, 1 over a lower 1, emblems below, die flaw by first I to rim, 7.99g (Marsh 57; MCE 535; S 3853B). *Rim nick on obverse, some other surface marks, one red spot on reverse, toned good extremely fine.* £400-500

Price Realised : £624

ex Douro Cargo, Spink Auction 118, 20-21 November 1996, lot 577 (part)
ex An Important Collection of Gold Sovereigns 1816-2000, offered as one lot, Sothebys, November 2000, lot 525 (part)
Calendar year mintage 2,368,215
See footnote for lot 1201, page 263, for a brief synopsis of the 1873 die numbers.

297 **Victoria,** Sovereign, 1873, die number 15, third young head left, W.W. in relief on truncation, date below, 1 doubled, light raised die flaws in date and legend both sides, D of DEI flawed to rim, some doubling in legend both sides, *rev* crowned quartered shield of arms within laurel wreath, die number 15 below, lightly die flawed, emblems below, 7.96g (Marsh 57; MCE 535; S 3853B). *Light nicks and other surface marks, almost extremely fine.* £300-350

Price Realised : £288

Calendar year mintage 2,368,215
See footnote for lot 1201, page 263, for a brief synopsis of the 1873 die numbers.

619 **Victoria,** Sovereign, 1873, die number 16, third young head left, W.W. in relief on truncation, date below, some light doubling on both sides, *rev* crowned quartered shield of arms within laurel wreath, die number 16 below, emblems below, some light raised die flaws in reverse legend, 7.95g (Marsh 57; MCE 535; S 3853B). *Some residual dirt on reverse rim and lettering, other surface marks, toned bold fine.* £300-350

Price Realised : £264

ex A H Baldwin & Sons Ltd, May 2006
Calendar year mintage 2,368,215
See footnote for lot 1201, page 263, for a brief synopsis of the 1873 die numbers.

1206 **Victoria,** Sovereign, 1873, die number 17, third young head left, W.W. in relief on truncation, date below, date and legend slightly doubled both sides, *rev* crowned quartered shield of arms within laurel wreath, die number 17 below, emblems below, some letters in legend die flawed, 7.98g (Marsh 57; MCE 535; S 3853B). *Scratch on cheek and by eye, some light surface marks, otherwise toned, extremely fine.* £300-400

Price Realised : £336

ex Randy Weir Numismatics, Unionville, Ontario, Canada, 12 November 1990
Calendar year mintage 2,368,215
See footnote for lot 1201, page 263, for a brief synopsis of the 1873 die numbers.

298 **Victoria,** Sovereign, 1873, die number 18, third young head left, W.W. in relief on truncation, date below, lightly die flawed, hint of doubling to date and legend both sides, *rev* crowned quartered shield of arms within laurel wreath, die number 18 below, lightly flawed as well as first I of legend, emblems below, 7.98g (Marsh 57; MCE 535; S 3853B). *Light nicks and surface marks, extremely fine.* £350-450

Price Realised : £360

Calendar year mintage 2,368,215
See footnote for lot 1201, page 263, for a brief synopsis of the 1873 die numbers.

620 **Victoria,** Sovereign, 1873, die number 20, third young head left, w.w. in relief on truncation, date below with hairline die flaw, some light doubling in legend, die flaw at O, *rev* crowned quartered shield of arms within laurel wreath, die number 20 below, emblems below, some light raised die flaws in reverse legend, 7.99g (Marsh 57; MCE 535; S 3853B). *Some light nicks and surface marks, extremely fine.* £300-400

Price Realised : £384

ex Randy Weir Numismatics, Unionville, Ontario, Canada, 6 February 1990
Calendar year mintage 2,368,215
See footnote for lot 1201, page 263, for a brief synopsis of the 1873 die numbers.

1207 **Victoria,** Sovereign, 1873, die number 21, third young head left, w.w. in relief on truncation, date below, last A die flawed to rim with other letters connected in last word, *rev* crowned quartered shield of arms within laurel wreath, die number 21 below, very thick tall 1, emblems below, some letters in legend die flawed, 7.98g (Marsh 57; MCE 535; S 3853B). *Hairlined, toned, very fine / extremely fine.* £250-300

Price Realised : £288

Calendar year mintage 2,368,215
See footnote for lot 1201, page 263, for a brief synopsis of the 1873 die numbers.

299 **Victoria,** Sovereign, 1873, die number 22 , third young head left, w.w. in relief on truncation, date below, raised die flaw to right of 3 from rim to neck, *rev* crowned quartered shield of arms within laurel wreath, die number 22 below, very thick 2's, emblems below, 7.97g (Marsh 57; MCE 535; S 3853B). *Surface marks and nicks, nearly very fine / good very fine.* £300-350

Price Realised : £288

ex Paul Davies Ltd. This coin was purchased from one of the groups of coins from the wreck of the RMS *Douro* that were not sold by auction and within the last 10 years.
Calendar year mintage 2,368,215
See footnote for lot 1201, page 263, for a brief synopsis of the 1873 die numbers.

1208 **Victoria,** Sovereign, 1873, die number 23, third young head left, w.w. in relief on truncation, date below, date and legend slightly doubled both sides, *rev* crowned quartered shield of arms within laurel wreath, die number 23 below, thick figures, emblems below, 7.98g (Marsh 57; MCE 535; S 3853B). *Dig on crown band, reverse rim nick, dig on cheek and other light surface marks, toned, good very fine / extremely fine.* £250-300

Price Realised : £288

Calendar year mintage 2,368,215
See footnote for lot 1201, page 263, for a brief synopsis of the 1873 die numbers.

621 **Victoria,** Sovereign, 1873, die number 24, third young head left, w.w. in relief on truncation, date below, some light doubling in date and legend, *rev* crowned quartered shield of arms within laurel wreath, die number 24 below, emblems below, some light raised die flaws in reverse legend, 7.95g (Marsh 57; MCE 535; S 3853B). *Some light scuffs and surface marks, toned very fine / good very fine.* £300-350

Price Realised : £288

ex Randy Weir Numismatics, Unionville, Ontario, Canada, 6 February 1990
Calendar year mintage 2,368,215
See footnote for lot 1201, page 263, for a brief synopsis of the 1873 die numbers.
This coin was purchased via Spink from one of the groups of coins from the wreck of the RMS *Douro* that were not sold by auction, bought in the last 10 years.

300 **Victoria,** Sovereign, 1873, die number 31, third young head left, w.w. in relief on truncation, date below, *rev* crowned quartered shield of arms within laurel wreath, die number 31 below, emblems below, 7.98g (Marsh 57; MCE 535; S 3853B). *Brilliant with light surface marks, extremely fine / good extremely fine.* £350-450

Price Realised : £480

Calendar year mintage 2,368,215
See footnote for lot 1201, page 263, for a brief synopsis of the 1873 die numbers.

1209 **Victoria,** Sovereign, 1873, die number 36, third young head left, w.w. in relief on truncation, date below, legend slightly doubled, *rev* crowned quartered shield of arms within laurel wreath, die number 36 below, emblems below, 7.98g (Marsh 57; MCE 535; S 3853B). *Some light digs and surface marks, toned, very fine / good very fine.* £250-300

Price Realised : £264

Calendar year mintage 2,368,215
See footnote for lot 1201, page 263, for a brief synopsis of the 1873 die numbers.

622 **Victoria,** Sovereign, 1873, die number 103, third young head left, w.w. in relief on truncation, hair bun die flawed to rim, date below, 1 of date die flawed to rim, some light doubling in date and legend both sides, last AT with die flaw to rim, hairline flaw in queen's name, *rev* crowned quartered shield of arms within laurel wreath, die number 103 below, die flawed number with the 0 over a lower 0, emblems below, some light raised die flaws in reverse legend, 7.99g (Marsh 57; MCE 535; S 3853B). *Some digs on neck and one by chin, otherwise extremely fine / good extremely fine.* £350-450

Price Realised : £456

ex Douro Cargo, Spink Auction 118, 20-21 November 1996, lot 1395 (part)
Calendar year mintage 2,368,215
See footnote for lot 1201, page 263, for a brief synopsis of the 1873 die numbers.

A Truly Fleur de Coin Example of a Victoria Die Number Sovereign

623 **Victoria,** Sovereign, 1873, die number 107, third young head left, w.w. in relief on truncation, die flaw from rear of neck onto field, date below lightly die flawed, some hairline flaws in legend, *rev* crowned quartered shield of arms within laurel wreath, die number 107 below, 1 of die number inverted and struck over a regular 1, emblems below, 7.99g (Marsh 57; MCE 535; S 3853B). *Prooflike FDC, seemingly an early strike.* £500-700

Price Realised : £3,120

ex Jacob Y Terner collection, Goldberg, Hollywood, USA, Sale 20, 26-27 May 2003
Calendar year mintage 2,368,215
See footnote for lot 1201, page 263, for a brief synopsis of the 1873 die numbers.
This coin is another example of as good a preservation of a Victorian Sovereign as one could wish for.

The Extremely Rare 1874 London Shield Reverse Sovereign Die Number 28

624 **Victoria,** Sovereign, 1874, die number 28, third young head left, w.w. in relief on truncation, date below, *rev* crowned quartered shield of arms within laurel wreath, die number 28 below, incomplete 2, emblems below, 7.94g (Marsh 58; MCE 537; S 3853B). *Some residual dirt on rim and lettering, some light scuffs and surface marks, otherwise almost very fine / very fine and extremely rare.* £2500-3000

Price Realised : £6,480

ex Spink and Son, January 2000
Calendar year mintage 520,713
This coin is die number 28 of a total of 3 different numbered dies in the Bentley Collection for 1874, running from 28 to 33. Marsh claims that 4 others exist, making a total of 7 possible dies for this rare shield reverse. There were also 1874 dated St George and Dragon reverse coins included in the output figure of just over a ½ million Sovereigns. This suggests very good die longevity indeed but most were likely to be the St George reverse in reality as the shield reverse of this date is very elusive. Neither the Bentley collector nor this cataloguer have ever seen any of the other four die numbers claimed to exist by Marsh.

The Extremely Rare 1874 London Shield Reverse Sovereign Die Number 32 of Queen Victoria

301 **Victoria,** Sovereign, 1874, die number 32, third young head left, w.w. in relief on truncation, raised die flaw from rear of neck to last word of legend, date below, date and legend with light raised die flaws, *rev* crowned quartered shield of arms within laurel wreath, die number 32 below, emblems below, 7.98g (Marsh 58; MCE 537; S 3853B). *Hairline scratch on neck, other light marks, toned, extremely fine and one of the finest examples available of this extremely rare "swan song" issue of the London shield die number series.* £5000-6000

Price Realised : £9,600

ex Spink Numismatic Circular, April 2000, item 3136
Calendar year mintage 520,713
This coin is die number 32 of a total of 3 different numbered dies in the Bentley Collection for 1874, running intermittently from 28 to 33. One of these rare pieces will be offered in each part of the Bentley sales. Marsh claims that four others exist, making a total of seven possible dies for this rare shield reverse. There were also 1874 dated St George and dragon reverse coins included in the output figure of just over half a million Sovereigns. This suggests very good die longevity indeed but most were likely the St George reverse in reality as the shield reverse of this date is very elusive. Neither the Bentley Collector, or this cataloguer have ever seen any of the die other four die numbers claimed to exist by Marsh.

The Very Rare Victoria 1874 Shield Reverse Sovereign, Die Number 33

1210 **Victoria,** Sovereign, 1874, die number 33, third young head left, w.w. in relief on truncation, date below, date and legend slightly doubled, *rev* crowned quartered shield of arms within laurel wreath, die number 33 below, 3's blundered and filled, emblems below, 7.98g (Marsh 58; MCE 537; S 3853B). *Dig near eye and scratch under date, numerous hairline scratches all over the obverse and one small scratch in reverse legend, otherwise very fine / good very fine and the rarest die number for 1874, still less than five known to the cataloguer, extremely rare.* £4000-5000

Price Realised : £5,520

ex Randy Weir, Unionville, Ontario, Canada, purchased 21 June 1995
Calendar year mintage 520,713
This coin is die number 33 of a total of 3 different numbered dies in the Bentley Collection for 1874, running intermittently from 28 to 33. Marsh claims that 4 others exist, making a total of 7 possible dies for this rare shield reverse. There were also 1874 dated St George and Dragon reverse coins included in the output figure of just over ½ million Sovereigns. This suggests very good die longevity indeed but most were likely the St George reverse in reality as the shield reverse of this date is very elusive. Neither the Bentley collector, or this cataloguer have ever seen any of the other 4 die numbers claimed to exist by Marsh.

The Unique 1870 Pattern Sovereign Muled with George III Style Reverse

1211 Victoria, Pattern Sovereign, 1870, engraved after William Wyon, second larger young head left, with double fillet, WW in relief without stops on truncation, date below, toothed border both sides, VICTORIA DEI GRATIA, some light doubling of legend, *rev* inverted die axis, mule with George III reverse, engraved after Benedetto Pistrucci, St George slaying dragon right with broken lance, groundline with BP incuse to left, all within horizontally ruled garter with buckle, W W P incuse on sides of buckle, garter motto HONI . SOIT . QUI . MAL . Y . PENSE ., some serifs weak in motto, edge milled with angled rims, 7.95g, 22mm (WR 313 R7, *this coin*; Douglas-Morris 208). *Has been lightly polished in fields, some heavy hairlines, tiny rim bruise at 7 o'clock on the obverse and a little dirt deposit further around, otherwise good extremely fine, the only Sovereign known muled between different reigns, unique.* £20,000-25,000

Price Realised : £30,000

ex Captain Vivian Hewitt collection, sold privately to Spink and Son Ltd, c.1969
ex Captain K J Douglas Morris collection, Sothebys, 26 November 1974, lot 208
ex Bank Leu, Zürich, 26 October 2004, lot 444, bought via Spink and Son Ltd
The date of this pattern piece coincides with the time of the introduction of the third type of young head obverse as defined in the Bentley Collection, though it happens to have the earlier second type bust as seen on the 1870 currency sovereign with die number 1 (see lot 1128, page 206).

Extremely Rare 1879 Pattern London Shield Reverse Sovereign of Queen Victoria

625 **Victoria,** Pattern Sovereign, 1879, engraved after William Wyon, third young head left, with double fillet, W.W. in relief on truncation, date below, toothed border and raised rim both sides, VICTORIA DEI GRATIA, *rev* struck with inverted die axis, engraved after Jean Baptiste Merlen, crowned shield of arms within laurel wreath tied with bow below shield, seven harp strings in Irish arms, left string emanates from scroll, emblems below, small rosette either side, BRITANNIARUM REGINA FID: DEF:, second word lightly doubled, edge milled, 8.00g, 22mm (WR 322 R7; DM -; Murdoch 511). *Well struck, four tiny black spots only, otherwise brilliant mint state and probably struck for display at the Melbourne International Exhibition in 1879, Australia, of the highest rarity.* £12,000-15,000

Price Realised : £48,000

ex Reginald Huth collection, Sothebys, 4 April 1927, lot 266A (part)
ex Sothebys, 9 October 1995, lot 827
Sovereigns of proof quality from highly polished dies would be struck as a matter of record for the mint and probably for presentation to highly important persons. It seems that in 1880 the Deputy Master of the Melbourne mint, V Delves Broughton, approached London requesting examples of coins and medals produced, for display at the International Exhibition in Melbourne. Mr C W Fremantle, the Comptroller at the Royal Mint, agreed to prepare two proof examples of each of the current coins of 1880 and earlier dates, which were struck in such quantity that when prepared for shipment weighed 2cwt and 19lb. The Museum of Victoria in Australia still retains one of the 1880 "Imperial Proof Sets" the other was seemingly traded after the exhibition for a collection of ancient coins. See lot 1212, page 274, for an 1880 proof shield sovereign, which may well emanate from the second set. The 1879 piece offered here may well be from the group of earlier date coins exhibited at Melbourne in 1880. It is so rare that not even an illustration was included in the Wilson Rasmussen publication.
For further reading on the subject of special strikings made by the mint for exhibition in Australia, see the Journal of the Numismatic Association of Australia, volume 2, article by John Sharples "The Numismatic Collection of the Museum of Victoria", available online at the Association website.

The Extremely Rare Proof 1880 Sovereign with Shield Reverse, Plain Edge

1212 **Victoria,** Pattern Sovereign, 1880, engraved after William Wyon, third young head left, with double fillet, W.W. in relief on truncation, date below, toothed border and raised rim both sides, VICTORIA DEI GRATIA, one light raised die flaw down cheek from hair, *rev* struck with en médaille die axis, engraved after Jean Baptiste Merlen, crowned shield of arms within laurel wreath tied with bow below shield, seven harp strings in Irish arms, left string emanates from scroll, emblems below, small rosette either side, BRITANNIARUM REGINA FID: DEF:, a couple of letters lightly doubled, edge plain, 7.95g, 21.8mm (WR 323 R5; Murdoch 513; Nobleman 273; Douglas-Morris 213). *Tiny red spot each side, cloudy tone, otherwise brilliant as struck and probably struck for display at the Melbourne International Exhibition in 1881 (Australia), extremely rare.* £15,000-20,000

Price Realised : £32,400

ex Virgil M Brand collection, d.1926, dispersed post mortem from c.1932
ex Spink Numismatic Circular, December 1992, item 7601
ex An Important Collection of Gold Sovereigns 1816-2000, offered as one lot, Sothebys, November 2000, lot 525 (part)
Sovereigns of proof quality from highly polished dies would be struck as a matter of record for the Mint and probably for presentation to highly important persons. It seems that in 1880 the Deputy Master of the Melbourne Mint, V Delves Broughton, approached London requesting examples of coins and medals produced for display at the International Exhibition in Melbourne. Mr C W Fremantle, the Comptroller at the Royal Mint, agreed to prepare two proof examples of each of the current coins of 1880 and earlier dates which were struck in such quantity that when prepared for shipment weighed 2cwt. and 19lb. The Museum of Victoria in Australia still retains one of the 1880 "Imperial Proof Sets", the other was seemingly traded after the exhibition for a collection of ancient coins and not long after found its way to the collection of Virgil Brand.
For further reading on the subject of special strikings made by the Mint for exhibition in Australia see the Journal of the Numismatic Association of Australia, vol 2, article by John Sharples, *The Numismatic Collection of the Museum of Victoria,* available online at the Association website.

Extremely Rare 1887 Pattern London Shield Reverse Sovereign of Queen Victoria

302 **Victoria,** Pattern Sovereign, 1887, engraved after William Wyon, third young head left, with double fillet, W.W. in relief on truncation, date below, toothed border and raised rim both sides, VICTORIA DEI GRATIA, *rev* struck with inverted die axis, engraved after Jean Baptiste Merlen, crowned shield of arms within laurel wreath tied with bow below shield, seven harp strings in Irish arms, left string emanates from scroll, emblems below, small rosette either side, BRITANNIARUM REGINA FID: DEF:, legend lightly doubled, edge milled, 8.05g, 22mm (WR 331 R5, *this coin illustrated*; DM 217). *Brilliant mint state and of the highest rarity.* £12,000-15,000

Price Realised : £33,600

ex Property of a Nobleman, Spink Auction 120, 9 July 1997, lot 634 – this coin illustrated in Wilson Rasmussen.
1887 is the final year for the young head design upon the coinage, so it seems natural that some young head Sovereigns of proof quality from highly polished dies would be struck as a matter of record for the Mint and probably for presentation to highly important persons, or as suggested in the Douglas Morris catalogue that it could be a trial for a Colonial Sovereign.

The Revival of the St George and the Dragon Reverse Sovereign

In 1871 there was a revival of the Pistrucci St George and the dragon reverse on the gold Sovereign which ran concurrently with the shield reverse Sovereign at the London Mint from 1871 till 1874 inclusive. This was in reaction to a wish expressed by the Queen herself and the Royal Mint Council was authorised to revive the St George reverse issued design on the 14 January 1871, and it was in use at London for currency until the 1885 dated coins. There are no issues of these London Sovereigns dated 1875, 1877, 1881, 1882, or 1883, though the *"Milled Coinage of England"* carries a ghost reference number "543" for the 1883, which was a repeated error it seems from "Brooke's English Coins" of an earlier era.

This reverse was issued in tandem with the Colonial Branch Mints in Australia, at Sydney from 1871 till 1887 and Melbourne, from 1872 till 1887 dated coins, as the new Mint there was not ready to operate in time in 1871 as intended. That is why the 1872 with 2 over 1 shield reverse Sovereign for Melbourne exists, but more information will be forthcoming about these Colonial pieces in that section of the Bentley Collection. The St George reverse had last been used in 1825, some 46 years earlier and contemporary thought on its revival can be found in the minutes of the proceedings of the Numismatic Society of London for meetings in 1871, where consternation is expressed about why an "old" design had been revived, and could the Mint have not done something more innovative, as surely the engravers were skilled enough to come up with something better. In fact the Reverend Asheton Pownall brought a brand new 1871 Sovereign to exhibit at the Numismatic Meeting on 16 February 1871, where such comments were garnered. This was just over a month since the revival was authorised at the Mint, and most interestingly it was noted the coin brought to the meeting appeared to have the 7 struck over a 2 suggesting the reuse of an old reverse die of 1821 which again was frowned upon. Such a variety on the 1871 Sovereign is not known today and it is hoped that as a result of this note, one will be discovered soon!

This is in stark contrast to today, for whenever we see the Royal Mint try something different in deference to what is today regarded as iconic design as St George (as has been done in some recent years, and most recently now in 2012 with a different stylistic interpretation of the reverse), we find these are often "one year wonders" before a quick return to the traditional design, which is now over 190 years old, with little variation since the 1821 version.

The Currency Sovereigns of Queen Victoria with St George and dragon reverse

The young head obverse most significantly no longer carries the date of the coin, which for the St George and dragon reverse after Pistrucci is always in the exergue on the reverse side. The obverse is therefore of a different design, though the rendering of the bust style is similar to that seen at the end of the die number series, well engraved with a complete hair "ponytail". This obverse was no doubt engraved by the Chief Engraver Leonard Charles Wyon, the son of William Wyon, working in the style of his Father and still acknowledging his design of the young head with the initials upon the neck. In fact the main difference with this bust design is upon the neck, where two distinct renderings of the WW initials occur once again. The first type to appear is the raised WW "buried" in the truncation, where the truncation appears literally too thin to support the large characters, and they only partially appear and meet the field below. In some cases as on some of the proof 1871 strikings this raised WW appears to be cut over the top of another even more partial raised WW right on the bottom edge of the truncation. Why this should be so rendered is a little mysterious, but could be as simple as correcting a first attempt at placing the initials, or more intriguingly perhaps Leonard C Wyon was acknowledging himself along with his Father, the twin WW's literally one within the other.

The second rendering of the raised WW complete on the truncation from 1880 is smaller and more neatly engraved. The legend is a longer and abbreviated one compared to the shield series and reads VICTORIA D: G: BRITANNIAR: REG: F: D: the tip of the neck usually points downwards, though there is one proof 1871 Sovereign where it distinctly points outwards (lot 1214, page 278). The finely toothed outer border is within twin linear concentric circles and an outer raised rim both sides.

The Sovereigns are struck with an inverted die axis and the reverse is as the 1821 design. The horse has a long tail with a three strand terminal, though this does vary later on. The horse tail length later in this series can be either short or long, and "spurs" of extra tail hair can appear below the top outside curve of the tail. The rendering of the dragon claws can also vary, at most it has four claws all attached on each foreleg. Sometimes one or two claws are detached and as dies start to wear they become more indistinct, being only a tiny detail on the coin. Sometimes the dragon has four claws on the left and three on the right, or three claws on each foreleg. St George himself can have a cloak with either a complete "hem-line" or sometimes it is partly broken and indistinct. The helmet streamer upon his head can also vary in its depiction. The WWP continues to appear in relief under the broken lance on the ground-line.

The most significant variation on the reverse though is the B.P. initials in the upper right of the exergue, which can be either large or small, mostly small in currency. They can be all there, or sometimes with absent stops though this is likely due to die degradation. This becomes more evident in coins where the letters themselves also become very indistinct and only partially there, until we see the "no B.P." varieties which again are likely due to blockages on the die, though there is a chance that one die may have had the initials left off at the design stage! The edges are always milled for currency as usual.

The Very Pleasing 1871 St George Proof Sovereign

1213 **Victoria,** Proof Sovereign, 1871, young head of third style left, WW buried over recut WW and more apparent in thin truncation in relief, tip of neck points downwards, finely toothed border within twin linear concentric circles and raised rim both sides, VICTORIA D: G: BRITANNIAR: REG: F: D:, *rev* struck en médaille, St George slaying dragon with sword, dragon claws thinner and some detached, three to left and three to right arm, horse with long tail ending in three strands no spurs of extra hair halfway, broken lance on ground-line to left, *WWP* in relief under lance, date in exergue, narrow date slightly doubled, tiny complete B.P. to upper right, edge plain, 8.00g, 21.8mm (WR 315 R4; Douglas-Morris 210-1). *Pleasing yellow gold tone, brilliant, well defined strike, a few light surface marks, black mark on reverse rim at top, hairline mark from neck to cheek, well frosted, practically as struck and very rare.* £6000-8000

Price Realised : £7,440

This is the slightly rarer type of 1871 Proof Sovereign encountered with the plain edge and the tiny B.P. initials in exergue. Some of the rarity ratings in the Wilson Rasmussen book seem jumbled in that this coin is rated slightly more common than it is in commerce, perhaps ratings were based on what was seen in Institutional collections only like with Peck's rating on the copper coins in the British Museum. This 1871 proof is one of six in total in the Bentley Collection of this date.

The Extremely Rare Milled Edge Proof Sovereign of 1871

1214 **Victoria,** Proof Sovereign, with milled edge, 1871, young head left of third style left, engraved after William Wyon, with double fillet in hair, WW buried over recut WW in thin truncation in relief and more apparent, tip of neck points outwards, nostril more rounded than the coin in lot 1213, finely toothed border within twin linear concentric circles and raised rim both sides, VICTORIA D: G: BRITANNIAR: REG: F: D:, letter A's and colons doubled, *rev* inverted die axis, engraved after Benedetto Pistrucci, St George slaying dragon with sword, horse with long tail ending in three strands, one extra spur of hair at top left of tail where it curves around, dragon claws all attached, four to left and three to right arm, broken lance on ground-line to left, *WWP* in relief under lance, date in exergue, wider date, no ghosting, larger B.P. to upper right, the B incomplete, edge milled, 8.00g, 22.1mm (WR 317 R5; Douglas-Morris 212; S 3856A). *Pleasing red copper tone, well defined strike, some hairlines, nick on chin, otherwise practically as struck and of extreme rarity.* £10,000-15,000

Price Realised : £12,600

ex Property of a Gentleman, Spink Auction 124, 18 November 1997, lot 2033
These extremely rare proofs were no doubt struck as a matter of record and for presentation to very important people upon the revival of the St George reverse design. The hardest coins to locate amongst these proofs are the milled edge varieties of which there are two types, the other type was previously offered in part one of the Bentley Collection and sold for £14,000 hammer. There are many subtle differences that occur with the designs of these proofs which perhaps is due to some being struck much later than others. With the obverse, the tip of the neck can point outward or downward, and the treatment of the WW on the neck can differ. On the reverse, the treatment of the horse's tail can differ, not only with its terminal strands but just around the outside curve of the tail at the top, a spur, or two spurs of extra tail hair can occur. The streamer on St George's helmet can differ in the depiction of the strands which is probably more due to die weakness, as can his cloak, where the hemline can be indistinct. The dragon's claws also can be all attached or some detached which again is due partly to progressive weakness in some dies, but there are at least two arrangements of the claws anyway. The most obvious difference is the treatment of the B.P. in exergue, which can be large or small and the date figures can be in or out of line. Some of these features are more differential in the succeeding currency pieces.

The Extremely Rare Milled Edge Proof St George Reverse Sovereign of 1871, Small B.P.

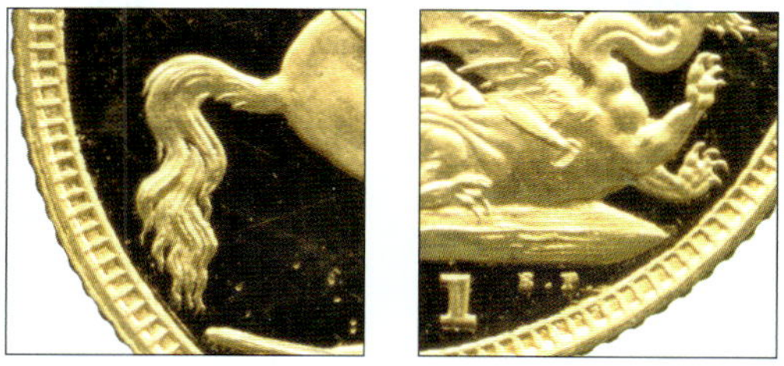

one extra hair spur on mid-left of tail **small B.P. dragon claws attached**

303 **Victoria (1837-1901),** Proof Sovereign, 1871, young head left of third style left, engraved after William Wyon, with double fillet in hair, WW buried over recut WW in thin truncation in relief and meeting field, tip of neck points outwards, finely toothed border within twin linear concentric circles and raised rim both sides, VICTORIA D: G: BRITANNIAR: REG: F: D:, obverse letter A's and colons doubled, *rev* struck en médaille, engraved after Benedetto Pistrucci, St George slaying dragon with sword, horse with long tail ending in three strands, one extra spur of hair at top left of tail where it curves around, dragon claws all attached, 4 to left and 3 to right foreleg, broken lance on ground-line to left, *WWP* in relief under lance, date in exergue, narrow date with slight die flaws, hint of doubling, tiny full B.P. to upper right, edge milled, 7.99g, 22.1mm (WR 318 R7; BM Collection 8465). *Pleasing red copper tone, a well defined strike, mint state and of extreme rarity.*

£10,000-12,000

Price Realised : £16,800

ex Dr. Jacob Y Terner collection, Goldberg, Hollywood, USA, 26-27 May 2003, lot 360 – previously graded as Proof 66 deep cameo by NGC.
See footnote for lot 1214, page 278.
The cataloguer would conclude that this milled edge piece was one of the earlier creations of the 1871 Proof.

A Very Rare Plain Edge Proof St George Reverse Sovereign of 1871, Large B.P.

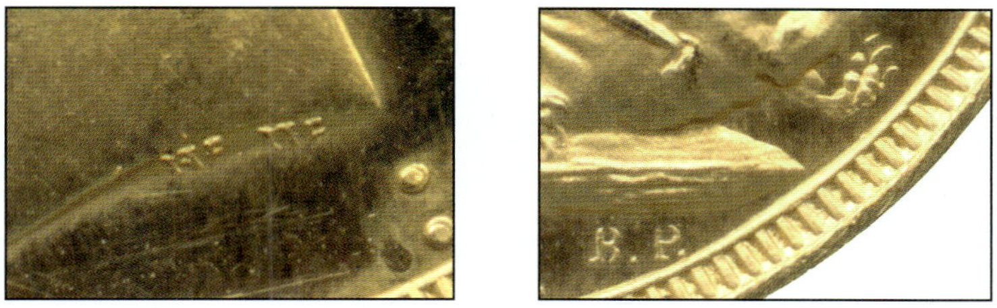

WW over WW less apparent and large incomplete B.P.

626 **Victoria,** Proof Sovereign, 1871, young head of third style left, WW buried under recut WW and less apparent in thin truncation in relief, tip of neck points outwards, finely toothed border within twin linear concentric circles and raised rim both sides, VICTORIA D: G: BRITANNIAR: REG: F: D:, obverse letter A's and colons doubled, *rev* struck en médaille, St George slaying dragon with sword, folds of cape not complete at hem, dragon with lower claws detached, four to left and three to right arm, horse with intermediate tail ending in two strands with traces of third, well defined tail with no spurs of extra hair, broken lance on ground-line to left, *WWP* in relief under lance, date in exergue, slightly doubled and widely spaced, the second 1 higher than the rest, large incomplete B.P. to upper right, edge plain, 8.00g, 21.8mm (WR 319 "R7"; BM Collection 8466; DM 212). *Tiny dig under second I of legend, otherwise lightly toned with underlying brilliance, as struck and very rare.*

£6000-8000

Price Realised : £7,440

ex Randy Weir Numismatics, Unionville, Ontario, Canada, unspecified date, c.1990
For more detailed reading about the introduction of the St George and dragon reverse and the proof strikings of it, please refer to lot 1214, page 278. It is interesting to note that this obverse die with the recut WW over the top of a lower WW always seems to have a little incuse dot on the upper part of each hair fillet near the top of the head.

A Very Rare Plain Edge Proof St George Reverse Sovereign of 1871, Large B.P.

WW over WW more apparent, large incomplete B.P.

627 **Victoria,** Proof Sovereign, 1871, young head of third style left, WW buried over recut WW and more apparent in thin truncation in relief, tip of neck points outwards, finely toothed border within twin linear concentric circles and raised rim both sides, VICTORIA D: G: BRITANNIAR: REG: F: D:, obverse letter A's and colons doubled, *rev* struck en médaille, St George slaying dragon with sword, folds of cape not complete at hem, dragon with lower claws attached, four to left and three to right arm, horse with intermediate tail ending in two strands with traces of two more, tail therefore more detached, no spurs of extra hair, broken lance on ground-line to left, *WWP* in relief under lance, date in exergue, slightly doubled, the second 1 higher than the rest, large incomplete B.P. to upper right, edge plain, 8.00g, 21.8mm (WR 319 "R7"; BM Collection 8466; DM 212). *Tiny dig in O of legend, otherwise brilliant as struck and very rare.* £6000-8000

Price Realised : £10,320

ex Winsor and Sons, Jamberoo, Australia, c.2005

For more detailed reading about the introduction of the St George and dragon reverse and the proof strikings of it, please refer to lot 1214, page 278. It is interesting to note that this obverse die with the recut WW over the tops of a lower WW always seems to have a little incuse dot on the upper part of each hair fillet near the top of the head.

This coin was used on the front cover of the Bentley Collection preview brochure (issued January 2012) and the auction catalogue for part two.

A Very Rare Plain Edge Proof St George Reverse Sovereign of 1871, Large B.P.

no hair spur on tail

large B.P.
dragon with different claws

304 **Victoria,** Proof Sovereign, 1871, young head of third style left, WW buried over recut WW and more apparent in thin truncation in relief, tip of neck points outwards, finely toothed border within twin linear concentric circles and raised rim both sides, VICTORIA D: G: BRITANNIAR: REG: F: D:, obverse letter A's and colons doubled, *rev* struck en médaille, St George slaying dragon with sword, dragon claws thinner and most detached, four to left and three to right foreleg, horse with intermediate tail ending in two strands with traces of two more between, one more defined than other, no spurs of extra hair, broken lance on ground-line to left, *WWP* in relief under lance, date in exergue, wider date out of line, no ghosting, large B.P. to upper right, with incomplete B, edge plain, 7.99g, 21.8mm (WR 319 R7; BM Collection 8466). *Pleasing yellow tone, brilliant, a well defined strike, a few light surface marks but practically mint state and very rare.* £6000-7000

Price Realised : £9,840

ex Stacks, 7-8 December 1994, lot 2460, previously graded as PF64 by NGC.
This is the more usual type of 1871 Proof Sovereign encountered with the plain edge and the large B.P. initials in exergue. Some of the rarity ratings in the Wilson Rasmussen book seem jumbled in that this coin is rated rarer than it is in commerce, perhaps ratings were based on what was seen in Institutional collections only like with Peck's rating on the copper coins in the British Museum. This 1871 proof has a very well defined strike though the dragon claws are detached and the horse tail strands differ from lot 303, page 279.

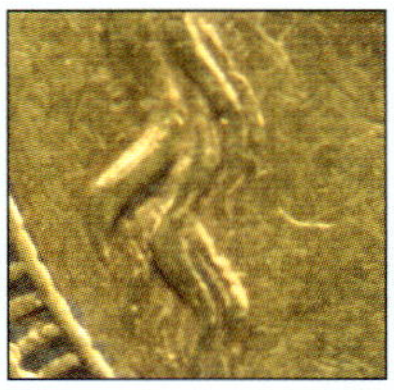

305 **Victoria,** Sovereign, 1871, young head left, WW buried in thin truncation in relief over trace of another WW, *rev* St George slaying dragon with sword, horse with short tail, two strand terminal with two other slightly shorter strands, no extra spur of hair, date in exergue, large B.P. mistruck to upper right, only a trace of left of B and trace of curve of P, 7.93g (Marsh 84A; MCE 532; S 3856). *Light scuffs and surface marks, toned, nearly very fine.* £300-350

Price Realised : £264

ex A H Baldwin & Sons Ltd sourced via Paul Davies Ltd, September 2006
Calendar year mintage 8,767,250
This Calendar output no doubt consists mainly of the shield reverse die number sovereigns.
The engraver initials on the exergue of the reverse seem to be quite haphazard in this issue whether large or small. They seem to have been quite susceptible to blockages on the die and often only a trace of the initials can be seen, more often seen with the small B.P. variety. In fact the so-called "no B.P. variety" may be the product of a blocked die rather than being unintentionally missed in punching the die.
Note also the very light weight of this piece which is on the limit of being non-legal tender.

1215 **Victoria,** Sovereign, 1871, young head left, WW buried in thin truncation in relief over trace of another WW, truncation points outwards, first D of legend die flawed to rim, other hairline flaws in some letters, further flaw on cheek, *rev* die axis inverted but slightly off-centre, St George slaying dragon with sword, horse with short tail, two strand terminal with two other slightly shorter strands, no extra spur of hair, wider date in exergue, large B.P. mistruck to upper right, only a trace of upper serifs to letters, hairline die flaw into field from claws area, 7.99g (Marsh 84A; MCE 532; S 3856). *Light hairlines and surface marks, toned, good extremely fine.* £300-350

Price Realised : £744

ex Randy Weir, Unionville, Ontario, Canada, purchased 13 August 1992
Calendar year mintage 8,767,250. See footnote for lot 305, page 281, for further reading.

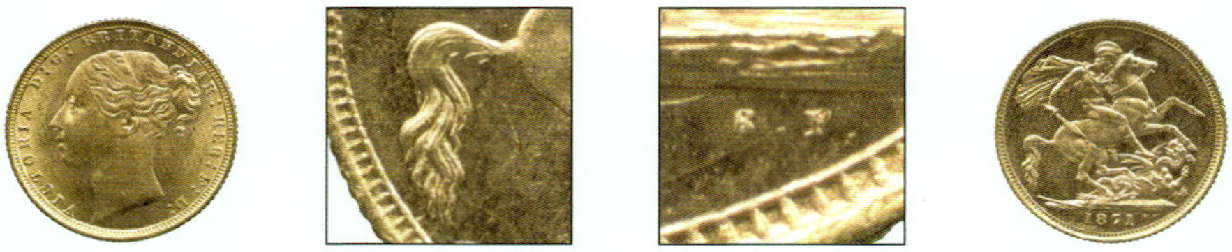

306 **Victoria,** Sovereign, 1871, young head left, ponytail slightly detached, WW buried in thin truncation in relief over trace of another WW, *rev* St George slaying dragon with sword, horse with long tail, three strand end to tail, one spur of extra hair on curve of tail, some dragon claws detached, date in exergue, narrower arrangement of figures, hairline die flaw in date, tiny B.P. to upper right, 7.99g (Marsh 84; MCE 532; S 3856A). *Several surface marks, slightly streaky tone, otherwise good extremely fine.* £350-400

Price Realised : £360

ex Randy Weir Numismatics, Unionville, Ontario, Canada, purchased 18 January 1990
Calendar year mintage 8,767,250
This Calendar output no doubt consists mainly of the shield reverse die number sovereigns, see footnote for lot 305, page 281.

1216 **Victoria,** Sovereign, 1871, young head left, trace of WW buried in thin truncation in relief, legend incomplete after F due to faulty strike, last A of legend die flawed to rim, *rev* St George slaying dragon with sword, horse with long tail, three strand terminal, no extra spur of hair, narrow date in exergue, small B.P. to upper right, 7.97g (Marsh 84; MCE 532; S 3856A). *Light hairlines and surface marks, about very fine.* £250-300

Price Realised : £216

ex St James's Auction 5, 27 September 2006, lot 674
Calendar year mintage 8,767,250

307 **Victoria,** Sovereign, 1872, young head left, ponytail slightly detached, WW buried in thin truncation in relief touches field, legend and date slightly doubled, *rev* St George slaying dragon with sword, die flaw from cloak to rim, horse with long tail, three strand end to tail, trace of one spur of extra hair on curve of tail, some dragon claws detached, date in exergue, tiny B.P. to upper right, 7.99g (Marsh 85; MCE 534; S 3856A). *Hairline marks on neck, otherwise good extremely fine.* £350-400

Price Realised : £1,860

ex Bruce Lorich, State College, Pennsylvania, USA, 8 July 2002
Calendar year mintage 13,486,708. This Calendar output no doubt consists mainly of the shield reverse die number sovereigns. This seems to be a different obverse with no trace of a WW under the other WW.

1217 **Victoria,** Sovereign, 1872, young head left, WW buried in thin truncation in relief, ponytail a little detached, last D of legend die flawed to rim, *rev* St George slaying dragon with sword, profile and date a little doubled, horse with long tail, three strand terminal, no extra spur of hair, narrow date in exergue, small B.P. to upper right, 7.98g (Marsh 85; MCE 532; S 3856A). *Light hairlines and surface marks, good extremely fine.* £300-400

Price Realised : £408

Calendar year mintage 13,486,708. This Calendar output no doubt consists mainly of the shield reverse die number sovereigns. This seems to be a different obverse with no trace of a WW under the other WW.

1218 **Victoria,** Sovereign, 1872, young head left, WW buried in thin truncation in relief, ponytail complete, mistruck first half of legend with only the initial V visible, *rev* St George slaying dragon with sword, profile and date a little doubled, horse with long tail, three strand terminal, one extra spur of hair, narrow date in exergue, small B.P to upper right, no second stop, 7.96g (Marsh 85; MCE 532; S 3856A). *Cleaned with hairlines and scuffs, good fine and unusual.* £250-300

Price Realised : £216

Calendar year mintage 13,486,708

1219 **Victoria,** Fantasy Uniface Reverse, dated 1872, struck in copper on an uneven flan of crude style, St George slaying dragon with sword, horse with long tail, broken lance on groundline to left, no WWP or BP, small date in exergue, beaded border, edge plain with bevelled rims, 4.66g, 22.4mm. *Good very fine.* £100-150

Price Realised : £432

Perhaps made by a practising forger or for a plaque

308 **Victoria,** Sovereign, 1873, young head left, ponytail complete, WW buried in thin truncation in relief touches field, *rev* St George slaying dragon with sword, horse with long tail, three strand end to tail, trace of one spur of extra hair on curve of tail, one dragon claw detached, date in exergue, small number 3, tiny B.P. to upper right, 7.98g (Marsh 86; MCE 536; S 3856A). *Very light surface marks, good extremely fine.* £300-350

Price Realised : £432

ex Randy Weir Numismatics, Unionville, Ontario, Canada, purchased 12 November 1990
Calendar year mintage 2,368,215
This Calendar output no doubt consists mainly of the shield reverse die number sovereigns.

309 **Victoria,** Sovereign, 1874, young head left, ponytail complete, WW buried in thin truncation in relief touches field, *rev* St George slaying dragon with sword, horse with long tail, three strand end to tail, one spur of extra hair on curve of tail, one dragon claw detached, date in exergue, tiny B.P to upper right, second stop absent, 7.98g (Marsh 87; MCE 538; S 3856A). *Reverse a little spotted, light surface marks and nicks, extremely fine.* £300-350

Price Realised : £384

Calendar year mintage 520,713
This Calendar output is very low and probably consists mainly of St George reverse Sovereigns as the shield reverse is extremely rare today. It is only marginally more than that in 1839! Note the blocked stop on the designer's initials on the reverse.

310 **Victoria,** Sovereign, 1876, young head left, ponytail complete, WW buried in thin truncation in relief, inner linear circle at border uneven, *rev* St George slaying dragon with sword, horse with long tail, three strand end to tail, one spur of extra hair on curve of tail, one dragon claw detached, date in exergue, tiny B.P. to upper right, 7.98g (Marsh 88; MCE 539; S 3856A). *Very light surface marks, extremely fine.* £300-350

Price Realised : £360

ex Steinbergs of North Carolina (formerly Florida), USA, 2 July 2001 – previously graded as MS64
Calendar year mintage 3,318,866
As there was no output of Sovereigns either side of 1876 it would seem prudent to think all of this number were 1876 dated sovereigns, unless of course any dies from 1874 were still in use.

1220 **Victoria,** Sovereign, 1876, date double struck, young head left, ponytail complete, WW buried in thin truncation in relief, ponytail a little detached, incomplete lower curl, *rev* St George slaying dragon with sword, horse with long tail, three strand end to tail, one spur of extra hair on curve of tail, one dragon claw detached, date in exergue, small number 3, tiny B.P. to upper right, 7.98g (Marsh 88; MCE 539; S 3856A). *Some dirt around rim, heavy surface marks and nicks with hairlines, very fine / good very fine.* £250-300

Price Realised : £288

purchased from Ebay, March 2008
Calendar year mintage 3,318,866

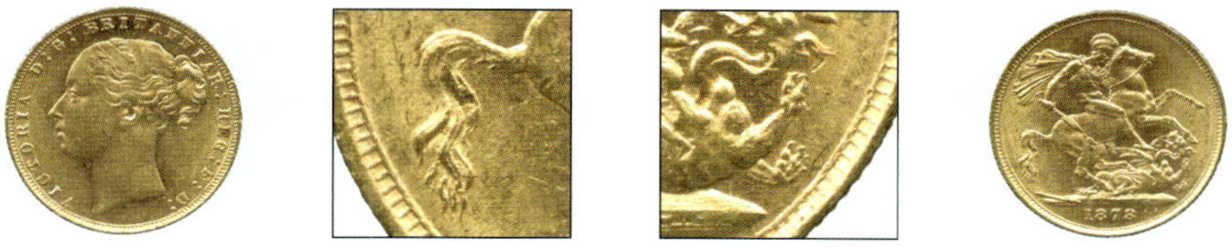

311 **Victoria,** Sovereign, 1878, young head left, ponytail complete, WW buried in thin truncation in relief, *rev* St George slaying dragon with sword, horse with long tail, three strand end to tail, trace of one spur of extra hair on curve of tail, dragon with two claws to left and four to right foreleg, some indistinct, date in exergue, only slight trace of B.P. to upper right, 7.98g (Marsh 89; MCE 540; S 3856A). *Tiny spot in legend, very light surface marks and nicks by dragon claws, otherwise practically extremely fine.* £300-350

Price Realised : £360

ex Reserve Bank of Australia sale, Downies, November 2005, lot 1428, via Winsor and Sons, Jamberoo, Australia, 4 December 2006
Calendar year mintage 1,091,275
Again it seems likely that most, if not all of this issue was 1878 dated coins, there being no 1877 issue and with the following year of 1879 being incredibly low in output and the dated 1879 coins today being extremely rare, it seems unlikely there was overlap either end of 1878 in striking coins of that date.

1221 **Victoria,** Sovereign, 1878, young head left, ponytail a little detached, WW buried in thin truncation in relief, *rev* St George slaying dragon with sword, horse with long tail, three strand end to tail, one spur of extra hair on curve of tail, dragon with three claws to left and four to right arm, some detached, date in exergue, only slight trace of B.P. to upper right, P only visible, 7.96g (Marsh 89; MCE 540; S 3856A). *Heavy surface marks and scuffs, otherwise fine.* £300-350

Price Realised : £216

ex Reserve Bank of Australia sale, Downies, November 2005, lot 1426, via Winsor & Sons, Jamberoo, Australia, December 2006
Calendar year mintage 1,091,275
Again it seems likely that most, if not all of this issue was 1878 dated coins, there being no 1877 issue and with the following year of 1879 being incredibly low in output and the dated 1879 coins today being extremely rare, it seems unlikely there was overlap either end of 1878 in striking coins of that date.

The Extremely Rare Victoria 1879 London St George Reverse Sovereign

312 **Victoria,** Sovereign, 1879, by William Wyon, young head left, ponytail complete, WW buried in thin truncation in relief, *rev* St George slaying dragon with sword, hem of cloak doubled, horse with long tail, three strand end to tail, trace of one spur of extra hair on curve of tail, dragon with four claws to left and three to right foreleg, one detached, date in exergue, date double struck, tiny B.P. to upper right, 7.99g (Marsh 90 R4; MCE 541; S 3856A). *Light surface marks mainly on obverse, nearly extremely fine / extremely fine and extremely rare.* £3000-4000

Price Realised : £3,120

ex Randy Weir Numismatics, Unionville, Ontario, Canada, purchased 3 August 1990
Calendar year mintage 20,013
This incredibly low mintage for the calendar year is perhaps indicative of how rare the 1879 Sovereign really is. This is one sixth of the output for 1841 and only six times higher than in 1819. Hardly any 1879 Sovereigns survive in higher grades than very fine. 1879 marks the year when Resident Engraver T J Minton dies and this post is then abolished.

Exceptional Pattern plain edge Victoria Sovereign 1880 with St George Reverse

313 **Victoria,** Proof Sovereign, 1880, engraved after William Wyon, young head left of third style, with double fillet, ponytail complete, WW buried in thin truncation in relief, finely toothed border within twin linear concentric circles and bevelled rim both sides, VICTORIA D: G: BRITANNIAR: REG: F: D:, *rev* struck en médaille, after Benedetto Pistrucci, St George slaying dragon with sword, horse with long tail, three strand end to tail, one spur of extra hair on curve of tail, dragon with four claws to left and three to right foreleg, all attached, broken lance on ground-line to left, *WWP* in relief under lance, date in exergue, tiny B.P. to upper right, edge plain, 7.98g, 21.8mm (WR 324 R5, *this coin illustrated*; Murdoch 512; Nobleman 274; DM 214). *Well defined strike with a pleasing red tone, mint state FDC and of the highest rarity.* £12,000-15,000

Price Realised : £24,000

Plate coin in Wilson and Rasmussen
presumably ex Capt. K J Douglas-Morris, Sothebys, 26 November 1974, lot 214
ex Spink Numismatic Circular, December 1992, item 7602
ex Spink Numismatic Circular, May 1993, item 2554
ex Spink Numismatic Circular, February 1994, item 169
This Proof is of the highest rarity and was perhaps struck by order of the Melbourne Mint for display at the International Exhibition in 1880 in Australia. Deputy Master of the Melbourne Mint, V Delves Broughton approached the London Royal Mint during 1879, and C W Fremantle, Deputy Master at London, supplied two specimen proofs of each coin in issue, one to display an obverse, the other to show a reverse. Note the bevelled finish to the usually raised rim.
For further reading see the Journal of the Australian Numismatic Association, Volume 2, 1986, article by John Sharples *"The Numismatic Collection of the Museum of Victoria."*

The Extremely Rare Milled Edge Proof Sovereign of 1880, St George Reverse

1222 **Victoria,** Proof Sovereign, 1880, engraved after William Wyon, young head left of third style, with double fillet, ponytail complete, WW buried in thin truncation in relief meets field, finely toothed border within twin linear concentric circles and bevelled rim both sides, VICTORIA D: G: BRITANNIAR: REG: F: D:, *rev* struck with inverted die axis, after Benedetto Pistrucci, St George slaying dragon with sword, horse with long tail, three strand end to tail, one spur of extra hair on curve of tail, dragon with four claws to left and three to right arm, all attached, broken lance on ground-line to left, *WWP* in relief under lance, date in exergue, tiny B.P. to upper right, edge milled, 7.97g, 22.1mm (WR 325 R6; Murdoch 514; Nobleman -; Douglas-Morris -). *Well defined strike from quite yellow gold with a nice cameo contrast between design and field, once polished with light surface marks and hairlines, otherwise practically as struck and of the highest rarity.* £12,000-15,000

Price Realised : £12,000

ex Spink Numismatic Circular, December 1992, item 7602
ex An Important Collection of Gold Sovereigns 1816-2000, offered as one lot, Sothebys, November 2000, lot 525 (part)
Interestingly the plate coin in Wilson and Rasmussen is a repeat of the plain edge piece on the page before (WR324), therefore no example of the milled edge proof could be photographed at the time the book was published, proving this coin perhaps rarer than its plain edge counterpart.
This Proof is of the highest rarity and was perhaps struck by order of the Melbourne Mint for display at the International Exhibition in 1880 in Australia. Deputy Master of the Melbourne Mint, V Delves Broughton, approached the London Royal Mint during 1879, and C W Fremantle, Deputy Master at London supplied two specimen proofs of each coin in issue, one to display an obverse, the other to show a reverse. For further reading see the Journal of the Australian Numismatic Association, vol 2, 1986, article by John Sharples, *The Numismatic Collection of the Museum of Victoria.*

314 **Victoria,** Sovereign, 1880, young head left, WW buried in thin truncation in relief touches field, trace of doubling in some letters of legend, *rev* St George slaying dragon with sword, incomplete hem to cloak, horse with short tail, three strand end to tail plus one higher, two spurs of extra hair on curve of tail, dragon with three claws to left and four to right foreleg, one detached, date in exergue, tiny indistinct BP to upper right, no stops visible, 7.99g (Marsh 91; MCE 542; S 3856B). *Many light surface marks, extremely fine.* £300-350

Price Realised : £408

ex Randy Weir Numismatics, Unionville, Ontario, Canada, purchased 9 June 1993
Calendar year mintage 3,650,080
A massive increase on the year before, many dies must have been engraved for 1880 and we have a different treatment of the horse tail, now shorter and with two spurs at the upper curve of the tail plus there is an incomplete hem to St George's cloak.

1223 **Victoria,** Sovereign, 1880, young head left, WW buried in thin truncation in relief touches field, trace of doubling in some letters of legend, *rev* St George slaying dragon with sword, incomplete hem to cloak, horse with short tail, three strand end to tail plus one higher, two spurs of extra hair on curve of tail, dragon with three claws to left and four to right arm, one detached, date in exergue, no BP to upper right, 7.98g (Marsh 91; MCE 542; S 3856B). *Many light surface marks and nicks, extremely fine.* £250-300

Price Realised : £360

ex Randy Weir Numismatics, Unionville, Ontario, Canada, purchased October 1990
Calendar year mintage 3,650,080
A massive increase on the year before, many dies must have been engraved for 1880 and we have a different rendering of the horse tail, now shorter and with two spurs at the upper curve of the tail plus there is an incomplete hem to St George's cloak.

The Victoria 8 Over 7, 1880 St George Reverse Sovereign

1224 **Victoria,** Sovereign, 1880, second 8 struck over 7, young head left, with double fillet, W.W. buried in thin truncation in relief, second W into field, first G of legend doubled, *rev* St George slaying dragon with sword, horse with long tail, three strand end to tail, one spur of extra hair on curve of tail, dragon with three claws to left and three to right arm, some claws detached, date in exergue lightly die flawed, tiny indistinct B.P. to upper right, 7.99g (Marsh 91A; MCE 542; S 3856D). *Red spot on neck, scuffed with some scratches behind bun of hair, some light surface marks, extremely fine, reverse better.* £300-400

Price Realised : £864

ex Douro Cargo, Spink Auction 118, 20-21 November 1996, lot 596
Calendar year mintage 3,650,080
It seems there were some unused reverse dies left due to the low mintage output of 1879. These dies obviously did not have the full date yet punched in but displayed merely "187" and were waiting in stock it seems, perhaps because of the lack of a couple of years striking in London in the 1870s. This unused die stock was converted for use in 1880 by punching an 8 over the 7 then finishing the date off with a 0. Other aspects of the reverse also match with characteristics of 1870s reverse dies of the long tail variety. This overdate was discovered for the first time in the Douro Cargo coins that were sold by auction in November 1996 by Spink and Son Ltd.

The Victoria 8 over 7, 1880 St George Reverse Sovereign

315 **Victoria,** Sovereign, 1880, second 8 struck over 7, young head left, with double fillet, ww buried in thin truncation in relief, legend with trace of doubling and some die flaws most evident at D:, *rev* St George slaying dragon with sword, horse with long tail, three strand end to tail, one spur of extra hair on curve of tail, dragon with four claws to left and three to right foreleg, one detached, date in exergue lightly die flawed, tiny B.P. to upper right, incomplete B, 7.99g (Marsh 91A; MCE 542; S 3856B). *Dig on neck above truncation, blemish by ear, slight scuff in reverse field and some light surface marks, extremely fine.* £300-400

Price Realised : £744

ex Douro Cargo, Spink Auction 118, 20-21 November 1996, lot 594
Calendar year mintage 3,650,080
It seems there were some unused reverse dies left due to the low mintage output of 1879. These dies obviously did not have the full date yet punched in but displayed merely "187" and were waiting in stock it seems, perhaps because of the lack of a couple of years striking in London in the 1870s. Therefore this unused die stock was converted for use in 1880 by punching an 8 over the 7 then finishing the date off with a 0. Other aspects of the reverse also match with characteristics of 1870s reverse dies of the long tail variety. This overdate was discovered for the first time in the Douro Cargo coins that were sold by auction in November 1996 by Spink and Son Ltd.

W.W. complete on truncation

316 **Victoria,** Sovereign, 1880, second young head left, W.W. complete on truncation in relief, second W intrudes field, hair with double fillet, ponytail with only a trace of the bottom curl, G of legend doubled, *rev* St George slaying dragon with sword, hemline of cloak is incomplete, horse with short tail, three strand end to tail plus one higher, two spurs of extra hair on curve of tail, dragon with three claws to left and three to right foreleg, two detached, date in exergue, no B.P. present, 7.98g (Marsh 91C; MCE 542; S 3856E). *Very light surface marks and nicks, good extremely fine.* £300-350

Price Realised : £660

ex Randy Weir Numismatics, Unionville, Ontario, Canada, purchased 20 November 1990
Calendar year mintage 3,650,080
In this higher calendar year output a new obverse become evident, the second to be coupled with the St George and dragon reverse. The most obvious feature is the initials on the truncation which are now fully complete with stops, but there is also a slight difference in the ponytail of hair. This particular coin is also coupled with the new short tail reverse although this one seems to have a totally blocked B.P. in exergue, probably not unintentionally omitted.

1225 **Victoria,** Sovereign, 1880, second young head left, W.W. complete on truncation in relief, second W intrudes field, hair with double fillet, ponytail with only a trace of the lower part of the curl, G of legend doubled, *rev* St George slaying dragon with sword, hemline of cloak is incomplete, horse with short tail, three strand end to tail plus one higher, two spurs of extra hair on curve of tail, dragon with three claws to left and three to right arm, two detached, date in exergue, only a trace of B.P. present no stops, 7.99g (Marsh 91E; MCE 542; S 3856F). *Very light surface marks and nicks, rim nicks, extremely fine.* £250-300

Price Realised : £360

ex Douro Cargo, Spink Auction 118, 20-21 November 1996, lot 598
Calendar year mintage 3,650,080
In this higher calendar year output a new obverse become evident, the second to be coupled with the St George and dragon reverse. The most obvious feature is the initials on the truncation which are now fully complete with stops, but there is also a slight difference in the ponytail of hair.

317 **Victoria,** Sovereign, 1884, young head left, WW buried in thin truncation in relief touches field, inner linear circle of border uneven, *rev* St George slaying dragon with sword, cloak with complete hemline, horse with short tail, three strand end to tail plus one higher, two spurs of extra hair on curve of tail, dragon with three claws to left and four to right foreleg, all attached, date in exergue, tiny BP to upper right, a little indistinct with blocked stops, 7.97g (Marsh 92; MCE 544; S 3856B). *Once cleaned with associated heavy surface marks and scuffs, extremely fine and rare.* £300-350

Price Realised : £312

ex Randy Weir Numismatics, Unionville, Ontario, Canada, purchased 14 June 1994
Calendar year mintage 1,769,635
Another high output at this time, there were no dated Sovereigns from the London Royal Mint for 1881, 1882 or 1883. This seems to be a better engraved short tail reverse die than previous as the claws and cloak hem are complete. Strangely it is coupled with an older first obverse for the St George type, perhaps using up older stock. Examples of this coupling have only been known for a few years and were only recently added to the *Standard Catalogue of British Coins.*

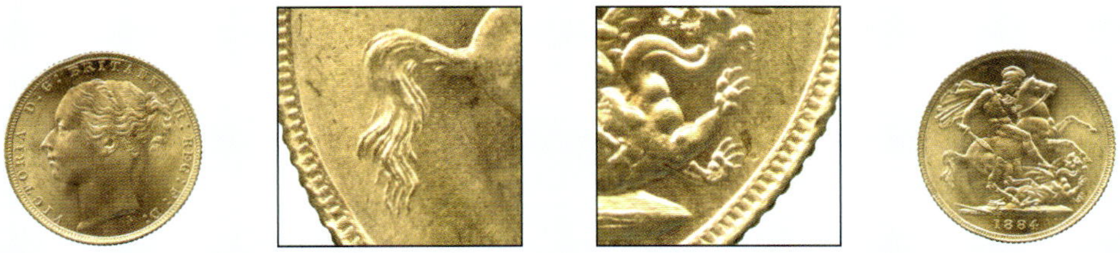

318 **Victoria,** Sovereign, 1884, second young head left, W.W. complete on truncation in relief, second W intrudes field, ponytail with only a trace of the bottom curl, G of legend doubled, *rev* St George slaying dragon with sword, horse with short tail, three strand end to tail with die flaws, one spur of extra hair on curve of tail, second indistinct, dragon with three claws to left and four to right foreleg, all attached, date in exergue, tiny BP to upper right, a little indistinct with blocked stops, 7.99g (Marsh 92; MCE 544; S 3856F). *Edge knock with light surface marks, good extremely fine.* £300-350

Price Realised : £1,104

ex Dr. Jacob Y Terner collection, Goldberg, Hollywood, USA, 26-27 May 2003, lot 379, previously graded MS64 by NGC.
Calendar year mintage 1,769,635
This coin couples the second young head for the St George reverse, with the short tail reverse which is becoming more flawed and weaker in parts.

319 **Victoria,** Sovereign, 1885, second young head left, w.w. complete on truncation in relief, second W intrudes field, ponytail complete, *rev* St George slaying dragon with sword, complete hemline to cloak, horse with short tail, three strand end to tail plus one higher, two spurs of extra hair on curve of tail, dragon with three claws to left and four to right foreleg, all attached, date in exergue, rim flaw to left side of exergue, tiny indistinct BP to upper right edge, P incomplete, 8.00g (Marsh 93; MCE 545; S 3856F). *Light surface marks, extremely fine.* £300-350

Price Realised : £384

ex Steinbergs of North Carolina (formerly Florida), USA, 2 July 2001, previously graded as MS62
Calendar year mintage 717,723
On the obverse this coin seems to demonstrate some "touching-up" of the design of the new second head, the ponytail is now complete.

1226 **Victoria,** Sovereign, 1885, second young head left, w.w. complete on truncation in relief, second W intrudes field, ponytail complete, lowest curl weak, some letters doubled, die flaw at EG of legend, *rev* St George slaying dragon with sword, complete hemline to cloak, horse with short tail, three strand end to tail plus one higher, two spurs of extra hair on curve of tail, dragon with three claws to left and four to right arm, one lower claw detached, date in exergue, rim flaw to left side of exergue, tiny indistinct BP to upper right edge, only B apparent, 7.99g (Marsh 93; MCE 545; S 3856F). *Scratch down bust, with nicks, surface marks and hairlines, extremely fine.* £250-300

Price Realised : £336

ex Randy Weir Numismatics, Unionville, Ontario, Canada, purchased October 1990
Calendar year mintage 717,723

Extremely Rare Victoria Young Head Proof Sovereign Dated 1887 St George Reverse

320 **Victoria,** Proof Sovereign, 1887, engraved after William Wyon, young head left of third rendering, hair with double fillet, WW buried in thin truncation in relief, finely toothed border within twin linear concentric circles and raised rim both sides, VICTORIA D: G: BRITANNIAR: REG: F: D:, the last letter doubled, *rev* struck with inverted die axis, after Benedetto Pistrucci, St George slaying dragon with sword, complete hem to cloak, horse with short tail, three strand end to tail plus one higher, two spurs of extra hair on curve of tail, dragon with three claws to left and four to right foreleg, all attached, broken lance on ground-line to left, *WWP* in relief under lance, date in exergue, tiny B P to upper right, no stops, the P incomplete, edge milled, 8.01g, 22.1mm (WR 332 R5; DM 218). *Brilliant mint state and of the highest rarity.* £12,000-15,000

Price Realised : £26,400

ex Grant Collection of English Milled Coins, Spink Auction 107, 22 November 1994, lot 434
The final year for the young head design upon the coinage was 1887, thus resulting in some young head Sovereigns of proof quality from highly polished dies being struck probably as a matter of record for the Mint and for presentation to highly important persons.

The Jubilee Style Bust Coinage For the Golden Jubilee of Queen Victoria

Much like today with our current Queen's Diamond Jubilee in 2012, preparations for Queen Victoria's Golden Jubilee of 1887 were underway years in advance. The Queen herself had first signified that she was willing for a change in portrait on the coinage as she had been most impressed by a portrait medal of her effigy by Mr Joseph Edgar Boehm RA (6 July 1834 - 12 December 1890) modelled from life. A large plaster model was prepared by Boehm in his studio, and from this metal copies were taken and then reduced for coinage. The first proposed coinage patterns appear from 1880 in base metals and silver, the Queen having sat for her portrait with Boehm in February of that year. The resulting currency coinage produced for 1887 included a commemorative gold Five Pound and Two Pound coin issued together for the first time since 1826. There were sets available in various guises officially for sale as proof or currency quality, with cases costing extra. The Jubilee coinage also marks for the first time in the British currency coinage the die axis being upright (en médaille). All die axes previously on coinage were of the inverted orientation and upright axis was reserved for medals or patterns. The obverse legend appears slightly more abbreviated than the last young head issue too. Apart from this, and the obvious bust change, the coinage is very similar to the previous young head St George type with a milled edge.
The story of the gestation of the coinage was revealed in a series of Royal Mint correspondence, the elements of which have been published in the British Numismatic Journal by G P Dyer and Mark Stocker in 1984. What can be seen is that the resulting currency coins were received with mixed reaction from the public, much to the consternation of C W Fremantle, the Deputy Master of the Mint who had fully supported the design. The populous accepted the change in celebration of the Jubilee, but more seriously criticism of the design was given by critics at the Royal Academy for the way the crown appeared upon the Queen's head, and the coinage was much discussed in Parliament. Comments ranged from such as "this toy crown" and "too small to be realistic," as had the Queen turned or moved the crown would have tumbled from her head.
More seriously, the Sixpence and Half-Sovereign coins being of similar dimensions and unfortunately of similar design, meant the Sixpences were quickly gilt by the unscrupulous and passed as gold coins. The Numismatic Society again were vocal about this, saying that the Mint had a precedent in 1821 when the Half Sovereign design had to be changed after one year as it was too similar to the sixpence. In 1887 the Sixpence became the withdrawn coin and the reverse design regressed to what it was before. The Numismatic Society and its President Sir John Evans, amongst others, continued to criticise the designs and the Jubilee portrait only lasted on British coins from 1887-1892 inclusive. Even the Queen herself had remarked on her displeasure of this coinage during 1888. In Melbourne and Sydney, Australia, the portrait continued briefly into 1893 on the gold coins. Boehm having died in 1890 was no longer around to see the change so soon after the Jubilee, and the criticism received may well have contributed to his demise, though he was kept very busy with his sculpture work.

For further reading see British Numismatic Journal 1984, p.274-288 "Edgar Boehm and the Jubilee Coinage" by G P Dyer and Mark Stocker.

321 **Victoria (1837-1901),** Pattern Sovereign, 1882, struck in silver, engraved by Joseph Edgar Boehm, large Jubilee older tall veiled bust left, veil touches end of legend, blank full truncation arcing round border, with small Imperial crown, cross on crown intrudes border, wearing 13 pearl necklace, and half a garter star visible on breast under sash intrudes field below, smaller breast brooch, square jewelled ear ring, VICTORIA D:G: BRITT: REG: F: D:, finely toothed border within twin linear concentric circles and raised rim both sides, *rev* struck en médaille, engraved after Benedetto Pistrucci, St George slaying dragon with sword, no streamer on helmet, with complete cloak hemline, horse with short tail, three strand end to tail, one spur of extra hair on curve of tail, dragon with three claws to left and four to right foreleg, all attached, broken lance on ground-line to left, *WWP* in relief under lance, date in exergue, trace of tiny BP to upper right, without stops, edge plain, 4.68g, 21.8mm (BNJ 1984, page 274, plate 2, no.16). *Attractively toned, mint state and of the highest rarity.* £5000-6000

Price Realised : £9,120

ex Baldwin's Auction 13, 28 May 1997, lot 2041
This early proposal in silver differs quite markedly from currency in the smaller details as described above. Additionally this bust is quite wide compared to the later currency bust. The St George and dragon reverse continues to be used for all Sovereigns up to the present century. For further reading see British Numismatic Journal 1984 - Edgar Boehm and the Jubilee Coinage, by G P Dyer and Mark Stocker.

Extremely Rare Silver Victoria Pattern Sovereign, dated 1885

1227 **Victoria,** Pattern Sovereign, 1885, struck in silver, engraved by Joseph Edgar Boehm, smaller narrower Jubilee, older veiled bust left, veil touches end of legend, blank full truncation arcing round border, with small Imperial crown with small trefoils, cross on crown meets border, wearing 12 pearl necklace, garter star visible on breast overlaps sash, just intrudes field below, smaller breast brooch further back on truncation, crenellated collar to dress, pearl drop ear ring, with less hair visible, VICTORIA D:G: BRITT: REG: F: D:, last colon clear of veil, veil decoration under crown, finely toothed border within twin linear concentric circles and raised rim both sides, *rev* struck en médaille, engraved after Benedetto Pistrucci, St George slaying dragon with sword, no streamer on helmet, with complete cloak hemline, horse with more mane hair and short tail, three strand end to tail, one spur of extra hair on curve of tail, dragon with three claws to left and four to right arm, all attached, broken lance on ground-line to left, *WWP* in relief under lance, date in exergue, full tiny BP to upper right, without stops, edge milled, 5.02g, 22mm (BNJ 1984, p.274, plate 2, no.13). *Attractively toned, a hint of cabinet friction, otherwise practically as struck and of the highest rarity.* £5000-6000

Price Realised : £7,200

ex Baldwin's Auction 13, 28 May 1997, lot 2042

This early proposal in silver differs quite markedly from currency in the smaller details as described above. The St George and dragon reverse continues to be used for all Sovereigns up to the present century. For further reading see British Numismatic Journal 1984 - Edgar Boehm and the Jubilee Coinage, by G P Dyer and Mark Stocker.

Extremely Rare Victoria Jubilee Type Pattern Sovereign, dated 1887

1228 **Victoria,** Pattern Sovereign, 1887, engraved by Joseph Edgar Boehm, Jubilee tall veiled bust left with older features, veil with two rows of crenellations, with small Imperial crown, large fleurs inside, top cross on crown meets the border, wearing 14 pearl necklace, brooch at front with incuse jewel, half a garter star at base of bust under sash, decorated border to dress bust, J.E.B. high on truncation into field with stops, angled J, second repositioned legend closer to crown, two bead pearl drop ear ring, VICTORIA D:G: BRITT: REG: F: D:, finely toothed border within twin linear concentric circles and raised rim both sides, outer rim blends with teeth, *rev* struck en médaille, after Benedetto Pistrucci, St George slaying dragon with sword, extra mane hair above hand holding rein, horse with short tail, three strand end to tail, two spurs of extra hair on curve of tail, dragon with three claws to left and four to right arm, one lower claw detached, broken lance on ground-line to left, *WWP* in relief under lance, date in exergue, complete tiny B.P. to upper right, edge milled, 7.89g, 22mm (Spink, *Numismatic Circular*, April 2001, article by S Hill, p.89; WR -; S -). *Some light handling marks, otherwise practically as struck and still one of only two known in private hands, of the highest rarity.* £4000-5000

Price Realised : £8,400

ex Spink Auction 1279, 12 July 2001, lot 167

This coin was the first to be discovered and is the same piece illustrated with enlargement in the Spink Circular article by S. Hill. The most obvious difference between this pattern and the adopted currency design is the extra pearl in the Queen's necklace.

The Proof Sovereign of 1887 Produced for Victoria's Golden Jubilee

322 **Victoria,** Proof Sovereign, 1887, engraved by Joseph Edgar Boehm, Jubilee tall veiled bust left with older features, veil with two rows of crenellations, with small Imperial crown, large fleurs inside, top cross on field within the border, wearing 13 pearl necklace, brooch at front with relief jewel, half a garter star at base of bust under sash, decorated border to dress bust, J.E.B. on edge of truncation into field with stops, angled J, repositioned second legend closer to crown, two pearl drop ear ring, VICTORIA D:G: BRITT: REG: F: D:, finely toothed border within twin linear concentric circles and raised rim both sides, outer rim blends with teeth, *rev* struck en médaille, after Benedetto Pistrucci, St George slaying dragon with sword, extra mane hair above hand holding rein, horse with short tail, three strand end to tail, two spurs of extra hair on curve of tail, dragon with three claws to left and three to right foreleg, trace of fourth claw, all attached, broken lance on ground-line to left, *WWP* in relief under lance, date in exergue, tiny B.P without final stop, incomplete P, to upper right, edge milled, 7.99g, 22.1mm (WR 333; S 3866B). *Brilliant mint state with just a few wispy hairlines.* £1000-1200

Price Realised : £3,360

English Silver Coinage quotes a figure of 797 Proof Sets with gold issued in 1887, no doubt Sovereigns and other coins from the set would have been available singly too, but the total issue of proof Sovereigns would be unlikely to exceed 1000 pieces as an educated guess.

The above proof Sovereign sets the standard description for the Jubilee type coinage. There are only really three major varieties in this coinage. Firstly the position of the obverse legend of which this proof is the so-called second type with the first half of the legend appearing closer to the crown on the Queen's head. The first type has the legend just over a millimetre further away.

The designer's initials on the truncation are the other area of variety on the obverse. The normal size initials always seem to have an angled letter J where the bottom is angled horizontally off the upright vertical. The smaller designer initials tend always to have a hooked J as you would expect. These initials can be differently arranged on the truncation of the bust, whether closer or spread and in line or in an arc, they can differ more on the Australian series coins.

The other difference is the horse's tail on the reverse, which becomes longer with different hair strand arrangements on some coins from 1891. Note with this proof the lack of a final stop after the initials in the exergue.

first type legend **normal initials – angled J**

323 **Victoria,** Sovereign, 1887, first legend, Jubilee veiled bust left, top cross on crown meets border, J.E.B. fully on truncation, angled J, first type legend further from crown, *rev* St George slaying dragon with sword, horse with short tail, date in exergue, weak 1 in date, tiny B.P. to upper right, all stops present, 7.98g (Marsh 125; MCE 547; S 3866). *Some light bagmarks, otherwise practically as struck.* £300-350

Price Realised : £432

ex Steinbergs of North Carolina (previously Florida), USA, bought 2 July 2001, when graded as MS64 by PCGS
Calendar year mintage 1,111,280
This coin depicts the first legend type further from the crown and the initials are fully on the truncation.

1229 **Victoria,** Sovereign, 1887, first legend, Jubilee veiled bust left, top cross on crown meets border, double struck J.E.B. fully on truncation, angled J, the E of the initials quite dramatically doubled, first type legend further from crown, hairline raised die flaw joins some letters in legend, *rev* St George slaying dragon with sword, horse with short tail, date in exergue, tiny B.P. to upper right, 7.98g (Marsh 125; MCE 547; S 3866). *Some light bagmarks, otherwise extremely fine and unusual.* £300-350

Price Realised : £408

ex Paul Davies Ltd, Ilkley, June 2008
Calendar year mintage 1,111,280
This coin depicts the first legend type further from the crown and the initials are fully on the truncation. For a full description of every aspect of a Jubilee type Sovereign, see lot 322 in part one of the Bentley Collection.

tiny initials – hooked J **cross meets border**

324 **Victoria,** Sovereign, 1887, tiny initials on truncation, Jubilee veiled bust left, top cross on crown meets border, tiny J.E.B. fully on truncation in arc, hooked type J lightly doubled, first type legend further from crown, *rev* St George slaying dragon with sword, hemline of cloak incomplete, horse with short tail, date in exergue, 7.99g (Marsh 125A; MCE 547; S 3866A). *Some light bagmarks and nicks, otherwise extremely fine and extremely rare.* £600-800

Price Realised : £1,320

ex Randy Weir Numismatics, Unionville, Ontario, Canada, purchased 13 June 1997
Calendar year mintage 1,111,280
The small curved initials with hooked J on the truncation are extremely rare. Only a small proportion of the calendar year output must have carried this obverse variety.

second type legend, cross on crown within border

325 **Victoria,** Sovereign, 1888, second legend, Jubilee veiled bust left, top cross on crown in field within border, J.E.B. on edge of truncation into field with stops, angled J, second repositioned legend closer to crown, *rev* St George slaying dragon with sword, hemline of cloak incomplete, no extra mane hair over rein hand, horse with short tail, the two extra spurs of tail hair quite long, date in exergue, tiny B.P to upper right, final stop absent as on the proof issue, 8.00g (Marsh 126; MCE 548; S 3866B). *Some light bagmarks and hairlines, extremely fine.* £300-350

Price Realised : £480

ex Steinbergs of North Carolina (previously Florida), USA, bought 21 March 2001, when graded as MS62 by PCGS
Calendar year mintage 2,277,424
The calendar year output probably includes many 1887 dated coins as is usual with special occasions, demand for the coin of the Jubilee year typically continues to be fulfilled into the following year at least for the first month or more.
Note the lack of the second stop on the designer's initials in the exergue which occurs intermittently.

B.P variety and full dragon claws

326 **Victoria,** Sovereign, 1889, second legend, Jubilee veiled bust left, top cross on crown in field within border, J.E.B. on edge of truncation into field with stops, angled J, second repositioned legend closer to crown, *rev* St George slaying dragon with sword, hemline of cape incomplete, no extra mane hair over rein hand, horse with short tail, fourth claw on right foreleg well defined on dragon, date in exergue, tiny B.P to upper right, final stop absent as on the proof issue, 7.99g (Marsh 127; MCE 549; S 3866B). *Some light bagmarks, good extremely fine.* £300-350

Price Realised : £432

Calendar year mintage 7,257,455
This is the highest calendar year output for the Jubilee head Sovereigns.

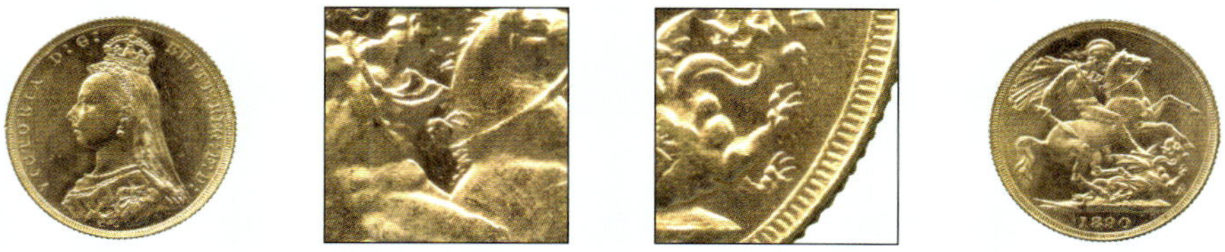

extra mane hair over rein hand and different dragon claw arrangement

327 **Victoria,** Sovereign, 1890, second legend, Jubilee veiled bust left, top cross on crown in field within border, J.E.B. on edge of truncation into field with stops, angled J, second repositioned legend closer to crown, *rev* St George slaying dragon with sword, hemline of cloak complete, with extra mane hair over rein hand, horse with short tail, left foreleg of dragon with only three claws, date in exergue, tiny B.P to upper right, final stop absent, 7.99g (Marsh 128; MCE 550; S 3866B). *Some light bagmarks, nicks and hairlines, good extremely fine.* £300-350

Price Realised : £432

Calendar year mintage 6,529,887

The Extremely Rare First Legend Jubilee Victorian Sovereign of 1890

328 **Victoria,** Sovereign, 1890, first legend, Jubilee veiled bust left, top cross on crown meets border, J.E.B. fully on truncation, angled J, first type legend further from crown, *rev* St George slaying dragon with sword, hemline of cloak complete, with extra mane hair over rein hand, horse with short tail, three strand end to tail, two spurs of extra hair on curve of tail, date in exergue, tiny B.P to upper right, final stop absent, 7.97g (cf Marsh 128; MCE 550; cf S 3866). *Some light bagmarks, good very fine and extremely rare.* £300-350

Price Realised : £504

Calendar year mintage 6,529,887
Looking at the high calendar year mintage it is perhaps not surprising that older first legend dies emerge from possible storage to strike Sovereigns.
Marsh discusses these variations briefly in the narrative of his book of ten years ago, but decided oddly not to include the variety in his tables at that time, as he could not gauge the rarity. However the fact he only found 12 first legend coins in a sample of 150 Jubilee type Sovereigns, most of them being 1887 or Australian issue, suggests they are at least 10 times rarer than second legend coins, this 1890 date even more so.
Incidentally the Spink Standard Catalogue still does not list 1890 for the first legend.

Extremely Rare Bronze Victoria Pattern Sovereign, dated 1891

1230 **Victoria,** Trial Striking in bronze from the Royal Mint presses of a forger's Sovereign, 1891, engraved in the style of Joseph Edgar Boehm, older veiled bust left, with small Imperial crown, top cross on crown in field within border, wearing 13 pearl necklace, half a garter star at base of bust under sash, sash touches linear circle then truncation, J.E.B. on edge of truncation, curvy hooked J, second repositioned legend, VICTORIA D:G: BRITT: REG: F: D:, finely toothed border, shorter teeth within twin linear concentric circles and raised rim both sides, *rev* struck en médaille, engraved in the style of Benedetto Pistrucci, St George slaying dragon with sword, different helmet streamer, one long thick strand, no upper or lower strands, cloak complete, no extra mane hair over rein hand, horse with very long tail, one strand terminal hair and no spurs above, dragon with three claws to left and two to right arm, broken lance on ground-line to left, no *WWP*, date in exergue out of line, full tiny close B.P. to upper right, edge plain, 4.18g, 22.2mm (ISBCC Bulletin, January 1978, vol 3, no.1). *Attractively toned, mint state and of the highest rarity.* £2000-2500

Price Realised : £7,440

ex Spink Auction 89, 25 November 1991, lot 138 (part)
ex Randy Weir Numismatics, Unionville, Ontario, Canada, purchased at NYINC, circa December 1995, Sheraton Hotel, New York

It has been proven by direct comparison physically that this striking in bronze and a companion piece struck in tin (lot 329) were struck from an unusual pair of dies still housed in the Royal Mint Museum along with another bronze striking in their collection. The circumstances behind their existence and why they had been kept by the Mint were lost to history until 1977, when the then Curator of the Mint Collection, Mr G P Dyer carried out some major research, the findings from which were revealed in an article prepared for the IBSCC Bulletin for January 1978, vol 3, no.1.

This research was sparked by Mr Dyer's curiosity as to why there was a ticket with the bronze specimen that stated it was struck from counterfeit dies, there being no such other striking of this nature in the Mint Collection. It turned out that the counterfeit dies that struck this specimen were still in the Museum collection, having been at times stored with the official tools of the Mint. The fact that there was a date on the ticket with the bronze specimen as to when it was struck made it easier to look into the Mint records to find out the purpose of the striking and this then led back to the story to how these well executed dies came to exist and why they were manufactured outside of the Mint.

Mr Dyer found that the details of the court case involving them was reported in detail in *The Times* newspapers of 8, 11 and 17 September 1891 where a Robert Schmidt, age 30, was sentenced to six months of penal servitude for being in the unlawful possession of a die for the purpose of making counterfeit sovereigns. He had approached a die-sinker Emil Schreier in May 1891 to order a pair of Sovereign dies. The die-sinker informed the Bank of England and the Treasury who instructed him to continue to make the dies and fulfil the order. Schmidt was arrested in a Victorian sting operation as he left the die-sinker's office, 5 September 1891, leading to the case as reported by *The Times.*

What is very significant is that the Royal Mint had never before taken trial strikes from counterfeit dies as a matter of record, such as the piece offered here and the tin piece previously offered in part one. Perhaps they were struck to demonstrate how good the counterfeiter's skill had become and as an example to all engravers employed within the Mint. The style and fabrication of the dies is first class and the design differs in only the smaller details from the current coinage. Had Schmidt's plan come to fruition, gun metal type blanks would have been cut by a lathe and a milled edge added mechanically, then gilded to bring them up to the full weight of a sovereign to pass into circulation.

The tin piece (lot 329) is the only known striking in this base metal, the Mint having easy access to tin on site at this time. The bronze specimen listed here and the other in the Mint Museum are the only ones known in that metal. One other specimen is known struck in lead that appeared in the Norweb Collection (part 4), 17 June 1987, lot 1680. This extreme rarity coupled with the history behind them makes them a significant part of the history of die-sinking, counterfeiting and the Mint.

329 **Victoria,** Sovereign, 1891, Trial Striking struck in Tin from the Royal Mint presses, engraved after Joseph Edgar Boehm, older veiled bust left, with small Imperial crown, top cross on crown in field within border, wearing 13 pearl necklace, half a garter star at base of bust under sash, sash touches linear circle then truncation, J.E.B. on edge of truncation, curvy hooked J, second repositioned legend, VICTORIA D:G: BRITT: REG: F: D:, finely toothed border, shorter teeth within twin linear concentric circles and raised rim both sides, *rev* struck en médaille, engraved after Benedetto Pistrucci, St George slaying dragon with sword, different helmet streamer, one long thick strand, no upper or lower strands, cloak complete, no extra mane hair over rein hand, horse with very long tail, one strand terminal hair and no spurs above, dragon with three claws to left and two to right foreleg, broken lance on ground-line to left, no *WWP*, date in exergue out of line, full tiny close B.P. to upper right, edge plain, 4.25g, 22.2mm (ESC -; cf WR 337). *Attractively toned, scuffs on cheek, otherwise practically as struck and of the highest rarity.* £1500-2000

Price Realised : £4,080

ex Spink Auction 89, 25 November 1991, lot 138 (part)
ex Randy Weir Numismatics, Unionville, Ontario, Canada, purchased December 1995, NYINC, Sheraton Hotel, New York.
See footnote to lot 1230 (page 296), for the full story behind this coin

The Extremely Rare Victoria Proof Sovereign of 1891 the "WR" Plate Coin

330 **Victoria,** Proof Sovereign, 1891, engraved after Joseph Edgar Boehm, Jubilee tall veiled bust left, with small Imperial crown, top cross on field within the border, wearing 13 pearl necklace, brooch at front with relief jewel, half a garter star at base of bust under sash, decorated border to dress bust, J.E.B. on edge of truncation into field with stops, angled J, repositioned second legend closer to crown, two pearl drop ear ring, VICTORIA D:G: BRITT: REG: F: D:, finely toothed border within twin linear concentric circles and raised rim both sides, outer rim blends with teeth, *rev* struck en médaille, engraved after Benedetto Pistrucci, St George slaying dragon with sword, different helmet streamer, one long incomplete strand, cloak complete, one strand of mane hair over rein hand, horse with long tail, three strand end to tail, two spurs of extra hair on curve of tail, dragon with four claws to left and three to right foreleg, one claw detached, broken lance on ground-line to left, *WWP* in relief under lance, date in exergue, wide spread full B.P. to upper right, edge milled, 7.97g, 22mm (WR 337 R7, *this coin illustrated;* DM 220). *Brilliant, just a few hairlines, otherwise mint state and extremely rare.* £10,000-12,000

Price Realised : £13,200

ex Randy Weir Numismatics, Unionville, Ontario, Canada, purchased December 1995, NYINC, Sheraton Hotel, New York.
This coin is the one used for illustration in the publication, English Pattern Trial and Proof Coins in Gold by Wilson and Rasmussen.
This coin is the initial issue of the new long tail reverse design for the Jubilee issue, perhaps it was commissioned in light of the demise of J E Boehm who was close to the Royal Family, having been with Princess Louise, Duchess of Argyll when he died.

Extremely Rare Victoria 1891 Currency Sovereign with Short Tail

short tail

331 **Victoria,** Sovereign, 1891, short tail reverse, Jubilee veiled bust left, top cross on crown in field within border, J.E.B. on edge of truncation into field with stops, angled J, second repositioned legend closer to crown, *rev* St George slaying dragon with sword, hemline of cloak complete, with extra mane hair over rein hand, horse with short tail, three strand end to tail, two spurs of extra hair on curve of tail, date in exergue, tiny B.P to upper right, final stop absent, 7.98g (Marsh 129; MCE 551; S 3866B). *Heavy surface marks and nicks, good fine, reverse stronger, extremely rare.* £400-500

Price Realised : £600

Calendar year mintage 6,329,476
This extremely rare variety of the short tail for 1891 was only discovered in 2004, it remains very elusive till this day. The tail lengths of these Jubilee head issues are all quite similar. It is the arrangement of the strands of tail hair and whether there is a spur or two of hair that really differs.

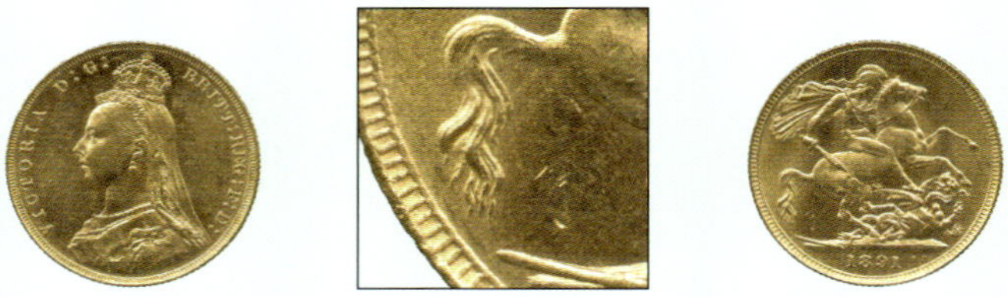

long tail

332 **Victoria,** Sovereign, 1891, long tail reverse, Jubilee veiled bust left, top cross on crown in field within border, J.E.B. on edge of truncation into field with stops, angled J, second repositioned legend closer to crown, *rev* St George slaying dragon with sword, helmet streamer with one long incomplete strand, horse with long tail, three strand end to tail, trace of one spur of extra hair on curve of tail, dragon with four claws to left and four to right foreleg, broken lance on ground-line to left, *WWP* in relief under lance, date in exergue, wide spread full B.P. to upper right, 7.99g (Marsh 129; MCE 551; S 3866C). *Some light bagmarks, extremely fine, reverse better.* £300-350

Price Realised : £360

ex Distinctive Coins, Downers Grove, Illinois, USA, purchased 29 January 2003
Calendar year mintage 6,329,476
This is the usual variety for the 1891 Sovereign.

333 **Victoria,** Sovereign, 1892, long tail reverse, Jubilee veiled bust left, J.E.B. on edge of truncation into field with stops, angled J, second repositioned legend closer to crown, *rev* St George slaying dragon with sword, helmet streamer with one long incomplete strand, horse with long tail, touch of mane hair above rein hand, no extra spur on curve of tail, dragon with three claws to right foreleg, one claw detached, date in exergue, full B.P. to upper right, 7.99g (Marsh 130; MCE 552; S 3866C). *Some light bagmarks, reverse rim nick, extremely fine, reverse better.* £300-350

Price Realised : £312

ex Randy Weir Numismatics, Unionville, Ontario, Canada, purchased 14 September 1993
Calendar year mintage 7,104,720
Another very high mintage this calendar year, little subtle differences occur between dies, but are only sub varieties in the series.

334 **Victoria,** Sovereign, 1892, Jubilee veiled bust left, J.E.B. on edge of truncation into field with stops, angled J, second repositioned legend closer to crown, *rev* St George slaying dragon with sword, helmet streamer with one long incomplete strand, horse with long tail, touch of mane hair above rein hand, no extra spur on curve of tail, dragon with three claws to each foreleg, one claw detached, date in exergue, full B.P. to upper right, 7.98g (Marsh 130; MCE 552; S 3866C). *Scuffed with some hairlines and bagmarks, nearly very fine and extremely rare.* £300-350

Price Realised : £264

Calendar year mintage 7,104,720
This year marks the death of Leonard Charles Wyon, Chief Engraver; his successor was George W De Saulles who was appointed in January 1893.

1231 **Victoria,** Sovereign, 1892, misstrike with plain part to edge milling, Jubilee veiled bust left, J.E.B. on edge of truncation into field with stops, angled J, second repositioned legend closer to crown, *rev* St George slaying dragon with sword, helmet streamer with one long incomplete strand, horse with long tail, touch of mane hair above rein hand, no extra spur on curve of tail, dragon with four claws to upper arm, top one detached, three claws to lower arm, one claw detached, date in exergue, full B.P. to upper right, edge milled with partial milling for one third of edge, 7.99g (Marsh 130; MCE 552; S 3866C). *Excess metal on rim due to the mistriking, otherwise practically as struck, highly unusual and rare.* £400-600

Price Realised : £1,860

Calendar year mintage 7,104,720

The Last Coinage of Queen Victoria

It was decided by a Royal Mint committee in February 1891 that the unpopular Jubilee portrait was no longer appropriate and something new was required. Fellows of the Royal Academy were called upon to submit ideas and designs, and the following made submissions:- Edward Onslow Ford ARA sculptor, Edward J Poynter RA painter, Henry N Armstead RA sculptor, Charles A Birch ARA sculptor, Thomas Brock RA sculptor, W Hamo Thornycroft RA sculptor. Interestingly Poynter had been one of the harsh critics of the Jubilee design, so now had a chance to literally prove how good a coin designer he himself was.

However, Thomas Brock's design won the day and the new older "widow" bust with heavy veil appeared for currency in 1893 to great acclaim. The design was engraved in metal from the designs by the Chief Engraver, George W De Saulles, who later went on to design the obverse for the King Edward VII coinage. Brock's initials appear below the bust and the titles now significantly include the Empress of India and read thus VICTORIA D:G: BRITT: REG: F: D: IND: IMP: again the coins are struck en médaille with an upright die axis and the St George reverse continues effectively unchanged except in the smallest details, which can vary from die to die. The edges are of course milled.

Excessively Rare Pattern Proposed for the Victoria 1893 Coinage by Allan Wyon

335 **Victoria (1837-1901),** Pattern Sovereign, 1893, engraved by Allan Wyon (1843-1907), old crowned and veiled bust left, with curved truncation, thick veil covers most of Order of India, sash covers most of Garter Star on breast, toothed border and raised rim both sides, VICTORIA D:G: BRITT: REG: F: D: IND: IMP:, *rev* struck en médaille, stylised St George attempting to slay dragon left with spear, ONE SOVEREIGN 1893 lightly doubled above, edge plain, 7.88g, 22mm (WR 339 R6, *this coin illustrated*). *Attractively toned, tiny red spot on ground on reverse, as struck and of the highest rarity.* £10,000-12,000

Price Realised : £18,000

ex George Hamilton Smith Collection, Glendining, 23 May 1927, lot 212
ex Baldwin's Hong Kong Coin Auction 42, 30 August 2007, lot 1146
This coin is the one used for illustration in the publication, English Pattern Trial and Proof Coins in Gold by Wilson and Rasmussen. The Baldwin copy of Hamilton-Smith notes three known as of 1927 with the milled edge.
In this stylised version of St George and the dragon, the dragon is unscathed and facing to the left rather than the conventional right of the traditional design. This gold pattern is struck to a lesser weight than the currency pieces as is often seen with new proposals which are not meant to be legal tender till designs and subsequent striking is approved. See lot 1232 for a silver striking of this pattern.

Extremely Rare Silver Victoria Pattern Sovereign, dated 1893

1232 **Victoria,** Pattern Sovereign, 1893, engraved by Allan Wyon (1843-1907), old crowned and veiled bust left, with curved truncation, thick veil covers most of Order of India, sash covers most of Garter Star on breast, toothed border and raised rim both sides, VICTORIA D:G: BRITT: REG: F: D: IND: IMP:, *rev* struck en médaille, stylised St George attempting to slay dragon left with spear, ONE SOVEREIGN 1893 lightly doubled above, edge milled, 5.19g, 22.1mm (cf WR 340). *Attractively toned, as struck and of the highest rarity.* £4000-5000

Price Realised : £9,360

ex Baldwin's Auction 13, 28 May 1997, lot 2045
See footnote to lot 335 (page 300), for further information on this design.

Proof Victoria 1893 Gold Sovereign by Thomas Brock

336 **Victoria,** Proof Sovereign, 1893, engraved by Thomas Brock, old veiled bust left, T.B. below, VICTORIA D:G: BRITT: REG: F: D: IND: IMP:, toothed border surrounding, *rev* struck en médaille, engraved after Benedetto Pistrucci, St George slaying dragon with sword, three strand streamer on helmet, horse with long tail, three strand end to tail, two spurs of extra hair on curve of tail, dragon with four claws on each foreleg, broken lance on ground-line to left, *WWP* in relief under lance, date in exergue, tiny B.P. to upper right, finely toothed border within twin linear concentric circles and raised rim, edge milled, 7.95g, 22.1mm (WR 341; Murdoch 496; Nobleman 277/9; S 3874). *Brilliant, mint state FDC.* £1200-1500

Price Realised : £3,360

Figures have been quoted of 556 Proof Sets with gold issued in 1893, no doubt Sovereigns and other coins from the set would have been available singly too, but the total issue of proof Sovereigns would be unlikely to exceed 750 pieces as an educated guess for this new coinage.

337

338

337 **Victoria,** Sovereign, 1893, old veiled bust left, T.B. below, first three words of legend die flawed, *rev* St George slaying dragon with sword, date in exergue, tiny B.P. to upper right, 7.98g (Marsh 145; MCE 553; S 3874). *Some light bagmarks, nicks and hairlines extremely fine.* £300-350

Price Realised : £456

Calendar year mintage 6,898,260

338 **Victoria,** Sovereign, 1894, old veiled bust left, *rev* St George slaying dragon with sword, date in exergue, 8.00g (Marsh 146; MCE 554; S 3874). *Previously graded by NGC as MS61, some light bagmarks, otherwise good extremely fine.* £300-350

Price Realised : £360

Ebay purchase, 8 February 2004
Calendar year mintage 3,782,611

339

340

341

339 **Victoria,** Sovereign, 1895, old veiled bust left, hairline raised die flaw in some lettering, *rev* St George slaying dragon with sword, top strand of streamer absent leaving two strands only, date in exergue, 7.98g (Marsh 147; MCE 555; S 3874). *Some light scuffs and surface marks, very fine / good very fine.* £300-350

Price Realised : £264

ex Spink and Son Ltd, December 2004
Calendar year mintage 2,285,317

340 **Victoria,** Sovereign, 1896, old veiled bust left, *rev* St George slaying dragon with sword, date in exergue, 7.98g (Marsh 148; MCE 556; S 3874). *Light bagmarks, otherwise extremely fine / good extremely fine.* £300-350

Price Realised : £384

ex Randy Weir Numismatics, Unionville, Ontario, Canada, purchased 12 November 1990
Calendar year mintage 3,334,065

341 **Victoria,** Sovereign, 1898, old veiled bust left, *rev* St George slaying dragon with sword, date in exergue, 7.98g (Marsh 149; MCE 557; S 3874). *A few trifling marks, spot on dragon claws and reverse field, otherwise good extremely fine.* £300-350

Price Realised : £1,080

ex American Heritage Minting, Jenkintown, Pennsylvania, USA, July 2002, previously graded as MS64 ny PCGS
Calendar year mintage 4,361,347
There were no Sovereigns issued in or dated 1897 at the Royal Mint London. We can therefore be fairly confident that the output of 1898 Sovereigns should be for all 1898 dated Sovereigns and it is unlikely old 1896 dated coins would have continued to be struck. That is not to say that 1898 dated coins could not have continued being struck into 1899 however!

342

343

344

342 **Victoria,** Sovereign, 1899, old veiled bust left, hairline raised die flaw in some lettering, *rev* St George slaying dragon with sword, date in exergue, 8.00g (Marsh 150; MCE 558; S 3874). *Some light bagmarks, extremely fine.* £300-350

Price Realised : £384

Calendar year mintage 7,515,978

343 **Victoria,** Sovereign, 1900, old veiled bust left, *rev* St George slaying dragon with sword, top strand of streamer absent leaving two strands only, horse tail with no extra spur on curve, date in exergue, 7.98g (Marsh 151; MCE 559; S 3874). *Some light bagmarks, otherwise good extremely fine.* £300-350

Price Realised : £432

ex Randy Weir Numismatics, Unionville, Ontario, Canada, purchased 26 September 1990
Calendar year mintage 10,846,741
This output for 1900 represents the zenith of the old head coinage of Victoria. Note the different streamer on the helmet of St George as seen on the 1895 Sovereign in lot 339 (above).

344 **Victoria,** Sovereign, 1901, old veiled bust left, *rev* St George slaying dragon with sword, only a trace of the top stand of the helmet streamer apparent, horse tail with no extra spur on curve, date in exergue, 7.99g (Marsh 152; MCE 560; S 3874). *Some light digs at base of bust, other bagmarks and nicks, otherwise good extremely fine.* £300-350

Price Realised : £432

ex Randy Weir Numismatics, Unionville, Ontario, Canada, purchased 19 October 1992
Calendar year mintage 1,578,948
The year that Queen Victoria died, 22 January 1901, represents the lowest mintage of Sovereigns no doubt as work would have transferred to preparing new coinage of Edward VII for 1902. Even though the mintage is lower, the 1901 Sovereigns do survive, as many more well to do people would have kept such coins as keepsakes of the late Queen.

The Reign of King Edward VII (1901-1910)

House of Saxe-Coburg and Gotha

Born: 9 November 1841

Accession: 22 January 1901

Married: Alexandra of Denmark 10 March 1863

Coronation: Saturday, 9 August 1902

Children: three sons, three daughters

Died: 6 May 1910, aged 68

The coinage of the reign of King Edward VII features a bare head portrait of the King facing to the right by George William De Saulles (4 February 1862 - 21 July 1903), who had been Chief Engraver since the death of Leonard Charles Wyon in 1892. De Saulles was authorised to execute new designs on 10 December 1901. His initials appear under the bust of the King and the titles now read EDWARDVS VII D: G: BRITT: OMN: REX F: D: IND: IMP: For the Sovereign the classic St George and dragon design continued, engraved after Pistrucci, still featuring the tiny WWP under the lance for William Wellesley Pole from his days of the Master-ship of the Mint about 1820. The reverse design still carries the inner linear circle and fine square teeth as used from the Jubilee head issue of Victoria through to the last issues of her reign. The coins have a milled edge.
De Saulles died suddenly in the Summer of 1903 after a short illness, at Chiswick whilst working upon and preparing models for the Great Seal of Edward VII which had to be executed by Frank Bowcher.

The New Sovereign of King Edward VII 1902 Struck to a Matt Finish

345 **Edward VII (1901-1910),** Matt Proof Gold Sovereign, 1902, engraved by George William De Saulles, bare head facing right, DES. below, toothed border and raised rim, EDWARDVS VII D: G: BRITT: OMN: REX F: D: IND: IMP:, *rev* struck en médaille, engraved after Benedetto Pistrucci, St George slaying dragon with sword, cloak with complete hemline, three stand helmet streamer, horse with long tail, ending in three strands, with one spur higher up at curve, broken lance on ground-line to left, *WWP* in relief under lance, date in exergue, tiny B.P. to upper right, finely toothed border within twin linear concentric circles and raised rim, edge milled, 7.99g (WR 408; S 3969). *Mint state with just a few little hairlines.* £350-400

Price Realised : £528

ex Randy Weir Numismatics, Unionville, Ontario, Canada, purchased 14 August 1992
According to English Silver Coinage, just over 15,000 matt proof sets were issued of one formation or the other, which included a matt proof gold Sovereign. Single coins may well have been available on request to, so the final figure could be around 15,500 struck.

346 **Edward VII,** Sovereign, 1902, bare head facing right, *rev* St George slaying dragon with sword, streamer on helmet weak in parts, date in exergue, 7.98g (Marsh 174; MCE 621; S 3969). *A few very light marks on obverse, tiny spot above head and under neck, otherwise mint state.* £300-350

Price Realised : £408

Calendar year mintage 4,737,796
We can assume that all of this output from the Mint will be 1902 dated coin of the new King. A very high output occurs the next year too, of which it can be assumed that many 1902 dated coins would be included, no doubt struck into the early part of the calendar year before the 1903 dated coins took over.

347 **Edward VII,** Sovereign, 1903, bare head facing right, *rev* St George slaying dragon with sword, date in exergue, 7.99g (Marsh 175; MCE 622; S 3969). *Lightly toned, three tiny digs over horse's lower front leg, other light bagmarks, otherwise good extremely fine.* £300-350

Price Realised : £408

ex Randy Weir Numismatics, Unionville, Ontario, undated invoice c.2000
Calendar year mintage 8,888,627

348 **Edward VII,** Sovereign, 1904, bare head facing right, *rev* St George slaying dragon with sword, date in exergue, 7.97g (Marsh 176; MCE 623; S 3969). *A few light bagmarks both sides and a light scratch behind head, otherwise good extremely fine.* £300-350

Price Realised : £336

ex Randy Weir Numismatics, Unionville, Ontario, Canada, purchased 2 June 1995
Calendar year mintage 10,041,369

349 **Edward VII,** Sovereign, 1904, off-centre striking, bare head facing right, *rev* St George slaying dragon with sword, date in exergue, 7.98g (Marsh 176; MCE 623; S 3969). *Struck off-centre 5% with excess metal on rim, short scratch over top leg of horse, some residual dirt on obverse rim, extremely fine and very rare.* £400-600

Price Realised : £624

ex St James's Auction 7, 8 February 2008, lot 682
Calendar year mintage 10,041,369
Mistakes do happen sometimes, especially in the years of high output, but are usually discovered and stopped from appearing in circulation, especially for a premium gold coin like the Sovereign. Such a misstrike is a very unusual occurrence.

350

351

352

350 **Edward VII,** Sovereign, 1905, bare head facing right, *rev* St George slaying dragon with sword, date in exergue, 7.98g (Marsh 177; MCE 624; S 3969). *Many light surface marks and nicks, extremely fine / good extremely fine.* £300-350

Price Realised : £384

ex Randy Weir Numismatics, Unionville, Ontario, Canada, purchased 23 April 1993
Calendar year mintage 5,910,403

351 **Edward VII,** Sovereign, 1906, bare head facing right, *rev* St George slaying dragon with sword, date in exergue, 7.98g (Marsh 178; MCE 625; S 3969). *Unevenly toned with some bagmarks, scuff by sword, good extremely fine.* £300-350

Price Realised : £336

ex An Important Collection of Gold Sovereigns 1816-2000, offered as one lot, Sothebys, 16-17 November 2000, lot 525 (part)
Calendar year mintage 10,466,981

352 **Edward VII,** Sovereign, 1907, bare head facing right, *rev* St George slaying dragon with sword, date in exergue, 8.00g (Marsh 179; MCE 626; S 3969). *Light surface marks, streak of tone above horse's head, nick on lance, extremely fine, reverse better.* £300-350

Price Realised : £288

ex Randy Weir Numismatics, Unionville, Ontario, undated invoice c.2000
Calendar year mintage 18,458,663
The highest output from the Mint of gold Sovereigns for 35 years at this time, the figure is nearly five million higher than 1872s record high.

353

354

355

353 **Edward VII,** Sovereign, 1908, bare head facing right, *rev* St George slaying dragon with sword, date in exergue, 7.98g (Marsh 180; MCE 627; S 3969). *Lightly toned with some surface marks, scratch on chin and nick on neck, spot on dragon's body, otherwise good extremely fine.* £300-350

Price Realised : £408

ex Randy Weir Numismatics, Unionville, Ontario, undated invoice c.2000
Calendar year mintage 11,729,006

354 **Edward VII,** Sovereign, 1909, bare head facing right, *rev* St George slaying dragon with sword, date in exergue, 7.99g (Marsh 181; MCE 628; S 3969). *Some nicks in obverse field, and surface marks, scratch on neck, otherwise extremely fine / good extremely fine.* £300-350

Price Realised : £288

ex Randy Weir Numismatics, Unionville, Ontario, Canada, purchased 12 November 1990
Calendar year mintage 12,157,099

355 **Edward VII,** Sovereign, 1910, bare head facing right, *rev* St George slaying dragon with sword, date in exergue, 7.98g (Marsh 182; MCE 629; S 3969). *Lightly toned, a few nicks and light surface marks, otherwise good extremely fine.* £300-350

Price Realised : £288

ex Randy Weir Numismatics, Unionville, Ontario, Canada, purchased 23 April 1993
Calendar year mintage 22,379,624
This mintage output for 1910 is the pinnacle of the reign of King Edward VII, the efficiency of the Mint and its striking machinery produced this highest output of the time, and never had consecutive years produced so many sovereigns. Higher outputs were still to come though in the reign of King George V.
King Edward VII died 6 May 1910.

The Reign of King George V (1910-1936)
House of Windsor

Born: 3 June 1865

Accession: 6 May 1910

Married: Mary of Teck, 6 July 1893

Coronation: Thursday, 22 June 1911, second Coronation as Emperor of India at the Delhi Durbar, Tuesday, 12 December 1911

Children: five sons, one daughter

Died: 20 January 1936, aged 70

The coinage of the reign of King George V features a bare head portrait of the King facing to the left by the Australian sculptor, Edgar Bertram Mackennal (12 June 1863 – 10 October 1931), whose initials appear on the truncation of the bust and with the titles GEORGIVS V D: G: BRITT: OMN: REX F: D: IND: IMP: Mackennal was famed for his artistic sculptures, but became more numismatically interesting, as the designer of the Olympic Medals for the London Olympic Games of 1908. This led to the commission for the Coronation Medallion for King George V, and he then successfully won the commission for the coinage and for postage stamp portraits. One other Royal commission was to design the tomb for King Edward VII at St George's Chapel, Windsor. He was also the first Australian citizen to be knighted, in 1921 and was admitted to the Royal Academy in 1922.

For the Sovereign the classic St George and dragon design continues engraved, after Pistrucci with his initials in the exergue, and amazingly still featuring the tiny WWP under the lance for William Wellesley Pole from his days of the Master-ship of the Mint circa 1820. Had the London Mint continued to produce gold Sovereigns from 1928, like some of the Colonial Mints did, then a smaller portrait of George V would no doubt have appeared as at Melbourne, Perth and Pretoria. More significantly, the reverses of these Colonial small head pieces are revised and the WWP initials disappear at last.

The Proof Sovereign of King George V for 1911

356 **George V (1910-1936),** Proof Sovereign, 1911, designed by Edgar Bertram Mackennal, bare head left, B.M. on truncation, toothed border and raised rim, GEORGIVS V D: G: BRITT: OMN: REX F: D: IND: IMP:, *rev* struck en médaille, engraved after Benedetto Pistrucci, St George slaying dragon with sword, helmet with three strand streamer, horse with long tail, ending in three strands, with one spur higher up at curve, broken lance on ground-line to left, *WWP* in relief under lance, date in exergue, tiny B.P. to upper right, finely toothed border within twin linear concentric circles and raised rim, edge milled, 7.98g, 21.9mm (WR 416; S 3996). *Black streak of tone on obverse and tiny spot on reverse, some hairlines with a red tone, otherwise mint state.* £500-600

Price Realised : £936

ex Spink and Son Ltd, August 2001
According to English Silver Coinage, 3764 proof sets were issued of one formation or the other, which included a proof gold Sovereign. Single coins may well have been available on request too, so the final figure could be around 4000 struck.
The reverse design continues from the reign of Edward VII still carrying the same outer border treatment as instigated in the reign of Queen Victoria.

357

358

359

357 **George V,** Sovereign, 1911, bare head left, *rev* St George slaying dragon with sword, date in exergue, 7.99g (Marsh 213; MCE 639; S 3996). *Slightly speckled, tiny piece of excess metal on rim below date, otherwise good extremely fine.* £300-350

Price Realised : £288

ex Randy Weir Numismatics, Unionville, Ontario, Canada, purchased May 1990
Calendar year mintage 30,044,105
Another record-breaking output year for the Mint appropriately for the first year of the new coinage of King George V.

358 **George V,** Sovereign, 1912, bare head left, *rev* St George slaying dragon with sword, raised die flaw in cloak and helmet streamer, flaw from lance to rim, date in exergue, 7.99g (Marsh 214; MCE 640; S 3996). *A few trifling nicks, otherwise uncirculated.* £300-350

Price Realised : £432

ex Randy Weir Numismatics, Unionville, Ontario, Canada, purchased May 1990
Calendar year mintage 30,317,921
This year represents the highest ever output of Sovereigns from the Royal Mint London, never equalled or bettered since.

359 **George V,** Sovereign, 1913, bare head left, *rev* St George slaying dragon with sword, date in exergue, 7.98g (Marsh 215; MCE 641; S 3996). *A couple of trifling bagmarks, otherwise good extremely fine.* £300-350

Price Realised : £432

This coin has been the longest owned piece in the collection bought c.1978
Calendar year mintage 24,539,672

360

361

362

360 **George V,** Sovereign, 1914, bare head left, *rev* St George slaying dragon with sword, date in exergue, 7.99g (Marsh 216; MCE 642; S 3996). *Very light cabinet friction, otherwise toned, as struck.* £300-350

Price Realised : £432

ex Randy Weir Numismatics, Unionville, Ontario, Canada, purchased 25 March 1992
Calendar year mintage 11,501,117
Mintage of gold still continued to be high even though World War I commenced during this year. Following the outbreak the Government issued Treasury banknotes to the value of Sovereigns and Half-Sovereigns ,which were convertible to gold on demand at the Bank of England. However the public were encouraged not to do this, as the gold was no doubt needed elsewhere for purchases of vital supplies from overseas.

361 **George V,** Sovereign, 1915, bare head left, *rev* St George slaying dragon with sword, date in exergue, 7.99g (Marsh 217; MCE 643; S 3996). *A few very light bagmarks, otherwise good extremely fine.* £300-350

Price Realised : £432

Calendar year mintage 20,295,280
This last very high mintage marks the end of higher production of gold at the Mint as Great Britain strengthened its reserves for payments under the duress of war. Most of the Sovereigns will not have been used by the public.
It is very interesting to note in the ten years from 1905 to 1915 Mint output was at its highest ever, and this total production was of a similar total of all the years from the Sovereign's inception, in 1817 until the previous record production total in 1872, a full 55 years of production.

362 **George V,** Sovereign, 1916, bare head left, *rev* St George slaying dragon with sword, date in exergue, 7.99g (Marsh 218; MCE 644; S 3996). *A few very light bagmarks and nicks, otherwise good extremely fine and rare.* £300-350

Price Realised : £720

ex Randy Weir Numismatics, Unionville, Ontario, Canada, purchased 18 September 1995
Calendar year mintage 1,554,120
Two years into war and still over one million Sovereigns were produced for the reserves of the Bank of England. Most of the 1916 issue and nearly all of the following 1917 issue were exported to America in lieu of payments. They were held probably at Fort Knox for many years until the USA passed the Gold Reserve Act at the time of the Great Depression in 1934, when all coin was converted to bars. See also footnote on lot 364.

The Extremely Rare George V 1917 London Mint Sovereign

363 **George V,** Sovereign, 1917, bare head left, B.M. on truncation, latter stop weak and smaller, toothed border and raised rim, GEORGIVS V D: G: BRITT: OMN: REX F: D: IND: IMP:, *rev* struck en médaille, St George slaying dragon with sword, horse with long tail, broken lance on ground-line to left, *WWP* in relief under lance, date in exergue, tiny B.P. to upper right, finely toothed border within twin linear concentric circles and raised rim, 7.99g (Marsh 219; MCE 645; S 3996). *Short scratch by mouth, nicks on neck and in field, other light bagmarks, otherwise extremely fine and one of the finest extant of this, the rarest London Mint Sovereign of the 20th Century.* £7000-8000

Price Realised : £13,200

ex Randy Weir Numismatics, Unionville, Ontario, Canada, purchased 29 January 1992
Calendar year mintage 1,014,714
Three years into war and still over one million Sovereigns were produced for the reserves of the Bank of England. Nearly all the 1917 issue were exported to America in lieu of payments and most were never seen by the public. They were held probably at Fort Knox for many years until the USA passed the Gold Reserve Act at the time of the Great Depression in 1934, when all coin was converted to bars. The only survivors we have today were those that ended up in overseas payment to other nations, other than the USA. See also footnote on lot 364.

364 **George V,** Sovereign, 1925, struck in the reign of George VI c.1949-1952, bare head left, B.M. recut on truncation, *rev* St George slaying dragon with sword, date in exergue, tiny B.P. very distinct to upper right, edge coarser milling with higher rims, 7.98g (Marsh 220; MCE 646; S 3996). *Toned, uncirculated.* £300-350

Price Realised : £312

ex Randy Weir Numismatics, Unionville, Ontario, Canada, purchased 23rd April 1993
Calendar year mintages: 1925 = 3,520,431; 1949 = 138,000; 1951 = 318,000; 1952 = 430,000
Total output dated 1925 = 4,406,431
When collectors started to collect the modern gold Sovereign just after World War II, the 1925 Sovereign was always a challenging coin to find, as its issue was for Bank of England gold reserves only. This, coupled with the Gold Standard Act of 1925 meant that the Treasury banknotes were no longer convertible to gold coin on demand, but the Bank was compelled to sell 400 ounce fine gold bars to any purchaser who asked for it at £3/17/10½d per ounce in legal tender money. This meant each bar would sell for £1560 and there was a demand as in 1929 and again in 1930 the Bank of England had to melt down a total of 91,350,000 Sovereigns from their stock, which no doubt included any 1916 or 1917 Sovereigns left and many other earlier dates or varieties.
The reissue of 1925 dated Sovereigns in the reign of George VI occurred because of a need for more coins in the gold reserve of the Bank of England. George VI dies were perhaps not used as the only issues of Sovereigns for the reign were commemorative patterns with plain edges in 1937 and so had never been authorised for currency, hence the 1925 George V designs were used again. These later coins eventually started to find their way into the hands of collectors and any premium on 1925 dated coins as a great rarity was soon eradicated.
The 1925 Sovereign as we have here has a high rim and recut initials on the truncation. If an original 1925 Sovereign could be found we would expect it to have a less prominent rim and shallower initials.
King George V died 20 January 1936. King Edward VIII ruled from this accession day until abdication, 11 December 1936, having never been crowned.

The Reign of King George VI (1936-1952)
House of Windsor

Born: 14 December 1895
Accession: 11 December 1936
Married: Lady Elizabeth Bowes-Lyon, 26 April 1923
Coronation: Wednesday, 12 May 1937
Children: two daughters
Died: 6 February 1952, aged 56

Thomas Humphrey Paget (September 1893-May 1974) was the designer of the coinage and postage stamps of not only King George VI but also for his elder brother King Edward VIII, who abdicated the throne in December 1936. Paget had prepared designs of Edward looking to the left like his Father King George V, therefore breaking with the tradition in place since the reign of Charles II, of succeeding monarchs facing in the opposite direction to their predecessor. He did not see why he should not face the same way as his Father, and seemed keen to break old-fashioned tradition when he could.

King George VI, was happy to follow the tradition of facing the opposite way to his predecessor on the coinage, and as Edward should have faced right he decided he would face left on his coinage. Gold coinage was no longer required for currency as Great Britain was no longer on the Gold Standard and so gold Five Pound, Two Pound, Sovereign and Half-Sovereign were only produced for the one occasion, the Coronation of 1937. The story of the design and gestation, to be struck as gold proof sets, was told in more detail in Baldwin's Auction 69, 3 May 2011, lot 754, where a matt proof gold set was sold. The Bentley Collection contains the other 1937 matt proof gold set in private hands, which is offered here.

Opportunity was also taken to recut a design after Pistrucci of the St George reverse, supposedly using the original matrix that was used for the gold Pattern Five Pounds of George III from dating to 1820, the main difference being that the WWP initials under the lance are now absent.

Extremely Rare George VI Matt Proof Coronation Gold Set, dated 1937

1233 **George VI (1936-1952),** Matt Proof Finish, Gold Set of Four Coins, dated 1937, consisting of Five-Pounds, Two-Pounds, Sovereign and Half-Sovereign, struck for photographic purposes at the Royal Mint, Tower Hill (London), with an experimental matt finish, each coin depicting bare head portrait of King George VI facing left, engraved by T Humphrey Paget, tiny HP below, legend in abbreviated Latin reads GEORGIVS VI D: G: BR: OMN: REX F: D: IND: IMP: and translates as "George VI, King of all the Britains, Defender of the Faith, Emperor of India", *rev* all struck with an "en médaille" die axis, each coin depicting St George slaying the dragon, after Benedetto Pistrucci, date in exergue with B.P. to upper right, all struck with plain edges in matt finished 22 carat gold (L&S 2; W&R 436 R6, 438 R7, 440 R7, 443 R7, *these coins illustrated*; K&M 858-861, *listed as unique*; S 4074-4077). *All in PCGS holders, graded PF64, matt finish applied individually to each coin, toned, as struck, one of only two complete sets in private hands, of the highest rarity.* (4) £60,000-80,000

Price Realised : £66,000

ex Goldberg Coin Auction 26, Hollywood, USA, 6 September 2004, lot 2296

Numismatic flash photography was still in its infancy c.1936, and accurate reproductions of the brilliant proof polished die designs for the new coinage of King George VI was impossible with the problems of reflection inherent in the metal. At that time the easiest way to achieve detailed photographic reproduction of the designs was to alter the surfaces of the subject matter to make them non-reflective to the latest flash photography method. For this reason, these experimental matt finish coins were produced from a sand-blasting process so that accurate photographic reproductions could be made to promote and display to the Press and to advertise the new coinage for sale to the Public. At the Royal Academy London it is a known fact that a matt gold set was displayed in the Summer Exhibition of 1937, part of a display of new Royal Mint product that occurred annually for many years after, but now sadly defunct. The matt finish coins were clearly suited to being viewed under the brilliant lighting of such a display, with no inherent reflections as would be experienced with brilliant proof gold coins. This matt sand-blasting solution was used again in the promotion and display of later sets in the reign of King George VI, first in 1950 to mark the Half Century, and then in 1951 for the Festival of Britain. The Royal Mint today confirm that 5501 gold sets were sold to the public, whether that figure includes the two matt gold sets is not confirmed but seems unlikely.

A H Baldwin & Sons Ltd, were privileged enough to have handled the other 1937 matt gold set in our Auction 69, 3 May 2011, lot 754, which sold for £108,000. That set was raw and ungraded, still in its original box with a photocopy of a Royal Mint letter. Please refer to that catalogue for a full write up of the history of that set which is also relevant to this set offered here. This is the only set so far graded by any commercial grading company.

365 **George VI,** Proof Gold Sovereign, 1937, by Thomas Humphrey Paget, bare head left, HP in relief below, GEORGIVS VI D: G: BRITT: OMN: REX F: D: IND: IMP:, finely toothed border within twin linear concentric circles and raised rim both sides, *rev* struck en médaille, by Benedetto Pistrucci, St George slaying dragon with sword, four strand streamer from helmet, no mane hair over rein hand, horse with long tail, ending in three strands, with one spur higher up at curve, broken lance on ground-line to left, date in exergue, tiny B.P. to upper right, edge plain, 8.00g (WR 439; S 4076). *Mint state with just a few hairlines.* £1500-1800

Price Realised : £1,920

ex Randy Weir Numismatics, Unionville, Ontario, Canada, purchased 6 February 1990

It is known that 5,501 gold Sovereigns were issued for the Coronation year.

King George VI died 6 February 1952 whilst his daughter Princess Elizabeth was away in Kenya.

The Reign of Queen Elizabeth II (1952-)
House of Windsor

Born: 21 April 1926

Accession: 6 February 1952

Married: Philip of Greece and Denmark, 20 November 1947

Coronation: Tuesday, 2 June 1953

Children: three sons, one daughter

Celebrating her Diamond Jubilee Year 2012

Queen Elizabeth II has ruled for sixty years in 2012 and is the second-longest reigning monarch in British history after Queen Victoria. If she rules beyond the 10 September 2015, Queen Elizabeth will become the longest reigning British monarch.

In her long reign Queen Elizabeth's coinage has been through several portrait changes, more so since decimalisation in February 1971. The scope of the Bentley Collection really ends at decimalisation with the more modern Sovereigns becoming perhaps too commemorative in their issue today. However the collection does include three coins of the "decimal" bust designed by Arnold Machin, two of which are of highest rarity.

The main portrait therefore present in the Bentley Collection is the young head type designed by Mary Gillick (1881 - 27 January 1965), the first woman sculptor to have an adopted design on a British coin. The master punch was engraved by Cecil Thomas, who designed the Coronation Crown of 1953. The young head portrait by Gillick continued on most issues until the 1967 dated coins, with one last final issue for a commemorative 1970 proof set. The Maundy coinage presented each Maundy Thursday continues to carry this young head portrait to the present time. It has become rather worn and touched up on the master tools and famously in 2002 when issued in gold for the Golden Jubilee proof sets, some of the Maundy Twopences literally had no nose on the portrait as the dies were engraved so weakly and shallow.

The first Sovereign of the reign was an excessively rare 1953 proof Sovereign as part of a set of record for Institutional collections only, consisting of a gold Five Pounds, Two Pounds, Sovereign and Half-Sovereign. One set was sold some decades ago by one of the Institutional owners, and has since been broken up into individual coins and sold, though the Bentley Collector has never had the opportunity to acquire one. At least two extra single proof Sovereigns are in private hands, though one of these was stolen and presumably melted many years ago. If one should ever come up for sale it would be one of the most valuable modern British gold Sovereigns.

Extremely Rare Proof Sovereign of Elizabeth II Dated 1957, Fine Milling

366 **Elizabeth II (1952-),** Proof Sovereign, 1957, designed by Mary Gillick, young laureate head right, tiny incuse M.G. on truncation, +ELIZABETH. II. DEI. GRATIA. REGINA. F: D:, finely toothed border within twin linear concentric circles and raised rim both sides, *rev* struck en médaille, engraved after Benedetto Pistrucci, St George slaying dragon with sword, three strand streamer from helmet, horse with long tail, ending with two finer strands, broken lance on ground-line to left, date in exergue, narrow tiny B.P. to upper right, edge finely milled, 7.97g (WR 449 R4; S 4124). *A few light surface marks, otherwise mint state and extremely rare.* £6000-8000

Price Realised : £9,840

These proof strikings were produced for special purposes as a matter of record or for presentation to very important persons. The 1957 issue is marked by very fine milling around the edge and lasts for this year only on the Sovereign.

367 **Elizabeth II,** Sovereign, 1957, by Mary Gillick, young laureate head right, tiny incuse M.G. on truncation, +ELIZABETH. II. DEI. GRATIA. REGINA. F: D:, finely toothed border both sides, *rev* struck en médaille, by Benedetto Pistrucci, St George slaying dragon with sword, horse with long tail, broken lance on ground-line to left, date in exergue, tiny B.P. to upper right, edge finely milled, 8.00g (Marsh 297; S4124). *A few light bagmarks, spot on T of obverse legend, good extremely fine.* £300-350

Price Realised : £264

ex Spink and Son Ltd, February 2005
Calendar year mintage 2,072,000

Extremely Rare Elizabeth II Specimen Satin Finish Sovereign, dated 1958

1234 Elizabeth II, Specimen Gold Sovereign, 1958, struck with a more uniform and textured matt finish, young laureate head right, designed by Mary Gillick, tiny incuse MG on truncation, +ELIZABETH. II. DEI. GRATIA. REGINA. F: D:, finely toothed border within twin linear concentric circles and raised rim both sides, *rev* struck en médaille, engraved after Benedetto Pistrucci, St George slaying dragon with sword, three strand streamer from helmet, horse with long tail, ending with two finer strands, broken lance on ground-line to left, date in exergue, narrow tiny B.P. to upper right, edge coarsely milled, 7.98g (Marsh -; WR -; S 4125). *As struck, unrecorded as a specimen and of the highest rarity.* £2500-3000

Price Realised : £6,720

This "specimen" finish Sovereign was located at A H Baldwin & Sons Ltd in May 2006
The finish on the coin is not dissimilar to other specimen strikings seen from the Colonial Mints, the 1911 Canada and 1918 India in the Bentley Collection.

Extremely Rare Proof Sovereign of Elizabeth II Dated 1958, Coarse Milling

368 **Elizabeth II,** Proof Gold Sovereign, 1958, designed by Mary Gillick, young laureate head right, tiny incuse M.G. on truncation, +ELIZABETH. II. DEI. GRATIA. REGINA. F: D:, finely toothed border within twin linear concentric circles and raised rim both sides, *rev* struck en médaille, by Benedetto Pistrucci, St George slaying dragon with sword, three strand streamer from helmet, horse with long tail, ending with two finer strands, broken lance on ground-line to left, date in exergue, narrow tiny B.P. to upper right, edge coarsely milled, 7.99g (WR 450 R4; S 4125). *Some light hairlines, otherwise mint state and extremely rare.* £6000-8000

Price Realised : £11,040

These proof strikings were produced for special purposes as a matter of record or for presentation to very important persons. The 1958 issue is marked by much coarser milling around the edge and continues for the rest of the pre-decimal Sovereigns.

369 **Elizabeth II,** Sovereign, 1958, young laureate head right, *rev* St George slaying dragon with sword, date in exergue, tiny B.P. to upper right, 7.99g (Marsh 298; S 4125). *A few light bagmarks and hairlines, good extremely fine.* £300-350

Price Realised : £264

ex Spink and Son Ltd, February 2005
Calendar year mintage 8,700,000

370 **Elizabeth II,** Specimen Gold Sovereign, 1959, struck with a more uniform and textured matt finish, young laureate head right, *rev* St George slaying dragon with sword, date in exergue, tiny B.P. to upper right, 7.99g (Marsh -; WR -; S 4125). *As struck and unrecorded as a specimen, of the highest rarity.* £3000-4000

Price Realised : £3,120

This "specimen" finish Sovereign was located at A H Baldwin and Sons Ltd in May 2006 after being looked after for some forty plus years, with many other unusual modern pattern and proof issues.
The finish on the coin is not dissimilar to other specimen strikings from the Colonial Mints, see the 1911 Canada and 1918 India Sovereigns.

Extremely Rare Elizabeth II Proof Sovereign, dated 1959

1235 **Elizabeth II,** Proof Gold Sovereign, 1959, designed by Mary Gillick, young laureate head right, *rev* struck en médaille, engraved after Benedetto Pistrucci, St George slaying dragon with sword, date in exergue, narrow tiny B.P. to upper right, edge coarsely milled, 7.98g (WR 451 R4; S 4125). *Practically as struck, mint state and extremely rare.* £6000-8000

Price Realised : £12,600

ex Dr Jacob Y Terner collection, Goldberg, Hollywood, USA, May 2003, lot 424, previously graded by PCGS as PF66 deep cameo
These proof strikings were produced for special purpose as a matter of record or for presentation to very important persons. The 1958 issue is marked by much coarser milling around the edge and continues for the rest of the pre-decimal Sovereigns.

371 **Elizabeth II,** Sovereign, 1959, young laureate head right, *rev* St George slaying dragon with sword, date in exergue, tiny B.P. to upper right, 7.99g (Marsh 299; S 4125). *A few light bagmarks, good extremely fine.* £300-350

Price Realised : £264

ex Spink and Son Ltd, February 2005
Calendar year mintage 1,385,368
For once it is known how much of this calendar year output was dated 1959 and how much was the overflow from 1958 due to the efforts of H G Stride in his co-authorship of the "History of the Gold Sovereign" with Sir Geoffrey Duveen. It turns out a mere 140 Sovereigns of this total were dated still as 1958 before the dies were changed over to 1959 dated coins.

372 **Elizabeth II,** Sovereign, 1962, young laureate head right, *rev* St George slaying dragon with sword, date in exergue, tiny B.P. to upper right, 8.00g (Marsh 300; S 4125). *A few light nicks and hairlines, rim nick on reverse, otherwise good extremely fine.* £300-350

Price Realised : £264

ex Spink and Son Ltd, February 2005
Calendar year mintage 3,000,000. The London calendar outputs from here onward are gleaned from Michael Marsh's *The Gold Sovereign*

373 **Elizabeth II,** Proof Gold Sovereign, 1963, designed by Mary Gillick, young laureate head right, tiny incuse M.G. on truncation, +ELIZABETH. II. DEI. GRATIA. REGINA. F: D:, finely toothed border within twin linear concentric circles and raised rim both sides, *rev* struck en médaille, engraved after Benedetto Pistrucci, St George slaying dragon with sword, three strand streamer from helmet, horse with long tail, ending with two finer strands, broken lance on ground-line to left, date in exergue, narrow tiny B.P. to upper right, edge coarsely milled, 8.01g (WR 452 R7; S 4125). *A few hairlines and some light speckling on reverse, otherwise mint state and extremely rare.* £6000-8000

Price Realised : £11,040

ex Dr. Jacob Y Terner collection, Goldberg, Hollywood, USA, 26-27 May 2003, lot 425 – previously graded as Proof 64 Cameo by NGC.
These proof strikings were produced for special purposes as a matter of record or for presentation to very important persons.

374 **Elizabeth II,** Sovereign, 1963, young laureate head right, *rev* St George slaying dragon with sword, date in exergue, tiny B.P. to upper right, 7.98g (Marsh 301; S 4125). *Spot on obverse legend, with a few light bagmarks, good extremely fine.* £300-350

Price Realised : £264

ex Spink and Son Ltd, February 2005
Calendar year mintage 7,400,000

1236 **Elizabeth II,** Sovereign, 1963, off-centre misstrike, young laureate head right, *rev* St George slaying dragon with sword, date in exergue, tiny B.P. to upper right, 8.00g (Marsh 301; S 4125). *Of slightly ovoid shape due to the misstrike, slight hairlines and tiny scratch under horse's front leg, obverse rim nick possibly caused by prising the coin off the die when the misstrike happened, spot on obverse and red tone, otherwise as struck and unusual.* £400-600

Price Realised : £1,980

ex Heritage auction, Long Beach Sale, 1 June 2006, lot 13179
Calendar year mintage 7,400,000

375 **Elizabeth II,** Sovereign, 1964, young laureate head right, *rev* St George slaying dragon with sword, date in exergue, tiny B.P. to upper right, 8.00g (Marsh 302; S 4125). *A few light bagmarks, light doubling of milling onto rim evident, good extremely fine.*
£300-350

Price Realised : £264

ex Spink and Son Ltd, February 2005
Calendar year mintage 3,000,000

Extremely Rare Elizabeth II Matt Proof Sovereign, dated 1965

1237 **Elizabeth II,** Matt Proof Sovereign, 1965, struck with a matt satin finish, young laureate head right, *rev* St George slaying dragon with sword, date in exergue, tiny B.P. to upper right, edge finely milled, 7.99g, 22.2mm (WR -; cf S 4125). *Bright frosted design, with satin matt fields, practically as struck and of the highest rarity.*
£8000-10,000

Price Realised : £14,400

ex Stacks, New York, 1 June 1997, lot 701
ex An Important Collection of Gold Sovereigns 1816-2000, offered as one lot, Sothebys, November 2000, lot 525 (part)
This coin was missed by the authors of *English Pattern, Trial and Proof Coins in Gold 1547-1968* when published in 2000. It is likely to be the only example in private ownership and should perhaps be rated R7 should it feature in any future edition or supplement.

376 **Elizabeth II,** Sovereign, 1965, young laureate head right, *rev* St George slaying dragon with sword, date in exergue, tiny B.P. to upper right, 7.99g (Marsh 303; S 4125). *A few light bagmarks, good extremely fine.*
£300-350

Price Realised : £264

ex Spink and Son Ltd, February 2005
Calendar year mintage 3,800,000

377 **Elizabeth II,** Sovereign, 1966, young laureate head right, *rev* St George slaying dragon with sword, date in exergue, tiny B.P. to upper right, 8.00g (Marsh 304; S 4125). *A few light bagmarks on obverse, good extremely fine.* £300-350

Price Realised : £264

ex Spink and Son Ltd, February 2005
Calendar year mintage 7,050,000

375

379

378 **Elizabeth II,** Sovereign, 1967, young laureate head right, *rev* St George slaying dragon with sword, date in exergue, tiny B.P. to upper right, 8.00g (Marsh 305; S 4125). *A few light bagmarks, good extremely fine.* £300-350

Price Realised : £264

ex Spink and Son Ltd, February 2005
Calendar year mintage 5,000,000

379 **Elizabeth II,** Sovereign, 1968, young laureate head right, *rev* St George slaying dragon with sword, date in exergue, tiny B.P. to upper right, 7.99g (Marsh 306; S 4125). *Some light bagmarks, extremely fine / good extremely fine.* £300-350

Price Realised : £264

ex Spink and Son Ltd, February 2005
Calendar year mintage 4,203,000

The Second Bust of Queen Elizabeth II

Decimalisation "D-Day" was 14 February 1971 and marked a change in the design of the coinage with new decimal reverses for the new denominations. A new obverse design of a more mature crowned portrait was also introduced. Arnold Machin (30 September 1911 - 9 March 1999) was the designer and also for the portrait upon the decimal stamps. His obverse lasted until 1984 dated coinage, 1985 marking the introduction of the portrait by Raphael David Maklouf. The Bentley collection is principally a pre-decimal Sovereign collection but does include a 1974 mistrike to be offered in part three, and the following two lots.

1238 **Elizabeth II (1952-),** Sovereign, 1974, struck without a retaining collar, designed by Arnold Machin, second crowned and draped bust right, ELIZABETH. II. DEI. GRATIA. REGINA. F: D:, finely toothed border within twin linear concentric circles and raised rim both sides, *rev* struck en médaille, engraved after Benedetto Pistrucci, St George slaying dragon with sword, horse with long tail, broken lance on ground-line to left, date in exergue, tiny B.P. to upper right, edge milled, 8.00g (S 4204). *Slightly ovoid in shape, light bagmarks on obverse, otherwise good extremely fine and highly unusual.* £300-400

Price Realised : £1,320

ex St James's Auction 4, 8 May 2006, lot 438

Unrecorded Pattern Elizabeth II 1976 Sovereign, One of Only Two in Existence

380 **Elizabeth II,** Pattern Sovereign, 1976, designed by Arnold Machin, experimental pattern struck with a totally brilliant finish without frosting, second crowned and draped bust right, ELIZABETH. II. DEI. GRATIA. REGINA. F: D:, finely toothed border within twin linear concentric circles and raised rim both sides, *rev* struck en médaille, engraved after Benedetto Pistrucci, St George slaying dragon with sword, horse with long tail, broken lance on ground-line to left, date in exergue, tiny B.P. to upper right, edge milled, 8.00g, 22.2mm (S 4204). *Brilliant mint state and one of only two specimens struck to proof quality with this brilliant finish, excessively rare.* £7000-9000

Price Realised : £19,200

ex Mark Rasmussen Numismatist via Spink and Son Ltd, May 2005
This intriguing coin has been seen and verified by the Royal Mint, though the letter from them has since gone astray. It basically confirmed that only two such coins were struck experimentally with a non-frosted finish to the design elements and legend. The other specimen of this is housed in the Royal Mint's own collection in Llantrisant in Wales. The only reference for this coin is the VIP Proof listing in the Spink Standard Catalogue, it only having come to light about 2004-2005.
The calendar year output for 1976 Sovereigns for currency is 4,045,056, a figure which probably includes this coin and the one in the Mint Collection.

381 **Elizabeth II,** Proof Sovereign, 1984, by Arnold Machin, with frosted design elements as usual, second crowned bust right, *rev* St George slaying dragon with sword, date in exergue, tiny B.P. to upper right, 7.99g, 22mm (S 4204). *Light thumbprint, otherwise practically as struck.* £300-350

Price Realised : £360

One of 12,880 issued, lacking certificate or box.
In modern decimal times the Mint has released figures of how many coins of a commemorative issue are actually "issued", rather than a calendar year output. These figures are useful, as often on certificates with these coins a "Limited Edition" figure is given which is the maximum number that could exist. The issue figure is often less than the limit of the edition, if an edition of coin is not a "sell-out"

Colonial Gold Issues

The entire Colonial branch mint section of the Bentley Collection is arranged in the chronological order of the opening of each branch of the Royal Mint. The exceptions to this being the Adelaide Pound token which pre-dates branch minting in Australia and the South African series of Ponds which are presented before the Imperial type George V South Africa Sovereigns. Additionally there are three Bombay mint (India), George V, 15-Rupee coins, dated 1918, which were issued in the same year as the Imperial type and whose face value directly equated with the gold sovereign at that time.

The running order for the Colonial section is as follows:-

AUSTRALIA
- Adelaide Pound type II 1852
- Sydney Branch Mint, "Australia" type reverse Sovereigns, first and second obverses 1855-1870
- Sydney Branch Mint, Imperial type Sovereigns from 1871 shield reverse followed by St George and dragon reverse to 1926
- Melbourne Branch Mint, Imperial type Sovereigns from 1872 shield reverse followed by St George and dragon reverse to 1931
- Perth Branch Mint, Imperial type Sovereigns 1899-1931

CANADA
- Ottawa Mint Imperial type Sovereigns 1908-1919

INDIA
- Bombay Branch Mint Imperial Sovereigns 1918 and companion 15 Rupee pieces dated 1918

SOUTH AFRICA
- President Thomas Burgers Ponds, Kruger type Ponds, Veldt Pond and varieties.
- Pretoria Branch Mint, Imperial type Sovereigns from 1923-1932

AUSTRALIA

References used in this section

McD Greg McDonald – *the Pocket Guide to Australian Coins and Banknotes*, 19th Edition 2012, valuations in Australian Dollars.

QM *The Quartermaster collection* – auction catalogue, 4 June 2009, issued by Monetarium (Australia) Pty Ltd, Kogarah, NSW, with expert cataloguing by Winsor & Sons of Jamberoo, NSW, Australia.

KM Krause and Mishler, valuations in American Dollars.

Fr Friedberg – *Gold Coins of the World,* valuations in American Dollars.

These are in addition to the Marsh and Spink references used in all sections of this catalogue.

Further Reading

The following publications have been consulted in relation to the Australian section in addition to those above:-

Coleman P Hyman, *An Account of the Coins, Coinages, and Currency of Australasia*, printed by Charles Potter, Sydney, 1893

Thomas Gill, *A Brief Sketch of the Coinage and Currency of South Australia*, printed by Vardon and Sons, Adelaide, 1912.

Dr Arthur Andrews, *Australasian Tokens and Coins, A Handbook*, published by William Applegate Gullick, 1921

J Hunt Deacon, *The "Ingots" and "Assay Office Pieces" of South Australia*, printed by the Hawthorn Press, Melbourne c.1955.

Robert L Clarke, *The Coins of British Oceania*, 2nd edition, 1964, South Pasadena, published by Dansco of Venice, California (USA) for American Collectors of Australian coins.

Captain J J Cullimore Allen, *Sovereigns of the British Empire*, published by Spink and Son, 1965

Royal Sovereign 1489-1989, edited by G P Dyer, published by the Royal Mint 1989

A Note on Grading

We wish to emphasise that the coins in this section have been graded according to strict British standards, which seem to compare differently to that used in Australia. This will become clear when coins with British grading here are actually nicer than a specimen in the Quartermaster collection which on the Australian system appears to be one whole grade higher. This occurs frequently and it would seem an Australian grading equivalent of the British standard is one grade step higher.

This is also demonstrated in the McDonald publication where valuations are quoted for three types of uncirculated coin, which is a direct reflection of the differing market-place between the UK and Australia for their collectible coinages. No UK coin catalogue has such degrees of valuation and the British standard prevails here with only one true grade of uncirculated. The grading of coins remains a subjective science especially when crossing to other continents.

SOUTH AUSTRALIA

The Adelaide Pound gold coin tokens issued by the South Australia Government Assay Office

Following the discovery of gold deposits at Ballarat in Victoria and near Bathurst in New South Wales, a gold rush caused the working man population of the townships of Southern Australia to deplete dramatically, leaving behind their businesses and families in the hope of striking it rich in the goldfields. This caused a massive drain on the economies of the towns as funds were withdrawn to finance travel and digging. Adelaide, the major town near the goldfields, suffered heavily with over half the male population effectively leaving town in a very short time and the town neared bankruptcy. However, gold mined from the fields began a sudden influx into the local economy as the first successful gold-diggers returned. A means of processing the gold was quickly required, preferably by refining and striking into coin. However the Lieutenant-Governor of South Australia, Sir Henry Young, knew a mint could not be set up without Royal approval from Great Britain and the logistics of obtaining such approval would take over six months with the distance involved. Sir Henry Young acted upon advice of George Tinline, the acting Manager of the South Australian Banking Company and the Colonial Treasurer, Robert Torrens about the understanding of a clause in the Bill affecting currency, which in part stated that "unless urgent necessity exists," effectively exposing a loophole in the Bill. This exploitation was used by the South Australian Legislative Council to pass the Bullion Act number 1, to produce gold ingots and later gold token coins.

Within hours of the Bullion Act being passed the Government Assay Office was set up and the refining of gold Ingots could commence. These excessively rare ingots were objects of necessity refined, weighed and stamped with the assay office hallmarks and their weight and fineness, a scant few survive today (Quartermaster collection lots 1 and 2 are two of a maximum of four examples in private hands). These ingots however did little to relieve the immediate problems in the town due to their variance in size, high value and the ease of which they could be faked. Criticism of the ingots by November of 1852 caused an amendment to be made to the Bullion Act authorising the issue of gold "coins" of Ten Shillings, One Pound, Two Pounds and Five Pounds, still without Royal approval and proclamation, therefore they were a token gold coinage. Dies were prepared by local die-sinker Joshua Payne for the Pound and Five Pound denominations and, by the time the amendments had been passed by the Council, coins had already been produced since late September. Payne probably also prepared the gold ingots that preceded the token coin issue.

The very first die for the gold pound failed after maybe no more than 30 strikes, but perhaps as many as 50, having seemingly started to crack as soon as the first piece was struck. No examples of the type one Pound are known today without some sign of the die crack and are of the highest rarity; the Bentley Collection does not contain an example of this coveted piece.

The Five Pound coin dies were purportedly used to strike six specimens and this is mentioned is sources as early as Hyman in 1893, however no survivors are known of these early pieces. The only Five Pound Adelaide gold tokens were six gold restrikes made from the dies in 1919 and a further one in 1929 for the National Gallery of South Australia. If an original Five Pound should ever turn up it would be a numismatic dream coin as would be a type I Pound with no sign of the die crack (perhaps the first coin struck).

The type II Pounds were struck more successfully in a larger quantity and were a great relief to the economy of Adelaide, but not many survive today and most that do have been mounted for jewellery. Minting had finished in February 1853 when nearly 25,000 had been struck. However, locals found the gold within the coin token was actually worth more than the face value and so many found their way at the time to the melting pot. The shortage of gold coin began to be relieved at this time as the Bank of New South Wales had placed a regular order of 3,000 sovereigns a month in London from August 1851, boosted to 50,000 a month in August 1852, with two special orders in the interim of 250,000 sovereigns each. The time of each order being placed until physical delivery would have been many months.

Royal disapproval followed by November 1853 and a great quantity of British gold Sovereigns were sent to circulate within the town to further alleviate any economic problems, probably from the quantities being supplied to the Bank of New South Wales.

Sir Henry Young went on to be Governor of Tasmania from 1854 and retired from that position in 1861. Robert Torrens who had suggested production of ingots initially was later knighted. George Tinline was awarded a solid gold plate and £2,500 for his effort and advice.

The legacy we have today are some very important gold Pound tokens dated 1852, a type II of which is listed below.

Very Rare Type II Adelaide Gold Pound 1852

628 **Adelaide,** gold token for a Pound, struck in 22 carat gold alloyed with copper, 1852, 2 of date with curly top, crown over date, beaded circle surrounding with dentilated pattern, GOVERNMENT ASSAY OFFICE, rosette either side, ADELAIDE below, very faint toothed border both sides, *rev* struck en médaille, ONE at centre, VALUE above, POUND below, beaded circle surrounding with dentilated pattern, WEIGHT. 5 DWT: 15 GRS: surrounding, rosette either side, 22 CARATS. below, 2's have plain tops, edge is not completely milled in that the reeding does not fully traverse the entire edge, 8.44g (McD page 40; QM 23 R3; KM 2; Fr 3). *Some light die striations showing through on rims both sides, light surface marks, weak on high points, otherwise extremely fine and very rare.* £20,000-25,000

Price Realised : £25,200

ex Monetarium, Kogarah, NSW Australia, purchased 7 March 2003
Total mintage 24,768, according to Hunt Deacon, which may include type I. The type I dies cracked immediately on use and broke purportedly after 30-40 pieces were struck.
The full weight of an Adelaide type II Pound as quoted on the coin equates to 8.7478g
The McDonald catalogue for 2012 rates an EF quality type II Pound at a valuation of AU$52,000 (or £35,000)

SYDNEY

The Sydney Branch Mint

The need for a Mint to produce coin in Australia and convert the local gold from the goldfields, without sending out of the country, finally came to fruition when an Order of Council was issued and ratified in the presence of the Queen at Osborne House on the Isle of Wight, 19 August 1853. Application and legislation to reach this point had been underway since at least 1851 and what with the escapades of Adelaide it became more apparent for the need that led to the Order of Council and building of a Mint on the site of the Old Rum Hospital in Macquarie Street, Sydney. Designs, dies and pattern coins were produced dated 1853, an example of which can be seen as QM24 in the Quartermaster collection. The Sydney mint opened 14 May 1855 and the first type design from the 1853 pattern was adopted for currency.

The design of the Sydney Sovereigns was to be quite different from the Imperial British type, as the original intention was for them to be only legal tender within Australia. This changed with the Colonial Branch Mint Act of 1866, when they became legal tender in the UK and other colonies too, which led directly to the harmonisation of the Imperial type designs at the Sydney mint. The 1855-1868 yellow gold Sovereigns of the Sydney mint that were alloyed with silver were most popular in export trade with India, where they were more revered than the British Sovereign for their yellow colour, signifying the more valuable alloy with silver as opposed to the red gold colour of the British Sovereign alloyed with copper. This changed in 1868, the first step towards harmonisation of the types of denomination, when Sydney mixed copper in the alloy, rather than silver, making some of the 1868 dated issue and all for 1870 of the red gold colour.

When the Sydney mint ceased minting gold Sovereigns in 1926, the total number of all Sovereigns struck of both Australia and Imperial types from 1855-1926, according to *Sovereigns of the British Empire*, stood at 144,435,550. However, this total is 50,000 pieces higher than the individually quoted calendar year outputs in this publication by Capt J J Cullimore Allen. Presumably this is the result of human error in adding all the individual calendar year outputs, it being such a round figure.

The Reign of Queen Victoria (1837-1901)
House of Hanover

Born: 24 May 1819
Accession: 20 June 1837
Married: Albert of Saxe-Coburg and Gotha, 10 February 1840
Coronation: Thursday 28 June 1838
Children: four sons, five daughters
Died: 22 January 1901, aged 81

The First Type "AUSTRALIA" Sovereign

There are two types of obverse, the first was engraved by James Wyon and appears on coins dated 1855 and 1856 as well as the initial pattern of 1853 (see QM24).

The second type obverse was engraved by Leonard Charles Wyon and appears on a pattern of 1855 (see QM26) and currency from 1857-1870.

The reverse design was by Leonard Charles Wyon and was unchanged from 1853-1870.

A Brilliant Example of the Extremely Rare 1855 Sovereign

629 **Victoria (1837-1901),** Sovereign, Sydney Branch mint, 1855, engraved by Joshua Payne, obverse designed by James Wyon, first young head left, with double fillet, small date below, toothed border and raised rim both sides, VICTORIA D: G: BRITANNIAR: REGINA: F: D:, *rev* struck with inverted die axis, reverse designed by Leonard Charles Wyon, AUSTRALIA at centre, crown above, within laurel wreath tied with bow at bottom, SYDNEY MINT above, ONE SOVEREIGN below, edge milled, 7.98g (McD 102; QM 25 R3; Marsh 360 R; KM 2; Fr 9). *Some scuffs and bagmarks both sides, some burnishing in obverse field around nose and lips, down to the chin, otherwise brilliant good extremely fine and on par with the Quartermaster specimen, being more choice though a little more surface marked.* £20,000-25,000

Price Realised : £20,400

ex Winsor and Sons, Jamberoo, NSW Australia, purchased January 2005
Calendar year mintage 502,000
The McDonald catalogue for 2012 rates an AUNC quality 1855 Sovereign at a valuation of AU$110,000 (or £74,000)

A Very Pleasing Example of the Last Year of the First Type Sydney Sovereign

630 **Victoria,** Sovereign, Sydney Branch mint, 1856, engraved by Joshua Payne, obverse designed by James Wyon, first young head left, with double fillet, small date below, toothed border and raised rim both sides, VICTORIA D: G: BRITANNIAR: REGINA: F: D: some letters doubled in legend, *rev* struck with inverted die axis, reverse designed by Leonard Charles Wyon, AUSTRALIA at centre, crown above, within laurel wreath tied with bow at bottom, SYDNEY MINT above, ONE SOVEREIGN below, edge milled, 7.98g (McD 103; QM 27 R3; Marsh 361 R; KM 2; Fr 9). *Some light nicks and surface marks both sides, with a little patchy deposit remaining in legend, otherwise extremely fine and very rare.* £6000-8000

Price Realised : £7,680

ex Kurt Jaggard Coins, Sydney, Australia, purchased 23 August 2002
Calendar year mintage 981,000
The McDonald catalogue for 2012 rates an EF quality 1856 Sovereign at a valuation of AU$19,500 (or £13,100)

The Second Type "AUSTRALIA" Sovereign

The second incarnation of the Sydney mint Sovereign occurs in 1857 for currency after a pattern submitted by Leonard C Wyon dated 1855. It seems Leonard's Father, William Wyon, perhaps influenced this portrait's style of hair, as the gathered hair is very similar to that seen on the British Gothic Florin and Crown from 1847 onward.

The full description for a second type Sovereign of the Sydney mint is as follows

Victoria (1837-1901), Sovereign, Sydney Branch mint, 1870, engraved by Joshua Payne, designed by Leonard Charles Wyon, second young head left, with hair gathered and plaited, looping under the ear and entwined into a looped bun at rear, wreath of banksia in hair, date below, toothed border and raised rim both sides, VICTORIA D: G: BRITANNIAR: REG: F: D:, *rev* struck with inverted die axis, AUSTRALIA at centre, crown above, within laurel wreath tied with bow at bottom, SYDNEY MINT above, ONE SOVEREIGN below, edge milled

A Pleasing Example of the First Year of the Second Type of Sydney Mint Sovereign

631 **Victoria,** Sovereign, Sydney Branch mint, 1857, second young head left, with hair gathered and plaited, wreath of banksia in hair, date below, legend surrounding with toothed border and rim, *rev* AUSTRALIA at centre, crown above, within laurel wreath tied with bow at bottom, SYDNEY MINT above, ONE SOVEREIGN below, edge milled, 7.99g (McD 104; QM 29 R3; Marsh 362 R; KM 4; Fr 10). *Once polished with associated light hairlines, otherwise a pleasing coin, good extremely fine and very rare.* £6000-8000

Price Realised : £6,480

ex Noble Numismatics, direct purchase, 16 January 2003
Calendar year mintage 449,000

Weak letter T in MINT on Reverse Sovereign of 1857

632 **Victoria,** Sovereign, Sydney Branch mint, 1857, second young head left, with wreath of banksia in hair, date below, letter F in legend slightly filled, *rev* crown and laurel wreath arranged around AUSTRALIA at centre, denomination below, legend above the word MINT with a very weak letter T, appears to read MIN, 7.96g (cf McD 104; QM 29 R3; Marsh 362 R; KM 4; Fr 10). *Scuffed with nicks and surface marks, otherwise very fine and very unusual.* £600-800

Price Realised : £624

ex Winsor and Sons, Jamberoo, NSW Australia, purchased c.2003
Calendar year mintage 449,000

A Well Preserved Example of the Extremely Rare 1858 Sovereign

633 **Victoria,** Sovereign, Sydney Branch mint, 1858, 5 die flawed closed, second young head left, with wreath of banksia in hair, date below, *rev* crown and laurel wreath arranged around AUSTRALIA at centre, denomination below, legend above, 7.97g (McD 105; QM 30 R3; Marsh 363 R; KM 4; Fr 10). *One light rim abrasion, other light bagmarks, otherwise toned, good extremely fine and pleasing, extremely rare.* £10,000-12,000

Price Realised : £9,600

ex Noble Numismatics, 25th Anniversary Sale 66, 28 March 2001, lot 1219
Calendar year mintage 1,101,500

634 **Victoria,** Sovereign, Sydney Branch mint, 1859, second young head left, with wreath of banksia in hair, date below, doubled date and legend, *rev* crown and laurel wreath arranged around AUSTRALIA at centre, denomination below, legend above, 7.99g (McD 106; QM 31 R2; Marsh 364; KM 4; Fr 10). *Some light surface marks and scuffing both sides, retaining mint brilliance and lustre, almost extremely fine / extremely fine and rare.* £1000-1500

Price Realised : £960

ex Monetarium, Kogarah, Australia, purchased 17 March 2003
Calendar year mintage 1,050,500

normal date

635 **Victoria,** Sovereign, Sydney Branch mint, 1860, clear open 6, second young head left, with wreath of banksia in hair, date below, *rev* crown and laurel wreath arranged around AUSTRALIA at centre, denomination below, legend above, 7.98g (McD 107; QM 32 R3; Marsh 365 R; KM 4; Fr 10). *Some light bagmarks, extremely fine / good extremely fine and rare.* £1000-1500

Price Realised : £9,600

ex Reserve Bank of Australia holdings via Winsor and Sons, Jamberoo, NSW Australia c.2003
Calendar year mintage 1,573,500

filled "6" in date

636 **Victoria,** Sovereign, Sydney Branch mint, 1860, slightly filled loop on 6, second young head left, with wreath of banksia in hair, date below, *rev* crown and laurel wreath arranged around AUSTRALIA at centre, denomination below, legend above, 7.99g (cf McD.107; QM 32 R3; Marsh 365 R; KM 4; Fr 10). *Heavily scuffed with surface marks, good fine.* £400-500

Price Realised : £504

ex Reserve Bank of Australia holdings via Winsor and Sons, Jamberoo, NSW Australia c.2003
Calendar year mintage 1,573,500

The Only Known High Grade Specimen of the 60 over 59 Dated Sydney Sovereign

"60" struck over "59"

637 **Victoria,** Sovereign, Sydney Branch mint, 1860, 60 struck over 59, second young head left, with wreath of banksia in hair, date below, *rev* crown and laurel wreath arranged around AUSTRALIA at centre, denomination below, legend above, 8.01g (McD 107a this coin illustrated p.57; QM-; Marsh -, KM 4; Fr 10). *Some light scuffing mainly on reverse, scratched by crown, otherwise good extremely fine and of the highest rarity.* £15,000-18,000

Price Realised : £16,800

ex Winsor and Sons, Jamberoo, NSW Australia, purchased c.2003
This is the plate coin in the McDonald catalogue, which suggests this is the highest grade example known and, possibly, the only example known.
Calendar year mintage 1,573,500
The McDonald catalogue for 2012 rates this coin as UNC at a valuation of AU$52,000 (or £35,000)

638 **Victoria,** Sovereign, Sydney Branch mint, 1861, second young head left, with wreath of banksia in hair, date below, doubled date with weakness to end of legend, *rev* crown and laurel wreath arranged around AUSTRALIA at centre, denomination below, legend above, NE of legend weaker than rest, 7.98g (McD 108; QM 33 R2; Marsh 366; KM 4; Fr 10). *Some light surface marks, retaining mint lustre, extremely fine / good extremely fine and very rare.* £1000-1500

Price Realised : £2,040

ex Winsor and Sons, Jamberoo, NSW Australia, purchased c.2003
Calendar year mintage 1,626,000

639 **Victoria,** Sovereign, Sydney Branch mint, 1861, with off-centre die axis, second young head left, with wreath of banksia in hair, date below, *rev* die axis slightly off-centre by a few degrees, crown and laurel wreath arranged around AUSTRALIA at centre, denomination below, letter V over a higher V, legend above, 7.97g (cf McD.108; QM 33 R2; Marsh 366; KM 4; Fr 10). *Some surface marks and digs, toned almost extremely fine and unusual.* £400-600

Price Realised : £624

Calendar year mintage 1,626,000

The Very Rare 1861 over-date Sovereign with 1 struck over 0

"1" struck over "0" in date

640 **Victoria,** Sovereign, Sydney Branch mint, 1861, 1 of date over 0 second young head left, with wreath of banksia in hair, date below, die flaw from second A of legend, *rev* crown and laurel wreath arranged around AUSTRALIA at centre, denomination below, legend above, 7.97g (McD 108a; QM 34 R6; Marsh -; KM 4; Fr 10). *Rim nick, some surface marks and digs, similar looking grade to Quartermaster specimen, though more surface marked, very fine and very rare, not many specimens extant.* £3000-4000

Price Realised : £3,120

Calendar year mintage 1,626,000
The McDonald catalogue for 2012 rates a VF quality 1 over 0 Sovereign at a valuation of AU$8,100 (or £5,400) with EF at $16,500 (or £11,000)

641 **Victoria,** Sovereign, Sydney Branch mint, 1862, second young head left, with wreath of banksia in hair, date lightly doubled below, incomplete 6, last part of legend doubled and some words on reverse, *rev* crown and laurel wreath arranged around AUSTRALIA at centre, denomination below, last N disjointed, legend above, 7.99g (McD 109; QM 35 R3; Marsh 367; KM 4; Fr 10). *A few light nicks and surface marks, light scratch in obverse field, retaining brilliance and lustre, otherwise extremely fine.* £2000-2500

Price Realised : £1,980

ex Noble Numismatics, Sale 66, 28 March 201, lot 1229
Calendar year mintage 2,477,500

hooked "6"

642 **Victoria,** Sovereign, Sydney Branch mint, 1863, second young head left, with wreath of banksia in hair, date below, hooked 6 without bulb at top, die flawed shut, no left serifs to second R in legend, last I struck over another I, *rev* crown and laurel wreath arranged around AUSTRALIA at centre, denomination below, legend above, some doubling in legend, 7.98g (McD 110; QM 36 R2; Marsh 368; KM 4; Fr 10). *Rim nick below date, some light surface marks and scuffs, otherwise nearly extremely fine.* £800-1000

Price Realised : £768

ex Noble Numismatics, direct purchase, 16 January 2003
Calendar year mintage 1,255,500

643 **Victoria,** Sovereign, Sydney Branch mint, 1863, second young head left, with wreath of banksia in hair, date below, hooked 6 without bulb at top, incomplete bottom serifs on second and third letter I's in legend, *rev* crown and laurel wreath arranged around AUSTRALIA at centre, denomination below, incomplete letter G, legend above, 7.97g (McD 110; QM 36 R2; Marsh 368; KM 4; Fr 10). *Rim nick on reverse, some light surface marks and heavier scuffs, some residual dirt, otherwise good fine and unusual.* £300-400

Price Realised : £288

ex A H Baldwin & Sons Ltd, purchased 13 April 2010
Calendar year mintage 1,255,500

644 **Victoria,** Sovereign, Sydney Branch mint, 1864, second young head left, with wreath of banksia in hair, date below, incomplete hooked 6, 8 doubled, *rev* crown and laurel wreath arranged around AUSTRALIA at centre, denomination below, incomplete letter G, legend above, die flaw across top of letters in SYDNEY, 7.99g (McD 111; QM 37 S; Marsh 369; KM 4; Fr 10). *Some scuffs and light digs with surface marks, otherwise extremely fine.* £500-600

Price Realised : £600

ex Randy Weir Numismatics, Unionville, Ontario, Canada, purchased 9 June 1993
Calendar year mintage 2,698,500

645 **Victoria,** Sovereign, Sydney Branch mint, 1865, second young head left, with wreath of banksia in hair, date below, curvy 6 with bulb top, *rev* crown and laurel wreath arranged around AUSTRALIA at centre, denomination below, legend above, 7.95g (McD 112; QM 38 R2; Marsh 370; KM 4; Fr 10). *Light scratch under N on reverse, lightly scuffed with surface marks, proof-like fields, good extremely fine, practically as struck.* £4000-5000

Price Realised : £4,560

ex Randy Weir Numismatics, Unionville, Ontario, Canada, purchased 17 March 1992
Calendar year mintage 2,130,500

646 **Victoria,** Sovereign, Sydney Branch mint, 1865, off-centre die-axis, second young head left, with wreath of banksia in hair, date below, *rev* die axis off by about 100 degrees, crown and laurel wreath arranged around AUSTRALIA at centre, denomination below, legend above, 7.94g (cf McD.112; QM 38 R2; Marsh 370; KM 4; Fr 10). *Heavily scuffed, almost fine to fine and unusual.* £300-400

Price Realised : £408

Calendar year mintage 2,130,500

The 1865 with "5" Struck Over "4" - One of Only Two Specimens Known

"5" struck over "4" in date

647 **Victoria,** Sovereign, Sydney Branch mint, 1865, with 5 struck over 4, second young head left, with wreath of banksia in hair, date below, last words of legend doubled, *rev* crown and laurel wreath arranged around AUSTRALIA at centre, denomination below, legend above, 7.95g (McD 112a; QM 39 R7; Marsh -; KM 4; Fr 10). *Heavy scuffs and surface marks, bold fine and one of only two specimens known, of highest rarity thus.* £4000-5000

Price Realised : £4,080

ex Reserve Bank of Australia holdings, direct purchase via Winsor and Sons, Jamberoo, Australia, 17 August 2005
Calendar year mintage 2,130,500. The McDonald catalogue for 2012 rates this coin as VF at a valuation of AU$11,750 (or £7,850)

648 **Victoria,** Sovereign, Sydney Branch mint, 1866, second young head left, with wreath of banksia in hair, date below, die flawed curvy 6's with bulbed tops, die flaw in REG: F:, the latter letter flawed to rim, *rev* crown and laurel wreath arranged around AUSTRALIA at centre, denomination below, legend above, 8.00g (McD 113; QM 40 S; Marsh 371; KM 4; Fr 10). *Light scuffs and surface marks, scratch in obverse field, good extremely fine and very pleasing.* £2000-2500

Price Realised : £2,760

ex Randy Weir Numismatics, Unionville, Ontario, Canada, purchased 17 March 1992
Calendar year mintage 2,911,000

649

650

649 **Victoria,** Sovereign, Sydney Branch mint, 1866, off-centre die-axis, second young head left, with wreath of banksia in hair, date below, curvy 6's with bulbed tops, *rev* die axis off by about 135 degrees, crown and laurel wreath arranged around AUSTRALIA at centre, denomination below, legend above, doubled DN in legend, 7.98g (cf McD.113; QM 40 S; Marsh 371; KM 4; Fr 10). *Some scuffs and digs, surface marks, toned very fine / good very fine and unusual.* £500-600

Price Realised : £552

ex Kurt Jaggard Coins, Sydney, Australia, purchased 30 May 2002
Calendar year mintage 2,911,000

650 **Victoria,** Sovereign, Sydney Branch mint, 1867, second young head left, with wreath of banksia in hair, date below, *rev* crown and laurel wreath arranged around AUSTRALIA at centre, denomination below, with incomplete letter E and N, legend above, with N doubled, 8.00g (McD 114; QM 41 S; Marsh 373; KM 4; Fr 10). *Light scuffs and surface marks, extremely fine, reverse better.* £1000-1500

Price Realised : £1,680

ex Kurt Jaggard Coins, Sydney, Australia, purchased 23 August 2002
Calendar year mintage 2,370,000

651

652

651 **Victoria,** Sovereign, Sydney Branch mint, 1868, struck in 22 carat gold alloyed with 8.33% silver, second young head left, with wreath of banksia in hair, date below, 6 flawed, *rev* crown and laurel wreath arranged around AUSTRALIA at centre, denomination below, legend above, legend with some doubling, 7.99g (McD 115; QM -; Marsh 373; KM 4; Fr 10). *A few very light marks, with yellow colour from the silver alloy, otherwise as struck and proof-like, very rare, the Quartermaster collection did not contain an example.* £2000-2500

Price Realised : £2,880

ex Winsor and Sons, Jamberoo, NSW Australia, purchased c.2005
Calendar year mintage 2,319,000 to which should be added that for calendar year 1869 of 1,202,000
The Sydney mint type Sovereigns are all struck in 22 carat gold and usually alloyed with 8.33% silver as demonstrated here. For an example of an 1868 Sovereign alloyed with copper and further information, see the next lot.

652 **Victoria,** Sovereign, Sydney Branch mint, 1868, struck in 22 carat gold alloyed with 8.33% copper, second young head left, with wreath of banksia in hair, date below, 6 flawed shut, light raised flaw in last two letters of legend, *rev* crown and laurel wreath arranged around AUSTRALIA at centre, denomination below, legend above, light raised flaws in some letters of legend with doubling, 8.00g (McD 115a; QM 43 S; Marsh 373; KM 4; Fr 10). *A few very light scuffs and surface marks, with red colour from the copper alloy, good extremely fine.* £1500-2000

Price Realised : £2,160

ex Winsor and Sons, Jamberoo, NSW Australia, purchased c.2005
Calendar year mintage 2,319,000 to which should be added that for calendar year 1869 of 1,202,000
The Sydney mint type Sovereigns are all struck in 22 carat gold and usually alloyed with 8.33% silver. The only variation to copper alloy is this 1868 issue coin and the issue of 1870. The cataloguer suspects that the copper alloy pieces were struck later than the silver alloy pieces. There are no known 1869 dated Australia Sovereigns though McDonald has a reference number 116 waiting in case one exists and Marsh has number 374. As the 1870 coins are alloyed with copper, this 1868 copper alloyed piece must have immediately preceded these and succeeded the silver alloy pieces. It might not be as clear cut as saying calendar year 1868 mintage was silver alloy and calendar year 1869 produced 1868 dated copper alloy coins, but it seems this would be the order of production.

A Superb 1870 Australia Sovereign

653 **Victoria,** Sovereign, Sydney Branch mint, 1870, struck in 22 carat gold alloyed with 8.33% copper, second young head left, with wreath of banksia in hair, date below, wispy raised flaw in legend and date, *rev* crown and laurel wreath arranged around AUSTRALIA at centre, denomination below, legend above, last N with incomplete limb, legend with doubling, 8.00g (McD 117; QM 44 S; Marsh 375; KM 4; Fr 10). *Tiny rim nick on obverse, otherwise as struck, with a brilliant red hue, very pleasing.* £2000-2500

Price Realised : £2,280

ex Noble Numismatics Sale 66, 28 March 201, lot 1344
Calendar year mintage 1,220,000

Imperial Type Sovereigns in Australia

With the very significant Coinage Act of 1870 in Great Britain came a sweeping change to harmonise the design of the coins minted from the Australian output of gold with that produced from the Royal Mint in London. The fact that the Australia design coins were legal tender only within Australia for their formative years had obviously affected export trade. The Colonial Branch Act of 1866 had made the Australia type coins legal tender in the UK and in trade, useful especially with closer neighbours in India and Asia. However the British Imperial gold Sovereign was already a respected trade coin with its shield reverse and more acceptable than the Australia type coins. This is what led to the design harmonisation as governed by the Act of 1870.

As briefly mentioned already in this catalogue (see page 204), the new third young head design was adopted from 1870 on British Sovereigns. This obverse, coupled with the shield reverse design, was deemed by the Act to be used at the Colonial branch mints in Sydney and the new Melbourne mint, which was being constructed and was hoped to be ready for operation in 1871. In fact it was 1872 before the Melbourne mint could start its operation and for further information about Melbourne please see the introduction before lot 744.

The Colonial branch Mints would add their own die letter beneath the shield design, under the junction of the laurel wreath. From 1871 the resurrection of the St George and dragon reverse Sovereigns occurred in Great Britain and at the Sydney mint, the latter having a letter S under the bust. Melbourne mint produced this reverse from 1872 and both of these branch mints struck both types of reverse for most years with the young head until 1887. The shield design was retained at the Australian branch mints as it was still the preferred coin in trade with India and Asia, while the St George reverse was preferred domestically. The mints were given the choice of which to strike according to demand, which is why some years do not exist for certain reverse types.

According to the publication *Royal Sovereign*, a Chinese General, Wong Yung Ho, visited the Melbourne mint in 1887 and confirmed that the shield design was preferred by the Indians when trading with the Orient. The Indians feared they would upset the Chinese if they paid for their wares with the St George reverse coin. This was because of the humiliating position of the Chinese national symbol the dragon under the horseman and therefore this reverse design was not generally seen in commerce in Asia.

The Quartermaster collection, sold in June 2009, with expert cataloguing by now retired dealer Barrie Winsor and Tony Richardson, revealed with detailed illustration for the first time in print the bust variations used on Australian shield reverse Sovereigns of Sydney and Melbourne. The 1871 S with WW incuse using the older style second type young head in the London series, with the subsequent third head style as mentioned previously in use on WW relief shield sovereigns from 1871 to 1880 at Sydney, with one further issue in 1882 and from 1872 to 1880 at Melbourne. However the Quartermaster collection transposes the naming of these busts, compared to that with which we are familiar in the British series. What is without doubt is that there is also a fourth bust variation with a higher hairline on the forehead, extra long hair behind the ear and variation again in the hair bun, which was used at Sydney and Melbourne from 1881 to 1887 and is illustrated and explained before the relevant lots. Additionally this bust was used on rare pattern or proof sovereigns of 1886 and 1887 without mint letter produced at the Royal Mint in London.

Sovereigns were produced for most years from 1855 to 1926 in one variety or another. The Half Sovereign was produced from 1855 too, and were last produced dated 1915.

The Bentley collection contains currency examples of all the known dates and practically all the reverse combinations, along with the sub-varieties known.

Sydney Mint Imperial Type Victoria Young Head Sovereigns, Shield Reverse

The full description for the majority of young head shield reverse Sovereign of the Sydney mint follows:-

Victoria (1837-1901), Sovereign, Sydney Branch mint, 1877 S, engraved after William Wyon, third young head style left, with double fillet, W.W. in relief on truncation, date below, toothed border and raised rim both sides, VICTORIA DEI GRATIA, *rev* struck with inverted die axis, engraved after Jean Baptiste Merlen, crowned quartered shield of arms within laurel wreath, tied with bow below shield, narrow crown arches not so acutely angled, each with eleven pearl adornment, five pearls vertically arranged on central upright, wreath of 24 leaves each side, each terminate with two leaves at top, seven harp strings in taller Irish arms, first left string from scroll at back of female figure, emblems below, small rosette either side, BRITANNIARUM REGINA FID: DEF: Mint letter M below, emblems below, edge milled

Abbreviated descriptions of the Sydney Sovereigns based on that above, follow here, the first coin of 1871 is somewhat different to the majority as demonstrated below.

The Initial Imperial Type Sovereign of the Sydney Mint

654 **Victoria (1837-1901),** Sovereign, 1871 S, young head left, the same as used in the second bust at the Royal Mint London, wide rear hair fillet with bottom line defined by a raised line, ww incuse without stops on truncation, date below, letter V slightly filled, raised die flaw from neck to rim to left of date, some light die flaws in legend both sides, *rev* crowned quartered shield of arms within laurel wreath, mint letter S below, emblems below, hint of doubling in legend, 7.99g (McD 118b; QM 46 S; Marsh 69; KM 6; Fr 11; S 3855). *Toned with some light surface marks, otherwise good extremely fine, on par with the Quartermaster collection example.* £400-600

Price Realised : £960

ex Kurt Jaggard Coins, Sydney, Australia, purchased 30 May 2002
Calendar year mintage 2,814,000 which includes St George reverse design pieces.
This obverse bust is the same as the second young head in the London series that was in use from 1848-1869. It is therefore a very late usage of this bust and the die may have been made much earlier than 1871 in anticipation of the new mint opening at Sydney, perhaps engraved during 1869 when this head was still in common use at the Royal Mint in London.

W.W. in relief truncation

655 **Victoria,** Sovereign, 1871 S, third young head left, more narrow rear hair fillet without defining line, w.w. in relief on truncation, date below, 7 over a lower 7, letter A's doubled, raised die flaw from D to rim and another from rim to neck at 1 of date, some die clashing evident with elements of reverse design showing as raised features on obverse, at bridge of nose and under chin, *rev* crowned quartered shield of arms within laurel wreath, mint letter S below, die flaw by mint mark and in parts of legend, 7.99g (McD 118a; QM 45 S; Marsh 69; KM 6; Fr 11; S 3855). *Toned with some light surface marks, otherwise good extremely fine and rare.* £400-600

Price Realised : £984

ex Randy Weir Numismatics, Unionville, Ontario, Canada, purchased 29 June 1990
Calendar year mintage 2,814,000 which includes St George reverse design pieces.

656 **Victoria,** Sovereign, 1872 S, third young head left, w.w. in relief on truncation, date below, raised die flaw from D to rim and C to rim, another from rim to neck at 1 of date, *rev* crowned quartered shield of arms within laurel wreath, mint letter S below, die flaw by mint mark and in parts of legend and wreath, 7.98g (McD 119; QM 47 S; Marsh 70; KM 6; Fr 11; S 3855). *Toned with some light surface marks, otherwise good extremely fine and scarce.* £400-600

Price Realised : £1,560

ex Kurt Jaggard Coins, Sydney, Australia, purchased 30 May 2002
Calendar year mintage 1,815,000 which includes St George reverse design pieces.

657 **Victoria,** Sovereign, 1873 S, third young head left, w.w. in relief on truncation, date below, raised die flaw at IA of queen's name, runs to rim from I, *rev* crowned quartered shield of arms within laurel wreath, mint letter S below, whole legend with light raised die flaws, 7.99g (McD 121; QM 50 S; Marsh 71; KM 6; Fr 11; S 3855). *Toned with some light surface marks, otherwise extremely fine / good extremely fine and scarce.* £400-600

Price Realised : £648

ex Randy Weir Numismatics, Unionville, Ontario, Canada, purchased 29 June 1990
Calendar year mintage 1,478,000 which includes St George reverse design pieces.

658 **Victoria,** Sovereign, 1875 S, third young head left, w.w. in relief on truncation, date below, *rev* crowned quartered shield of arms within laurel wreath, mint letter S below, 7.98g (McD 123; QM 52 S; Marsh 72; KM 6; Fr 11; S 3855). *A couple of tiny digs and some light surface marks, otherwise extremely fine / good extremely fine and scarce.* £400-600

Price Realised : £576

ex Randy Weir Numismatics, Unionville, Ontario, Canada, purchased 13 August 1992
Calendar year mintage 2,122,000 which includes St George reverse design pieces. There were no 1876 S Shield reverse sovereigns struck, only St George type.

low letter "S" touches rose

659 **Victoria,** Sovereign, 1877 S, third young head left, w.w. in relief on truncation, date below, die flaws in parts of last two words, penultimate I flawed to rim, *rev* crowned quartered shield of arms within laurel wreath, mint letter S below lower touching rose, some doubling in legend, 7.98g (McD 124; QM 53 S; Marsh 73; KM 6; Fr 11; S 3855). *Some light bagmarks, otherwise good extremely fine and scarce.* £400-600

Price Realised : £744

ex Randy Weir Numismatics, Unionville, Ontario, Canada, purchased 18 January 1990
Calendar year mintage 1,590,000 all shield type as no St George reverse was struck this year or the next.

660 **Victoria,** Sovereign, 1878 S, third young head left, w.w. in relief on truncation, date below, lightly die flawed, V slightly filled, *rev* crowned quartered shield of arms within laurel wreath, mint letter S below, 7.97g (McD 125; QM 54 S; Marsh 74; KM 6; Fr 11; S 3855). *Once polished with associated light surface marks, otherwise good very fine / extremely fine and scarce.* £300-400

Price Realised : £264

ex Randy Weir Numismatics, Unionville, Ontario, Canada, purchased 18 July 1990
Calendar year mintage 1,259,000 all shield type as no St George reverse was struck this year or the previous.

661 **Victoria,** Sovereign, 1878 S, third young head left, W.W. in relief on truncation, date below, die flaw like a stop after V of queen's name so it appears to read V.ICTORIA, *rev* crowned quartered shield of arms within laurel wreath, mint letter S below, 7.95g (cf McD.125; QM 54 S; Marsh 74; KM 6; Fr 11; S 3855). *Some light deposit around rim, light scuffs and surface marks, good fine and an oddity.* £300-400

Price Realised : £264

ex St James's Auction 6, 8 June 2007, lot 577
Calendar year mintage 1,259,000 all shield type as no St George reverse was struck this year or the previous.
The pellet type die flaw is reminiscent of some other similar varieties seen in the British series, most notably the O.NE Penny of 1897 which sells for quite a premium.

"S" struck over a higher "S"

662 **Victoria,** Sovereign, 1879 S, third young head left, W.W. in relief on truncation, date below, open C in queen's name, *rev* crowned quartered shield of arms within laurel wreath, mint letter S below, S appears to be over a higher S, 7.95g (McD 126; QM 55 S; Marsh 75; KM 6; Fr 11; S 3855). *Surface marks, good fine to almost very fine and unusual.* £300-400

Price Realised : £312

ex A H Baldwin & Sons Ltd, purchased November 2008
Calendar year mintage 1,366,000 which includes St George reverse design pieces.

so-called "C" over "O" variety

663 **Victoria,** Sovereign, 1879 S, so-called C over O variety, third young head left, W.W. in relief on truncation, date below, lightly die flawed, letter C in queen's name appears die flawed as does letter T, letter D and penultimate A both with die flaws to rim like the C, *rev* crowned quartered shield of arms within laurel wreath, mint letter S below, 7.99g (McD 126, note d and p.57; QM 56 R7; Marsh 75; KM 6; Fr 11; S 3855). *Light surface marks, good extremely fine and finer than the Quartermaster specimen which in 2009 was thought to be unique, this cataloguer has seen three specimens thus far, extremely rare variation of which this is the best that he has seen.* £1000-1500

Price Realised : £1,380

Calendar year mintage 1,366,000 which includes St George reverse design pieces.
This "variety" was catalogued in the Quartermaster collection for the first time and now appears in the McDonald publication as "two known" with a valuation in VF at AUD$9,500 (or £6,350). However, this cataloguer has seen three specimens. Rather than being a definite letter O under the C, it appears more likely that the C is die flawed closed as the raised die flaw continues from the top of the C to the rim. This is not the only letter to demonstrate a flaw from its top to rim as the dies were weakening and beginning to break down. The variety nevertheless is little known and seems to sell for a premium as an interesting variation to a normal 1879 S shield sovereign.

664 **Victoria,** Sovereign, 1880 S, third young head left, w.w. in relief on truncation, date below, lightly flawed on figure 1, letter G die flawed to rim, *rev* crowned quartered shield of arms within laurel wreath, mint letter S below, S flawed as is last letter D of legend, 7.99g (McD 127; QM 57 S; Marsh 76; KM 6; Fr 11; S 3855). *Light surface marks, extremely fine.* £300-400

Price Realised : £384

ex Noble Numismatics Sale 66, 28 March 2001, lot 1264
Calendar year mintage 1,459,000 which includes St George reverse design pieces.

The Extremely Rare Inverted A in VICTORIA 1880 Sydney Sovereign

inverted "A" for "V"

665 **Victoria,** Sovereign, 1880 S, inverted A for V in legend, third young head left, w.w. in relief on truncation, date below, some light die flaws in legend and date both sides, *rev* crowned quartered shield of arms within laurel wreath, mint letter S below, 7.99g (McD 127a; QM 58 R5; cf Marsh 76; KM 6; Fr 11; S 3855). *Light surface marks, brilliant good extremely fine and appears to be on par with the Quartermaster specimen of this great rarity.* £3000-4000

Price Realised : £7,200

ex Spink and Son, purchased 6 February 2002
Calendar year mintage 1,459,000 which includes St George reverse design pieces.
This is a genuine legend error and truly rare variety that is still only demonstrated by a few specimens. The engraver in haste, or due to lack of sharpness in eyesight or poor daylight, has clearly selected an A punch rather than a V when stamping in the letters onto the obverse die; or perhaps the correct punch could not be located in time. He and his superiors either did not notice or could not afford to waste a valuable die for a tiny error, the legacy of which has passed to us as an interesting true variety in the coinage of 1880. Similar inverted A for V varieties occur in the British Sovereign series too and it is one of the more spectacular variations that can occur on a coin and of great rarity.
The McDonald catalogue for 2012 rates this coin as AUNC at a valuation of AU$17,000 (or £11,350)

A New Style Portrait at the Sydney Mint

From 1881-1887, with the shield reverse, the fourth bust style comes into use at Sydney and at Melbourne. The main defining characteristics are the much higher hairline, which if extended up would meet the centre of the letter A in the legend. Behind the ear there is a distinctly longer curling strand of hair compared to those either side of it. The hair at the rear of the hair bun is perhaps a little finer engraved in the strands and there is a slightly larger gap from the G of legend to the hair bun. Additionally the tip of the neck at the front is more sharply pointed than the previous busts. Note that for 1882 dated shield reverse coins at Sydney that this new bust and the previous one exist together.

666 **Victoria,** Sovereign, 1881 S, fourth young head left, w.w. in relief on truncation which is more truncated with a pointed tip at front, hair behind ear with longer strand, hairline higher on forehead, date below, lightly flawed on figure 1 from neck to rim, last letter I die flawed to rim, *rev* crowned quartered shield of arms within laurel wreath, mint letter S below, 7.99g (McD 129; QM 60 S; Marsh 77; KM 6; Fr 11; S 3855). *Light surface marks, dusky tone, good extremely fine and scarce.* £300-400

Price Realised : £480

Calendar year mintage 1,360,000 which includes St George reverse design pieces.

667 **Victoria,** Sovereign, 1882 S, fourth young head left, w.w. in relief on truncation, date below, *rev* crowned quartered shield of arms within laurel wreath, mint letter S below, first letters R and E of legend die flawed, 7.97g (McD 131; QM -; Marsh 78; KM 6; Fr 11; S 3855). *Obverse rim nick and nick in cheek, otherwise extremely fine / good extremely fine and scarce.* £300-400

Price Realised : £384

ex Randy Weir Numismatics, Unionville, Ontario, Canada, purchased 18 July 1990
Calendar year mintage 1,298,000 which includes St George reverse design pieces.
It is interesting to note the Quartermaster collection did not contain an example of the newer portrait 1882 S shield sovereign QM62, by contrast the Bentley Collection does not contain the 1882 S shield with the earlier third head obverse, one of the few varieties not present in the Australian currency shield reverse series.

668 **Victoria,** Sovereign, 1883 S, fourth young head left, w.w. in relief on truncation, date below, *rev* crowned quartered shield of arms within laurel wreath, mint letter S below, low mint letter near rose, 7.97g (McD 133; QM 64 S; Marsh 79; KM 6; Fr 11; S 3855). *Struck from very yellow coloured gold, suggesting high silver content in the alloy, dig on 8 of date other light marks, otherwise good extremely fine and unusual, scarce.* £300-400

Price Realised : £408

ex Randy Weir Numismatics, Unionville, Ontario, Canada, purchased 31 July 1990
Calendar year mintage 1,108,000 which includes St George reverse design pieces.

669

670

669 **Victoria,** Sovereign, 1884 S, fourth young head left, w.w. in relief on truncation, date below, lightly die flawed date and legend both sides, *rev* crowned quartered shield of arms within laurel wreath, mint letter S below, 7.98g (McD 135; QM 66 C; Marsh 80; KM 6; Fr 11; S 3855). *Toned with light surface marks, good extremely fine and scarce.* £300-400

Price Realised : £552

Calendar year mintage 1,595,000 which includes St George reverse design pieces.

670 **Victoria,** Sovereign, 1885 S, fourth young head left, w.w. in relief on truncation, date below, lightly die flawed legend both sides, D flawed to rim, *rev* crowned quartered shield of arms within laurel wreath, mint letter S below, low mint letter near rose, 7.99g (McD 137; QM 68 S; Marsh 81; KM 6; Fr 11; S 3855). *Very attractive tone, some light bagmarks, otherwise practically as struck and scarce.* £600-800

Price Realised : £648

ex Randy Weir Numismatics, Unionville, Ontario, Canada, purchased 18 January 1990
Calendar year mintage 1,486,000 which includes St George reverse design pieces.

671

672

671 **Victoria,** Sovereign, 1886 S, fourth young head left, w.w. in relief on truncation, date below, lightly die flawed 6, last R flawed to rim, *rev* crowned quartered shield of arms within laurel wreath, mint letter S below, 7.99g (McD 139; QM 70 S; Marsh 82; KM 6; Fr 11; S 3855). *Light surface marks and hairlines, a few scratches on obverse, good extremely fine and scarce.* £400-500

Price Realised : £480

ex Randy Weir Numismatics, Unionville, Ontario, Canada, purchased 22 March 1990
Calendar year mintage 1,667,000 which includes St George reverse design pieces.

672 **Victoria,** Sovereign, 1887 S, fourth young head left, w.w. in relief on truncation, date below, lightly die flawed 7 to rim, *rev* crowned quartered shield of arms within laurel wreath, mint letter S below, 7.98g (McD 141; QM 72 S; Marsh 83; KM 6; Fr 11; S 3855). *Light surface marks and uneven tone, otherwise practically as struck and scarce.* £400-600

Price Realised : £1,920

ex International Acquisitions, Wellington, New Zealand, 22 January 2002
Calendar year mintage 1,000,000 which includes St George reverse design pieces.

Sydney Mint Imperial Type Victoria Young Head Sovereigns, St George and Dragon Reverse

The new St George and dragon reverse, a design resurrected from the reign of George IV, was introduced at Sydney in 1871 and Melbourne in 1872. Variation can occur in the portrait at the truncation, where the initials W.W. can either be "buried" within the truncation in relief without stops and therefore not fully apparent, or later versions which have the W.W. complete on truncation with stops and in relief.

The reverses show a lot more variation, only at Sydney the dates can appear to be more spread or closer in arrangement and the B.P. initials can vary in size. At both Sydney and Melbourne the initials can be complete or so incomplete that merely a trace exists. Some varieties have no trace of B.P. at all and the stop distances can vary too. Moving on from the exergue, St George can either have a cape with a complete hem line or some detachment. The dragon itself has varying claw arrangements between the upper and lower front arms both in number, shape and length, whether attached or not. Also earlier date coins have straighter claws, whereas some later dies have more curved claws. It is only from study of the Bentley collection herewith that the make-up of the die varieties has finally been determined.

The most major variation in the reverse designs is in the horse tails, till recently thought of as being either long tail or short tail. From research in the last decade in Australia and published properly in the Quartermaster collection catalogue, a so-called intermediate tail variety has become apparent. However from further study this cataloguer has determined that the medium tail should more correctly be termed a variation on the long tail specifically. It is evident that as the years passed by that the transfer from the master die of the St George long tail design became less well defined and the elements of the lowest strands of the tail and significantly the spur in the recess of the tail become much weaker. The lack of the strand terminals on the end of the tail make the distance from the lance larger, the hem of the cape on these pieces is less complete and the B.P. initials are also mere traces. The dragon claws can be more detached too, which explains why the short tail makes an appearance later as a new master die must have been employed. There are also two variations of the short tail design and the horse tail spurs, which can be thick or thin with single or multi-strands of hair. Some strands can curve either in towards or away from the main body of the tail. As mentioned above, the dragon will vary too in the claw arrangements, when there is a tail variation.

A full description of the St George reverse Sydney Sovereign is as follows

Victoria (1837-1901), Sovereign, 1871 S, young head of third style left, engraved after William Wyon, bound with two fillets, letter S below, WW buried in truncation in relief, VICTORIA D: G: BRITANNIAR: REG: F: D: finely toothed border within twin linear concentric circles and raised rim both sides, *rev* inverted die axis, engraved after Benedetto Pistrucci, St George slaying dragon with sword, dragon claws four to left and four to right arm, the second on upper arm detached, horse with long tail ending in three strands, upper curve of tail with one spur of hair, broken lance on ground-line to left, *WWP* in relief under lance, date in exergue, tiny B.P. to upper right, edge milled

Note that the hem of the cape of St George can be complete or a little disjointed too.

The One Year Only Type Large B.P. 1871 Sydney Sovereign

claws of 4/3 arrangement, short tail horse and wider date and large B.P.

673 **Victoria (1837-1901),** Sovereign, 1871 S, short tail horse, young head of third style left, letter S below close to neck, WW buried in truncation in relief, trace of top of another WW at bottom, some letter R's with lower serifs joined, *rev* St George slaying dragon with sword, dragon claws four to left and three to right arm, the first on lower arm detached, horse with short tail ending in three strands, no spur of hair at upper curve of tail, date in exergue, widely spaced the 8 higher than rest, large B.P. to upper right, 7.98g (McD 143; QM 74 S; Marsh 110A; KM 7; Fr 15; S 3858). *Some light bagmarks, very fine and scarce, appears to compare well with the Quartermaster coin.* £300-400

Price Realised : £552

ex Winsor and Sons, Jamberoo, NSW Australia, purchased January 2005
Calendar year mintage 2,814,000 which includes shield reverse design pieces.
The large B.P. variety only occurs at Sydney mint for this date, it is a one year only type, and is in combination with a more spread date. The obverse has a more defined WW buried in the truncation with a trace of another lower WW.

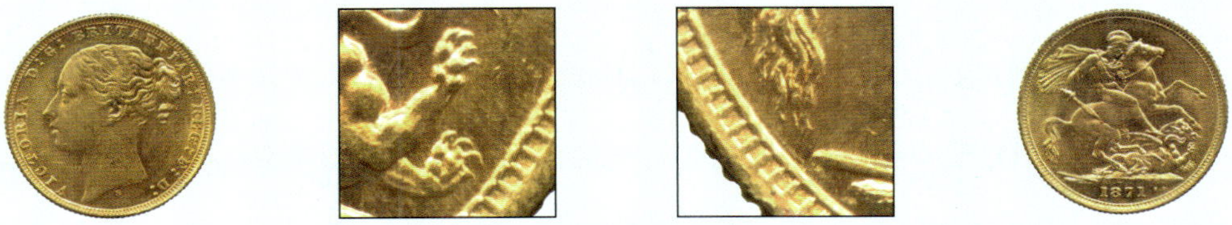

claws of 4/4 arrangement and long tail horse

674 **Victoria,** Sovereign, 1871 S, long tail horse, young head of third style left, letter S below close to neck, WW buried in truncation in relief, all letter R's with lower serifs joined, *rev* St George slaying dragon with sword, dragon claws four to left and four to right arm, the second on upper arm detached, the lowest claw on lower arm very short, horse with long tail ending in three strands, upper curve of tail with one spur of hair, date in exergue, tiny B.P. to upper right, 7.98g (McD 143a; QM 75 R2; Marsh 110; KM 7; Fr 15; S 3858A). *Some light bagmarks and hairlines, appears to be on par with the Quartermaster specimen, good extremely fine and very rare.* £1000-1500

Price Realised : £984

ex Kurt Jaggard Coins, Sydney, Australia, purchased 30 May 2002
Calendar year mintage 2,814,000 which includes shield reverse design pieces.
The McDonald catalogue for 2012 rates this coin as AUNC at a valuation of AU$4,900 (or £3,300)

one stop only in B.P

675 **Victoria,** Sovereign, 1872 S, young head of third style left, letter S below close to neck, WW buried in truncation in relief, *rev* St George slaying dragon with sword, horse with long tail, upper curve of tail with one weak spur of hair, date in exergue, tiny B.P to upper right, last stop absent, 7.97g (McD 144; QM 76 S; Marsh 111; KM 7; Fr 15; S 3858A). *Some light bagmarks, otherwise good extremely fine and scarce.* £350-450

Price Realised : £480

ex Randy Weir Numismatics, Unionville, Ontario, Canada, purchased 2 June 1995
Calendar year mintage 1,815,000 which includes shield reverse design pieces.

676 **Victoria,** Sovereign, 1873 S, young head of third style left, letter S below, WW buried in truncation in relief, *rev* St George slaying dragon with sword, horse with long tail, upper curve of tail with one spur of hair, date in exergue, lightly die flawed date, tiny B.P to upper right, last stop absent, 7.98g (McD 146; QM 78 S; Marsh 112; KM 7; Fr 15; S 3858A). *Some light bagmarks, otherwise extremely fine and scarce.* £300-400

Price Realised : £384

ex Randy Weir Numismatics, Unionville, Ontario, Canada, purchased 19 October 1991
Calendar year mintage 1,478,000 which includes shield reverse design pieces.

677 **Victoria,** Sovereign, 1874 S, young head of third style left, letter S below, WW buried in truncation in relief, last letter I flawed from rim to neck, all letter R's with lower serifs joined, *rev* St George slaying dragon with sword, horse with long tail, upper curve of tail with one spur of hair, date in exergue, 4 slightly doubled, tiny B.P. to upper right, last stop distant, 7.99g (McD 148; QM 80 R; Marsh 113; KM 7; Fr 15; S 3858A). *Some light bagmarks and surface marks, otherwise extremely fine and rare.* £300-400

Price Realised : £984

ex Randy Weir Numismatics, Unionville, Ontario, Canada, purchased 2 June 1995
Calendar year mintage 1,899,000 presumably mostly St George as there are no shield sovereigns of Sydney dated 1874.

678 **Victoria,** Sovereign, 1875 S, young head of third style left, letter S below, WW buried in truncation in relief, all letter R's with lower serifs joined, *rev* St George slaying dragon with sword, horse with long tail, upper curve of tail with one spur of hair, date in exergue, tiny B.P. to upper right, last stop distant, 7.98g (McD 150; QM 82 S; Marsh 114; KM 7; Fr 15; S 3858A). *Some light bagmarks, otherwise toned extremely fine and scarce.* £300-400

Price Realised : £840

ex Randy Weir Numismatics, Unionville, Ontario, Canada, purchased c.1997
Calendar year mintage 2,122,000 which includes shield reverse design pieces.

679 **Victoria,** Sovereign, 1876 S, young head of third style left, letter S below doubled, WW buried in truncation in relief, all letter R's with lower serifs joined, some light raised die flaws in first half of legend, *rev* St George slaying dragon with sword, horse with long tail, upper curve of tail with one spur of hair, date in exergue, lightly die flawed date, tiny B.P. to upper right, last stop distant, 7.98g (McD 152; QM 84 S; Marsh 115; KM 7; Fr 15; S 3858A). *Light bagmarks, otherwise extremely fine and scarce.* £300-400

Price Realised : £768

ex Randy Weir Numismatics, Unionville, Ontario, Canada, purchased 21 August 1992
Calendar year mintage 1,613,000 presumably mostly St George as there are no shield sovereigns of Sydney dated 1874. There are no St George reverse Sydney mint Sovereigns for both 1877 and 1878.

"S" further from neck

680 **Victoria,** Sovereign, 1879 S, young head of third style left, letter S below further from neck, WW buried in truncation in relief, *rev* St George slaying dragon with sword, horse with long tail, upper curve of tail with one spur of hair, date in exergue, tiny B.P. to upper right, last stop doubled, 8.00g (McD 156; QM 88 R; Marsh 116; KM 7; Fr 15; S 3858A). *Some light bagmarks and other surface marks, otherwise extremely fine / good extremely fine and very rare.* £1000-1500

Price Realised : £1,980

ex Monetarium, Kogarah, Australia, purchased 17 March 2003
Calendar year mintage 1,366,000 which includes shield reverse design pieces.
The McDonald catalogue for 2012 rates this coin as EF at a valuation of AU$3,400 (or £2,300)

"S" distant from neck and long tail with trace of one single strand spur

681 **Victoria,** Sovereign, 1880 S, young head of third style left, letter S below further from neck, WW buried in truncation in relief, *rev* St George slaying dragon with sword, horse with long tail, upper curve of tail with one spur of hair, date in exergue, tiny B.P. to upper right, 7.99g (McD 158; QM 91 S; Marsh 117; KM 7; Fr 15; S 3858A). *Some light bagmarks, otherwise good extremely fine and scarce.* £300-400

Price Realised : £528

ex Monetarium, Kogarah, Australia, purchased 17 March 2003
Calendar year mintage 1,459,000 which includes shield reverse design pieces.

short tail with two short spurs and no B.P. variety

682 **Victoria,** Sovereign, 1880 S, short tail and no B.P. variety, young head of third style left, letter S below further from neck, WW buried in truncation in relief, some light flaws in parts of obverse legend, *rev* St George slaying dragon with sword, horse with short tail, upper curve of tail with two short spurs of hair, date in exergue, blank exergue to upper right, 7.96g (McD 158a; QM -; Marsh 117; KM 7; Fr 15; S 3858B). *Scuffed with surface marks, almost very fine and very rare, no example present in the Quartermaster collection.* £300-500

Price Realised : £672

ex Reserve Bank of Australia Sale, Downies, November 2005, lot 1885, purchased through Winsor and Sons, December 2005
Calendar year mintage 1,459,000 which includes shield reverse design pieces.

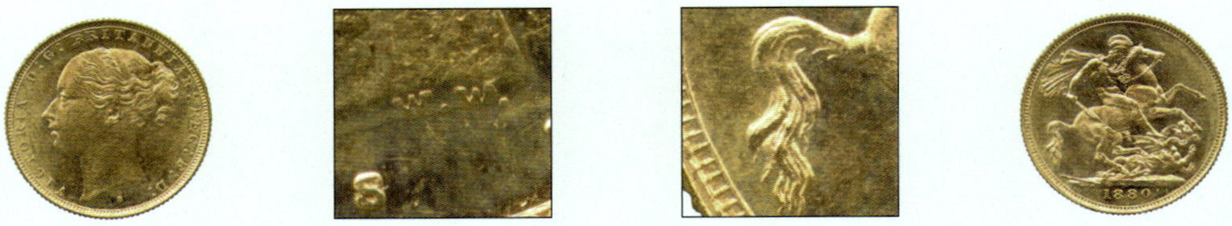

W.W. complete on truncation and long tail with weak single strand spur at upper curve of tail

683 **Victoria,** Sovereign, 1880 S, second young head of third style left, letter S below further from neck, W.W. complete truncation in relief, *rev* die axis slightly off-centre, St George slaying dragon with sword, horse with long tail, upper curve of tail with one weak single strand spur of hair, incomplete hem to cape, date in exergue, incomplete BP to upper right widely spaced no stops, 7.99g (McD 158b; QM 92 S; Marsh 117; KM 7; Fr 15; S 3858C). *A few light nicks and surface marks, appears to be finer than the example in the Quartermaster collection, good extremely fine and rare.* £400-600

Price Realised : £696

ex Monetarium, Kogarah, Australia, purchased 17 March 2003
Calendar year mintage 1,459,000 which includes shield reverse design pieces.

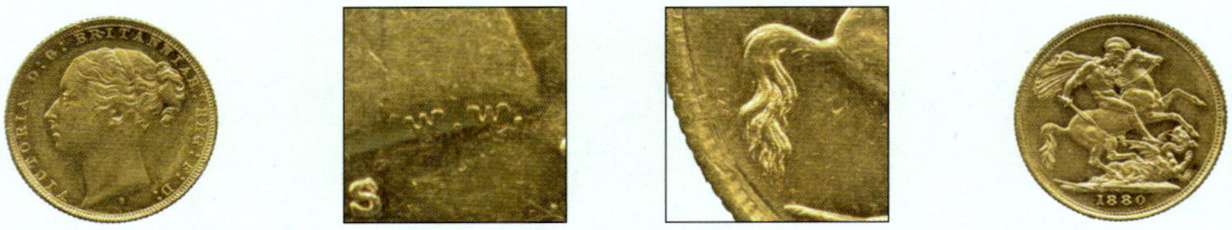

W.W. complete on truncation and long tail with single strand spur at upper curve of tail

684 **Victoria,** Sovereign, 1880 S, second young head of third style left, letter S below further from neck, W.W. complete truncation in relief, *rev* St George slaying dragon with sword, horse with long tail, upper curve of tail with one single strand spur of hair, date in exergue, a mere trace of BP to upper right, 7.98g (cf McD.158c; QM 93 S; Marsh 117B; KM 7; Fr 15; S 3858F). *A few light nicks and surface marks, obverse rim nick, appears to be the same variety and finer than the example in the Quartermaster collection, a pleasing extremely fine and rare.* £400-600

Price Realised : £672

ex Kurt Jaggard Coins, Sydney, Australia, purchased 22 October 2001
Calendar year mintage 1,459,000 which includes shield reverse design pieces.
The no BP varieties are usually blocked or weak BP dies, there are very few coins on which the BP is definitely absent like the coin in the next lot.

no BP variety and short tail with two short single strand spurs

685 **Victoria,** Sovereign, 1881 S, short tail and no B.P. variety, young head of third style left, letter S below further from neck, WW buried in truncation in relief, *rev* St George slaying dragon with sword, cape hem complete, some light die flaws in field, horse with short tail, upper curve of tail with two single strand spurs of hair, date in exergue, blank exergue to upper right, 7.98g (McD 160; QM 95 S; Marsh 118B; KM 7; Fr 15; S 3858B). *Some bagmarks, extremely fine / good extremely fine and appears finer than the Quartermaster collection coin and rare.* £350-450

Price Realised : £432

ex Randy Weir Numismatics, Unionville, Ontario, Canada, purchased 29 June 1990
Calendar year mintage 1,459,000 which includes shield reverse design pieces.

no B.P. variety and short tail with two short single strand spurs

686 **Victoria,** Sovereign, 1881 S, short tail and no B.P. variety, second young head of third style left, letter S below further from neck, W.W. complete truncation in relief, hint of some doubling in legend, *rev* St George slaying dragon with sword, horse with short tail, upper curve of tail with two single strand spurs of hair, date in exergue, blank exergue to upper right, 7.99g (McD 160a; QM 96 S; Marsh 118B; KM 7; Fr 15; S 3858D). *Some bagmarks, otherwise good extremely fine and appears finer than the Quartermaster collection coin and rare.* £400-600

Price Realised : £840

ex Monetarium, Kogarah, Australia, purchased 17 March 2003
Calendar year mintage 1,459,000 which includes shield reverse design pieces.

short tail with thick multi-strand spur

687 **Victoria,** Sovereign, 1882 S, short tail with BP variety, second young head of third style left, letter S below further from neck, lightly die flawed, W.W. complete truncation in relief, third and fourth colons of legend die flawed to rim, *rev* St George slaying dragon with sword, horse with short tail, upper curve of tail with thick spur of hair consisting of two strands, date in exergue, B with incomplete P to upper right, no stops, 7.98g (McD 162a; QM 101 S; Marsh 119; KM 7; Fr 15; S 3858E). *Some bagmarks, otherwise good extremely fine and appears finer than the Quartermaster collection coin and rare.* £400-600

Price Realised : £696

ex Monetarium, Kogarah, Australia, purchased 17 March 2003
Calendar year mintage 1,298,000 which includes shield reverse design pieces.

thick multi-strand spur at upper curve of tail and weaker hem to cape

688 **Victoria,** Sovereign, 1882 S, short tail with no BP variety, second young head of third style left, letter S below further from neck, W.W. complete truncation in relief, D G doubled, *rev* St George slaying dragon with sword, horse with short tail, upper curve of tail with thick spur of hair consisting of two strands, weak hem to cape, date in exergue, 2 rotated out of line slightly, blank to upper right, no stops, 7.99g (McD 162; QM 100 S; Marsh -; KM 7; Fr 15; S 3858D). *Some bagmarks and digs, dig by first 8, otherwise extremely fine / good extremely fine and appears finer than the Quartermaster collection coin and rare.* £400-600

Price Realised : £432

ex Randy Weir Numismatics, Unionville, Ontario, Canada, purchased 18 September 1995
Calendar year mintage 1,298,000 which includes shield reverse design pieces.

spur of two parallel strands of hair at upper curve of tail and complete hem to cape

689 **Victoria,** Sovereign, 1883 S, short tail with BP variety, second young head of third style left, letter S below, W.W. complete truncation in relief, die flaw near initials, another flaw to left of third I, D G doubled, *rev* St George slaying dragon with sword, horse with short tail, upper curve of tail with spur of hair consisting of two long parallel strands, complete hem to cape, date in exergue, BP with no stops, 7.98g (McD 164; QM 105 R; Marsh 120; KM 7; Fr 15; S 3858E). *Some light marks and digs, otherwise extremely fine / good extremely fine and appears to be on par with the Quartermaster collection coin and rare.* £400-600

Price Realised : £432

ex Randy Weir Numismatics, Unionville, Ontario, Canada, purchased 7 January 1995
Calendar year mintage 1,108,000 which includes shield reverse design pieces.

short horse tail with thin hair spur in upper curve

690 **Victoria,** Sovereign, 1884 S, short tail with BP variety, second young head of third style left, letter S below, W.W. complete truncation in relief, light flaw to left of fourth I, D G doubled, light flaw in queen's name, *rev* St George slaying dragon with sword, horse with short tail, upper curve of tail with thin strand of hair and trace of another higher one, complete hem to cape, date in exergue, BP incomplete with no stops, 7.98g (McD 166; QM 109 S; Marsh 121; KM 7; Fr 15; S 3858E). *Some light marks and hairlines, otherwise good extremely fine and appears to be more attractive than the Quartermaster collection coin and scarce.* £400-600

Price Realised : £480

ex Randy Weir Numismatics, Unionville, Ontario, Canada, purchased 18 January 1990
Calendar year mintage 1,595,000 which includes shield reverse design pieces.

short horse tail with thin hair spur angled more outward

691 **Victoria,** Sovereign, 1885 S, short tail with BP variety, second young head of third style left, letter S below, W.W. complete truncation in relief, *rev* St George slaying dragon with sword, horse with short tail, upper curve of tail with thin strand of hair angled more outward, complete hem to cape, date in exergue, BP with no stops, 7.99g (McD 168; QM 112 S; Marsh 122; KM 7; Fr 15; S 3858E). *Some light bagmarks, nicks and hairlines, otherwise good extremely fine and appears to be finer than the Quartermaster collection coin and scarce.* £400-600

Price Realised : £432

ex Randy Weir Numismatics, Unionville, Ontario, Canada, purchased 2 June 1995
Calendar year mintage 1,486,000 which includes shield reverse design pieces.
This reverse die has a different treatment to the 1884 in the preceding lot, the thin strand spur of hair halfway up the tail is angled more outwards, with a thin short strand above it, unlike the 1884 which is less angled with a mere stump of hair above. The tail terminates in three strands of hair and to the left of this is a strand of shorter hair and folded towards the three strands at termination.

692

693

692 **Victoria,** Sovereign, 1886 S, short tail with BP variety, second young head of third style left, letter S below, W.W. complete truncation in relief, some light die flaws in letters at beginning and end of legend, D G doubled, *rev* St George slaying dragon with sword, horse with short tail, upper curve of tail with thin strand of hair and trace of another higher one, complete hem to cape, date in exergue, BP with no stops, the P weak and incomplete, 7.98g (McD 170; QM 116 S; Marsh 123; KM 7; Fr 15; S 3858E). *Some light bagmarks, obverse rim nick, reverse brilliant, otherwise good extremely fine and appears to be on par with the Quartermaster collection coin but with a better reverse, scarce.* £400-600

Price Realised : £696

ex Randy Weir Numismatics, Unionville, Ontario, Canada, purchased 12 November 1990
Calendar year mintage 1,667,000 which includes shield reverse design pieces. This 1886 reverse has the same tail arrangement as the 1884 in lot 690.

693 **Victoria,** Sovereign, 1887 S, short tail with BP variety, second young head of third style left, letter S below, W.W. complete truncation in relief, light die flaws in some letters in legend, *rev* St George slaying dragon with sword, die flaw from St George helmet to rim, horse with short tail, upper curve of tail with thin strand of hair and trace of another higher one, complete hem to cape, date in exergue, the 7 with a serif foot at top right, BP with no stops, the P weak and incomplete, 7.98g (McD 172; QM 118 S; Marsh 124; KM 7; Fr 15; S 3858E). *Some light bagmarks, otherwise extremely fine / good extremely fine and appears to be on par with the Quartermaster collection coin, scarce.* £400-600

Price Realised : £648

ex Randy Weir Numismatics, Unionville, Ontario, Canada, purchased 18 July 1990
Calendar year mintage 1,000,000 which includes shield reverse design pieces. This 1887 reverse has the same tail arrangement as the 1884 in lot 690 and 1886 in the preceding lot.
The Melbourne mint St George Sovereign of 1887 in Lot 786 also has this 7 with the extra serif foot at top. The same punch must have been used to prepare both dies at the Royal Mint in London.

Sydney Mint Victoria Jubilee Type Sovereigns

The Golden Jubilee of Victoria's reign occurred in 1887, bringing a change to the coinage with a more up to date and mature portrait of the Queen wearing a tiny crown with veil. Both the Sydney and Melbourne mints seamlessly swapped over to the new design, with the same quirks as the London mint pieces, in that there are two varieties of legend spacing in relation to the bust which has its own variations on the initials on the truncation. The reverses also venture through two different types of tail.

The standard full description for a Jubilee type Sovereign of Queen Victoria at the Sydney mint is as follows:-

Victoria (1837-1901), Sovereign, 1887 S, Sydney mint, engraved by Joseph Edgar Boehm, Jubilee tall veiled bust left with older features, veil with two rows of crenellations, with small Imperial crown, large fleurs inside, top cross on field intrudes the border, wearing 13 pearl necklace, brooch at front with relief jewel, half a garter star at base of bust under sash, decorated border to dress bust, small spread J.E.B. fully on truncation arranged in a straight line with a hooked J, first type legend further from crown, two pearl drop ear ring, VICTORIA D:G: BRITT: REG: F: D:, finely toothed border within twin linear concentric circles and raised rim both sides, outer rim blends with teeth, *rev* struck en médaille, after Benedetto Pistrucci, St George slaying dragon with sword, streamer to helmet, complete hem to cape, extra mane hair above hand holding rein, horse with short tail, three strand end to tail, two spurs of extra hair on curve of tail, dragon with three claws to left and three to right arm, trace of fourth claw, all attached, broken lance on ground-line to left, *WWP* in relief under lance, S mint mark at centre of ground, date in exergue, tiny B.P. to upper right, edge milled

An Extremely Rare Proof 1887 Sydney Mint Sovereign

694 **Victoria (1837-1901),** Proof Specimen Sovereign, 1887 S, Jubilee tall veiled and crowned bust left with older features, top cross of crown touches linear circle, wearing 13 pearl necklace, initials J.E.B. fully on truncation in a straight line but curving up towards shoulder, hooked J doubled, first type legend with G: further from crown, finely toothed border within twin linear concentric circles and raised prominent rim both sides, *rev* struck en médaille, St George slaying dragon with sword, streamer to helmet, horse with short tail, three strand end to tail, two extra spurs of hair on upper curve of tail, dragon with three claws to upper and four to lower arm, the second lower claw detached, S mint mark at centre of ground, date in exergue, tiny B.P. to upper right, edge milled, 7.97g (McD 174; QM -; Marsh -; KM 10; Fr 19; cf S 3868A). *Two tiny rim nicks on reverse, very light scratch in hair, perhaps from light polishing, more yellow to orange colour than a currency piece, well defined and otherwise good extremely fine and extremely rare.* £15,000-25,000

Price Realised : £12,000

ex An Important Collection of Gold Sovereigns 1816-2000, offered as one lot, Sothebys, November 2000, lot 525 (part)
The McDonald catalogue for 2012 rates this coin as Proof at a valuation of AU$195,000 (or £131,000). This coin has seen light polishing, hence the low estimate, but it is extremely rare and the Quartermaster collection did not contain an example. The Bentley Collection contains two examples.

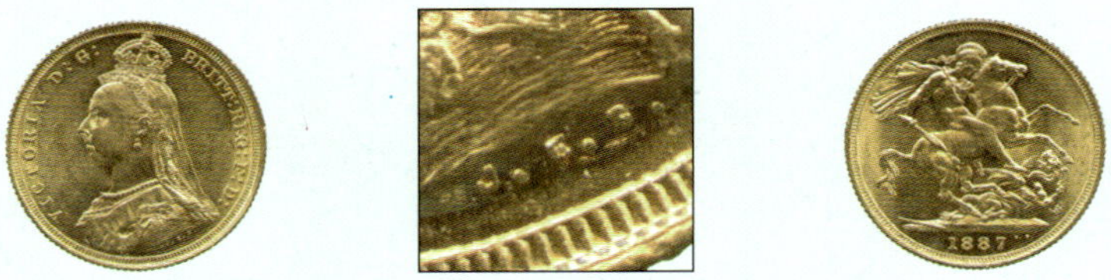

tiny small spread J.E.B. with hooked "J"

695 **Victoria,** Sovereign, 1887 S, Jubilee crowned bust left, tiny initials J.E.B. fully on truncation arcing towards perimeter, hooked J with doubled B, first type legend with G: further from crown, some light die flaws in parts, *rev* St George slaying dragon with sword, streamer to helmet, horse with short tail, dragon with three / four arrangement of claws, S mint mark at centre of ground, date in exergue, tiny B.P. to upper right, 7.98g (McD 174; QM 124 R; Marsh 138A; KM 10; Fr 19; S 3868). *Some light surface marks, a pleasing extremely fine / good extremely fine and rare.* £400-600

Price Realised : £1,032

Calendar year mintage 1,002,000

Proof-like 1887 Sydney Mint Sovereign with JEB initials in arc

696 **Victoria,** Sovereign, 1887 S, Jubilee tall veiled and crowned bust left with older features, top cross of crown touches linear circle, wearing 13 pearl necklace, small initials J.E.B. fully on truncation, arranged in a slight arc, hooked J with doubled B and therefore larger, the E a little blundered, first type legend with G: further from crown, finely toothed border within twin linear concentric circles and raised prominent rim both sides, *rev* St George slaying dragon with sword, streamer to helmet, horse with short tail, dragon with three / four arrangement of claws, S mint mark at centre of ground, date in exergue, tiny B.P. to upper right, edge milled, 7.99g (McD 174; QM 124 R; Marsh 138A; KM 10; Fr 19; S 3868). *Toned a few very light marks, otherwise as struck with a specimen-like finish and rare.* £600-800

Price Realised : £5,040

Calendar year mintage 1,002,000
This coin is not dissimilar to the specimen listed as lot 694 (above) on account of the overall finish of the coin. However it is not quite as well defined in the smallest detail of the design, the J.E.B. is malformed and the brooch above is also unclear.

larger repositioned J.E.B. with hooked J and larger stops

697 **Victoria,** Sovereign, 1887 S, Jubilee crowned bust left, larger initials J.E.B. fully on truncation in a straight line, hooked J with large stops, first type legend with G: further from crown, *rev* St George slaying dragon with sword, horse with short tail, S mint mark at centre of ground, date in exergue, tiny B.P. to upper right, 7.98g (McD 174; QM -; cf Marsh 138A; KM 10; Fr 19; S 3868). *Patchy red tone, light surface marks, almost extremely fine / extremely fine and rare, no matching type in the Quartermaster collection.* £350-450

Price Realised : £384

Calendar year mintage 1,002,000

B.P initials – no second stop

698 **Victoria,** Sovereign, 1888 S, Jubilee crowned bust left, small spread J.E.B. fully on truncation, reading in a straight line towards shoulder, hooked J, first type legend with G: further from crown, *rev* St George slaying dragon with sword, die flaw from rim to top of horse head, horse with short tail, S mint mark at centre of ground, date in exergue, tiny B.P to upper right, the last stop absent, 7.98g (McD 176; QM 129 S; Marsh 139; KM 10; Fr 19; S 3868A). *Some hairline scratches on reverse, otherwise weak extremely fine to extremely fine and scarce.* £300-400

Price Realised : £288

Calendar year mintage 2,187,000

normal J.E.B. with angled "J" fully on truncation

699 **Victoria,** Sovereign, 1888 S, Jubilee crowned bust left, J.E.B. fully on truncation with right-angled J, first type legend with G: further from crown, *rev* St George slaying dragon with sword, horse with short tail, S mint mark at centre of ground, date in exergue, tiny B.P to upper right, the last stop absent, 7.99g (McD 176b; QM 131 S; Marsh 139; KM 10; Fr 19; S 3868). *Some light bagmarks and other surface marks, otherwise weak extremely fine to extremely fine and scarce.* £300-400

Price Realised : £312

Calendar year mintage 2,187,000

second repositioned legend detail

700 **Victoria,** Sovereign, 1888 S, second legend, Jubilee crowned bust left, J.E.B. fully on truncation with right-angled J, second type legend with G: closer to crown, which does not intrude border circle, *rev* St George slaying dragon with sword, horse with short tail, S mint mark at centre of ground, date in exergue, tiny B.P to upper right, the last stop absent, 7.99g (McD 176c; QM 132 C; Marsh 139; KM 10; Fr 19; S 3868B). *Rim nick on reverse and other very light marks, otherwise weak extremely fine / good extremely fine.* £300-400

Price Realised : £336

ex Ebay purchase, 21 February 2002
Calendar year mintage 2,187,000

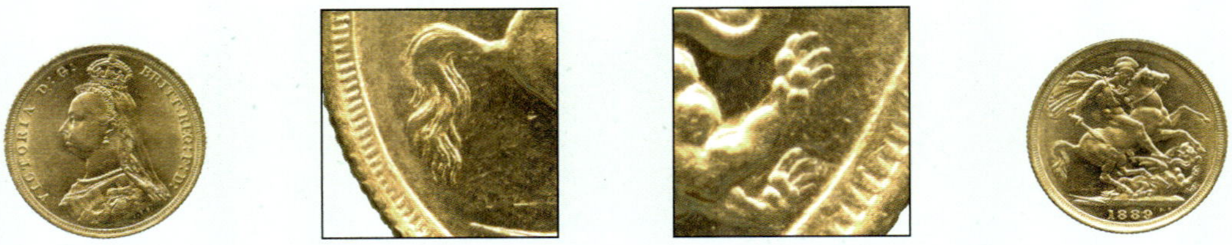

thick tail spur of twin strands and dragon claws of 4/4 arrangement

701 **Victoria,** Sovereign, 1889 S, first legend, Jubilee crowned bust left, J.E.B. fully on truncation with right-angled J, first type legend with G: further from crown, some light die flaws in latter half of legend, *rev* St George slaying dragon with sword, horse with short tail, now with one thick spur of hair at upper curve made up of two strands of hair, dragon claws fully attached, with four claws on both arms, S mint mark at centre of ground, date in exergue, tiny B.P to upper right, the last stop absent, 7.99g (McD 178; QM 135 S; cf Marsh 140; KM 10; Fr 19; S 3868A). *Some light surface marks, otherwise good extremely fine and scarce.* £400-600

Price Realised : £600

ex Ebay purchase, 21 February 2002. Calendar year mintage 3,262,000

lower arm, fourth claw weaker

702 **Victoria,** Sovereign, 1889 S, second legend, Jubilee crowned bust left, J.E.B. fully on truncation with right-angled J, second type legend with G: closer to crown, *rev* St George slaying dragon with sword, horse with short tail, now with one thick spur of hair at upper curve, lower arm of dragon with weak fourth claw, S mint mark at centre of ground, date in exergue, tiny B.P to upper right, the last stop absent, 7.99g (McD 178a; QM -; cf Marsh 140; KM 10; Fr 19; S 3868A). *Some light bagmarks, otherwise practically as struck and extremely rare, no specimen present in the Quartermaster collection.* £400-600

Price Realised : £840

Calendar year mintage 3,262,000

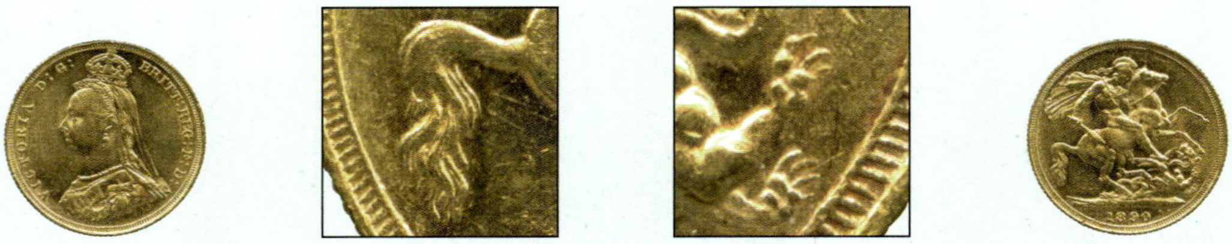

two extra spurs of hair on tail and dragon claws of 3/4 arrangement, the second lower detached

703 **Victoria,** Sovereign, 1890 S, first legend, Jubilee crowned bust left, J.E.B. fully on truncation with right-angled J, first type legend with G: further from crown, some light die flaws in legend, *rev* St George slaying dragon with sword, horse with short tail, with two extra spurs of hair at upper curve, dragon claws with three on upper and four on lower arms, the second claw on the lower arm detached, S mint mark at centre of ground, date in exergue, tiny B.P to upper right, the last stop absent, 7.99g (McD 180; QM 139 S; Marsh 141; KM 10; Fr 19; S 3868A). *Once cleaned, with light surface marks, a weak extremely fine and rare.* £300-400

Price Realised : £360

ex A H Baldwin & Sons Ltd sourced via Paul Davies Ltd, September 2006. Calendar year mintage 2,808,000

704 **Victoria,** Sovereign, 1890 S, second legend, Jubilee crowned bust left, J.E.B. fully on truncation with right-angled J, second type legend with G: closer to crown, *rev* St George slaying dragon with sword, horse with short tail, with two extra spurs of hair at upper curve, S mint mark at centre of ground, date in exergue, tiny B.P to upper right, the last stop absent, 7.99g (McD 180a; QM 140-1 S; Marsh 141; KM 10; Fr 19; S 3868B). *Some light bagmarks, otherwise good extremely fine and scarce.* £300-400

Price Realised : £600

ex Randy Weir Numismatics, Unionville, Ontario, Canada, purchased 12 November 1990. Calendar year mintage 2,808,000

doubled "S" resembles a figure "9"

705 **Victoria,** Sovereign, 1890 S, second legend, Jubilee crowned bust left, J.E.B. fully on truncation with right-angled J, second type legend with G: closer to crown, *rev* St George slaying dragon with sword, horse with short tail, with two extra spurs of hair at upper curve, S mint mark at centre of ground flawed and resembling a number 9, date in exergue, tiny B.P to upper right, the last stop absent, 7.95g (cf McD 180a; QM 140-1 S; Marsh 141; KM 10; Fr 19; S 3868B). *Toned with many surface marks, good fine and unusual.* £300-350

Price Realised : £288

Calendar year mintage 2,808,000

longer strands in helmet streamer and four curved claws attached to each arm

706 **Victoria,** Sovereign, 1891 S, long horse tail, Jubilee crowned bust left, J.E.B. fully on truncation with right-angled J, second type legend, light die flaws in queen's name, *rev* St George slaying dragon with sword, helmet streamer consists of longer strands, light die flaw from rim to helmet, horse with long tail, with one extra spur of hair at upper curve, dragon claws now with four curved claws on each arm all attached, S mint mark at centre of ground, date in exergue, tiny complete B.P. to upper right, 7.98g (McD 182; QM 143 C; Marsh 142; KM 10; Fr 19; S 3868C). *Light bagmarks and surface marks, extremely fine / good extremely fine.* £300-400

Price Realised : £504

ex Randy Weir Numismatics, Unionville, Ontario, Canada, purchased December 1990
Calendar year mintage 2,596,000. The legend type from 1891-1893 is always of the second repositioned type.

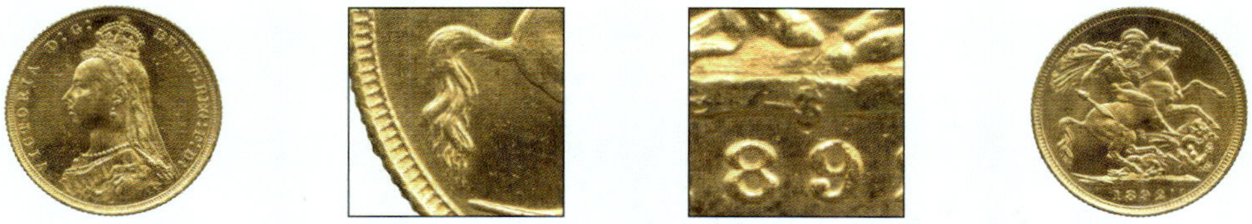

long horse tail with one extra spur and "S" struck over a lower "S"

707 **Victoria,** Sovereign, 1892 S, long horse tail, Jubilee crowned bust left, J.E.B. fully on truncation with right-angled J, second type legend, *rev* St George slaying dragon with sword, horse with long tail, with one extra spur of hair at upper curve, dragon claws now with four curved claws on each arm all attached, S mint mark at centre of ground, S struck over a lower S, date in exergue, widely spread figures, tiny complete B.P. to upper right, 7.98g (McD 184; QM 146 S; Marsh 143; KM 10; Fr 19; S 3868C). *Some light bagmarks and hairlines, otherwise good extremely fine.* £300-400

Price Realised : £456

ex Randy Weir Numismatics, Unionville, Ontario, Canada, purchased 12 November 1990
Calendar year mintage 2,837,000

B.P. complete

708 **Victoria,** Sovereign, 1893 S, long horse tail, Jubilee crowned bust left, J.E.B. fully on truncation with right-angled J, second type legend, *rev* St George slaying dragon with sword, horse with long tail, with one extra spur of hair at upper curve, S mint mark at centre of ground, S struck over a lower S, date in exergue, date lower in exergue than previous years appearing more spread, tiny complete B.P. to upper right, 7.99g (McD 186; QM 148-9 S; Marsh 144; KM 10; Fr 19; S 3868C). *Some light bagmarks, scratch on cheek, otherwise good extremely fine.* £300-400

Price Realised : £504

ex Charles Stueve, Abbeygate Coins, Westhampton Beach, New York, c.1990
Calendar year mintage 1,498,000. The Jubilee head at Sydney and Melbourne both occur dated 1893, whereas London does not, having already swapped to the new old head design entirely by 1893. The Colonial Branch mints in Australia did not receive their old head dies until much later than the local demand dictated for the striking of gold. Therefore these two mints carried on with the Jubilee head production in 1893. At Sydney there were more Jubilee head pieces dated 1893 than the new old head pieces. It was the other way around for these types at Melbourne.

Sydney Mint Victoria Old Head Type Sovereigns

The old head type design commenced on the coinage in 1893 after a gestation of just over two years. This was a direct reaction to public criticism of the Jubilee type design, culminating in comment from the Queen herself on her own displeasure of the small crowned bust. The British Royal Mint introduced the new design on coinage dated from 1893 and whole proof sets containing all the designs were available to purchase.
For more information on the design process of the old head see part one of the Bentley Collection, before Lot 335. At this time the only Colonial Branch Mints in operation were the Sydney and Melbourne mints. They received the new design much later in the year and had already struck many Sovereigns of the older Jubilee type design in both mints. Sydney in fact struck more of the old design than the new old head for coins dated 1893, Melbourne vice versa. The full description of such a coin is as follows.

Victoria (1837-1901), Sovereign, 1896 S, Sydney Branch mint, engraved by Thomas Brock, old veiled bust left, T.B. below, VICTORIA D:G: BRITT: REG: F: D: IND: IMP:, toothed border surrounding, *rev* struck en médaille, engraved after Benedetto Pistrucci, St George slaying dragon with sword, three strand streamer on helmet, horse with long tail, three strand end to tail, one spur of extra hair on curve of tail, dragon with four claws on each arm, broken lance on ground-line to left, *WWP* in relief under lance, S mint mark at centre of ground, date in exergue, tiny B.P. to upper right, finely toothed border within twin linear concentric circles and raised rim, edge milled

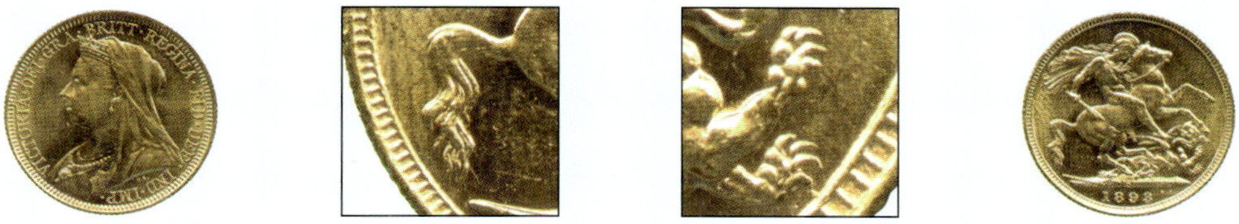

one extra spur of hair in upper curve of tail and four long curved claws on each arm

709 **Victoria (1837-1901),** Sovereign, 1893 S, old veiled bust left, T.B. below, toothed border surrounding, raised die flaws in some words in legend, *rev* St George slaying dragon with sword, horse with long tail, one spur of extra hair on curve of tail, dragon with four curved claws attached on each arm, S mint mark at base of ground, date in exergue, tiny B.P. to upper right, finely toothed border within twin linear concentric circles and raised rim, 7.99g (McD 189; QM 151 C; Marsh 162; KM 13; Fr 23; S 3877). *Some light bagmarks, otherwise good extremely fine and appears to be on par with the Quartermaster coin.* £300-350

Price Realised : £528

ex Randy Weir Numismatics, Unionville, Ontario, Canada, purchased 7 June 1996
Calendar year mintage 1,346,000. This coin shares the same reverse die as the Jubilee head issue and is technically a mule.

710 **Victoria,** Sovereign, 1894 S, old veiled bust left, T.B. below, toothed border surrounding, *rev* St George slaying dragon with sword, horse with long tail, tiny thin hair spur in upper curve of tail, dragon with four shorter curved claws attached on each arm, die flaw at front raised leg of horse, S mint mark on ground, date in exergue, tiny B.P. to upper right, 8.00g (McD 191; QM 153 C; Marsh 163; KM 13; Fr 23; S 3877). *Some light bagmarks, otherwise good extremely fine and appears to be on par with the Quartermaster coin.* £300-350

Price Realised : £312

ex Randy Weir Numismatics, Unionville, Ontario, Canada, purchased 29 June 1990
Calendar year mintage 3,067,000

711 **Victoria,** Sovereign, 1895 S, old veiled bust left, T.B. below, toothed border surrounding, *rev* St George slaying dragon with sword, horse with long tail, S mint mark on ground, date in exergue, tiny B.P. to upper right, 7.98g (McD 193; QM 155 C; Marsh 164; KM 13; Fr 23; S 3877). *Some light bagmarks, otherwise good extremely fine and appears to be on par with the Quartermaster coin.* £300-350

Price Realised : £456

ex Randy Weir Numismatics, Unionville, Ontario, Canada, purchased 29 June 1990
Calendar year mintage 2,758,000

712 **Victoria,** Sovereign, 1896 S, old veiled bust left, T.B. below, toothed border surrounding, *rev* St George slaying dragon with sword, horse with long tail, raised die flaw from lance to rim, S mint mark on ground, date in exergue, tiny B.P. to upper right, 7.98g (McD 195; QM 158 S; Marsh 165 S; KM 13; Fr 23; S 3877). *Some light bagmarks, dig on right side of ground-line, otherwise brilliant good extremely fine and appears to be finer than the Quartermaster coin.* £300-350

Price Realised : £528

ex David L Cannon collection, Cincinnati, Ohio, USA, purchased 19 September 1989
Calendar year mintage 2,544,000

713 **Victoria,** Sovereign, 1897 S, old veiled bust left, T.B. below, toothed border surrounding, *rev* St George slaying dragon with sword, horse with long tail, S mint mark on ground, date in exergue, tiny B.P. to upper right, 7.98g (McD 197; QM 161 S; Marsh 166; KM 13; Fr 23; S 3877). *Some light bagmarks, otherwise good extremely fine and appears to be finer than the Quartermaster coin.* £300-350

Price Realised : £624

Calendar year mintage 2,532,000

714

715

714 **Victoria,** Sovereign, 1898 S, old veiled bust left, T.B. below, toothed border surrounding, *rev* St George slaying dragon with sword, horse with long tail, S mint mark on ground, date in exergue, tiny B.P. to upper right, 7.99g (McD 199; QM 163 S; Marsh 167; KM 13; Fr 23; S 3877). *Some light bagmarks and nicks, otherwise good extremely fine and appears to be on par with the Quartermaster coin.* £300-350

Price Realised : £984

Calendar year mintage 2,548,000

715 **Victoria,** Sovereign, 1899 S, old veiled bust left, T.B. below, toothed border surrounding, *rev* St George slaying dragon with sword, horse with long tail, S mint mark on ground, date in exergue, tiny B.P. to upper right, 7.99g (McD 201; QM 165 C; Marsh 168; KM 13; Fr 23; S 3877). *Quite bagmarked, otherwise brilliant good extremely fine and appears to be on par with the Quartermaster coin.* £300-350

Price Realised : £552

ex Randy Weir Numismatics, Unionville, Ontario, Canada, purchased 29 June 1990
Calendar year mintage 3,259,000

716

717

716 **Victoria,** Sovereign, 1900 S, old veiled bust left, T.B. below, toothed border surrounding, some light die flaws in first half of obverse legend, *rev* St George slaying dragon with sword, horse with long tail, only a trace of extra spur of hair at upper curve, S mint mark at base of ground, date in exergue, tiny B.P. to upper right, 7.98g (McD 204; QM 168 C; Marsh 169; KM 13; Fr 23; S 3877). *Some light bagmarks, otherwise good extremely fine and appears to be on par with the Quartermaster coin.* £300-350

Price Realised : £336

ex Randy Weir Numismatics, Unionville, Ontario, Canada, purchased October 1990
Calendar year mintage 3,586,000. This represents the highest calendar year output for the old head design in the Sydney series.

717 **Victoria,** Sovereign, 1901 S, old veiled bust left, T.B. below, toothed border surrounding, *rev* St George slaying dragon with sword, horse with long tail, S mint mark on ground, date in exergue, tiny B.P. to upper right, 7.98g (McD 207; QM 171 C; Marsh 170; KM 13; Fr 23; S 3877). *Quite bagmarked, otherwise brilliant good extremely fine and appears to be finer than the Quartermaster coin.* £300-350

Price Realised : £408

ex Randy Weir Numismatics, Unionville, Ontario, Canada, purchased October 1990
Calendar year mintage 3,012,000
Queen Victoria died on 22 January 1901

The Reign of King Edward VII (1901-1910)
House of Saxe-Coburg and Gotha

Born: 9 November 1841

Accession: 22 January 1901

Married: Alexandra of Denmark 10 March 1863

Coronation: Saturday, 9 August 1902

Children: three sons, three daughters

Died: 6 May 1910, aged 68

718

719

720

718 **Edward VII (1901-1910),** Sovereign, 1902 S, Sydney mint, engraved by George William De Saulles, bare head facing right, DES. below, toothed border and raised rim, EDWARDVS VII D: G: BRITT: OMN: REX F: D: IND: IMP:, *rev* struck en médaille, engraved after Benedetto Pistrucci, St George slaying dragon with sword, cloak with complete hemline, two stand helmet streamer, horse with long tail, ending in three strands, with one spur higher up at curve, broken lance on ground-line to left, *WWP* in relief under lance, S mint mark on ground, date in exergue, tiny B.P. to upper right, finely toothed border within twin linear concentric circles and raised rim, edge milled, 7.98g (McD 210; QM 178 (part); KM 15; Fr 32; Marsh 204; S 3973). *A myriad of nicks and surface marks mainly on obverse, dig by cape, otherwise extremely fine / good extremely fine.* £300-350

Price Realised : £312

ex David L Cannon collection, Cincinnati, Ohio, USA, purchased 19 September 1989
Calendar year mintage 2,813,000

719 **Edward VII,** Sovereign, 1903 S, bare head facing right, DES. below doubled, *rev* St George slaying dragon with sword, S mint mark on ground, date in exergue, tiny B.P. to upper right, 7.99g (McD 213; QM 179 (part); KM 15; Fr 32; Marsh 205; S 3973). *Unevenly toned with light bagmarks, two short scratches on beard, otherwise good extremely fine.* £300-350

Price Realised : £336

Calendar year mintage 2,806,000

720 **Edward VII,** Sovereign, 1904 S, bare head facing right, DES. below, raised die flaw at top of second D and RE of legend, *rev* St George slaying dragon with sword, S mint mark on ground, date in exergue, tiny B.P. to upper right, 7.99g (McD 216; QM 180 (part); KM 15; Fr 32; Marsh 206; S 3973). *Rim nick on reverse, surface marks and hairlines, otherwise good extremely fine.* £300-350

Price Realised : £528

ex Robert Reed collection, Los Angeles, USA c.1990
Calendar year mintage 2,986,000

721

722

721 **Edward VII,** Sovereign, 1905 S, bare head facing right, DES. below, *rev* St George slaying dragon with sword, S mint mark on ground, date in exergue, tiny B.P. to upper right, some light die flaws around date and initials, 8.00g (McD 219; QM 181 (part); KM 15; Fr 32; Marsh 207; S 3973). *Serious obverse bagmarks, scuffed, otherwise extremely fine / good extremely fine.* £300-350

Price Realised : £312

Calendar year mintage 2,778,000

722 **Edward VII,** Sovereign, 1906 S, bare head facing right, DES. below, light raised die flaw in REX, *rev* St George slaying dragon with sword, S mint mark on ground, date in exergue, light die flaw at top of 0, tiny B.P. to upper right, 7.98g (McD 222; QM 182 (part); KM 15; Fr 32; Marsh 208; S 3973). *A few light bagmarks and nicks, otherwise good extremely fine.* £300-350

Price Realised : £768

ex Robert Reed collection, Los Angeles, USA c.1990
Calendar year mintage 2,792,000.

723

724

723 **Edward VII,** Sovereign, 1907 S, bare head facing right, DES. below, *rev* St George slaying dragon with sword, S mint mark on bottom of ground, date in exergue, tiny B.P. to upper right, 7.99g (McD 225; QM 183 (part); KM 15; Fr 32; Marsh 209; S 3973). *A few light bagmarks, nicks and other marks, larger scuff on cheek, lovely reverse, otherwise good extremely fine.* £300-350

Price Realised : £312

ex Randy Weir Numismatics, Unionville, Ontario, Canada, purchased September 1991
Calendar year mintage 2,539,000

724 **Edward VII,** Sovereign, 1908 S, bare head facing right, DES. below, *rev* St George slaying dragon with sword, S mint mark on ground, date in exergue, raised die flaw from lance to rim, tiny B.P. to upper right, 7.98g (McD 228; QM 184 (part); KM 15; Fr 32; Marsh 210; S 3973). *A few light surface marks and nicks, scratch by initial E of legend, with a superb reverse, otherwise good extremely fine.* £300-350

Price Realised : £408

Calendar year mintage 2,017,000

725

726

725 **Edward VII,** Sovereign, 1909 S, bare head facing right, DES. below, *rev* St George slaying dragon with sword, S mint mark on ground, date in exergue, tiny B.P. to upper right, 7.99g (McD 231; QM 185 (part); KM 15; Fr 32; Marsh 211; S 3973). *A few light bagmarks, nicks and hairlines, otherwise extremely fine.* £300-350

Price Realised : £312

Calendar year mintage 2,057,000

726 **Edward VII,** Sovereign, 1910 S, bare head facing right, DES. below, light die flaw at second D of legend and following word, *rev* St George slaying dragon with sword, S mint mark on ground, date in exergue, tiny B.P. to upper right, 7.99g (McD 234; QM 186 (part); KM 15; Fr 32; Marsh 212; S 3973). *A few light nicks and hairlines, lightly scratched at rear of ear, otherwise good extremely fine.* £300-350

Price Realised : £312

Calendar year mintage 2,135,000. King Edward VII died on 6 May 1910

The Reign of King George V (1910-1936)
House of Windsor

Born: 3 June 1865

Accession: 6 May 1910

Married: Mary of Teck, 6 July 1893

Coronation: Thursday, 22 June 1911, second Coronation as Emperor of India at the Delhi Durbar, Tuesday, 12 December 1911

Children: five sons, one daughter

Died: 20 January 1936, aged 70

727 **George V (1910-1936),** Sovereign, 1911 S, Sydney mint, designed by Edgar Bertram Mackennal, bare head left, B.M. on truncation, toothed border and raised rim, GEORGIVS V D: G: BRITT: OMN: REX F: D: IND: IMP:, *rev* struck en médaille, engraved after Benedetto Pistrucci, St George slaying dragon with sword, helmet with three strand streamer, horse with long tail, ending in three strands, with one spur higher up at curve, broken lance on ground-line to left, *WWP* in relief under lance, S mint mark on ground, date in exergue, tiny B.P. to upper right, finely toothed border within twin linear concentric circles and raised rim, edge milled, 7.98g (McD 237; QM 187; KM 29; Fr 38; Marsh 271; S 4003). *A few light bagmarks, otherwise practically as struck.*
£300-400

Price Realised : £336

ex Randy Weir Numismatics, Unionville, Ontario, Canada, purchased 14 January 1992
Calendar year mintage 2,519,000

728 **George V,** Sovereign, 1912 S, bare head left, B.M. on truncation, *rev* St George slaying dragon with sword, S mint mark on ground, date in exergue, tiny B.P. to upper right, 7.99g (McD 240; QM 188; KM 29; Fr 38; Marsh 272; S 4003). *A few light hairlines and surface marks, otherwise good extremely fine.* £300-400

Price Realised : £312

ex Randy Weir Numismatics, Unionville, Ontario, Canada, purchased 14 January 1992
Calendar year mintage 2,227,000

729 **George V,** Sovereign, 1913 S, bare head left, B.M. on truncation, *rev* St George slaying dragon with sword, S mint mark on ground, date in exergue, tiny B.P. to upper right, 7.99g (McD 243; QM 189; KM 29; Fr 38; Marsh 273; S 4003). *Some very light marks, uncirculated, previously graded by PCGS as MS64.* £300-400

Price Realised : £480

ex Ebay purchase 2002
Calendar year mintage 2,2349,000

730 **George V,** Sovereign, 1914 S, bare head left, B.M. on truncation, latter stop weak and smaller, *rev* St George slaying dragon with sword, S mint mark on ground, date in exergue, tiny B.P. to upper right, 7.99g (McD 246; QM 190; KM 29; Fr 38; Marsh 274; S 4003). *Some light nicks on neck and reverse field, otherwise practically as struck.* £300-400

Price Realised : £624

ex Randy Weir Numismatics, Unionville, Ontario, Canada, purchased 10 June 1991
Calendar year mintage 1,774,000

731 **George V,** Sovereign, 1915 S, bare head left, B.M. on truncation, latter stop weak and smaller, lightly die flawed in some letters of legend, *rev* St George slaying dragon with sword, S mint mark on ground, date in exergue, tiny B.P. to upper right, 7.99g (McD 249; QM 191; KM 29; Fr 38; Marsh 275 S; S 4003). *Some light nicks on neck, otherwise good extremely fine.* £300-400

Price Realised : £312

ex Randy Weir Numismatics, Unionville, Ontario, Canada, purchased 10 June 1991
Calendar year mintage 1,346,000

732 **George V,** Sovereign, 1916 S, bare head left, B.M. on truncation, latter stop weak and smaller, *rev* St George slaying dragon with sword, S mint mark on ground, date in exergue, tiny B.P. to upper right, 7.98g (McD 252; QM 192; KM 29; Fr 38; Marsh 276; S 4003). *Some light marks on head, reverse rim nick, otherwise extremely fine / good extremely fine.* £300-350

Price Realised : £312

ex Randy Weir Numismatics, Unionville, Ontario, Canada, purchased c.1997
Calendar year mintage 1,242,000

733 **George V,** Sovereign, 1917 S, bare head left, B.M. on truncation, latter stop weak and smaller, *rev* St George slaying dragon with sword, S mint mark on ground, date in exergue, tiny B.P. to upper right, 7.99g (McD 255; QM 193; KM 29; Fr 38; Marsh 277; S 4003). *Bagmarks and nicks both sides, scratch on cloak, otherwise good extremely fine.* £300-400

Price Realised : £288

ex Randy Weir Numismatics, Unionville, Ontario, Canada, purchased 10 June 1991
Calendar year mintage 1,666,000

734 **George V,** Sovereign, 1918 S, bare head left, B.M. on truncation, latter stop weak and smaller, *rev* St George slaying dragon with sword, S mint mark on ground, date in exergue, tiny B.P. to upper right, 7.99g (McD 258; QM 194; KM 29; Fr 38; Marsh 278; S 4003). *Just a few light hairlines, very pleasing, uncirculated.* £300-400

Price Realised : £360

ex Randy Weir Numismatics, Unionville, Ontario, Canada, purchased c.1997
Calendar year mintage 3,716,000

735 **George V,** Sovereign, 1919 S, bare head left, B.M. on truncation, latter stop weak and smaller, *rev* St George slaying dragon with sword, S mint mark on ground, date in exergue, tiny B.P. to upper right, 7.99g (McD 261; QM 195; KM 29; Fr 38; Marsh 279; S 4003). *Some light surface marks and bagmarks, good extremely fine.* £300-400

Price Realised : £864

Calendar year mintage 1,835,000

The Legendary 1920 Sydney Mint Sovereign

736 **George V,** Sovereign, 1920 S, Sydney mint, by Edgar Bertram MacKennal, bare head left, B.M. on truncation, latter stop weak and smaller, toothed border on obverse, GEORGIVS V D. G. BRITT: OMN: REX F. D. IND: IMP:, *rev* struck en médaille, by Benedetto Pistrucci, St George slaying dragon with sword, horse with long tail, broken lance on ground-line to left, *WWP* in relief under lance, S in relief on ground-line at centre, date in exergue, tiny B.P. to upper right, grained border in linear circle surrounding, edge milled, 7.99g, 22.1mm (McD 264; cf Quartermaster 196; KM 29; Fr 38; Marsh 280 R4; S 4003). *Struck from a rusted reverse die as usual for this rarest of the rare currency issues from the Sydney mint, tiny scratch on face of St George, with a few other light handling marks, tiny reverse rim nick and another tiny nick on the obverse, otherwise practically as struck, of the highest rarity and the crowning piece in the collection.* £300,000-400,000

Price Realised : £780,000
New World Record

ex Jaggards, Sydney Australia, retail list, February 1979
ex Kurt Jaggard Monetary Auction Sale 2, Sydney, Australia, 11 April 2006, lot 404, sold for AU$582,500 (£392,000)
purchased by Winsor and Sons, Jamberoo, NSW Australia as detailed in McDonald footnote (a) and p.71

Calendar year mintage 360,000 – but 1920 dated coins must statistically be a small fraction of this judging from the tiny number of survivors that have ever appeared for sale on dealers lists or in public auction.
The 1920 S is the rarest date and mint combination in the gold Sovereign series of the British Empire. Much rarer than the London 1819 Sovereign, the key piece of the Great Britain Sovereign series of which there are about 10-12 specimens in commerce.
The McDonald catalogue for 2012 rates UNC quality 1920S Sovereign at a valuation of AU$900,000 (or £606,000 at the current exchange rate)

Other examples traced of the 1920 Sydney mint Sovereign in chronological order of date sold publicly.

1. Spink and Son (Australia) Pty Ltd, Sydney, Australia, Sale 2, 2 November 1978, lot 631, "nearly EF" sold for AU$3,600 hammer price (estimate AU$3,000), ex A H F Baldwin collection.

Spink and Son, London, Auction 90, "The Property of a Lady", 15 March 1992, lot 438, "good EF" sold for £104,000 hammer price – the second highest price ever achieved for a British coin at that time (estimate £20,000-25,000). This collection was once that of Capt J J Cullimore Allen, author of *Sovereigns of the British Empire*, published in 1965, in which from his narrative it does not sound as though he owned a 1920 S at that time. He died in 1970 but Mr D G Liddel of Spink and Son fulfilled one last promise to obtain this coin for the collection to make it complete in 1978.

2. Noble Numismatics, Sydney, Australia, Sale 50 – 20th Anniversary Sale, 20-22 March 1996, lot 1470, "EF" quality, sold for AU$135,000 hammer price (estimate AU$100,000).

3. Specimen / Proof Striking sold in the Quartermaster collection, Monetarium (Australia) Pty Ltd, Kogarah, 4 June 2009, lot 196, "Finest known example FDC" sold for AU$800,000 hammer price (estimate AU$750,000-850,000). This coin has been struck from a good reverse die as opposed to the other three which all appear to be from a rusty reverse die.

There was a 1920 S Sovereign sold through Spink and Son, circa November 1973, having been bought in the Wallis and Wallis Sale (CM43) of 23 October 1973, however a catalogue of this sale has not been available to consult further. It is suspected that that coin could be the one offered for sale here, as there was a detailed report of the coin prepared by the Royal Mint certifying it genuine with its distinctive "pickled" reverse. The weight of the coin was exactly the same as the coin offered here and therefore may be some earlier provenance for this piece. This makes a total of only three different currency examples that have passed through public auction, which have the rusted reverse die, and the one specimen proof that was sold at the Quartermaster sale. The first Sovereign listed above has since been housed in an institutional collection and is therefore far less likely to appear again for sale, as opposed to those that are privately owned. There is also a currency 1920 S Sovereign with the distinctive "pickled" reverse certified genuine and housed in the Royal Australian Mint Collection, another institutional piece unlikely ever to be on the market. This coin came from the Reserve Bank of Australia, to whom it had been handed in 1931, when Australia left the Gold Standard and law dictated that gold was to be sold to the Central Bank by private individuals from 1929.

The story of the 1920 dated Sydney mint Sovereign is one steeped in mystery; why is it so rare and elusive today?

Firstly, it is interesting to note at this decade change that very few other denominations exist as 1920 dated coins from the Sydney mint. In fact it is only the bronze Penny that seems to have been issued for currency dated that year with some from Sydney, probably more from Melbourne, with a total output of over nine million pieces. According to McDonald all the currency Halfpennies dated 1920 were produced at Melbourne (a pattern only existing for Sydney), as opposed to Krause that lists them as being from Sydney with a mintage just over four million. However, what is more striking is the lack of silver currency from the Sydney mint dated 1920, there being only some extremely rare patterns of the Florin and Shilling but no Sixpences or Threepences. This was because of the price fluctuation in silver following World War I, which culminated in the price reaching a major high in sterling on 11 February 1920 of 89.5pence an ounce. For this reason, manufacturing coin was totally uneconomical before you even consider the additional costs of smelting and minting. There were also no gold Half-Sovereigns produced from Sydney at this time, as reported in the Royal Mint report for 1921, reviewing production in 1920.

Contemporary surviving records from the Sydney mint are sketchy and what survives on record at the Royal Mint is only of what dies were produced to send to Sydney and the calendar year output figures.

Because the calendar year output figure has always been quoted as 360,000 pieces from the mint record as evidenced in publications like "Sovereigns of the British Empire" by Capt J J Cullimore Allen, it was only ever suspected to be a "rare" year, as this output was much lower than the seven figure sums produced in each year of the preceding decade. In fact Cullimore Allen compared the rarity equally to a 1922 Sydney, which had a slightly higher output year and did not even individually value the coin on a tentative price list, dated 25 February 1965 and included with the book, which rates Burgers Ponds at £350-400, when a lowly Sydney George V Sovereign is rated "from £4". It must also be remembered that information at that time from Australian researchers and collectors was rare, as the Australian law dictated that private individuals could not legally retain gold coins.

It should be additionally borne in mind that the output figure given by the mint is for the total of Sovereigns produced in a calendar year and does not necessarily correlate with the date upon each coin. Most of the 360,000 produced could well have been 1919 dated which is suggested by the few surviving currency specimens dated 1920 that have been publicly sold.

It seems clear there was a major issue with the condition of the reverse dies received at the Sydney mint, which would have been shipped from London in advance of the new date being produced.

The fact that three of the 1920 Sovereigns ever sold by auction, and the example in the Royal Australian Mint, have the unusual reverse does suggest that the dies as received were not in usable condition, which is evident from the fact of the "pickled" surface state of the dies used to strike the currency pieces surviving today. This "rusted" appearance seems, perhaps, to be a result of the original packing grease used to transport the dies becoming encrusted and / or baked onto the dies and giving them a rough texture which transmitted to the coins as the "rusted" look on all the known currency pieces evident today. More research needs to be done to find a record of the passage of the dies from the mint in London to Sydney by ship, especially if the voyage had interruption or the cargo hold had a problem. Either a large quantity was produced from these faulty reverse dies and later melted down after scrutiny from quality control, leaving some scant few survivors (which seems highly unlikely in practice, especially with gold coinage) or a small quantity only was ever struck as a matter of record or for a special purpose, once it was realised that full scale production of coins dated 1920 would not be possible.

From some limited research in collaboration with Mr G P Dyer, former Curator of the Royal Mint, it has been possible to glean that a total of 22 reverse dies dated 1920 left the mint office for packing and shipping in November 1919. Research compiled over the years by Mr Dyer from the literally scraps of information left of what was the Sydney mint record, it seems only two of these dies were used in 1920, having been received in January of that year in Sydney. Therefore it could be concluded that 20 of the 22 reverse dies were unusable. Furthermore, the 360,000 Sovereigns struck in 1920 were produced initially on two dates in January to a total of £220,000, and latterly two dates in June to a total of £140,000. The January "journeys" (a days work in the mint) were most likely 1919 dated coins. The two journeys of June 1920 could have been produced from the two reverse dies of the 22 received, but further confirmation is required. Presumably 22 reverse dies, if they had all been used, would have been enough to strike up to four million sovereigns, if demand and capability dictated it. Mintage output in calendar year 1918 was nearly of that quantity and later for the calendar year 1925 at Sydney broke five million output for one time only.

So from the scant evidence, it seems possible that a maximum 140,000 Sovereigns of the 360,000 produced in the year 1920 could have been dated 1920. However, the physical survivors that have appeared suggest a very low mintage indeed. This cataloguer feels that they must have been struck to order for a special event in 1920 without the time available to restore the reverse dated die to a proper usable state.

The specimen strike as the Quartermaster coin (No.3 above) was probably struck later, perhaps to mark the closure of the Sydney mint in 1926, when more care and attention could be made with one of the dies to finally obliterate the rusty texture upon it.

The small number of surviving coins in commerce strongly suggest a very small mintage and therefore it would seem much if not all the quantity struck in the calendar year 1920 were probably dated 1919. The intriguing story of the 1920 dated coins being struck for a prominent special occasion seems somehow more likely, and further research could be very valid and hopefully very fruitful.

A 1920 Sydney Sovereign will always be a piece of Australian numismatic history and, for now, an enigma.

The Very Rare 1921 Sydney Sovereign

737 **George V,** Sovereign, 1921 S, bare head left, B.M. on truncation, latter stop absent, *rev* St George slaying dragon with sword, S mint mark on ground, date in exergue, tiny B.P. to upper right, 7.98g (McD 267; QM 199 S; KM 29; Fr 38; Marsh 281 R3; S 4003). *Reverse rim nick, nick on tip of neck, weaker reverse strike around ground-line, otherwise good extremely fine and very rare.* £1500-2000

Price Realised : £1,980

ex Winsor and Sons, Jamberoo, NSW Australia, purchased 2005
Calendar year mintage 839,000
The McDonald catalogue for 2012 rates AUNC quality 1921S Sovereign at a valuation of AU$3,500 (or £2,350)

The Extremely Rare 1922 Sydney Sovereign

738 **George V,** Sovereign, 1922 S, bare head left, B.M. on truncation, latter stop very weak, *rev* St George slaying dragon with sword, small raised die flaw from tail to lance, S mint mark on ground, date in exergue, tiny B.P. to upper right, 7.98g (McD 270; cf.QM.202; KM 29; Fr 38; Marsh 282 R3; S 4003). *A myriad of bagmarks, mainly on obverse, otherwise extremely fine and extremely rare.* £10,000-15,000

Price Realised : £17,400

ex Jaggards of Sydney, invoiced 13 June 2001
Calendar year mintage 578,000
The McDonald catalogue for 2012 rates EF quality 1922S Sovereign at a valuation of AU$35,750 (or £24,075). Curiously the Quartermaster collection only had an example of the even rarer specimen proof striking.

The Extremely Rare 1923 Sydney Sovereign with a Satin Finish

739 **George V,** Specimen Sovereign, 1923 S, struck to proof quality, bare head left, B.M. on truncation, latter stop absent, *rev* St George slaying dragon with sword, S mint mark on ground, date in exergue, tiny B.P. to upper right, 7.97g (McD 273; QM 205 R7; KM 29; Fr 38; Marsh 283 R5; S 4003). *One nick in obverse field and one speck of dirt on reverse rim, otherwise with a satin finish, compares very well with the Quartermaster collection specimen striking, of the highest rarity.* £30,000-40,000

Price Realised : £30,000

ex Winsor and Sons, Jamberoo, NSW Australia, purchased 2005
Calendar year mintage 416,000

The Rare 1924 Sydney Sovereign

740 **George V,** Sovereign, 1924 S, bare head left, B.M. on truncation, latter stop weak and smaller, small raised die flaw from rim to neck, *rev* St George slaying dragon with sword, S mint mark on ground, date in exergue, tiny B.P. to upper right, raised die flaw by lance, 7.98g (McD 276; QM 208 S; KM 29; Fr 38; Marsh 284 R3; S 4003). *Unevenly toned on reverse, other light marks in obverse field, extremely fine and very rare* £1200-1500

Price Realised : £2,160

ex Randy Weir Numismatics, Unionville, Ontario, Canada, purchased September 1991
Calendar year mintage 394,000
The McDonald catalogue for 2012 rates the EF quality 1924S Sovereign at a valuation of AU$2,250 (or £1,500)

741 **George V,** Sovereign, 1925 S, bare head left, B.M. on truncation, latter stop weak and smaller, small raised die flaw under 2 of date to rim, *rev* St George slaying dragon with sword, S mint mark on ground, date in exergue, tiny B.P. to upper right, 7.99g (McD 279; QM 211; KM 29; Fr 38; Marsh 285 S; S 4003). *Reverse rim nick, otherwise practically as struck* £300-400

Price Realised : £384

ex Randy Weir Numismatics, Unionville, Ontario, Canada, purchased September 1991
Calendar year mintage 5,632,000. This is the highest calendar year output ever from the Sydney mint for a gold Sovereign.

The Extremely Rare 1926 Sydney Currency Sovereign

742 **George V,** Sovereign, 1926 S, bare head left, B.M. on truncation, M very weak and latter stop absent, *rev* St George slaying dragon with sword, small raised die flaw from tail to lance, S mint mark on ground, date in exergue, tiny B.P. to upper right, 7.98g (McD 282; QM 214 R3; KM 29; Fr 38; Marsh 286 R4; S 4003). *Some light marks, a little weak of strike on reverse and some nicks in the exergue, appears to be finer than the Quartermaster collection coin, lightly toned good extremely fine, practically as struck and extremely rare.* £20,000-25,000

Price Realised : £22,800

ex Winsor and Sons, Jamberoo, NSW Australia, purchased c.2004
Calendar year mintage 1,031,050
The McDonald catalogue for 2012 rates UNC quality 1926S Sovereign at a valuation of AU$58,000 (or £39,000)

The Extremely Rare Specimen Striking of the 1926 Sydney Sovereign

743 **George V,** Specimen Sovereign, 1926 S, struck to proof quality, bare head left, B.M. on truncation, latter stop weak and smaller, *rev* St George slaying dragon with sword, S mint mark on ground, date in exergue, tiny B.P. to upper right, 7.98g, 22.3mm (McD 282; QM -; KM 29; Fr 38; Marsh -; S 4003). *One light rim nick on reverse and nick on body of horse, tiny speck on king's cheek, otherwise toned practically as struck and of the highest rarity.* £30,000-40,000

Price Realised : £33,600

ex Noble Numismatics Sale 66, 28 March 2001, lot 1318
Perhaps the odd 50 in the calendar year mintage of 1,031,050 were some of these specimen strikings which were struck to mark the closure of the Sydney mint along with other later strikings of Sydney mint coins like the 1902 gold Five Pounds and Two Pounds amongst others.
For further reading on the subject of the closure of the mint see the Journal of the Numismatic Association of Australia, volume 2, article by John Sharples "The Numismatic Collection of the Museum of Victoria" available online at the Association website.
Specimen strikes were produced as a matter of record for institutional collections and for rare presentation to very important persons.
The McDonald catalogue for 2012 rates the Proof quality 1926S Sovereign at a valuation of AU$195,000 (or £131,000)

MELBOURNE

The Melbourne Mint

Colonel Edward Ward, the first Deputy Master at Melbourne, originally anticipated the new Melbourne mint would open as early as 1870. However, due to circumstances somewhat beyond control, the mint opened late for operation, 12 June 1872, in William Street. It was later considered one of the six best buildings in the City. This tardiness was mostly because the ship *Rangoon* had sunk near Galle Harbour in Ceylon while carrying all the new 1871 dated dies from the mint in London. A very limited number of the dies were salvaged and these later came into use with the overdate 1872 over 1, which is explained in more detail in lot 746. Colonel Ward was already experienced, having previously been Deputy Master at Sydney and it was through his leadership that the difficulties were overcome at Melbourne. By the end of 1872 nearly three quarters of a million sovereigns of the shield reverse had been produced, all with the mint letter M under the wreath on the reverse. St George reverse Sovereigns and gold Half Sovereigns were also introduced to production from 1873 with mint letter M, and both shield and St George reverse coins were produced in most years until 1887. The shield design was retained at the Australian branch mints only, as it was still the preferred coin in trade with India and Asia, and the St George reverse was preferred domestically. The mints were given the choice of which to strike according to demand, which is why some years do not exist for certain reverse types.

According to the publication *Royal Sovereign*, a Chinese General, Wong Yung Ho, visited the Melbourne mint in 1887 and confirmed that the shield design was preferred by the Indians when trading with the Orient. The Indians feared they would upset the Chinese if they paid for their wares with the St George reverse coin. This was because of the humiliating position of the Chinese national symbol the dragon under the horseman and therefore this reverse design was not generally seen in commerce in Asia. Half Sovereigns were last produced dated 1915 and the Sovereigns were last struck dated 1931.

According to *Sovereigns of the British Empire* by Capt J J Cullimore Allen, when the Melbourne mint ceased minting Imperial type gold Sovereigns dated 1931, the total quantity of all Sovereigns at this branch mint stood at 147,282,731 pieces, including those sent for pyx trial assay. This was the highest total of gold sovereigns from the three branch mints based in Australia. However the individual year by year breakdowns quoted in this publication, including the pyx or assay totals, come to 59,436 coins less than the quoted total, showing some inaccuracy in the quoted figures or more likely a lack of completeness in the year breakdowns in the earlier period of the mint operation, perhaps in the young head series where some uncertainty lies.

The Reign of Queen Victoria (1837-1901)
House of Hanover

Born: 24 May 1819

Accession: 20 June 1837

Married: Albert of Saxe-Coburg and Gotha, 10 February 1840

Coronation: Thursday 28 June 1838

Children: four sons, five daughters

Died: 22 January 1901, aged 81

Melbourne Mint Imperial Type Victoria Young Head Sovereigns, Shield Reverse
The full description for the young head shield reverse Sovereign of the Melbourne mint is as follows

Victoria (1837-1901), Sovereign, Melbourne Branch Mint, 1872 M, engraved after William Wyon, third young head left, with double fillet, w.w. in relief on truncation, date below, toothed border and raised rim both sides, VICTORIA DEI GRATIA, *rev* struck with inverted die axis, engraved after Jean Baptiste Merlen, crowned quartered shield of arms within laurel wreath, mint letter M below, emblems below, edge milled

744 **Victoria (1837-1901),** Sovereign, 1872 M, third young head left, w.w. in relief on truncation, date below, trace of doubling in date and legend both sides, raised die flaw from D of legend to head, *rev* crowned quartered shield of arms within laurel wreath, mint letter M below, emblems below, 8.00g (McD 120; QM 48 S; Marsh 59 R; KM 6; Fr 12; S 3854). *Some light surface marks, otherwise good extremely fine and rare.* £400-600

Price Realised : £720

ex Kurt Jaggard Coins, Sydney, Australia, purchased 30 May 2002
Calendar year mintage 748,180 which includes St George reverse design pieces.

745 **Victoria,** Sovereign, 1872 M, struck with an en médaille die axis, third young head left, w.w. in relief on truncation, date below, raised die flaw from neck to rim by 7 of date, *rev* struck with an upright die axis, crowned quartered shield of arms within laurel wreath, mint letter M more slender and tall below, emblems below, 7.98g (cf McD.120; QM 48 S; Marsh 59 R; KM 6; Fr 12; S 3854). *A few tiny nicks on head and neck, tiny red spots on reverse, otherwise extremely fine / good extremely fine, very unusual and rare.* £600-800

Price Realised : £1,800

ex Douro Cargo, Spink Auction 118, 20-21 November 1996, lot 1045 (part)
Calendar year mintage 748,180 which includes St George reverse design pieces.

"2" struck over "1"

746 **Victoria,** Sovereign, 1872 M, 2 struck over 1, third young head left, hair in bun more disjointed, weak bridge to nose, w.w. in relief on truncation, date below, raised die flaw to left of date to rim, raised die flaw to left of D in legend to head, further flaw at penultimate A of legend, *rev* crowned quartered shield of arms within laurel wreath, mint letter M below touches left ribbon, emblems below, 7.97g (McD 120 note c; QM 49 S; Marsh 59A R4; KM 6; Fr 12; S 3854). *Some tiny black spots in upper right quarter of reverse, otherwise weak extremely fine / good extremely fine and very rare.* £1200-1500

Price Realised : £3,240

ex Randy Weir Numismatics, Unionville, Ontario, Canada, purchased September 1991
Calendar year mintage 748,000 which includes St George reverse design pieces, 180 of this total went for pyx trial.
According to McDonald and the Quartermaster catalogues, these overdate pieces were struck for only a few days in September 1872 when 1872 dated dies were expended unexpectedly early before a new batch of dies could be received from England. A local engraver, Julius Hogarth, was employed to change unused 1871 dated dies to show 1872. The new 1872 dies from England arrived in early October but, what is more interesting is that, the 1871 dated dies had already been to the bottom of the sea and back. They had been sent over the previous year when it was anticipated that the Melbourne mint would be ready on schedule for operation. However, the ship carrying the 1871 dies ,the *Rangoon* hit rocks and sank near Galle Harbour on the last leg of the journey from Ceylon. Some of the dies were evidently salvaged and it seems Julius Hogarth made at least one usable with the overdate engraving.
It seems that for 1873 only St George reverse designs were produced.

747 **Victoria,** Sovereign, 1874 M, third young head left, w.w. in relief on truncation, date below, trace of doubling in date and legend both sides, raised die flaw from D of legend to head, *rev* crowned quartered shield of arms within laurel wreath, mint letter M below, emblems below, 7.98g (McD 122; QM 51 S; Marsh 59 R; KM 6; Fr 12; S 3854). *Some light surface marks, a little weakly struck at centre, red tone, otherwise good extremely fine.* £600-800

Price Realised : £624

ex Randy Weir Numismatics, Unionville, Ontario, Canada, purchased September 1991
Calendar year mintage 1,373,000 which includes St George reverse design pieces, 298 of this total went for pyx trial. There were no shield Sovereigns issued from Melbourne in the preceding year 1873.

748 **Victoria,** Sovereign, 1874 M, third young head left, w.w. in relief on truncation, date below, *rev* crowned quartered shield of arms within laurel wreath, mint letter M taller and slender below, emblems below, 7.98g (McD 122; QM 51 S; Marsh 59 R; KM 6; Fr 12; S 3854). *Patches of silver colour showing through on reverse, perhaps surface enrichment of residual silver solder and gilding, other surface marks, very fine.* £300-350

Price Realised : £288

ex Randy Weir Numismatics, Unionville, Ontario, Canada, purchased April 1992
Calendar year mintage 1,373,000 which includes St George reverse design pieces, 298 of this total went for pyx trial.
This piece was originally bought for the Bentley Collection as a piece seemingly demonstrating a silver alloy in the mix with the gold content. There are no shield Sovereigns from the Melbourne mint from 1875-1879 inclusive.

The Extremely Rare 1880 M shield Sovereign

749 **Victoria,** Sovereign, 1880 M, third young head left, w.w. in relief on truncation, date below, trace of doubling in date and legend both sides, raised die flaw from D of legend to head, *rev* crowned quartered shield of arms within laurel wreath, mint letter M below, die flaw running through some letters, emblems below, 7.98g (McD 128; QM 59 R3; Marsh 61 R2; KM 6; Fr 12; S 3854). *Rim nick on obverse and one on reverse, light bagmarks, toned good extremely fine and extremely rare, this coin appears to be finer than the Quartermaster example.* £5000-6000

Price Realised : £7,440

ex Douro Cargo, Spink Auction 118, 20-21 November 1996, lot 1074
Calendar year mintage 3,052,800 which includes St George reverse design pieces, 654 of this total went for pyx trial.
The McDonald catalogue for 2012 rates an AUNC quality 1880M shield Sovereign at a valuation of AU$11,250 (£7,500)

A New Style Portrait at the Melbourne Mint

From 1881 till 1887 with the shield reverse the fourth bust style comes into use at Melbourne just like at Sydney. The main defining characteristics are the much higher hairline which if extended up would meet the centre of the letter A in the legend. Behind the ear there is a distinctly longer curling strand of hair compared to those either side of it. The hair at the rear of the hair bun is perhaps a little more finely engraved in the strands and there is a slightly larger gap from the G of legend to the hair bun. Additionally the tip of the neck at the front is more sharply pointed than the previous busts.

A Wonderful Example of the 1881 M Shield Sovereign

750 **Victoria,** Sovereign, 1881 M, fourth young head left, w.w. in relief on truncation which is more truncated with a pointed tip at front, hair behind ear with longer strand, hairline higher on forehead, date below, *rev* crowned quartered shield of arms within laurel wreath, mint letter M below, right foot near to ribbon, emblems below, 7.99g (McD 130; QM 61 S; Marsh 62 R; KM 6; Fr 12; S 3854). *Rim nick, a few light handling marks, otherwise as struck and very pleasing with a proof-like hue, appears finer than the Quartermaster specimen.* £2000-2500

Price Realised : £4,320

ex Kurt Jaggard Coins, Sydney, Australia, purchased 30 May 2002
Calendar year mintage 2,324,800 which includes St George reverse design pieces, 503 of this total went for pyx trial.
The McDonald catalogue for 2012 rates an UNC quality 1881M shield Sovereign at a valuation of AU$5,000 (or £3,350)

751 **Victoria,** Sovereign, 1882 M, fourth young head left, w.w. in relief on truncation, date below, *rev* crowned quartered shield of arms within laurel wreath, mint letter M below, right foot touches ribbon, emblems below, 7.98g (McD 132; QM 63 S; Marsh 63; KM 6; Fr 12; S 3854). *Surface marks and rim nicks, extremely fine, reverse better and scarce.* £500-600

Price Realised : £480

ex Randy Weir Numismatics, Unionville, Ontario, Canada, purchased October 1991
Calendar year mintage 371,400 of which 531 went for pyx trial.

The Extremely Rare 1883 M Shield Sovereign

752 **Victoria,** Sovereign, 1883 M, fourth young head left, w.w. in relief on truncation, date below, *rev* crowned quartered shield of arms within laurel wreath, mint letter M below, left foot touches ribbon, emblems below, 7.98g (McD 134; QM 65 R2; Marsh 64 R2; KM 6; Fr 12; S 3854). *Toned with two tiny black specks on reverse shield, otherwise uncirculated and finer than the Quartermaster example, extremely rare.* £2500-3000

Price Realised : £4,800

ex Randy Weir Numismatics, Unionville, Ontario, Canada, purchased October 1991
Calendar year mintage 427,000 of which 450 went for pyx trial.

753 **Victoria,** Sovereign, 1884 M, fourth young head left, w.w. in relief on truncation, date below, *rev* crowned quartered shield of arms within laurel wreath, mint letter M below, right foot near to ribbon, emblems below, 7.98g (McD 136; QM 67 S; Marsh 65; KM 6; Fr 12; S 3854). *Light surface marks and hairlines, bagmarks and a few nicks, otherwise good extremely fine and scarce.* £800-1000

Price Realised : £768

ex Randy Weir Numismatics, Unionville, Ontario, Canada, purchased 5 December 1989
Calendar year mintage 2,942,000 which includes St George reverse design pieces, 630 of this total went for pyx trial.

754 **Victoria,** Sovereign, 1884 M, fourth young head left, w.w. in relief on truncation, date below, *rev* crowned quartered shield of arms within laurel wreath, mint letter M below, right foot touches ribbon, emblems below, 7.98g (McD 136; QM 67 S; Marsh 65; KM 6; Fr 12; S 3854). *Some light nicks and surface marks, prooflike and obviously a very early strike, good extremely fine, reverse as struck and rare.* £1000-1200

Price Realised : £1,032

ex A H Baldwin & Sons Ltd, November 2008
Calendar year mintage 2,942,000 which includes St George reverse design pieces, 630 of this total went for pyx trial.
This coin could even have be struck from the proof dies after they had served their purpose in striking proof coins and therefore retaining some of the proof qualities on the surfaces. The coin is at least an early striking showing sharp definition of the design.

755 **Victoria,** Sovereign, 1885 M, fourth young head left, w.w. in relief on truncation, date below, *rev* crowned quartered shield of arms within laurel wreath, mint letter M below, emblems below, 7.99g (McD 138; QM 69 S; Marsh 66; KM 6; Fr 12; S 3854). *Quite bagmarked and scuffed, with reverse rim nick, dig on cheek, extremely fine, reverse better, rare.* £400-600

Price Realised : £432

ex Randy Weir Numismatics, Unionville, Ontario, Canada, purchased 18 January 1990
Calendar year mintage 2,966,500 which includes St George reverse design pieces, 643 of this total went for pyx trial.

The Extremely Rare 1886 M Shield Sovereign

756 **Victoria,** Sovereign, 1886 M, fourth young head left, w.w. in relief on truncation, date below, *rev* crowned quartered shield of arms within laurel wreath, mint letter M below, emblems below, 7.98g (McD 140; QM 71 R4; Marsh 67 R3; KM 6; Fr 12; S 3854). *Light scratch in field, and another under chin intruding neck with other light surface marks, black speck on Irish harp, extremely fine, reverse better, less surface marked than the Quartermaster coin and appears to be of commensurate quality and extremely rare.* £8000-10,000

Price Realised : £8,880

ex Noble Numismatics, Sale 66, 28 March 2001, lot 1268
Calendar year mintage 2,901,500 which includes St George reverse design pieces, 631 of this total went for pyx trial.
The McDonald catalogue for 2012 rates an EF quality 1886M shield Sovereign at a valuation of AU$34,900 (or £23,500)

The Extremely Rare 1887 M Shield Sovereign

757 **Victoria,** Sovereign, 1887 M, fourth young head left, w.w. in relief on truncation, date below, *rev* crowned quartered shield of arms within laurel wreath, mint letter M below, left foot touches ribbon, emblems below, 7.98g (McD 142; QM 73 R3; Marsh 68 R3; KM 6; Fr 12; S 3854). *Very light surface marks, otherwise toned, as struck, and appears on par with the Quartermaster example, if not better, extremely rare.* £7000-9000

Price Realised : £7,440

ex Kurt Jaggard Coins, Sydney, Australia, purchased 30 May 2002
Calendar year mintage 1,916,424 which includes St George reverse design pieces, 624 of this total (probably all shield reverses) went for pyx trial.
The McDonald catalogue for 2012 rates an UNC quality 1887M shield Sovereign at a valuation of AU$19,500 (or £13,100)

Melbourne Mint Imperial Type Victoria Young Head Sovereigns, St George and Dragon Reverse

The new St George and dragon reverse, a design resurrected from the reign of George IV, was introduced at Sydney in 1871 and Melbourne in 1872. Variation can occur in the portrait at the truncation, where the initials W.W. can either be "buried" within the truncation in relief without stops and therefore not fully apparent, or later versions which have the W.W. complete on truncation with stops and in relief.

For more information on the varieties of this type, please see lot 672, page 340.

A note on the Pyx Trial Totals Quoted for the Melbourne Mint

Capt Cullimore Allen in his publication *Sovereigns of the British Empire* gives calendar year outputs for the Melbourne mint for every year of its existence and a separate figure each time for "Assay Pieces" which were those set aside for the annual trial of the Pyx in London. Cullimore Allen does not make it quite clear whether this figure is included in the calendar year output totals or whether it is in addition to. Earlier in the publication it is suggested that the pyx assay number is included in the year total as the Deputy Master of the Melbourne mint seems to have been instructed to always finish a years output on a round number figure. Pyx Trial coins by their very nature are intended to be circulation strikes and in the modern coinage are not additions to a total production run, so it seems to make sense that the Assay figure must be included in the output total for the year. It is not as if once the Trial of the Pyx on these coins has taken place that they would not have been released into circulation anyway, if they were not there would be thousands of sovereigns gathering in storage somewhere from these annual trials. However later in the book Cullimore Allen, just before Edward VII, specifically says that the assay total needs to be added to the still round figured calendar year totals. This is in reaction to correspondence he had with the Deputy Master at the Melbourne mint c.1960, who quoted an old correspondent from 1909. To this cataloguer something in this information seems to have been lost in the passage of time and through more than one correspondent. The round figure totals make more sense, Sydney mint carried out the same round total practice and the same Deputy Master was responsible for this at the start, so the Assay trial pieces we feel must be already included in the Melbourne totals, which is why the totals quoted here are also different to the Marsh publication, as he added the Pyx trial piece numbers on top.

A full description of the St George reverse Melbourne Sovereign is as follows

Victoria (1837-1901), Sovereign, 1874 M, young head of third style left, engraved after William Wyon, bound with two fillets, letter M below, WW buried in truncation in relief, VICTORIA D: G: BRITANNIAR: REG: F: D:, finely toothed border within twin linear concentric circles and raised rim both sides, *rev* inverted die axis, engraved after Benedetto Pistrucci, St George slaying dragon with sword, dragon claws four to left and four to right arm, the second on upper arm detached, horse with long tail ending in three strands, tail with extra single stand spur at upper curve of tail, broken lance on ground-line to left, *WWP* in relief under lance, date in exergue, tiny B.P. to upper right, edge milled.

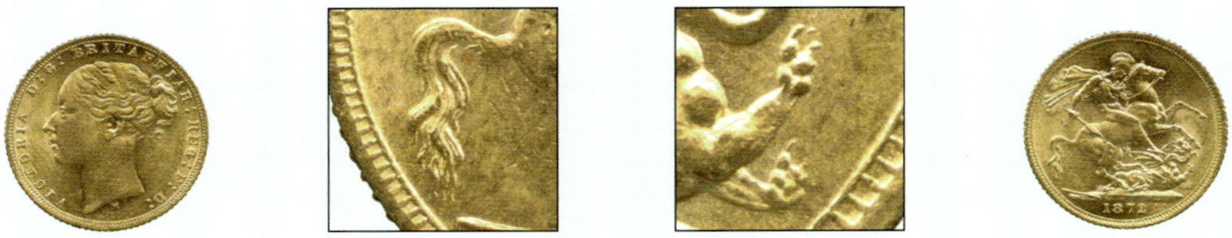

some dragon claws absent

758 **Victoria (1837-1901),** Sovereign, 1872 M, young head of third style left, letter M below, ww buried in truncation in relief, VICTORIA D: G: BRITANNIAR: REG: F: D:, die flaw between N's in legend, *rev* St George slaying dragon with sword, some dragon claws absent, three to left and one to right arm, the second on upper arm detached, horse with long tail ending in three strands, tail with extra single stand spur at upper curve of tail, date in exergue, tiny B.P. to upper right, 8.00g (McD 145; QM 77 R2; Marsh 94; KM 7; Fr 16; S 3857). *Some light bagmarks, appears to be finer than the Quartermaster specimen, good extremely fine and very rare.* £1500-2000

Price Realised : £4,560

ex Kurt Jaggard Coins, Sydney, Australia, purchased 30 May 2002
Calendar year mintage 748,180 which includes shield reverse design pieces.
The dragon claws are not fully evident on this 1872 sovereign, it should be the usual 4/4 arrangement but where there should be claws are mere stumps and only 3/1 are visible.
The McDonald catalogue for 2012 rates an AUNC quality 1872M St George Sovereign at a valuation of AU$6,500 (or £4,375)

weak dragon claws of 4/4 arrangement

759 **Victoria,** Sovereign, 1872 M, with misstruck reverse rim, young head of third style left, letter M below, ww buried in truncation in relief, *rev* St George slaying dragon with sword, mere trace of spur on long horse tail, dragon claws of 4/4 arrangement but most very weak, date in exergue, tiny B.P. with faint stops to upper right, rim and border misstruck appearing thicker than usual, 7.98g (cf McD 145; QM 77 R2; Marsh 94; KM 7; Fr 16; S 3857). *Cleaned with surface marks, otherwise very fine, very rare and unusual.* £300-400

Price Realised : £360

ex A H Baldwin & Sons Ltd, June 2008
Calendar year mintage 748,000 which includes St George reverse design pieces, 180 of this total went for pyx trial.

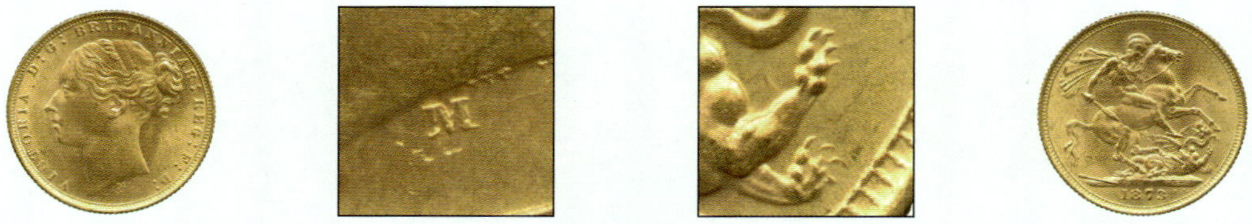

high letter "M" under neck and dragon claws 4/4 arrangement

760 **Victoria,** Sovereign, 1873 M, young head of third style left, letter M below nearly touches neck, ww buried in truncation in relief, first G in legend die flawed to rim, *rev* St George slaying dragon with sword, long tail with trace of hair spur in upper curve of tail, dragon claws all present of 4/4 arrangement, the last a stub claw, date in exergue, tiny B.P. to upper right, 8.00g (McD 147; QM 79 R; Marsh 95; KM 7; Fr 16; S 3857). *Light bagmarks, mainly near to horse tail, otherwise toned, good extremely fine and appears to be on par with the Quartermaster coin, if not more attractive, rare.* £400-500

Price Realised : £1,920

ex Randy Weir Numismatics, Unionville, Ontario, Canada, purchased 12 November 1990
Calendar year mintage 752,000 presumably all St George reverse of which 199 went for pyx trial.

761 **Victoria,** Sovereign, 1874 M, young head of third style left, letter M below near neck, WW buried in truncation in relief, *rev* St George slaying dragon with sword, long tail with single hair spur in upper curve of tail, dragon claws all present of 4/4 arrangement, date in exergue, tiny B.P. to upper right, 7.98g (McD 149; QM 81 R; Marsh 96; KM 7; Fr 16; S 3857). *Light bagmarks on obverse, appears to be finer than the Quartermaster coin, toned practically as struck and rare.* £1000-1200

Price Realised : £984

ex Randy Weir Numismatics, Unionville, Ontario, Canada, purchased 18 July 1990
Calendar year mintage 1,373,000 which includes shield reverse design pieces, 298 of this total went for pyx trial.
The McDonald catalogue for 2012 rates an UNC quality 1874M St George Sovereign at a valuation of AU$3,550 (or £2,400)

762 **Victoria,** Sovereign, 1874 M, struck with an off-centre die axis, young head of third style left, letter M below, WW buried in truncation in relief, light raised die flaws in queen's name, *rev* die axis about 45 degrees off-centre, St George slaying dragon with sword, long tail with single hair spur in upper curve of tail, dragon claws all present of 4/4 arrangement, date in exergue, tiny B.P. to upper right, 7.96g (cf McD.149; QM 81 R; Marsh 96; KM 7; Fr 16; S 3857). *Heavy surface marks and scuffs both sides, nearly very fine and unusual.* £400-500

Price Realised : £408

ex Randy Weir Numismatics, Unionville, Ontario, Canada, purchased 18 July 1990
Calendar year mintage 1,373,000 which includes shield reverse design pieces, 298 of this total went for pyx trial.

Transitional 1875 Reverse
Showing elements of Long Tail and so-called Medium Tail Design

no spur of hair on long tail

763 **Victoria,** Sovereign, 1875 M, young head of third style left, letter M below near neck, WW buried in truncation in relief, *rev* St George slaying dragon with sword, absent spur on long tail, only a mere stub apparent, dragon with 4/4 claw arrangement, date in exergue, tiny B.P. to upper right, 7.99g (cf McD.151a/151b; QM 83 S; Marsh 97; KM 7; Fr 16; S 3857). *Red spot on cheek and tiny spot on reverse rim, other light surface marks and bagmarks, good extremely fine and unusual.* £400-500

Price Realised : £1,128

ex Randy Weir Numismatics, Unionville, Ontario, Canada, purchased October 1991
This coin appears to be a transitional piece between the long tail and so-called medium tail which proves the medium is a variation of the long tail. Elements of the long tail type still vaguely show under scrutiny of the coin and it is therefore a hybrid of McDonald 151a and 151b, the latter being newly discovered.
Calendar year mintage 1,888,000 presumably all St George reverse of which 405 went for pyx trial.

Transitional 1876 Reverse with elements of Long Tail and so-called Medium Tail Design

no spur apparent on long tail and weak dragon claws

764 **Victoria,** Sovereign, 1876 M, young head of third style left, letter M below near neck, WW buried in truncation in relief, *rev* St George slaying dragon with sword, spur absent but terminal strands of long tail evident, raised die flaw at top of tail, dragon claws weak at top arm, arrangement 4/4 but some merely stumps, date in exergue, lightly die flawed figures, tiny B.P. to upper right, 8.00g (cf McD 153; QM 85 S; Marsh 98; KM 7; Fr 16; S 3857). *Very yellow gold, with a few light bagmarks, seems to be on par with the Quartermaster example, weakly struck, good extremely fine.* £400-500

Price Realised : £1,152

ex Randy Weir Numismatics, Unionville, Ontario, Canada, purchased 9 September 1997
This coin appears to be another transitional piece between the long tail and so-called medium tail which proves the medium is a variation of the long tail. Elements of the long tail type still vaguely show under scrutiny, in this case the terminal strands.
Calendar year mintage 2,124,000 presumably all St George reverse of which 445 went for pyx trial.

Transitional 1877 Reverse with elements of Long Tail and so-called Medium Tail Design

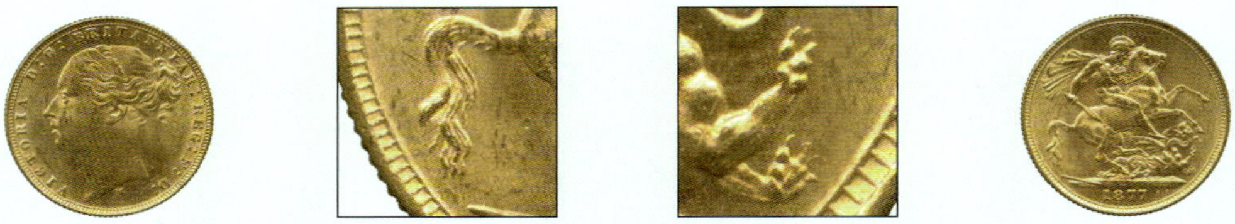

no spur apparent on long tail and weak dragon claws

765 **Victoria,** Sovereign, 1877 M, young head of third style left, letter M below near neck, WW buried in truncation in relief, *rev* St George slaying dragon with sword, spur absent but terminal strands of long tail evident, no hair spur, some raised die flaws in field, dragon claws with some absence and stumps, upper arm with two attached and trace of a detached third claw, lower arm with one attached and three detached, date in exergue, lightly die flawed figures, tiny B.P. to upper right, 7.98g (McD 154; QM 86 R; Marsh 99; KM 7; Fr 16; S 3857). *Streaky tone to reverse, extremely fine/good extremely fine and on par with the Quartermaster specimen which also lacks the spur.* £400-500

Price Realised : £576

ex Randy Weir Numismatics, Unionville, Ontario, Canada, purchased 12 November 1990
Calendar year mintage 1,487,000 presumably all St George reverse of which 316 went for pyx trial.

thin strand spur halfway up tail, all dragon claws apparent and large stops on B.P.

766 **Victoria,** Sovereign, 1878 M, young head of third style left, letter M below lower, WW buried in truncation in relief, some doubling of legend, BR and E out of alignment, *rev* St George slaying dragon with sword, horse with long tail, thin single strand of hair in upper curve of tail, dragon claws of 4/4 arrangement and all apparent, date in exergue, second 8 slightly rotated, tiny B.P. to upper right with large stops, 7.99g (McD 155; QM 87 R; Marsh 100; KM 7; Fr 16; S 3857). *Light bagmarks, brilliant good extremely fine, appears to be finer than the Quartermaster coin.* £400-600

Price Realised : £600

ex Randy Weir Numismatics, Unionville, Ontario, Canada, purchased 12 November 1990
Calendar year mintage 2,171,000 presumably all St George reverse of which 457 went for pyx trial.

weak B.P. with incomplete "B"

767 **Victoria,** Sovereign, 1879 M, young head of third style left, letter M below lower, WW buried in truncation in relief, some doubling of legend, with some letters out of alignment, *rev* St George slaying dragon with sword, weak tail spur with long tail, dragon claws of 4/4 arrangement and all apparent, date in exergue, second 8 slightly rotated, weak B.P. to upper right, incomplete B, 7.99g (McD 157; QM 90 S; Marsh 101; KM 7; Fr 16; S 3857). *Uneven tone, light bagmarks, good extremely fine.* £400-600

Price Realised : £504

ex Randy Weir Numismatics, Unionville, Ontario, Canada, purchased 18 July 1990
Calendar year mintage 2,740,000 presumably all St George reverse of which 594 went for pyx trial.

so-called medium tail variety, no stops in BP and weak dragon claws

768 **Victoria,** Sovereign, 1879 M, so-called medium tail, young head of third style left, letter M below near neck, WW buried in truncation in relief, some doubling of legend, with some letters out of alignment, *rev* St George slaying dragon with sword, absent tail spur with "medium" tail, three strand terminal to tail, shorter strand to left curves outward, dragon claws of 4/4 arrangement but with two upper arm claws detached, two lower claws weak, date in exergue, die flaw in date, weak BP to upper right, incomplete B and stops absent, 7.98g (McD 157a; QM 89 S; Marsh 101; KM 7; Fr 16; S 3857D). *Attractively toned, some light bagmarks, a pleasing extremely fine on par with the Quartermaster coin.* £800-1000

Price Realised : £960

This coin demonstrates the traits of the "medium" tail, which would seem to be a weaker rendition of the long tail when transferred from the master die. It is not the strike of the actual coins that is weak, but the engraving process of the dies used to strike these coins, the detail is therefore different giving the "medium" tail characteristics, a variation on the long tail.
Calendar year mintage 2,740,000 presumably all St George reverse of which 594 went for pyx trial.

last stop in B.P. larger with short dragon claws

769 **Victoria,** Sovereign, 1879 M, so-called medium tail, struck with an off-centre die axis, young head of third style left, letter M below near neck, WW buried in truncation in relief, with some letters out of alignment, *rev* die axis at 8 o'clock rotation, St George slaying dragon with sword, absent tail spur with "medium" tail, three strand terminal to tail, shorter strand to left curves outward, dragon claws of 4/4 arrangement but short and stubby, date in exergue, die flaw in date, weak B.P. to upper right, last stop larger, incomplete B, 7.97g (McD 157a; QM 89 S; Marsh 101; KM 7; Fr 16; S 3857D). *Surface marks, nicks and hairlines, rim nick on reverse, very fine, reverse better and unusual.* £300-400

Price Realised : £312

For further information on the medium tail See footnote for lot 768
Calendar year mintage 2,740,000 presumably all St George reverse of which 594 went for pyx trial.

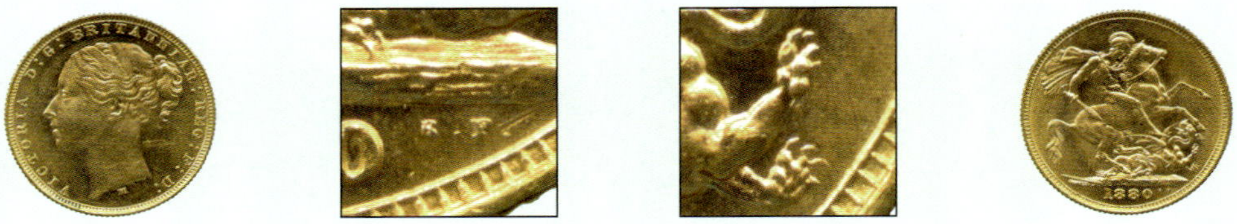

complete B.P. small stops and thin dragon claws

770 **Victoria,** Sovereign, 1880 M, horse with long tail, young head of third style left, letter M below, ww buried in truncation in relief, *rev* St George slaying dragon with sword, horse with long tail, one single strand hair spur in upper curve of tail, three strand terminal with shorter strand to left curving towards, dragon claws of 4/4 arrangement some very thin, date in exergue, tiny B.P. to upper right, 7.98g (McD 159; QM 94 S; Marsh 102; KM 7; Fr 16; S 3857). *Dig on 1 of date, light bagmarks and other hairlines, brilliant, good extremely fine and on par with the Quartermaster example.* £400-600

Price Realised : £1,104

ex Randy Weir Numismatics, Unionville, Ontario, Canada, purchased 22 March 1990
Calendar year mintage 3,052,800 which includes shield reverse design pieces, 654 of this total went for pyx trial.

so-called medium tail variety

771 **Victoria,** Sovereign, 1880 M, horse with medium tail, young head of third style left, letter M below touches neck, ww buried in truncation in relief, some letters in legend out of alignment, *rev* St George slaying dragon with sword, absent tail spur with "medium" tail, three strand terminal to tail, shorter strand to left curves outward, dragon claws of 4/4 arrangement but weak and some detachment, date in exergue, tiny B.P. to upper right with weak stops, 7.99g (McD 159a; QM -; Marsh 102; KM 7; Fr 16; S 3857D). *With nicks and light bagmarks, good extremely fine and very rare, no example present in the Quartermaster collection.* £800-1000

Price Realised : £960

Calendar year mintage 3,052,800 which includes shield reverse design pieces, 654 of this total went for pyx trial.

very low letter "M" mintmark

772 **Victoria,** Sovereign, 1881 M, horse with medium tail, young head of third style left, letter M below very low, ww buried in truncation in relief, *rev* St George slaying dragon with sword, absent tail spur with "medium" tail, three strand terminal to tail, shorter strand to left curves outward, dragon claws of 4/4 arrangement with some detachment, date in exergue, tiny B.P. to upper right, 7.99g (McD 159a; QM -; Marsh 102; KM 7; Fr 16; S 3857D). *Light bagmarks, otherwise brilliant, practically as struck and unusual with the low mint letter.* £400-600

Price Realised : £1,152

ex Randy Weir Numismatics, Unionville, Ontario, Canada, purchased 10 July 1993
Calendar year mintage 2,324,800 which includes shield reverse design pieces, 503 of this total went for pyx trial.

short tail variety, long attached dragon claws and no BP variety

773 **Victoria,** Sovereign, 1881 M, short tail and no BP variety, young head of third style left, letter M below, WW buried in truncation in relief, *rev* St George slaying dragon with sword, horse with short tail, with two single strand spurs in upper curve of tail, dragon claws of 3 / 4 arrangement long attached and distinct, date in exergue, no BP to upper right, 7.99g (McD 161a; QM 98 S; Marsh 103B R; KM 7; Fr 16; S 3857A). *Brilliant with some light hairlines and nick on cheek, practically as struck and finer than the Quartermaster coin, very rare.* £1000-1200

Price Realised : £1,104

ex Kurt Jaggard Coins, Sydney, Australia, purchased 30 May 2002
Calendar year mintage 2,324,800 which includes shield reverse design pieces, 503 of this total went for pyx trial.

a fourth tail variety – thick multi-strand spur of hair in upper curve of tail

774 **Victoria,** Sovereign, 1882 M, horse with "medium" tail, young head of third style left, letter M below, WW buried in truncation in relief, some letters in legend out of alignment, last letter I and G doubled, *rev* St George slaying dragon with sword, horse with medium tail with more short tail characteristics, one thicker spur made up of multiple strands of hair, dragon claws of 3 / 4 arrangement long attached and distinct, date in exergue, tiny incomplete BP to upper right, stops absent, 7.99g (McD 163a; QM 103 S; Marsh 104; KM 7; Fr 16; S 3857D). *With light bagmarks and hairlines, otherwise extremely fine / good extremely fine, appears to be on par with the Quartermaster collection.* £500-700

Price Realised : £432

ex Randy Weir Numismatics, Unionville, Ontario, Canada, purchased 12 November 1990
This variety is not detailed in any of the publications, but was present in the Quartermaster collection and is a variation on the so-called medium tail, representing a transitional die between the long and short tails with more characteristics towards being a short tail type such as the dragon claws. The larger thicker spur is the main defining characteristic.
Calendar year mintage 2,093,850

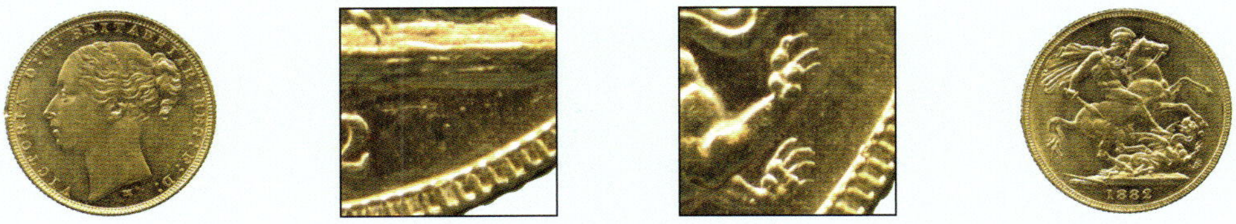

mere trace of BP in exergue and dragon claws 3/4, long and attached

775 **Victoria,** Sovereign, 1882 M, horse with "medium" tail, young head of third style left, letter M below, WW buried in truncation in relief, some letters in legend out of alignment, last EG doubled, *rev* St George slaying dragon with sword, horse with medium tail with more short tail characteristics, one thicker spur made up of multiple strands of hair, dragon claws of 3 / 4 arrangement long attached and distinct, date in exergue, figure 2 slightly rotated right, a mere trace of BP only, 7.98g (cf McD 163/163a; QM 102 S; Marsh 104; KM 7; Fr 16; S 3857D). *With light bagmarks and hairlines, otherwise brilliant extremely fine / good extremely fine, appears to be finer than the Quartermaster collection example, which may also have the trace BP rather than none, rare.* £500-700

Price Realised : £480

ex Randy Weir Numismatics, Unionville, Ontario, Canada, purchased 12 November 1990
Calendar year mintage 2,093,850

W.W. complete on truncation

776 **Victoria,** Sovereign, 1882 M, second young head of third style left, letter M below low down, W.W. complete on truncation in relief with stops, some letters in legend doubled, *rev* St George slaying dragon with sword, horse with short tail, one thicker spur made up of multiple strands of hair, dragon claws of 3 / 4 arrangement long attached and distinct, date in exergue, incomplete BP, stops absent, 7.98g (McD 163b; QM 104 R; Marsh 104; KM 7; Fr 16; S 3857C). *With light bagmarks mainly on reverse, otherwise brilliant practically as struck and appears to be finer than the Quartermaster collection example, rare.* £800-1000

Price Realised : £1,740

ex Randy Weir Numismatics, Unionville, Ontario, Canada, purchased c.1997
Calendar year mintage 2,093,850

short horse tail with two spurs of hair in upper curve

777 **Victoria,** Sovereign, 1883 M, first young head of third style left, letter M below low down, WW buried in truncation in relief, *rev* St George slaying dragon with sword, horse with short tail, two well defined separate spurs of hair in upper curve of tail, dragon claws of 3 / 4 arrangement long attached and distinct, date in exergue, incomplete BP, stops absent, 7.98g (McD 165a; QM 107 C; Marsh 105; KM 7; Fr 16; S 3857C). *With light bagmarks, nicks and hairlines, extremely fine / good extremely fine, appears to be on par with the Quartermaster collection example, with a better looking reverse.* £400-600

Price Realised : £456

ex Monetarium, Kogarah, Australia, purchased 17 March 2003
Calendar year mintage 1,623,000
This coin marks the appearance of a new reverse die at Melbourne with the short tail and two spurs of hair in the curve. It is well defined and looks fresh even today, it seems that the same care in engraving was not applied to the initials in the exergue however.

incomplete BP, stops absent

778 **Victoria,** Sovereign, 1883 M, second young head of third style left, letter M below low down, W.W. complete on truncation in relief with stops, *rev* St George slaying dragon with sword, horse with short tail, two wispy separate spurs of hair in upper curve of tail, date in exergue, dragon claws of 3 / 4 arrangement long attached and distinct, incomplete BP, stops absent, 7.99g (McD 165b; QM 108 C; Marsh 105; KM 7; Fr 16; S 3857C). *With light bagmarks and scuffs, obverse rim nick, otherwise good extremely fine, appears to be on par with the Quartermaster collection example.* £300-500

Price Realised : £384

ex Randy Weir Numismatics, Unionville, Ontario, Canada, purchased 18 July 1990
Calendar year mintage 1,623,000
This coin is a variation on the short tail type in the lot above, the tail is more "wispy" and with thinner definition in its strands though of the same basic make up. Incidentally the calendar year mintages for both 1882 and 1883 are the only two years of production at the Melbourne mint where mintage of St George reverse is separately known to that of the shield reverse, though of course these figures are not necessarily representative of what the dates were on those coins struck within that calendar year. This is especially true with Colonial Branch Mints, as there could be long delays in receiving dies for striking from Great Britain.

short horse tail with one spur of hair in upper curve

779 **Victoria,** Sovereign, 1884 M, second young head of third style left, letter M below low down, W.W. complete on truncation in relief with stops, D G of legend doubled, *rev* St George slaying dragon with sword, horse with short tail, one single strand spur of hair in upper curve of tail, dragon claws of 3 / 4 arrangement long attached and distinct, date in exergue, date figures out of line, tiny BP with stops absent, 7.98g (McD 167b; QM 111 S; Marsh 106; KM 7; Fr 16; S 3857C). *Light bagmarks, tone spot on obverse, good extremely fine.* £300-500

Price Realised : £360

ex Randy Weir Numismatics, Unionville, Ontario, Canada, purchased 18 July 1990
Calendar year mintage 2,942,000 which includes shield reverse design pieces, 630 of this total went for pyx trial.
This coin is another version of the short tail type, the tail is well defined with only one spur of hair in the upper curve of the tail.

"M" mintmark nearer to neck

780 **Victoria,** Sovereign, 1884 M, first young head of third style left, letter M below nearer neck, WW buried in truncation in relief, last F of legend doubled, light die flaw in latter part of queen's name, *rev* St George slaying dragon with sword, horse with short tail, one weak strand spur of hair in upper curve of tail, dragon claws of 3 / 4 arrangement long some detachment, date in exergue, only a mere trace of BP to right, 7.98g (McD 167a; QM 110 S; Marsh 106; KM 7; Fr 16; S 3857B). *Light bagmarks, good extremely fine.* £300-500

Price Realised : £504

Calendar year mintage 2,942,000 which includes shield reverse design pieces, 630 of this total went for pyx trial.

"M" mintmark further from neck

781 **Victoria,** Sovereign, 1884 M, first young head of third style left, letter M below lower down, WW buried in truncation in relief, *rev* St George slaying dragon with sword, horse with short tail, one single strand spur of hair in upper curve of tail, dragon claws of 3 / 4 arrangement long attached and distinct, date in exergue, tiny BP with stops absent, 7.98g (McD 167a; QM 110 S; Marsh 106; KM 7; Fr 16; S 3857B). *With light surface marks, good extremely fine.* £300-500

Price Realised : £384

ex Reserve Bank of Australia Sale, Downies, November 2005, lot 1978, purchased through Winsor and Sons, December 2005
Calendar year mintage 2,942,000 which includes shield reverse design pieces, 630 of this total went for pyx trial.

incomplete BP without stops

782 **Victoria,** Sovereign, 1885 M, first young head of third style left, letter M below, WW buried in truncation in relief, *rev* St George slaying dragon with sword, horse with short tail, one single strand spur of hair in upper curve of tail, dragon claws of 3 / 4 arrangement long attached and distinct, date in exergue, incomplete B with a trace only of P in exergue, 7.97g (McD 169a; QM 114 R; Marsh 107; KM 7; Fr 16; S 3857B). *With light surface marks, dig on cheek, good very fine.* £300-350

Price Realised : £384

Calendar year mintage 2,966,500 which includes shield reverse design pieces, 643 of this total went for pyx trial.

783 **Victoria,** Sovereign, 1885 M, first young head of third style left, letter M below, WW buried in truncation in relief, first D doubled, second R die flawed on lower right foot, *rev* St George slaying dragon with sword, horse with short tail, one single strand spur of hair in upper curve of tail, dragon claws of 3 / 4 arrangement long attached and distinct, date in exergue, 5 die flawed shut at top, incomplete B without P in exergue, 7.98g (McD 169a; QM 114 R; Marsh 107; KM 7; Fr 16; S 3857B). *With surface marks, scratch on neck, dig by first* T *in legend, good very fine.* £300-350

Price Realised : £288

ex Reserve Bank of Australia Sale, Downies, November 2005, lot 2001, purchased through Winsor and Sons, December 2005
Calendar year mintage 2,966,500 which includes shield reverse design pieces, 643 of this total went for pyx trial.

W.W. complete on truncation”

784 **Victoria,** Sovereign, 1885 M, second young head of third style left, letter M below low down, W.W. complete on truncation in relief with stops, *rev* St George slaying dragon with sword, horse with short tail, one single strand spur of hair in upper curve of tail, dragon claws of 3 / 4 arrangement long attached and distinct, date in exergue, only a mere trace of BP to right, 7.98g (McD 169c; QM 115 R; Marsh 107; KM 7; Fr 16; S 3857C). *With light bagmarks and nicks, otherwise, good extremely fine.* £400-600

Price Realised : £360

Calendar year mintage 2,966,500 which includes shield reverse design pieces, 643 of this total went for pyx trial.

short single strand with shorter one above in upper tail curve

785 **Victoria,** Sovereign, 1886 M, second young head of third style left, letter M below low down, W.W. complete on truncation in relief with stops, *rev* St George slaying dragon with sword, horse with short tail, one short single spur of hair in upper curve of tail, smaller shorter strand above, dragon claws of 3 / 4 arrangement, long claws with second on lower arm detached, date in exergue, BP to right, incomplete P stops absent, 7.99g (McD 171; QM 117 S; Marsh 108; KM 7; Fr 16; S 3857C). *With light bagmarks and a little weak on high points, otherwise, good extremely fine, appears to be on par with the Quartermaster collection example.* £400-600

Price Realised : £480

ex Steinbergs of Vermont, purchased 2 July 2001
Calendar year mintage 2,901,500 which includes shield reverse design pieces, 631 of this total went for pyx trial.

short tail, trace of spur of hair

786 **Victoria,** Sovereign, 1887 M, second young head of third style left, letter M below low down, W.W. complete on truncation in relief with stops, *rev* St George slaying dragon with sword, horse with short tail, trace stub spur of hair in tail, date in exergue, the figure 7 with an extra serif foot at top right of 7, dragon claws of 3 / 4 arrangement long attached and distinct, BP to right, incomplete P stops absent, 7.98g (McD 173; QM 119 S; Marsh 109; KM 7; Fr 16; S 3857C). *With light bagmarks and a little weak on high points, otherwise, very attractive good extremely fine, appears to be finer than the Quartermaster collection example.* £400-600

Price Realised : £432

Calendar year mintage 2,901,500 which includes shield reverse design pieces, 631 of this total went for pyx trial.
The Sydney mint St George Sovereign of 1887 in Lot 693 also has this 7 with the extra serif foot at top. The same punch must have been used to prepare both dies at the Royal Mint in London.

Melbourne Mint Victoria Jubilee Type Sovereigns

The Golden Jubilee of Victoria's reign occurred in 1887, bringing a change to the coinage with a more up to date and mature portrait of the Queen wearing a tiny crown with veil. Both the Sydney and Melbourne mints seamlessly swapped over to the new design, with the same quirks as the London mint pieces, in that there are two varieties of legend spacing in relation to the bust which has its own variations on the initials on the truncation. The reverses also venture through two different types of tail.

The standard full description for a Jubilee type Sovereign of Queen Victoria is as follows:-

Victoria (1837-1901), Sovereign, 1887 M, Melbourne mint, engraved by Joseph Edgar Boehm, Jubilee tall veiled bust left with older features, veil with two rows of crenellations, with small Imperial crown, large fleurs inside, top cross on field intrudes the border, wearing 13 pearl necklace, brooch at front with relief jewel, half a garter star at base of bust under sash, decorated border to dress bust, J.E.B. on edge of truncation into field with stops, angled J, first type legend further from crown, two pearl drop ear ring, VICTORIA D:G: BRITT: REG: F: D:, finely toothed border within twin linear concentric circles and raised rim both sides, outer rim blends with teeth, *rev* struck en médaille, after Benedetto Pistrucci, St George slaying dragon with sword, streamer to helmet, complete hem to cape, extra mane hair above hand holding rein, horse with short tail, three strand end to tail, two spurs of extra hair on curve of tail, dragon with three claws to left and three to right arm, trace of fourth claw, all attached, broken lance on groundline to left, *WWP* in relief under lance, M mint mark at centre of ground, date in exergue, tiny B.P. to upper right, edge milled

Unique Silver Striking of an 1887 Melbourne Mint Sovereign

787 **Victoria (1837-1901),** Pattern Sovereign,1887 M, struck in silver, engraved by Joseph Edgar Boehm, Jubilee tall veiled bust left with older features, veil with two rows of crenellations, with small Imperial crown, large fleurs inside, top cross of crown touches linear circle, wearing 14 pearl necklace, brooch at front with relief jewel, almost full garter star at base of bust under sash, decorated border to dress bust, prominent and robust J.E.B. fully on truncation, hooked J doubled, repositioned second legend closer to crown, two pearl drop ear ring, VICTORIA D:G: BRITT: REG: F: D:, finely toothed border within twin linear concentric circles and raised prominent rim both sides, *rev* struck en médaille, after Benedetto Pistrucci, St George slaying dragon with sword, no streamer to helmet as young head reverses, extra mane hair above hand holding rein, horse with short tail, three strand end to tail, no extra hair on curve of tail, dragon with three claws to upper and four to lower arm, shorter fourth claw, all attached, broken lance on ground-line to left, *WWP* in relief under lance, M mint mark at centre of ground, date in exergue, 7 of date with upper right serif with foot, tiny BP without stops to upper right, edge plain, 4.66g, 21.8mm (McD 175c and note *this coin*; QM -). *Very attractively toned, mint state proof and the only known specimen, unique.* £20,000-30,000

Price Realised : £15,600

ex A H F Baldwin collection
ex Spink Australia Sale 2, 2 November 1978, lot 613
ex Noble Numismatics Sale 70, 9-11 July 2002, lot 1232, sold for $26,500
The McDonald catalogue for 2012 rates lists this coin in proof quality at a valuation of AU$190,000 (or £128,000) the same as many of the gold proof Sovereigns.

small J.E.B. fully on truncation with a hooked "J"

788 **Victoria,** Sovereign, 1887 M, Jubilee style bust left, small J.E.B. fully on truncation with a hooked J, necklace of 13 pearls, first type legend further from crown, cross on crown crosses linear circle, raised die flaw in ITT of legend, *rev* St George slaying dragon with sword, helmet with streamer, complete hem to cape bar one intrusion, horse with short tail, two small spurs of extra hair at upper curve, M mint mark at centre of ground, date in exergue, B.P. complete to upper right, 7.99g (McD 175; QM 126 S; Marsh 131A R; KM 10; Fr 20; S 3867). *A little weak of strike, a few tiny light surface marks, otherwise toned, as struck and far superior to the Quartermaster example, rare.* £400-600

Price Realised : £1,320

Calendar year mintage 940,000

larger J.E.B. fully on truncation with a right-angled "J"

789 **Victoria,** Sovereign, 1887 M, Jubilee style bust left, J.E.B. fully on truncation with an angled J, first type legend further from crown, *rev* St George slaying dragon with sword, helmet with more wispy streamer, weak hem to cape, horse with short tail, two small spurs of extra hair at upper curve, M mint mark at centre of ground, date in exergue, B.P. complete to upper right, 7.98g (McD 175a; QM 127 C; Marsh 131; KM 10; Fr 20; S 3867A). *A number of light hairlines and surface marks, some bagmarks, extremely fine and on par with the Quartermaster example.* £300-350

Price Realised : £384

Calendar year mintage 940,000

790 **Victoria,** Sovereign, 1887 M, struck with an off-centre die axis, Jubilee style bust left, J.E.B. fully on truncation with an angled J, first type legend further from crown, *rev* die axis off by about 45 degrees, St George slaying dragon with sword, helmet with streamer, horse with short tail, two small spurs of extra hair at upper curve, M mint mark at centre of ground, date in exergue, B.P. complete to upper right, 7.96g (cf McD.175a; QM 127 C; Marsh 131; KM 10; Fr 20; S 3867A). *A little weak of strike, heavily scuffed and surface marked, good fine to almost very fine and very unusual.* £300-350

Price Realised : £360

ex Robert Reed collection, Los Angeles, USA, c.1990
Calendar year mintage 940,000

first type legend further from crown

791 **Victoria,** Sovereign, 1887 M, Jubilee style bust left, J.E.B. fully on truncation with an angled J, first type legend further from crown, raised die flaw from rim down into crown and into veil, *rev* St George slaying dragon with sword, helmet with streamer, raised die flaw to weak hem to cape, horse with short tail, two small spurs of extra hair at upper curve, M mint mark at centre of ground, date in exergue, B.P. complete to upper right, 7.99g (McD 175a; QM 127 C, *this coin*; Marsh 131; KM 10; Fr 20; S 3867A). *Lightly hairlined, good extremely fine.* £350-450

Price Realised : £600

ex Reserve Bank of Australia, Downies, 29-30 November 2005, lot 2050
ex Quartermaster collection, Monetarium, 4 June 2009, lot 127
Calendar year mintage 940,000

second type legend closer to crown

792 **Victoria,** Sovereign, 1887 M, Jubilee style bust left, J.E.B. on edge of truncation with an angled J, the letters intrude the field, second type legend with G: closer to crown, the top cross clear of the border circle, *rev* St George slaying dragon with sword, helmet with streamer, complete hem to cape, horse with short tail, two small spurs of extra hair at upper curve, M mint mark at centre of ground, date in exergue, B.P. complete to upper right, 7.98g (McD 175b; QM 128 S; Marsh 131; KM 10; Fr 20; S 3867B). *Some light bagmarks, otherwise practically as struck.* £400-600

Price Realised : £1,176

Calendar year mintage 940,000

J.E.B. on edge of truncation, very die flawed

793 **Victoria,** Sovereign, 1887 M, Jubilee style bust left, J.E.B. on edge of truncation with an angled J, the letters intrude the field, die flaw from rim onto bust through jewel and letter B and onto veil, second type legend, *rev* St George slaying dragon with sword, complete hem to cape with some die flaws, horse with short tail, two small spurs of extra hair at upper curve, M mint mark at centre of ground, date in exergue, B.P. complete to upper right, 7.98g (McD 175b; QM 128 S; Marsh 131; KM 10; Fr 20; S 3867B). *Once polished with associated hairlines, now with a red tone, good very fine , reverse better and a spectacular die flaw.* £300-400

Price Realised : £360

ex A H Baldwin & Sons Ltd, purchased August 2007
Calendar year mintage 940,000

J.E.B. fully on truncation

794 **Victoria,** Sovereign, 1888 M, Jubilee style bust left, J.E.B. fully on truncation with an angled J, first type legend further from crown, *rev* St George slaying dragon with sword, hem of cape complete, horse with short tail, two small spurs of extra hair at upper curve, M mint mark at centre of ground, date in exergue, last 8 of date higher, B.P to upper right, no final stop, 7.98g (McD 177; QM 133 R; Marsh 132; KM 10; Fr 20; S 3867A). *Some light bagmarks, good very fine and finer than the Quartermaster example.* £300-350

Price Realised : £384

ex A H Baldwin & Sons Ltd sourced via Paul Davies Ltd, September 2006
Calendar year mintage 2,830,000 of which 612 went for pyx trial.

J.E.B. on edge of truncation

795 **Victoria,** Sovereign, 1888 M, Jubilee style bust left, J.E.B. on edge of truncation with an angled J, the letters intrude the field, second type legend with G: closer to crown, some die flaws in legend, *rev* St George slaying dragon with sword, weak hem to cape, horse with short tail, two small spurs of extra hair at upper curve, M mint mark at centre of ground, date in exergue, B.P to upper right, no final stop, 7.99g (McD 177a; QM 134 S; Marsh 132; KM 10; Fr 20; S 3867B). *Some light bagmarks, spot by elbow on reverse, toned, otherwise practically as struck and more attractive than the Quartermaster example.* £350-450

Price Realised : £624

ex Randy Weir Numismatics, Unionville, Ontario, Canada, purchased 12 November 1990
Calendar year mintage 2,830,000 of which 612 went for pyx trial.

The Extremely Rare 1888 Melbourne Proof Sovereign with second legend

796 **Victoria,** Sovereign, 1888 M, Jubilee style bust left, J.E.B. on edge of truncation with an angled J, the letters intrude the field, second type legend with G: closer to crown, the top cross clear of the border circle, *rev* St George slaying dragon with sword, complete hem to cape, horse with short tail, two small spurs of extra hair at upper curve, dragon with all claws attached, three to upper arm, four to lower arm, M mint mark at centre of ground, date in exergue, B.P. complete to upper right, 7.98g (cf McD.177b; QM -; Marsh -; KM 10; Fr 20; cf S 3867B). *Toned as struck FDC and of the highest rarity, a beautiful coin.* £30,000-40,000

Price Realised : £34,800

ex Paul Davies Ltd, purchased before 2005
For another example of one of these rare proofs of this second legend type see KJC Inaugural Monetary Auction, 10 June 2005, lot 809. These were struck in reaction to a request from the new Deputy Master, George Anderson, who wanted to mount a display of coins at the 1888 International Exhibition in Melbourne, following in the tradition of a display at the 1880 Exhibition by his predecessor. He made a request to the Royal Mint London to supply these proofs which was at first refused because C W Fremantle in London envisaged the request as a restrike of what had already been struck in 1880. However, Anderson reassured the mint he merely wanted examples of what may already be available in stock from 1880, rather than fresh strikes and other current productions as and when the mint could strike for them. Fremantle was happier with this second request and supplied Melbourne with specimen proof strikings from this date forward as long as they paid the face value for them. This started with the Colonial coins of 1888, including examples like this 1888 Proof Sovereign. For further reading on the subject of special strikings made by the mint for exhibition in Australia see the Journal of the Numismatic Association of Australia, volume 2, article by John Sharples "The Numismatic Collection of the Museum of Victoria" available online at the Association website.
The McDonald publication for 2012 only lists the 1888M with the first type legend, probably a misprint as this proof of the second legend was listed as McD177a. Nevertheless the 1888M Proof is a major rarity and the variety listed by McDonald has a valuation in Proof quality of AU$180,000 (or £121,000)

thick hair spur on short horse tail

797 **Victoria,** Sovereign, 1889 M, Jubilee style bust left, J.E.B. on edge of truncation with an angled J, the letters intrude the field, second type legend with G: closer to crown, *rev* St George slaying dragon with sword, complete hem to cape, horse with short tail, with thick spur of extra hair at upper curve, dragon with all claws attached, four claws to each arm, M mint mark at centre of ground, date in exergue, B.P to upper right, no final stop, 7.99g (McD 179a; QM 137-8 C; Marsh 133; KM 10; Fr 20; S 3867B). *Some light bagmarks, brilliant, good extremely fine and finer than the Quartermaster example.* £350-450

Price Realised : £360

ex Randy Weir Numismatics, Unionville, Ontario, Canada, purchased 5 December 1989
Calendar year mintage 2,732,000 of which 590 went for pyx trial.

all dragon claws attached 4/4

798 **Victoria,** Sovereign, 1889 M, Jubilee style bust left, J.E.B. fully on truncation with an angled J, first type legend further from crown, *rev* St George slaying dragon with sword, hem of cape complete, horse with short tail, with thick spur of extra hair at upper curve, dragon with all claws attached, four claws to each arm, M mint mark at centre of ground, date in exergue, last 8 of date higher, B.P to upper right, no final stop, 7.98g (McD 179; QM 136 S; cf Marsh 132; KM 10; Fr 20; S 3867A). *Some light bagmarks, extremely fine / good extremely fine and scarce.* £300-350

Price Realised : £312

ex Spink and Son, purchased November 2003
Calendar year mintage 2,732,000 of which 590 went for pyx trial.

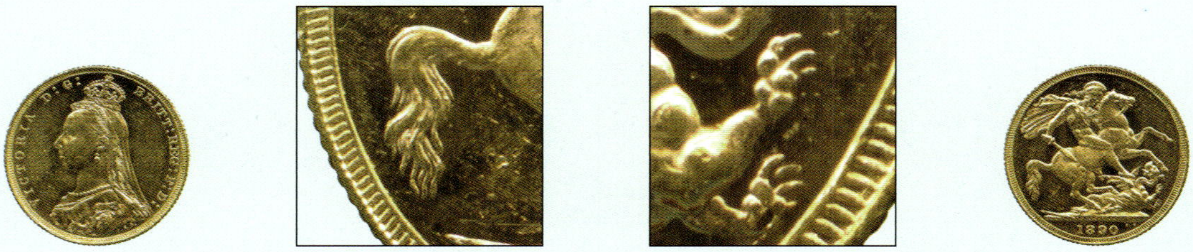

two extra spurs of hair on short horse tail and one dragon claw detached 3 / 4

799 **Victoria,** Sovereign, 1890 M, Jubilee style bust left, second type legend, *rev* St George slaying dragon with sword, complete hem to cape, horse with short tail, two spurs of extra hair at upper curve, dragon with one lower claw detached, three to upper arm, four to lower arm, M mint mark to right of centre of ground, date in exergue, B.P to upper right, no final stop, 7.99g (McD 181; QM 142 S; Marsh 134; KM 10; Fr 20; S 3867B). *Some light bagmarks, otherwise practically as struck and scarce.* £350-450

Price Realised : £432

Calendar year mintage 2,473,000 of which 537 went for pyx trial.

longer strands in streamer, long tail of horse and curvy dragon claws

800 **Victoria,** Sovereign, 1891 M, long tail reverse, Jubilee style bust left, second type legend, die flaws at both letter D's in legend, *rev* St George slaying dragon with sword, longer individual strands in helmet streamer, heavier engraved rendition of cape, horse with long tail, with one light spur of extra hair at upper curve, dragon with four curved claws to each arm, M mint mark at centre of ground, date in exergue, B.P to upper right, no final stop, 7.99g (McD 183a; QM 145 S; Marsh 135; KM 10; Fr 20; S 3867C). *Some light bagmarks, spot in legend, good extremely fine and scarce.* £350-450

Price Realised : £360

Calendar year mintage 2,749,000 of which 592 went for pyx trial.

dragon claws with one detached

801 **Victoria,** Sovereign, 1891 M, short tail reverse, Jubilee style bust left, second type legend, *rev* St George slaying dragon with sword, complete hem to cape, horse with short tail, two spurs of extra hair at upper curve, dragon with one lower claw detached, three to upper arm with trace of a fourth, four to lower arm, M mint mark, date in exergue, B.P to upper right, no final stop, 7.97g (McD 183; QM 144 S; Marsh 135; KM 10; Fr 20; S 3867B). *Surface marks, good very fine to extremely fine and scarce.* £300-400

Price Realised : £288

ex Reserve Bank of Australia Sale, Downies, November 2005, lot 2129, purchased through Winsor and Sons, December 2005
Calendar year mintage 2,749,000 of which 592 went for pyx trial.

full B.P. in exergue

802 **Victoria,** Sovereign, 1892 M, long tail reverse, Jubilee style bust left, second type legend, *rev* St George slaying dragon with sword, longer individual strands in helmet streamer, horse with long tail, with one spur of extra hair at upper curve, dragon with four curved claws to each arm, M mint mark at centre of ground, date in exergue, full B.P. to upper right, 7.99g (McD 185; QM 147 C; Marsh 136; KM 10; Fr 20; S 3867C). *Some light bagmarks, nicks and scuffs, otherwise brilliant, good extremely fine and scarce.* £350-450

Price Realised : £360

ex Randy Weir Numismatics, Unionville, Ontario, Canada, purchased 12 November 1990
Calendar year mintage 3,488,000 of which 750 went for pyx trial. This is the highest calendar year output for the Melbourne mint in the Jubilee issue.

803 **Victoria,** Sovereign, 1893 M, long tail reverse, Jubilee style bust left, second type legend, *rev* St George slaying dragon with sword, horse with long tail, with one light spur of extra hair at upper curve, dragon with four curved claws to each arm, M mint mark at centre of ground, date in exergue, full B.P. to upper right, 7.99g (McD 188; QM 150 S; Marsh 137; KM 10; Fr 20; S 3867C). *Some light bagmarks, good extremely fine and on par with the Quartermaster collection example, scarce.* £350-450

Price Realised : £384

ex Charles Stueve, Abbeygate Coins, Westhampton Beach, New York, c.1990
Calendar year mintage 1,649,000 of which 352 went for pyx trial.
See footnote for Lot 707 for more information about the use of the Jubilee head type for 1893 at the Branch Mints. There were less 1893 dated Jubilee Sovereigns struck at Melbourne than there were of the old head dated 1893.

Melbourne Mint Victoria Old Head Type Sovereigns

The old head type design commenced on the coinage in 1893 after a gestation of just over two years. This was a direct reaction to public criticism of the Jubilee type design, culminating in comment from the Queen herself on her own displeasure of the small crowned bust. The British Royal Mint introduced the new design on coinage dated from 1893 and whole proof sets containing all the designs were available to purchase.
For more information on the design process of the old head see page 300.
At this time the only Colonial Branch Mints in operation were the Sydney and Melbourne mints. They received the new design much later in the year and had already struck many Sovereigns of the older Jubilee type design in both mints. Sydney in fact struck more of the old design than the new old head for coins dated 1893, Melbourne vice versa. The full description of such a coin is a follows.

Victoria (1837-1901), Sovereign, 1896 M, Melbourne Branch Mint, engraved by Thomas Brock, old veiled bust left, T.B. below, VICTORIA D:G: BRITT: REG: F: D: IND: IMP:, toothed border surrounding, *rev* struck en médaille, engraved after Benedetto Pistrucci, St George slaying dragon with sword, three strand streamer on helmet, horse with long tail, three strand end to tail, one spur of extra hair on curve of tail, dragon with four claws on each arm, broken lance on ground-line to left, *WWP* in relief under lance, M mint mark at centre of ground, date in exergue, tiny B.P. to upper right, finely toothed border within twin linear concentric circles and raised rim, edge milled

The 1893 M Old Head Sovereign muled with the reverse of the 1893 M Jubilee head issue

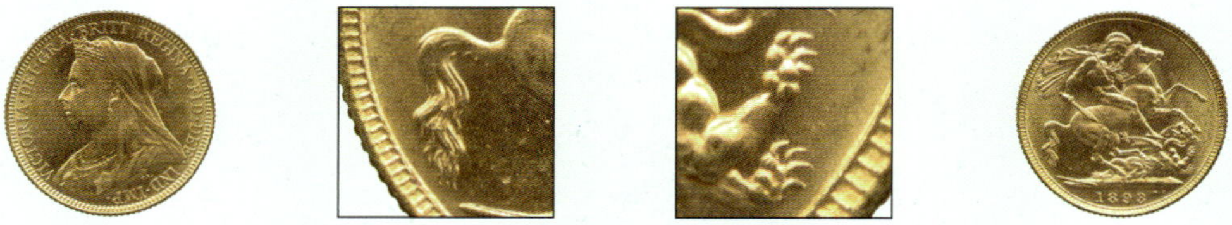

one extra spur of hair in upper curve of tail and four long curved claws on each arm

804 **Victoria (1837-1901),** Sovereign, 1893 M, old veiled bust left, T.B. below, toothed border surrounding, *rev* St George slaying dragon with sword, horse with long tail, one spur of extra hair on curve of tail, dragon with four curved claws attached on each arm, M mint mark at centre of ground, date in exergue, tiny B.P. to upper right, finely toothed border within twin linear concentric circles and raised rim, 8.00g (McD 190; QM 152 S; Marsh 153; KM 13; Fr 24; S 3875). *Some light bagmarks, otherwise good extremely fine and appears to be finer than the Quartermaster coin, scarce.* £300-400

Price Realised : £528

ex Randy Weir Numismatics, Unionville, Ontario, Canada, purchased 14 August 1992
Calendar year mintage 1,914,000 of which 400 went for pyx trial. This coin shares the same reverse die as the Jubilee head issue and is technically a mule.

four short claws on each arm

805 **Victoria,** Sovereign, 1894 M, old veiled bust left, T.B. below, *rev* St George slaying dragon with sword, horse with long tail, trace of a weak spur of extra hair on curve of tail, dragon with short claws of a 4/4 arrangement, M mint mark at centre of ground, date in exergue, tiny B.P. to upper right, 7.99g (McD 192; QM 154 C; Marsh 154; KM 13; Fr 24; S 3875). *Some light bagmarks, scratch on cheek, otherwise good extremely fine.* £300-350

Price Realised : £288

ex Randy Weir Numismatics, Unionville, Ontario, Canada, purchased 5 December 1989
Calendar year mintage 4,166,000 of which 874 went for pyx trial.

four curved claws on each arm

807 **Victoria,** Sovereign, 1896 M, old veiled bust left, T.B. below, *rev* St George slaying dragon with sword, horse with long tail, one distinct spur of extra hair on curve of tail, dragon with more curved claws of a 4/4 arrangement, M mint mark at centre of ground, date in exergue, tiny B.P. to upper right, 7.99g (McD 196; QM 159 C; Marsh 156; KM 13; Fr 24; S 3875). *Some light bagmarks, otherwise good extremely fine and appears to be finer than the Quartermaster coin.* £300-400

Price Realised : £504

ex Randy Weir Numismatics, Unionville, Ontario, Canada, purchased 29 August 1990
Calendar year mintage 4,456,000 of which 932 went for pyx trial.

808

809

808 **Victoria,** Sovereign, 1897 M, old veiled bust left, T.B. below, *rev* St George slaying dragon with sword, horse with long tail, one distinct spur of extra hair on curve of tail, dragon with more curved claws of a 4/4 arrangement, M mint mark at centre of ground, date in exergue, tiny B.P. to upper right, 7.98g (McD 198; QM 162 C; Marsh 157; KM 13; Fr 24; S 3875). *Some light bagmarks, otherwise good extremely fine and appears to be finer than the Quartermaster coin.* £300-400

Price Realised : £360

ex Randy Weir Numismatics, Unionville, Ontario, Canada, purchased 29 June 1990
Calendar year mintage 5,129,500 of which 1,065 went for pyx trial.

809 **Victoria,** Sovereign, 1897 M, old veiled bust left, very sharply defined T.B. below, *rev* St George slaying dragon with sword, horse with long tail, one distinct spur of extra hair on curve of tail, very sharply defined curved dragon claws, M mint mark at centre of ground, date in exergue, tiny B.P. to upper right, 7.99g, 22mm (McD 198; cf QM 162 C; Marsh 157; KM 13; Fr 24; S 3875). *Proof-like, struck from dies with a frosted design and legend, if not struck from proof dies, this must be a very early striking with a currency style rim and edge, scuffed in the fields otherwise brilliant as struck and very unusual.* £400-600

Price Realised : £2,640

ex Randy Weir Numismatics, Unionville, Ontario, Canada, purchased 12 November 1990
Calendar year mintage 5,129,500 of which 1,065 went for pyx trial. These unusually prooflike pieces tend to appear from the Sydney mint for 1893 only and the Melbourne Mints for each year of the old head series. According to McDonald there are proof specimens struck for every year of the Melbourne mint, which concurs with the agreement between the Deputy Master Anderson and the Royal Mint London to supply proof specimens each year, as detailed by John Sharples in his article on the Museum of Victoria in the Journal of the Numismatic Association of Australia, volume 2. McDonald values each year in Proof condition at $180,000 (or £121,000) each for 2012.

810

811

810 **Victoria,** Sovereign, 1898 M, old veiled bust left, T.B. below, *rev* St George slaying dragon with sword, horse with long tail, one weak spur of extra hair on curve of tail, dragon with weaker curved claws of a 4/4 arrangement, M mint mark at centre of ground, date in exergue, tiny B.P. to upper right, raised die flaw to right of initials, 7.98g (McD 200; QM 164 C; Marsh 158; KM 13; Fr 24; S 3875). *Some light bagmarks, dig in hair, otherwise good extremely fine and appears to be on par with the Quartermaster coin.* £300-350

Price Realised : £360

ex Ebay purchase, 2 April 2003
Calendar year mintage 5,508,000 of which 1,138 went for pyx trial.

811 **Victoria,** Sovereign, 1899 M, old veiled bust left, T.B. below, raised die flaw on C of queen's name, *rev* St George slaying dragon with sword, horse with long tail, one weak spur of extra hair on curve of tail, dragon with curved claws of a 4/4 arrangement, M mint mark at centre of ground, date in exergue, tiny B.P. to upper right, last sop more distant, 7.98g (McD 202; QM 166 C; Marsh 159; KM 13; Fr 24; S 3875). *Some light bagmarks, otherwise extremely fine.* £300-350

Price Realised : £384

ex Randy Weir Numismatics, Unionville, Ontario, Canada, purchased 13 August 1992
Calendar year mintage 5,578,000 of which 1,157 went for pyx trial. This year represents the highest calendar year output of an old head design at the Melbourne mint. In fact it is the highest output ever from this mint for any gold Sovereign from 1872-1931.

812 **Victoria,** Sovereign, 1900 M, old veiled bust left, T.B. below, *rev* St George slaying dragon with sword, horse with long tail, very weak spur of extra hair on curve of tail, dragon with curved claws of a 4/4 arrangement, M mint mark at centre of ground, date in exergue, tiny B.P. to upper right, 7.99g (McD 205; QM 169 C; Marsh 160; KM 13; Fr 24; S 3875). *Some light bagmarks, softly struck, otherwise good extremely fine.* £300-350

Price Realised : £288

ex Randy Weir Numismatics, Unionville, Ontario, Canada, purchased October 1990
Calendar year mintage 4,305,000 of which 904 went for pyx trial.

813 **Victoria,** Sovereign, 1901 M, old veiled bust left, T.B. below, heavy die flaw across FID: DEF: of legend, *rev* St George slaying dragon with sword, horse with long tail, one spur of extra hair on curve of tail, dragon with curved claws of a 4/4 arrangement, M mint mark at centre of ground, date in exergue, tiny B.P. to upper right, 7.99g (McD 208; QM 172 C; Marsh 161; KM 13; Fr 24; S 3875). *Some light bagmarks, a little weak of strike, otherwise brilliant good extremely fine and appears to be finer than the Quartermaster coin.* £300-400

Price Realised : £528

Calendar year mintage 3,986,000 of which 1,701 went for pyx trial. 1901 marks the year that the highest ever number of such pieces were set aside for this purpose.
Queen Victoria died on 22 January 1901

The Reign of King Edward VII (1901-1910)
House of Saxe-Coburg and Gotha

Born: 9 November 1841

Accession: 22 January 1901

Married: Alexandra of Denmark 10 March 1863

Coronation: Saturday, 9 August 1902

Children: three sons, three daughters

Died: 6 May 1910, aged 68

814 **Edward VII (1901-1910),** Sovereign, 1902 M, Melbourne mint, engraved by George William De Saulles, bare head facing right, DES. below, toothed border and raised rim, EDWARDVS VII D: G: BRITT: OMN: REX F: D: IND: IMP:, *rev* struck en médaille, engraved after Benedetto Pistrucci, St George slaying dragon with sword, cloak with practically complete hemline, two thick stand helmet streamer, horse with long tail, ending in three strands, with one spur higher up at curve, broken lance on ground-line to left, *WWP* in relief under lance, M mint mark on ground, date in exergue, tiny B.P. to upper right, finely toothed border within twin linear concentric circles and raised rim, edge milled, 7.99g (McD 211; QM 178 (part); KM 15; Fr 33; Marsh 186; S 3971). *Some light bagmarks, otherwise good extremely fine.* £300-350

Price Realised : £312

Calendar year mintage 4,265,000 of which 2,157 went for pyx trial. This marks the highest calendar year mintage at the Melbourne mint in the reign of King Edward VII.

815 **Edward VII,** Sovereign, 1903 M, bare head facing right, DES. below, *rev* St George slaying dragon with sword, M mint mark on ground, date in exergue, tiny B.P. to upper right, 7.99g (McD 214; QM 179 (part); KM 15; Fr 33; Marsh 187; S 3971). *Some light bagmarks across face, otherwise good extremely fine.* £300-350

Price Realised : £288

ex Randy Weir Numismatics, Unionville, Ontario, Canada, purchased 6 February 1990
Calendar year mintage 3,520,000 of which 1,780 went for pyx trial.

816 **Edward VII,** Sovereign, 1904 M, bare head facing right, DES. below, *rev* St George slaying dragon with sword, M mint mark on ground, date in exergue, tiny B.P. to upper right, 7.99g (McD 217; QM 180 (part); KM 15; Fr 33; Marsh 188; S 3971). *Streak of tone on reverse with a few light bagmarks, otherwise good extremely fine.* £300-350

Price Realised : £432

ex Randy Weir Numismatics, Unionville, Ontario, Canada, purchased 6 February 1990
Calendar year mintage 3,742,000 of which 1,897 went for pyx trial.

817 **Edward VII,** Sovereign, 1905 M, bare head facing right, DES. below, *rev* St George slaying dragon with sword, M mint mark on ground, date in exergue, tiny B.P. to upper right, 7.99g (McD 220; QM 181 (part); KM 15; Fr 33; Marsh 189; S 3971). *A few light bagmarks, otherwise good extremely fine, a little weaker on the reverse.* £300-350

Price Realised : £312

ex Randy Weir Numismatics, Unionville, Ontario, Canada, purchased c.1998
Calendar year mintage 3,632,000 of which 1,838 went for pyx trial.

818 **Edward VII,** Sovereign, 1906 M, bare head facing right, DES. below, *rev* St George slaying dragon with sword, M mint mark on ground, date in exergue, tiny B.P. to upper right, 7.99g (McD 223; QM 182 (part); KM 15; Fr 33; Marsh 190; S 3971). *A few light bagmarks, otherwise good extremely fine.* £300-350

Price Realised : £312

ex David L Cannon collection, Cincinnati, Ohio, USA, purchased 19 September 1989
Calendar year mintage 3,656,000 of which 1,853 went for pyx trial.

819 **Edward VII,** Sovereign, 1907 M, bare head facing right, DES. below, *rev* St George slaying dragon with sword, M mint mark on ground, date in exergue, tiny B.P. to upper right, 7.99g (McD 226; QM 183 (part); KM 15; Fr 33; Marsh 191; S 3971). *A few light bagmarks, hairline scratch on the reverse, otherwise good extremely fine.* £300-350

Price Realised : £312

ex Randy Weir Numismatics, Unionville, Ontario, Canada, purchased c.1998
Calendar year mintage 3,331,000 of which 1,691 went for pyx trial.

820 **Edward VII,** Sovereign, 1908 M, bare head facing right, DES. below, *rev* St George slaying dragon with sword, M mint mark on ground, date in exergue, tiny B.P. to upper right, 7.98g (McD 229; QM 184 (part); KM 15; Fr 33; Marsh 192; S 3971). *A few light bagmarks and other surface marks, otherwise good extremely fine.* £300-350

Price Realised : £312

ex Randy Weir Numismatics, Unionville, Ontario, Canada, purchased c.1998
Calendar year mintage 3,078,500 of which 1,648 went for pyx trial.

821 **Edward VII,** Sovereign, 1909 M, bare head facing right, DES. below, raised die flaw to right of second R in legend from rim to head, *rev* St George slaying dragon with sword, M mint mark on ground, date in exergue, tiny B.P. to upper right, 7.98g (McD 232; QM 185 (part); KM 15; Fr 33; Marsh 193; S 3971). *A few light bagmarks, otherwise good extremely fine.* £300-350

Price Realised : £288

ex David L Cannon collection, Cincinnati, Ohio, USA, purchased 19 September 1989
Calendar year mintage 3,028,000 of which 1,538 went for pyx trial.

822 **Edward VII,** Sovereign, 1910 M, bare head facing right, DES. below, *rev* St George slaying dragon with sword, M mint mark on ground, date in exergue, tiny B.P. to upper right, 7.98g (McD 235; QM 186 (part); KM 15; Fr 33; Marsh 194; S 3971). *A few light bagmarks and hairlines, otherwise extremely fine to good extremely fine.* £300-350

Price Realised : £288

Calendar year mintage 3,053,000 of which 1,547 went for pyx trial.
King Edward VII died on 6 May 1910

The Reign of King George V (1910-1936)
House of Windsor

Born: 3 June 1865

Accession: 6 May 1910

Married: Mary of Teck, 6 July 1893

Coronation: Thursday, 22 June 1911, second Coronation as Emperor of India at the Delhi Durbar, Tuesday, 12 December 1911

Children: five sons, one daughter

Died: 20 January 1936, aged 70

823 **George V (1910-1936),** Sovereign, 1911 M, Melbourne mint, designed by Edgar Bertram Mackennal, bare head left, B.M. on truncation, toothed border and raised rim, GEORGIVS V D: G: BRITT: OMN: REX F: D: IND: IMP:, *rev* struck en médaille, engraved after Benedetto Pistrucci, St George slaying dragon with sword, helmet with three strand streamer, horse with long tail, ending in three strands, with one spur higher up at curve, broken lance on ground-line to left, *WWP* in relief under lance, M mint mark on ground, date in exergue, tiny B.P. to upper right, finely toothed border within twin linear concentric circles and raised rim, edge milled, 7.99g (McD 238; QM 187; KM 29; Fr 39; Marsh 229; S 3999). *Scratch in field by forehead, otherwise good extremely fine.* £300-400

Price Realised : £336

ex VP Coins, Maryborough, Queensland, 8 October 2001
Calendar year mintage 2,850,000 of which 1,451 went for pyx trial.

824 **George V,** Sovereign, 1911 M, struck with an off-centre die-axis, obverse a little off-centre with a thick rim, bare head left, B.M. on truncation, *rev* struck at a 45 degree die axis, St George slaying dragon with sword, M mint mark on ground, date in exergue, tiny B.P. to upper right, 7.98g (McD 238; QM 187; KM 29; Fr 39; Marsh 229; S 3999). *Surface marks and hairlines, good very fine and unusual.* £300-400

Price Realised : £312

ex Paul Davies Ltd, purchased June 2008
Calendar year mintage 2,850,000 of which 1,451 went for pyx trial.

825 **George V,** Sovereign, 1912 M, head left, B.M. on truncation, *rev* St George slaying dragon with sword, M mint mark on ground, date in exergue, tiny B.P. to upper right, 7.98g (McD 241; QM 188; KM 29; Fr 39; Marsh 230; S 3999). *Surface marks, three small nicks on head, good extremely fine.* £300-400

Price Realised : £360

Calendar year mintage 2,468,000 of which 1,257 went for pyx trial.

826 **George V,** Sovereign, 1913 M, head left, B.M. on truncation, *rev* St George slaying dragon with sword, M mint mark on ground, date in exergue, tiny B.P. to upper right, 7.99g (McD 244; QM 189; KM 29; Fr 39; Marsh 231; S 3999). *Surface marks and nicks, small scratch on neck, slightly weaker strike on reverse with an uneven tone, otherwise extremely fine.* £300-350

Price Realised : £288

Calendar year mintage 2,322,000 of which 1,180 went for pyx trial.

827 **George V,** Sovereign, 1914 M, head left, B.M. on truncation, latter stop weaker and smaller, *rev* St George slaying dragon with sword, M mint mark on ground, date in exergue, tiny B.P. to upper right, 7.99g (McD 247; QM 190; KM 29; Fr 39; Marsh 232; S 3999). *Softly struck, some residual dirt in the milling, attractively toned practically as struck.* £300-400

Price Realised : £312

Calendar year mintage 2,011,000 of which 1,029 went for pyx trial.

828 **George V,** Sovereign, 1915 M, head left, B.M. on truncation, latter stop weaker and smaller, die flaw from tip of neck, other light flaws at first D and second T of legend, *rev* St George slaying dragon with sword, M mint mark on ground, date in exergue, tiny B.P. to upper right, 7.99g (McD 250; QM 191; KM 29; Fr 39; Marsh 233; S 3999). *Softly struck, some surface marks, otherwise good extremely fine.* £300-350

Price Realised : £312

Calendar year mintage 1,637,000 of which 839 went for pyx trial.

829 **George V,** Sovereign, 1916 M, head left, B.M. on truncation, latter stop weaker and smaller, *rev* St George slaying dragon with sword, M mint mark on ground, date in exergue, tiny B.P. to upper right, 7.99g (McD 253; QM 192; KM 29; Fr 39; Marsh 234; S 3999). *Softly struck, surface marks and nicks, otherwise good extremely fine.* £300-350

Price Realised : £312

Calendar year mintage 1,272,000 of which 634 went for pyx trial.

830 **George V,** Sovereign, 1917 M, head left, B.M. on truncation, *rev* St George slaying dragon with sword, M mint mark on ground, date in exergue, tiny B.P. to upper right, 7.98g (McD 256; QM 193; KM 29; Fr 39; Marsh 235 S; S 3999). *Well struck, some surface marks and hairlines, otherwise extremely fine to good extremely fine.* £300-350

Price Realised : £288

Calendar year mintage 934,000 of which 469 went for pyx trial.

831 **George V,** Sovereign, 1918 M, head left, B.M. on truncation, light raised die flaw at first D of legend, *rev* St George slaying dragon with sword, M mint mark on ground, date in exergue, tiny B.P. to upper right, 7.98g (McD 259; QM 194; KM 29; Fr 39; Marsh 236; S 3999). *Reverse rim nick, black spot on dragon shoulder, some bagmarks, otherwise good extremely fine.* £300-350

Price Realised : £288

Calendar year mintage 4,907,000 of which 2,493 went for pyx trial. This represents the highest calendar year output of Sovereigns for the Melbourne mint in the reign of George V.

832 **George V,** Sovereign, 1919 M, head left, B.M. on truncation, *rev* St George slaying dragon with sword, M mint mark on ground, date in exergue, tiny B.P. to upper right, 7.99g (McD 262; QM 195; KM 29; Fr 39; Marsh 237 S; S 3999). *Light surface marks, good extremely fine and rare.* £400-600

Price Realised : £768

Calendar year mintage 514,000 of which 257 went for pyx trial.

The Very Rare 1920 Melbourne Mint George V Sovereign

833 **George V,** Sovereign, 1920 M, head left, B.M. on truncation, *rev* St George slaying dragon with sword, M mint mark on ground, date in exergue, tiny B.P. to upper right, 7.98g (McD 265; QM 197 R; KM 29; Fr 39; Marsh 238 R2; S 3999). *Light surface marks and nicks, good extremely fine and very rare.* £4000-5000

Price Realised : £6,240

ex Winsor and Sons, Jamberoo, NSW Australia, purchased c.2004
Calendar year mintage 530,000 of which 266 went for pyx trial.
The McDonald catalogue for 2012 rates AUNC quality 1920M Sovereign at a valuation of AU$11,750 (or £7,900)

The Extremely Rare 1921 Melbourne Mint George V Sovereign

834 **George V,** Sovereign, 1921 M, head left, B.M. on truncation, *rev* St George slaying dragon with sword, M mint mark on ground, date in exergue, tiny B.P. to upper right, 7.99g (McD 268; QM 200 R3; KM 29; Fr 39; Marsh 239 R3; S 3999). *Light surface marks, good extremely fine, compares well with the Quartermaster collection coin and is less surface marked, therefore perhaps better, extremely rare.* £10,000-12,000

Price Realised : £15,600

ex Noble Numismatics Sale 66, 28 March 2001, lot 1302
Calendar year mintage 240,000 of which 121 went for pyx trial.
The McDonald catalogue for 2012 rates AUNC quality 1921M Sovereign at a valuation of AU$38,000 (or £25,600)

The Very Rare 1922 Melbourne Mint George V Sovereign

835 **George V,** Sovereign, 1922 M, head left, B.M. on truncation, *rev* St George slaying dragon with sword, M mint mark on ground, date in exergue, light die flaw from date figures to ground line, tiny B.P. to upper right, 7.99g (McD 271; QM 203 R2; KM 29; Fr 39; Marsh 240 R2; S 3999). *Light surface marks and nicks, short light scratch on rump of horse, otherwise good extremely fine, appears to be on par with the Quartermaster collection coin, very rare.* £7000-9000

Price Realised : £13,200

ex Jaggards, Sydney, Australia, purchased 13 June 2001
Calendar year mintage 608,000 of which 306 went for pyx trial.
The McDonald catalogue for 2012 rates AUNC quality 1922M Sovereign at a valuation of AU$23,000 (or £15,500)

836

837

836 **George V,** Sovereign, 1923 M, head left, B.M. on truncation, *rev* St George slaying dragon with sword, M mint mark on ground, date in exergue, tiny B.P. to upper right, 7.99g (McD 274; QM 206 C; KM 29; Fr 39; Marsh 241 R; S 3999). *Light surface marks and nicks, a little residual dirt in obverse legend, good extremely fine.* £300-400

Price Realised : £336

ex Randy Weir Numismatics, Unionville, Ontario, Canada, purchased 13 June 1997
Calendar year mintage 510,870 of which 259 went for pyx trial.

837 **George V,** Sovereign, 1924 M, head left, B.M. on truncation, slight raised die flaw in part of king's name, *rev* St George slaying dragon with sword, M mint mark on ground, date in exergue, tiny B.P. to upper right, 7.99g (McD 277; QM 209 C; KM 29; Fr 39; Marsh 242 R; S 3999). *Some obverse rime nicks, light surface marks, otherwise practically as struck* £300-400

Price Realised : £504

ex Randy Weir Numismatics, Unionville, Ontario, Canada, purchased December 1990
Calendar year mintage 278,000 of which 140 went for pyx trial.

838 **George V,** Sovereign, 1925 M, head left, B.M. on truncation, *rev* St George slaying dragon with sword, M mint mark on ground, date in exergue, tiny B.P. to upper right, 7.99g (McD 280; QM 212 C; KM 29; Fr 39; Marsh 243; S 3999). *A few tiny marks otherwise good extremely fine, practically as struck.* £300-400

Price Realised : £552

Calendar year mintage 3,310,000 of which 1,662 went for pyx trial.

839 **George V,** Sovereign, 1926 M, head left, B.M. on truncation, *rev* St George slaying dragon with sword, M mint mark on ground, date in exergue, tiny B.P. to upper right, 7.98g (McD 283; QM 215 S; KM 29; Fr 39; Marsh 244 R; S 3999). *Reverse rim nick, some light surface marks, otherwise good extremely fine.* £300-400

Price Realised : £336

ex Randy Weir Numismatics, Unionville, Ontario, Canada, purchased 13 June 1997
Calendar year mintage 211,000 of which 107 went for pyx trial. This is the lowest calendar year output for the Melbourne mint under George V. However there are no examples known of 1927 dated Melbourne mint sovereigns, though output continued in the calendar year for 1927 to the tune of 310,000 pieces. Therefore probably most, if not all were dated 1926, of these 156 went for pyx trial. This explains why the 1926 M is not such a rare date as other years with higher calendar year outputs. Strangely, Marsh lists a 1927 M as number 245 rated R2, probably as an assumption of existence as it is almost certain he never saw a specimen.

The Rare 1928 Melbourne Mint George V Sovereign

840 **George V,** Sovereign, 1928 M, head left, B.M. on truncation, *rev* St George slaying dragon with sword, M mint mark on ground, date in exergue, tiny B.P. to upper right, 7.99g (McD 287; QM 218 R; KM 29; Fr 39; Marsh 246 R2; S 3999). *Light surface marks, brilliant good extremely fine and rare.* £2000-2500

Price Realised : £2,280

Calendar year mintage 413,000 of which 208 went for pyx trial.
The McDonald catalogue for 2012 rates AUNC quality 1928M Sovereign at a valuation of AU$5,250 (or £3,500)

The Rare 1929 Melbourne Mint George V Sovereign

841 **George V,** Sovereign, 1929 M, second smaller head left, BM on truncation, no stops, linear outer circle with grained border teeth compartments and rim both sides, *rev* slightly smaller design therefore with a deeper exergue, St George slaying dragon with sword, no *WWP* initials under lance anymore, M mint mark on ground, date in exergue, tiny B.P. to upper right, 7.98g (McD 289; QM 220 R; KM 29; Fr 39; Marsh 247 R3; S 4000). *Spot in obverse field, hairlined, otherwise toned, good extremely fine and rare.* £2000-2500

Price Realised : £2,160

ex Noble Numismatics Sale 66, 28 March 2001, lot 1320
Calendar year mintage 436,719 of which 219 went for pyx trial.
The McDonald catalogue for 2012 rates AUNC quality 1929M Sovereign at a valuation of AU$5,200 (or £3,500)

The Extremely Rare Proof 1929 Melbourne Mint George V Sovereign

842 **George V,** Proof Sovereign, 1929 M, second smaller head left, BM on truncation, *rev* smaller St George slaying dragon with sword, M mint mark on ground, date in exergue, tiny B.P. to upper right, 7.99g, 22.1mm (McD 289; QM -; KM 29; Fr 39; Marsh -; S 4000). *Lightly toned, as struck and of the highest rarity, there being no specimen in the Quartermaster collection.* £30,000-40,000

Price Realised : £40,800

The McDonald catalogue for 2012 rates Proof quality 1929M Sovereign at a valuation of AU$195,000 (or £131,000)

843 **George V,** Sovereign, 1930 M, second smaller head left, BM on truncation, *rev* smaller St George slaying dragon with sword, M mint mark on ground, date in exergue, tiny B.P. to upper right, 7.99g (McD 291; QM 222 S; KM 29; Fr 39; Marsh 248 R; S 4000). *Small dig on second O in legend and other light marks, otherwise proof-like, practically as struck and scarce.* £300-400

Price Realised : £408

Calendar year mintage 77,547 of which 41 went for pyx trial.

844 **George V,** Sovereign, 1931 M, second smaller head left, BM on truncation, *rev* smaller St George slaying dragon with sword, M mint mark on ground, date in exergue, tiny B.P. to upper right, 7.98g (McD 293; QM 224 S; KM 29; Fr 39; Marsh 249 R2; S 4000). *Some light marks and nicks, otherwise practically as struck and scarce.* £400-600

Price Realised : £600

ex Charles Stueve, Abbeygate Coins, Westhampton Beach, New York, c.1990
Calendar year mintage 57,779 of which 30 went for pyx trial. This is the smallest and final calendar year output of gold sovereigns at the Melbourne mint. It is not a great rarity today, as usually last issues of a coin become somewhat symbolic and were probably kept as souvenirs of the Melbourne mint.

PERTH

The Perth Mint

The Reign of Queen Victoria (1837-1901)
House of Hanover

Born: 24 May 1819

Accession: 20 June 1837

Married: Albert of Saxe-Coburg and Gotha
10 February 1840

Coronation: Thursday 28 June 1838

Children: four sons, five daughters

Died: 22 January 1901, aged 81

Perth Mint Victoria Old Head Type Sovereigns

Gold was first discovered in Western Australia around Hall's Creek in 1884 and gold mines became established at Kimberley in 1886. Production increased until in 1892 over £226,000 was produced from the Western goldfields alone. That year a new goldmine was discovered at Coolgardie and in the next two years the production of gold increased to over one million pounds in value. The Colony in Western Australia had been granted Government in 1890, with John Forrest as the first Premier and Treasurer and it was he who was instrumental in establishing the Perth mint to follow suit with the Sydney and Melbourne branches.

Permission was granted for a mint from London in 1894, as long as certain conditions were adhered to. The Perth mint Bill went through Assembly in July 1895 and a design with requirements for the new two storey building to house the Mint was prepared by Horace Seymour, the Deputy Master of the Royal Mint in London. The drawings by the Public Works Department were contracted and signed off 12 June 1896 with builders for a sum of £22,000 to be completed in 12 months, but this was put on hold till the architect returned in 1897 and a renegotiation was necessary with a new completion date of 1 January 1898. A Proclamation for the new Mint was ratified by Queen Victoria 13 October 1897, that all gold coins to be struck would carry the mint letter P.

However, as usual with all large building projects, there were some delays, and the Perth mint building was finally completed 17 October 1898. The keys were handed over for the empty building officially to the Deputy Master John Francis Campbell in November 1898, at which point the fitting of the minting machinery commenced. The mint was ready to go as of June 1899 and the very first Perth mint Sovereign was struck 20 June 1899 and presented to the Governor, Sir Gerard Smith.

When the Perth mint ceased minting Imperial type gold Sovereigns dated 1931, the total quantity of all Sovereigns at this branch mint stood at 106,384,197 pieces, including those sent for pyx trial assay. This figure is quoted by Capt J J Cullimore Allen, along with the individual year totals of coins issued. When added the individual totals equal the overall quantity.

845 **Victoria (1837-1901),** Sovereign, 1899 P, Perth mint, engraved by Thomas Brock, old veiled bust left, T.B. below, VICTORIA D:G: BRITT: REG: F: D: IND: IMP:, toothed border surrounding, *rev* struck en médaille, engraved after Benedetto Pistrucci, St George slaying dragon with sword, three strand streamer on helmet, horse with long tail, three strand end to tail, one spur of extra hair on curve of tail, dragon with four short curved claws on each arm, broken lance on ground-line to left, *WWP* in relief under lance, P mint mark at bottom of ground, date in exergue, tiny B.P. to upper right, finely toothed border within twin linear concentric circles and raised rim, edge milled, 7.99g (McD 203; QM 167 S; Marsh 171 R; KM 13; Fr 25; S 3876). *Some light bagmarks, otherwise weak extremely fine / good extremely fine and rare.* £400-600

Price Realised : £552

ex Monetarium, Kogarah, Australia, purchased 17 March 2003
Calendar year mintage 690,992.

846 **Victoria,** Sovereign, 1900 P, old veiled bust left, raised die flaw in part of queen's name, *rev* St George slaying dragon with sword, P mint mark on ground, date in exergue, tiny B.P. to upper right, 7.98g (McD 206; QM 170 S; Marsh 172; KM 13; Fr 25; S 3876). *Some light bagmarks, otherwise good extremely fine and appears to be finer than the Quartermaster example, scarce.* £300-400

Price Realised : £576

ex Randy Weir Numismatics, Unionville, Ontario, Canada, purchased 23 April 1993
Calendar year mintage 1,886,089

847 **Victoria,** Sovereign, 1901 P, old veiled bust left, *rev* St George slaying dragon with sword, P mint mark on ground, date in exergue, tiny B.P. to upper right more rounded distinctive stops, 7.98g (McD 209; QM 173 S; Marsh 173; KM 13; Fr 25; S 3876). *Some light bagmarks, otherwise good extremely fine and appears to be on par with the Quartermaster example, scarce.* £300-400

Price Realised : £744

ex Randy Weir Numismatics, Unionville, Ontario, Canada, purchased 29 June 1990
Calendar year mintage 2,889,333
Queen Victoria died on 22 January 1901

The Reign of King Edward VII (1901-1910)
House of Saxe-Coburg and Gotha

Born: 9 November 1841

Accession: 22 January 1901

Married: Alexandra of Denmark 10 March 1863

Coronation: Saturday, 9 August 1902

Children: three sons, three daughters

Died: 6 May 1910, aged 68

848 **Edward VII (1901-1910),** Sovereign, 1902 P, Perth mint, engraved by George William De Saulles, bare head facing right, Des. below, toothed border and raised rim, EDWARDVS VII D: G: BRITT: OMN: REX F: D: IND: IMP:, *rev* struck en médaille, engraved after Benedetto Pistrucci, St George slaying dragon with sword, cloak with complete hemline, two stand helmet streamer, horse with long tail, ending in three strands, with one spur higher up at curve, broken lance on ground-line to left, *WWP* in relief under lance, P mint mark on ground, date in exergue, tiny B.P. to upper right, finely toothed border within twin linear concentric circles and raised rim, edge milled, 8.00g (McD 212; QM 178 (part); KM 15; Fr 34; Marsh 195; S 3972). *Some light bagmarks, otherwise attractively toned good extremely fine.* £300-350

Price Realised : £408

ex Randy Weir Numismatics, Unionville, Ontario, Canada, purchased 23 April 1993
Calendar year mintage 4,289,122

849

850

849 **Edward VII,** Sovereign, 1903 P, bare head facing right, Des. below doubled, *rev* St George slaying dragon with sword, P mint mark on ground, date in exergue, tiny B.P. to upper right, 7.98g (McD 215; QM 179 (part); KM 15; Fr 34; Marsh 196; S 3972). *Some light bagmarks, black spot on ground-line, otherwise good extremely fine.* £300-350

Price Realised : £336

Calendar year mintage 4,674,783

850 **Edward VII,** Sovereign, 1904 P, bare head facing right, Des. below, *rev* St George slaying dragon with sword, P mint mark on ground, date in exergue, tiny B.P. to upper right, 7.98g (McD 218; QM 180 (part); KM 15; Fr 34; Marsh 197; S 3972). *Rim nick on the reverse, some surface marks and hairlines, otherwise good extremely fine.* £300-350

Price Realised : £360

ex Randy Weir Numismatics, Unionville, Ontario, Canada, purchased 2 June 1995
Calendar year mintage 4,506,756

851

852

853

851 **Edward VII,** Sovereign, 1905 P, bare head facing right, DES. below, *rev* St George slaying dragon with sword, P mint mark on ground, date in exergue, tiny B.P. to upper right, some light die flaws around date and initials, 7.98g (McD 221; QM 181 (part); KM 15; Fr 34; Marsh 198; S 3972). *A few light bagmarks, otherwise good extremely fine.* £300-350

Price Realised : £360

ex Randy Weir Numismatics, Unionville, Ontario, Canada, purchased 23 April 1993
Calendar year mintage 4,876,193

852 **Edward VII,** Sovereign, 1906 P, bare head facing right, DES. below, *rev* St George slaying dragon with sword, P mint mark on ground, date in exergue, tiny B.P. to upper right, 7.99g (McD 224; QM 182 (part); KM 15; Fr 34; Marsh 199; S 3972). *A few light bagmarks, a pleasing extremely fine.* £300-350

Price Realised : £552

ex Randy Weir Numismatics, Unionville, Ontario, Canada, purchased c.1998
Calendar year mintage 4,829,817

853 **Edward VII,** Sovereign, 1907 P, bare head facing right, DES. below, *rev* St George slaying dragon with sword, P mint mark on ground, date in exergue, tiny B.P. to upper right, 7.99g (McD 227; QM 183 (part); KM 15; Fr 34; Marsh 200; S 3972). *A few light bagmarks and dig under chin in field, otherwise good extremely fine.* £300-350

Price Realised : £312

ex Randy Weir Numismatics, Unionville, Ontario, Canada, purchased 6 February 1990
Calendar year mintage 4,972,289. This calendar year represents the pinnacle of Perth mint Sovereign production.

854

855

856

854 **Edward VII,** Sovereign, 1908 P, bare head facing right, DES. below, *rev* St George slaying dragon with sword, P mint mark on ground, date in exergue, tiny B.P. to upper right, 7.99g (McD 230; QM 184 (part); KM 15; Fr 34; Marsh 201; S 3972). *A few light surface marks and nicks, otherwise good extremely fine.* £300-350

Price Realised : £312

ex Randy Weir Numismatics, Unionville, Ontario, Canada, purchased 23 April 1993
Calendar year mintage 4,875,617

855 **Edward VII,** Sovereign, 1909 P, bare head facing right, DES. below, *rev* St George slaying dragon with sword, P mint mark on ground, date in exergue, tiny B.P. to upper right, 7.99g (McD 233; QM 185 (part); KM 15; Fr 34; Marsh 202; S 3972). *A few light bagmarks, very softly struck otherwise good extremely fine for a weak strike.* £300-350

Price Realised : £288

Calendar year mintage 4,524,241

856 **Edward VII,** Sovereign, 1910 P, bare head facing right, DES. below, *rev* St George slaying dragon with sword, P mint mark on ground, date in exergue, tiny B.P. to upper right, 7.98g (McD 236; QM 186 (part); KM 15; Fr 34; Marsh 203; S 3972). *A few light nicks and hairlines, otherwise unevenly toned, good extremely fine.* £300-350

Price Realised : £336

ex Randy Weir Numismatics, Unionville, Ontario, Canada, purchased 23 April 1993
Calendar year mintage 4,690,625
King Edward VII died on 6 May 1910

The Reign of King George V (1910-1936)
House of Windsor

Born: 3 June 1865

Accession: 6 May 1910

Married: Mary of Teck, 6 July 1893

Coronation: Thursday, 22 June 1911, second Coronation as Emperor of India at the Delhi Durbar, Tuesday, 12 December 1911

Children: five sons, one daughter

Died: 20 January 1936, aged 70

857 **George V (1910-1936),** Sovereign, 1911 P, Perth mint, designed by Edgar Bertram Mackennal, bare head left, B.M. on truncation, toothed border and raised rim, GEORGIVS V D: G: BRITT: OMN: REX F: D: IND: IMP:, *rev* struck en médaille, engraved after Benedetto Pistrucci, St George slaying dragon with sword, helmet with three strand streamer, horse with long tail, ending in three strands, with one spur higher up at curve, broken lance on ground-line to left, *WWP* in relief under lance, P mint mark on ground, date in exergue, lightly die flawed figures, tiny B.P. to upper right, finely toothed border within twin linear concentric circles and raised rim, edge milled, 7.99g (McD 239; QM 187; KM 29; Fr 40; Marsh 250; S 4001). *A few tiny bagmarks, otherwise good extremely fine.* £300-400

Price Realised : £312

ex Randy Weir Numismatics, Unionville, Ontario, Canada, purchased 23 April 1993
Calendar year mintage 4,373,165

858

859

858 **George V,** Sovereign, 1912 P, bare head left, B.M. on truncation, *rev* with die axis slightly off-centre, St George slaying dragon with sword, P mint mark on ground, date in exergue, tiny B.P. to upper right, 7.99g (McD 242; QM 188; KM 29; Fr 40; Marsh 251; S 4001). *A few surface marks and nicks, otherwise good extremely fine.* £300-400

Price Realised : £312

ex Randy Weir Numismatics, Unionville, Ontario, Canada, purchased 23 April 1993
Calendar year mintage 4,278,144

859 **George V,** Sovereign, 1913 P, bare head left, B.M. on truncation, *rev* with die axis slightly off-centre, St George slaying dragon with sword, P mint mark on ground, date in exergue, tiny B.P. to upper right, 8.00g (McD 245; QM 189; KM 29; Fr 40; Marsh 252; S 4001). *A few light surface marks, otherwise good extremely fine.* £300-400

Price Realised : £288

ex Noble Numismatics Sale 66, 28 March 2001, lot 1297
Calendar year mintage 4,635,287

860

861

862

860 **George V,** Sovereign, 1914 P, bare head left, B.M. on truncation, latter stop weak and small, *rev* with die axis slightly off-centre, St George slaying dragon with sword, P mint mark on ground, date in exergue, tiny B.P. to upper right, 7.99g (McD 248; QM 190; KM 29; Fr 40; Marsh 253; S 4001). *A few light hairlines and surface marks, otherwise good extremely fine.* £300-400

Price Realised : £576

ex Randy Weir Numismatics, Unionville, Ontario, Canada, purchased 23 April 1993
Calendar year mintage 4,815,996

861 **George V,** Sovereign, 1915 P, bare head left, B.M. on truncation, latter stop weak and small, *rev* with die axis slightly off-centre, St George slaying dragon with sword, P mint mark on ground, date in exergue, tiny B.P. to upper right, 7.98g (McD 251; QM 191; KM 29; Fr 40; Marsh 254; S 4001). *Some bagmarks and surface marks with nicks, red tone, otherwise good extremely fine.* £300-400

Price Realised : £288

ex Randy Weir Numismatics, Unionville, Ontario, Canada, purchased 23 April 1993
Calendar year mintage 4,373,596

862 **George V,** Sovereign, 1916 P, bare head left, B.M. on truncation, latter stop weak and small, *rev* with die axis slightly off-centre, St George slaying dragon with sword, P mint mark on ground, date in exergue, tiny B.P. to upper right, 7.98g (McD 254; QM 192; KM 29; Fr 40; Marsh 255 S; S 4001). *A few light surface marks, otherwise good extremely fine.* £300-400

Price Realised : £288

ex Randy Weir Numismatics, Unionville, Ontario, Canada, purchased 23 April 1993
Calendar year mintage 4,096,771

863

864

865

863 **George V,** Sovereign, 1917 P, bare head left, B.M. on truncation, latter stop weak and small, *rev* with die axis slightly off-centre, St George slaying dragon with sword, P mint mark on ground, filled in upper part, date in exergue, tiny B.P. to upper right, 7.98g (McD 257; QM 193; KM 29; Fr 40; Marsh 256 S; S 4001). *A few light surface marks, some spots, otherwise practically as struck.* £300-400

Price Realised : £336

ex Ebay purchase, 21 August 2001
Calendar year mintage 4,110,286

864 **George V,** Sovereign, 1918 P, bare head left, B.M. on truncation, latter stop weak and small, *rev* with die axis slightly off-centre, St George slaying dragon with sword, P mint mark on ground, date in exergue, tiny B.P. to upper right, 7.98g (McD 260; QM 194; KM 29; Fr 40; Marsh 257; S 4001). *A few light surface marks, otherwise practically as struck.* £300-400

Price Realised : £312

ex Randy Weir Numismatics, Unionville, Ontario, Canada, purchased c.1997
Calendar year mintage 3,812,884

865 **George V,** Sovereign, 1919 P, bare head left, B.M. on truncation, latter stop absent, *rev* with die axis slightly off-centre, St George slaying dragon with sword, P mint mark on ground, date in exergue, tiny B.P. to upper right, 7.98g (McD 263; QM 195; KM 29; Fr 40; Marsh 258; S 4001). *A few light surface marks, otherwise good extremely fine, practically as struck.* £300-400

Price Realised : £312

ex Randy Weir Numismatics, Unionville, Ontario, Canada, purchased October 1991
Calendar year mintage 2,995,216

866

867

868

866 **George V,** Sovereign, 1920 P, bare head left, B.M. on truncation, latter stop weak and small, *rev* with die axis slightly off-centre, St George slaying dragon with sword, P mint mark on ground, date in exergue, tiny B.P. to upper right, 8.00g (McD 266; QM 198; KM 29; Fr 40; Marsh 259; S 4001). *A few light surface marks, unevenly toned, otherwise good extremely fine.* £300-400

Price Realised : £288

ex Randy Weir Numismatics, Unionville, Ontario, Canada, purchased c.1997
Calendar year mintage 2,421,196

867 **George V,** Sovereign, 1921 P, bare head left, B.M. on truncation, latter stop absent, *rev* with die axis slightly off-centre, St George slaying dragon with sword, P mint mark on ground, date in exergue, tiny B.P. to upper right, 7.98g (McD 269; QM 201; KM 29; Fr 40; Marsh 260; S 4001). *Blemish by mouth with some hairlines, otherwise practically as struck.* £300-400

Price Realised : £312

ex Randy Weir Numismatics, Unionville, Ontario, Canada, purchased 23 April 1993
Calendar year mintage 2,314,360

868 **George V,** Sovereign, 1922 P, bare head left, B.M. on truncation, latter stop absent, *rev* with die axis slightly off-centre, St George slaying dragon with sword, P mint mark on ground, date in exergue, tiny B.P. to upper right, 7.99g (McD 272; QM 204; KM 29; Fr 40; Marsh 261; S 4001). *A few light surface marks and a little softly struck, otherwise practically as struck.* £300-400

Price Realised : £288

ex Randy Weir Numismatics, Unionville, Ontario, Canada, purchased 23 April 1993
Calendar year mintage 2,298,884

869

870

871

869 **George V,** Sovereign, 1923 P, bare head left, B.M. on truncation, latter stop weak and small, *rev* with die axis slightly off-centre, St George slaying dragon with sword, P mint mark on ground, date in exergue, tiny B.P. to upper right, 7.99g (McD 275; QM 207; KM 29; Fr 40; Marsh 262; S 4001). *A few light surface marks, otherwise uncirculated.* £300-400

Price Realised : £288

ex Randy Weir Numismatics, Unionville, Ontario, Canada, purchased October 1991
Calendar year mintage 2,124,154

870 **George V,** Sovereign, 1924 P, bare head left, B.M. on truncation, latter stop very weak and small, *rev* with die axis slightly off-centre, St George slaying dragon with sword, P mint mark on ground, date in exergue, tiny B.P. to upper right, 7.98g (McD 278; QM 210; KM 29; Fr 40; Marsh 263; S 4001). *A few light surface marks, otherwise good extremely fine.* £300-400

Price Realised : £312

ex Randy Weir Numismatics, Unionville, Ontario, Canada, purchased 23 April 1993
Calendar year mintage 1,464,416

871 **George V,** Sovereign, 1925 P, bare head left, B.M. on truncation, latter stop absent, parts of legend lightly die flawed, *rev* with die axis slightly off-centre, St George slaying dragon with sword, P mint mark on ground, date in exergue, tiny B.P. to upper right, 7.98g (McD 281; QM 213 S; KM 29; Fr 40; Marsh 264 S; S 4001). *A few light surface marks, dark tone, otherwise good extremely fine and scarce.* £400-600

Price Realised : £480

ex Randy Weir Numismatics, Unionville, Ontario, Canada, purchased 23 April 1993
Calendar year mintage 1,837,901

872

873

874

872 **George V,** Sovereign, 1926 P, bare head left, B.M. on truncation, latter stop weak and small, *rev* with die axis slightly off-centre, St George slaying dragon with sword, P mint mark on ground, date in exergue, tiny B.P. to upper right, 7.99g (McD 284; QM 216 S; KM 29; Fr 40; Marsh 265 R; S 4001). *A few light surface marks, light tone, otherwise good extremely fine and the rarest date to find for the George V Perth mint series.* £1500-2000

Price Realised : £1,620

ex Randy Weir Numismatics, Unionville, Ontario, Canada, purchased 4 November 2000
Calendar year mintage 1,313,578
The McDonald catalogue for 2012 rates AUNC quality 1926P Sovereign at a valuation of AU$3,600 (or £2,400)

873 **George V,** Sovereign, 1927 P, bare head left, B.M. on truncation, latter stop weak and small, parts of legend lightly die flawed, *rev* with die axis slightly off-centre, St George slaying dragon with sword, P mint mark on ground, date in exergue, tiny B.P. to upper right, 7.99g (McD 286; QM 217 S; KM 29; Fr 40; Marsh 266 S; S 4001). *Lightly toned, practically as struck and scarce.* £400-600

Price Realised : £624

ex Randy Weir Numismatics, Unionville, Ontario, Canada, purchased October 1991
Calendar year mintage 1,383,544

874 **George V,** Sovereign, 1928 P, bare head left, B.M. on truncation, latter stop very weak and small, parts of legend lightly die flawed, *rev* with die axis slightly off-centre, St George slaying dragon with sword, P mint mark on ground, date in exergue, tiny B.P. to upper right, 7.99g (McD 288; QM 219 S; KM 29; Fr 40; Marsh 267 S; S 4001). *A few light marks, practically as struck and scarce.* £300-400

Price Realised : £312

ex Randy Weir Numismatics, Unionville, Ontario, Canada, purchased 23 April 1993
Calendar year mintage 1,333,417

875

876

877

875 **George V,** Sovereign, 1929 P, second smaller head left, BM on truncation, no stops, linear outer circle with grained border teeth compartments and rim both sides, *rev* slightly smaller design therefore with a deeper exergue, St George slaying dragon with sword, no *WWP* initials under lance anymore, P mint mark on ground, date in exergue, tiny B.P. to upper right, 7.98g (McD 290; QM 221; KM 29; Fr 39; Marsh 268 S; S 4002). *A few light surface marks, extremely fine to good extremely fine.* £300-400

Price Realised : £312

ex Randy Weir Numismatics, Unionville, Ontario, Canada, purchased 23 April 1993
Calendar year mintage 1,606,625

876 **George V,** Sovereign, 1930 P, second smaller head left, BM on truncation, some light die flaws in legend, *rev* smaller St George slaying dragon with sword, P mint mark on ground, date in exergue, tiny B.P. to upper right, 7.99g (McD 292; QM 223; KM 29; Fr 39; Marsh 269 R; S 4002). *A few light surface marks, otherwise uncirculated.* £300-400

Price Realised : £288

ex Randy Weir Numismatics, Unionville, Ontario, Canada, purchased October 1991
Calendar year mintage 1,915,352

877 **George V,** Sovereign, 1931 P, second smaller head left, BM on truncation, some light die flaws in legend, *rev* smaller St George slaying dragon with sword, P mint mark on ground, date in exergue, tiny B.P. to upper right, 8.00g (McD 294; QM 225; KM 29; Fr 39; Marsh 270 S; S 4002). *A few light surface marks, otherwise good extremely fine.* £300-400

Price Realised : £288

ex Ebay purchase from Queensland, Australia, 21 August 2001
Calendar year mintage 1,173,568. This is the lowest and final calendar year output for Sovereigns during the reign of George V.

The Extremely Rare 1931 Perth Mint Proof Sovereign

878 **George V,** Proof Sovereign, 1931 P, second smaller head left, BM on truncation, no stops, linear outer circle with grained border teeth compartments and rim both sides, *rev* slightly smaller design therefore with a deeper exergue, St George slaying dragon with sword, no *WWP* initials under lance, P mint mark on ground, date in exergue, tiny B.P. to upper right, 7.98g (McD 294 and note; QM -; KM -; Fr 39; Marsh -; S 4002). *Mint state and of the highest rarity.* £30,000-40,000

Price Realised : £52,800

ex Mr Agnew collection, Director of Channon Consolidated Goldfields, c.1931
ex Agnew Family collection, sold to Spink and Son privately c.1994
ex An Important Collection of Gold Sovereigns 1816-2000, offered as one lot, Sothebys, November 2000, lot 525 (part)
No doubt these proofs were struck to mark the end of the production of gold Sovereigns at the Perth mint and were a VIP gift to prominent people involved in the mining and minting process. The cataloguer was present when this coin changed hands, c.1994, and the grandfather of the vendor was one of the Agnew family who was a Director of Channon Consolidated Goldfields at the time of the coins issue. This company was a conglomerate first formed in 1887 and eventually bought out by Hanson plc in 1988.
This coin is mentioned in the footnote of the McDonald publication and is apparently one of only two specimen proofs in private hands. The McDonald catalogue gives this proof coin of 1931 at Perth a valuation of AU$210,000 (or £141,150).

CANADA

Ottawa, Canada Mint

Following the discovery of gold deposits in the Yukon in 1900, the Canadian Government requested a right to coin the gold into Sovereigns. The new mint would have to be a Branch of the Royal Mint and in 1901 the Canadian House of Commons allowed funding for a branch at Ottawa and Royal assent was received. This caused some consternation, as gold was not common in trade as a whole and was really only seen on the western side of the country. Building did not actually start until 1905 and took nearly three years, opening 2 January 1908 with the economist James Bonar (1852-1941) as Deputy Master. Production from then onwards was sporadic at best, until an end in 1919 with less than one million gold Sovereigns struck in total and no half-sovereigns. The Branch Mint status was retained until the last year that British Imperial Sovereigns were struck in Australia in 1931, when it became the Royal Canadian Mint in its own right. The total output of gold Sovereigns issued in the entire period was a mere 627,834 pieces, including 318 pieces for pyx trial; miniscule compared to Australian branch mints.

The Reign of King Edward VII (1901-1910)
House of Saxe-Coburg and Gotha

Born: 9 November 1841

Accession: 22 January 1901

Married: Alexandra of Denmark 10 March 1863

Coronation: Saturday, 9 August 1902

Children: three sons, three daughters

Died: 6 May 1910, aged 68

The Extremely Rare 1908 Canada Sovereign
Struck to a Satin Specimen Finish

879 **Edward VII (1901-1910),** Satin Finish Proof Sovereign, 1908 C, Ottawa, Canada mint, engraved by George William de Saulles, bare head facing right, DES. below, toothed border and raised rim, EDWARDVS VII D: G: BRITT: OMN: REX F: D: IND: IMP:, *rev* struck en médaille, engraved after Benedetto Pistrucci, St George slaying dragon with sword, cloak with complete hemline, two stand helmet streamer, horse with long tail, ending in three strands, with one spur higher up at curve, broken lance on ground-line to left, *WWP* in relief under lance, C mint mark on ground, date in exergue, tiny B.P. to upper right, finely toothed border within twin linear concentric circles and raised rim, edge milled, 8.00g (KM 14; Fr 1; Marsh 183 R6; S 3970). *One tiny spot after VII of legend, otherwise superb with a wonderful satin finish, mint state and extremely rare.* £4000-5000

Price Realised : £8,400

ex Randy Weir Numismatics, Unionville, Ontario, Canada, purchased 19 September 1992
Calendar year mintage 636 pieces including 10 which were sent for pyx trial.
All the 1908 Canada specimens were struck to this satin finish in commemoration of the inauguration of the Ottawa Mint.

The Excessively Rare 1909 Canada Sovereign Struck to a Satin Specimen Finish

880 **Edward VII,** Satin Finish Proof Sovereign, 1909 C, bare head facing right, DES. below, *rev* St George slaying dragon with sword, C mint mark on ground, date in exergue, tiny B.P. to upper right, 7.99g (KM 14; Fr 1; Marsh -; S 3970). *One tiny spot after D: G: of legend, one very small rim bruise, otherwise superb with a wonderful satin finish, mint state and of the highest rarity.* £6000-8000

Price Realised : £9,360

ex Randy Weir Numismatics, Unionville, Ontario, Canada, purchased 19 September 1992
This amazing coin was struck with the same proof satin finish as the 1908 pieces and was therefore probably struck at the beginning of the run of 1909 dated Sovereigns. It stands out when comparing the coin side by side with a regular 1909 currency piece and clearly matches the finish on the 1908 Sovereign in the previous lot.

881 **Edward VII,** Sovereign, 1909 C, bare head facing right, DES. below, *rev* St George slaying dragon with sword, C mint mark on ground, date in exergue, tiny B.P. to upper right, 7.98g (KM 14; Fr 1; Marsh 184 R2; S 3970). *Some very light surface marks, otherwise good extremely fine and very rare.* £400-500

Price Realised : £888

ex Randy Weir Numismatics, Unionville, Ontario, Canada, purchased 27 January 1994
Calendar year mintage 16,273 pieces including 27 which were sent for pyx trial.

882 **Edward VII,** Sovereign, 1910 C, bare head facing right, DES. below, *rev* St George slaying dragon with sword, C mint mark on ground, date in exergue, tiny B.P. to upper right, 7.99g (KM 14; Fr 1; Marsh 185 R2; S 3970). *Some very light surface marks, otherwise as struck and very rare.* £500-600

Price Realised : £1,260

ex Randy Weir Numismatics, Unionville, Ontario, Canada, purchased 22 March 1990
Calendar year mintage 28,012 pieces including 8 which were sent for pyx trial.
King Edward VII died on 6 May 1910

The Reign of King George V (1910-1936)
House of Windsor

Born: 3 June 1865

Accession: 6 May 1910

Married: Mary of Teck, 6 July 1893

Coronation: Thursday, 22 June 1911, second Coronation as Emperor of India at the Delhi Durbar, Tuesday, 12 December 1911

Children: five sons, one daughter

Died: 20 January 1936, aged 70

The Extremely Rare Specimen Striking of the First Canadian Sovereign of George V

883 **George V (1910-1936),** Specimen Sovereign, 1911 C, Ottawa, Canada mint, struck to a specimen satin finish, designed by Edgar Bertram Mackennal, bare head left, B.M. on truncation, toothed border and raised rim, GEORGIVS V D: G: BRITT: OMN: REX F: D: IND: IMP:, *rev* struck en médaille, engraved after Benedetto Pistrucci, St George slaying dragon with sword, helmet with three strand streamer, horse with long tail, ending in three strands, with one spur higher up at curve, broken lance on ground-line to left, *WWP* in relief under lance, C mint mark on ground, date in exergue, tiny B.P. to upper right, finely toothed border within twin linear concentric circles and raised rim, edge milled, 7.98g, 21.9mm (KM 20; Fr 2; Marsh -; cf S 3997). *Listed by KM with no valuation, slight red patches of tone on rump of horse and reverse rim, otherwise mint state as struck, previously graded by PCGS as SP67, and of the highest rarity.* £8000-10,000

Price Realised : £10,440

ex Proof Positive Coins, Nova Scotia, Canada, 3 August 2002
PCGS show a total of 11 pieces in specimen grade on their population report.

884 **George V,** Sovereign, 1911 C, bare head left, B.M. on truncation, *rev* St George slaying dragon with sword, C mint mark on ground, date in exergue, tiny B.P. to upper right, 8.00g (KM 20; Fr 2; Marsh 221 S; S 3997). *Some nicks in obverse field and over St George helmet, otherwise good extremely fine, practically as struck.* £300-400

Price Realised : £408

ex Randy Weir Numismatics, Unionville, Ontario, Canada, purchased 14 August 1992
Calendar year mintage 256,946 pieces including 102 which were sent for pyx trial.

885 **George V,** Sovereign, 1913 C, bare head left, B.M. on truncation, *rev* St George slaying dragon with sword, C mint mark on ground, date in exergue, tiny B.P. to upper right, 7.99g (KM 20; Fr 2; Marsh 222 R4; S 3997). *Some light hairlines, light streak of tone under neck on obverse, otherwise good extremely fine, rare.* £1200-1500

Price Realised : £1,800

ex Randy Weir Numismatics, Unionville, Ontario, Canada, purchased 31 July 1990
Calendar year mintage 3,715 pieces including 2 which were sent for pyx trial.

886 **George V,** Sovereign, 1914 C, bare head left, B.M. on truncation, *rev* St George slaying dragon with sword, C mint mark on ground, date in exergue, tiny B.P. to upper right, 7.98g (KM 20; Fr 2; Marsh 223 R3; S 3997). *Some light surface marks both sides, scratch below chin, otherwise good extremely fine, scarce.* £500-600

Price Realised : £960

ex Randy Weir Numismatics, Unionville, Ontario, Canada, purchased 6 April 1990
Calendar year mintage 14,891 pieces including 9 which were sent for pyx trial.

The Key Date to the Canadian Sovereign Series the George V 1916 C

887 **George V,** Sovereign, 1916 C, bare head left, B.M. on truncation, *rev* St George slaying dragon with sword, C mint mark on ground, date in exergue, tiny B.P. to upper right, 7.99g (KM 20; Fr 2; Marsh 224 R5; S 3997). *A few very tiny light marks, otherwise as struck and extremely rare, the key date.* £10,000-12,000

Price Realised : £22,800

ex Randy Weir Numismatics, Unionville, Ontario, Canada, purchased 6 April 1990
Calendar year mintage 6,111 pieces including 8 which were sent for pyx trial.

888 **George V,** Sovereign, 1917 C, bare head left, B.M. on truncation, *rev* St George slaying dragon with sword, C mint mark on ground, date in exergue, tiny B.P. to upper right, 7.98g (KM 20; Fr 2; Marsh 225 R; S 3997). *Tiny spot near B of legend, otherwise practically as struck.* £300-400

Price Realised : £432

ex Randy Weir Numismatics, Unionville, Ontario, Canada, purchased 6 April 1990
Calendar year mintage 58,845 pieces including 30 which were sent for pyx trial.

889 **George V,** Sovereign, 1918 C, bare head left, B.M. on truncation, *rev* St George slaying dragon with sword, C mint mark on ground, date in exergue, tiny B.P. to upper right, 7.98g (KM 20; Fr 2; Marsh 226 S; S 3997). *Once cleaned with some heavy bagmarks and scuffs, otherwise extremely fine, scarce.* £300-350

Price Realised : £384

ex David L Cannon collection, Cincinnati, Ohio, 19 September 1989
Calendar year mintage 106,516 pieces including 54 which were sent for pyx trial.

890 **George V,** Sovereign, 1919 C, bare head left, B.M. on truncation, *rev* St George slaying dragon with sword, C mint mark on ground, date in exergue, tiny B.P. to upper right, 7.99g (KM 20; Fr 2; Marsh 227 S; S 3997). *Some light surface marks both sides, patchy red tone, otherwise good extremely fine, scarce.* £300-350

Price Realised : £504

ex Randy Weir Numismatics, Unionville, Ontario, Canada, purchased 17 August 1996
Calendar year mintage 135,889 pieces including 68 which were sent for pyx trial.

BRITISH INDIA

Bombay, India Mint (now Mumbai)

The Bombay Branch Mint had been proposed since the late 19th Century and was prompted by an active export trade, which demanded to finance heavy movements of coin and also for disbursements to Indian troops. Building and installation commenced from 21 December 1917 and the new mint struck its first Sovereigns 15 August 1918 with the last on 22 April 1919, closing in May 1919. In just over eight months of output it issued more Imperial type Sovereigns than the Ottawa branch mint did in its entire tenure from 1908-1919. The gold blanks were supplied by the domestic Indian mints at Bombay and Calcutta and the face value of a gold Sovereign was set at a direct exchange value of 15-Rupees which is why the Bentley Collection also contains gold 15-Rupees dated to this significant year.

The Reign of King George V (1910-1936)
House of Windsor

Born: 3 June 1865

Accession: 6 May 1910

Married: Mary of Teck, 6 July 1893

Coronation: Thursday, 22 June 1911, second Coronation as Emperor of India at the Delhi Durbar, Tuesday, 12 December 1911

Children: five sons, one daughter

Died: 20 January 1936, aged 70

The Extremely Rare Specimen Striking of the First Indian Imperial Sovereign of George V

891 **George V (1910-1936),** Specimen Sovereign, 1918 I, Bombay, India Mint, struck to a specimen satin finish, well defined striking, designed by Edgar Bertram Mackennal, bare head left, B.M. on truncation, toothed border and raised rim, GEORGIVS V D: G: BRITT: OMN: REX F: D: IND: IMP:, *rev* struck en médaille, engraved after Benedetto Pistrucci, St George slaying dragon with sword, helmet with three strand streamer, horse with long tail, ending in three strands, with one spur higher up at curve, broken lance on ground-line to left, *WWP* in relief under lance, I mint mark on ground, date in exergue, tiny B.P. to upper right, finely toothed border within twin linear concentric circles and raised rim, edge milled, 7.98g (KM 525A; Fr 1609; Marsh -; cf S 3998). *Listed in KM without a valuation, toned as struck and of the highest rarity.* £8000-10,000

Price Realised : £13,200

ex Randy Weir Numismatics, Unionville, Ontario, Canada, purchased 17 August 1996

892 **George V,** Sovereign, 1918 I, bare head left, B.M. on truncation, *rev* St George slaying dragon with sword, I mint mark on ground, date in exergue, tiny B.P. to upper right, 7.99g (KM 20; Fr 2; Marsh 228; S 3997). *Toned as struck.* £300-400

Price Realised : £648

ex Randy Weir Numismatics, Unionville, Ontario, Canada, purchased 18 April 1994
Total mintage of gold Sovereigns 1,295,372 pieces.

893 **George V,** Fifteen Rupees, 1918, crowned bust left, GEORGE V KING EMPEROR thick toothed border, *rev* struck en médaille, horizontal line at centre 15 RUPEES INDIA 1918, beaded border surrounding, outer pattern with floral ornamentation, 7.99g, 22.1mm (KM 525; Fr 1608). *Some weakness in striking, otherwise toned as struck.* £300-400

Price Realised : £3,360

ex Randy Weir Numismatics, Unionville, Ontario, Canada, purchased 17 August 1996

894 **George V,** Proof Fifteen Rupees, 1918, restrike (c.1955), crowned bust left, GEORGE V KING EMPEROR, thick toothed border, *rev* struck en médaille, horizontal line at centre 15 RUPEES INDIA 1918, beaded border surrounding, outer pattern with floral ornamentation, 8.00g, 22.2mm (KM 525; Fr 1608a). *Hairlined, brilliant fields and obverse design, reverse design and letters frosted, otherwise as struck.* £300-400

Price Realised : £3,120

ex Randy Weir Numismatics, Unionville, Ontario, Canada, purchased 17 August 1996

895 **George V,** Proof Fifteen Rupees, 1918, restrike (c.1968-1670), crowned bust left, GEORGE V KING EMPEROR, thick toothed border, *rev* struck en médaille, horizontal line at centre 15 RUPEES INDIA 1918, beaded border surrounding, outer pattern with floral ornamentation, 8.00g, 22.3mm (KM 525; Fr 1608a). *Very yellow coloured gold, design and fields all brilliant with hairlines, otherwise as struck.* £300-400

Price Realised : £2,760

ex Randy Weir Numismatics, Unionville, Ontario, Canada, purchased 17 August 1996

SOUTH AFRICA

The Bentley Collection contains a run of the gold "Ponds" of the Transvaal – The Zuid Afrikaansche Republiek (ZAR), both those first issued under President Thomas Burgers and the later issues from Paul Kruger. This collecting pattern follows the influence of the publication *Sovereigns of the British Empire* by Capt J J Cullimore Allen in 1965, which included the earlier South African gold pieces that were not Sovereigns. They were included for sake of completeness as they had emanated from the same mint at Pretoria.

The Pretoria Mint

The first coin ever struck for the South African government was the Thomas Francois Burgers (1834-1881) gold "Ponds" minted from gold from the initial source discovered in South Africa, with the effigy of Burgers, who was President from 1872-1877. They were a coin of great pride and endeavour. Burgers himself having visited the goldfields in early 1874, purchased a quantity of alluvial gold. This gold was despatched to the Republic's Consul-General in London, Mr J J Pratt, along with designs for Burger's portrait and the reverse coat of arms. Burgers had already declared British sterling as the currency for the Zuid Afrikaanse Republiek (ZAR) and therefore requested that this gold be turned into Staatsponden with the same intrinsic value as the British sovereign. Burgers hoped that finished coins would be available when the Volksraad next met in May of 1874. However, the alluvial gold only reached London in the middle of May and first had to be refined by Johnson and Matthey. The working dies were engraved by Leonard Charles Wyon with the blessing of the Royal Mint. The gold and the dies were transported to Birmingham for striking of the coins by Ralph Heaton and Sons. It was hoped at least a few finished coins might accompany Mrs Burgers and family on their way home from England at Southampton in early July, however the obverse die had broken, rendering such a delivery impossible. Eventually a total of 695 pieces were received by Pratt on 25 July, which were despatched to South Africa in early August 1874 as there were concerns over the copper tint of the coins. Since the breakage, a new die had been engraved, on which the President's beard was rendered in a more coarse style and employed to mint a total of 142 coins.

This group of 142 pieces was sent 20 September minus four pieces, it seems, which were kept back for Mr Pratt, Mr Wyon, Messrs. Johnson Matthey and Messrs. Heaton. This second group of fine beard coins reached South Africa 23 October 1874. The first had arrived in mid-September all much later than President Burgers had originally anticipated, and at a much greater cost as the price of manufacture exceeded the face value of the coins. President Burgers first produced the coins at the meeting of the Volksraad on Tuesday, 22 September 1874, as an item off the agenda. He announced the coins as the first ever struck for South Africa and handed £50 worth to the Chairman of the meeting, to loud cheers, however the fact his effigy appeared on the coin did not seem to go down well with some members, to the extent Burgers claimed his effigy appeared against his wishes. Later the Executive Council presented President Burgers with one of the Staatsponds and the Volksraad did the same. Burgers himself bought a further eight specimens to give to his family. Designs were prepared for a series of other denominations, but the Volksraad seems to have voted against any further coin issues. A fuller account of all the events of this time and facsimile copies of original correspondence are to be found in *South Africa's First Gold Coin* by Matthy Esterhuysen.

The South African Republic coinage was first recorded in print in an anonymous article in the Numismatic Chronicle published in London in 1900, no author's name was given as the subject matter was controversial because of the Boer War. This narrative had resulted from a presentation given at one of the Society meetings back in 1894, and it later became apparent the author was Sir Augustus Prevost.
A total of 837 gold Staatsponden were struck of both varieties bearing the effigy of Burgers

Reference guide

Hern	Hern, *Handbook on South African Coins and Patterns*
Kaplan	Stan Kaplan, *The coins of South Africa by Alec Kaplan*
Esterhuysen	Matthy Esterhuysen, *South Africa's First Gold Coin*, published by Purnell 1976

Very Rare South Africa 1874 Fine Beard Pond

fine beard points

896 **ZAR,** President Thomas Francois Burgers (1872-1877), Gold Pond, 1874, spread date, fine point bearded bust of Burgers left, date below, THOMAS FRANÇOIS BURGERS, toothed border both sides, *rev* struck with inverted die axis, oval shield of arms divided in three, lion passant to upper left, Boer with rifle to upper right, ox wagon at bottom, with an escutcheon of an upright anchor, all upon frame surmounted by eagle, three "vierkleur" flags either side, three full flagpoles visible each side, the lower left pole appears disjointed, motto on scroll below in larger letters EENDRAGT MAAKT MAGT, large stop below, ZUID AFRIKAANSCHE REPUBLIEK, edge milled, 7.99g, 22.3mm (Hern B1; KM 1.2; Fr 1; Kaplan 2). *Lightly toned, mint state and very rare.* £40,000-50,000

Price Realised : £45,600

ex Knightsbridge Coins, London, purchased on advice of Randy Weir 15 October 1999
Mintage 695 pieces according to Esterhuysen and Hern.
The dies for this extremely rare issue were engraved by Leonard C Wyon and resulting gold coins struck by Ralph Heaton and Sons of Birmingham, who had the order to produce these coins from gold mined in the Lydenburg district. This was the first source of gold mined in South Africa
The specimen here is a particularly fine one and appears to compare very well with one sold by DNW as MS65 in June 2011 for a hammer price of £70,000.

Excessively Rare Pattern 1874 Fine Beard Pond
Struck in White Metal on a thick flan

897 **ZAR,** President Thomas François Burgers (1872-1877), Pattern Pond, struck in white metal on a thick flan, 1874 closer date, fine point bearded bust of Burgers left, date below, THOMAS FRANÇOIS BURGERS, larger teeth in toothed border both sides, *rev* struck with inverted die axis, oval shield of arms with escutcheon and frame surmounted by eagle, three "vierkleur" flags either side, three full flagpoles visible each side, the lower left pole appears disjointed, motto on scroll below in larger letters EENDRAGT MAAKT MAGT, large stop below, ZUID AFRIKAANSCHE REPUBLIEK, edge milled, 2.06g, 22.5mm, thickness 3mm (Hern B10; KM Pn21; cf Kaplan 2). *Some light corrosion evident in hair and on rim, otherwise as struck and excessively rare.* £8000-10,000

Price Realised : £7,200

Extremely Rare South Africa 1874 Coarse Beard Pond

coarse beard points

898 **ZAR,** President Burgers, Gold Pond, 1874, closer date, 8 doubled, short coarse bearded bust of Burgers left, date below, THOMAS FRANÇOIS BURGERS, toothed border and raised rim both sides, *rev* struck with inverted die axis, oval shield of arms divided in three, lion passant to upper left, Boer with rifle to upper right, ox wagon at bottom, with an escutcheon of an upright anchor, all upon frame surmounted by eagle, three "vierkleur" flags either side, three full flagpoles visible each side, the lower left pole appears disjointed, motto on scroll below EENDRAGT MAAKT MAGT, stop below, ZUID AFRIKAANSCHE REPUBLIEK, edge milled, 7.99g, 22.3mm (Hern B2; KM 1.1; Fr 1a; Kaplan 1). *With attractive red tone, with only a touch of wear in the toning to highest points, otherwise as struck and extremely rare.*

£80,000-100,000

Price Realised : £78,000

ex Knightsbridge Coins, London, purchased on advice of Randy Weir, 15 October 1999
Mintage 142 pieces according to Hern and Cullimore Allen, Krause gives 174 as the total.
The specimen here is a particularly fine one and appears to compare very well with one sold by DNW as MS64 in June 2011 for a hammer price of £180,000.

Extremely Rare Pattern Struck in Bronze of the 1874 Coarse Beard Pond

899 **ZAR,** President Burgers, Pattern Pond, struck in bronze, 1874, spread date, weak serifs in date, short coarse bearded bust of Burgers left, date below, THOMAS FRANÇOIS BURGERS, toothed border and raised rim both sides, *rev* struck with inverted die axis, oval shield of arms divided in three, lion passant to upper left, Boer with rifle to upper right, ox wagon at bottom, with an escutcheon of an upright anchor, all upon frame surmounted by eagle, three "vierkleur" flags either side, only two full flagpoles visible each side, the third lowest flagpole behind flag with only tip showing, motto on scroll below EENDRAGT MAAKT MAGT, stop below, ZUID AFRIKAANSCHE REPUBLIEK, edge milled, 4.16g, 22.1mm (Hern B7/6; KM Pn19; cf Kaplan 1). *A few light hairlines, tiny short scratch by pellet stop, with a bluish tone, otherwise practically as struck and extremely rare.* £10,000-12,000

Price Realised : £14,400

ex Randy Weir Numismatics, Unionville, Ontario, Canada, purchased 10th June 1993.

The specimen here is a particularly fine one and appears to compare better than the one sold by Dix Noonan and Webb graded good extremely fine in November 2011 for a hammer price of £22,000

The Very Rare Erroneous Design Double Shaft 1892 Pond

double shaft wagon

900 **ZAR,** President Stephanus Johannes Paulus Kruger, Gold Pond, 1892, double shaft variety, bearded bust of President Kruger left, O.S. artist initials raised on truncation, fine toothed border and rim both sides, ZUID AFRIKAANSCHE REPUBLIEK, *rev* struck en médaille, oval shield of arms divided in three, lion passant to upper left, Boer with rifle to upper right, ox wagon at bottom with two shafts and wheels of same size, with an escutcheon of an upright anchor, all upon frame surmounted by large eagle, overlapping three "vierkleur" flags either side, motto on scroll below EENDRAGT MAAKT MAGT, floral emblems below, 1 POND * 1892 * surrounds upper portion, stops are mullets, edge milled, 7.99g, 21.9mm (Hern Z44; KM 10.1; Fr 2; Kaplan 11). *A few trifling marks and nicks both sides, otherwise as struck and extremely rare.* £6000-8000

Price Realised : £6,000

ex Randy Weir Numismatics, Unionville, Ontario, Canada, purchased 14 August 1992
Mintage issued 15,650 of which most were recalled and melted down to be reissued as single shaft reverse coins. These dies were engraved by Otto Schultz and the coins struck by the Berlin Mint (Germany), who unfortunately took the design of the ox wagon to be not unlike that in common use in the American west pulled by a horse, which have twin shafts. These American wagons also had the wheels front and back of similar size, however, the traditional African ox wagon has smaller front wheels and one central shaft to lash the oxen to. These were major errors and went unnoticed until after issue of the coin. It is significant to note a similar error occurred on the design of postage stamps for 1894 with a two shaft wagon. Stamp issues of 1869-1893 are all depicted with the traditional single shaft ox wagon.
This error of design was coupled with an unfortunate coincidence on the obverse. The engraver's initials, OS, form the word "ox" in Dutch or Afrikaans, effectively branding the President, who had already objected to the inclusion of the initials anyway, as explained in the Numismatic Chronicle account of the Coinage of the South African Republic published anonymously in 1900.
Many of the first issue coins were withdrawn from circulation and melted down. Upon the subsequent order to the Berlin Mint, changes were made to the design of the wagon and the initials were dropped from the obverse effigy.

The Extremely Rare Single Shaft Pond of 1892

single shaft wagon, smaller front wheel

901 **ZAR,** President Kruger, Gold Pond, 1892, single shaft variety, bearded bust of President Kruger left, plain truncation, *rev* Transvaal Arms with ox wagon with correct single shaft and smaller front wheel, arms surmounted by large eagle, overlapping three "vierkleur" flags either side, motto on scroll below, 7.98g, 21.9mm (Hern Z45; KM 10.2; Fr 2; Kaplan 12). *Some tiny light surface marks, otherwise as struck and rare.*

£20,000-25,000

Price Realised : £38,400

ex Spink Auction 1237, 22 March 2000, lot 721

Mintage is combined in records with that of 1893 date at 61,926 pieces issued over two years, the majority presumably dated 1893.

This coin is the correct reverse for the Arms of the South African Republic, it was struck to replace the erroneous issue in the preceding lot. However it is the rarer type today for the 1892 dated gold Pond.

The specimen here is a particularly fine one and appears to compare better than the one sold by Heritage (graded MS61) in January 2012 for a hammer price of US$37,500.

902 **ZAR,** President Kruger, Gold Pond, 1893, bearded bust of President Kruger left, *rev* Transvaal Arms with "vierkleur" flags either side, 7.99g (Hern Z46; KM 10.2; Fr 2; Kaplan 13). *Some tiny light marks, otherwise as struck and rare.*

£5000-6000

Price Realised : £9,840

ex Knightsbridge Coins, London, purchased on advice of Randy Weir, 15 October 1999

Mintage is combined in records with that of 1893 date at 61,926 pieces issued over two years.

The specimen here is a particularly fine one and appears to be much better than the one sold by Heritage (graded XF45) in January 2011 for a hammer price of US$16,000.

903 **ZAR,** President Kruger, Gold Pond, 1894, bearded bust of President Kruger left, *rev* Transvaal Arms with "vierkleur" flags either side, 8.00g (Hern Z47; KM 10.2; Fr 2; Kaplan 14). *Some tiny light marks, otherwise as struck and scarce.* £5000-6000

Price Realised : £18,000

ex Knightsbridge Coins, London, purchased on advice of Randy Weir, 15 October 1999
Mintage issued 317,723 pieces.
The specimen here is a particularly fine one and appears to compare well with the one sold by Heritage (graded MS62) in January 2011 for a hammer price of US$12,000.

904 **ZAR,** President Kruger, Gold Pond, 1895, bearded bust of President Kruger left, *rev* Transvaal Arms with "vierkleur" flags either side, 7.99g (Hern Z48; KM 10.2; Fr 2; Kaplan 15). *Some tiny light marks, otherwise good extremely fine and rare.* £4000-5000

Price Realised : £4,560

ex Reserve bank of Australia sale, Downies, November 2005, lot 37, via Winsor and Sons, Jamberoo, NSW Australia, December 2005
Mintage issued 336,000 pieces.

905 **ZAR,** President Kruger, Gold Pond, 1896, bearded bust of President Kruger left, *rev* Transvaal Arms with "vierkleur" flags either side, 7.98g (Hern Z 49; KM 10.2; Fr 2; Kaplan 16). *Hairline scratch under the bust and a few tiny marks, otherwise extremely fine / good extremely fine and scarce.* £3000-4000

Price Realised : £2,640

ex Spink Auction 1237, 22 March 2000, lot 722
Mintage issued 235,000 pieces.

906 **ZAR,** President Kruger, Gold Pond, 1897, bearded bust of President Kruger left, *rev* Transvaal Arms with "vierkleur" flags either side, 7.98g (Hern Z 50; KM 10.2; Fr 2; Kaplan 17). *A few bagmarks, otherwise extremely fine / good extremely fine and scarce.* £3000-4000

Price Realised : £3,240

ex Spink Auction 1237, 22 March 2000, lot 723
Mintage issued 310,980 pieces.

907 **ZAR,** President Kruger, Gold Pond, 1898, slightly larger bearded bust of President Kruger left, *rev* Transvaal Arms with "vierkleur" flags either side, 7.98g (Hern Z 51; KM 10.2; Fr 2; Kaplan 18). *A few tiny marks, previously graded by NGC as MS64, otherwise as struck and rare.* £2000-3000

Price Realised : £1,920

ex Steinbergs, Vermont, USA, purchased 8 July 2001
Mintage issued 136,870 pieces.

The Extremely Rare 99 counterstamp 1898 gold Pond

908 **ZAR,** President Kruger, Gold Pond, 1898, with "99" counterstamp incuse below bust, slightly larger bearded bust of President Kruger left, *rev* Transvaal Arms with "vierkleur" flags either side, 7.98g, 21.9mm (Hern Z 52; KM 10.2; Fr 2; Kaplan 19 RRRR). *A few tiny spots and light surface marks, good extremely fine and extremely rare, one of the great rarities in the South African series.* £40,000-50,000

Price Realised : £79,200

ex Knightsbridge Coins, London, purchased on advice of Randy Weir, 15 October 1999
Mintage issued 130 pieces
The only rarer currency gold coin of South Africa is the single 9 incuse counterstamp which is unique and not present in the Bentley Collection. 1898 dies had to be used in the calendar year 1899 and it was decided to stamp these with, at first, the single 9 incuse stamp, but latterly the twin 9 stamp as demonstrated here.

909 **ZAR,** President Kruger, Gold Pond, 1900, slightly larger bearded bust of President Kruger left, *rev* Transvaal Arms with "vierkleur" flags either side, 8.00g (Hern Z 53; KM 10.2; Fr 2; Kaplan 20). *A few light marks and nicks, otherwise extremely fine / good extremely fine.* £1500-2000

Price Realised : £1,680

ex Knightsbridge Coins, London, purchased on advice of Randy Weir, 15 October 1999
Mintage issued 788,000 pieces.

Extremely Rare Obverse Brockage of a President Kruger Gold Pond

910 **ZAR,** President Kruger, Gold Pond, undated, c.1898-1900, obverse brockage, slightly larger bearded bust of President Kruger left, legend and design doubled with a high rim, *rev* incuse impression of the obverse design in reverse, 7.99g (KM 10.2; Fr 2). *Some light bruises, otherwise toned as struck and a good on target brockage of highest rarity.* £8000-10,000

Price Realised : £15,600

ex DNW auction, 17 December 2007, lot 375 and back cover illustration
A true one-off. A brockage occurs when the striking process goes awry. When a coin is struck one die is static and fixed in position, usually the obverse, as is the case here c.1898-1900. The glitch in the process occurs with the feeding in of the coin blanks. A blank flan previous to the brockage we have here would have entered the striking chamber and, not seated quite on target, it would be unable to exit easily after striking. The blank adhered to the moving reverse die. The next blank gold flan to be struck, our soon-to-be-brockage coin, will have entered the chamber and the reverse die with the previous coin stuck to it will have struck this new flan with an incuse obverse impression on its reverse, it receiving the obverse impression from the lower die as usual. At this point the problem in the process is usually discovered. Brockages are often spectacular and occur in gold coinage with much less frequency than the silver and copper, due to the higher quality control in working with gold. For another brockage in the British gold Sovereign series dated 1856, see lot 76, page 91.

This concludes the output of regular "Kruger" ponds, after what Cullimore Allen claims totals 2,203,265 pieces. However, on adding all the individual figures given plus one for the unique single 9 counterstamp we make a total of 2,202,280 pieces. Perhaps the discrepancy is explained by the "blank" issue ponds with or without rim as offered over the next seven lots. These were partly prepared coins which were hurriedly removed from the mint at Pretoria in 1900 when the British occupied the area as part of the conflict of the Boer War of 1899-1902.

911

912

911 **ZAR,** blank Gold Pond, undated, with raised rim both sides, 7.99g, 21.6mm (Hern Z56; Kaplan 22). *Slight surface marks, otherwise as struck and very rare.* £600-800

Price Realised : £1,920

ex Knightsbridge Coins, London, purchased on advice of Randy Weir, 15 October 1999

912 **ZAR,** blank Gold Pond, undated, without raised rim both sides, 7.99g, 22.1mm (Hern Z55; Kaplan 21). *With concentric turning circles across surfaces on both sides, as struck and very rare.* £600-800

Price Realised : £1,920

ex Randy Weir Numismatics, Unionville, Ontario, Canada, purchased 23 April 1993

Hand Inscribed Blank Gold Ponds with Rim

913 **ZAR,** blank Gold Pond, hand-engraved inscriptions, dated 1900 by hand, with raised rim both sides, COINED / BY BOERS / AT / MACHADODORP / 1900, place name with twin curved lines above and below, *rev* blank, 7.94g, 21.6mm (cf Hern Z56; Kaplan 22). *Very fine, as made and very rare.* £600-800

Price Realised : £1,560

ex W V Royle Baldwin collection, purchased via A H Baldwin & Sons Ltd, 2006

914 **ZAR,** blank Gold Pond, hand-engraved inscriptions, dated 1900 by hand, with raised rim both sides, KRUGERS / LAST COIN / 1900, first word in a curving arc, surrounded by curved lines and decoration, further decoration either side of date, *rev* blank, 7.96g, 21.6mm (cf Hern Z56; Kaplan 22). *Extremely fine, as made and very rare.* £1000-1500

Price Realised : £2,160

ex Morton and Eden auction, 10 June 2009, lot 232, purchased via A H Baldwin & Sons Ltd
This lot is accompanied by a contemporary letter dated 3 October 1900 on note paper from the Victoria Club, Maritzburg, signed by Lt Col R Sandwith which reads "This gold disc represents one of Oom Paul's last attempts at coining – it was made out of stolen gold" the letter goes on to record the provenance of the piece as being from Mr Wolmarans of the late Transvaal Executive at Delagon Bay. The letter concludes "They were struck about July or Aug. 1900 at Machadodorf" with a postscript anticipating the possibility of future forgery.

915 **ZAR,** blank Gold Pond, hand-engraved inscriptions, dated 1900, with raised rim both sides, *BRITISH OCCUPATION* around upper half in arc, OF / MACHADODORP in two lines at centre, linear curve ruled above and below, AUGUST 28th 1900 in arc around lower half, asterisk at left and right, *rev* blank, 7.73g, 21.6mm (cf Hern Z56; Kaplan 22). *Almost very fine, otherwise as made and very rare.* £600-800

Price Realised : £1,380

ex A H Baldwin & Sons Ltd, 2007

A Blank Gold Pond without Rim Hand Inscribed Both Sides

916 **ZAR,** blank Gold Pond, hand-engraved inscriptions both sides, dated 1900, rimless both sides, SOVEREIGN ISSUED around upper half in arc, BY / KRUGER / PRETORIA / 1900 in four lines, *rev* SENT HOME around upper half in arc, BY / F. S. MAUDE., 7.79g, 22.1mm (cf Hern Z55; Kaplan 21). *Pierced good very fine, otherwise as made and very rare.*
£600-800

Price Realised : £1,176

ex W V Royle Baldwin collection, purchased via A H Baldwin & Sons Ltd, 2006

A Hand Inscribed Blank Gold Pond without Rim

917 **ZAR,** blank Gold Pond, hand-engraved inscription in Gothic script, undated, rimless both sides, "Kruger's / Last / Issue", 7.95g, 22.1mm (cf Hern Z55; Kaplan 21). *With concentric turning circles across surfaces both sides, as made and very rare.*
£800-1000

Price Realised : £840

ex W V Royle Baldwin collection, purchased via A H Baldwin & Sons Ltd, 2006

The Very Rare Gold Veldt Pond of 1902

918 **ZAR,** Gold Veldt Pond, 1902, struck by hand at Pilgrims Rest, late 1902 by P J Kloppers acting Mint Master, ZAR in script, date below, *rev* inverted die axis, EEN / POND in two lines, raised rim both sides, edge thickly milled, 8.33g, 22.7mm (Hern Z54; KM 11; Fr 4; Kaplan 23). *Lightly toned, practically as struck and extremely rare.*
£20,000-25,000

Price Realised : £20,400

ex Randy Weir Numismatics, Unionville, Ontario, Canada, purchased 31 July 1993
Mintage of 986 pieces struck by hand in a dormant workshop on the Transvaal Gold Mining Estate by P J Kloppers, a former head teacher at the De Kaap Government School. This issue was produced on the recommendation of General Christian Muller, the assistant-commandant-general, and authorised by Schalk Burger, acting President of the Republic after Paul Kruger had left the country on 19 October 1900.
The specimen here is a particularly fine one and appears to compare well with the one sold by Heritage (graded MS64) in January 2012 for a hammer price of US$42,500

Branch Mint of the Royal Mint at Pretoria South Africa

With the Unification of South Africa into a Dominion under the establishment of British rule, the Pretoria mint became a further Branch mint of the Royal Mint. Gold sovereigns of the Imperial design were issued, dating from 1923 to 1932 inclusive, the latter year being the last date issued by any branch mint. There were no more gold Sovereigns issued from branch mints and the next gold Sovereign was struck in London as a commemorative issue in 1937, for the Coronation of King George VI (1936-1952). Gold was struck once again at Pretoria under the Union of South Africa in 1952, when a proof issue of the "Pound" was struck for sets of coins which then continued yearly into the start of the reign of Queen Elizabeth II. The Bentley Collection does not contain any of these later coins. Once a former branch mint loses its Royal Mint affiliation, it also loses the right to strike gold Sovereigns, therefore later production must have gold denominations of an alternative name.

The Pretoria Branch Mint for South Africa was the last such mint established and opened for turning locally mined gold into coin in 1923. The first Deputy Master was R G J Pearson who had been Assistant Assayer at Melbourne Branch in Australia from 1897 to 1907 and afterwards Assayer at Ottawa, Canada. In Pretoria he presided over the refining of more than 20 million ounces of gold.

The Reign of King George V (1910-1936)
House of Windsor

Born: 3 June 1865

Accession: 6 May 1910

Married: Mary of Teck, 6 July 1893

Coronation: Thursday, 22 June 1911, second Coronation as Emperor of India at the Delhi Durbar, Tuesday, 12 December 1911

Children: five sons, one daughter

Died: 20 January 1936, aged 70

The Very Rare 1923 South Africa Proof Sovereign

919 **George V (1910-1936),** Proof Sovereign, 1923 SA, Pretoria, South Africa mint, designed by Edgar Bertram Mackennal, bare head left, BM on truncation, no stops as the initials are placed too low on the truncation, toothed border and raised rim, GEORGIVS V D: G: BRITT: OMN: REX F: D: IND: IMP:, *rev* struck en médaille, engraved after Benedetto Pistrucci, St George slaying dragon with sword, helmet with three strand streamer, horse with long tail, ending in three strands, with one spur higher up at curve, broken lance on ground-line to left, *WWP* in relief under lance, SA mint mark on ground, date in exergue, tiny B.P. to upper right, finely toothed border within twin linear concentric circles and raised rim, edge milled, 7.99g, 22.2mm (Hern S338; KM 21; Fr 5; Marsh -; S 4004). *Small spot of red wax by rear leg of horse, otherwise brilliant as struck and rare.* £800-1000

Price Realised : £2,520

ex An Important Collection of Gold Sovereigns 1816-2000, offered as one lot, Sothebys, November 2000, lot 525 (part)
Mintage 655 pieces as part of the proof sets of all denominations dated for the initial year of operation of the Imperial Pretoria Mint.

The Extremely Rare 1923 South Africa Currency Sovereign

920 **George V,** Sovereign, 1923 SA, Pretoria, South Africa mint, bare head left, B.M. on truncation, *rev* die axis a touch off-centre, St George slaying dragon with sword, SA mint mark on ground, date in exergue, tiny B.P. to upper right, 8.00g (Hern S338 and note; Kaplan 100 RRRR; KM 21; Fr 5; Marsh 287 R6; S 4004). *Small red spot behind neck and some other tiny red spots both sides, otherwise brilliant proof-like as struck and extremely rare.* £5000-7000

Price Realised : £13,200

ex "A small group of coins from the family of Raoul Robellaz Kahan", Glendinings, 9 December 1992, lot 457 or 458
purchased via Randy Weir Numismatics, Unionville, Ontario, Canada, 14 November 1994
Calendar year mintage 719 pieces.
A small group of coins from the family of Raoul Robellaz Kahan, a long term employee of the Royal Mint in the Branch Mint at Perth Australia, and later Deputy Master for one year at the Bombay Mint (India), 1918-1919, during the striking of the Sovereigns and the 15-Rupee pieces (see lots 891-895, pages 419-420).
Kahan was later responsible for the construction of the Rand Refinery, Germiston (South Africa), which received its first consignment of gold in December 1921. By 1924 the Transvaal Chamber of Commerce had received over 10,000 ounces of fine gold. This is why he would have had access to 1923 SA Sovereigns at source and is probably the mint official mentioned in Hern's note above this listing, who obtained a number of brand new 1923 SA Sovereigns in proof-like preservation.
The low mintage of 1923SA Sovereigns was dictated entirely by how much gold was brought in to refine in its first months of operation. Only enough gold came in to mint up to 719 pieces for currency circulation in the calendar year 1923. Sources vary in their quotes for the mintage, some say incorrectly as few as 64, which has been arrived at by taking 719 totalled here minus the 655 proofs, which is wrong. Marsh quotes 406 pieces. The 719 figure comes from earlier sources and is later quoted in the South African based publications.
It is significant to note that the Important Collection of Gold Sovereigns 1816-2000, offered as one lot, Sothebys, 16-17 November 2000, lot 525, did not contain an example of the 1923 SA currency Sovereign, the only other coin not present in that collection in currency was the 1920 Sydney.

The Extremely Rare 1924 South Africa Currency Sovereign

921 **George V,** Sovereign, 1924 SA, Pretoria, South Africa mint, bare head left, B.M. on truncation, latter stop weak and small, *rev* St George slaying dragon with sword, SA mint mark on ground, date in exergue, tiny B.P. to upper right, 7.99g (Hern S339; Kaplan 101 RRR; KM 21; Fr 5; Marsh 288 R5; S 4004). *Some hairlines on reverse, a little scuffed on neck, otherwise good extremely fine and extremely rare.* £4000-5000

Price Realised : £10,560

ex Randy Weir Numismatics, Unionville, Ontario, Canada, purchased 9 November 1991
Calendar year mintage 3,184 pieces. Again sources disagree on the number struck and again we have quoted the earlier source with the higher number from *Sovereigns of the British Empire* by Capt J J Cullimore Allen with which Hern agrees. Marsh quotes the number at 2,660.

922 923 924 925

922 **George V,** Sovereign, 1925 SA, Pretoria, South Africa mint, bare head left, B.M. on truncation, latter stop weak and small, *rev* St George slaying dragon with sword, small raised die flaw from tip of lance, SA mint mark on ground, date in exergue, tiny B.P. to upper right, 7.99g (Hern S340; Kaplan 102; KM 21; Fr 5; Marsh 289; S 4004). *Some nicks on neck, red tone, practically as struck.* £300-350

Price Realised : £408

ex Randy Weir Numismatics, Unionville, Ontario, Canada, purchased 10 June 1991
Calendar year mintage 6,086,264 pieces.

923 **George V,** Sovereign, 1926 SA, Pretoria, South Africa mint, bare head left, B.M. on truncation, latter stop weak and small, *rev* St George slaying dragon with sword, SA mint mark on ground, date in exergue, tiny B.P. to upper right, 7.99g (Hern S341; Kaplan 103; KM 21; Fr 5; Marsh 290; S 4004). *Slightly streaky tone both sides, a few light marks, good extremely fine.* £300-350

Price Realised : £432

ex Randy Weir Numismatics, Unionville, Ontario, Canada, purchased 10 June 1991
Calendar year mintage 11,107,611 pieces.

924 **George V,** Sovereign, 1927 SA, Pretoria, South Africa mint, bare head left, B.M. on truncation, latter stop absent, *rev* St George slaying dragon with sword, SA mint mark on ground, date in exergue, tiny B.P. to upper right, 7.99g (Hern S342; Kaplan 104; KM 21; Fr 5; Marsh 291; S 4004). *Slightly streaky tone both sides, some bagmarks, good extremely fine.* £300-350

Price Realised : £312

ex Randy Weir Numismatics, Unionville, Ontario, Canada, purchased 10 January 1991
Calendar year mintage 16,379,704 pieces.

925 **George V,** Sovereign, 1928 SA, Pretoria, South Africa mint, bare head left, B.M. on truncation, latter stop absent, *rev* St George slaying dragon with sword, SA mint mark on ground, date in exergue, tiny B.P. to upper right, 7.99g (Hern S343; Kaplan 105; KM 21; Fr 5; Marsh 292; S 4004). *A few light bagmarks, otherwise practically as struck.* £300-350

Price Realised : £408

ex Randy Weir Numismatics, Unionville, Ontario, Canada, purchased 24 May 1990
Calendar year mintage 18,235,057 pieces. This represents the highest mintage from the Pretoria mint of Imperial type gold Sovereigns.

The Excessively Rare South African Matt Proof Sovereign of 1928

926 **George V,** Matt Proof Sovereign, 1928 SA, Pretoria, South Africa mint, bare head left, B.M. on truncation, distinct and clear, *rev* St George slaying dragon with sword, SA mint mark on ground, date in exergue, tiny B.P. to upper right, 7.98g, 22mm (Hern S343 proof; Kaplan -; KM 21; Fr 5; Marsh -; S 4004). *Light hairline from head to legend to rim, a few tiny nicks on head, wispy hairline on reverse above lance, otherwise an impressive coin toned with the matt satin finish and otherwise as struck, probably unique, Hern lists this coin as the only specimen known.* £15,000-20,000

Price Realised : £33,600

ex An Important Collection of Gold Sovereigns 1816-2000, offered as one lot, Sothebys, November 2000, lot 525 (part)
This satin matt proof piece was probably struck to mark the end of the larger bust design of George V, before the change to the small head design from 1929, see the next lot for a proof of the small head.

The Excessively Rare South African Proof Sovereign of 1929 Small Head

927 **George V,** Proof Sovereign, 1929 SA, Pretoria, South Africa mint, second smaller bare head left, BM on truncation, no stops, linear outer circle with grained border teeth compartments and rim both sides, *rev* slightly smaller design therefore with a deeper exergue, St George slaying dragon with sword, no *WWP* initials under lance anymore, SA mint mark on ground, date in exergue, tiny B.P. to upper right, 7.98g (Hern -; Kaplan -; KM 21; Fr 5; Marsh -; S 4005). *Mint state, toned as struck and probably unique, not recorded by Hern, excessively rare.* £12,000-15,000

Price Realised : £52,800

ex Spink and Son, c.1996, via Randy Weir Numismatics, Unionville, Ontario, Canada
This specimen of the 1929 proof was probably struck to mark the start of the small head design from this year at the Pretoria mint.

928 **George V,** Sovereign, 1929 SA, Pretoria, South Africa mint, second smaller bare head left, BM on truncation, no stops, *rev* smaller St George slaying dragon with sword, SA mint mark on ground, date in deeper exergue, tiny B.P. to upper right, 7.99g (Hern S344; Kaplan 106; KM 21; Fr 5; Marsh 293; S 4005). *A few tiny nicks at top of head, otherwise practically as struck.* £300-350

Price Realised : £552

Calendar year mintage 12,024,107 pieces.

929 **George V,** Sovereign, 1930 SA, Pretoria, South Africa mint, second smaller bare head left, BM on truncation, no stops, *rev* smaller St George slaying dragon with sword, SA mint mark on ground, date in deeper exergue, tiny B.P. to upper right, 7.99g (Hern S345; Kaplan 107; KM 21; Fr 5; Marsh 294; S 4005). *A few tiny marks with an uneven tone, otherwise practically as struck.* £300-350

Price Realised : £360

ex Randy Weir Numismatics, Unionville, Ontario, Canada, purchased 10 June 1991
Calendar year mintage 10,027,756 pieces.

930 **George V,** Sovereign, 1931 SA, Pretoria, South Africa mint, second smaller bare head left, BM on truncation, no stops, light raised die flaw at M to rear of neck, *rev* smaller St George slaying dragon with sword, SA mint mark on ground, date in deeper exergue, tiny B.P. to upper right, 8.00g (Hern S346; Kaplan 108; KM 21; Fr 5; Marsh 295; S 4005). *A few tiny marks, otherwise practically as struck.* £300-350

Price Realised : £432

ex Randy Weir Numismatics, Unionville, Ontario, Canada, purchased 10 June 1991
Calendar year mintage 8,511,792 pieces.

931 **George V,** Sovereign, 1932 SA, Pretoria, South Africa mint, second smaller bare head left, BM on truncation, no stops, *rev* smaller St George slaying dragon with sword, SA mint mark on ground, date in deeper exergue, tiny B.P. to upper right, 7.99g (Hern S347; Kaplan 109; KM 21; Fr 5; Marsh 296; S 4005). *A few light bagmarks, otherwise as struck.* £300-350

Price Realised : £480

ex Randy Weir Numismatics, Unionville, Ontario, Canada, purchased 27 September 1990
Calendar year mintage 1,066,680 pieces. This marks the last year of operation for minting gold Sovereigns of the Imperial type at any of the Branch Mints, a total of 83,442,874 Sovereigns were struck from 1923-1932 under King George V.

Bibliography

Abbreviated references used in the cataloguing:-

DM	Douglas-Morris, *Captain K J Douglas-Morris Collection of British Gold Coins*, sold by Sothebys, 26 November 1974
Esterhuysen	Matthy Esterhuysen, *South Africa's First Gold Coin*, published by Purnell 1976
Forrer	Leonard Forrer, *Biographical Dictionary of Medallists*, six volumes and two supplements, published by Spink & Son Ltd, reprinted by Baldwin's with an index, France, 1904-1930
Fr	A Friedberg, *Gold Coins of the World*
Hern	Hern, *Handbook on South African Coins and Patterns*
Kaplan	Alec Kaplan, *The coins of South Africa*, published by Stan Kaplan
KM	Krause and Mishler, *Standard Catalog of World Coins*, 19th and 20th Century Editions, published by Krause Publications
Marsh	Michael A Marsh, *The Gold Sovereign*, Golden Jubilee Edition, Cambridge (publications), 2002
McD	Greg McDonald – *the Pocket Guide to Australian Coins and Banknotes*, 19th Edition 2012, valuations in Australian Dollars.
MCE	*Milled Coinage of England 1662-1946*, gold section by D G Liddell, published Spink & Son, 1950
Montagu	*Mr Montagu's Collection of Coins from George I to Victoria*, Spink & Son Catalogue, published as a fixed price list, London 1891
Murdoch	*John G Murdoch Collection, Third Portion George I to Victoria*, Sothebys, 15 March 1904
Nobleman	*Baron Ferrari Philipe de la Renotière as "A Nobleman" recently deceased*, Sothebys, 27 March 1922
QM	*The Quartermaster collection* – auction catalogue, 4 June 2009, issued by Monetarium (Australia) Pty Ltd, Kogarah, NSW, with expert cataloguing by Winsor & Sons of Jamberoo, NSW, Australia.
S	*Spink Standard Catalogue of British Coins*, edited by P Skingley, 2012 edition
WR	A Wilson and M Rasmussen, *English Pattern Trial and Proof Coins in Gold*, Alexander Publishing, 2000

Other references cited in footnotes and for further reading:-

Royal Sovereign 1489-1989, edited by G P Dyer, Royal Mint Publication, 1989
The History of the Gold Sovereign, by Sir Geoffrey Duveen and H G Stride, published Oxford University Press, 1962
Sovereigns of the British Empire, by Captain J. J. Cullimore Allen O.B.E. published Spink & Son, 1965
The Pound Sterling – A History of English Money, by Sir Albert Feavearyear, edited by E Victor Morgan, published at Oxford Clarendon Press, 1963
The History of the Currency, by W A Shaw MA, published by Clement Wilson, 1896
"The Numismatic Collection of the Museum of Victoria" article by John Sharples, in the Journal of the Numismatic Association of Australia, vol.2
"The Coinage of the South African Republic" anonymous article, chapter XIV, Numismatic Chronicle 1900, 3rd Series, vol.20
Journal of the Numismatic Society, London, published by Bernard Quaritch

Appendix 1

BENTLEY COLLECTION OF SOVEREIGNS - Overview of Prices Achieved

	Low Estimate.	High Estimate	Hammer	Total (with Premium)	Quantity of Lots/Coins
Whole Bentley Collection	£2,388,025	£3,088,250	£3,377,795	£4,053,354	1241
Part One	£545,125	£677,750	£749,455	£899,346	382
Part Two	£1,287,450	£1,679,350	£1,883,970	£2,260,764	549
Part Three	£555,750	£731,550	£704,370	£845,244	310
London Mint Coins	£1,295,525	£1,661,000	£1,731,205	£2,077,446	938
Highest London Coin	£150,000	£200,000	£155,000	£186,000	1819, lot 941
Colonial Mint Coins	£1,092,800	£1,427,650	£1,606,590	£1,927,908	303
WORLD RECORD PRICE	£300,000	£400,000	£650,000	£780,000	1920S, lot 736
Australia Mint Coins S M P A	£752,300	£999,000	£1,145,020	£1,374,024	251
Adelaide	£20,000	£25,000	£21,000	£25,200	1
Sydney Mint all	£525,250	£700,250	£885,240	£1,062,288	115
Sydney "AUSTRALIA" type	£85,300	£107,900	£86,190	£103,428	25
Sydney Young Head Shield Rev.	£10,200	£14,200	£16,790	£20,148	19
Sydney Young Head St George	£8,800	£12,800	£12,190	£14,628	21
Sydney Jubilee Head	£19,850	£31,600	£19,620	£23,544	15
Sydney Older head	£2,700	£3,150	£3,940	£4,728	9
Sydney Edward VII	£2,700	£3,150	£3,000	£3,600	9
Sydney George V	£395,700	£527,450	£743,510	£892,212	17
Melbourne Mint all	£165,650	£218,800	£183,470	£220,164	101
Melbourne Young Head Shield Rev.	£30,300	£37,950	£35,220	£42,264	14
Melbourne Young Head St George	£14,500	£19,600	£20,390	£24,468	29
Melbourne Jubilee Head	£55,050	£76,550	£48,420	£58,104	17
Melbourne Older head	£2,800	£3,600	£4,900	£5,880	9
Melbourne Edward VII	£2,700	£3,150	£2,380	£2,856	9
Melbourne George V	£60,000	£77,550	£72,160	£86,592	22
Perth Mint all	£41,400	£54,950	£55,310	£66,372	34
Perth Older head	£1,000	£1,400	£1,560	£1,872	3
Perth Edward VII	£2,700	£3,150	£2,720	£3,264	9
Perth George V	£37,700	£50,400	£51,030	£61,236	22
Canada Mint Coins all C	£31,800	£39,750	£48,030	£57,636	12
Canada Edward VII	£10,900	£14,100	£16,590	£19,908	4
Canada George V	£20,900	£25,650	£31,440	£37,728	8
India Mint Coins I - George V	£9,200	£11,600	£19,240	£23,088	5
South African Imperial SA George V	£39,200	£50,800	£96,270	£115,524	13
South Africa Republic Burgers/Kruger	£260,300	£326,500	£298,030	£357,636	23
All Gold Pattern and Proofs	£916,750	£1,192,700	£1,223,520	£1,468,224	78
All Other Patterns / trials	£75,700	£100,450	£86,940	£104,328	20
Highlight Brochure Coins	£1,417,000	£1,849,000	£2,109,550	£2,531,460	69
Highest non-highlight coin	£20,000	£25,000	£32,000	£38,400	1892, lot 901
Statistics by Monarchs					
George III Coinage	£294,850	£391,300	£345,970	£415,164	32
George IV Coinage	£118,550	£146,150	£141,500	£169,800	29
William IV Coinage	£69,550	£91,700	£99,680	£119,616	20
Victoria all Coinage of Period	£913,025	£1,172,150	£1,220,505	£1,464,606	969
Victoria London Mint all	£662,525	£838,400	£950,285	£1,140,342	807
Victoria Young Head Shield rev.	£277,050	£352,900	£448,770	£538,524	158
Victoria Die Number Coins	£199,425	£248,450	£212,225	£254,670	582
Victoria Young Head St George	£136,750	£175,650	£210,360	£252,432	37
Victoria Jubilee Head London	£31,700	£39,600	£50,170	£60,204	19
Victoria Older Head London	£17,600	£21,800	£28,760	£34,512	11
Edward VII all Coinage of Period	£22,450	£27,700	£28,270	£33,924	42
Edward VII London	£3,450	£4,150	£3,580	£4,296	11
George V all Coinage of Period	£572,300	£754,500	£1,027,970	£1,233,564	96
George V London	£9,600	£11,050	£14,320	£17,184	9
George VI	£61,500	£81,800	£56,600	£67,920	2 lots,5 coins
Elizabeth II	£51,500	£66,450	£78,510	£94,212	21

Appendix 2

BENTLEY COLLECTION OF SOVEREIGNS – Top 50 Ranked Lots by Price Achieved

No.	Date	Type	Low Estimate	Price Realised (with Premium)	RANK
736	**1920**	**Sydney**	**£300,000**	**£780,000**	**1**
941	1819	London	£150,000	**£186,000**	2
908	1898	Pond 99 overstamp	£40,000	**£79,200**	3
898	1874	Proof Pond	£80,000	**£78,000**	4
1233	1937	Matt Set gold	£60,000	**£66,000**	5
878	1931	Perth Proof	£30,000	**£52,800**	6
927	1929	SA Proof	£12,000	**£52,800**	6
625	1879	Pattern	£12,000	**£48,000**	7
896	1874	Proof Pond	£40,000	**£45,600**	8
957	1830	Proof en medaille	£25,000	**£43,200**	9
842	1929	Melbourne Proof	£30,000	**£40,800**	10
901	1892	Pond	£20,000	**£38,400**	11
796	1888	Melbourne Proof	£30,000	**£34,800**	12
302	1887	Pattern	£12,000	**£33,600**	13
743	1926	Sydney Specimen	£30,000	**£33,600**	13
926	1928	SA Matt Proof	£15,000	**£33,600**	13
966	1837	Pattern	£15,000	**£33,600**	13
1212	1880	Pattern	£15,000	**£32,400**	14
739	1923	Sydney	£30,000	**£30,000**	15
1211	1870	Pattern	£20,000	**£30,000**	15
33	1837	Pattern	£15,000	**£28,800**	16
3	1817	Proof	£15,000	**£27,600**	17
252	1871	Pattern	£15,000	**£26,400**	18
320	1887	Proof milled	£12,000	**£26,400**	18
940	1818	Proof	£15,000	**£26,400**	18
382	1816	Pattern	£15,000	**£25,200**	19
397	1837	Pattern	£15,000	**£25,200**	19
628	1852	Adelaide Pound	£20,000	**£25,200**	19
34	1838	Pattern	£15,000	**£24,000**	20
313	1880	Proof PE	£12,000	**£24,000**	20
887	1916	Canada	£10,000	**£22,800**	21
742	1926	Sydney	£20,000	**£22,800**	21
934	1816	Pattern	£15,000	**£22,800**	22
970	1841	normal A's	£10,000	**£22,800**	22
2	1816	Pattern	£15,000	**£21,600**	23
38	1838	narrow shield	£10,000	**£21,600**	23
45	1843	narrow shield	£12,000	**£20,400**	24
629	1855	Sydney type	£20,000	**£20,400**	24
918	1902	Veld Pond	£20,000	**£20,400**	24
16	1825	Proof 1st	£18,000	**£19,200**	25
35	1838	Proof	£12,000	**£19,200**	25
380	1976	Specimen	£7,000	**£19,200**	25
394	1830	Pattern	£10,000	**£19,200**	25
932	1816	Pattern	£8,000	**£18,600**	26
961	1832	Proof 1st	£10,000	**£18,600**	26
14	1823	George IV	£8,000	**£18,000**	27
335	1893	Pattern A Wyon	£10,000	**£18,000**	27
903	1894	Pond	£5,000	**£18,000**	27
1017	1863	827 truncation	£8,000	**£18,000**	27
738	1922	Sydney	£10,000	**£17,400**	28
40	1839	Proof ME	£10,000	**£16,800**	29
65	1853	Proof	£10,000	**£16,800**	29
303	1871	Proof milled	£10,000	**£16,800**	29
637	1860	60 over 59 Sydney	£15,000	**£16,800**	29
385	1820	Proof	£15,000	**£15,600**	30
426	1859	Ansell	£6,000	**£15,600**	30
787	1887	M silver pattern	£20,000	**£15,600**	30
834	1921	Melbourne	£10,000	**£15,600**	30
910	undated	brockage Pond	£8,000	**£15,600**	30
76	1856	Brockage	£2,000	**£15,000**	31
959	1831	Proof 1st	£6,000	**£15,000**	31
31	1836	N in shield	£12,000	**£14,400**	32
213	1870	die 1 WW raised	£8,000	**£14,400**	32
899	1874	Pattern Pond bronze	£10,000	**£14,400**	32
1237	1965	Matt Proof	£8,000	**£14,400**	32
21	1828	George IV	£12,000	**£13,200**	33
106	1863	827 trun die 22	£8,000	**£13,200**	33
212	1869	24 Carat Proof	£8,000	**£13,200**	33
330	1891	Proof Jubilee	£10,000	**£13,200**	33
363	1917	London	£7,000	**£13,200**	33
891	1918	I Specimen	£8,000	**£13,200**	33
835	1922	Melbourne	£7,000	**£13,200**	33
920	1923	South Africa	£5,000	**£13,200**	33
1214	1871	Proof large BP	£10,000	**£12,600**	34
1235	1959	Proof	£6,000	**£12,600**	34
694	1887	Sydney Proof	£15,000	**£12,000**	35
1222	1880	Proof milled	£12,000	**£12,000**	35
368	1958	Proof	£6,000	**£11,040**	36
373	1963	Proof	£6,000	**£11,040**	36
935	1817	uniface trial	£10,000	**£11,040**	36
921	1924	South Africa	£4,000	**£10,560**	37
960	1831	WW no stops	£3,000	**£10,560**	37
883	1911	C Specimen	£8,000	**£10,440**	38
627	1871	Proof	£6,000	**£10,320**	39
17	1825	Proof 2nd	£8,000	**£10,080**	40
304	1871	Proof extra strands	£6,000	**£9,840**	41
366	1957	Proof	£6,000	**£9,840**	41
902	1893	Pond	£5,000	**£9,840**	41
301	1874	London die 32	£5,000	**£9,600**	42
633	1858	Sydney type	£10,000	**£9,600**	42
635	1860	Sydney type	£1,000	**£9,600**	42
391	1825	Proof 2nd ME	£6,000	**£9,360**	43
880	1909	C obv specimen	£6,000	**£9,360**	43
1232	1893	Pattern silver	£4,000	**£9,360**	43
321	1882	Jubilee Pattern silver	£5,000	**£9,120**	44
55	1848	1st head	£4,000	**£8,880**	45
400	1839	Proof	£4,000	**£8,880**	45
756	1886	Melbourne	£8,000	**£8,880**	45
41	1841	unbarred A's	£6,000	**£8,640**	46
879	1908	C Specimen	£4,000	**£8,400**	47
1228	1887	Pattern 14 pearls	£2,500	**£8,400**	47
933	1816	Pattern	£4,000	**£8,160**	48
6	1818	descending colon	£4,000	**£7,680**	49
630	1856	Sydney type	£6,000	**£7,680**	49
626	1871	Proof	£6,000	**£7,440**	50
749	1880	Melbourne	£5,000	**£7,440**	50
757	1887	Melbourne	£7,000	**£7,440**	50
952	1825	first type	£4,000	**£7,440**	50
969	1839	Proof	£4,000	**£7,440**	50
1213	1871	Proof tiny BP	£6,000	**£7,440**	50
1230	1891	Pattern bronze	£2,000	**£7,440**	50
		Total Values	£1,792,500	£3,126,480	

Appendix 3

BENTLEY COLLECTION OF SOVEREIGNS – Top Highlights in All Areas

Top 10 Ranked London Sovereigns

No.	Date	Type	Low Estimate	Price Realised (with Premium)	RANK
941	**1819**	**London**	**£150,000**	**£186,000**	1
1233	1937	Matt Set gold	£60,000	£66,000	2
625	1879	Pattern	£12,000	£48,000	3
957	1830	Proof en medaille	£25,000	£43,200	4
302	1887	Pattern	£12,000	£33,600	5
966	1837	Pattern	£15,000	£33,600	5
1212	1880	Pattern	£15,000	£32,400	6
1211	1870	Pattern	£20,000	£30,000	7
33	1837	Pattern	£15,000	£28,800	8
3	1817	Proof	£15,000	£27,600	9
252	1871	Pattern	£15,000	£26,400	10
		Total Values	**£354,000**	**£555,600**	

Top 10 Ranked Non-UK Coins

No.	Date	Type	Low Estimate	Price Realised (with Premium)	RANK
736	**1920**	**Sydney type**	**£300,000**	**£780,000**	1
908	1898	Pond 99 overstamp	£40,000	£79,200	2
898	1874	Proof Pond	£80,000	£78,000	3
878	1931	Perth Proof	£30,000	£52,800	4
927	1929	SA Specimen	£12,000	£52,800	4
896	1874	Proof Pond	£40,000	£45,600	5
842	1929	Melbourne Proof	£30,000	£40,800	6
901	1892	Pond	£20,000	£38,400	7
796	1888	Melbourne Proof	£30,000	£34,800	8
926	1928	SA Matt Proof	£15,000	£33,600	9
743	1926	Sydney Specimen	£30,000	£33,600	9
739	1923	Sydney	£30,000	£30,000	10
		Total Values	**£657,000**	**£1,299,600**	

Top 10 Ranked Australian Sovereigns

No.	Date	Type	Low Estimate	Price Realised (with Premium)	RANK
736	**1920**	**Sydney type**	**£300,000**	**£780,000**	1
878	1931	Perth Proof	£30,000	£52,800	2
842	1929	Melbourne Proof	£30,000	£40,800	3
796	1888	Melbourne Proof	£30,000	£34,800	4
743	1926	Sydney Specimen	£30,000	£33,600	5
739	1923	Sydney	£30,000	£30,000	6
628	1852	Adelaide Pound	£20,000	£25,200	7
742	1926	Sydney	£20,000	£22,800	8
629	1855	Sydney type	£20,000	£20,400	9
738	1922	Sydney	£10,000	£17,400	10
		Total Values	**£520,000**	**£1,057,800**	

Top 10 Ranked Sydney Mint Sovereigns

No.	Date	Type	Low Estimate	Price Realised (with Premium)	RANK
736	**1920**	**S**	**£300,000**	**£780,000**	1
743	1926	S Specimen	£30,000	£33,600	2
739	1923	S specimen	£30,000	£30,000	3
742	1926	S	£20,000	£22,800	4
629	1855	Sydney type	£20,000	£20,400	5
738	1922	S	£10,000	£17,400	6
637	1860	60 over 59	£15,000	£16,800	7
694	1887	S Proof	£15,000	£12,000	8
633	1858	Sydney type	£10,000	£9,600	9
635	1860	Sydney type		£9,600	9
630	1856	Sydney type		£7,680	10
		Total Values		**£952,200**	

Top 10 Ranked Melbourne Mint Sovereigns

No.	Date	Type	Low Estimate	Price Realised (with Premium)	RANK
842	**1929**	**M Proof**	**£30,000**	**£40,800**	1
796	1888	M Proof	£30,000	£34,800	2
787	1887	M silver pattern	£20,000	£15,600	3
834	1921	M	£10,000	£15,600	3
835	1922	M	£7,000	£13,200	4
756	1886	M	£8,000	£8,880	5
749	1880	M	£5,000	£7,440	6
757	1887	M	£7,000	£7,440	6
833	1920	M	£4,000	£6,240	7
752	1883	M	£2,500	£4,800	8
758	1872	M St George	£1,500	£4,560	9
750	1881	M	£2,000	£4,320	10
		Total Values	**£127,000**	**£163,680**	

Top 10 Ranked Perth Mint Sovereigns

No.	Date	Type	Low Estimate	Price Realised (with Premium)	RANK
878	**1931**	**P Specimen**	**£30,000**	**£52,800**	1
872	1926	P	£1,500	£1,620	2
847	1901	P	£300	£744	3
873	1927	P	£400	£624	4
846	1900	P	£300	£576	5
860	1914	P	£300	£576	5
845	1899	P	£400	£552	6
852	1906	P	£300	£552	6
871	1925	P	£400	£480	7
848	1902	P	£300	£408	8
850	1904	P	£300	£360	9
851	1905	P	£300	£360	9
849	1903	P	£300	£336	10
		Total Values	**£35,100**	**£59,988**	

Top 10 Ranked South African Coins

No.	Date	Type	Low Estimate	Price Realised (with Premium)	RANK
908	**1898**	**Pond 99 overstamp**	**£40,000**	**£79,200**	1
898	1874	Proof Pond	£80,000	£78,000	2
927	1929	SA Specimen	£12,000	£52,800	3
896	1874	Proof Pond	£40,000	£45,600	4
901	1892	Pond	£20,000	£38,400	5
926	1928	SA Matt Proof	£15,000	£33,600	6
918	1902	Veld Pond	£20,000	£20,400	7
903	1894	Pond	£5,000	£18,000	8
910	-	Pond brockage	£8,000	£15,600	9
899	1874	Pattern Pond bronze	£10,000	£14,400	10
		Total Values	**£250,000**	**£396,000**	

Top Ranked Canada Mint Sovereigns

No.	Date	Type	Low Estimate	Price Realised (with Premium)	RANK
887	**1916**	**C**	**£10,000**	**£22,800**	1
883	1911	C Specimen	£8,000	£10,440	2
879	1908	C Specimen	£4,000	£8,400	3
880	1909	C obv specimen	£6,000	£9,360	4
		Total Values	**£28,000**	**£51,000**	

Top Ranked India Mint Coins

No.	Date	Type	Low Estimate	Price Realised (with Premium)	RANK
891	**1918**	**I Specimen**	**£8,000**	**£13,200**	1
893	1918	15 Rupees	£300	£3,360	2
894	1918	restrike 15R	£300	£3,120	3
895	1918	restrike 15R	£300	£2,760	4
		Total Values	**£8,900**	**£22,440**	

Top 10 Ranked George III Sovereigns

No.	Date	Type	Low Estimate	Price Realised (with Premium)	RANK
941	**1819**	**London**	**£150,000**	**£186,000**	**1**
3	1817	Proof	£15,000	£27,600	2
940	1818	Proof	£15,000	£26,400	3
382	1816	Pattern	£15,000	£25,200	4
934	1816	Pattern	£15,000	£22,800	5
2	1816	Pattern	£15,000	£21,600	6
932	1816	Pattern	£8,000	£18,600	7
935	1817	uniface	£10,000	£11,040	8
933	1816	Pattern	£4,000	£8,160	9
6	1818	descending colon	£4,000	£7,680	10
		Total Values	**£251,000**	**£355,080**	

Top 10 Ranked George IV Sovereigns

No.	Date	Type	Low Estimate	Price Realised (with Premium)	RANK
957	**1830**	**Proof en medaille**	**£25,000**	**£43,200**	**1**
16	1825	Proof 1st	£18,000	£19,200	2
14	1823	first type	£8,000	£18,000	3
21	1828	2nd type	£12,000	£13,200	4
17	1825	Proof 2nd	£8,000	£10,080	5
391	1825	Proof 2nd ME	£6,000	£9,360	6
952	1825	first type	£4,000	£7,440	7
392	1826	Proof	£3,000	£6,960	8
11	1821	Proof	£4,000	£6,000	9
949	1821	Proof AE	£3,000	£5,040	10
		Total Values	**£91,000**	**£138,480**	

Top 10 Ranked William IV Sovereigns

No.	Date	Type	Low Estimate	Price Realised (with Premium)	RANK
394	**1830**	**Pattern**	**£10,000**	**£19,200**	**1**
961	1832	Proof 1st	£10,000	£18,600	2
959	1831	Proof 1st	£6,000	£15,000	3
31	1836	N in shield	£12,000	£14,400	4
960	1831	WW no stops	£3,000	£10,560	5
26	1831	2nd bust	£5,000	£6,960	6
24	1831	Proof 2nd	£4,000	£5,520	7
25	1831	1st bust	£2,750	£3,840	8
965	1837	unusual WW	£1,500	£3,240	9
27	1832	1st bust	£2,000	£3,120	10
28	1832	2nd	£2,000	£3,120	10
		Total Values	**£58,250**	**£103,560**	

Top 10 Ranked Victorian Sovereigns

No.	Date	Type	Low Estimate	Price Realised (with Premium)	RANK
625	**1879**	**Pattern**	**£12,000**	**£48,000**	**1**
796	1888	M Proof	£30,000	£34,800	2
302	1887	Pattern	£12,000	£33,600	3
966	1837	Pattern	£15,000	£33,600	3
1212	1880	Pattern	£15,000	£32,400	4
1211	1870	Pattern	£20,000	£30,000	5
33	1837	Pattern	£15,000	£28,800	6
252	1871	Pattern	£15,000	£26,400	7
320	1887	Proof milled	£12,000	£26,400	7
397	1837	Pattern	£15,000	£25,200	8
34	1838	Pattern	£15,000	£24,000	9
313	1880	Proof PE	£12,000	£24,000	9
970	1841	normal A's	£10,000	£22,800	10
		Total Values	**£198,000**	**£390,000**	

Top 10 Ranked Victorian London Sovereigns

No.	Date	Type	Low Estimate	Price Realised (with Premium)	RANK
625	1879	Proof shield rev.	£12,000	£48,000	1
302	1887	Pattern	£12,000	£33,600	2
966	1837	Pattern	£15,000	£33,600	2
1212	1880	Pattern	£15,000	£32,400	3
1211	1870	Pattern	£20,000	£30,000	4
33	1837	Pattern	£15,000	£28,800	5
252	1871	Pattern	£15,000	£26,400	6
320	1887	Proof milled	£12,000	£26,400	6
397	1837	Pattern	£15,000	£25,200	7
34	1837	Pattern	£15,000	£24,000	8
313	1880	Proof PE	£12,000	£24,000	8
970	1841	normal A's	£10,000	£22,800	9
38	1838	narrow shield	£10,000	£21,600	10
		Total Values	**£178,000**	**£21,600**	

Top 10 Ranked Victoria Sydney Mint Sovereigns

No.	Date	Type	Low Estimate	Price Realised (with Premium)	RANK
629	**1855**	**Sydney type**	**£20,000**	**£20,400**	**1**
637	1860	60 over 59 Sydney	£15,000	£16,800	2
694	1887	Sydney Proof	£15,000	£12,000	3
633	1858	Sydney type	£10,000	£9,600	4
635	1860	Sydney type	£1,000	£9,600	4
630	1856	Sydney type	£6,000	£7,680	5
665	1880	S inv A for V	£3,000	£7,200	6
631	1857	Sydney type	£6,000	£6,480	7
696	1887	S 1st JEB	£600	£5,040	8
645	1865	Sydney type	£4,000	£4,560	9
647	1865	5 over 4	£4,000	£4,080	10
		Total Values	**£84,600**	**£103,440**	

Top 10 Ranked Victoria Melbourne Mint Sovereigns

No.	Date	Type	Low Estimate	Price Realised (with Premium)	RANK
796	**1888**	**Melbourne Proof**	**£30,000**	**£34,800**	**1**
787	1887	M silver pattern	£20,000	£15,600	2
756	1886	Melbourne	£8,000	£8,880	3
749	1880	Melbourne	£5,000	£7,440	4
757	1887	Melbourne	£7,000	£7,440	4
752	1883	Melbourne	£2,500	£4,800	5
758	1872	M St George	£1,500	£4,560	6
750	1881	Melbourne	£2,000	£4,320	7
746	1872	M 2 over 1	£1,200	£3,240	8
809	1897	Melbourne	£400	£2,640	9
760	1873	Melbourne	£400	£1,920	10
		Total Values	**£78,000**	**£95,640**	

Top 10 Ranked Edward VII Sovereigns

No.	Date	Type	Low Estimate	Price Realised (with Premium)	RANK
880	**1909**	**C obv specimen**	**£6,000**	**£9,360**	**1**
879	1908	C Specimen	£4,000	£8,400	2
882	1910	Canada	£500	£1,260	3
881	1909	Canada	£400	£888	4
722	1906	Sydney	£300	£768	5
349	1904	off centre	£400	£624	6
852	1906	Perth	£300	£552	7
345	1902	Matt Proof	£350	£528	8
720	1904	Sydney	£300	£528	8
346	1902	London	£300	£408	9
347	1903	London	£300	£408	9
353	1908	London	£300	£408	9
848	1902	Perth	£300	£408	9
724	1908	Sydney	£300	£408	9
350	1905	London	£300	£384	10
		Total Values	**£14,350**	**£25,332**	

Top 10 Ranked George V Sovereigns

No.	Date	Type	Low Estimate	Price Realised (with Premium)	RANK
736	**1920**	**Sydney**	**£300,000**	**£780,000**	**1**
878	1931	P Specimen	£30,000	£52,800	2
927	1929	SA Specimen	£12,000	£52,800	2
842	1929	M Proof	£30,000	£40,800	3
743	1926	S Specimen	£30,000	£33,600	4
926	1928	SA Matt Proof	£15,000	£33,600	4
739	1923	Sydney	£30,000	£30,000	5
887	1916	Canada	£10,000	£22,800	6
742	1926	Sydney	£20,000	£22,800	6
738	1922	Sydney	£10,000	£17,400	7
834	1921	Melbourne	£10,000	£15,600	8
363	1917	London	£7,000	£13,200	9
891	1918	I Proof	£8,000	£13,200	9
835	1922	Melbourne	£7,000	£13,200	9
920	1923	South Africa	£5,000	£13,200	9
921	1924	SA	£4,000	£10,560	10
		Total Values	**£528,000**	**£1,165,560**	

Top Ranked George VI Sovereigns

No.	Date	Type	Low Estimate	Price Realised (with Premium)	RANK
1233	**1937**	**Matt Set gold**	**£60,000**	**£66,000**	**1**
365	1937	Proof	£1,500	£1,920	2
		Total Values	**£61,500**	**£1,920**	

Top 10 Ranked Elizabeth II Sovereigns

No.	Date	Type	Low Estimate	Price Realised (with Premium)	RANK
380	**1976**	**Specimen**	**£7,000**	**£19,200**	**1**
1237	1965	Matt Proof	£8,000	£14,400	2
1235	1959	Proof	£6,000	£12,600	3
368	1958	Proof	£6,000	£11,040	4
373	1963	Proof	£6,000	£11,040	5
366	1957	Proof	£6,000	£9,840	6
1234	1958	Specimen	£2,500	£6,720	7
370	1959	Specimen	£3,000	£3,120	8
1236	1963	off centre	£400	£1,980	9
1238	1974	no collar strike	£300	£1,320	10
		Total Values	**£45,200**	**£91,260**	

Victorian Breakdown

Top 10 Ranked Victoria Die Number type Sovereigns

No.	Date	Type	Low Estimate	Price Realised (with Premium)	RANK
213	**1870**	**die 1 WW raised**	**£8,000**	**£14,400**	**1**
106	1863	827 trun die 22	£8,000	£13,200	2
212	1869	24 Carat PF64	£8,000	£13,200	2
301	1874	32	£5,000	£9,600	3
624	1874	243	£2,500	£6,480	4
1210	1874	33	£4,000	£5,520	5
225	1871	die 1	£2,000	£3,360	6
623	1873	107	£500	£3,120	7
289	1872	109	£600	£2,880	8
202	1869	34	£800	£2,040	9
1180	1872	49	£600	£1,980	10
		Total Values	**£40,000**	**£75,780**	

Top 10 Ranked Victoria Young Head Shield Reverse Sovereigns

No.	Date	Type	Low Estimate	Price Realised (with Premium)	RANK
625	**1879**	**Pattern**	**£12,000**	**£48,000**	**1**
302	1887	Pattern	£12,000	£33,600	2
966	1837	Pattern	£15,000	£33,600	2
1212	1880	Pattern	£15,000	£32,400	3
33	1837	Pattern	£15,000	£28,800	4
252	1871	Pattern	£15,000	£26,400	5
397	1837	Pattern	£15,000	£25,200	6
34	1838	Pattern	£15,000	£24,000	7
970	1841	normal A's	£10,000	£22,800	8
38	1838	narrow shield	£10,000	£21,600	9
45	1843	narrow shield	£12,000	£20,400	10
		Total Values	**£146,000**	**£316,800**	

Top 10 Ranked Victoria Young Head St George Reverse Sovereigns

No.	Date	Type	Low Estimate	Price Realised (with Premium)	RANK
1211	**1870**	**Pattern**	**£20,000**	**£30,000**	**1**
320	1887	Proof milled	£12,000	£26,400	2
313	1880	Proof PE	£12,000	£24,000	3
303	1871	Proof milled	£10,000	£16,800	4
1214	1871	Proof large BP	£10,000	£12,600	5
1222	1880	Proof milled	£12,000	£12,000	6
627	1871	Proof	£6,000	£10,320	7
304	1871	Proof extra strands	£6,000	£9,840	8
626	1871	Proof	£6,000	£7,440	9
1213	1871	Proof tiny BP	£6,000	£7,440	9
758	1872	M St George	£1,500	£4,560	10
		Total Values	**£101,500**	**£161,400**	

Top 10 Ranked Victoria Jubilee head Sovereigns

No.	Date	Type	Low Estimate	Price Realised (with Premium)	RANK
796	**1888**	**M Proof**	**£30,000**	**£34,800**	**1**
787	1887	M silver pattern	£20,000	£15,600	2
330	1891	Proof LT 2nd legend	£10,000	£13,200	3
694	1887	S Proof	£15,000	£12,000	4
321	1882	Jubilee Pattern silver	£5,000	£9,120	5
1228	1887	Pattern 14 pearls	£2,500	£8,400	6
1230	1891	Pattern bronze	£2,000	£7,440	7
1227	1885	Pattern silver	£5,000	£7,200	8
329	1891	Pattern aluminium	£2,000	£4,080	9
322	1887	Proof	£1,000	£3,360	10
		Total Values	**£92,500**	**£115,200**	

Top 10 Ranked Victoria older veiled head Sovereigns

No.	Date	Type	Low Estimate	Price Realised (with Premium)	RANK
335	**1893**	**Pattern A Wyon**	**£10,000**	**£18,000**	**1**
1232	1893	Pattern silver	£4,000	£9,360	2
336	1893	Proof	£1,200	£3,360	3
809	1897	Melbourne	£400	£2,640	4
341	1898	London	£300	£1,080	5
714	1898	Sydney	£300	£984	6
847	1901	Perth	£300	£744	7
713	1897	Sydney	£300	£624	8
846	1900	Perth	£300	£576	9
715	1899	Sydney	£300	£552	10
845	1899	Perth	£400	£552	10
		Total Values	**£17,800**	**£38,472**	

Appendix 4

BENTLEY COLLECTION OF SOVEREIGNS – Top Proof Sovereigns

Table of Gold Proof Sovereigns

No.	Date	Type	Low Estimate	Price Realised (with Premium)	RANK (78 Pieces)
898	**1874**	**Proof Pond**	**£80,000**	**£78,000**	**1**
1233	1937	Matt Set gold	£60,000	£66,000	2
878	1931	P Specimen	£30,000	£52,800	3
927	1929	SA Specimen	£12,000	£52,800	3
625	1879	Pattern	£12,000	£48,000	4
896	1874	Proof Pond	£40,000	£45,600	5
957	1830	Proof en medaille	£25,000	£43,200	6
842	1929	M Proof	£30,000	£40,800	7
796	1888	M Proof	£30,000	£34,800	8
302	1887	Pattern	£12,000	£33,600	9
743	1926	S Specimen	£30,000	£33,600	9
926	1928	SA Matt Proof	£15,000	£33,600	9
966	1837	Pattern	£15,000	£33,600	9
1212	1880	Pattern	£15,000	£32,400	10
1211	1870	Pattern	£20,000	£30,000	11
33	1837	Pattern	£15,000	£28,800	12
3	1817	Proof	£15,000	£27,600	13
252	1871	Pattern	£15,000	£26,400	14
320	1887	Proof milled	£12,000	£26,400	14
940	1818	Proof	£15,000	£26,400	14
382	1816	Pattern	£15,000	£25,200	15
397	1837	Pattern	£15,000	£25,200	15
34	1837	Pattern	£15,000	£24,000	16
313	1880	Proof PE	£12,000	£24,000	16
934	1816	Pattern	£15,000	£22,800	17
2	1816	Pattern	£15,000	£21,600	18
16	1825	Proof 1st	£18,000	£19,200	19
35	1838	Proof	£12,000	£19,200	19
380	1974	Specimen	£7,000	£19,200	19
394	1830	Pattern	£10,000	£19,200	19
932	1816	Pattern	£8,000	£18,600	20
961	1832	Proof 1st	£10,000	£18,600	20
335	1893	Pattern A Wyon	£10,000	£18,000	21
40	1839	Proof ME	£10,000	£16,800	22
65	1853	Proof	£10,000	£16,800	22
303	1871	Proof milled	£10,000	£16,800	22
385	1820	Proof	£15,000	£15,600	23
959	1831	Proof 1st	£6,000	£15,000	24
213	1870	die 1 WW raised	£8,000	£14,400	25
1237	1965	Matt Proof	£8,000	£14,400	25
212	1869	24 Carat PF64	£8,000	£13,200	26
330	1891	Proof LT 2nd legend	£10,000	£13,200	26
891	1918	I Specimen	£8,000	£13,200	26
1214	1871	Proof large BP	£10,000	£12,600	27
1235	1959	Proof	£6,000	£12,600	27
694	1887	S Proof	£15,000	£12,000	28
1222	1880	Proof milled	£12,000	£12,000	28
368	1958	Proof	£6,000	£11,040	29
373	1963	Proof	£6,000	£11,040	29
935	1817	uniface trial	£10,000	£11,040	29
883	1911	C Specimen	£8,000	£10,440	30
627	1871	Proof	£6,000	£10,320	31
17	1825	Proof 2nd	£8,000	£10,080	32
304	1871	Proof extra strands	£6,000	£9,840	33
366	1957	Proof	£6,000	£9,840	33
391	1825	Proof 2nd ME	£6,000	£9,360	34
880	1909	C obv specimen	£6,000	£9,360	34
879	1908	C Specimen	£4,000	£8,400	35
1228	1887	Pattern 14 pearls	£2,500	£8,400	35
626	1871	Proof	£6,000	£7,440	36
969	1839	Proof	£4,000	£7,440	36
1213	1871	Proof tiny BP	£6,000	£7,440	36
392	1826	Proof	£3,000	£6,960	37
1234	1958	Specimen	£2,500	£6,720	38
11	1821	Proof	£4,000	£6,000	39
399	1839	Proof	£3,500	£6,000	39
39	1839	Proof	£4,000	£5,760	40
24	1831	Proof 2nd	£4,000	£5,520	41
322	1887	Proof	£1,000	£3,360	42
336	1893	Proof	£1,200	£3,360	42
370	1959	Specimen	£3,000	£3,120	43
894	1918	restrike 15R	£300	£3,120	43
895	1918	restrike 15R	£300	£2,760	44
919	1923	SA Proof	£800	£2,520	45
365	1937	Proof	£1,500	£1,920	46
356	1911	Proof	£500	£936	47
345	1902	Matt Proof	£350	£528	48
381	1984	Proof	£300	£360	49
		Total Values	**£916,750**	**£1,468,224**	

Table of Silver and Base Metal Pattern and Proof Sovereigns

No.	Date	Type	Low Estimate	Price Realised (with Premium)	RANK (20 Pieces)
787	**1887**	**M silver pattern**	**£20,000**	**£15,600**	**1**
899	1874	Pattern Pond bronze	£10,000	£14,400	2
1232	1893	Pattern silver	£4,000	£9,360	3
321	1882	Jubilee Pattern silver	£5,000	£9,120	4
933	1816	Pattern	£4,000	£8,160	5
1230	1891	Pattern bronze	£2,000	£7,440	6
897	1874	Pattern Pond aluminium	£8,000	£7,200	7
1227	1885	Pattern silver	£5,000	£7,200	7
1	1816	Pattern	£4,000	£5,040	8
949	1821	Proof AE	£3,000	£5,040	8
954	1825	Proof AE	£3,000	£4,800	9
329	1891	Pattern aluminium	£2,000	£4,080	10
95	1863	copper Pattern	£1,500	£2,160	11
1016	1863	uniface bronze	£600	£1,056	12
981	1847	Copper	£300	£816	13
951	1824	uniface lead	£800	£744	14
936	1817	uniface lead	£800	£720	15
947	1821	uniface lead	£800	£720	15
1219	1872	uniface copper	£100	£432	16
948	1821	uniface lead	£800	£240	17
		Total Values	**£75,700**	**£104,328**	

Appendix 5

BENTLEY COLLECTION OF SOVEREIGNS – Results for Coins Featured in the Promotional Brochure

Results for Coins Illustrated in Promotional brochure in price order
Coins in bold are pattern/proof issues, others are currency

No.	Date	Type	Low Estimate	Price Realised (with Premium)	RANK
736	1920	S	£300,000	£780,000	1
941	1819	London	£150,000	£186,000	2
908	1898	99 overstamp Pond	£40,000	£79,200	3
898	**1874**	**Coarse Pond**	**£80,000**	**£78,000**	**4**
1233	**1937**	**Matt Set gold**	**£60,000**	**£66,000**	**5**
878	**1931**	**Perth Proof**	**£30,000**	**£52,800**	**6**
927	**1929**	**South Africa Proof**	**£12,000**	**£52,800**	**6**
625	**1879**	**Pattern shield**	**£12,000**	**£48,000**	**7**
896	**1874**	**Fine Pond**	**£40,000**	**£45,600**	**8**
957	**1830**	**Proof George IV**	**£25,000**	**£43,200**	**9**
842	**1929**	**Melbourne Proof**	**£30,000**	**£40,800**	**10**
796	**1888**	**Melbourne Proof**	**£30,000**	**£34,800**	**11**
302	**1887**	**Pattern Shield**	**£12,000**	**£33,600**	**12**
743	**1926**	**Sydney Proof**	**£30,000**	**£33,600**	**12**
926	**1928**	**South Africa Proof**	**£15,000**	**£33,600**	**12**
966	**1837**	**Pattern Victoria**	**£15,000**	**£33,600**	**12**
1212	**1880**	**Pattern shield**	**£15,000**	**£32,400**	**13**
1211	**1870**	**Pattern St George**	**£20,000**	**£30,000**	**14**
33	**1837**	**Pattern Victoria**	**£15,000**	**£28,800**	**15**
3	**1817**	**Proof**	**£15,000**	**£27,600**	**16**
252	**1871**	**Pattern shield**	**£15,000**	**£26,400**	**17**
320	**1887**	**Proof St George**	**£12,000**	**£26,400**	**17**
382	**1816**	**Pattern**	**£15,000**	**£25,200**	**18**
397	**1837**	**Pattern Victoria**	**£15,000**	**£25,200**	**18**
628	1852	Adelaide Pound	£20,000	£25,200	18
34	**1838**	**Pattern Victoria**	**£15,000**	**£24,000**	**19**
313	**1880**	**Proof St George**	**£12,000**	**£24,000**	**19**
887	1916	Canada	£10,000	£22,800	20
934	**1816**	**Pattern**	**£15,000**	**£22,800**	**20**
970	1841	normal A's	£10,000	£22,800	20
38	1838	narrow shield	£10,000	£21,600	21
45	1843	narrow shield	£12,000	£20,400	22
629	1855	Sydney	£20,000	£20,400	22
16	**1825**	**Proof 1st type**	**£18,000**	**£19,200**	**23**
35	**1838**	**Proof**	**£12,000**	**£19,200**	**23**
394	**1830**	**William IV Pattern**	**£10,000**	**£19,200**	**23**
932	**1816**	**Pattern**	**£8,000**	**£18,600**	**24**
961	**1832**	**Proof 1st bust**	**£10,000**	**£18,600**	**24**
14	1823	George IV	£8,000	£18,000	25
1017	1863	827 truncation	£8,000	£18,000	25
40	**1839**	**Proof milled**	**£10,000**	**£16,800**	**26**
65	**1853**	**Proof**	**£10,000**	**£16,800**	**26**
303	**1871**	**Proof milled**	**£10,000**	**£16,800**	**26**
426	1859	Ansell	£6,000	£15,600	27
834	1921	Melbourne	£10,000	£15,600	27
959	**1831**	**Proof 1st bust**	**£6,000**	**£15,000**	**28**
31	1836	N in shield	£12,000	£14,400	29
1237	**1965**	**Matt Proof**	**£8,000**	**£14,400**	**29**
21	1828	George IV	£12,000	£13,200	30
106	1863	827 trun die 22	£8,000	£13,200	30
212	**1869**	**24 Carat PF64**	**£8,000**	**£13,200**	**30**
330	**1891**	**Proof Jubilee**	**£10,000**	**£13,200**	**30**
363	1917	London	£7,000	£13,200	30
891	**1918**	**India Proof**	**£8,000**	**£13,200**	**30**
920	1923	South Africa	£5,000	£13,200	30
694	**1887**	**Sydney Proof**	**£15,000**	**£12,000**	**31**
935	**1817**	**uniface reverse**	**£10,000**	**£11,040**	**32**
883	**1911**	**Canada Specimen**	**£8,000**	**£10,440**	**33**
301	1874	London die 32	£5,000	£9,600	34
633	1858	Sydney	£10,000	£9,600	34
391	**1825**	**Proof**	**£6,000**	**£9,360**	**35**
880	**1909**	**Canada Proof**	**£6,000**	**£9,360**	**35**
55	1848	1st head	£4,000	£8,880	36
879	**1908**	**Canada Proof**	**£4,000**	**£8,400**	**37**
1228	**1887**	**Pattern 14 pearls**	**£2,500**	**£8,400**	**37**
757	1887	Melbourne shield	£7,000	£7,440	38
11	**1821**	**Proof**	**£4,000**	**£6,000**	**39**
312	1879	London St George	£3,000	£3,120	40
872	1926	Perth	£1,500	£1,620	41

Appendix 6

BENTLEY COLLECTION OF SOVEREIGNS - Index

593	Page 246
594	Page 247
595	Page 248
596	Page 248
597	Page 249
598	Page 250
599	Page 251
600	Page 252
601	Page 253
602	Page 253
603	Page 254
604	Page 254
605	Page 255
606	Page 256
607	Page 256
608	Page 258
609	Page 258
610	Page 259
611	Page 260
612	Page 260
613	Page 261
614	Page 263
615	Page 264
616	Page 265
617	Page 266
618	Page 266
619	Page 267
620	Page 268
621	Page 269
622	Page 269
623	Page 270
624	Page 270
625	Page 273
626	Page 279
627	Page 280
628	Page 322
629	Page 324
630	Page 324
631	Page 325
632	Page 326
633	Page 326
634	Page 326
635	Page 327
636	Page 327
637	Page 327
638	Page 328
639	Page 328
640	Page 328
641	Page 329
642	Page 329
643	Page 329
644	Page 329
645	Page 330
646	Page 330
647	Page 330
648	Page 330
649	Page 331
650	Page 331
651	Page 331
652	Page 331
653	Page 332
654	Page 334
655	Page 334
656	Page 334
657	Page 335
658	Page 335
659	Page 335
660	Page 335
661	Page 336
662	Page 336
663	Page 336
664	Page 337
665	Page 337
666	Page 338
667	Page 338
668	Page 339
669	Page 339
670	Page 339
671	Page 339
672	Page 339
673	Page 341
674	Page 341
675	Page 342
676	Page 342
677	Page 342
678	Page 342
679	Page 343
680	Page 343
681	Page 343
682	Page 343
683	Page 344
684	Page 344
685	Page 344
686	Page 345
687	Page 345
688	Page 345
689	Page 346
690	Page 346
691	Page 346
692	Page 347
693	Page 347
694	Page 348
695	Page 348
696	Page 348
697	Page 349
698	Page 349
699	Page 349
700	Page 349
701	Page 350
702	Page 350
703	Page 350
704	Page 351
705	Page 351
706	Page 351
707	Page 351
708	Page 352
709	Page 353
710	Page 353
711	Page 353
712	Page 353
713	Page 354
714	Page 354
715	Page 354
716	Page 354
717	Page 354
718	Page 355
719	Page 355
720	Page 355
721	Page 356
722	Page 356
723	Page 356
724	Page 356
725	Page 356
726	Page 356
727	Page 357
728	Page 358
729	Page 358
730	Page 358
731	Page 358
732	Page 359
733	Page 359
734	Page 359
735	Page 359
736	Page 360
737	Page 362
738	Page 362
739	Page 363
740	Page 363
741	Page 363
742	Page 364
743	Page 365
744	Page 367
745	Page 367
746	Page 368
747	Page 368
748	Page 368
749	Page 369
750	Page 370
751	Page 370
752	Page 370
753	Page 371
754	Page 371
755	Page 371
756	Page 372
757	Page 372
758	Page 374
759	Page 374
760	Page 374
761	Page 375
762	Page 375
763	Page 375
764	Page 376
765	Page 376
766	Page 376
767	Page 377
768	Page 377
769	Page 377
770	Page 378
771	Page 378
772	Page 378
773	Page 379
774	Page 379
775	Page 379
776	Page 380
777	Page 380
778	Page 380
779	Page 381
780	Page 381
781	Page 381
782	Page 381
783	Page 382
784	Page 382
785	Page 382
786	Page 383
787	Page 384
788	Page 384
789	Page 385
790	Page 385
791	Page 385
792	Page 386
793	Page 386
794	Page 386
795	Page 387
796	Page 387
797	Page 388
798	Page 388
799	Page 388
800	Page 389
801	Page 389
802	Page 389
803	Page 389
804	Page 390
805	Page 391
807	Page 391
808	Page 391
809	Page 391
810	Page 392
811	Page 392
812	Page 392
813	Page 392
814	Page 393
815	Page 393
816	Page 394
817	Page 394
818	Page 394
819	Page 394
820	Page 395
821	Page 395
822	Page 395
823	Page 396
824	Page 397
825	Page 397
826	Page 397
827	Page 397
828	Page 398
829	Page 398
830	Page 398
831	Page 398
832	Page 398
833	Page 399
834	Page 399
835	Page 400
836	Page 400
837	Page 400
838	Page 401
839	Page 401
840	Page 401
841	Page 401
842	Page 402
843	Page 402
844	Page 402
845	Page 404
846	Page 404
847	Page 404
848	Page 405
849	Page 405
850	Page 405
851	Page 406
852	Page 406
853	Page 406
854	Page 406
855	Page 406
856	Page 406
857	Page 407
858	Page 407
859	Page 407
860	Page 408
861	Page 408
862	Page 408
863	Page 408
864	Page 408
865	Page 408
866	Page 409
867	Page 409
868	Page 409
869	Page 409
870	Page 409
871	Page 409
872	Page 410
873	Page 410
874	Page 410
875	Page 410
876	Page 410
877	Page 410
878	Page 411
879	Page 413
880	Page 414
881	Page 414
882	Page 414
883	Page 415
884	Page 416
885	Page 416
886	Page 416
887	Page 417
888	Page 417
889	Page 417
890	Page 417
891	Page 419
892	Page 419
893	Page 420
894	Page 420
895	Page 420
896	Page 422
897	Page 423
898	Page 424
899	Page 425
900	Page 426
901	Page 427
902	Page 427
903	Page 428
904	Page 428
905	Page 428
906	Page 428
907	Page 429
908	Page 429
909	Page 430
910	Page 430
911	Page 431
912	Page 431
913	Page 431
914	Page 431
915	Page 431
916	Page 432
917	Page 432
918	Page 432
919	Page 433
920	Page 434
921	Page 434
922	Page 435
923	Page 435
924	Page 435
925	Page 435
926	Page 435
927	Page 436
928	Page 436
929	Page 437
930	Page 437
931	Page 437
932	Page 15
933	Page 16
934	Page 17
935	Page 19
936	Page 19
937	Page 21
938	Page 21
939	Page 21
940	Page 22
941	Page 24
942	Page 27
943	Page 28
944	Page 29
945	Page 30
946	Page 30
947	Page 32
948	Page 32
949	Page 33
950	Page 34
951	Page 35
952	Page 36
953	Page 38
954	Page 39
955	Page 41
956	Page 41
957	Page 43
958	Page 45
959	Page 46
960	Page 47
961	Page 49
962	Page 50
963	Page 51
964	Page 51
965	Page 52
966	Page 55
967	Page 58
968	Page 58
969	Page 60
970	Page 63
971	Page 64
972	Page 66
973	Page 67
974	Page 68
975	Page 69
976	Page 70
977	Page 72
978	Page 71
979	Page 72
980	Page 74
981	Page 75
982	Page 77
983	Page 77
984	Page 78
985	Page 79
986	Page 80
987	Page 81
988	Page 83
989	Page 82
990	Page 84
991	Page 85
992	Page 84
993	Page 86
994	Page 88
995	Page 89
996	Page 90
997	Page 90
998	Page 93
999	Page 93
1000	Page 92
1001	Page 94
1002	Page 95
1003	Page 95
1004	Page 97
1005	Page 98
1006	Page 99
1007	Page 101
1008	Page 99
1009	Page 100
1010	Page 103
1011	Page 100
1012	Page 100
1013	Page 106
1014	Page 105
1015	Page 107
1016	Page 108
1017	Page 109
1018	Page 115
1019	Page 115
1020	Page 116
1021	Page 117
1022	Page 117
1023	Page 118
1024	Page 120
1025	Page 120
1026	Page 122
1027	Page 122
1028	Page 123
1029	Page 124
1030	Page 125
1031	Page 126
1032	Page 127
1033	Page 128
1034	Page 129
1035	Page 130
1036	Page 130
1037	Page 131
1038	Page 132
1039	Page 133
1040	Page 134
1041	Page 135
1042	Page 135
1043	Page 137
1044	Page 137
1045	Page 138
1046	Page 139
1047	Page 140
1048	Page 140
1049	Page 141
1050	Page 142
1051	Page 142
1052	Page 144
1053	Page 144
1054	Page 145
1055	Page 146
1056	Page 146
1057	Page 147
1058	Page 148
1059	Page 149
1060	Page 151
1061	Page 151
1062	Page 151
1063	Page 152
1064	Page 153
1065	Page 154
1066	Page 154
1067	Page 155
1068	Page 156
1069	Page 157
1070	Page 158
1071	Page 159
1072	Page 160
1073	Page 160
1074	Page 161
1075	Page 162
1076	Page 162
1077	Page 163
1078	Page 164
1079	Page 165
1080	Page 166
1081	Page 166
1082	Page 167
1083	Page 168
1084	Page 168
1085	Page 169
1086	Page 170
1087	Page 171
1088	Page 171
1089	Page 172
1090	Page 173
1091	Page 174
1092	Page 174
1093	Page 175
1094	Page 176
1095	Page 177
1096	Page 177
1097	Page 178
1098	Page 179
1099	Page 180
1100	Page 181
1101	Page 182
1102	Page 183
1103	Page 183
1104	Page 184
1105	Page 185
1106	Page 185
1107	Page 186
1108	Page 187
1109	Page 188
1110	Page 188
1111	Page 189
1112	Page 190
1113	Page 191
1114	Page 192
1115	Page 192
1116	Page 194
1117	Page 195
1118	Page 196
1119	Page 196
1120	Page 197
1121	Page 198
1122	Page 199
1123	Page 199
1124	Page 200
1125	Page 200
1126	Page 201
1127	Page 202
1128	Page 206
1129	Page 206
1130	Page 207
1131	Page 208
1132	Page 209
1133	Page 210
1134	Page 211
1135	Page 211
1136	Page 212
1137	Page 213
1138	Page 213
1139	Page 214
1140	Page 215
1141	Page 216
1142	Page 217
1143	Page 217
1144	Page 218
1145	Page 219
1146	Page 220
1147	Page 220
1148	Page 221
1149	Page 222
1150	Page 223
1151	Page 224
1152	Page 224
1153	Page 224
1154	Page 225
1155	Page 227
1156	Page 227
1157	Page 228
1158	Page 229
1159	Page 230
1160	Page 231
1161	Page 231
1162	Page 232
1163	Page 233
1164	Page 234
1165	Page 235
1166	Page 236
1167	Page 236
1168	Page 238
1169	Page 238
1170	Page 239
1171	Page 240
1172	Page 240
1173	Page 241
1174	Page 242
1175	Page 243
1176	Page 244
1177	Page 244
1178	Page 245
1179	Page 246
1180	Page 246
1181	Page 247
1182	Page 248
1183	Page 249
1184	Page 249
1185	Page 251
1186	Page 252
1187	Page 252
1188	Page 253
1189	Page 254
1190	Page 255
1191	Page 255
1192	Page 257
1193	Page 257
1194	Page 258
1195	Page 259
1196	Page 259
1198	Page 261
1199	Page 261
1200	Page 262
1201	Page 263
1202	Page 264
1203	Page 264
1204	Page 265
1205	Page 266
1206	Page 267
1207	Page 268
1208	Page 268
1209	Page 269
1210	Page 271
1211	Page 272
1212	Page 274
1213	Page 278
1214	Page 278
1215	Page 282
1216	Page 282
1217	Page 283
1218	Page 283
1219	Page 283
1220	Page 284
1221	Page 285
1222	Page 286
1223	Page 287
1224	Page 287
1225	Page 289
1226	Page 290
1227	Page 292
1228	Page 292
1229	Page 294
1230	Page 296
1231	Page 299
1232	Page 301
1233	Page 310
1234	Page 313
1235	Page 315
1236	Page 316
1237	Page 317
1238	Page 318

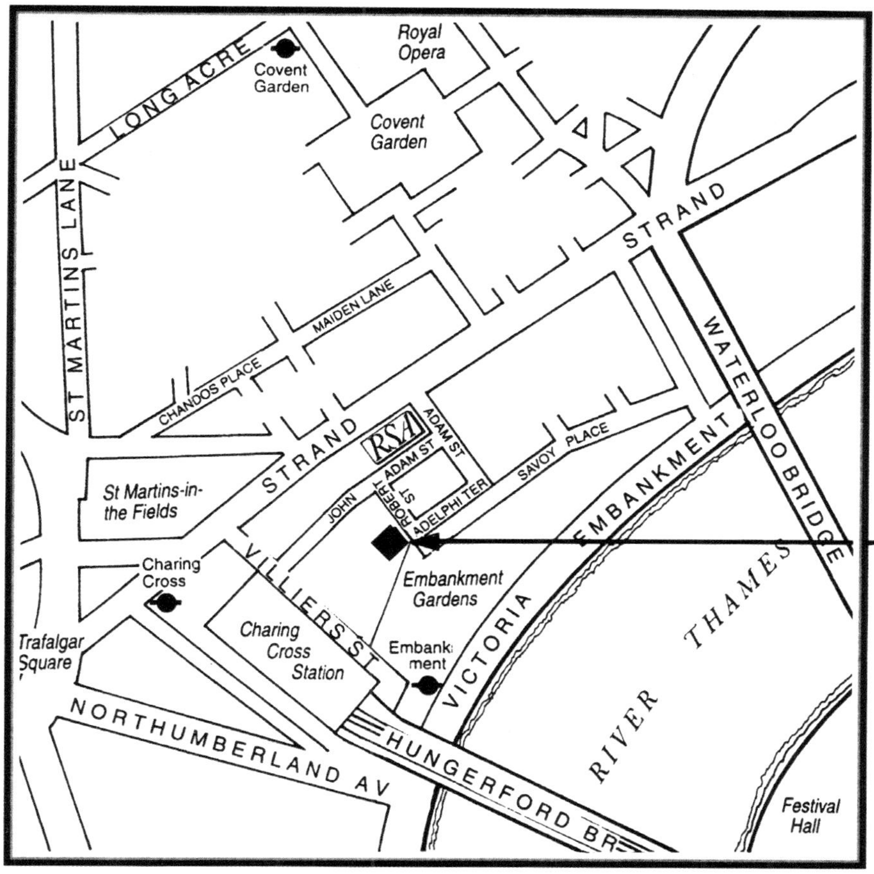

Baldwin's
11 Adelphi Terrace
London WC2N 6BJ

OUR SPECIALIST TEAM

Ian Goldbart	Managing Director	Ian@baldwin.co.uk
Edward Baldwin	Chairman European, Russian, Colonial and Oriental Coins Military Medals and Decorations, Books	Edward@baldwin.co.uk
Seth Freeman	Director Tokens and Banknotes	Seth@baldwin.co.uk
Steve Hill	Director English hammered and milled Coins	Steve@baldwin.co.uk
Dimitri Loulakakis	Director English, European and Latin American Coins, modern Greek Coins	Dimitri@baldwin.co.uk
Andre de Clermont	Islamic Coins	Andre@baldwin.co.uk
Graham Byfield	Ancient Coins, Indian and Islamic Coins, Commemorative Medals	Graham@baldwin.co.uk
Paul Hill	Ancient Greek, Roman and Byzantine Coins	Paul@baldwin.co.uk
Caroline Holmes	Numismatic Books	Caroline@baldwin.co.uk
David Kirk	Military Medals and English Coins	David@baldwin.co.uk
Julie Lecoindre	Numismatic Specialist	Julie@baldwin.co.uk
Matt Curtis	Auction Office Manager	Matt@baldwin.co.uk
Sam Weedall	Auction Co-Ordinator	Sam@baldwin.co.uk
Domoni Mainstone	Auction Administrator	Domoni@baldwin.co.uk
Caroline Newton	PR and Marketing Manager	CarolineNewton@baldwin.co.uk

EXTERNAL CONSULTANTS

Daniel Fearon	Commemorative Medals	Daniel@baldwin.co.uk
Stan Goron	Indian Coins	Stan@baldwin.co.uk
Brian Kemp	Banknotes	BrianKemp@baldwin.co.uk
Peter Donald	Byzantine Coins	Peter@baldwin.co.uk

WORLDWIDE REPRESENTATIVES

Mr Randy Weir	P O Box 64577, Unionville, Ontario, L3R 0M9, Canada	RandyWeir@baldwin.co.uk
Mr Ma Tak Wo	Unit 2A, 9th Floor, China Insurance Building, 48 Cameron Road Tsim Sha Tsui, Kowloon, Hong Kong	MaTakWo@baldwin.co.uk